Understanding the UK Economy

MACMILLAN TEXTS IN ECONOMICS

Understanding the UK Economy is the first of a new generation of economics textbooks from Macmillan developed in conjunction with a panel of distinguished editorial advisers:

David Greenaway, Professor of Economics, University of Nottingham
Gordon Hughes, Professor of Political Economy, University of Edinburgh
David Pearce, Professor of Economics, University College London
David Ulph, Professor of Economics, University of Bristol

Future Macmillan Texts in Economics cover the core compulsory and optional courses in economics at first-degree level and will include:

International Finance: Keith Pilbeam ⎫
Macroeconomics: Nicholas Rau   ⎬ *forthcoming*
Monetary Economics: Stuart Sayer   ⎭

Introductory Principles ⎫
Comparative Economics
Development Economics
Econometrics
Financial Economics
Industrial Economics   ⎬ *in preparation*
Labour Economics
Microeconomics
Public Sector Economics
Quantitative Methods
Welfare Economics   ⎭

Series Standing Order

If you would like to receive future titles in this series as they are published, you can make use of our standing order facility. To place a standing order please contact your bookseller or, in case of difficulty, write to us at the address below with your name and address and the name of the series. Please state with which title you wish to begin your standing order. (If you live outside the United Kingdom we may not have the rights for your area, in which case we will forward your order to the publisher concerned.)

Customer Services Department, Macmillan Distribution Ltd, Houndmills, Basingstoke, Hampshire, RG21 2XS, England.

Understanding the UK Economy

Edited by

Peter Curwen

Contributors:
David Gowland and Stephen James
Keith Hartley and Nick Hooper
Brian McCormick
Paul Marshall
Bob Sedgwick

MACMILLAN

First published 1990
Reprinted 1990

Published by
MACMILLAN EDUCATION LTD
Houndmills, Basingstoke, Hampshire RG21 2XS
and London
Companies and representatives
throughout the world

Typeset by Latimer Trend & Company Ltd, Plymouth

Printed and bound in Great Britain by
Butler & Tanner Ltd, Frome and London

British Library Cataloguing in Publication Data
Understanding the UK economy—(Macmillan texts in
economics).
1. Great Britain. Economic conditions
I. Curwen, Peter J. (Peter Jeremy), 1945–
330.941
ISBN 0–333–51104–2 (hardcover)
ISBN 0–333–51105–0 (paperback)

To Ben and Alex

Hello

Ben s my friend.
So s Alc

Contents

List of Figures

List of Tables

Preface

We very much hope that the justification for writing a book of this kind is self-evident. If this is not the case, then we simply wish to point out that economic literacy remains at far too low a level in the UK. In seeking to enhance this literacy we like to think that this book will be of interest to a very wide-ranging audience, but we recognise that, in practice, almost all those who read it will be studying a parallel course in economic principles, either at 'A' level or as undergraduates, or will already be acquainted with economic issues either through their work or their reading of the financial press. We hope that the book is sufficiently challenging to interest readers who are already conversant with economics, but not so challenging as to prevent readers who are not conversant with economic theory from following the discussion.

We have tried to strike an acceptable balance between **analysis** and **description**. It is obviously necessary, in a book of this kind, to describe how the UK functions at the present time, and also how it has functioned in the past where this has been different. It is, however, unilluminating simply to explain what is done in policy terms without simultaneously explaining **why**, and the reasons why are also to be found in the book where appropriate. It should be noted that the kinds of models to be found in textbooks may often fail to explain why many policies are being pursued, because the real world may be evolving very rapidly and be using fairly crude rules of thumb whilst coming to terms with these changes. It is accordingly our intention to concentrate upon the real world, and to give short shrift to textbook models which cannot shed much light upon it.

Most readers familiar with economics will have been taught the subject as a succession of separate boxes labelled 'employment', 'inflation', and so on. There is, as a consequence, a preference for applica-tions to be organised into similar boxes, to be dipped into one by one as appropriate. We do not care for this approach because, first, it fails to emphasise the **fundamental linkages** between the various parts of the economy; secondly, it fails to deliver a satisfactory **historical perspective**; and thirdly, it permits the authors covering the content of separate boxes to offer a **subjective interpretation** of events which conflicts with that to be found in other boxes. Rather oddly, some books consider this latter point to be a virtue, and express distaste for the imposition of monolithic structures. Our view is that this is very much a vice, and is indicative of lack of editorial control. This book is accordingly approached from precisely the opposite viewpoint – namely, that individual authors should work to a carefully predetermined structure and that stylistic differences should be kept to a minimum. In particular, each author has been asked to set out the pros and cons of every policy debate without prejudice. This does not mean that the authors do not have strong preferences concerning the conduct of policy, nor indeed that they have refrained from expressing them, but rather that they do not seek to persuade by omitting to mention what the counter-arguments are.

The issue concerning the need to provide a framework which integrates individual sections has been difficult to resolve. One innovative feature in this respect is the introductory chapter which seeks to provide both a philosophical basis and an historical perspective for all that follows. A second innovation is to set the discussion of fiscal and monetary policy at the end of the book, in Chapter 9, so that it draws together the macroeconomic threads from previous chapters, with Chapter 8 doing the same for the microeconomic threads. The early chapters presume least prior knowledge, but where necessary they are extensively cross-referenced to later points in the text where the missing information is to be found. Issues which can broadly be said to concern welfare have been allocated a chapter of their own (Chapter 7), rather than ignored altogether or dispersed in brief and unrelated sections throughout the text.

Certain themes inevitably appear under several chapter headings – for example, the development of the Single European Market. Generally speaking they are left dispersed, but cross-referenced to other parts of the book where the same themes recur. However, in certain cases – for example, agriculture – it has made more sense to collect the themes together under one heading in order to avoid duplication and the loss of continuity in the discussion. For these reasons, the structure of the book may at first sight appear unusual, but we believe firmly that it does, in fact, make better sense than the structures to be found in other texts, and we leave it to the readers to judge for themselves (and hopefully to let us know their opinions on the matter in due course).

Whilst the book is essentially about the UK economy, it has a stronger international flavour than is commonly associated with books on this topic. This reflects a whole host of developments, such as the Single European Market and deregulation in general, which are making it increasingly inappropriate to view policy within the physical confines of the UK alone. Since this is very much a feature of ongoing policy we have deliberately set up our discussion so that it offers clear pointers towards the future, and we have chosen to compensate for this by saying much less than is usual about the more distant past.

In our opinion the election of the current government was a significant watershed in policy terms, for reasons set out in the Introduction. Each chapter is accordingly structured to say relatively little about the period before 1969; to provide a fairly detailed review of the decade 1969–79; and to focus primarily upon the decade 1979–89 and especially upon how it has compared with the decade which preceded it.

All this places great demands upon the handling of data. We have tried to introduce as much data as possible, and to locate it all within the appropriate context rather than relegate it to appendixes. Equally, we recognise that tabular material can be boring – and, at times, a poor means of communication – so where appropriate other methods of presentation have been used. A point to be emphasised is that data is expressed in the form normally used by government and reported in the media. Thus, for example, the Public Sector Borrowing Requirement (PSBR) is not simply stated as an absolute number but as a percentage of GDP. Much of the data is adjusted for inflation, and whenever space permits the comparable data for other countries is also included.

The contributors to this book (other than the editor) have been chosen because they are knowledgeable in their fields. However, too much knowledge can be a vice as well as a virtue when it comes down to the need to compress a great deal of information into a small space, and the authors are commended to you not so much because they are 'specialists' but because they have proved in their previously published work that they have the facility to communicate to the target audience for this book. We hope that it makes enjoyable reading. No doubt you will let us know if that is not the case. One way or the other the editor is more than happy to accept ultimate responsibility for the entire finished product, although individual authors are responsible only for the chapters which bear their name.

Finally, I would like to thank Gordon Hughes and the other five anonymous reviewers for their thorough dissection of the text in its varying stages of completion. There is a myth – propagated, one suspects, by those who write only short articles – that textbooks are not refereed adequately, but that has been far from the reality in this particular case. Whilst some suggestions for improvement have been set aside for this edition, it is anticipated that they will be incorporated in the second edition. Any restructuring of the text in subsequent editions will be determined entirely by the suggestions of users, and these are accordingly welcomed by the editor.

PETER CURWEN

List of Abbreviations

ACAS	Arbitration, Conciliation and Advisory Service
ACT	Advance Corporation Tax
AFBD	Association of Futures Brokers and Dealers
APC	Average Propensity to Consume
ATM	Automated Teller Machine
BBC	British Broadcasting Corporation
BES	Business Expansion Scheme
BIS	Bank For International Settlements
BoP	Balance of Payments
BSA	Building Society Association
CAP	Common Agricultural Policy
CBI	Confederation of British Industry
CCC	Competition and Credit Control
CD	Certificate of Deposit
CFF	Compensatory Financing Facility
CGT	Capital Gains Tax
CR	Concentration Ratio
CSO	Central Statistical Office
CTT	Capital Transfer Tax
DCE	Domestic Credit Expansion
DHSS	Department of Health and Social Security
DIB	Defence Industrial Base
DM	Deutsch Mark
DTI	Department of Trade and Industry
EAGGF	European Agricultural Guarantee and Guidance Fund
EAP	Enlarged Access Policy
EC	European Community
ECU	European Currency Unit
EEA	Exchange Equalisation Account
EEC	European Economic Community
EER	Effective Exchange Rate
EFF	Extended Fund Facility
EFL	External Financing Limit
EFTPOS	Electronic Funds Transfer at Point of Sale
ELs	Eligible Liabilities
EMCF	European Monetary Co-operation Fund
EMS	European Monetary System
EMU	European Monetary Union
ERI	Effective Exchange Rate Index
ERM	Exchange Rate Mechanism
ET	Employment Training
FES	Family Expenditure Survey
FIMBRA	Financial Intermediaries and Brokers Regulatory Association
FIS	Family Income Supplement
FMI	Financial Management Initiative
FRN	Floating-rate Note
FSBR	Financial Statement and Budget Report
GAB	General Agreements to Borrow
GATT	General Agreement on Tariffs and Trade
GDFCF	Gross Domestic Fixed Capital Formation
GDP	Gross Domestic Product
GNP	Gross National Product
HMSO	Her Majesty's Stationary Office
HP	Hire Purchase
IBA	Independent Broadcasting Association
IBELs	Interest Bearing Eligible Liabilities
IDC	Industrial Development Certificate
IGA	Inter-governmental Agreements
IMF	International Monetary Fund
IMRO	Investment Management Regulatory Organisation
ISDA	International Swap Dealers Association
LAUTRO	Life Assurance and Unit Trust Regulatory Organisation
LDC	Less Developed Country

LDMA	London Discount Market Association	PPP	Purchasing Power Parity
LIBOR	London Inter-bank Offered Rate	PPS	Perpetual Preferred Stock
LIFFE	London International Financial Futures Exchange	PRT	Petroleum Revenue Tax
MCA	Monetary Compensatory Amount	PSBR	Public Sector Borrowing Requirement
MERM	Multilateral Exchange Rate Model	PSDR	Public Sector Debt Repayment
MLR	Minimum Lending Rate	R & D	Research and Development
MMC	Monopolies and Mergers Commission	RDG	Regional Development Grant
MoD	Ministry of Defence	RER	Real Exchange Rate
MPC	Marginal Propensity to Consume	RPI	Retail Prices Index
MSC	Manpower Services Commission	RPM	Resale Price Maintenance
MTFS	Medium Term Financial Strategy	RSA	Regional Selective Assistance
NBFI	Non-bank Financial Intermediaries	RSSL	Recruitment Subsidy for School Leavers
NDP	Net Domestic Product	SDR	Special Drawing Right
NHS	National Health Service	SEA	Single European Act
NI	National Income	SERPS	State Earnings Related Pension Scheme
NICs	National Insurance Contributions	SFF	Supplementary Financing Facility
NNDI	Net National Disposable Income	SIB	Securities and Investments Board
NNP	Net National Product	SRO	Self Regulatory Organisation
NSB	National Savings Bank	TB	Treasury Bill
OECD	Organisation for Economic Co-operation and Development	TEC	Training and Enterprise Council
		TFE	Total Final Expenditure
OFGAS	Office of Gas Supply	TPI	Tax and Price Index
OFT	Office of Fair Trading	TSA	The Securities Association
OFTEL	Office of Telecommunications	TSB	Trustee Savings Bank
OMO	Open-market Operation	UAA	Utilised Agricultural Area
OPEC	Organisation of Petroleum Exporting Countries	USM	Unlisted Securities Market
		VAT	Value Added Tax
OTC	Over the Counter	VER	Voluntary Export Restraint
PAYE	Pay As You Earn	YES	Youth Employment Subsidy
PDI	Personal Disposable Income	YOP	Youth Opportunity Programme
PEP	Personal Equity Plan	YTS	Youth Training Scheme

Acknowledgements

The authors and publishers wish to thank the following for permission to use copyright material:

Bank of England for Tables 1.12, 1.13, 4.1, 4.3, 4.9, and Figures 1.7, 2.1, 4.4, and 9.1.

Barclays Bank for Table 9.6 and Figure 9.2.

Controller of Her Majesty's Stationery Office for Tables 1.1 to 1.9, 1.11, 3.1, 3.2, 3.4, 4.2, 4.4 to 4.8, 5.3, 6.1 to 6.5, 6.7, 6.8, 7.1 to 7.3, 7.5, 8.1, 8.2, 8.5, 8.6, 8.8, 8.9, 8.12, 9.1, 9.3 to 9.5; and Figures 1.5, 1.6, 1.8, 1.11, 1.12, 3.1 to 3.5, 3.7, 4.1 to 4.3, 6.1 to 6.8, 7.3 to 7.6.

Council of Mortgage Lenders for Table 2.3 and Figure 2.2.

Financial Times for Table 7.8 and Figures 1.2 and 5.2.

Information Division, HM Treasury for Tables 1.10 and Figures 1.3, 1.4, 1.9, 1.10 and 5.4.

Institute for Fiscal Studies for Table 7.9 and Figure 7.4.

Organisation for Economic Co-operation and Development for Table 4.10 and Figure 5.3.

Statistical Office of the European Communities for Tables 5.1, 5.2, 5.4 and 5.5.

The Independent for Figure 3.6.

UBS Phillips & Drew for Figure 4.5.

Every effort has been made to trace all the copyright-holders, but if any have been inadvertently overlooked the publishers will be pleased to make the necessary arrangement at the first opportunity.

Introduction
Peter Curwen

Our purpose in this Introduction is to set the scene for the detailed analysis of the UK economy which is the subject matter of this book. The teaching of economics has arguably become increasingly pseudo-scientific, content to build ever more sophisticated models which are judged on virtually any criterion other than the amount of light which they shed upon the behaviour of economic agents in the real world. This, in its turn, has tended to detract from the need to study the historical and political context within which policy-making actually takes place. This book, however is entirely about the real world, and therefore requires the reader to have at least a rudimentary understanding of economic history and political systems. This Introduction sets out to provide this understanding and may, therefore, readily be omitted by those already conversant with its context.

It has become the practice of late to talk about a 'Thatcherite' revolution in the manner in which the UK is governed, and if such a revolution has indeed occurred then it must have had its primary impact upon economic policy. But a revolution in policy presupposes the prior existence of a revolutionary change in the **ideas which lie behind it**, and it is helpful, therefore, to begin by addressing this particular matter.

Economic ideas, in common with those of many other disciplines, tend to pass through successive phases of revolution and evolution. The revolutionary phases are often associated with a particular event, such as the publication of a book, although the seeds of the ideas may have been sown a great many years earlier awaiting the ideal moment for germination. Furthermore, it is not altogether easy to pinpoint when a revolution is set in motion since there is inevitably a great deal of inertia before revolutionary ideas gain widespread acceptance. The subsequent discussion is concerned primarily with the Keynesian and monetarist revolutions. The former is generally associated with the publication of the *General Theory* in 1936, but for our purposes is more sensibly seen in policy terms as underpinning the significant changes which took place between 1944 and 1949. The monetarist revolution flowered during the 1970s and came of age during the early years of the period of Conservative rule commencing in 1979, and it is indeed for this reason that 1979 is treated as the watershed year for the text as a whole.

The evolutionary phase of Keynesianism lasted broadly from 1950 to 1970, at which point events (discussed below) conspired to bring about its

1

steady demise until its official replacement by monetarism. Monetarism, on the other hand, barely had the chance to evolve at all before significant aspects were consigned to virtual oblivion, leaving the UK in a kind of policy limbo – part-monetarist, part-Keynesian and with a heavy dose of what might best be called 'pragmatism' thrown in for good measure.

It is important to appreciate, to begin with, that there are two quite divergent ways of looking at those economic models which are put into practice. The first, clearly enunciated by Keynes himself and generally favoured by the kind of intellectual circles in which he moved, is that the ideas of economists and political philosophers are the **driving force behind the implementation of policy**. Support for this viewpoint can be found in the influential doctrine of laissez-faire during the nineteenth century, and more recently in the writings of Keynes himself. The opposing doctrine is that economists have a barely detectable influence on society as a whole, since the popularity of particular ideas ultimately depends upon their compatibility with economic and political circumstances at the time. In other words, the broad direction in which economic policy moves is determined by the ways in which **interest groups in society respond to changing economic opportunities**, and economic models are chosen because they lend intellectual support to the behaviour of those groups.

The debate between these two schools of thought will, naturally, never be satisfactorily resolved because it is hard to see how either case can be 'proved' to everyone's satisfaction. An interesting current illustration of this debate relates to the case of privatisation, where it is possible to argue, on the one hand, that the policy was adopted as a result of years of ear-bending in influential Conservative circles by the Institute of Economic Affairs and other like-minded groups and, on the other, that once the decision had been taken to reduce the role of government and to cut public expenditure, asset sales were simply one available means to achieve these goals.

A variety of economic models are analysed in the chapters which follow. However, it is at best unhelpful simply to model the economy at a specific point in time, as though it can be divorced from the historical and political context which shaped it over a period of many decades. Indeed, it is possible to argue that many of the key influences moulding the way the economy behaves today have their origins well back into the nineteenth century, but a shortage of space does not permit us to examine these other than in a fairly cursory way.

The neo-classical world

At the end of the nineteenth century the **forces of the market place** still largely held sway over economic life. Certainly, government had been taking on board ever wider responsibilities which needed to be financed through taxation, but macroeconomic management of the kind practised after 1945 was incompatible with the prevailing 'neo-classical' orthodoxy.

This held true, for example, with respect to unemployment. The mechanisation of agriculture at the turn of the century forced large numbers of people off the land and into towns and cities. There were, understandably, difficulties in absorbing this inflow of labour into the industrial workforce, and the prevailing orthodoxy therefore needed to explain the adjustment process whereby the level of employment would be restored to equilibrium. The line taken by the neo-classical school was that, in a competitive market system such as characterised the UK economy at the time, the **equilibrium condition was one of full employment**. In other words, any imbalances between the supply of, and demand for, a factor of production such as labour could be only temporary, since any imbalance between the two would automatically trigger forces in the market place which would bring them back into balance. The forces in question were **changes in relative prices**, such that if there was excess demand for a factor of production its price (its wage in the case of labour) would be driven upwards until the point was reached at which potential purchasers would be induced to switch over from demanding the new, relatively expensive, factor of production, to others which in the process had become relatively cheap. Likewise, the price of a factor of production in excess supply would be driven steadily downwards, until a level was reached at which all that was being supplied at the price level was purchased.

Given its resurgence in the modern context of **supply-side economics**, it is important to appreciate what interpretation this line of argument placed upon the concept of full employment. What the neo-classical model was effectively saying was that, if the market for labour was left to its own devices, a wage rate would be established such that anyone who was willing to work would have a job to go to, and employment would in that sense be permanently 'full'. By implication, all unemployment could be treated as **voluntary** because the individuals in question must either be unwilling to work at **any** wage rate, or willing to work, but only at a wage rate higher than that the market was prepared to pay. There would always be enough potential jobs to employ everyone willing to work, it was simply a question of finding the market-clearing wage. However, if some individuals chose not to accept that wage, then clearly they were preventing the market from functioning smoothly, in which case they were themselves the **cause** of the problem of unemployment. Since they were the cause, and a cure was readily available were they willing to accept a reduction in their target wage rate, it could not by implication be anyone else's responsibility to deal with unemployment. Hence there was no need for governments to intervene in the labour market.

and would be employed in preference to capital. This would be wholly unaffected by a doubling of the **general price level**, with the prices above rising to £2 and £4 respectively, since labour would remain one half of the price of capital per unit employed, and indeed this would hold true were prices in general to rise by a multiple of 100 or 1000 times. The **volume** of labour would remain constant whilst the total monetary **value** of labour used would vary enormously.

It followed that there was no direct link between the general level of prices and the level of employment. Nevertheless, there had to be a reason why the general price level showed considerable volatility over time, and the reason was called the **Quantity Theory of Money**. The original, or 'old' version of the Quantity Theory was formulated within the context of a monetary system called the gold standard. This meant that the total amount of money available was directly related to the available stock of gold − originally on a one-to-one basis but, subsequent to the widespread adoption of the principle of credit creation, in a fixed proportionate relationship. Hence, if more gold was put into circulation, but no more real goods and services, prices in general would be driven upwards in order to ensure that the available stock of money would remain just sufficient, **and no more**, to purchase the available stock of goods and services. This applied equally well in reverse, with prices falling when the output of goods and services increased but no new supply of gold became available.

Real and money magnitudes

Within the neo-classical model a crucial distinction was made between **real** and **money** magnitudes. The total **volume** of labour − or of any other factor of production − in employment at any one time was regarded as a real magnitude, governed by the price of one factor relative to that of others. If a unit of labour cost £1 whilst a unit of machinery cost £2, then labour was half the price of capital

The neo-classical 1930s

The return of the labour force from active military duty after 1918 coincided with a sharp downturn in economic activity resulting from a combination of matters such as an overvalued exchange rate, ageing technology and increased world-wide competition. Industries such as coal-mining suffered badly. Motive power was switching from coal to oil, and deep-mining in Britain was very expensive compared to the costs of newly-opened mines elsewhere. The coal-mine owners sought to re-solve the problem by forcing their coal-miners to take a reduction in their wages. However, the miners resisted, going on strike in 1921 and triggering the General Strike of 1926. They were ultimately defeated (hindered, in part, by the lack of a welfare system to fall back on in hard times) but many mines were nevertheless forced to shut down. This was paralleled in other industries and, as a result, there was widespread unemployment in the UK at a time when other economies were booming.

Although the depression in the UK from 1919 onwards was by no means typical (the overvalued currency was a critical factor not found elsewhere), it did provide food for thought for many econo-mists brought up in the neo-classical orthodoxy, amongst them John Maynard Keynes. The neo-classical model was steadily amended and refined, and within Keynes's *Treatise on Money*, published in 1930, one can detect a distinct step forward along the evolutionary path of the existing ortho-doxy at precisely the point in history when events conspired to expose the model's inadequacies, for in 1929 there occurred the Wall Street Crash.

Unfortunately, the response of most govern-ments after the Great Crash was to do all the wrong things. In particular, America rapidly intro-duced an era of trade protectionism to which other countries responded in kind, with the result that the total volume of world trade fell sharply. It has also been argued by writers such as Milton Fried-man that the American Federal Reserve System deliberately engineered a shortage of liquidity, thereby making it very difficult for debtors to obtain the money they needed to settle their debts. Irrespective of the causes, the effects were straight-forward enough. Unemployment rose sharply throughout the Western World, the impact falling particularly upon towns and regions overdepen-dent upon traditional heavy industries such as shipbuilding.

In the face of mass unemployment the neo-classical orthodoxy effectively broke down. To argue that millions of people could be got back to work simply by lowering the wage rate, thereby restoring equilibrium in the labour market, seemed

futile in the extreme. But on the subject of what else could be done the model was largely silent. The time was at last ripe for the seed of revolution to grow.

The Keynesian revolution

This revolution was associated with the work of Keynes, and in particular with the ideas expressed in the *General Theory of Employment, Interest and Money*, published in 1936. The *General Theory* is a book of baffling obscurity – which some argue was deliberately introduced in order to get the central, simple, propositions accepted whilst the arguments raged about interpreting the complexities. The standard textbook version is based on a simplified interpretation introduced after the Second World War, and it is certainly only fair to argue that Keynes himself, who died in 1946, would have made significant alterations to his text had he lived longer. Nevertheless, there can be little dispute about his main lines of attack upon the neo-classical orthodoxy.

In the *General Theory*, Keynes set out to demon-strate that the level of National Income – and hence effectively of output and employment – was determined by the **interaction of changes in both real and monetary variables**, and also that there was a direct link between decisions taken by **individual households and firms** and the effect upon the **economy as a whole**. The cornerstone of Keynes's work was the refutation of the logical reasoning which led in the neo-classical model to the automatic restoration of full employment and, having set out an alternative theory which in the general case would generate less than full employ-ment, the use of that theory to explain how unemployment could be cured.

One of the main innovations of the Keynesian model was its stress upon the role of **expectations in the face of uncertainty**. Keynes felt that decisions with respect to the expansion or curtail-ment of output were to a considerable degree dependent upon the prevailing set of expectations about the future held by households and firms. In the event, for example, that firms in general did not expect an early recovery from a period of recession, their natural reaction would be to hold back from producing output which they did not expect to be able to sell, and to lay off workers whom they could no longer gainfully employ. The consequence of such a policy would be significantly to reduce the amount of money which households had to spend since, insofar as it existed, state assistance was not as rewarding as full-time employment. The consequent cut-back in consumption spending would adversely affect retail outlets, which in turn would reduce orders from wholesalers, and the latter would cut back orders from manufacturers.

The curtailment of output and employment undertaken in the expectation of a fall in demand for goods and services would thus itself create the expected circumstances of reduced consumption. In other words, expectations have an in-built tendency to be **self-fulfilling**, and in so doing they inevitably help to generate a further set of **similar expectations**. The confirmation of a firm's expectations that it would not be able to sell what it produced would thus probably cause the firm to curtail output and employment still further. The link between decisions taken by households and firms, and their consequences for the economy as a whole are, therefore, plain to see.

This line of reasoning tends to imply that the level of employment is fundamentally affected by the prevailing set of expectations. But there seems little enough reason to suppose that the prevailing state of expectations will always be such as to secure full employment. The neo-classical model argued that full employment could always be restored by reducing the wage rate. But suppose the wage rate was indeed to fall as it recommended, the result would logically be a reduction in the amount of money available for current consumption, which in turn would lead inevitably to a reduction in sales and profits. The Keynesian model argued that firms would respond by **cutting** output and employment. Since this was exactly the opposite conclusion to that postulated in the neo-classical model, the inevitable conclusion was that full employment could not, in fact, be restored through changes in relative prices.

The one undisputed fact of the early 1930s was that the Great Crash and its aftermath had resulted in depressed expectations. It was not that firms did not want to expand on an individual basis, but if one firm produced more output, created new jobs and paid out more in wages at a time when other firms did not follow suit, then almost all of the extra wages would be spent on the output of other firms rather than that of the firm paying out the wages, thereby inevitably driving it into bankruptcy. Of course, if all firms chose to expand simultaneously there would be enough extra wages in circulation to keep them all in business, but that could happen only if their expectations were simultaneously to improve, and in the climate of the early 1930s that was simply not going to happen.

It followed logically from this that full employment could be restored if either households unilaterally decided to spend more money — for example, by running down accumulated savings — or firms decided to invest in more capital machinery. But if neither group was willing to behave in this way, the needed improvement in the climate or expectations would have to be engineered by some other party. Clearly, the only other party capable of achieving this was the **government**.

The implication was that full employment could be restored only if the government created a demand for goods and services. This, however, flew straight in the face of the neo-classical orthodoxy and, somewhat curiously, given the part played by Keynes in this tale, the UK government was particularly disinclined to accept the need for increased government spending.

A matter of debt

But what other objections, apart from a simple-minded belief in the neo-classical model, were there to increased government spending? The answer was that increased spending not covered by increased taxation meant that the indebtedness of the government would have to increase. If the spending was productive, and earned a good rate of return, then the economy would grow as a consequence, and in later years there would be more resources to tax, thereby allowing the debt to be repaid. But if the money was spent unproductively – for example, on national defence – then the debt would never be repaid. However, this would, for example, increase the burden of financing the debt borne by future generations; hence balancing the fiscal books was held to be the only sound way to behave.

In advocating government spending in excess of tax revenue, Keynes was not, however, suggesting that borrowing to get the economy on the move again was to be regarded as anything other than a temporary measure. The idea was that once public spending had generated more optimistic expectations, the simultaneous expansion of private sector organisations would once again be restored as the driving force behind economy activity, thereby allowing the government to cut back its own operations and to use revenue from the newly expanded tax base to redeem at least part of the outstanding debt.

In fairness to Keynes, it should be said that his view of the world was one in which a small group of public-spirited intellectuals would operate economic policy with wisdom, discretion and foresight. His was not a world of fiscal profligacy; debt was perfectly sensible so long as there was an intention to repay, to balance the books over the longer haul. But spending other people's money proved to be fun, especially as it helped to keep politicians in elected office, so acceptance of the belief that there was nothing particularly immoral about debt *per se* was turned around and used in evidence against him. Politicians in office all agreed that debt **ought** to be repaid, but they could not see any political advantage in doing so, especially as the interest payments might fall due during another political party's period in office.

Neo-classicism in decline

At this juncture it is important to remind the reader that models such as the neo-classical orthodoxy do not simply disappear when a revolution in thought occurs. They stand in the wings, changing their shape to fit the times, awaiting the opportunity to leap back upon the stage when the facade of the new orthodoxy shows signs of cracking.

An illustration of what we mean can be seen in what is commonly referred to as the **crowding-out** debate. The neo-classical orthodoxy held, as we have seen above, that changes in relative prices determined what happened in the real economy. Full employment could thus be addressed not simply in terms of the relative price of labour, but also in terms of the relative price of loanable funds (**savings**). It was argued that a fall in household expenditure would indeed initially cause a loss of output and employment. But given that income must either be spent or saved, the cut in spending would result in increased savings. This in turn would cause interest rates – the price of savings – to fall, and thereby cheapen the cost of borrowing for investment by firms. This would result in an expansion of investment which would provide new employment opportunities for those laid-off by the decline in the consumer goods sector, and full employment would ultimately be restored.

There was, however, one obvious drawback to this argument – namely, that the private sector might hold back investment decisions for considerable periods of time if their expectations about the future state of the economy were depressed. In the face of uninvested savings you could reduce the rate of interest, but firms would still not borrow the money unless they expected to earn a rate of return higher than the borrowing cost of capital. In the midst of a major recession firms might refuse to invest on the scale needed to get the economy growing again, in which case public sector investment would be a more than acceptable substitute, at least in the short term. Indeed, contracts placed by public sector bodies would provide work for the private sector and crowd them in rather than out.

It is of significance to note that the necessity for investment in infrastructure projects such as roads, hospitals and schools was not of itself the issue, but rather whether the private sector could be relied upon to invest on the necessary scale. The fact that there clearly was a need for public sector investment in the 1930s, given the prevailing set of private sector expectations, appeared to have driven another nail into the coffin of the neo-classical orthodoxy, but again it is easy in retrospect to see how acceptance of the desirability of public sector **investment** spending could easily slide into acceptance of the desirability of public sector spending **of any kind**.

In practice, it is probably fair to argue that it was the Second World War, rather than the *General Theory*, which accounted for the demise of neo-classicism in the UK. Elsewhere the Nazis in Germany were behaving in a thoroughly Keynesian way by the mid-1930s, and the New Deal was implemented in the USA, albeit with far less effect because the desire to help the disadvantaged had to compete with the desire not to run budget deficits. However, unemployment remained extremely high in the UK, especially on a regional basis (thereby providing further 'evidence' of labour market inflexibility), until the government was forced, despite itself, to rearm. Even then it was well into 1941, the second year of the War, before all of the unemployed could be absorbed into 'productive' work.

The new order cometh

By the end of the Second World War the Keynesian revolution had inexorably entered into its 'orthodoxy' phase, common to all advanced Western economies for roughly 25 years. Not surprisingly, the sacrifices of the war years served to speed up enormously the process of social change. Under no circumstances was there to be a re-run of the 1930s, which meant that a clear priority had to be given to the eradication of unemployment. On the whole, the expectation was that, once the economy was restored to a peacetime footing, there would be considerable problems in switching the labour force into civilian occupations. The concept of 'full' employment was not, therefore, an immediate objective. The *White Paper on Employment* in 1944 talked in terms of something less ambitious, but for once the reality was an improvement upon the expectation. Naturally, the initial period of postwar reconstruction was bound to generate exceptionally high levels of demand in the short term. But the maintenance of demand in the longer term would obviously need the government to play a more active role via demand management, which would have the characteristics established in the Keynesian model, namely short-term, counter-cyclical fiscal policy. Monetary policy would also need to be short-term and counter-cyclical, but would have little to do bar keeping down the interest rate in order to cheapen the cost of borrowing for investment.

But the Keynesian revolution was not simply an issue of macroeconomic objectives and instruments. It was an era in which voters turned away from markets, which were perceived as **efficient** but **inequitable**, in order to create a fairer and more just society. Although Churchill, who had led the wartime government, was a Conservative, and what in modern parlance would be called a 'wet', there was nevertheless a massive swing towards the Labour Party, which had almost completely displaced the Liberals. The era of the Welfare State had arrived.

Efficiency versus equity

The postwar years have been characterised by contradictions within the processes of macroeconomic control, but one must not lose sight of the underlying debate about the role of market mechanisms. The Keynesian model effectively discarded the view that a modern advanced economy could be left to its own devices, and ushered in the era of the 'mixed economy'. But there are clearly an enormous variety of ways in which one can draw the boundaries between private and public sectors, and a great deal therefore hinges upon the balance between efficiency and equity at the microeconomic level. At the end of the day there are very few goods and services which cannot be supplied efficiently by the market mechanism – in the sense of maximising output for given inputs – but the amounts of goods and services produced, and their allocation between households, may be considered inequitable from a wider social perspective. One may naturally respond by arguing that concentration upon the issue of equity does not of itself necessitate any conflict with the objective of maximum efficiency, and indeed it is clear that the introduction of the Welfare State presupposed that no serious conflict would occur. But efficiency in the market is dependent upon the profit motive, and the profit motive has to be subjugated to the wider 'public interest' if equity issues are to be given greater priority.

This line of argument can best be clarified by a concrete example. Before the Second World War the health service largely required payment to be made at the point of consumption. Its size, therefore, depended upon people's willingness and ability to pay, but insofar as there was a demand for the service it could be provided very efficiently. The National Health Service (NHS) was introduced because this level of provision was felt to be both inadequate and inequitable, but equity — or so it was thought — could be maximised only by providing health care free at the point of consumption. Theoretically, there was no reason why this expanded provision could not be delivered as efficiently as before, but logically this would be true only if the motivation towards efficiency was generated as strongly by the pursuit of the public interest as by the pursuit of profit. At the time this was taken for granted, because it was felt that there was a consensus within society that the public interest should transcend private interests. In setting up the NHS, in expanding education and welfare services and in taking industries into public ownership, very little thought was thus given to the issue of objectives, and how best to achieve them.

In retrospect this was, at best, unfortunate, but it reflected the widely held view at the time that a transfer of ownership from private to public sector would be sufficient to guarantee an improvement in performance. For example, there was bound to be a better relationship between managers and workers in an industry once it had been transferred to public ownership, since the owners would no longer be seeking to squeeze every drop of profit out of the workers. There would be no more General Strikes, no more trouble in the coal industry, the long-term future of which would now be assured. Regrettably, hardly anyone observed that the coal-miners themselves had no greater personal stake in the industry post-nationalisation than they

had had previously. Indeed, if anything, they had even less of a stake since wages and jobs were no longer directly related to the profitability of the industry. It would thus be in their personal interests to try to raise their wages even if it resulted in the industry making losses. They might well prefer not to take this action because, for example, there was a government in power which had their wholehearted support. But if another, less appealing, government took power, or if the economic environment became so problematic that any government would be forced to try to control wages, then confrontation would almost inevitably occur. In such a situation it would be vital for someone to re-establish control, whether management or ultimately government. Yet to **re**-establish control there needed to be an **effective** system of control established in the first place, which even a cursory glance at the statutes governing the nationalised industries or the NHS demonstrates not to have been the case.

A further aspect of the 'efficiency versus equity' debate to which insufficient attention is paid relates to the distributions of income and wealth, and their implications for tax regimes. So far we have discussed the Keynesian orthodoxy largely from the expenditure side, but if public spending is to rise appreciably then it will be necessary to raise taxes, in which case one needs to stress the issue of **whom or what to tax**, and how onerously the individual taxes are to be applied. Once one starts out with the premise that a greater degree of equity is needed, it follows logically that the primary purpose of taxation, other than simply to finance expenditure, is to **redistribute**. That requires a strong element of progressivity to be present, most obviously in the income tax and inheritance tax schedules. But this in turn has implications for efficiency, since it affects the incentives to work and to take risks.

One further point is worth emphasising at this stage, before we return to the historical narrative. No matter what macroeconomic control system is adopted, it must send out both explicit and implicit signals at a microeconomic level. In a market system the signals are primarily in the form of **changing prices**, and this will remain true of many goods and services which are publicly provided, even though the prices in question are not market prices. The **absence** of a price – as in the provision of health care – sends out an equally strong signal. When one compares different societies with roughly equal wealth, one should **expect** to find different consumption patterns. This is because in one society a good may be taxed or subsidised where in the other society it is not. If, for example, mortgages and pension contributions are subject to tax relief, one should hardly be surprised to discover that the most popular forms of wealth are houses and pensions.

To summarise this part of the argument, what we are saying is that the macroeconomic model, whether Keynesian or otherwise, requires one to look deeply into its microeconomic implications, and this is why in later chapters we will be looking at tax regimes, industrial policy, welfare provision and other related matters.

Employment, trade and inflation

As we have indicated above, the primary focus of the Keynesian model was upon the level of unemployment. However, it follows logically that if there is insufficient demand for private sector goods and services, and a consequent falling off in the level of employment, then the new jobs created by public spending in order to maintain full employment will largely be in the public sector – that is, in central government, local government and the nationalised industries. And if the prevailing orthodoxy holds that any shortcomings in the operations of private sector bodies need to be remedied by government in order to promote the cause of **social justice** (and sometimes **efficiency**), then the mix of the mixed economy is logically going to become weighted increasingly towards the public sector and away from the private sector. But the Keynesian model does not of itself imply any such outcome, since public expenditure is meant to come to the fore only during recessions. When the economy is booming it may even be necessary for the public sector to cut back in order to dampen down excess demand in the private sector.

So why did the upsurge in public spending happen in every major European economy? One obvious reason is that elected politicians see themselves as elected to change things for the better, and this is bound to cost money. Furthermore, a consensus about the desirability of improving equity and welfare is incompatible with sharp cuts in public spending, since no element of such spending can be cut without causing someone somewhere a great deal of anguish. Yet if the government cannot bring itself to make cuts, the political opposition has little choice but to differentiate its product by promising to spend even more, and to resist any cuts which are on the agenda.

This argument has particular implications for employment policy. In principle, the objective of giving everyone a job can be fulfilled independently of locational issues. In other words, if an industry shuts down in the North and another simultaneously expands in the South, full employment can be maintained by moving the redundant workers to the new location. However, this inevitably means both short-term hardship for those required to move, and probably long-term decline in the areas where firms shut down. In countries such as West Germany these consequences did not trouble politicians overmuch, but in the UK they were considered to be unacceptable, and steps were taken, even by Conservative governments ostensibly dedicated to free market principles, to prevent them – through, for example, the rescue of lame duck industries.

The according of primacy to the objective of full employment also created other kinds of difficulty. The maintenance of high levels of demand in order to sustain full employment had implications for other important policy objectives, in particular for inflation and for the external trading position as reflected in the balance of payments. The existence of inflation and of deficits in the balance of payments needed to be examined from the point of view both of cause and of cure. Unfortunately, the Keynesian model had nothing useful to say about inflation because it had been formulated during an historical period when prices were tending to fall rather than to rise, and there seemed to be no obvious reason in theory why the demand for labour could not be expanded to absorb the available supply without bidding up its price.

Nevertheless, inflation did exist throughout the 1950s and 1960s, albeit at a fairly modest level, so in many ways the simplest thing to do was to ignore it and to hope it would go away. Every now and again prices would rise unusually sharply, and something would need to be done about it, but on the whole there were more important things to worry about. In particular, high levels of demand tended to be associated with high levels of imports, the more so as the UK became increasingly unable to compete internationally with respect to her manufactured goods. Now a balance of payments deficit can be dealt with in a number of different ways:

1. the **domestic economy can be deflated** (expenditure reducing) so that there is less demand to spill over into imports
2. the **price of imports can be raised**, and that of exports lowered, via an alteration in the exchange rate (expenditure switching)
3. **artificial restraints on trade** can be introduced, such as tariffs and quotas on imports or subsidies to exports.

In the event the remedy mentioned in 3 was available on only a short-term emergency basis, because the UK was a member of GATT (General Agreement on Tariffs and Trade) which required free trade to be pursued whenever possible. Solution 2 was available within the terms and conditions of the adjustable-peg exchange rate regime introduced near the end of the Second World War (1944) at Bretton Woods. Unfortunately, it was considered to be a sign of failure for a country to lower its exchange rate, and so it was a policy to be avoided except as a last resort for fear that the government so doing would lose votes. But this left only solution 1, although its implementation meant that the level of aggregate demand would have to be cut back, thereby adversely affecting output and employment.

Given the higher priority assigned to full employment than to the external balance this could obviously be tolerated only for the minimum period compatible with restoring the balance of payments into better shape, whereupon demand would need to be expanded again in order to restore full employment. However, since this procedure had done nothing to deal with the underlying causes of the problem – namely an uncompetitive economy – but only with its symptoms in the form of a balance of payments deficit, the symptoms were obviously going to recur once the economy was back at full employment again. A succession of periods of demand expansion to create jobs, followed by demand reduction to control imports, thus became the dominant characteristic, known as **stop-go**, of UK economic policy during the 1950s and 1960s.

Fiscal versus monetary policy

As we have indicated, the level of aggregate demand was largely manipulated via **fiscal means**, and monetary policy had relatively little to do. However, its assigned role – namely, low interest rates to foster investment – was somewhat incompatible with a world in which inflation was a persistent phenomenon, since rising prices implied the need to **raise** interest rates to deter consumption financed by credit.

In the USA during the late 1950s, Professor Milton Friedman at Chicago University and others began publishing material which indicated that the money supply was the all-important monetary aggregate on which the authorities would have to concentrate their attention if they wished to have any meaningful control over economic activity. Friedman argued, in particular, that the role of monetary policy during the Great Depression had been widely misunderstood. The orthodox version of events held that the US monetary authorities had pursued aggressively expansionary monetary policies between 1929 and 1933, but that these policies had proved ineffectual. Friedman, on the other hand, contended that the monetary authorities had pursued highly **deflationary** policies. According to his research, the quantity of money in the United States fell by one-third during the course of the Depression, thereby providing clear evidence that monetary policy was extremely effective in regulating the level of economic activity rather than the reverse.

At the heart of Friedman's work lay the **New Quantity Theory** which represented a modernised version of the neo-classical model, linking the money supply to **money national income** (the volume of (real) output at current prices). In his model, most commonly known as **Monetarism**, real output resulted from decisions taken primarily by households and firms in the private sector, and could not be adjusted by demand management. Since real magnitudes were ultimately unaffected by the supply of money, the latter was directly linked only to the rate of inflation, and became its primary cause. However, the fact was that, in trying to elevate inflation to become the primary focus of economic policy, Friedman's time had not yet arrived, particularly where the UK was concerned, although his ideas caught on more quickly elsewhere. Just as the Keynesian revolution had to wait for the neo-classical orthodoxy to break down in the face of mass unemployment, so the monetarist revolution had to wait upon a breakdown of the Keynesian orthodoxy. But for the moment at least, the Keynesian facade seemed impregnable. Quite simply, in an atmosphere of 'you've never had it so good', one does not seriously question the view that the prevailing orthodoxy has helped to bring this about. True, the UK economy had grown slowly by comparison with most other comparable countries, but growth was rapid by comparison with previous periods in the UK. True, there were periodic balance of payments crises which deflected the economy off course, and inflation was also ever-present. But jobs were freely available for those who wanted to work, and most people's standard of living was rising steadily. It was not a time for revolution, even in ideas.

The issue of inflation remained largely ignored, both in academic and political circles. This passive view of the problem was reinforced when, in 1957, A. W. Phillips published an article discussing what henceforth became universally known as the **Phillips Curve**. The Phillips Curve suggested that inflation need not be considered as an independent problem, but its real importance lay in the fact that up until that point in time the Keynesian model contained no theory of inflation. Given that inflation was treated with rather more indifference than it merited, this missing link did not prevent the model operating to most people's satisfaction. Nevertheless, the apparent message of the Phillips

Curve that there was a predictable trade-off between employment and inflation (thereby offering, in effect, a 'menu' of choices between combinations of employment and inflation) appeared considerably to simplify economic policy. The government simply had to choose the particular **level of aggregate demand** which would generate the **target level of employment**, and a predetermined amount of inflation would simultaneously be generated. The price level could, therefore, be regulated to a lowly place in the pecking order of economic objectives, since in choosing the target value for the primary objective one could not be thrown off course by an unforseen rate of inflation as one could by the balance of payments.

Unfortunately, at the end of the 1960s the situation began to deteriorate alarmingly. The rate of inflation began to rise sharply, and to register a value well above what had been predicted on the basis of the Phillips Curve. At first the authorities understandably treated this as an aberration, arguing that the original relationship between unemployment and inflation would shortly be restored. But when unemployment was allowed to rise slightly to help rein back inflation, it had precisely the opposite effect, and a new phenomenon appeared known as **stagflation** — namely, rising prices at the same time as rising unemployment. This phenomenon clearly needed to be explained within the context of the Keynesian model, but the model was found wanting. After 25 years its Achilles heel had been exposed.

Rather ironically, it was precisely at this point in time, at the beginning of the 1970s, that the exchange rate mechanisms introduced at Bretton Woods began to break down, to the point at which the UK felt obliged, in 1972, to move over to a floating rate (albeit a 'managed' one). This meant that balance of payments crises could now be dealt with via the exchange rate rather than via deflation (given the political will to accept currency depreciation), and thus allowed more freedom for demand to be managed in order to maintain full employment. But raising demand at a time when inflation was roaring ahead was not really a sensible option, and the quadrupling of oil prices by OPEC helped send the inflation rate soaring to 24 per cent in 1975, as well as causing significant damage to the balance of payments. The Labour government in power at the time was unable to cope with these pressures, particularly as the foreign currency reserves were inadequate for the purpose, and turned for help to the International Monetary Fund (IMF), a body which was sympathetic to the monetarist doctrines now coming into vogue. The price exacted in return for assistance was that the UK economy would have to be subjected to a dose of monetarism, with tight control over the money supply and a tight fiscal policy keeping demand in check.

It was rather ironic that a Labour government should be the first to apply monetarist doctrines, since its underlying philosophy was hardly right-wing. Nevertheless, it was as much imposition as choice at the time (or at least that was how the government excused its behaviour) and an inevitble effect was what, from the government's point of view, was a highly undesirable further upturn in unemployment. Indeed, the attempt to impose fiscal discipline, and to control inflation via a prices and incomes policy, ultimately led to the 'winter of discontent' and to the government's downfall. It was replaced in 1979 by the first Thatcher government, which for the first time deliberately chose to make a version of monetarism the key plank of UK economic policy.

The brief reign of monetarism

As previously indicated, the Keynesian orthodoxy collapsed in the face of a persistent rate of inflation well above the rate predicted by the Phillips Curve, and into the vacuum created by the failure of the model stepped the monetarist 'revolution'. It is important to remember that monetarism was a reworking of the neo-classical model rather than a totally new approach, and that it was not 'invented' after 1970. As with the Keynesian model, it had been advocated for many years prior to that, but few people were altogether persuaded by it. In particular, it must be borne in mind that its underlying philosophy placed particular emphasis upon **markets**, and played down very heavily the role of government as prime mover in the economy.

It would be fair to argue that the Conservative government under Edward Heath was sympathetic to the doctrine of the free market, but at the end of the day it did not have the conviction to let markets have their head. Indeed, it is an interesting aspect of the Heath government that it took Rolls Royce and British Leyland **into** public ownership rather than let them be destroyed by the forces of the market, thereby demonstrating that expediency was often a stronger factor than polemic in political manifestos. The Thatcher government was different in that it set out determinedly to apply monetarism as a philosophy, relying heavily upon the evidence that the lax monetary policy introduced during the Heath government's term of office had been responsible for the inflationary boom of the early 1970s. However, what the Thatcher government did not at first realise was just how difficult this was going to be. Because monetarism is about markets, it is clearly much more than simply a statement about the money supply and the macroeconomy, and in that respect it becomes difficult to form a judgement as to its success or failure, since some parts of the philosophy may work quite well whilst others may need to be discarded as unworkable. Whether what remains at the end of this process is still monetarism is, therefore, highly debatable, and we need to shed some light on this issue below.

Viewed in terms of macroeconomic policy monetarism is fairly straightforward. It contends that the price level is the most important economic objective because real variables such as employment can best be stimulated in the context of a non-inflationary environment. However, whilst zero (or near-zero) rates of inflation assist in the generation of employment through their positive impact upon the prospects of the private sector, demand management is either self-defeating (because of crowding out) or a recipe for accelerating inflation. The only way to control the price level is via the money supply. Hence it follows that the growth of the money supply should be geared to the expected growth rate of real output, which thereby makes it possible to buy any extra output at the **existing** level of prices. The balance of payments can be left to its own devices by allowing the exchange rate to float freely, thereby ensuring a tendency for it to self-equilibrate.

However, certain points flow obviously from the above. First, governments must resist the temptation to create money by **spending more than they earn** (running a PSBR), so fiscal policy must be viewed from the point of view of its consequences for the money supply rather than as a set of instruments to be managed in their own right. Fiscal policy becomes **subordinate** to money supply control, thereby reversing the logic of the Keynesian model. Fiscal conservatism means balancing government spending against taxation. But markets are much better at determining what people want to consume than the bureaucrats in local and central government, so public spending must be kept under tight control. This in turn will permit taxes to be cut, which will leave more of their incomes in people's pockets and provide the incentive for them to work harder, thereby generating economic growth. This growth will eventually provide new jobs in areas of the economy where there is genuine private demand, represented by direct spending by consumers, rather than an artificial demand generated by government spending designed, for example, to keep technologically backward and internationally uncompetitive industries in business.

This approach is generally known as 'supply-side economics' because it rests upon the assumption that **supply must be created before demand** if there is to be non-inflationary growth within the economy (see Chapter 1 for a fuller discussion of these matters). At the microeconomic level, the philosophy has far-reaching effects. Individual households and firms must be made to stand on their own feet, to succeed or fail as the market for what they provide dictates. Those who fail may need to be helped by the government within reason, but not to the point at which failure seems to be a soft option. In particular, the loss of a job is dependent upon the forces of the market. Jobs may need to be preserved by workers taking wage cuts, workers may need to retrain or they may need to move to where the work is (possibly on their bicycles). If institutions such as trade unions are less than keen about these developments then their power to prevent them must be destroyed, and

that applies to professional bodies as well as to craft unions.

Not surprisingly these doctrines seem firmly rooted in the neo-classical orthodoxy where the individual is responsible for his or her own predicament, and it is not the job of government to get him or her out of it. In other words, the postwar swing from efficiency to equity must be put into reverse gear. Efficiency is once again to be king, and those who are productive will be allowed to enjoy the fruits of their labour. To be rich is no longer socially unacceptable; to be poor is unnecessary, so poverty must be pushed back into decent obscurity.

The Thatcher years

As will be discussed below, as well as in the body of the text, the Thatcher years in office have been — and increasingly are — open to a variety of interpretations. On the one hand, there has been a renewed debate about the theoretical underpinnings of both the Keynesian and monetarist models, and on the other there has been an increasingly bitter debate about the picture presented by the statistical data generated both by the government and by other sources.

We have already referred to the debate between demand-siders and supply-siders, but there has also been a reinterpretation of the Keynesian model in order to make it more compatible with the observed phenomena of the 1970s and 1980s. The adherents of this approach are usually known as new, neo- or radical Keynesians. In addition, there has arisen a school of thought known as 'New Classical Economics', which has much in common with monetarism but which differs with respect to, for example, the role of expectations. It is also probably fair to say that many economists take an eclectic view of the proceedings, accepting parts but not all of any one viewpoint. Under the circumstances it is hardly surprising that the government receives conflicting advice, and that it is never exactly clear which model — if any! — of the economy it is trying to implement. At various stages in the main text these models will be introduced and analysed briefly, although it is not the primary purpose of an applied text such as this to analyse these models in detail. Accepting for the moment that economic policy may, therefore, be driven as often by short-term expediency as by the logic of a specific model, it is nevertheless desirable to provide a summary of recent experience in the light of the apparent switch to a monetarist orthodoxy in the early 1980s. One unchanging point of reference, explored fully in Chapter 9, has been the priority accorded to the **control of inflation**. In the early Thatcher years this was seen as the task assigned to the money supply, but that has now altered insofar as control of the money supply is widely (but not universally) seen as a failure. Indeed, the government itself declared, in June 1989, that it no longer intended even to compile the money supply measure favoured during the early 1980s called M_3. For some time now the government has relied upon the **interest rate** as its primary means of regulating demand, a policy which has brought many attendant problems in its wake and which may or may not prove to be successful. In this latter respect it is important to note that there is no unanimity about the meaning of the term 'success'. For example, it is possible to argue simultaneously that the UK's growth record is good because it has been positive and high by international standards for many years, and that it is bad because the level of output only recently rose above the level achieved at the time the government first took office. Equally, the inflation rate did fall to well below 5 per cent at one stage, the soaring money supply notwithstanding, but it never showed any sign of getting down to below 1 per cent, remained above that of many of the UK's main competitors and has recently begun to rise quite sharply.

The government has certainly achieved its aim of fiscal conservatism, turning its borrowing requirement into a debt repayment. However, there remains a body of opinion which believes that such behaviour is wholly inappropriate (see the discussion concerning the repayment of debt in Chapter 9), and it is significant to note that this has not resulted from the intended reduction in government spending combined with a reduction in taxation. Rather, in absolute terms, even after allowing for inflation, government spending has risen with tax revenue rising even faster due to the phenomenon known as **fiscal drag** (all of which matters are discussed in detail in Chapter 3).

The **exchange rate** has also been a matter of some ambiguity. The one certainty is that it has never been permitted to float freely as it should in a basic monetarist model – which permits the advocates of such a model to contend that it has never been properly tested – but there has been an increasingly acrimonious debate about whether the UK should join the European Monetary System (EMS) (see Chapter 5) and also about what kind of exchange rate policy – if any – the UK has been using over the past few years. Here again, therefore, it is difficult to know how to measure 'success' or 'failure'.

At the microeconomic level there has been a real attempt to deregulate or free up markets – indeed the UK is generally acknowledged to be the world leaders in this respect, although Americans might remark that it would have been better not to have created so many areas which needed deregulating in the first place. Unfortunately, it is also the case that some of the worst rigidities (such as are manifested in the housing market) have not been addressed at all successfully, and perhaps more importantly that the overriding impression given by the government has been its interventionist and centralising stance in a wide variety of markets. At heart this reflects one of the most awkward realities of economic life – namely, the fact that since free markets are subject to abuse, the more free the markets the more they need to be regulated. This issue is addressed at various points in the text, for example with respect to financial markets in Chapter 2, and particularly in Chapter 8.

At the macroeconomic level, as already indicated, the government has come to suffer from a shortage of instruments to control the economy, and hence it has come to overuse – and arguably abuse – those that are favoured. Here again it is much easier to explain where the government has gone wrong than to provide a convincing alternative approach.

As has been noted above, the Keynesian model broke down in the face of exceptionally high levels of inflation. It can just as easily be argued, however, that the most telling indictment of monetarism has been its failure to reduce unemployment to acceptable levels, although even here, as demonstrated in Chapter 6, the acceptability (or otherwise) of the current level of unemployment is subject to heated debate. The fact that during the Keynesian orthodoxy governments chose to live with permanently rising prices, and that during the monetarist orthodoxy they chose to live with heavy unemployment, may be put down to the forces of democracy − at the end of the day the electorate must vote for one particular party − but even democracy can be made to mean all things to all men, and it is possible to argue that votes are not so much cast in favour of policy packages as against the alternatives which are viewed as wholly unacceptable. Some reflections on political processes are contained in the section which follows, and also in Chapter 8. For the moment it is necessary only to reflect that the movement away from any kind of established orthodoxy and towards what may best be termed pragmatism may be the only way forward. As will constantly be reiterated in the course of the text, the world's economies are evolving very rapidly, and the model of last year's behaviour may provide a poor guide to the current year, let alone to the future. In the UK, the Keynesian orthodoxy lasted for three decades whilst the monetarist experiment lasted for well under one decade. For the moment revolution is unfashionable and evolution is the name of the game. How long will it be, one wonders, before another orthodoxy comes to the fore?

The political context

It is a reasonable expectation of a so-called 'democracy' that its citizens will constantly consider it to be their right − and possibly their duty − to exhort the government to adopt this or that economic strategy. However, what they often fail to appreciate is that in order to deliver economic policies one must first create a **political system** with that end in mind, and since there are many ways of devising such a system, its precise form is ultimately of great consequence. One simple point to make in this context is to ask whether the 'Thatcherite revolution' would have occurred in any of

the other seven major industrial countries had it not occurred in the UK − to which the answer must be a firm negative because it was critically dependent upon the political context of the UK. When, in the course of time, Mrs Thatcher's full term in office is retrospectively compared with that, for example, of President Reagan, there can be no doubt as to which of them will be judged to have had a more revolutionary impact upon their respective economies. However, as we shall argue below, the odds were stacked in her favour before she began.

A crucial − though by no means unique − feature of the UK political system is that it involves a race to be 'first past the post' between a very small number of very strong contenders and a number of 'also-rans'. Each constituency race produces a single Member of Parliament who may well fail to be supported by a majority of those casting their vote, let alone of those eligible to vote. However, the fact that the majority of voters do not actively support the government's policies is not of itself the issue, but rather that this system permits of a government being formed by a political party with more MPs than any other party, irrespective of whether it has been supported by the largest aggregate number of voters, and that once a government has been formed the level of electoral support is technically a non-issue until the electoral term is over.

On occasion, the combination of a strong opposition party and the also-rans may muster enough MPs to outvote the largest party, but again the key issue is that this generally is not the case in practice, and that even when it is, the opposition parties are generally less than fully united in their political goals. The style of political debate is also inevitably highly adversarial, but this should again not be allowed to conceal the key point that when the fire and fury has died down, and the vote is taken, a government with an **absolute majority of MPs is always the official winner**.

Clearly, this system delivers extraordinary powers to a majority government. Constitutionally, the monarchy has no power of veto, nor does the House of Lords (the upper chamber) which can only debate and recommend. A simple majority of one seat in the House of Commons is thus sufficient (provided, of course, every MP is available to vote) to permit the government to steamroller through any legislation that it wishes, irrespective of whether or not it was mentioned in the campaign manifesto issued to voters. It is true that individual MPs can refuse to vote in accord with their party line, but the rules disallowing the use of private monies to 'buy votes' effectively mean that an MP who rejects a 'three-line whip' will lose the support of the party machine and later, if not sooner, lose his seat. It follows that, especially when a party has a small overall majority, MPs toe the line almost without fail rather than bring down their own government. As a consequence, backbench MPs have little effective power over economic policy, whilst a small section amongst them, appointed to the Cabinet, have a great deal. Furthermore, a Prime Minister, elected from within the ranks of MPs and hence inseparable from the party in power, can exercise exceptional power by using the threat of dismissal from the Cabinet to force recalcitrant members to do what he or she wishes.

This ability to steamroller policy through Parliament is both a virtue and a vice. It obviously permits of very strong government, and there can be no doubt that voters prefer a government with a clear sense of purpose, and a determination to put it into practice, to one which is constantly vulnerable to losing on a vote of confidence. But such power can easily be abused, and it follows that other parties can appeal successfully to voters only by differentiating their policies to a considerable degree from those of the government. Irrespective of how it intends to behave in practice, a party must in principle appear to be either right-wing or left-wing, so voters have no opportunity to opt for a package containing combinations of the two. Thus if the party in power advocates public ownership, opposition parties may feel obliged to advocate denationalisation, and vice versa.

Other political systems

We will return subsequently to comment upon the performance of government in the UK, but first it is salutary to compare the above analysis to political systems elsewhere. In the USA, which has a two main party, first-past-the-post system, the President is not, however, the leader of the party in power in the House of Representatives (often called 'the House'), but elected independently, and may well belong to the other party. If the House is unsympathetic he may, therefore, find it very difficult to get his Bills enacted. He, in his turn, has considerable power to veto Bills emanating from the House, so one rebuff may well be repaid in kind. The upper chamber (the Senate) is a powerful body in its own right, and may well be controlled by the opposite party to the House. A President, House and Senate (which together constitute the Congress) belonging to the same party is possible, but unlikely. In any event, because election is as much a function of the wealth and prestige of the individual as of the party machine, individual Congressmen and Senators quite frequently vote against their own party line. All this prevents the accumulation of too much power in too few hands, as was precisely the original intention, but it is not exactly designed to deliver priorities, such as cuts in government spending, since every politician, irrespective of party, in an area adversely affected by such cuts will automatically vote against the strategy.

In continental Europe there is **proportional representation** (seats allocated in proportion to votes cast). This effectively prevents any one party from getting an absolute majority over all others, which on the face of it should lead to weak government. On the other hand, it follows that, as a general rule, a coalition must reach agreement on priorities which are common to all parties if it wishes to avoid government by crisis, and the important policies may, therefore, get carried out with all-party support even when there is fundamental disagreement about other matters. The obvious drawback is that these shared priorities invariably sit somewhere near the political centre, and if voters are unhappy about that they can express their disapproval only by voting for someone or something on the extreme of the political spectrum (fascist or communist).

Judging by results

If, on the other hand, the UK government thinks the electorate want privatisation, then it can be delivered by the system. The problem is that the government can also deliver privatisation whether the electorate want it or not. It follows that the only way to judge political systems, and interpretations of democracy, is by results. Which economies work well and which do not? During the 1960s and 1970s the UK performed badly whilst Germany, for example, performed very well, so coalitions come out on top. However, the situation has reversed itself somewhat during the 1980s, with the UK providing a political lead which other countries wish they could follow. Altogether, then, case not proven either way is the only sensible verdict.

One further comment of some importance is that adversarial politics in the UK are not as 'adversarial' as one might imagine. As we have indicated, each party must differentiate its product in principle, but what happens in practice may be a totally different matter. When one examines the economic records dating back to the Second World War, it is very difficult to pinpoint the years in which there was a change in the party in power. This arises for a number of reasons. In the first place, many priorities are shared. Until recently, there was little dispute about the need to keep down unemployment to its lowest possible level. The Welfare State was not imposed against the wishes of any major party, nor is the current view that the public sector has failed to deliver the exclusive preserve of 'dry' Tories. There may be disagreement about causes and cures, but that is bound to be true even within the ranks of a coalition government. In the second place, governments are by no means all-powerful, and may be forced to take involuntary actions. This may arise simply because the UK is not a particularly big player on the world stage, and cannot, therefore, be insulated from the forces which buffet the world economy. No matter how healthy the underlying economy, the UK cannot expect to grow much – if at all – at a time when other advanced economies are sliding into recession. More generally, the government may find itself in a losing battle with the forces of the market place. The government may, for example, wish to see the exchange rate rise, but if the foreign exchange market wishes to see the exchange rate fall that may well prove to be the ultimate outcome.

To sum up this brief discussion, the overall picture with respect to the UK is that it has a political system with enormous potential power to direct economic policy. The system could result in enormous swings in the direction of policy as each successive government seeks to undo what its predecessor has done, but this is unlikely to happen because many priorities are shared, and the external environment may not permit it. It should finally be remembered that for a government to spend its time in office removing its predecessor's legislation from the statute book is not merely very unconstructive, but may leave little time to enact new policies. In any event, many policies which the political system requires the opposition party to oppose may privately be approved of. Thus, for example, the Labour Party currently have no desire whatsoever to undo all the trade union legislation put in place by the Conservatives, although they do intend to undo some of it on a very selective basis. It is equally true that some desirable policies are simply too expensive to implement. For example, no future government could possibly afford to repurchase the shares of privatised companies even if, as is unlikely, they were prepared to devote scarce parliamentary time to that end.

1

The Macroeconomy

Bob Sedgwick

Introduction   *Peter Curwen*

In the course of this book we will be examining a great many facets of the aggregate economy. Certain of these require detailed consideration, and hence have an entire chapter given over to their analysis. A number, however, require less detailed treatment, and it is our main purpose in Chapter 1 to bring them together at an early stage in our overall discussion. Whilst this necessarily means that Chapter 1 is less cohesive than those that

follow, it is important to see its component parts as part of a 'macroeconomic jigsaw puzzle', which cannot fully be appreciated until every piece is put into its alloted place.

Some idea of the nature of this jigsaw puzzle can be obtained by reference to a schematic representation of the UK economy such as that depicted in **Figure 1.1**. Despite its apparent complexity, it is intended to be a highly simplified version of the reality. The so-called 'Treasury' model of the economy, used by the majority of groups which

Figure 1.1 A schematic representation of the UK economy

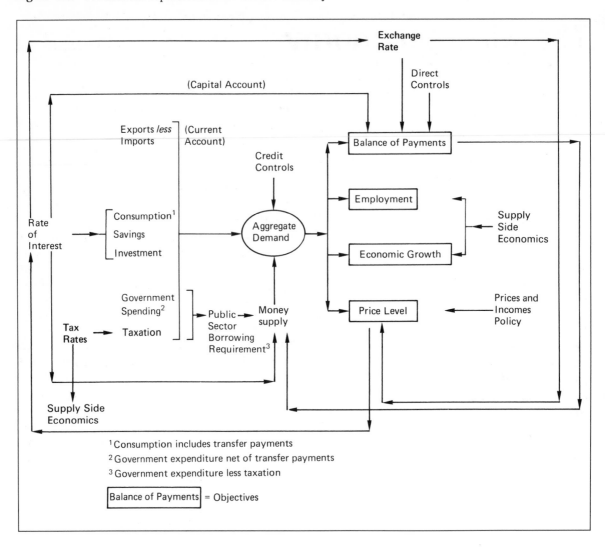

¹ Consumption includes transfer payments
² Government expenditure net of transfer payments
³ Government expenditure less taxation

Balance of Payments = Objectives

seek to forecast the future behaviour of the UK economy, contains several hundred equations. However, its recent record in forecasting such variables as the level of employment and the rate of inflation has been less than inspiring of confidence, so our simplified model may not necessarily be improved by the addition of further variables. One obvious reason for this is that the behaviour of economic agents such as households and firms is constantly evolving, whilst the only known data must be derived from behaviour in past periods.

Policy objectives

At the heart of our model lie the main **objectives** of economic policy – the balance of payments; employment; economic growth; and the price level. It is for the government of the day to decide both the rank ordering of priorities – **which** objective is most important, which least – and to determine the **desired value** for each objective. It is to be noted that we do not seek at this juncture to specify what these might be. Whilst introductory textbooks often tend to talk in terms of 'full' employment we do not do so here since for many years past there has been no consensus about what the term 'full' means.

One further reservation is in order. It is evident that there is a consensus about the desirability of maintaining 'high' levels of employment in the UK, as indeed there is about maintaining a low rate of inflation. There is, however, always some element of ambiguity even in the assertion that it is a 'good' thing for the UK economy to attain these objectives. A reduction in the price of raw material imports, for example, represents 'good' news for a manufacturing nation such as the UK since it helps to hold down inflation. It must, however, be extremely damaging to a less-developed country exporting the materials. Such a country may subsequently be unable to repay its international debts which may partly be owed to the UK government and partly to UK banks. Once a debt default becomes a real possibility, it obviously gives one cause to wonder whether the original price reduction was, after all, such a good thing for the UK.

As shown in **Figure 1.1**, the most direct route to the policy objectives passes through the circle labelled aggregate demand (*AD*). Clearly, aggregate demand can be moved in only one direction at any one time, but this immediately begs the question as to whether all four specified objectives will be improved or made worse simultaneously. As we will discover, this is not the case in practice. Thus, for example, an increase in *AD* can be expected to increase the level of employment, but only at the expense of rising prices and a weakening of the balance of payments. Part of our task below is, therefore, to identify these **trade-offs in policy objectives**, and to form a view as to their likely significance. However, it is evident that, if one objective can be satisfied only at the expense of another if a single pathway is followed through the model, this drawback can be largely avoided where the latter objective can be improved by following a route which does not pass through the *AD* circle. Thus, as shown in **Figure 1.1**, it is possible, at least in theory, to hold down prices during a period of buoyant demand through the use of a prices and incomes policy. Equally, the balance of payments can be improved either through manipulation of the exchange rate or by the use of direct controls. Where, on the other hand, *AD* is being held down with a view to controlling inflation, the reduction in employment which would otherwise have been expected to transpire can be offset by so-called 'supply-side' policies.

Whether these independent pathways to specified objectives actually work in practice is a matter of some dispute, as we will discover below. However, irrespective of whether they are workable or not, it is clear from **Figure 1.1** that there is more than one way to pass through the *AD* circle. One pathway joins *AD* to a set of variables labelled exports *less* imports $(X - M)$; consumption (*C*); savings (*S*); investment (*I*); government spending (*G*); and taxation (*T*). These variables constitute the building blocks of the Keynesian model. However, an alternative route is via the money supply (also somewhat confusingly labelled (*M*)) and constitutes the key pathway of the monetarist model. It may immediately be noted that (*G*) and (*T*) are directly linked into the money supply via the public sector borrowing requirement (PSBR), emphasising the point that the PSBR is simultaneously a component of both **fiscal** and **monetary** policy.

It is important to note that all the variables such as taxation and the money supply are simply absolute magnitudes. Their size is predetermined in the model by prior decisions about the desired value for employment, the price level and other objectives. However, at any point in time the value of, for example, (*T*) or (*G*) may be incompatible with those objectives, and it becomes necessary to change something in order to change the value of (*T*). This something is called a policy **instrument**. In the case of (*T*) a suitable instrument might be a change in the rate at which a tax is applied, or in a tax threshold. In the case of the money supply a change in the rate of interest may be required as part of the process by which an open market operation is used to transfer cash or liquidity between the Bank of England and the non-bank private sector (see **pp. 82–3**).

Policy instruments

Policy instruments appear at the other end of our model from policy objectives. What lies in between can be called **intermediate targets**. It is evident from our simplified model that an instrument can normally be expected to affect more than one intermediate target, and for most intermediate targets to affect more than one further intermediate target or objective. In every case, for the model to be useful as a predictor of the future behaviour of the economy, the form of all of these relationships needs to be known as precisely as possible. If the standard rate of income tax is lowered by 1 per cent, for example, by how much will total tax receipts rise or fall? In this particular case the answer is indeed known with some accuracy, because the Inland Revenue keeps detailed records on all taxpayers. However, if the rate of interest were to be raised or lowered by 1 per cent, the effect upon savings and investment would be far less predictable.

Furthermore, instruments do not have an immediate impact upon intermediate targets. When the rate of interest is altered, households and firms are unlikely to change their behaviour until some (possibly considerable) time has elapsed. Once a household has decided, for example, to buy a settee, it is unlikely to forgo that purchase on account of a marginal increase in the interest rate, although this may reasonably be expected to affect future decisions about other consumption items.

So far, we have said very little about the external sector. At any point in time UK residents will be buying goods and services emanating from abroad, whilst foreign residents will be buying UK goods and services. In a simple sense it is immaterial whether a UK good is bought by a UK or foreign resident since the effect upon aggregate demand is identical. However, the obvious complexity introduced by foreign trade is that more than one currency has to be involved and a **currency exchange** must occur. The **rate of exchange** is, therefore, a critical variable in the model since it can be manipulated in order to alter the relative price of UK and foreign goods and services. This inevitably affects more than one objective, as shown in **Figure 1.1**, but this is by no

means the entire story. In the first place, the exchange rate is itself closely linked to the interest rate. Secondly, when the flow of currency moving between two countries to settle trade debts is affected by the exchange rate, this does not merely affect the balance of payments but also the supply of sterling in the UK. But the money supply is itself an intermediate target in the model, and if is altered there may well be a subsequent effect upon, for example, the price level, which in turn may affect the interest rate, and so on.

It can be seen, therefore, that it is an oversimplification to say that a change in an instrument leads eventually to a change in one or more objectives, and there the matter ends. In reality, a further set of ripples will be sent flowing across the economy, and it is almost impossible to determine when this process has finally come to rest. By now, the reader should have come to appreciate why economic forecasts are so often wrong! Nevertheless, a good deal is known about how the UK economy works, and it is now our task to discuss each piece of the system so that, by the time we reach Chapter 9, we will be able to present a reasonably informed view of how the economy actually does work.

The national accounts

The basic building-blocks

Data on UK aggregate economic activity is published annually in the UK *National Accounts* by the Central Statistical Office (CSO), and quarterly estimates are made available in issues of *Economic Trends* and CSO press releases. Before looking at how the accounts are compiled and what they show, we will first define the most frequently used terms. The most important aggregate income variable for macroeconomic theory and policy is a measure of the **total output of goods and services in the economy**. This is termed **Gross Domestic Product** or **GDP**. It differs from total sales in the economy because this total includes **intermediate sales**, or transactions between producers — for example, purchases of steel, plastics, glass and tyres by car manufacturers. GDP is a measure of **final output**, since it is this which corresponds to income. To add together **all** transactions in the economy would involve **double counting**; GDP is thus a measure of the **value added** by producers at each stage of the production process. The sum of value added by each producer gives a measure of final output, and is equal to the value of sales by each producer *minus* their purchase of inputs from other producers and imports. The value of final output or the total of value added is thus identical to the sum of each firm's labour costs plus its trading profits.

GDP, and other measures of total output or income, can be recorded in several ways. GDP at **market prices** is final output valued at the market prices at which it sold. This can differ from the true cost of production or value added because of sales taxes, such as value added tax (VAT), which make market prices greater than the cost of production. In some cases market prices are below production costs because of subsidies paid to producers by the government. GDP at **factor cost** is final output measured in terms of costs of production. It is equal to GDP at market prices *less* **total indirect taxes** and *plus* **subsidies**. The sum of indirect taxes and subsidies is termed **net indirect taxes** in the national accounts.

The data in the accounts is valued using the measuring rod of money. Unlike a standard metre or unit of weight, the value of money – the purchasing power of the pound sterling – is not constant but alters with changes in the general level of prices. This is the problem of inflation discussed on **pp. 52–61**. The consequence is that measured GDP can alter over time not because more real output is actually being produced but simply because an unchanged level of output is being sold at higher prices. Changes in money GDP can thus reflect inflation rather than real changes. In order to overcome this difficulty GDP, and the other measures of aggregate output, are measured in inflation-adjusted or **constant price** terms, so that any change in the data reflects a change in quantities and not in the general level of prices. At present, the base year used in calculating GDP at constant prices is **1985** – that is, all the data for each year is valued in terms of the prices prevailing in one year, in this case 1985.

GDP measures the income from economic activity in the economy, and needs to be adjusted for any additional income received by UK citizens in the form of returns on overseas investments, *less* similar payments made to overseas holders of UK assets, in order to arrive at a figure for the total income available to UK citizens. The resultant figure is referred to as **Gross National Product (GNP)**. It is equal to GDP *plus* **net property income from abroad**.

Both GDP and GNP overstate the true income available to UK citizens because they make no allowance for the using up, or depreciation, of the stock of physical capital in the process of producing output – that is, the wear and tear of machines, vehicles and buildings and obsolesence. This **capital consumption** has to be made good out of current output if the economy is to maintain its capacity to produce. An allowance for capital consumption is thus deducted from the estimates of GDP and GNP in order to produce **net** figures for income. These are referred to respectively as **Net Domestic Product (NDP)**, and **Net National Product (NNP)**. These indicate the amount of income available for consumption and additions to the stock of capital through investment. Net National Product expressed at factor cost is what is correctly termed **National Income (NI)**.

National Income is the total income of all residents of the UK derived from their economic activity in the UK and from their ownership of assets abroad after making allowance for capital consumption. However, this is not the same as their total income available for expenditure. As a consequence of gifts or transfers either made overseas or received from overseas, total disposable income can differ from National Income. To obtain the correct figure **net current transfers paid abroad** need to be deducted from National Income in order to arrive at **Net National Disposable Income (NNDI)**.

As with the other aggregate income measures, from which it is derived, NNDI does not record the value of the many non-market transactions which are a source of satisfaction to those involved, such as work in the home or work done for free for friends and neighbours. It also makes no allowance for the external effects associated with production,

Table 1.1   *National product and GDP, 1988*

(a)   1988 national product by category of expenditure at current prices (£ billion)

	Consumers' expenditure	293.6
plus	General government final consumption	91.8
plus	Investment expenditure	
	of which:	93.1
	Gross domestic fixed capital formation (88.8)	
	Value of physical increase in stocks and work in progress (4.3)	
equals	Total domestic expenditure	478.5
plus	Exports of goods and services	108.6
minus	Imports of goods and services	− 125.2
equals	Gross domestic product (GDP) at market prices:	461.9
minus	Taxes on expenditure	− 75.0
plus	Subsidies	5.9
equals	Gross domestic product (GDP) at factor cost:	392.8
plus	Net property income from abroad:	5.6
equals	Gross national product (GNP) at factor cost:	398.4
minus	Capital consumption:	− 54.8
equals	Net national product (NNP) at factor cost or national income (expenditure estimate)	343.6
plus	Statistical discrepancy (expenditure adjustment)	2.0
equals	Net national product (NNP) at factor cost or national income (average estimate)	345.6

Source: UK National Accounts 'Blue Book', CSO, 1989, Table 1.2.

some of which may be beneficial but most of which are usually bad (such as environmental pollution). Nor does it value leisure time.

The measurement of GDP is based on the equivalence of aggregate income, production and expenditure in the circular flow of income. GDP can − and is − measured by valuing all factor incomes as **GDP (I)**, by valuing all final output or value added as **GDP (O)** and by valuing all final expenditure as **GDP (E)**. In principle, all three measures should be the same because they are equal **by definition**, but in practice they differ. The differences arise because of omissions in data

coverage and errors in data collection and processing. For this reason the three separate measures are combined to produce an average estimate called **GDP (A)**. It needs to be emphasised that the task of collecting all the many different kinds of data required for an economy as complex as that of the UK is exceptionally difficult, and hence some errors are unavoidable. The problem is complicated by the fact that in many cases individuals and firms have an incentive to provide misleading data − usually as an understatement of the true figure − in order to avoid paying income tax, corporation tax and VAT. In addition, illegal or **black economy**

Table 1.1 *Cont.*

(b) *1988 GDP by category of income at current factor cost (£ billion)*

Factor Incomes	
Income from employment	249.8
Income from self-employment	42.6
Gross trading profits of companies[1,2]	70.2
Gross trading surplus of public corporations and general government enterprises	7.3
Rent	27.4
Imputed charge for consumption of non-trading capital	3.4
Total domestic income[2]	400.7
minus Stock appreciation	− 6.1
equals Gross domestic product (income based)	394.6
plus Statistical discrepancy (income adjustment)	0.2
equals Gross domestic product, at factor cost, average estimate	394.8
plus Net property income from abroad	5.6
minus Capital consumption	− 54.8
equals Net national product at factor cost or national income (average estimate)	345.6

Notes:
[1] Before providing for (deducting) stock appreciation.
[2] Before providing for (deducting) capital consumption.
Source: UK National Accounts 'Blue Book', CSO, 1989, Table 1.3.

productive activity generates income, but goes unrecorded in the official estimates of GDP. For all these, and other, reasons the different measures of GDP need to be reconciled through a statistical adjustment. They are also subject to frequent, and at times large, revisions at later dates. Some components of the aggregate figures, such as imports, exports and saving are especially subject to very large errors and require correspondingly large revisions over time.

The expenditure approach

The calculation of GDP, GNP and NI using the expenditure approach involves the measurement of all categories of expenditure in the economy.

The sum of consumer's expenditure, investment expenditure (or gross domestic fixed capital formations (GDFCF), as it is referred to in the national accounts), additions to stocks and work in progress and general government final consumption is equal to **Total Domestic Expenditure**. Adding the value of total exports of goods and services to this gives **Total Final Expenditure** (TFE). Since expenditure on imports represents an outflow of money from the UK, the total value of such expenditure has to be deducted from TFE in order to arrive at the value of total expenditure in the domestic circular flow of income. This figure measures GDP. It is appropriate when estimating GDP from the side of expenditure to value it in terms of the prices actually paid for goods and services. This yields an estimate of GDP at **market prices**. To convert this to a measure of output in terms of costs requires indirect taxes to be deducted and subsidies to be added, a factor cost adjustment, to give GDP at factor cost. Adding Net Property Income from Abroad to this gives GNP at factor cost. The final step to arrive at an estimate of National Income is to deduct an estimate of capital consumption from GNP at factor cost to give NNP at factor cost or National Income (NI) **expenditure based**.

This is summarised in **Table 1.1**.

The income approach

Table 1.1 also shows the alternative way of calculating GDP and NI in terms of income. Total Domestic Income is the sum of all incomes from employment; incomes from self-employment; gross trading profits of companies; gross trading surplus of public corporations; gross trading profits of general government enterprises; rent; and other (imputed) incomes. Any increase in the money value of stocks of output and materials is deducted from the figure for Total Domestic Income to give a measure of income attributable to activity in the current period. The resultant figure is GDP. Because the estimation of GDP in this way is based on incomes (payments for factor services) it is valued at factor cost. To reconcile the income-based measure of GDP with the expenditure-based measure a statistical adjustment or residual error term is added. The resultant figure is then identical to the expenditure-based measure and estimates of GNP and NNP or NI are derived from it in exactly the same way as with the expenditure-based estimate.

Estimates of UK National Product for 1988 based on the measurement of expenditure are given in **Table 1.1**.

In 1988 GDP valued at market prices amounted to £461.9 bn. The largest category of expenditure in this total was consumers' expenditure of £293.6 bn, constituting 63.5 per cent of GDP. Government expenditure on goods and services accounted for another 20.0 per cent and total gross investment expenditure for 20.1 per cent. The open nature of the UK economy is clearly revealed by the figures for exports of good and services of £108.6 bn (23.5 per cent), and expenditure on imports of goods and services of £125.2 bn (27.1

per cent). In adding all these percentages together, that for imports has a negative sign so that the total figure does sum to 100 per cent. Deducting Net Indirect Taxes of £69.1 bn gives GDP at factor cost of £392.8 bn. Thus net indirect taxes accounted for 15 per cent of GDP at market prices Net property income from abroad amounted to £5.6 bn in 1988 and thus gives a figure for GNP at factor cost of £398.4 bn.

The scale of the annual using up of physical capital in producing the year's output is shown by the provision of £54.8 bn for capital consumption. This was equivalent to 14 per cent of GDP at factor cost. Subtracting this from GDP gives NNP or National Income of £343.6 bn. The statistical discrepancy or expenditure adjustment reconciles this figure with the average estimate of National Income, NNP(A), of £345.6 bn.

The estimates of UK National Product in 1988 using the income approach are given in **Table 1.1**. Total Domestic Income, before deducting stock appreciation, was at £400.7 bn. Of this total, income from employment was £249.8 bn, or 62.3 per cent. Subtracting the figure for stock appreciation from Total Domestic Income gives an estimate of GDP at factor cost of £304.6 bn. This differs from the estimate obtained using the expenditure approach of £392.8 bn. To reconcile the two estimates requires a statistical discrepancy or income adjustment of £0.2 bn to give a figure of GDP(A) of £394.8 bn. The addition of Net Property Income From Abroad and the subtraction of capital consumption from GDP(A) gives a NNP (A) of £345.6 bn, the same as previously.

The output approach

Estimates of GDP using the output approach, GDP(O), based on survey returns from producers and estimates of production in physical terms, are available before estimates based on the other two approaches and provide the best indication of aggregate economic activity in the short run. A provisional estimate of GDP(O) is published quarterly by the CSO some weeks after the end of the quarter to which it relates, and several weeks ahead of the more complete estimates based on the other

Table 1.2 *GDP at constant factor cost: output based measure, index numbers of output by sector (1985 = 100)*

	1985 weight in total output	1977	1978	1979	1980	1981	1982	1983	1984	1985	1986	1987	1988
Agriculture, forestry and fishing	19	72.4	78.0	76.8	85.3	87.5	94.8	89.7	105.4	100.0	98.9	99.3	100.5
Energy and water supply	106	61.7	69.8	82.5	82.6	86.5	91.6	96.8	88.8	100.0	105.0	103.9	99.4
Manufacturing	238	105.5	106.0	105.9	96.7	90.9	91.1	93.7	97.6	100.0	101.0	106.6	114.0
Total production	363	92.7	95.3	9.0	92.5	89.6	91.3	94.7	94.9	100.0	102.2	105.8	109.5
Construction	59	87.3	93.6	94.2	89.1	82.1	88.6	94.3	98.6	100.0	101.1	109.0	117.0
Services:													
Distribution, hotels, etc.	134	85.8	89.8	92.4	86.7	85.4	87.1	90.9	95.7	100.0	103.6	110.6	118.0
Transport and communication	70	86.1	88.7	92.2	90.5	90.7	89.8	92.5	96.8	100.0	104.0	112.5	119.1
Other	374	83.4	85.8	88.0	89.8	90.8	92.4	95.1	97.6	100.0	103.7	108.8	113.6
Total services	578	84.4	87.1	89.6	89.2	89.5	90.8	93.8	97.1	100.0	103.8	109.7	115.3
Gross domestic product (output based)	1,000	87.2	90.2	92.9	90.2	89.0	91.0	94.0	96.6	100.0	103.0	108.1	113.1

Source: UK National Accounts 'Blue Book', CSO, 1989, Table 1.5

methods. The output estimates are subject to error and later revision. In recent years the estimate has indicated faster growth than the expenditure estimates of GDP, and for this reason has been subject to less upward revision than the other estimates. The reasons for the size and divergence of the differences in the estimates based on the different approaches is not completely clear, and reinforces the point that the UK National Income estimates are far from perfect. This can be a serious source of error in government macroeconomic policy because the government's assessment of the state of the economy and the required policy response is dependent upon the accuracy of this data.

Because of the nature of the underlying data used in constructing the output estimate of GDP(O), it is more meaningful to express the data in index number form. **Table 1.2** contains data for GDP(O) in index number form, based on 1985 = 100, for the period 1977–88. **Table 1.2** also contains index numbers of the output of different sectors of the economy for the same period.

The first column is on the left-hand side of **Table 1.2** shows the weights (which sum to 1000) given to each sector and are proportional to the distribution of net output across the sectors in 1985. That is, they represent each sector's contribution to total output in that year. Total production, for example, has a weight of 344 or 34.4 per cent of total GDP. Total provision of services has a weight of 578 or 57.8 per cent of total GDP and signifies that, contrary to popular misconceptions, the UK is no longer primarily a manufacturing economy. The greater importance of service industries or the **tertiary sector** in the economy relative to traditional manufacturing or the **secondary sector** is in line with the structure of the other economically advanced economies. The UK creates the main part of its annual output or income from non-manufacturing activities.

A more detailed breakdown of total output by industry in 1987 is given in **Table 1.3**.

The data in **Table 1.3**, while it relates to production or output, is derived in a different way to that in **Table 1.1**. The data in **Table 1.3** is constructed by estimating the **value added** by each sector, but this is measured in terms of each

Table 1.3   *UK GDP by industry[1] 1988 (£ billion)*

Industry category		Net output
Agriculture, forestry and fishing		5.6
Energy and water supply		21.9
Of which:		
Extraction of mineral oil and natural gas	7.6	
Coal and coke	2.8	
Manufacturing		93.5
Construction		25.7
Distribution, hotels and catering; repairs		55.1
Transport and communication		28.7
Banking, finance, insurance, business services and leasing[2]		76.9
Ownership of dwellings (rent)		21.4
Public administration, national defence and compulsory social security		27.0
Education and health services		35.2
Other services		25.8
Total		416.8
Adjustment for financial services[3]		−22.2
Gross domestic product (income based)		394.6
Statistical discrepancy (income component)		0.2
Gross domestic product at factor cost (average estimate)		394.8

Notes:
[1] The contribution of each industry to the gross domestic product (its value added), net of stock appreciation but before providing for (= deducting) capital consumption.
[2] Including net interest receipts by financial companies.
[3] The same as net interest receipts by financial companies.
Source: UK National Accounts 'Blue Book', CSO, 1989, Tables 2.1 and 2.2.

sector's total labour costs and total trading profits. This data is obtained from special surveys of labour costs and by using information provided by tax offices – that is, it is not based on the extensive use of direct measures of physical output. Because

Table 1.4 *GDP, output based measure – growth of output by sector, 1980–88*

	(1) 1985 weight in total output[1]	(2) Percentage change from 1980 to 1988	(3) Contribution to change in output 1980 to 1988 ((1) × (2))	(4) Percentage share of total change
Agriculture, forestry and fishing	1.9	17.8	33.8	1.4
Energy and water supply	10.6	20.1	213.2	8.4
Manufacturing	23.8	17.7	421.0	16.6
Construction	5.9	31.3	184.5	7.3
Services	57.8	29.2	1687.5	66.3
Total	100.0	25.4	2540.0	100.0

Note:
[1] Expressed as % of total weights in Table 1.2.
Source: UK National Accounts 'Blue Book', CSO, 1989, Table 1.5.

of the way it is derived the figure for GDP given in **Table 1.3** is equivalent to GDP(A) at factor cost and is the same as that given in **Table 1.1**.

The Energy and Water Supply industries are combined into one sector and had a total output of £21.9 bn or 5.5 per cent of GDP(A) in 1988. Within this total the oil and gas industries accounted for £8.9 bn or 41 per cent and contributed 2.3 per cent of GDP(A). The importance of oil production for the economy since the mid-1970s can be judged from the fact that its contribution is greatly in excess of that of the combined output of Agriculture, Forestry and Fishing of £5.6 bn or 1.4 per cent of GDP(A). Even this low share overstates the importance of the agricultural sector since much of its production is heavily subsidised and would cease if the subsidies and special tax incentives given to farmers and the forestry industry were removed.

The nature and importance of the service sector is revealed more clearly by the data in **Table 1.3**. Banking, Finance, Insurance and Business Services, which is just one part of the service sector, accounted for £76.9 bn, before deducting their net interest receipts, or 19.5 per cent of GDP(A). This compares with the total contribution from manu-

facturing of £93.5 bn or 23.7 per cent. Manufacturing is an indispensible part of the economy's structure but in relative terms is likely to continue its long-term decline in relation to the overall service sector. This has an important consequence for the discussion of unemployment in Chapter 6.

Table 1.4 shows the growth of output by the main sectors of the economy between 1980 and 1988. It is based on the data given in **Table 1.2**.

The left-hand column in **Table 1.4** gives the percentage share of each sector in total output using the weights given in **Table 1.3**. Total output increased by 25.4 per cent in real terms between 1980 and 1988. Within this aggregate total, the growth of output by each sector is given in column (2). Agriculture, Forestry and Fishing increased its output by 17.8 per cent over the period and hence grew at a slower rate than output as a whole. Likewise, the growth of output by the manufacturing sector was below average at 17.7 per cent as was the growth of output by the Energy and Water sector of 20.1 per cent. However, that by the Construction sector of 31.3 per cent and by the Services sector of 29.2 per cent were both above the average. The high growth of output by the Energy and Water sector until 1987 was mainly

Table 1.5 *UK real domestic product by category of expenditure at 1985 prices¹, 1977–89 (£ billion)*

	1977	1978	1979	1980	1981	1982	1983	1984	1985	1986	1987	1988	1989²
Consumers' expenditure	176.0	186.7	194.9	195.0	195.2	197.1	205.5	209.2	217.0	229.1	241.4	258.0	264.1
General government final consumption	66.9	68.5	69.9	71.0	71.3	71.8	73.2	73.9	74.0	75.4	76.3	76.7	77.1
Gross domestic fixed capital formation	53.3	54.9	56.5	53.4	48.3	50.9	53.5	58.0	60.3	61.5	66.9	75.6	77.6
Value of increase in stocks and work in progress	3.2	2.9	3.3	−3.4	−3.2	−1.3	1.3	1.1	0.6	0.7	1.0	3.5	−0.2
Exports of goods and services	84.0	85.8	88.8	89.0	88.2	89.0	91.0	96.9	102.6	107.0	112.4	113.2	116.3
Imports of goods and services	−73.7	−76.6	−84.0	−81.2	−78.9	−82.8	−88.1	−96.7	−99.2	−105.9	−113.9	−127.8	−132.7
GDP (expenditure based) at market prices	310.2	322.6	330.1	323.7	320.2	324.5	336.4	342.4	355.3	367.8	384.1	399.2	402.2
Statistical discrepancy	−1.1	−1.7	−0.2	−1.0	−1.7	−0.4	−0.8	0.3	0.0	−0.2	0.9	1.8	5.8
GDP (average estimate) at market prices	309.1	320.9	329.9	322.7	318.5	324.1	335.6	342.7	355.3	367.6	385.0	401.0	408.0
Factor cost adjustment	−41.1	−45.2	−46.6	−45.3	−44.2	−44.9	−46.4	−48.4	−49.5	−52.0	−55.2	−56.9	−58.1
GDP at factor cost	267.5	275.7	283.3	277.4	274.4	279.2	289.2	294.3	305.8	315.6	329.8	344.1	349.9
Index of GDP at factor cost, 1985 = 100	87.2	90.2	92.6	90.7	89.7	91.3	94.6	96.2	100.0	103.2	107.8	111.5	114.7

Notes:
¹ For the years before 1983, totals differ from the sum of their components.
² Forecast.
Source: UK National Accounts 'Blue Book', CSO, 1989, Table 1.6.
Economic Trends (March 1989) p. 111.

due to the contribution from North Sea oil and gas and the high growth of output by the Construction sector reflected a boom in company investment expenditure and in the private housing market from 1984 onwards. The rapid growth in output by the Services sector reflected a number of factors including the structural transformation of the economy away from manufacturing towards services and the growing impact of the current revolution in computing and telecommunications technologies on the nature of economic activity: especially in the field of financial services, it is one of the consequences of the 'information technology revolution'.

The contribution of each sector's growth in output to the overall change in calculated by multiplying the figure in column (2) by its weight in total output, column (1), and is given in column (3) as an absolute figure and in column (4) as a percentage share. Of the overall growth in total output of 25.4 per cent during this period, Agriculture and manufacturing contributed relatively little of the total change, whilst services contributed the bulk of the total change.

National income and output, 1977–88

Examining the composition of GDP in terms of categories of expenditure, income and output in any one year is necessary for an understanding of how the national accounts are constructed, and to obtain an understanding of the structure of the economy and the relative importance of different kinds of activities in it. A major use of the accounts is, however, to study the performance and changing structure of the economy over time. This information provides the basis for identifying macroeconomic problems and for assessing the effectiveness of macroeconomic and other economic policies designed to deal with them.

Data for UK Domestic Product, by category of expenditure at 1985 constant prices, is given in **Table 1.5** for the period of 1977–89. The last row in **Table 1.5** expresses GDP(A), at factor cost, in

index number form since it makes for easier comprehension of changes in the data.

In money terms GDP at factor cost increased by a staggering 173.3 per cent between 1977 and 1987. Unfortunately, this large increase is due more to rising prices than to the growth of real output — that is, it merely serves to indicate that the UK experienced high rates of inflation in this period, especially between 1977 and 1982.

A more accurate picture of the growth of output during this period is provided by the constant price data in **Table 1.5**. Between 1977 and 1987 real GDP(A) increased by 22.4 per cent. This implies a much lower annual rate of increase over the period as a whole, and clearly indicates a very different picture to that suggested by the growth of nominal income.

The data in **Table 1.5** also show how the main categories of expenditure have altered in real terms in this period, and provide a clear indication of the nature of some of the UK's macroeconomic problems.

The most serious problem was the severe economic recession between 1979 and 1981. This is most readily apparent from inspection of the index number series for real GDP(A) given at the bottom of **Table 1.5**. Real GDP increased between 1977 and 1979 and then declined for two years as the economy went into recession. During 1982 GDP started to increase again, but did not exceed the level reached in 1979 until 1983. Thereafter, real GDP increased every year. A very dramatic indication of the severity of the 1979–81 recession is provided by the graph of capacity utilisation shown in **Figure 1.2**.

Capacity utilisation

The graph in **Figure 1.2** is based on the responses to the Confederation of British Industry, (CBI) survey of business conditions and expectations; it shows the percentage of firms answering 'NO' to the question: 'Is your present level of output below your capacity output level?'. The degree of capacity utilisation revealed by the answers to this

Figure 1.2   *Capacity utilisation*

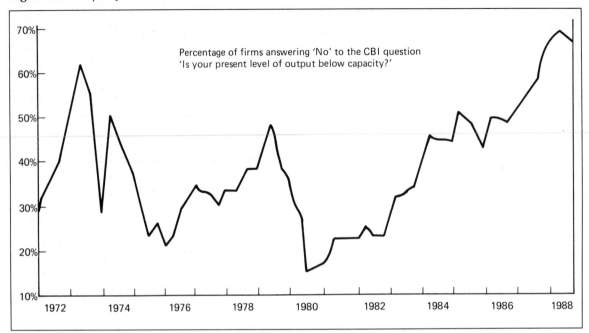

Percentage of firms answering 'No' to the CBI question
'Is your present level of output below capacity?'

Source: Financial Times, 16 February 1989

question provides a very good indication of the strength of aggregate demand in the economy. In 1979, 50 per cent of the firms surveyed reported full capacity working. While this may seem low, it indicates a high level of demand and represented the highest level obtained since the 1970–73 boom. The rapid decline in the degree of capacity utilisation in 1980 was the sharpest recorded in the period 1972–89 and also the lowest level with 85 per cent of firms reporting below-capacity output in 1980. The subsequent slow recovery to 1983 is clearly shown, as is the much stronger recovery in 1984–85. By 1985 capacity working was above the 1979 level, and this was followed by further continued growth of demand leading to the highest level of capacity utilisation (at 70 per cent) for the entire period from 1972. The high level of capacity utilisation in 1988 points to a very high level of aggregate demand in the economy and indicates the likelihood of both increasing inflationary pressure and a worsening balance of trade deficit.

Consumers' expenditure and investment

Despite the economic recession between 1979 and 1981, the data in **Table 1.5** reveals that real consumers' expenditure did not show a corresponding decline but rather continued to increase, albeit by a small amount, between 1979 and 1981. This is not really surprising since consumers' expenditure is one of the most stable components of aggregate demand. This is discussed in more detail on **pp. 41–3**.

A similar picture is revealed by the data for real General Government Final Expenditure, and again is not really surprising given the role of government policy in stabilising demand and its use of the level of its own expenditure for this purpose.

The behaviour of real GDFCF and changes in the value of stocks and work in progress are, on the other hand, much more volatile. According to the theory of national income determination it is fluctuations in this expenditure and in exports, magnified by the multiplier process, which lead to the overall variability of national output unless offset by counterbalancing changes in government expenditure.

From a peak of £56.5 bn in 1979 real investment expenditure declined to £48.3 bn in 1981. It increased again in 1982 and 1983 but in the latter year exceeded the 1980 figure only by £50 mn. Thereafter the recovery in real GDFCF was much stronger and stood at £75.6 bn in 1988. This represented an increas of 39.4 per cent over the period 1977–88 but of much less if 1988 is excluded. Given the importance of investment in determining future levels of income and growth, this increase was quite modest and only exceeded the increase in real GDP at factor cost when the sharp upsurge in 1988 is taken into account.

Investment in stocks and work in progress or inventory investment is even more variable than investment in fixed assets because, to a great extent, it acts as a buffer against variations in aggregate demand. It is also responsive to changes in the level of interest rates. This variability is reflected in the data on the real value of increases in stocks and work in progress. During 1977–79 such inventory investment averaged £3.1 bn a year. In 1980, in response to the recession in the economy and the very high level of interest rates, the level of stocks and work in progress was cut drastically by £3.4 bn. The course and severity of the recession is shown by the further reductions in stocks and work in progress which took place in 1981 and 1982. The subsequent recovery in demand and in output is seen in the addition to stocks and work in progress during 1983 and the following years. Of interest is the fact that the average value of changes in stocks and work in progress in the period 1985–87 is only £566 mn as compared with over £3 bn in the three years prior to 1980. This could reflect both the changed nature of the structure of the economy – that is, the relative decline in the importance of manufacturing – and a change in stockholding behaviour in response to high interest rates. Investment is examined in more detail later in this chapter.

Exports and imports

In the three years from 1979 the real value of exports of goods and services increased. A slight decrease was recorded in 1981 but the upward trend in exports was resumed from 1982 onwards. This pattern reflects two main factors. For a given exchange rate, the level of exports is dependent on the level of demand in the rest of the world, and this remained buoyant while the UK economy went into recession. The level of UK exports in this period also included a significant contribution from exports of North Sea oil, the production of which was unaffected by the recession in the rest of the economy, especially that in manufacturing. The severity of the latter is revealed by the index of real output for the manufacturing sector. Based on 1985 = 100, this index stood at 106 in 1979, fell to 91 in 1981, increased slightly in 1982 to 91.2 and grew in each of the following years. However, such was the impact of the recession on the manufacturing sector that despite continued increases from 1982 onwards it remained below the level reached in 1979 until 1987 when the index stood at 106.6.

The pattern of real expenditure on imports, on the other hand, shows clearly that the economy went into recession during 1979–81. From a pre-recession peak figure of £84.0 bn in 1979 the real value of imports of goods and services declined in 1980 and again in 1981 to £78.9 bn.

This decline reflected the fact that the level of real expenditure on imports is positively related to the level of real national income and additions to stocks, so that as these declined with the recession, imports also fell. The increase in real expenditure on imports in 1982, and the continued growth thereafter, signified the recovery from the recession and subsequent growth in real national income. After the recession the growth of imports exceeded that of exports, and in 1987 the current account of the balance of payments moved into deficit. This deterioration in the trade balance reflects several factors including the high level of demand in the economy, especially investment expenditure, and the shortage of productive capacity and skilled labour.

Table 1.6   *Investment (GDFCF) by type of asset and by sector as a % of GDP, 1977–88*[1]

	1977	1978	1979	1980	1981	1982	1983	1984	1985	1986	1987	1988
GDFCF as a per cent of GDP	17.7	17.1	17.2	16.6	15.2	15.8	16.0	17.0	17.0	16.7	17.3	19.0
GDFCF excluding dwellings as a per cent of GDP	13.1	13.1	13.1	12.7	12.0	12.4	12.3	13.3	13.7	13.3	13.8	15.3
Private sector investment as a per cent of GDP	11.2	12.0	12.3	12.0	11.3	12.0	11.7	12.8	13.6	13.3	14.4	16.4
General government investment as a per cent of GDP	2.8	2.4	2.2	2.0	1.4	1.3	1.8	1.9	1.9	1.9	1.8	1.5
Public corporation investment as a per cent of GDP	3.0	2.7	2.6	2.6	2.4	2.4	2.5	2.2	1.6	1.5	1.2	1.1
Stocks and work in progress as a per cent of GDP	1.0	0.9	1.0	−1.0	−1.0	−0.4	0.4	0.3	0.2	0.2	0.2	0.2

Note:
[1] For the years before 1983, totals may not equal the sum of their components, because of the method used in rebasing to 1985 prices.
Source: Economic Trends, Annual Supplement (1988).
Economic Trends, CSO, (July 1989).

Investment

The role of investment

The level of investment expenditure has a twofold importance. In the short run, fluctuations in the level of GDFCF and inventory investment cause fluctuations in the level of aggregate demand, and hence in GDP. In the longer run, the level of investment determines the rate of growth of the stock of capital and this is a major determinant of the rate of growth of real income. In comparison with the more successful OECD countries the UK invests too little both in absolute terms and as a proportion of GDP. The **quality** and **nature of investment** is also important. In the period since 1945 a high proportion of UK investment has been of questionable value in terms of its contribution to economic growth and economic performance. Unlike countries such as Japan and W. Germany the UK has devoted a disproportionately large fraction of its investment expenditure to the defence industries. Whatever the value of this in terms of national defence the investment has produced a poor return in terms of industrial performance, jobs and exports. Similarly, such prestige projects as the UK nuclear energy programme and Concorde have accounted for very high proportions of UK investment expenditure without producing much of lasting value in terms of internationally competitive industries, employment and exports. In those countries which have not been handicapped in this way, investment has been concentrated in those areas of manufacturing such as vehicles, consumer electronics, computers and modern machine tools which have experienced a high rate of growth of world demand. Since the early 1980s, as a result of changes in government policy and the state of the economy, there appears to have been an improvement in the quality of investment in the UK as indicated by a significant increase in productivity.

Definition of investment

'Investment' in this context refers to investment in **physical assets** or **fixed capital formation** rather than investment in financial assets. This form of investment – in contrast to the acquisition of financial assets and consumption – adds to the country's stock of physical productive capital and yields a flow of productive services in the future as well as in the period in which it takes place. Total investment (GDFCF) consists of **replacement investment** and **net investment**. Replacement investment is required to make good the depreciation of the stock of capital which results through wear and tear in the use of capital to produce the annual flow of output. The more intensively the existing stock of capital is used in a given period, the greater the rate of depreciation, and the greater the flow of replacement investment required to maintain the size of the stock of capital – and hence output – in the following period. **Net investment** is investment in excess of that required to make good depreciation and increases the total stock of physical capital in the country. The rate of growth of the stock of physical capital is an important determinant of the rate of growth of real national income. Replacement investment also affects the rate of growth of real income to the extent that the replacement capital is better and more productive than that which it replaced because it incorporates technical progress.

Between 1977 and 1988, GDFCF measured in constant 1985 prices increased from £53.3 bn to £75.6 bn. As a percentage of GDP, however, this represented only a modest increase from 17.7 per cent to 19.0 per cent. Furthermore 1988 was the only year subsequent to 1977 that the ratio stood noticeably above the level achieved in that year. The annual variation in this investment ratio over the period since 1977 is given in **Table 1.6**.

Investment in **physical assets** covers many different types of capital items. These can be categorised into private dwellings, other building and work, vehicles, ships and aircraft, and plant and machinery. All investment expenditure adds to aggregate demand but investment by the personal sector on private dwellings has no direct effect on productivity. For this reason, when looking at the relationship between investment and economic performance, it is better to consider the figure for GDFCF *minus* expenditure on dwellings. This data is given in the second row of **Table 1.6**. GDFCF excluding dwellings increased slightly between 1977 and 1987 from 13.1 per cent to 13.8 per cent. This compares with an average for the whole period of 12.9 per cent. The average is depressed because of the recession in 1980–81 during which the ratios of GDFCF and GDFCF excluding dwellings to GDP declined. The recovery from this recession and the subsequent period of growth in real GDP are marked by an increase in the investment ratios, especially during 1988.

According to the elementary theory of income determination investment expenditure is an injection into the circular flow of income. Changes in the level of such expenditure lead, via the multiplier process, to larger changes in the level of national income. It is important to realise, however, that the decline in real investment expenditure and share of investment in GDP which occurred in 1980 and 1981 cannot be taken as evidence of this process at work. Data analysis and interpretation is full of pitfalls. The data in **Table 1.6** is annual, and such a frequency of observation is too low to draw statistical inferences about causation. A proper analysis of the influence of changes in investment expenditure on the level of demand in the economy requires quarterly or monthly data and the use of sophisticated statistical techniques. The pattern shown by the annual data in **Table 1.6** could indicate either that lower investment leads to lower income or that a decline in income leads to lower investment!

The striking features of the figures for the shares of GDFCF and GDFCF excluding dwellings in GDP between 1977 and 1987 are their relative stability over the period as a whole and their steady recovery from the trough of the recession in 1981. While no inference can be drawn at this stage about causation, the period since 1982 has also been characterised by sustained and relatively stable growth of demand and output.

Business investment

The behaviour of total business investment in real terms from 1965 to the second half of 1988 is plotted in **Figure 1.3**.

Business investment refers to investment by the trading sector of the economy. It thus includes all investment by public corporations, such as nationalised industries, but excludes general government investment. Personal sector investment in dwellings is excluded by definition. The trading sector includes production and service industries and is much broader than the manufacturing sector. Investment by the trading sector is correspondingly much greater than investment by the manufacturing sector, as is shown in the lower part of **Figure 1.3**. For example, in 1987 manufacturing investment accounted for only about 26 per cent of business investment. In 1987 investment by the business sector accounted for about 65 per cent of GDFCF while investment by the manufacturing sector was less than 16 per cent of GDFCF.

The trend of total business investment in real terms was static between 1973 and 1979. This implies that it declined as a per cent of GDP. It fell sharply in the recession years of the early 1980s but in the period since 1982 has shown a marked upward trend. Between 1982 and 1987 the annual average rate of growth was 5 per cent. More importantly, the annual rate of growth increased rather than decreased in the same period and towards the end of this period exceeded the growth of consumption. This implies that a larger share of demand was being devoted to improving productive potential and efficiency. The failure to do this in a consistent pattern in previous decades was one of the factors contributing to poor economic performance and relative industrial decline. The large peak in business investment at the end of 1984, and the similar peak in manufacturing investment, was caused by the bringing forward of investment to avoid changes in the tax system in 1985 designed to discourage certain forms of investment undertaken to gain a tax advantage.

In contrast with business investment, real investment in manufacturing has remained fairly static over the whole period covered by **Figure 1.3**. As a consequence it has declined as a percentage of total business investment as well as of GDFCF and of GDP. In 1987 it accounted for only 26 per cent of business investment compared with 34 per cent in 1970. This decline reflects structural changes in the pattern of productive activity. Total real expenditure on investment has increased over

Figure 1.3 *Total business investment*

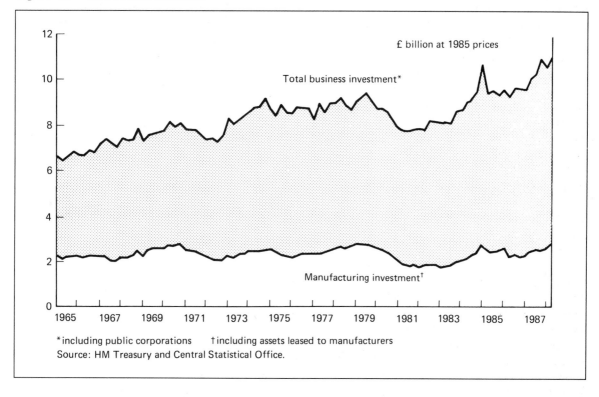

£ billion at 1985 prices

Total business investment*

Manufacturing investment†

*including public corporations   †including assets leased to manufacturers
Source: HM Treasury and Central Statistical Office.

Source: Reproduced from *Economic Progress Report*, 199 (December 1988)

time and the share of investment in GDP has remained fairly constant so that the behaviour of investment in manufacturing reflects changes in demand rather than an overall lack of investment.

While the overall picture concerning investment in the period since the late 1970s is one of relative stability in contrast to greater variability in the past, some significant changes have occurred within the total. Some of these are shown by the data in **Table 1.6**.

The pattern of investment

Private sector investment as a proportion of GDP increased from 11.2 per cent in 1977 to 16.4 per cent in 1988. This growth has been at the expense of General Government Investment and Public Corporation Investment. The former declined as a proportion of GDP from 2.8 per cent in 1977 to 1.5 per cent in 1988, the latter from 3.0 per cent in 1977 to 1.1 per cent in 1988. In interpreting these changes, however, a note of caution is required since some of the change reflects the government's privatisation programme which has caused the transfer of some major public corporations to the private sector. Nevertheless, as shown by the decline in general government investment expenditure as a percentage of GDP, and the growth of business investment, an overall shift in the pattern of investment expenditure in favour of the private sector has taken place since the early 1980s. This is another indication of the changes in government policy towards the economy in this period and of the shift away from demand management to supply-side policies.

Another new and significant change in the

Table 1.7 *Investment by type of asset as a % of GDFCF*[1]

	1977	1978	1979	1980	1981	1982	1983	1984	1985	1986	1987	1988
Investment in dwellings as a per cent of GDFCF	24.0	23.5	23.7	23.2	21.1	21.4	22.8	21.7	19.7	21.1	20.4	19.6
Investment in other new buildings and work as a per cent of GDFCF	32.0	30.4	28.7	28.7	30.8	32.2	31.2	31.2	30.2	30.3	30.7	30.1
Investment in plant and machinery as a per cent of GDFCF	32.1	33.3	34.9	36.9	37.9	36.3	36.3	36.7	39.3	39.5	39.9	40.3
Investment in vehicles, ships and aircraft	12.2	13.1	13.3	11.8	10.1	9.8	9.7	10.5	10.6	9.2	9.5	10.1

Note:
[1] For the years before 1983, totals may not equal the sum of their components, because of the method used in rebasing the original data to 1985 prices.
Source: UK National Accounts 'Blue Book', CSO, (1989) Table 13.2.

pattern of investment since the late 1970s is revealed by the data in **Table 1.7**.

Table 1.7 gives the share of each of the four main classes of fixed investment as a proportion of GDFCF. Investment in dwellings declined from 24 per cent to 19.6 per cent between 1977 and 1988. A similar, although less pronounced, decline also occurred in investment in other buildings and work, down from 32 per cent to 30.1 per cent in 1988. Investment in vehicles, ships and aircraft also declined from 12.2 per cent to 10.1 per cent. The relative decline in these three categories of fixed investment is matched by a correspondingly large increase in the share of investment devoted to plant and equipment. This increased from 32.1 per cent in 1977 to just over 40 per cent in 1988. The growth of investment in plant and equipment is important because is is through this form of investment more than any other that new technologies are introduced into business and productivity increased.

Within the period 1977–88 the respective shares of the four categories of investment exhibit some variation which can be explained in terms of specific factors. For example, the relative decline in investment in dwellings in 1981–82 was due to the economic recession in that period and the high level of mortgage interest rates. The large jump in investment in plant and machinery in 1985 from 36.7 per cent of total investment to 39.3 per cent was due in part to measures announced in the 1984 Budget concerning the lowering of the rate of corporation tax and the reduction of first-year investment allowances. Clearly, however, the longer-term trends shown by the data for this period must reflect the operation of more fundamental factors. The longer-term decline in the share of investment going to dwellings is due in part to the decline in the rate of inflation from the high levels of the mid-1970s. Inflation increases the attraction of property as a form of investment because property prices rise in line with inflation, and this maintains the real value of investment. In contrast, the real value of money and many financial assets declines with inflation. The decline in investment in dwellings also reflects demographic changes, a decline in the rate of population growth, and a sharp reduction in council spending on housing caused by changes in long-term government policy.

Company profitability

The long-term increase in the share of investment in plant and machinery combined with the increase in the share of private sector investment in GDP is also an indication of a fundamental shift in government policy away from demand management to supply-side policies. Supply-side policies include the removal of distortions in the tax system which encourage investment for short-term financial gain rather than long-term real economic benefit. They also include reductions in the rate of company taxation which increase the after-tax return on investment. Such changes were introduced in the UK in this period, especially after the 1984 Budget. In addition, other supply-side policies, in particular those relating to trade unions and industrial relations, have led to changed work practices and an improvement in the quality of investment. All of these have contributed to an increase in the net rate of return on capital received by companies which has encouraged further company investment and increased the availability of internal funds to finance the additional investment. The long-term behaviour of companies' net rates of return on capital is shown in **Figure 1.4**.

The trend in company profitability was sharply downwards from the early 1960s to the mid-1970s. Thereafter the trend was reversed, and since the early 1980s company profitability has increased almost continuously to levels comparable with those of the early 1960s. Given the positive relationship between the level of return on investment and the willingness to invest, the sustained rise in net return on company investment after 1981 helps to account for the changed pattern of investment in this period.

Stocks

One last category of investment remains to be considered. Fixed investment does not include investment in stocks or inventories. Although the

Figure 1.4   *Companies' net rate of return on capital*

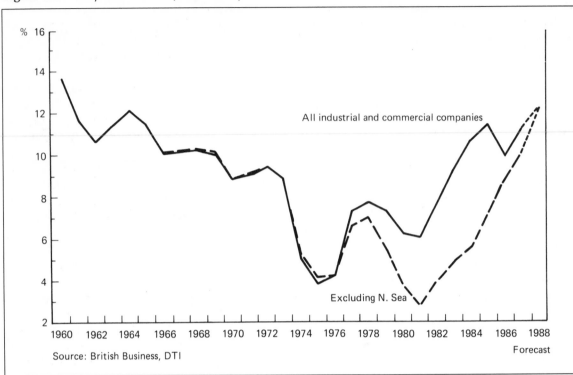

Source: British Business, DTI

Source: Reproduced from *Economic Progress Report*, 199 (December 1988).

scale of investment in stocks is small in comparison with GDFCF, the behaviour of stocks is of considerable importance because changes in the level of investment in stocks both reflects changes in the level of demand and causes such changes. The bottom row in **Table 1.6** shows the ratio of stocks to GDP.

Without stocks of raw materials, work in progress and finished goods the economy as we know it could not function. Nor could the income multiplier process operate. This is because in many cases sales are met out of stocks rather than current production to order. The main exceptions to this are the production of services and items of fixed capital equipment. Imagine the problem and frustration of going to a shop to buy food for your lunch or the latest hit CD, or of going to a pub on a very hot day for a pint of lager, and being told to come back a few days later to give the relevant producer time to make what you wanted!

Stocks are a residual or buffer between sales and production which makes it possible for demand to be satisfied when it occurs. A rise in sales relative to production is possible if stocks exist but means a decline in the level of stocks. This, however, acts as a signal to producers to increase output if the increased demand is expected to continue. Conversely, a rise in stocks relative to production, unless it is planned by producers in anticipation of a higher level of future sales, signals a reduction in demand and the need to cut back production if the reduced demand is expected to continue.

The greater the variability of sales the greater the level of stocks and the greater the variability of the ratio of stocks to GDP. The more stable the growth of sales and hence output the lower the variability of the ratio of stocks to GDP and the lower the absolute level of stocks because of the more certain environment in which firms operate. This is seen in the behaviour of the ratio of stocks to GDP in the period since 1983. This stability is in marked contrast to the very volatile behaviour of the stock ratio in the 1970s. The significance of this is that the stability of the ratio of stocks to GDP is not just a consequence of a more stable growth path of real GDP but also an important source of such stability.

Changes in the level of stocks as firms alter the level of production to match actual or **expected** changes in sales have a multiplier effect on the level of demand in the economy and intensify and/ or prolong economic fluctuations. That is, changes in expectations about future levels of sales are translated through changes in stock levels, and magnified by the multiplier process, into actual fluctuations. Economic policies and conditions which produce expectations of steady growth thus lead to stability in stock levels which contribute to the attainment and continuation of stable real income growth. The stability of the ratio of stocks to GDP in the UK after 1983 may be due in some way to the switch in policy away from demand management towards greater emphasis on supply-side policies.

Personal income, consumption and saving *Peter Curwen*

Personal income

Personal income consists of wages and salaries, employers' contributions, current grants from general government and other personal income. In total these constitute much the largest element of national income. However, the term 'personal' is somewhat ambiguous in that it refers not merely to individuals but to unincorporated businesses, private non-profit-making bodies and life assurance and pension funds. The latter three elements are largely excluded in data for 'household' incomes, but in making this distinction there are particular difficulties with, for example, the earnings of entrepreneurs who are, in effect, individual person and business rolled into one. **Figure 1.5** contains quarterly data for personal income before tax at current prices since 1977, and these show a steady upwards progression throughout the whole period

at an average annual rate of around 10 per cent.

Personal income net of income taxes, social security contributions and transfer payments is called personal disposable income (PDI), which is also shown at current prices in **Figure 1.5**. Whilst this is understandably more volatile than pre-tax personal income given that tax regimes can be altered at specified points in time, the longer-term trend is very similar and exhibits an almost identical average rate of growth. The individual components of pre-tax personal income can mostly be measured quite accurately (± 3 per cent or less), and the same is true for income taxes and social security contributions. However, the subtraction of the latter from the former inevitably renders PDI less accurate than either ($\pm$ between 3 and 10 per cent).

Consumers' expenditure

Consumers' expenditure represents the consumption not merely of households but of the other non-household parts of the personal sector. Nevertheless, household consumption constitutes 90 per cent of the total, and it is reasonable to treat one as a close approximation of the other. Consumption expenditure is also plotted at current prices in **Figure 1.5**, where the quarterly data are seasonally adjusted. This is necessary since consumption always surges in the final quarter of each year due to Xmas shopping, and the unadjusted data give the false impression that this heralds an ongoing upturn in expenditure.

Figure 1.6 gives a breakdown of real consumers's expenditure (at 1985 prices) in 1988. The brackets contain, sequentially, the equivalent figures for 1975 and 1980. As can be seen, there has been a **significant** drop in the shares taken by both food and alcoholic drink and tobacco. This was to be expected as individuals become better off over time, but it is also the case that smoking has recently become less socially acceptable. The general tendency for purchases of durable and other goods to rise as a proportion of the total was equally to be expected, but the outstanding feature has been the sharp upsurge in the share taken by consumption of other services in recent years. In

Figure 1.5   *Personal income, 1977–89, quarterly, at current prices*

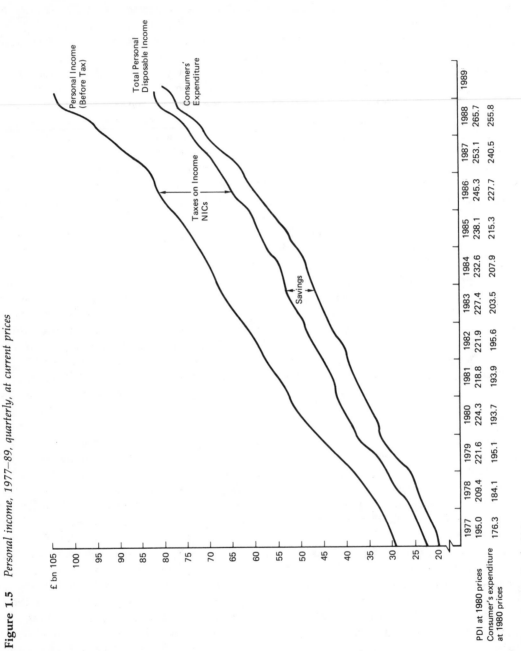

	1977	1978	1979	1980	1981	1982	1983	1984	1985	1986	1987	1988	1989
PDI at 1980 prices	195.0	209.4	221.6	224.3	218.8	221.9	227.4	232.6	238.1	245.3	253.1	265.7	
Consumer's expenditure at 1980 prices	176.3	184.1	195.1	193.7	193.9	195.6	203.5	207.9	215.3	227.7	240.5	255.8	

Source: Economic Trends, CSO

Figure 1.6 *Share of consumers' expenditure, 1988, 1985 prices*

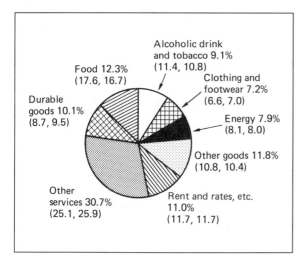

Alcoholic drink
and tobacco 9.1%
(11.4, 10.8)

Food 12.3%
(17.6, 16.7)

Clothing and
footwear 7.2%
(6.6, 7.0)

Durable
goods 10.1%
(8.7, 9.5)

Energy 7.9%
(8.1, 8.0)

Other goods 11.8%
(10.8, 10.4)

Other
services 30.7%
(25.1, 25.9)

Rent and rates, etc.
11.0%
(11.7, 11.7)

Source: Financial Statistics, CSO

absolute terms, real spending on food and on alcohol and tobacco has remained remarkably stable for roughly 15 years – hence their declining share of a growing total. Absolute real energy consumption has also remained stable. The durable goods and clothing and footwear categories are fairly small components of total spending, so that modest increases in their shares of a growing total represent quite significant growth rates in absolute spending. It is reasonable to project these trends forward into the 1990s, provided real PDI continues to grow.

It is also worth noting that attention in the media is sometimes addressed to trends in retail sales as a guide to trends in consumers' expenditure, since the former are published on a provisional basis much earlier than the latter. However, it must be borne in mind that, for example, whilst food represents 12–13 per cent of consumers' expenditure, it represents roughly 40 per cent of retail sales which exclude energy, rent and rates and other services. Hence, in the short term, retail sales may prove a very unreliable guide to trends in the larger aggregate.

As can be seen from **Table 1.8** PDI is, by definition, either **consumed** or **saved**. The propor-

tion saved (saving ratio) is specified in **Table 1.8**, and it follows that the proportion consumed, known technically as the average propensity to consume (APC), is given by the formula (1 − saving ratio). Currently, this stands at well over 90 per cent and, taking the official data at face value, has been increasing during most of the 1980s.

It is interesting to note that, because consumption is determined by PDI rather than gross income, savings tend to fall somewhat when the tax and national insurance burden rises. Between 1983 and 1987, for example, total deductions rose from 21.20 to 21.45 per cent of total income, whereas the saving ratio fell sharply other than in 1984, the only year in which total deductions fell as a proportion of gross income. Whilst this relationship must be treated with caution, it does suggest that when the government removes demand from the economy via taxation, consumption steps into the breach to maintain demand. During the period covered by **Table 1.8**, consumers' expenditure rose by 74 per cent whilst PDI rose by 67 per cent. It appears that consumers have recently not merely spent the whole of their PDI, but borrowed in order to finance yet further consumption.

For the past decade, with the sole exception of the recession year of 1981, real PDI adjusted for inflation has risen. This is shown by the data for real PDI at the foot of **Figure 1.5**. Recent years have seen quite substantial increases, although none has been as large as occurred in each of the two years 1978 and 1979. Unfortunately, it is not altogether clear whether rising real PDI stimulates or depresses consumption. Evidence from the USA, where the saving ratio is exceptionally low, suggests that once real incomes rise to the point at which most people have satisfied their desire to own assets such as a house and some company shares, they see no further point in saving for the future and opt instead for additional current consumption. However, it is most unlikely that the UK has reached the same stage, as yet, and there was every sign in the booming housing market of 1988 that saving for asset accumulation was as popular as ever.

A related issue, of increasing importance given the present government's supply-side strategy, is the effect of reductions in the rates of income tax,

Table 1.8   *Personal income, expenditure and saving* (£ billion)

	1983	1984	1985	1986	1987	1988
Wages and salaries	145.5	155.1	168.6	182.7	198.7	221.8
Employers' contributions	24.1	25.0	26.0	27.0	28.0	29.8
Current grants	39.9	43.0	46.8	50.8	52.5	54.4
Other personal income	51.9	56.0	59.9	65.3	70.6	79.7
Total income	261.4	279.1	301.3	325.8	349.8	385.7
Less deductions:						
Taxes on income	33.2	34.6	37.6	40.8	43.7	48.5
Social security contributions	20.8	22.3	24.2	26.1	28.4	31.6
Transfers	1.4	1.4	1.7	1.9	2.1	2.2
Personal disposable income (PDI)	206.0	220.8	237.8	257.0	275.6	303.4
Less consumers' expenditure	184.6	197.5	215.3	237.4	259.3	289.8
Balance: personal saving	21.4	23.3	22.5	19.6	16.3	13.6
Saving ratio %[1]	10.4	10.5	9.5	7.6	5.9	4.5

Note:
[1] Saving as % of PDI
Source: Financial Statistics, Table 9.1.
Economic Trends, CSO Table A7 (July 1989).

especially those in excess of the standard rate. In the Keynesian model, taxing high income earners and redistributing the proceeds to those on low incomes is expected to raise the marginal propensity to consume (MPC) and to reduce the saving ratio. The recent reductions in the upper rates of income tax should thus have the opposite effect, given that they redistribute in favour of higher income groups. It is as yet impossible to form a judgement on the matter, but it will be a useful addition to our knowledge about consumption to discover whether this extra money will be spent or saved.

Saving

National saving is the sum of private (personal and company) saving and public saving. **Personal saving** is the difference between PDI and consumers' expenditure. In principle it is equal to personal investment plus the personal sector's acquisition of financial assets *net* of personal borrowing. **Company saving** is the residual income of companies net of tax, profits remitted abroad, transfers and payments of interest and dividends. Company expenditure on durable goods in the form of fixed investment and stocks is **not** deducted from their income in measuring company saving, but depreciation is. **Public saving** is the difference between the public sector's current receipts and current expenditure, and is broadly equivalent to public sector net investment *less* public sector borrowing (or *plus* public sector debt repayment).

The discussion of saving in the media is concerned primarily with the personal sector, although as we will note later this may be misguided. Unfortunately, personal sector saving is a very unreliable statistic (potentially up to 20 per cent inaccurate in either direction) as it is the difference between two somewhat inaccurate figures for PDI and consumers' expenditure respectively. Furthermore, the distinction between consumption expenditure on durable goods and saving can be a fine one. Whilst, for example, the purchase of a car is treated as current consumption in the statistics, many purchasers would see the accumulation of a deposit and the repayment of the residual purchase price as an act of **saving**. On occasion, the CSO redefines consumption as saving (for example, DIY expenditure in 1984), and more generally the saving ratio tends to be retrospectively adjusted in each year's 'Blue Book'. The ratios recorded during the 1970s have in recent years thus been much reduced − with, for example, a downgrading of each of the previous seven years' ratios by almost 1 per cent in the 1987 'Blue Book'.

One other consideration bedevils the meaning of saving, namely that whilst personal payments into a private pension fund are counted as saving, contributions to the government's pension and social security schemes are not. Obviously, if the latter were not deducted from gross income both PDI and the saving ratio (including such payments) would be considerably larger.

Why the saving ratio varies over time
It is important to explain why the personal saving ratio (and hence, by implication, the APC) should vary over time. It is useful to start with the relationship between inflation and consumption/saving behaviour. The traditional view was that once people came to realise that the value of money would be adversely affected by inflation, they would rush out to spend it as quickly as possible. This view was broadly supported by behaviour during the overseas hyperinflations of the prewar period, but the relatively modest price rises manifested in the UK since 1970 appear to have stimulated more mixed behaviour, with the saving ratio rising during the high (by UK standards) inflation of the 1970s, then falling with inflation in the 1980s. There are a number of ways of explaining this, and their relative merits are unlikely ever to be satisfactorily distinguished since they are, in any event, significantly interdependent.

For example, if a person sets out to maintain the **real**, rather than the **nominal**, value of his savings,

he or she will be obliged to increase the nominal value of those savings at the same rate as prices are rising. Furthermore, since high rates of inflation generally go hand in hand with rising unemployment, people who fear they may lose their jobs may try to build up a pool of savings in order to cushion their potential loss of income. Equally, if prices of consumer goods are rising so rapidly that people feel that they will never be able to afford to buy them, they may decide to give up trying to do so and save instead.

The role of interest rates in all this is hard to divine. Since interest rates, in nominal terms, tend to rise with inflation, the sacrifice in terms of interest foregone when buying consumer goods must itself be rising. However, the inflation-adjusted real rate of interest was negative during the mid-1970s, at a time of very high nominal rates, and positive in the mid-1980s, at a time of lower nominal rates, so one could have expected savings to be higher rather than lower in the latter period (assuming, of course, that savers were not suffering in the 1970s from **money illusion** − the illusion that nominal and real rates are the same). In fact, correlating savings against real rates of interest appears to indicate a rather weak relationship. This may, in turn, reflect the fact that financial deregulation has made it increasingly easy for people to borrow, and therefore the principle that one has to save before one buys a costly item has been steadily eroded. Rather perversely at first sight, people may continue to put increasingly large sums of money into life assurance and pension funds and simultaneously borrow to finance additional current consumption. Savings are defined net of borrowing, so increased borrowing reduces the saving ratio. However, the borrower himself is unlikely to view borrowing as dissaving. Indeed, of course, pension fund contributions may well be compulsory rather than voluntary. In 1980, after adjusting for contributions to life insurance and pension funds, the personal sector still placed 30 per cent of its savings on a discretionary basis, but by 1986 this latter figure had become negative. In particular, it should be borne in mind that employers' social security contributions are open-ended, and therefore rise rapidly with gross incomes.

A broader view of these factors may be termed the 'wealth effect'. Over the long haul – and, indeed, in most individual years – the value of property has tended to rise faster than prices in general. Equally, the value of company shares has easily outstripped inflation over the past decade, and more recently, though not previously, post-tax rates of interest have also outstripped inflation. As a result, people who own assets (currently, in practice, the great majority) will tend to feel wealthier as time passes, and hence feel less need to convert current income into wealth via saving. This will also reflect the increased probability of inheritance.

The age structure of the population also links in with this analysis. The bulk of savings are accumulated by people between the ages of 45 and 65. Younger people have heavy outgoings incurred in setting up homes and raising families, whilst the elderly earn little and may need to eat into past savings. The high birth rate immediately after the Second World War has produced an exceptionally large generation approaching its period of high savings, which could well cause savings to rise again in the 1990s.

All this is, understandably, confusing enough, but it is additionally important not to interpret saving purely within the context of the personal sector. **Figure 1.7**, based on a somewhat different approach to the calculation of savings from that used previously, incorporates the savings of the personal sector, company sector and public sector, all expressed as a percentage of GDP at factor cost. As can be seen on the left-land side of **Figure 1.7**, the decline in personal saving was offset by an increase in company saving from 1979 to 1987, whilst the saving of the public sector remained consistently negative throughout the same period. As a result, total savings at current prices showed a remarkable degree of stability from 1980 to 1987. Whilst this data is unavailable beyond 1987, CSO statistics indicate that the public sector moved into surplus in 1988, whilst the personal sector followed up a substantial deficit in 1988 with an even more substantial one in 1989. Clearly, these trends have offset each other to a considerable extent.

Adjusting the data for inflation, as shown on the right-hand side of **Figure 1.7**, has no effect upon this general proposition, although the sectoral shares are very different. This arises because, when inflation is rapid, a sector with positive net assets has an artificially increased income and saving rate, and vice versa. As result, the conventional national accounts misallocate savings among the sectors when inflation is high. The high nominal saving ratio of the personal sector in 1979 was thus in reality negative after adjusting for inflation, and exceeded 2 per cent only in the period 1982–84. In real terms the 1986 figure of 1 per cent was little less than the 1980 figure of 16 per cent. On the other hand, the real saving of the company sector was slightly higher than its nominal saving in every year except 1985 when it was identical. In the case of the public sector the real saving ratio was positive, but rapidly declining, between 1979 and 1982, and marginally negative thereafter.

Given the evident constancy of national savings it is understandable that the government does not believe it necessary to take remedial action to boost savings, and indeed it may be reasonable to expect personal sector saving to rise again once the message is absorbed that the real wealth of the personal sector is no longer rising at all rapidly due to the slowdown in the housing market. Nevertheless, international comparisons emanating from the OECD in the form of the ratio of saving (gross of capital consumption but net of stock appreciation) to GDP/GNP, paint a more mixed picture. At around 19 per cent for the past three years the UK ratio compares well with that of the USA (12–13 per cent), but lies below the OECD average and well below the ratio in West Germany (24 per cent) and Japan (32 per cent).

However, there are those (at Morgan Grenfell, for example) who prefer to define personal sector savings in terms of the net acquisition of financial assets (bank deposits and purchases of securities, *less* borrowing), and who calculate accordingly that the saving ratio for this sector has held steady at around 14 per cent after a sharp drop at the beginning of the 1980s. If this calculation is correct then the OECD figure for the UK is clearly a serious underestimate. This must be seen as an issure of some importance, since if savings are already quite buoyant there is less reason to expect households to rein back their consumption expen-

Figure 1.7   *Total domestic saving[1] as % of GDP at factor cost*

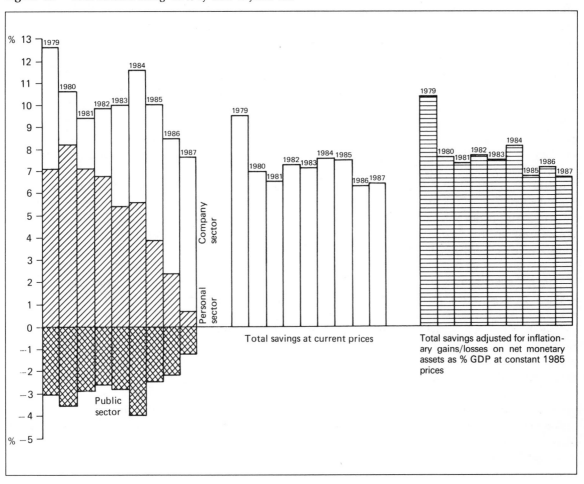

Note:

[1] After providing for stock appreciation and capital consumption at replacement cost and *plus* net capital transfers.

Source: Bank of England Quarterly Bulletin (May 1988) p. 234, and (May 1989) p. 250

diture. No doubt, in 10 years' time, it will be possible to take retrospective measurements of savings and to resolve the issue as to whether they have fallen or not, but this is of little consolation to the Chancellor at the present time. All things considered, he has little choice but to adopt a pragmatic approach, in this case based upon the use of interest rates, which is less concerned with the initial size of the propensities to consume and save than with how they are changing over time as interest rates are raised or lowered.

Economic performance

Introduction

Any assessment of the UK's recent economic performance needs to be placed in an historical context for it to be meaningful. This raises the question of the time period over which performance should be assessed and against which earlier time period it should be judged. Depending upon the choice of time periods very different pictures of recent economic performance can be created. As always statistics – and especially those extending over time – need to be treated with caution. The particular problem which arises in the present context is the performance of the economy between 1970 and the end of 1973. The UK economy experienced a very strong policy-created boom in this period which culminated in the highest level of demand and economic activity the economy had ever known. Although the level of real output achieved in this period was very high, and the level of unemployment correspondingly low, the economy was operating beyond its sustainable level of output (its natural rate), and the level of performance was thus atypical. Indeed, the boom broke at the end of 1973 and with its end came a collapse of the property market, a secondary banking crisis which nearly caused a collapse of the entire banking system and the highest rates of inflation experienced in the UK this century. To try to achieve a more balanced picture of long-run or sustainable economic growth and employment this period needs either to be given less weight or placed in a much longer historical perspective so that it ceases to distort the data.

This section will focus mainly on economic performance since 1979. This date represents a major shift in macroeconomic policy following the change of government in that year and the start of the Thatcher economic experiment. It also provides a period of nearly 10 years which is long enough to reveal the underlying changes in performance of the economy.

1979 also marks a break with the turbulent years of the 1970s which witnessed several major structural changes and shocks in the world economy as well as a number of structural changes specific to the UK. In the early 1970s the post-1944 Bretton Woods fixed exchange rate system was abandoned in favour of a floating rate system. The world economy was subject to two major OPEC oil price increases. The UK joined the European Community (EC), which had major implications for the pattern of its international trade flows. By the end of the 1970s the UK had changed from being an oil importing country to become a major net exporter of oil.

International comparisons

The choice of 1979 as the starting date for this assessment of economic performance is significant in another major respect. From the early 1980s onwards the UK has witnessed a complete turnaround in its economic performance. Before 1980 the UK's economic performance in terms of real growth, living standards, productivity growth, unemployment level and inflation rate was decidedly poor by international standards. Since 1981 the relative decline of the UK economy has come to an end, and on a whole range of macroeconomic indicators the economy has improved its international position by a substantial margin and outperformed the other major OECD countries with the exception of Japan. Such was the magnitude of its relative decline in the 1960s and 1970s that, despite its recent impressive performance, the UK still lags behind the other main economic powers, but at least the gap has started to be narrowed. More significantly, the improved performance of the UK since 1981 stands in sharp contrast with the deterioration in performance by the other major OECD countries. This change in performance coincides with a shift in macroeconomic policy away from the short-term demand management policies of the 1960s and 1970s, which has produced a series of 'stop–go' cycles in activity but had done nothing to reverse the process of long-run decline, to much greater emphasis on longer-term supply-side policies.

During 1979–81 the UK economy experienced a severe recession and with it a large increase in unemployment and a decline in the manufacturing sector. While severe, the rise in unemployment and the decline in manufacturing did not represent a new trend but rather the acceleration of trends clearly established in the 1960s. By 1983 the economy had moved out of recession, and between 1983 and 1988 it experienced sustained and rapid economic growth. Since 1988 the pace of growth has slackened but still remains high by past standards. However, also since 1988, the ability of the economy to sustain its high rate of growth looks increasingly doubtful with the emergence of clear signs of excess demand pressure. The annual rate of inflation has started to show a strong upward trend and the current account of the balance of payments, if the figures are to be believed, shows the largest deficit ever recorded.

Figure 1.8 *Real GDP, 1981–87, average measure, factor cost*

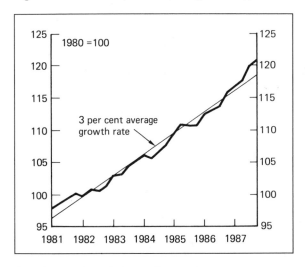

Source: Economic Progress Report, 196 (June 1988)

Over the period 1981–88 real output rose at an average rate of just over 3 per cent per annum. In 1988 the rate of growth was 3.7 per cent. **Figure 1.8** shows the path of real growth between 1981 and 1987. The yearly growth rates for 1982–88 are given in **Table 1.9**.

Although the annual rate of growth has varied during this period around the overall trend of 3 per cent, the striking feature is that the variations have been limited with no pronounced deviations from trend. Such steady growth is important in itself and contrasts sharply with previous experience. In particular, steady growth in this period has enabled firms to expand output without marked fluctuations in the level of stocks and work in progress. This distinctive feature of the 1980s has already been noticed when examining the components of GDP earlier in the chapter. The relative stability of additions to stocks is not only a consequence of steady growth but also a contributor to such stability. In earlier periods large fluctuations in stocks and work in progress, magnified by the multiplier process, have been a major cause of economic instability. The change in the pattern of additions to stocks, and its impact on GDP growth, is shown clearly in **Figure 1.9**.

Growth in the longer term

The steady, sustained, pattern of growth since the early 1980s is placed in its longer-term perspective in **Figure 1.10**. **Figure 1.10** is based on the Treasury's latest estimates of annual GDP growth since 1949. The data has been used to calculate overlapping six-year period growth rates, rather than annual growth rates, in order to facilitate direct comparison with the six-year period 1981–87. **Figure 1.10** includes the Treasury's estimate of growth in 1988 which, in the event, was greater than predicted.

Figure 1.10 shows that in the 1950s and 1960s successive six-year periods had annual real growth rates of between 2.5 and 3.5 per cent. The changed

Table 1.9 *Real GDP growth*

% Average measure, factor cost						
1982	1983	1984	1985	1986	1987	1988
1.6	3.3	2.4	3.7	3.0	4.4	3.7

Average growth 3.2

Source: Economic Progress Report, 196 (June 1988).
Economic Trends, Table 2 (July 1989)

Figure 1.9   *Annual contribution of stockbuilding to GDP growth*

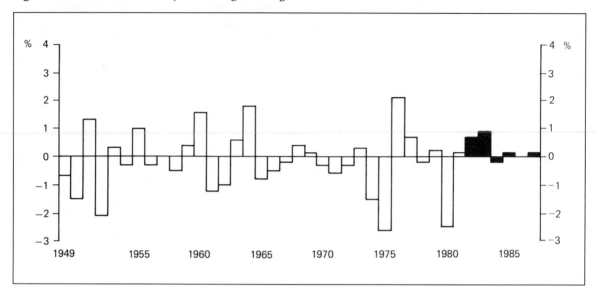

Source: *Economic Progress Report*, 196 (June 1988)

economic conditions of the 1970s and the deterioration in economic performance after the 1970–73 boom stand out clearly. During the 1970s the six-year average growth rate declined to less than 2 per cent. Growth was even lower in the 1979–81 recession but it recovered after 1981 and during 1983–88 the UK experienced the highest sustained rate of growth since 1949–54.

The distinct improvement in the UK's economic performance since the early 1970s is significant not just in comparison with the performance of the 1970s but also in relation to that of the major OECD countries.

During the period 1960–87 the UK's annual average *per capita* real GDP growth rate was 2.1 per cent. This was slightly higher than the US growth rate during the same period but below that of the other major OECD countries and decidedly poor in comparison with Japan's 5.5 per cent growth rate. For the sub-period 1960–68 the UK came out bottom of the international comparison with an average growth rate of 2.4 per cent. During 1968–73, which covers the period of the 1970–73 boom, the average real rate of growth

rose to 2.9 per cent, ahead of the USA which achieved an average growth rate of only 1.8 per cent, but still failed to match the high rates achieved in the other OECD countries. In the sub-period 1973–79 average real *per capita* GDP growth rates declined in all the major OECD countries as a consequence of the first OPEC oil price increase and the subsequent decline in world trade. The UK's average real growth rate slumped to 1.5 per cent, still ahead of the USA but still behind the others. In the period from 1979 to 1987 the picture changed. With the exception of Japan and the UK, the other major OECD countries continued to experience a deterioration in their growth performance while the UK improved its average real growth rate to reach second place behind Japan. Between 1981 and 1987, following the UK's recession, performance was even better. The UK achieved an average real *per capita* growth rate of 2.9 per cent, as high as its past best between 1968–73, and significantly ahead of all the other major OECD countries with the continued exception of Japan, which achieved a growth rate of 3 per cent.

Figure 1.10 *Average growth for six-year periods, 1949–54 to 1983–88*

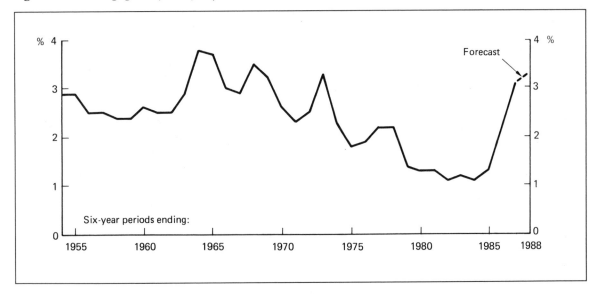

Source: Economic Progress Report, 196 (June 1988)

The recovery in the UK's real *per capita* GDP growth since the early 1980s stands in sharp contrast with the poor performance of most of the other OECD countries and is equally remarkable in relation to the low growth rates of the 1970s. However, it still leaves the UK behind most of the other OECD countries in terms of the absolute level of real *per capita* GDP (see NEDC, 1988).

In 1966 the UK was second only to the USA in terms of real *per capita* GDP, but since then all the other OECD countries, except Italy, have overtaken the UK. Japan, which had the lowest real standard of living among the major OECD countries in 1966, moved ahead of the UK in 1980 and now ranks second with Germany behind the USA. The UK clearly still has a lot of ground to make good if it is to move back up the league table of real living standards, but its recent economic performance would seem to indicate that there is nothing inevitable about the kind of relative economic decline experienced in the 1960s and 1970s. Since 1981 the UK economy has demonstrated its potential to match and exceed the performance of the other OECD countries.

Productivity

Underlying the UK's improved economic performance since 1981 is a significant and sustained improvement in productivity. The striking nature of this turnaround on past poor performance is brought out in **Table 1.10**.

Over the whole period 1960–88 all the major OECD countries suffered from a decline in productivity growth as measured by real output per worker employed. In the sub-period 1960–70 the UK had a productivity growth rate of 2.4 per cent per annum. This was higher than the United States' rate of increase but substantially behind the rates achieved by most other OECD countries. During 1970–80 all the OECD countries suffered a very sharp decline in productivity growth in the aftermath of the first OPEC oil price increase. The rate declined to 1.3 per cent per annum in the UK. This was higher than that achieved by the USA and Sweden but still significantly less than that achieved in the other OECD countries. During 1980–88 this pattern is broken. The UK achieved an annual average growth rate of 2.5 per cent

Table 1.10 *Output per person employed (average annual percentage changes)*

Whole economy	1960-70	1970-80	1980-88
UK	2.4	1.3	2.5
US	2.0	0.4	1.2
Japan	8.9	3.8	2.9
Germany	4.4	2.8	1.8
France	4.6	2.8	2.0
Italy	6.3	2.6	2.0
Canada	2.4	1.5	1.4
G7 average	**3.5**	**1.7**	**1.8**

UK data from Central Statistical Office. Other countries' data from OECD except 1988 which are calculated from national GNP or GDP figures and OECD employment estimates.

Manufacturing industry	1960-70	1970-80	1980-88
UK	3.0	1.6	5.2
US	3.5	3.0	4.0
Japan	8.8	5.3	3.1
Germany	4.1	2.9	2.2
France	5.4	3.2	3.1
Italy	5.4	3.0	3.5
Canada	3.4	3.0	3.6
G7 average	**4.5**	**3.3**	**3.6**

UK data from Central Statistical Office. Other countries' data from OECD, except France and Italy which use IMF employment data. 1988 data for France and Italy cover first three quarters only.

Sources: CSO, OECD, IMF; Reproduced from *Treasury Economic Progress Report,* 201, (April 1989).

which placed it second to Japan and ahead of the other OECD countries which it had lagged behind for nearly two decades.

Economic growth depends upon the **growth of capital and labour** and the **efficiency** with which these are used. The latter is referred to as 'total factor productivity'. It is the improvement in this which largely accounts for the UK's better performance since 1980. According to one set of estimates (Muellbauer, 1986) the trend total factor productivity growth rate for UK manufacturing was 2.76 per cent per annum between the second

half of 1980 and 1986. This exceeds the figure of 2.63 per cent for the period 1959–72 and is much higher than the comparable figure for the 1970s.

Many factors account for this change but high among them is the much greater emphasis given to supply-side factors in government economic policy since 1979. These include changes to the tax system, trade union reforms, privatisation of nationalised industries and greater emphasis on vocational training as detailed on **pp. 61–8**. Another factor was the improvement in management forced on companies by the severity of the 1979–81 recession.

The obvious over-heating of the economy in 1988–89 indicates, however, that if the improvement in productivity growth and economic performance is to be maintained then much more still needs to be done to restructure the economy. In particular, a much higher level of physical investment in new equipment and technologies is required, along with greatly improved vocational training and investment in education. More expenditure on research and development in areas other than defence is also called for along with continued improvements to management and labour relations to make more effective use of these investments.

Inflation *(with Peter Curwen)*

Since the late 1940s the UK economy has experienced a succession of severe macroeconomic problems punctuated by short periods of more favourable economic performance. The same four main problems occur with a disturbing persistence even though at particular times one dominates. These are a low rate of growth of real GDP, high unemployment, persistent inflation and balance of payments deficits. The most serious and protracted problem in the 1970s was that of inflation. In 1975, at the height of the inflationary process, the annual rate of inflation exceeded 24 per cent. The seriousness of the problem is brought out by the fact that the inflation rate in 1975 was higher than at any other time this century. The economic performance of the economy in the 1980s has been dictated by the measures adopted to eradicate the high inflation of the 1970s.

Measurement of inflation

'Inflation' refers to a rise in the general level of prices, or in an average measure of prices in the economy, rather than to the behaviour of the price of an individual good or service. Inflation becomes a serious problem when the general level of prices rises persistently and unpredictably. The rate of inflation is calculated using an index of the general price level, or some other relevant concept of prices, and the index is constructed as a weighted average of the relevant prices. The question of relevant prices highlights the fact that different groups of people are interested in the behaviour of different sets of prices, for example a manufacturer may be concerned about the rate of increase of the price of fuel and raw materials, while a consumer will be more interested in retail prices. For this reason the CSO publishes several different price indices or measures of inflation.

The most widely used of these is the Retail Prices Index (RPI) which is published by the Department of Employment. This is a weighted average of prices for a basket of 600 goods and services consumed by a 'typical' household. The total weights of 1000 are distributed so as to reflect the pattern of spending as revealed by the Family Expenditure Survey (FES), and a new set of weights is introduced at the beginning of each year. Over time the weights assigned to different groups of goods and services can vary considerably, and it is also necessary periodically to alter the main categories of weights in order to reflect major changes in spending patterns. In January 1987 a significant amendment was made to the categories which had been in force since 1974 in order to take account of such items as holiday expenditure and the cost of financial services. The four largest categories are currently housing (175), food (154) which is shrinking continuously, consumer durables (135) and motoring expenditure (128). These weights exclude the spending of high income earners and of pensioner households, the latter having their own independent RPI which is used in order, for example, to index-link pensions.

The RPI for the period since 1975, based upon 1980 = 100, is shown in **Table 1.11**. However, most interest is focussed upon the ongoing rate of inflation, which is expressed most commonly as an annual rate of change. Thus, for example, the annual rate for calendar 1987 can be calculated from **Table 1.11** by the formula $159.9 - 152.4 \div 152.4 \times 100$ per cent which equals 4.9 per cent. When this is repeated on a monthly basis the resulting pattern is as shown in **Figure 1.11**.

The RPI measures only the prices of final goods and services. It thus excludes the prices of intermediate products, but includes the effects of alterations in indirect taxes and in excise duties. There are obviously other ways of going about measuring inflation, and a number of other measures in common usage are set out in **Table 1.11**. The Tax and Price Index (TPI) has been published since August 1979. The general idea was to take account of changes in income taxes and National Insurance Contributions (NICs) which were expected to fall thereby leaving households with more real spending power than appeared to be the case after adjusting gross incomes for changes in the RPI. This was expected to exert downward pressure on wage demands. However, as it turned out the TPI promptly rose more rapidly than the RPI as a result of the 1980 Budget and was put into abeyance, a position it has continued to occupy ever since even though the TPI has risen somewhat more slowly than the RPI since April 1983. The Producer Price Index, previously known as the Wholesale Price Index, is divided into an index covering the prices of materials and fuel and an index covering the prices of home sales of manufactured products ('factory gate' prices). These indices respond to inflationary pressures earlier than the RPI and hence can be useful in providing prior warning of an upsurge in retail prices. As shown in **Table 1.11**, the RPI shadows factory gate prices very closely whereas the index for materials and fuel is relatively volatile and (as in 1986) can occasionally fall. As will be reiterated below, a combination of falling input prices and rising output prices is evidence of a sharp rise in profit margins.

Although these are the only price indices which are widely reported, much of the adjustment from nominal to real magnitudes is done using so-called price 'deflators'. The best-known of these is the index of total home costs, commonly referred to as

Figure 1.11   *The Retail Prices Index*

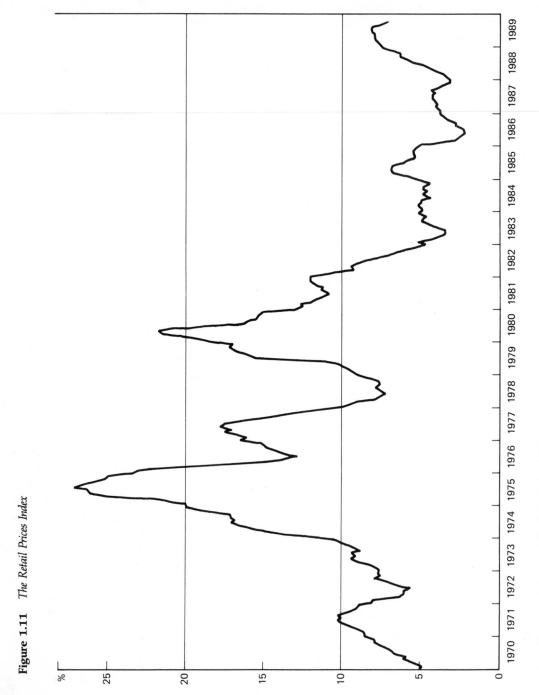

Source: Department of Employment Gazette (September 1989)

Table 1.11 *Assorted price indices (1980 = 100)*

| Year | General index of retail prices | Tax and price index | Producer price index | | GDP deflator[1] |
			Materials and fuel	Manufactured (home sales)	
1975	51.1 (24.2)[2]	54.4	54.9	52.4	52.0
1976	59.6 (16.5)	64.5	68.4	60.9	59.4
1977	69.0 (15.7)	73.9	78.9	72.0	66.7
1978	74.7 (8.2)	76.1	81.6	79.1	74.6
1979	84.8 (13.4)	85.2	92.2	87.7	84.2
1980	100.0 (18.0)	100.0	100.0	100.0	100.0
1981	111.9 (11.9)	114.8	109.3	109.5	110.6
1982	121.5 (8.6)	126.1	117.2	118.0	117.9
1983	127.1 (4.6)	131.1	125.3	124.4	124.7
1984	133.4 (5.0)	136.2	136.4	132.1	130.8
1985	141.5 (6.1)	143.3	137.7	139.4	138.4
1986	146.3 (3.4)	145.9	126.6	145.7	142.2
1987	152.4 (4.2)	147.9	130.4	151.2	149.3
1988	159.9 (4.9)	155.0	134.6	158.0	158.2

Notes:
[1] GDP at current factor cost ÷ GDP at constant factor cost.
[2] Figures in brackets represent the percentage increase on the previous year.
Sources: Department of Employment Gazette.
Economic Trends.
Monthly Digest of Statistics.

the 'implicit' price deflator, which is also recorded in **Table 1.11**. This index measures the change of all prices in the economy as reflected in changes in the cost of producing all of the components of GDP.

All of the main measures of inflation tell much the same story in the longer term, although monthly and quarterly figures can deviate quite appreciably (which is a good reason for not paying too much attention to them). However, the recorded figures for inflation have a significant impact upon financial markets so there is political capital to be made out of the exclusion from the RPI of any components which are rising undesirably fast from the government's point of view. Controversy has recently surfaced in this respect concerning the treatment of housing costs in the RPI.

Because the RPI is used as an indicator of changes in the cost of living it includes as one component the rate of interest paid on mortgage loans for house purchase. Since in most cases the mortgage rate moves in line with other interest rates, this means that each time interest rates rise the RPI – and hence the annual rate of inflation – also increases. Some, including the government, argue that such interest rate induced changes in the RPI are unrepresentative of the 'true' rate of inflation and that the cost of mortgage funds should be excluded from the index. This argument can be rejected on the grounds that if the RPI is meant to be representative of the cost of living it should include the cost of home ownership. If all property was rented a rise in rents would unquestionably imply an increase in the cost of living and would be incorporated in the RPI. An increase in the mortgage rate has exactly the same effect on someone buying their own house and hence should also be included in the RPI, at least until such time as an alternative proxy for housing costs comes into widespread acceptance.

The reasons for inflation

The contrast between the inflationary experience of the 1970s and the 1980s is shown clearly by the annual inflation rate data. Between 1971 and 1979 the annual rate of inflation ranged between 7.1 and 24.2 per cent, with an average value of 13.3 per cent. Between 1982 and 1988 the annual rate of inflation ranged between 3.4 and 8.6 per cent, and the average value had come down to 5.3 per cent. This latter figure is high both by past standards, and in comparison with some of the other major OECD countries, but represents a significant achievement in comparison with the inflationary experience of the 1970s.

The 18 per cent annual rate of inflation in 1980 is out of line with the generally downward trend in inflation after 1979, and shows, *inter alia*, the consequence of an increase in the rate of VAT to 15 per cent which had a once-and-for-all effect on the rate of inflation for one year.

After 1980 the annual rate of inflation declined to 3.4 per cent in 1986, which was the lowest annual rate of inflation recorded since the 1960s. Unfortunately, the trend rate of inflation subsequently moved upwards again, indicating that the earlier success in bringing inflation under control had not permanently removed the threat of inflation from the economy.

Why did the UK experience such high rates of inflation in the 1970s and how was it reduced, but not apparently defeated, in the 1980s? There are no simple answers to these questions and this section focuses only on some general aspects of inflation during this period.

Discussions of the causes and remedies for inflation abound with dozens of different and apparently conflicting explanations of inflation, and help to create the impression that economists are unable to agree on anything. The majority of the explanations offered for inflation by economists, businessmen and politicians are at best incomplete, usually based on faulty logic and frequently at variance with the facts. Explanations often appear to be contradictory because of a failure to make explicit or define the sense in which the term 'cause' is used.

For example, the centuries-old Quantity Theory of Money, and the modern monetarist version of the Quantity Theory, explain inflation in terms of the rate of growth of the nominal quantity of money. According to this analysis, sustained inflation is always and everywhere caused by excess monetary expansion and the only effective and lasting cure for inflation is control of the rate of growth of the nominal quantity of money. This view appears to stand in sharp contrast to the large class of explanations which place primary emphasis on cost-push pressure – especially increasing money wage rates – as the main cause of inflation. However, just as a car will eventually come to a halt if it runs out of fuel no matter how much pressure is put on the accelerator, so a process of inflation can not continue unless it is fuelled by continuous increases in the nominal quantity of money. The issues here are: is cost-push pressure independent of the state of demand or a consequence of excess demand caused by monetary expansion, and why is it that on some occasions independent cost-push pressure is supported by sufficient monetary expansion to allow accelerating inflation? Put differently, to say that inflation is caused by excessive monetary expansion, and that the government is ultimately responsible for this since it controls the printing presses, leaves unanswered the question of why governments on some occasions undertake excessive monetary expansion. If one of the reasons is their unwillingness to face the political consequences of resisting wage-push pressure, especially from trade unions in the public sector, the apparent conflict between cost-push and money supply explanations is resolved.

International factors

The other factor which needs to be considered in explaining inflation is the extent to which an explanation is general in nature or specific to an individual country. Given that many different kinds of country experienced a severe inflation problem in the 1970s, any explanation of UK inflation which depends solely upon factors specific to the UK is seriously incomplete and probably erroneous. The correct explanation must also account for the fact that many other countries experienced the same problem at the same time.

The similarity of the inflationary experience of the major OECD countries, as measured by the annual average rate of increase in the consumer prices index, is represented graphically in **Figure 1.12**.

All six countries shown in **Figure 1.12** had a rising rate of inflation during 1966–72. The rates differed, with the UK at the top of the range, but the pattern of movement was essentially similar. All six countries experienced a significant increase in the rate of inflation after 1972, with a sharp peak in 1974/75 followed by a period of high but declining rates of inflation with a smaller peak in 1980. In most cases inflation declined after 1980 to levels below those experienced in the late 1960s.

The UK and Japan were very close in terms of inflation rates until 1973. From 1973 until the end of 1981 the UK, while following the pattern in other countries, achieved the distinction of a significantly higher annual rate while Japan achieved the lowest. From 1981 onwards the pattern for all six countries is similar, but in this period the UK achieved a lower average rate than Italy, France and West Germany combined.

The common factor in explaining the inflationary experience of different countries in the 1970s is the behaviour of the price of **crude oil** and hence of other energy sources. The first substantial increase in the price of oil, the first OPEC oil price 'shock', occurred in 1973 and accounts for the upturn in inflation in 1974 and 1975. The second, smaller, OPEC oil price shock occurred in 1979 and this is seen in **Figure 1.12** in the upturn in inflation rates in 1980. The substantial and unexpected increase in the price of energy in the 1970s combined with sharp increases in the prices of

Figure 1.12 *Consumer price indices, selected countries, 1975–88*

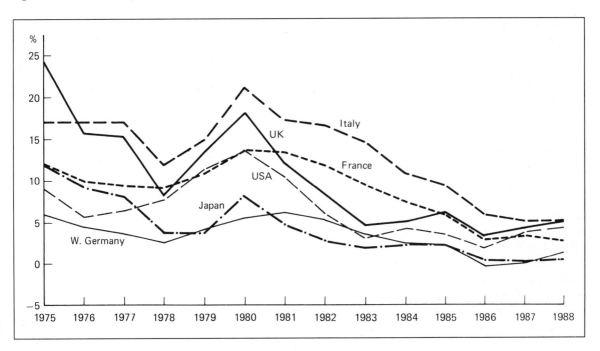

Sources: OECD, Main Economic Indicators; *Department of Employment Gazette*

other commodities and the feed-on effects of this on other costs and prices, accounts for the broad pattern of the inflationary experience of the 1970s, but clearly fails to explain why the UK had much higher inflation rates than other countries. The latter is the more surprising in that compared with Italy, W. Germany, France and Japan the UK was much less dependent on imported energy supplies.

Experience during the 1970s

Periods of sustained inflationary pressure, such as that experienced by the UK during the 1970s, are always associated with sustained monetary expansion. Excess monetary expansion is usually the cause of inflation in the sense that increases in the rate of growth of the nominal quantity of money precede increases in the rate of inflation. The process linking changes in monetary growth to changes in the rate of inflation involves long and variable lags and can be obscured for periods of one, two or even three years, especially at times of structural change in the financial system, but is clearly observable in the longer run.

The UK's inflationary experience since the early 1970s offers some support for the long-run Quantity Theory relationship. Uncontrolled and largely unplanned expansion of the money supply following the reform of the system of monetary control in 1971, known as Competition and Credit Control (CCC), set in motion a process of accelerating inflation before the OPEC oil price shock had its inflationary impact. Over the period 1969–73 the annual rate of growth of broad money supply, $\pounds M_3$, increased from 2.2 per cent to 27 per cent in 1972 and 1973. These unprecedented rates of monetary expansion fed through into inflation with a lag, and added significantly to the inflationary pressure caused by the oil price increase. This combination of events explains why the UK suffered much higher rates of inflation after 1973 than the other major OECD countries.

With the rapid acceleration of the rate of inflation to over 24 per cent in 1975, inflationary expectations became an important determinant of economic behaviour, and long-established empiri-

cal economic relationships, such as the Phillips Curve relationship between unemployment and inflation, ceased to hold. Indeed, the 1970s proved to be the critical testing ground for many previously cherished macroeconomic theories. The Phillips Curve and the associated idea of using an expansion of government expenditure permanently to reduce unemployment did not survive the test of experience in this period.

During 1973–77 the annual rate of increase of the broad money supply, $\pounds M_3$, was reduced to a range of 6–11 per cent. The deliberate reduction and control of the rate of growth of the money supply was due to an increasing, if reluctant, acceptance of the link between monetary expansion and inflation and the need to control the rate of growth of the money supply as an essential prerequisite for the successful control of inflation. This policy was formalised in 1976 with the introduction of annual monetary targets for the rate of growth of the money supply. This policy was adopted partly as a condition imposed by the IMF in return for granting the UK a loan to help deal with its exchange rate problem. The irony of this was that if monetary targets had been introduced early, as part of a programme of restraining monetary growth and inflation, the exchange rate would not have depreciated and hence there would have been no need to borrow from the IMF. In the event the IMF loan proved to be unnecessary because of the UK's emergence as a net oil exporter, which quickly led to upward pressure on the exchange rate. However, the legacy of monetary targets remained.

Monetary growth was restrained for two years following the introduction of monetary targets, but relaxed subsequently as attention shifted from reducing inflation to reducing unemployment, which increased almost continuously following the 1974 recession. Thus between 1977 and 1980 the annual rate of growth of the money supply went up from 9 per cent to nearly 20 per cent. However, the 20 per cent figure in 1980 is misleading as to the underlying position with regards to monetary conditions. It reflects a once-and-for-all adjustment in the financial system and volume of banking business following the abolition of the Supplementary Special Deposit Scheme, the 'Corset', and the introduction of yet another new system of monetary control.

Experience since 1979

From 1979 onwards the main priority of government economic policy was the elimination of inflation, and effective control of the rate of growth of the money supply was seen as one of the main means of achieving this objective. To this end annual monetary targets were announced each year in the Chancellor's Budget Statement and used to signal the government's firm commitment to the eradication of inflation (see **pp. 322–5**). Between 1982 and 1984 this policy met with some success in that the annual rate of increase of £M$_3$ was in the range of 9–10 per cent and the annual rate of inflation declined to 5 per cent in 1984.

Monetary policy was much tighter in the early 1980s than in the 1970s and achieved the desired reduction in inflation. It also, however, led to very high real interest rates and a substantial appreciation of the exchange rate (which was appreciating anyway as a result of growing net oil exports) which combined to plunge the economy into recession during 1979–81. The recession served to reduce inflationary expectations and combined with the government's supply-side policies, particularly trade union reform, brought inflation down to levels comparable with those of the UK's main overseas competitors for the first time in twenty years. The recession also saw unemployment reach levels hitherto unimaginable in the post-1945 period. The persistence of very high unemployment levels in the following period of low inflation and economic recovery, as well as the nature of this unemployment, suggests some kind of fundamental structural change in the economy. The 1979–81 recession caused by the new government's economic policy and tight control of the money supply thus served to reveal the full extent of a more deep-seated economic problem rather than comprising the cause of the problem itself.

The severity of the recession, combined with the persistence of high levels of unemployment, led the government to alter the basis of its monetary policy after 1982. In a small open economy the government can control one, and only one, of the following target variables: the money supply, the rate of interest and the exchange rate. The emphasis on monetary targets after 1979 contributed to the sharp appreciation of the exchange rate and hence to the loss of exports and the rise in unemployment. This also helped to bring inflation down through a fall in the price of imports. Once inflation was down, however, government policy switched towards targeting the exchange rate, especially the critical sterling–Deutsch Mark (DM) rate, in an attempt to reduce imports and boost exports and by this means reduce unemployment. At the time, the switch of policy target was not admitted publicly, and the government still announced annual target ranges for the rate of growth of the money supply as an indicator of its continued commitment to an anti-inflation strategy. The practical implications of the unannounced official switch in target was that the growth of the money supply exceeded the government's target range by an increasingly large amount (see **pp 324–5**). Given the achievement of low rates of inflation in the mid-1980s, little concern was expressed by the government and others about the failure to meet the money supply targets.

To some commentators this simply revealed yet again how quickly the lessons of recent history could be forgotten. They observed that between 1984 and 1988 the annual rate of growth of M$_3$ increased from 10 per cent to 23 per cent. They accordingly argued that, taken in conjunction with a lag which was long in comparison with the experience of the mid-1970s (though not when taking a longer-term perspective), the uncontrolled growth of the money supply after 1985 fed through into increasing inflationary pressure and rising inflation. The lagged effect was to cause inflation to bottom out at 3.4 per cent in 1986, subsequently increasing in each of the following years until it had returned to its 1982 rate by mid-1989. This alleged cause and effect relationship between broad money and inflation enjoyed some support in both government circles and elsewhere, although much criticism was also voiced over the fact that the relationship had been far too erratic in the past to provide anything akin to 'proof' that inflation was essentially an issue of too much money chasing too few goods.

It is possible to analyse what happened by reference to **Table 1.12** and **Table 1.13**. As shown in **Table 1.12**, the ongoing rises in labour costs which have always been a characteristic of the UK economy, were mostly compensated by rises in labour productivity with the result that unit labour costs rose very little after 1982. The biggest contributor to manufacturing output prices since 1982 has clearly been changes in domestic profit margins. These appear to have risen exceptionally sharply in 1986, although much less of late. It has been argued that companies basically apply a mark-up to their expected long-run costs, which does explain the rise in margins in 1986 when oil input prices fell sharply, but is less plausible in terms of later years.

Table 1.13 takes into account the effects upon output prices of competitiveness and capacity

Table 1.12 *Contributions to output prices in manufacturing[1] from changes in cost components (%)*

	Labour productivity (increase −) (1)	Labour costs (2)	Unit labour costs (3 = 1 + 2)	Input prices (4)	Bought-in services (5)	Margins (residual) (6) = (7 − 3 + 4 + 5)	Output prices (7)
1980	1.8	8.0	9.9	3.7	5.2	− 3.4	15.4
1981	− 2.0	6.3	4.2	2.9	2.7	− 2.4	7.4
1982	− 3.0	4.4	1.3	2.3	1.1	2.2	6.9
1983	− 3.8	3.7	− 0.1	2.6	0.9	2.0	5.4
1984	− 2.7	3.4	0.6	3.0	1.0	0.5	5.1
1985	− 1.4	3.5	2.1	1.0	1.2	1.4	5.7
1986	− 1.5	3.1	1.6	− 3.4	1.0	4.9	4.1
1987	− 3.1	3.4	0.2	1.7	0.9	1.6	4.4
1988	− 2.5	3.5	1.0	1.6	1.4	0.8	4.8

Note:
[1] Excluding food, drink and tobacco.
Source: Bank of England Quarterly Bulletin (May 1989) p. 229.

Table 1.13 *Estimated contributions to the growth in output prices (%)*

	Unit labour costs	Input price proxy	Bought-in services	Competi-tiveness	Capacity utilisation	Residual	Output prices
1980	9.3	3.0	5.7	− 2.3	− 1.2	1.0	15.4
1981	8.7	1.3	7.1	− 3.1	− 3.6	− 3.0	7.4
1982	2.7	0.8	5.0	− 1.0	0.5	− 1.1	6.9
1983	− 0.4	0.2	2.1	1.1	1.6	0.8	5.4
1984	− 0.6	1.1	1.1	1.4	2.4	− 0.2	5.1
1985	1.3	1.0	1.4	1.0	1.7	− 0.5	5.7
1986	2.7	− 4.7	1.8	—	0.1	4.1	4.1
1987	0.8	− 0.4	1.7	0.7	0.1	1.5	4.4
1988	0.6	0.9	1.7	0.3	1.3	—	4.8

Source: Bank of England Quarterly Bulletin (May 1989) p. 232.

utilisation, both of which are correlated with profit margins. The residual indicates that the specified contributions did not account exactly for the measured output prices, with the large residuals in 1986 and 1987 indicating that manufacturers took advantage of an unexpected fall in input prices. It is clear from **Table 1.13** that, for example, whereas companies were constrained in their ability to put up their prices because of competitive pressures in the early 1980s, they felt able to take advantage of their improved competitiveness thereafter. It is also clear that as spare capacity was used up there was a tendency to take advantage of the shortage of supply by raising margins.

At the present time, it would appear that margins are roughly comparable with past experience. It is obviously possible to argue that inflation would have been rather lower if companies had resisted the urge to raise prices at every opportunity, but it must also be recognised that they could not have been expected to leave their margins at the depressed levels of the early 1980s. The most interesting lesson is possibly that UK manufacturers will have to emulate their Japanese and W. German rivals in being prepared to cut margins in order to maintain competitiveness.

One factor which may well have some significant bearing on this issue is the somewhat ominous recent upturn in earnings. The Department of Employment publishes an average earnings index for all employees in Great Britain. Starting at a 17 per cent increase during the 12-month period ending in January 1981, the index fell progressively for two years, at which point the underlying increase for the 12-month period to January 1983 stood at 8 per cent. It remained absolutely constant at 7.5 per cent from July 1984 to March 1987, and reached 8 per cent once again in October 1987. The underlying rate subsequently rose to stand at 9·25 per cent in August 1988, and it has remained at roughly that level for the past year.

At one stage the remarkable stability of the underlying rate was one of the most remarked-upon features of inflation – although as already noted it was generally matched by the underlying increase in productivity. The upturn since 1988 has therefore recreated the fear in some circles that stagflation may reappear. At this juncture it is difficult to be certain either way since the underlying rate has remained fairly stable for many months, but there can be no doubt that a rise to over 10 per cent will cause much dismay in financial circles.

Clearly, the rise in earnings reflects pressure in the labour market and a general shortage of supply. The best hope in seeking to mitigate inflationary pressures must therefore lie in generating additional capacity since manufacturers are clearly able to sell more than they can currently supply whilst maintaining an historically acceptable profit margin. The issue of how to increase supply is primarily a matter of raising the level of investment, but there are also wider issues to which we must now turn.

Supply-side economics   *Peter Curwen*

During the long period of Keynesian orthodoxy it was widely accepted both that government intervention was desirable *per se* and also that the purpose of macroeconomic intervention was primarily to maintain demand during recessions in order to boost output and employment. In terms of a standard economic model this is best viewed as a shift to the right of the aggregate demand curve. However, it follows that if prices are to remain stable (as measured in aggregate by a price index) then aggregate supply must increase at the same rate as aggregate demand. In a recession, with machinery and men lying idle, this seems a reasonable proposition, but in practice it is open to a number of objections. In the first place the labour supply, for example, may be inflexible because it is geographically located in a different place to where the demand is being created, or it may possess skills which are unsuitable or alternatively no skills at all. It is possible to argue that regional policy can resolve the former difficulty by moving work to the workers, although as we shall see (on **pp. 295–6**) this may be both inefficient and expensive, but the latter problem is likely to prove more intractable. Equally, there is the issue of 'crowding out' whereby government spending may to a greater or lesser degree simply displace private sector spending.

But if aggregate supply is inflexible then a surge in aggregate demand is almost certainly going to create excess demand and hence drive up prices, thereby creating the kind of trade-off between employment and inflation enshrined in the Phillips Curve. Faced with this phenomenon, the logical response might be to try to suppress the inflationary pressure whilst maintaining high levels of aggregate demand – in which case inflation cannot be suppressed by reducing aggregate demand itself. This suggests that a prices and incomes policy should be used in order to prevent, by law, the onset of both price and wage inflation, but since this does nothing of itself to reduce the excess demand it is unlikely to have lasting effects (see **pp. 338–9**).

This being so, logic indicates that if output and employment are to be fostered without creating inflationary pressures, then the model must be made to work the other way around – that is, by holding aggregate demand in check in order to prevent it spilling over into higher prices, whilst simultaneously increasing aggregate supply. Indeed, if aggregate supply increases whilst aggregate demand remains constant, then not only do output and employment rise but downwards pressure is also exerted on prices. It may, of course, be argued that aggregate demand cannot be held back that successfully in the face of rising aggregate supply, at least not in the context of the UK, but so long as supply moves first and demand merely keeps pace with it, rising output and employment are compatible with stable prices. It is possible to set some of the subsequent discussion in the context of this simple model. In particular, monetarism can best be viewed as the attempt to rein back aggregate demand after 1979 in order to control inflation whilst supply-side economics got on with the task of creating output and jobs. It is clear that both needed to work in tandem, or alternatively that some other mechanism for reining in demand such as high interest rates be introduced instead of money supply control.

The Achilles heel of such an approach is straightforward – if demand moves ahead of supply, which could most easily happen when supply runs up against capacity constraints, then rising output and employment will be accompanied by rising prices, and if prices rise too quickly demand may have to be reined in so sharply that a recession is caused. The issue of whether demand can be adequately reined in is discussed in detail in Chapter 9. For the moment the concern is to address how a supply-side policy has been introduced in the UK since 1979.

It is important to appreciate that aggregate supply is dependent upon supply at a microeconomic level. The bottom line is that individuals must be given incentives to work harder and to behave in an entrepreneurial manner. This can happen only if markets are allowed to work as freely as possible, hence the main task of government is to create an environment in which effort is rewarded rather than to take decisions on behalf of individuals. From this it follows that governments should reduce their share of total expenditure and so reform the fiscal system that the total tax burden is reduced and disincentive effects are kept to a minimum.

It is, however, slightly ironic that, at least in the medium term, it is incumbent upon the government to take a great deal of (often legislative) action in order to get the supply side of the economy to work. Thus, for example, the failure of the private sector to deal adequately with the training of the labour force has left the government with much of the responsibility for improving the quality of the labour supply. Equally, deregulation of markets has generally brought regulation hard on its heels (see, for example, **pp. 98–9**). The wide range of governmental initiatives which may reasonably be considered as supply-side policies is set out in **Appendix 1.2.** It is not possible to comment on all of these in detail, but it should be noted that some, for example, are directed at removing the 'unemployment trap' – that is, the tendency for certain people to find themselves no better off financially when in employment than when out of employment; some at encouraging workers to price themselves back into jobs, mainly by curbing the power of trade unions to push up wages; some to improve the quality of the labour force; some to deregulate markets; and some to transfer activity back from the unofficial (black) economy to the official economy.

It is extremely difficult to judge whether these

policies have been successful, partly because insufficient time has passed since their introduction and partly because it is never possible to be certain what would have happened in their absence. Obviously such indicators as the rate of growth offer some support for the efficacy of supply-side measures, and there is widespread agreement that the labour market works rather better than it did 10 years ago. But whether cuts in tax rates have achieved anything is at best open to doubt, particularly since, as will be shown on **p. 112**, the aggregate tax burden has not decreased in line with falling tax rates.

Appendix 1.1   Say's Law, the Laffer Curve and the Gutman Effect

Say's Law

Supply-side economics has its roots in the work of J. B. Say (1767–1832) who is best-known for coining the expression 'supply creates its own demand', an opinion shared by many neo-classical economists. Say's basic argument was that if there was an increase in the numbers of those seeking work then competition among the suppliers of labour would drive down the real wage to the point at which employers would be willing to buy any available labour which had not already chosen to be self-employed. In the process of using these labour inputs to make products, payments would have to be made for both labour and other inputs in the form of interest, dividends and profits. The value of output is thus exactly matched by an equal amount of factor payments sufficient to buy everything which has been produced. Hence **supply creates its own demand**.

During the Keynesian orthodoxy Say's Law came to be held in low esteem once it became widely accepted that there could be a deficiency of effective demand (see discussion in the Introduction). Say's Law came back into fashion along with the Quantity Theory when a solution was sought to the problem of 'stagflation'.

The Laffer Curve

The Curve, associated with the work of A. Laffer in the mid-1970s but which can be traced back to the ideas of Adam Smith (1776) among others, correlates tax rates with tax revenue. The Curve begins with zero revenue at a zero rate of tax, rises to a peak at some positive rate of less than 100 per cent (which can be determined only empirically) and subsides back to zero revenue at a tax rate of 100 per cent. This latter point is supposed to be the consequence of the total disincentive effect of such a tax rate, although it seems extremely implausible once one accepts that most tax revenue is returned to workers as benefits of one kind or another. However, the key issue is that if tax rates are raised continuously then eventually tax revenue will begin to fall, which implies the need to keep the rate below the threshold rate that triggers the fall in revenue. It follows logically that if tax rates start above this threshold then lowering them will increase tax revenue. Just what is going to happen if tax rates are lowered when they are already below the threshold is somewhat less clear-cut, but the benefits are likely to be rather greater if tax-deductible allowances such as mortgage interest relief are simultaneously phased out. In the case of the UK there is considerable disagreement about the exact shape of the Laffer Curve.

The Gutman Effect

This phenomenon, named after P. Gutman, essentially arises when reductions in the rate of tax induce transactions occurring previously in the black economy, and hence generating no tax revenue, to enter the official economy because the possibility of fines or imprisonment is no longer warranted given the relatively small deduction in tax if transactions are declared to the tax authorities. Hence the tax base is widened if tax rates are reduced and tax revenue rises accordingly. This effect will operate in conjunction with the Laffer Curve.

Appendix 1.2   Supply-Side Measures

The measures outlined below are all associated in one way or another with the supply side of the economy. In other words, they were introduced either wholly or partly in order to **help markets work better**. A fuller version can be obtained from the *Economic Progress Report* (November/December 1984; November/December 1985; October 1987; August 1988; and August 1989).

From 1979 to 1984 the government was slowly evolving its supply-side strategy, which is assembled under broad heads below. However, the pace picked up after 1985 as much supply-side legislation reached the statute books, so information is assembled by year thereafter.

1979–84

(1) In the **labour** market the main tax changes came in the 1979 Budget with the basic rate of income tax reduced to 30 per cent, higher rates of tax brought down sharply, and VAT raised to 15 per cent.

(a) Personal allowances rose by 16 per cent in real terms over the whole period.

(b) National Insurance surcharge reduced, then abolished in 1984 Budget.

(c) Encouragement of profit sharing and share option schemes.

(d) Earnings-related supplement to unemployment benefit was abolished.

(e) Enterprise Allowance scheme to foster self-employment for the unemployed.

(f) Reduction in stamp duty on house purchase.

(g) Right to buy for council house tenants.

(h) 1946 Fair Wages Resolution rescinded and statutory provisions for setting pay solely on comparability grounds repealed.

(i) Alteration to legislation on unfair dismissal.

(2) Also legislation to shift balance back towards the individual and to promote democracy within trade unions.

(a) Financial assistance provided for union ballots.

(b) Secret ballots to be held (i) before industrial action is taken if unions to retain immunity against legal proceedings, (ii) to 'approve' closed shop agreements, and (iii) from October 1985 for elections to the governing bodies of trade unions.

(c) Secondary picketing made subject to civil litigation.

(3) White Paper on *Training for Jobs*.

(a) Youth Training Scheme.

(b) Manpower Services Commission's 'Open Tech' initiative on 'distance learning'.

(c) Young Workers Scheme 1982.

(d) Enterprise Allowance Scheme.

(4) In the **capital** market foreign exchange controls abolished in 1979.

(a) Dividend controls abolished in 1979.

(b) Hire purchase controls abolished in 1982.

(c) Controls on bank lending abolished in 1980.

(5) Simplification of planning controls.

(a) Public sector bodies encouraged to make land available for development.

(b) System of industrial development certificates relaxed in 1979 and suspended in 1982.

(c) Office development permits abolished.

(d) Stringent limitations upon industrial subsidies and other measures of regional policy.

(e) Creation of Enterprise Zones.

(f) Loan Guarantee Scheme.

(g) Business Expansion Scheme 1983.

(6) Tax changes affecting companies included:

(a) 1980 Budget – initial allowance of 50 per cent for industrial buildings increased to 100 per cent for small industrial buildings.

(b) 1981 Budget – initial allowances for industrial buildings increased from 50 per cent to 75 per cent.

(c) Capital allowances of 75 per cent introduced for the first year only for the construction of properties for letting.

(d) 1984 Budget – phasing out of initial allowances of 100 per cent for plant and machinery and of 75 per cent for industrial buildings by 1986.

(7) Abolition of pay and price controls in 1979.

(a) Competition Act 1980.

(b) *Report of the Committee of Inquiry into Proposals to amend the Shops Acts*, Cmnd 9376 (1984)

(c) Privatisation programme.

(d) Contracting out in local authorities and National Health Service.

Budget

1985

Main personal allowances raised by double the rate of inflation.

National Insurance contributions rate reduced for low paid workers and upper limit on employees' contributions for higher paid workers abolished.

Expansion of Youth Training Scheme.

Expansion of Community Programme.

1986

Basic rate of income tax reduced from 30 per cent to 29 per cent, also small companies' rate of corporation tax.

Capital transfer tax (now inheritance tax) reformed to encourage lifetime gifts.

Improvements in tax incentives for employee share schemes.

Restart programme extended nationwide.

Enterprise Allowance Scheme expanded.

Stamp duty on share transactions reduced from 1 per cent to 0.5 per cent.

Personal Equity Plan (PEP) scheme announced.

Other Measures

1985

Social Security Act 1985 improved occupational pension rights of 'early leavers'.

Solicitors' near-monopoly of conveyancing reduced by Administration of Justice Bill 1985.

White Paper *Lifting the Burden* (Cmnd 9571) issued in July, listing some 80 proposals for deregulating business activities.

New policy on support for industrial research and development announced March 1985.

Setting up of Enterprise and Deregulation Unit (EDU) for three years.

1986/87

Social Security Act 1986 introduced greater flexibility into pension arrangements to help to alleviate the 'unemployment trap'.

Housing and Planning Act 1986 encouraged more home purchases by public sector tenants.

Green Paper *Trade Unions and their members* Cm 95, issued in February 1987, contained further proposals to improve democracy and members' rights in trades unions.

White Paper *Building businesses. . . not barriers* Cmnd 9794 issued in May 1986, listed some 80 proposals for lifting administrative and legal burdens on businesses.

Business Expansion Scheme's life extended indefinitely.

Life of Loan Guarantee Scheme extended and premium reduced.

1987

Basic rate of income tax reduced from 29 per cent to 27 per cent.

Small companies' corporation tax rate reduced to 27 per cent.

New tax regime for personal pensions to give greater freedom of choice.

Tax relief for retraining employees changing jobs.

Profit-related pay encouraged by tax relief.

Business Expansion Scheme altered to ease equity raising throughout the year.

VAT arrangements changed to reduce the burden on small businesses.

1988

Basic rate of income tax reduced from 27 per cent to 25 per cent.

Main personal allowances raised by double the rate of inflation.

Higher rates of income tax above 40 per cent abolished.

Small companies' rate of corporation tax cut to 25 per cent.

Capital gains taxation reformed.

Business Expansion Scheme extended to companies' specialising in letting residential property.

Capital duty abolished.

VAT registration arrangements modified.

Wages Act 1986 reduced the scope of the Wages Councils' activities.

Technical and Vocational Education initiative extended nationwide.

City Technology Colleges proposed.

Further employment measures introduced, including expansion of the Community Programme, the Restart programme, increased number of Jobclubs, and a new Job Training Scheme.

Building Societies Act 1986 allowed building societies to diversify.

Financial Services Act 1986 introduced new system of regulation for financial services industry.

Banking Act 1987 strengthened framework for banking supervision.

Local Enterprise Agency Grant Scheme introduced.

White Paper *Housing, the Government's proposals*, Cm 214, issued in September 1987, outlined the reform of the rented housing sector.

May 1987 Report to Parliament *Encouraging Enterprise* set out proposals for deregulating business activities.

1988

White Paper *Training for Employment* announced a new employment training programme (incorporating existing programmes) to improve skills of long-term unemployed.

Career Development Loan Scheme extended nationally.

Legislation covering investor protection in financial markets came into effect in April 1988.

January 1988 *Enterprise Initiative* White Paper sets up Business Development Initiative to provide subsidised consultancy to small firms. It also revised regional assistance.

Loan Guarantee Scheme extended in inner city task force areas from June 1988.

1989

Reform of NICs

Small companies upper limit for 25 per cent corporation tax raised.

Abolition of retirement pensioners earnings rule.

New tax incentives for share ownership, including major improvements to PEPs.

In April 1988, under the Social Security Act 1986, family credit replaced family income supplement.

From July 1988 Social Security Act 1986 gave right to join personal pension schemes.

Education Reform Act 1988 provided for national curriculum; open enrolment; ceding of school budget responsibility to heads and governors; abolition of ILEA.

White Paper *Releasing Enterprise* (Cmnd 512) issued in November 1988, specified 80 new deregulation proposals, including review of SIB rule book. EDU to survive until at least April 1990.

References

1 Cm 95 (1987)   *Trade Unions and their members* (HMSO) (Feb-May).
2 Cm 214 (1987)   *Housing, the Government's proposals* (HMSO) (September).
3 Cmnd 9571 (1985)   *Lifting the Burden* (HMSO) (July).
4 Cmnd 9794 (1986)   *Building businesses . . . not barriers* (HMSO) (May).
5 Cmnd 512 (1988)   *Releasing Enterprise* (HMSO) (November).
6 Muellbauer, J. (1986)   'The Assessment: productivity and Competitiveness in British Manufacturing', *Oxford Review of Economic Policy* (Autumn) pp. i–xxv.
7 NEDC (1988)   *British Industrial Performance.*
8 A useful summary of recent publications on growth in the UK and elsewhere is to be found in Wolf, M. (1988)   'Is There a British Miracle?', *Financial Times*, 16 June, p. 27.

2

The Financial System

Peter Curwen

Financial intermediation

In a primitive economic world those who have saved part of their income and who wish to **on-lend their savings** (the ultimate lenders), will meet together with those who wish to **borrow** for varous reasons (the ultimate borrowers) and arrange a mutually agreeable price for the transfer of funds between them. However, in a sophisticated world such transfers are beset with difficulties. The lenders and borrowers may be geographically dispersed; the amounts which lenders wish to make available may not match the amounts which borrowers wish to borrow; and the term to maturity of

funds on offer may not match borrowers' requirements. In principle, the price charged for transfers of funds – the interest rate – can be adjusted to overcome most of these difficulties, but in many cases a mutually agreeable interest rate will not be forthcoming, and the transfers will not take place even though lenders wish to lend and borrowers wish to borrow. Financial intermediaries are needed to overcome this problem.

Any lender who has decided to hold a portfolio of financial assets has to balance a number of considerations in deciding which assets to hold. In the first place, he or she is concerned with the **risk** element in the loan, which arises because the loan may not be repaid at all; because he or she may need cash prior to an asset's redemption date; or because even if an asset can be redeemed before maturity this may involve a partial capital loss. Furthermore, if relatively small sums are involved, these can generally be turned into only one or two different types of asset, thereby preventing the lender from holding a sufficiently diversified portfolio of assets to protect against a particularly bad performance by one type of asset held. Secondly, the lender is unlikely to want to lend for long periods, partly for the reasons mentioned above, and partly because it constrains his ability to spend as the opportunity arises.

Finally, the individual lender is unlikely to be well-informed. It may prove a time-consuming and expensive process to find a borrower willing to match the characteristics of the loan, and indeed the lender may ultimately fail to do so.

It is equally true that a potential borrower may be unable to find a lender willing and able to match his requirements – which generally include a desire to borrow for long periods of time. At the end of the day these considerations, combined with the fact that the lender obviously wants to maximise the interest rate whilst the borrower wants to minimise it, severely constrain the volume of funds transferred directly between individuals.

It is also necessary to take account of **liquidity considerations**. 'Liquidity' is concerned primarily with the speed with which any instrument can be turned into cash, or wholly liquid, form. But it is also important that the value of the instrument is preserved in the process. It is possible to sell most financial instruments in the open market for cash, but there is no guarantee that the exact face-value of the instrument will be repaid to its holder unless it is held to maturity. If it is sold prior to maturity, then its face-value will be determined by the face-value of newly-issued instruments having the same characteristics with respect to – for example – yield, maturity and risk. An early sale of any instrument may thus result in either a capital gain or a capital loss. Conventionally, any instrument issued with an original life-span of no more than 91 days is considered to be liquid, and this term also applies to any instrument which, irrespective of its

original term to maturity, has less than 91 days left to maturity.

These issues can be addressed by an intermediary. The law of large numbers operates such that, whilst some liabilities to depositors need to be kept in cash or near-cash form to meet daily cash withdrawals, the rest can be on-lent to borrowers as long-term lending. As a consequence, the intermediary, unlike an individual, can create a balance sheet with its liabilities in relatively liquid forms and its assets (representing its claims on those to whom it lends) in relatively illiquid forms. Because it handles large numbers of loans, an intermediary must expect some borrowers to default. However, such defaults are very unlikely to put the intermediary at risk of going out of business. Hence, whilst the ultimate lender, in lending directly to one or a few individuals, faces the possibility of a total default, he generally runs the risk of losing no more than a small proportion of his funds if the intermediary he deposits them with gets into difficulties. Furthermore, the rate of interest can be adjusted to take account of different degrees of risk when lending to different intermediaries.

It is important to note from this discussion that when funds are deposited with an intermediary the money is not, in the majority of cases, on-lent in exactly the same form to the ultimate borrower. Instead, the process of 'funds transformation' takes place whereby the intermediary creates liabilities, in the form of claims against itself by the ultimate lender, having different characteristics to its assets in the form of its own claims against the ultimate borrowers. Sometimes one intermediary may on-lend to another, with the result that funds transformation takes place on more than one occasion as funds flow through the financial system, and in the process the ultimate lender becomes increasingly separated from the ultimate borrower.

In summary, the process of intermediation is as beneficial to lenders as it is to borrowers. On the one hand, as discussed above, the lender faces a reduced risk; he can withdraw his money on demand or by giving relatively short periods of notice; he has no need to choose between a host of ultimate borrowers but between only a small number of intermediaries; and he effectively obtains a share in a much more diversified portfolio than he could hold as an individual. On the other hand, the borrower knows where to go to get funds, and there are more funds available.

One final point which should be noted is that whilst in principle the use of an intermediary might be expected to cause interest rates paid to depositors to fall, and those charged to borrowers to rise (since the intermediary exists to make a profit by selling its services), this may well not happen in practice. The depositor faces a reduced risk of default, and therefore should accept a lower reward for the risk-taking element of the loan, so that even after adding the intermediary's mark-up the cost to the borrower may be lower than for a direct transfer from the ultimate lender.

Classifying financial intermediaries

The range of financial intermediaries in the UK is unusually varied. The first task is, therefore, to determine the most coherent way to arrange them in classes for further analysis. There are two main considerations here. In the first place, monetary controls operate through intermediaries, and it would seem helpful to divide up intermediaries into those which are affected by controls (particularly over the money supply) and those which are not. In this respect it was traditionally argued that intermediaries which can create credit (**banks**) should be distinguished from those which cannot create credit (**non-banks**). In practice, however, such distributions are always rather unsatisfactory. Let us assume, for example, that an individual transfers money from his or her bank deposit account to a building society, and that this money is then redeposited by the society into a current account at the same bank. Since its total deposits are unaffected the bank can create as much credit as previously, but in addition the building society can now offer additional mortgage loans on the basis of its new deposits.

The second consideration is that it is necessary to lay down in law what, for example, is or is not a bank so that appropriate prudential supervision can be exercised by the Bank of England (see discus-

sion of the Banking Act 1987 below). Historically, these considerations did not create particular difficulties, but the 1980s has seen much blurring of traditional distinctions between intermediaries, partly as a result of attempts to regulate particular institutions in the pursuit of money supply control (see **pp. 86** and **312**). The Banking Act 1979 created a now obsolete distinction between banks and licensed deposit-takers, but in September 1983 the Bank of England introduced a new classification system for banks which created three categories of **British bank**. The first category comprises the **retail** banks, as listed below. The second, categorised as **other British banks**, comprises primarily the subsidiaries of the clearing banks, whilst the third category comprises the **British merchant banks**. All other banks are categorised as **overseas banks**.

The banks can also be divided into those which conduct business primarily in the **retail** market — that is, branch banks handling vast numbers of small accounts — and those which conduct **wholesale** business involving small numbers of very large transactions. The retail banks are all British, whilst the wholesale banks are primarily foreign. Most banks fall partly into both categories, so their classification is determined by their predominant form of business. The **discount houses** retain a separate classification.

However, many intermediaries are not banks as defined above. Whilst these can be lumped together as non-bank financial intermediaries (NBFI), some closely resemble banks in that they take in deposits, often via branch networks, and indeed may in individual cases ultimately need to be reclassified as banks as discussed below, whilst others conduct their business in quite different ways. Table 2.1 shows the full classification.

We now need to examine, albeit briefly, the individual components of the monetary sector. At the heart of the sector lies the Bank of England, so we will start by discussing its role, subsequently moving on to look at the banks, both retail and wholesale, and the non-bank financial intermediaries. We will then examine the capital market where equities and bonds are traded, before completing the discussion with an overview of how the sector

Table 2.1 *Financial intermediaries*

Banks	
Retail banks:	London clearing banks (5)
	Scottish clearing banks (3)
	Northern Ireland banks (4)
	Trustee Savings Banks (3)
	Co-operative Bank plc
	Yorkshire Bank plc
	Girobank plc
	Bank of England Banking Department
Wholesale banks:	Other British banks
	British Merchant banks
	Overseas banks
Discount houses	
Non-bank financial intermediaries	
Other deposit-takers:	Building societies
	National Savings Bank
	Finance houses
other NBFI:	Insurance companies
	Pension funds
	Investment trusts
	Unit trusts

has evolved in recent years and the changes that can be expected to take place in the near future.

The Bank of England

The Bank of England (the Bank) is the central bank of the UK. It started life as a joint stock company in 1694, and in return for a large loan to the government was put in a privileged position which enabled it to become the largest private bank. It was subsequently authorised to hold the gold reserves of the banking system. In 1844 note issuing powers were terminated other than via the Bank, which gradually became a monopoly supplier (other than in Scotland). It also increasingly stood prepared to maintain liquidity in the banking system. Whilst not technically a public sector body until the passing of the Bank of England Act 1946, it had long been under the control of the Treasury (Chancellor of the Exchequer). It still retains today

the residual part of its private sector clientele. It is managed by a Court of Directors, headed by the Governor, who are appointed by the Crown.

The Bank's balance sheet has since 1844 been somewhat artificially divided into two halves, namely the **Issue Department** which is concerned with the issue of notes by the Bank, and the **Banking Department** which is concerned with everything else. Issue Department liabilities consist of £14 bn of notes in circulation, and its assets consist of an equivalent amount of government and other securities. Banking Department liabilities consist of public deposits (accounts of the government), bankers' deposits and reserves and other accounts. Bankers' deposits are either **operational** and used for inter-bank clearing; to equalise cash-flows between banks and the government; or to pay for the purchase of notes and coin, or **non-operational** cash-ratio deposits to comply with monetary control requirements. Banking Department assets (of £3 bn) consist of government securities; advances and other accounts; and premises, equipment and other securities which are primarily in the form of commercial bills.

Functions of the Bank of England

The Bank performs a wide variety of functions. It:

(a) is responsible for the issue of notes and coins
(b) acts as banker to the central government
(c) acts as banker to the banking system
(d) manages the Exchange Equalisation Account (EEA)
(e) advises the government on, and on behalf of the government carries out, its monetary policy
(f) supervises the financial system.

These days notes and coins are the proverbial 'small change' of the financial system, and are produced to meet demand rather than to implement policy. As banker to the government the Bank handles the daily net balances of government departments, financing them when they show a deficit and converting any surplus into repayments of debt. The balance sheet item 'public deposits' is normally kept as small as possible in order to minimise the need to issue – and pay interest on – new national debt. The Bank is responsible not only for debt transactions which arise in the present period, but also for managing all the outstanding debt from previous periods. This requires a continuous stream of transactions in both the bill market and in the market for longer-dated government securities, known as **gilt-edged** (or gilts for short). All government debt instruments can be freely traded on the Stock Exchange and money markets, and can therefore be controlled for policy purposes as set out below.

All clearing banks keep an account at the Bank through which pass, first, daily transfers of funds between public deposits and the accounts of the banks' customers and, secondly, daily transfers of funds from one bank to another for bank clearing purposes (plus the occasional purchase of notes and coins). These transfers utilise the bankers' operational balances at the Bank, which do not need to be particularly large as all daily cash flows are netted out.

The **Exchange Equalisation Account** contains the UK's gold and foreign currency reserves. These reserves are used periodically for intervention purposes in order to maintain the value of the exchange rate for sterling in accordance with the wishes of the government. If sterling is considered to be too low the Bank will buy sterling and sell other currencies as appropriate, and if it is considered to be too high the Bank will sell sterling and buy foreign currencies. Sterling required for this purpose is obtained from the National Loans Fund which forms part of the public deposits. The Bank therefore needs to keep accounts with a large number of overseas central banks.

Altogether, the Bank operates in three separate markets – **gilt-edged; discount**; and **foreign exchange**. These operations collectively constitute the government's monetary policy. The Bank has always had the right to use its expertise to give advice to the government concerning the conduct of monetary policy, but it is nevertheless only the government's agent, and it is the Chancellor of the Exchequer, acting via the Treasury, who has ultimate responsibility for such policy. Confusion may arise in this respect because it is inevitably reported in the news that the Bank has taken particular actions in the gilt-edged or currency markets, but in so doing it is simply following instructions. Market interventions are, however, best performed at particular times and on a particular scale, and the Bank has considerable discretion in this respect since the Chancellor has better things to do than keep the markets under continuous scrutiny.

The Bank has an important role to play in the gilt-edged market. The Bank not merely issues gilts on behalf of the government, but underwrites the issues in that any unsold gilts are bought in by the Issue Department for future resale. It buys and sells on a daily basis in order to ensure that there is a receptive market for large-scale holders of gilts, especially insurance companies and pension funds, which may wish to adjust their portfolios. The Bank's operations also inevitably affect gilt-edged prices, and hence long-term interest rates. Until recently this was considered of great importance, because sales of gilts reduce the liquidity of the private sector and hence help to control the money supply. However, the volume of gilt sales has dropped sharply over the past two years (see **pp. 94–5**).

The final, but increasingly vital, role for the Bank is to supervise the **financial system**. With such vast sums at stake confidence is all-important, and it is the Bank's job to set the rules and ensure fair play. There has never been any need to question the Bank's ability to achieve this in the banking sector, but the increasing sophistication and diversity of non-banking activity has recently forced the Bank to permit other regulatory bodies to take over some of its responsibilities, for example the Securities and Investments Board (SIB) under the terms of the Financial Services Act 1986 (see **pp. 97–8**).

Banking supervision was first formalised under the Banking Act 1979 which allowed the Bank to authorise recognised banks and licensed deposit takers which offered a narrower range of services. However, the collapse of Johnson Matthey Bankers in September 1984 set in train a reappraisal which resulted in the passing of the Banking Act 1987, which now treats all banks in a uniform category. In order for a bank to be authorised it is required in particular that every director, controller and manager shall be a fit and proper person to hold his position; that the business of the bank be conducted prudently especially in respect of capital adequacy, liquidity, and bad and doubtful debt provision; that proper systems of accounting and control are maintained; and that net assets are at least £1 mn. If necessary, required standards can be adjusted in individual cases. The Bank can object to take-overs and mergers involving banks, and has done so recently on several occasions. The Bank must be notified if a bank becomes over-exposed (borrowing in excess of 25 per cent of bank capital) to an individual borrower. A Board of Banking Supervision has been set up to give guidance on the development of the supervisory system.

Traditionally monetary policy was heavily dependent upon **liquidity ratio controls**. This is no longer the case, and since 1982 no such controls have been enforced by the Bank. Individual banks are expected to maintain what they themselves consider to be a prudent level of liquidity, but the Bank requires that banks maintain systems for keeping proper checks on liquidity, and reserves the right to check up that this is the case. However, the Bank issued a consultative paper in 1988 which contained a new set of tough proposals concerning bank liquidity.

The Financial Services Act 1986 also led to a more formal regulation of the wholesale money markets. To become an approved institution a bank must pass a 'fit and proper' test covering ability to manage and capital adequacy, and agreement to abide by the 'London Code of Conduct'. The Bank also runs the scheme which insures depositors against the failure of an authorised bank.

The banking sector

As previously discussed, there are two ways in which the banking sector can usefully be divided up for analytic purposes – namely, British/overseas and retail/wholesale. **Table 2.2**, parts (a) and (b), sheds considerable light on why these distinctions are useful. As shown in part (a), the total deposit liabilities of the UK banking sector are close to £1,000 bn. Of this total, over £950 bn is recorded separately either as sterling or foreign currency liabilities, whilst the rest is in a mixture of currencies. To those unfamiliar with the Eurocurrency markets (discussed below), it may come as a surprise to note that over 60 per cent of the £950 bn is in the form of non-sterling deposits. The proportions are in practice somewhat variable, because they are a snapshot of the picture on one particular day which may be unrepresentative of the days which both precede and follow it. One reason for this is that wholesale banking tends to respond to **demand** – in other words, if there is a potential borrower for a very large sum of foreign currency at a particular point in time, the wholesale banks will go out and attract deposits of the same magnitude. One must also bear in mind that the valuation of foreign currency deposits varies according to movements in the exchange rate. It is thus quite possible to find the ratio between sterling and non-sterling deposits standing as low as 30:70.

This ratio disguises the fact that the retail banks, which are primarily British banks with branch networks, conduct much more of their business in sterling than the wholesale banks. As shown in part (**b**) of **Table 2.2**, sterling deposits are almost equally divided between retail and wholesale banks, whilst the latter takes in over 90 per cent of foreign currency deposits. It is somewhat surprising to learn that wholesale banks take in three-quarters of all deposits in the UK. Since the wholesale banks are mostly subsidiaries of foreign banks, it follows that the latter must take in the majority of all deposits, and as shown in **Table 2.2** the proportion is roughly 65 per cent of the total. Here again the distinction between British banks taking in most of the sterling deposits, and overseas banks taking in an even bigger proportion of the foreign currency deposits, is particularly notable.

Retail banks

The retail banking sector comprises primarily the **clearing banks in England, Scotland and Northern Ireland**. There are also the **Trustee Savings Banks** and the **Girobank** which have recently become clearing banks and provide very similar

Table 2.2 (*a*) *UK monetary sector[1] deposit liabilities at 30 September 1988*

	Sterling deposit liabilities (a)		Foreign currency deposit liabilities (b)		Total deposit liabilities
	£bn	%[2]	£bn	%	£bn[3]
Retail banks	187.1	79.9	47.0	20.1	281.8
British merchant banks[5]	20.7	59.1	14.3	40.9	40.1
Other British banks	43.5	64.7	23.7	35.3	78.9
American banks	16.7	17.5	78.7	82.5	100.4
Japanese banks	25.6	9.9	233.7	90.1	261.8
Other overseas banks[4]	73.0	27.2	195.4	72.8	278.0
Total	363.6	38.0	592.8	62.0	1041.0

Notes:
[1] As a result of the changes in the monetary sector culminating in the conversion of the Abbey National Building Society into a bank on 12 July 1989, the term 'monetary sector' is to be replaced by 'banks in the United Kingdom' or simply 'banks'.
[2] Expressed as percentage of (a) + (b) only.
[3] Including items in suspense and transmission, capital and other funds.
[4] Including consortium banks listed separately prior to August 1987.
[5] Members of British Merchant Banking and Securities Houses Association (formerly the Accepting Houses Committee).
Source: Calculations based on data in *Bank of England Quarterly Bulletin.*

(*b*)

	% UK monetary sector sterling deposits	% UK monetary sector foreign currency deposits	% UK monetary sector total deposits[1]
Retail banks	51.4	7.9	24.5
Wholesale banks	49.6	92.1	75.5
British banks	49.1	14.3	35.2
Overseas banks	30.9	85.7	64.8

Note:
[1] Excluding items in suspense and transmission, capital and other funds.
Source: Calculations based on data in *Bank of England Quarterly Bulletin.*

services. The odd man out is the Bank of England Banking Department, which gets included in the statistics despite its quite different role which has been discussed above.

The typical retail bank is a clearing bank which provides services to individuals and firms through a branch network. The traditional side of the business is represented by current (sight) and deposit (time) accounts; the provision of cheque books; clearing of cheques; overdraft facilities and personal loans; small currency transactions; and a wide range of financial advice. More recently, there has been considerable innovation in the way that traditional services are provided, such as cheque-guarantee cards; automated teller machines; and Eurocheques, and most recently new lines of business have been developed such as large-scale mortgage lending on a regular basis; managed unit trusts; and share dealing services.

All retail banks publish balance sheets to a set pattern, and their combined balance sheet as at 31 December 1987 and 1988 is set out in **Figure 2.1**. Retail banks do an increasing amount of wholesale business, as discussed below, but this is not distinguished separately in the balance sheet.

The balance sheet ultimately represents a trade-off between a number of contradictory forces. On the one hand, retail banks are, with minor exceptions, obliged to make profits for shareholders, and high rates of return can be earned only by lending for longish periods of time and by taking a certain amount of risk. On the other hand, account holders constantly require cash to be made available, and other low return assets may need to be held either for prudential reasons to avoid a possible loss of confidence by depositors, or because it is so required by the Bank of England.

The balance sheet, both liabilities and assets, is divided into sterling and foreign currency categories. **Sterling deposits** are heavily dominated by the sight and time deposits of individuals and companies in the UK. Traditionally, the latter paid interest whilst the former did not, but sight deposits remained in the majority because they offered instant access whilst time deposits required notice of withdrawal. However, factors such as the provision of interest-bearing instant-access accounts by building societies eventually persuaded large numbers of depositors that only minimum sums should be kept in bank current accounts, and the banks were forced to respond by offering to forgo charges on such accounts provided, typically, they were kept in credit. As a result, time deposits lost their appeal, and sight deposits once again became equally popular.

In 1987 the Midland Bank introduced a **Vector account** which paid interest on accounts held in credit, but attracted few customers because interest earned was largely offset by account charges. The decision by Lloyds Bank in October 1988 to offer all of its customers an interest-bearing current account came as a considerable surprise, but it is clear that, since the Midland, Barclays, Royal Bank of Scotland and TSB have followed suit, this process is now unstoppable. Indeed, in January 1989 Barclays went one stage further by abolishing charges for transactions on current accounts such as standing orders and cheques even if they do go into overdraft. The distinction between sight and time deposits will thus eventually appear to be no more than an historical anachronism, especially when it is borne in mind that the retail banks' wholesale business largely comprises interest-bearing sight deposits.

Wholesale deposits and deposits from overseas in sterling are currently of equal value. Wholesale deposits have fixed terms to maturity varying from days to years, and are paid a market-determined rate of interest which may therefore differ considerably from interest rates paid to individuals. Whilst wholesale deposits, are still fairly modest, it must be recognised that there is intense competition for retail deposits, and the retail banks, like all other intermediaries, can no longer rely on a sufficiently large inflow of retail deposits to meet their needs for on-lending particularly in, for example, the mortgage market. Wholesale deposits can, therefore, be expected to continue their relatively rapid growth.

Certificates of Deposit (CDs) are fixed-term deposits which are exchanged for a certificate issued by the bank which can be traded in the open market. Hence, although the deposit itself cannot be withdrawn before maturity, the original depositor can get at his cash much earlier by selling his CD, although he may well be obliged to sell it for less than its face value if interest rates have risen.

The large item '**sterling and other currencies**' includes items in suspense because, for example, of uncertainty about ownership; items being transferred between accounts; and the capital injected into the banks by shareholders *plus* liabilities to bond holders. It is also the custom to itemise 'eligible' liabilities. These comprise all sterling deposits from non-bank sources with an original maturity of no more than two years; net inter-bank lending in sterling; sterling CDs issued *less* sterling CDs held; any net deposit liabilities in sterling to overseas offices; and any net liabilities in currencies other than sterling – *less* 60 per cent of the net value of transit items. Eligible liabilities were first

Figure 2.1 *Retail banks, balance sheet*

	31/12/87 £m	31/12/88 £m
Sterling Liabilities		
Notes issued	1 266	1 407
Deposits: UK monetary sector	14 953	20 165
UK public sector	3 323	4 185
UK private sector	115 162	137 362
Overseas	14 623	17 609
Certificates of deposit	9 657	11 965
Other Currency Liabilities		
Deposits: UK monetary sector	6 700	6 373
Other UK	6 609	6 883
Overseas	25 216	26 437
Certificates of deposit[1]	4 287	3 549
Sterling and Other Currencies[2]	39 875	47 038
TOTAL LIABILITIES[3]	241 671	282 974
Sterling Assets		
Notes and Coins	2 963	3 375
Balances with Bank of England[4]	625	749
Market loans: Secured money with LDMA	5 190	5 220
Other UK monetary sector	18 354	17 639
UK monetary sector CDs	3 309	4 201
UK local authorities	963	738
Overseas	3 594	3 573
Bills: Treasury bills	669	1 502
Eligible local authority bills	423	388
Eligible bank bills	4 931	6 060
Other	259	137
Advances: UK public sector	571	702
UK private sector	111 854	147 920
Overseas	4 441	5 284
Banking Dept. lending to central government (net)	820	956
Investments: UK government stocks	5 593	3 547
Others	4 259	5 122
Other Currency Assets		
Market loans and advances: UK monetary sector	10 380	10 007
UK monetary sector CDs	288	178
UK public sector	66	—
UK private sector	6 246	7 648
Overseas	30 796	30 391
Bills	176	436
Investments	5 722	6 198
Miscellaneous (all currencies)	19 179	20 999
TOTAL ASSETS	241 671	282 974

Source: Bank of England Quarterly Bulletin
[1] And other short-term paper issued.
[2] Items in suspense and transmission, capital and other funds.
[3] Of which eligible liabilities amounted to £127 bn at end-1987 and £160 bn at end-1988.
[4] Including cash ratio deposits.

introduced in 1971 for the purposes of monetary control, and since August 1981 all banks with eligible liabilities in excess of £10 million must hold 0.5 per cent of their eligible liabilities in the form of non-interest bearing balances at the Bank of England. Whilst these were originally intended to operate as a cash-ratio monetary control mechanism (see **p. 313**), they currently serve only to provide the Bank of England with a free source of income to pay for its functions as the central bank.

Overall, the preponderance of instant-access or short-notice deposits means that retail bank liabilities are exceptionally liquid, and this inevitably has to be reflected in their asset portfolios. Of late some 25 per cent of all assets have been liquid (three months or less to maturity). This category includes, first, notes and coins (till money) plus balances at the Bank of England – which are partly involuntary to finance the Bank, and partly voluntary to facilitate inter-bank clearing. Sterling market loans represent short-term money market lending, either (**a**) to the discount houses, (**b**) to the inter-bank market, (**c**) to another bank in return for that bank's CD, (**d**) to local authorities, or (**e**) to overseas individuals and banks.

Of these, inter-bank lending is by far the most important, although it is only recently that it has become so dominant. It represents transfers from banks which temporarily have an excess of liquidity to those which are temporarily short of funds (an especially useful practice in the days when monetary controls operated on bank liquidity, although this is no longer of any relevance). There is a speculative element, insofar as any bank which expects interest rates to rise can borrow for long periods in the hope that the money can be on-lent for an initial short period at current interest rates, and then relent subsequently for successive periods at higher rates, thereby earning a speculative profit. If interest rates are expected to fall, successful speculation would require the bank to borrow short, and subsequently to reborrow more cheaply, whilst lending long at current rates.

Eligible bank bills are also prominent in the balance sheet. An eligible bill is one which the Bank of England will buy, via the discount houses, in order to make good a shortfall of cash in the banking sector. Only the bills issued by private

companies, called commercial bills, which have been 'accepted' (guaranteed to be redeemed at face value) by major banks which fulfil specified requirements laid down by the Bank of England, acquire the status of eligible bank bills. The government's own bills (Treasury bills) are obviously also eligible, as are certain bills issued by local authorities.

It is worth noting that when a bank buys a bill it is not redeemed at face value *plus* interest by its issuer, but rather the bank buys the bill at a discount to its face value and when it matures its issuer redeems it at face value. The difference between the price paid and the face value can then be divided by the price paid in order to convert the discount into a conventional rate of interest. Any discounted bill can be rediscounted any number of times – that is, it can be resold at a different price to another party who subsequently is paid the bill's face value if it is held to maturity. By rediscounting bills a bank can, therefore, hold a portfolio of bills some part of which matures on any given day of the year.

The bulk of bank lending to private individuals and firms is represented by UK **private sector advances**. Public sector advances are insignificant because lending to the government and local authorities is largely via discounting their bills, money market loans and the purchase of long-dated government securities (gilt-edged). Private sector advances are linked to bank base rates where modest sums are involved, but large loans are commonly linked to the central money market interest rate known as the London Inter-Bank Offered Rate (LIBOR). It is important also to note that traditionally the pattern of private sector sterling deposits and advances was one where the deposits of individuals were recycled into loans to firms. In 1978 individuals deposited three times as much as they borrowed. By 1988 these deposits had trebled, but their borrowing had risen nearly tenfold, and marginally exceeded these deposits. Since 1983 they have borrowed more than firms in aggregate.

Banking Department lending to central government represents the net contribution to the retail banking sector of the Banking Department of the Bank of England. As it retains certain long-standing private individual accounts these do need to be itemised as retail bank assets, but the major part, which represents transactions with government departments, is something of an anachronism in the balance sheet. This item is quite often negative, which simply means that government departments have more money on deposit than they are borrowing at that point in time.

Foreign currency assets are almost entirely in the form of inter-bank lending within the UK and of lending to overseas residents, companies and especially banks. It may finally be noted that the fixed assets of retail banks, in the form primarily of property, are not separately itemised because of their relatively modest value.

In conclusion, we may note that the pattern of the retail banks' balance sheet is constantly evolving. In particular, the difficulty of attracting adequate retail funds has driven banks into the wholesale markets where interest rates are linked to LIBOR, and this has to be balanced by increased LIBOR-linked lending. The problem is accentuated by the need to pay interest on sight deposits which were traditionally a free source of funds. Furthermore, the retail banks are obliged to hold some non-interest earning assets in the form of bankers' balances. These factors, combined with a very expensive branch network and with severe losses on many of their loans to sovereign countries (see **p. 169**), have understandably made considerable inroads into their profitability, and they have increasingly seen the solution as a movement away from traditional banking services and towards other financial services − that is, banks as financial supermarkets.

Amongst the retail banks two organisations warrant a brief individual mention.

Girobank plc

This started out life in 1968 as the National Giro in an attempt to get at those without bank accounts, comprising some 25 per cent of the adult population. Since these individuals were accustomed to using Post Offices on a regular basis, the existing very large branch network seemed ideal for the purpose of providing money transmission services at a modest price. However, whilst there was considerable initial growth in deposits, there were a number of serious hindrances in the form of a competing bank giro; current account facilities at the TSBs; increasing use of credit cards; and a

continuing desire on the part of a very large number of individuals to deal only in cash transactions.

During the 1970s the range of banking services steadily improved, and deposits gradually built up to a current value of over £1½ bn held in 2 mn accounts. However, this is still a very small-scale operation. Renamed the National Girobank in 1978, the organisation subsequently became Girobank plc in 1985 and in April 1989 was sold off to the Alliance and Leicester, the fifth biggest building society. It has had full clearing bank status since 1983, and should be able to hold its own on a modest scale in future years.

TSB Group plc

Originally there were large numbers of local savings banks which were administered by the National Debt Commissioners, and which provided depositors with a simple money in−money out service. Even cheque books did not come into use until 1965, and the Central Trustee Savings Bank was then established as a member of the Bankers Clearing House to clear cheques on behalf of all the individual banks. The TSB Act 1976 authorised the development of a full range of banking services, subject to a requirement that the smaller banks merged together. Subsequently, the decision was taken to privatise the remaining banks, and although the sale proceeds were arguably the entitlement of the government, they were put straight into the TSB Group plc balance sheet. This is rather unusual compared to other retail banks in that, for historical reasons, most of the deposits are time deposits and a disproportionate share of the assets are held in the form of public sector debt. The TSB Group has found it difficult to find creditworthy borrowers so advances are relatively low as a share of assets, and there is no sovereign country debt.

Wholesale banks

As shown in **Table 2.2(a)** the total deposit liabilities of the wholesale banks amount to some £750 bn, of which some £640 bn is held at overseas banks. Collectively, therefore, wholesale banks greatly outweigh retail banks, but as there are 600 or so such banks currently in operation in the UK, their individual portfolios are on average much smaller than those of the typical retail bank.

Wholesale banks concern themselves with small numbers of large-scale transactions. Deposits of less than £100,000 are unlikely to be accepted, and these deposits are often parcelled up into even larger loans. Deposits are not normally withdrawable on demand, so there is no need to keep anything like the same degree of cash and near-cash reserves as retail banks. Furthermore, it is possible to supplement liquidity by borrowing in the inter-bank market or through issuing certificates of deposit, with the result that, for example, British merchant banks keep only some £50 mn, and other British banks some £110 mn, in the form of notes and coin and of balances with the Bank of England. Because each deposit is in a specific currency (mostly non-sterling – see **pp. 90–2** for a discussion of the Eurocurrency markets), and the depositor can specify the term to maturity, wholesale banks need to find borrowers who want the same currencies for as near as possible the same periods of time. A perfect match between assets and liabilities is, however, rarely possible because of the preference among lenders to lend for periods of time which are shorter than the periods over which borrowers prefer to borrow, and there are obvious problems in matching currencies. The characteristic transaction of a wholesale bank is, therefore, quite different from that of a retail bank, but this has led to the main retail banks setting up wholesale banking subsidiaries in order to diversify their pattern of business, so there are in practice more links between the two banking sectors than may at first seem apparent.

British Merchant banks

The British Merchant banks are distinguished from other British wholesale banks by virtue of their membership of the British Merchant Banking and Securities Houses Association. Their former name of 'accepting houses' arose from the traditional practice of 'accepting' commercial bills, which effectively guarantees repayment in full upon maturity, and hence makes the bills easier to market and reduces the interest rate which needs to be offered. Some bills are retained for their own portfolios, but this type of agency business is no longer all that important, acceptances representing only some 12–15 per cent of total liabilities at the present time.

The now more significant banking activity is almost entirely wholesale rather than retail. The total deposit liabilities of £40 bn are modest by wholesale banking standards, and are generally divided between sterling and foreign currencies in approximately a 60:40 ratio. Both deposits originating overseas and from the inter-bank markets (UK monetary sector) have become increasingly prominent. Assets are correspondingly distributed, with the bulk of sterling assets in the form of loans to the UK inter-bank market and advances to UK borrowers, and the greater part of foreign currency assets in the form of lending abroad, especially to foreign banks. Lending to non-bank customers is relatively unimportant and, as indicated above, very little cash is held.

British Merchant banks are also significant providers of financial services. Many undertake responsibility for all the administrative aspects of issuing new equity; provide a wide range of banking services for companies and some wealthy individuals; act as management consultants with respect to, for example, mergers and take-overs; and provide portfolio management services for pension funds and, in certain cases, unit trusts and investment trusts.

Other British banks

The typical other British bank, so categorised because whilst registered in the UK it does most of its business with overseas clients, is considerably smaller than the typical British Merchant bank. Of the 200 or more such banks, the core group comprises long-standing institutions originally set up to facilitate retail banking in British colonies. This has understandably not been a growth area for some time, and this category now includes a number of the smaller UK banks which offer a restricted range of services, including some which, although not officially Merchant banks, provide almost identical services. Since the Banking Act 1979 took them within its provisions, many former finance houses have also operated in this category, competing directly with organisations listed separately under that heading.

The total deposit liabilities of other British banks are twice those of the British Merchant banks, but there are considerable similarities in the respective balance sheets. Other British banks do not, however, hold many acceptances.

Overseas banks

A number of American and European banks have had a London office for many decades in order to provide services for their customers whilst in the UK. However, the number of overseas banks has grown enormously over the past two decades, initially as a result of the growth of the Eurocurrency markets, and very recently as a result of financial deregulation. There are currently some 450 overseas banks in London, a gain of 100 on the figure only two years ago. The invasion has been spearheaded from America and Japan, and, as can be seen in **Table 2.2(a)**, whilst the American banks alone have deposit liabilities of £100 bn, equal to over 80 per cent of the combined liabilities of British Merchant banks and other British banks, this represents only 40 per cent of the liabilities of the Japanese banks which are almost all comparative newcomers to London. The Japanese banks, surprisingly, have deposit liabilities virtually equal to those of the retail banks, and doubtless will soon overtake them, and there are as many deposits again held at the other (non-American) overseas banks.

The Eurocurrency markets are discussed separately below, and it is necessary to note at this stage only that the enormous growth in **international money** (for example, dollars traded outside America) was particularly centred in London, so all the important overseas banks necessarily had to open an office there to participate on any scale in these markets. American banks, in particular, were drawn to London by a desire to avoid the much tighter regulations in their domestic market. Because American and Japanese banks have been at the forefront of developments in electronic banking, they have been particularly well placed to take advantage of the recent deregulation of financial services, and their recent movement into, for example, the mortgage market has had profound effects upon traditional practices in the UK. No doubt they will steadily encroach upon other areas of business, such as corporate finance, and given that their deposits are backed by the vastly greater assets of the parent companies, they look set to streamroller everything in their path.

As shown in **Table 2.2(a)**, the overseas banks do the vast bulk of their business in **foreign currencies**. Their deposits, unsurprisingly, largely come from overseas, and mostly from parent organisations. Around one-third of their sterling deposits also come from overseas, and most of what remains is borrowed in the UK inter-bank markets which also provide over 15 per cent of foreign currency deposits. On the assets side of the balance sheet there are minimal amounts of cash and balances held at the Bank of England, but massive amounts of foreign currency lending to overseas residents, a great deal of which is routed via overseas banks. Inter-bank lending is very important, both in sterling and foreign currencies. As with other categories of wholesale banks, almost exactly the same amount is borrowed from the inter-bank markets as is lent to them. Apart from the modest net effect of retail bank operations in the inter-bank markets, it is simply a matter of definition that total lending must be equal to total borrowing, and the very large sums being transferred represent either portfolio adjustments by individual banks (for example, adjustment of maturity profiles) or simply opportunities which individual banks have to borrow from other banks with no immediate customers and to on-lend at a profit. Because wholesale banking is in aggregate so much larger than retail banking, the small proportion of assets held in sterling still represents a far from modest £50 bn of lending. Whilst they are clearly more than happy to compete for sterling business in the UK, they do not as yet show any real interest in moving out of London, and this is why one gets the impression, even in the largest provincial cities, that the UK retail banks are the only major banking intermediaries.

Since August 1987 the other overseas banks category has included the operations of the **consortium banks**. These are independent banks, jointly owned by other banks and/or financial intermediaries located in a variety of countries, with no single parent body having a majority share in the consortium. They were often set up because individual small banks could not afford a London operation, and the combined status of the parent bodies could be expected to attract more business than their individual operations added together. By combining together they could move into areas of business beyond their individual means, and also operate outside the control of their domestic regulations. They operate entirely in wholesale markets, and 80 per cent of their assets are in foreign currencies. It is no longer worth listing consortium banks separately because, unlike other overseas banks, their growth is insignificant. Many consortium members have become a strong enough to stand alone, whilst others have grown reluctant to let other banks involve them in overly risky ventures. There is also no longer the need to avoid regulations in many domestic markets. Nevertheless, there are always small institutions wishing to have a share in a London-based operation, so as consortium members withdraw others take their place, and the number of consortia has tended to remain stable at a figure of 23 since 1981.

Discount market

The discount market is a money market, the membership of which was until very recently restricted to the eight (currently nine) discount houses which were members of the London Discount Market Association (LDMA). The nature of their business can be clearly seen in the LDMA balance sheet, which at 30 January 1989 showed total liabilities of £13.1 bn, of which sterling liabilities constituted £12.6 bn. Of these, £11.5 bn were funds borrowed 'at call' (recallable without notice) and overnight. These funds, as we have seen, represent the most liquid asset bar cash itself in the retail banks' balance sheet. On the assets side of the balance sheet are to be found very little bar sterling denominated short-term assets, largely in the form of commercial bills (£5 bn) and certificates of deposit (£5 bn).

It follows logically that the functions of the discount market are to make a market in bills of all kinds; to give the banking sector a means by which they can replenish their cash holdings virtually on demand; and to assist in the financing of short-term

trade debts through the purchase of discounted commercial bills from banks and their customers. The discount houses are also committed to tender for the whole of every issue of Treasury Bills (TBs) in order to guarantee that government departments can pay their way, but they can be out-bid, and indeed holdings of TBs have fallen to quite insignificant levels (less than £100 mn during most of 1988).

The LDMA, in essence, exists to maintain liquidity in the financial system. There are vast amounts of short-term instruments in existence, and the LDMA effectively guarantees that they can be bought and sold freely, thereby greatly reducing the need for cash holdings. At the end of daily cheque clearing, for example, some banks will have cash surpluses which can earn interest, albeit at very low rates, by being placed in the discount market, whilst the others can find the cash on the spot which is needed to settle deficits.

The discount market also has an important role to play in the conduct of monetary policy. Every day, money flows between government departments and the clearing banks via accounts held at the Bank of England. On any given day this may result in a very large net cash flow in one direction or the other. If government departments have drawn heavily on cash held at the clearing banks, they will immediately have to go to the discount market to replenish their cash holdings. With cash in short supply, short-term interest rates will have to rise rapidly to attract sufficient cash into the market. Conversely, if the clearing banks are flush with cash which is then deposited in the discount market, the LDMA will have to bid for short-term assets, causing their prices to rise and their yields (face value *less* price paid) to fall.

If short-term interest rates become very volatile, this will quickly be transmitted to longer-term interest rates and to the exchange rate. In order to avoid this, the Bank of England stands ready to smooth cash flows between government departments and the clearing banks. If the banks have too much cash the Bank will mop it up by selling eligible bills to the LDMA, whilst if there are cash shortages the Bank will buy eligible bills in return for cash. This is called an **open-market operation** (OMO). Whilst it is the case that the Bank of

England is willing on occasion to deal directly with financial intermediaries other than the LDMA, it is formally the case that only the LDMA may go to the Bank for funds when they cannot be obtained from any other source.

An OMO in the discount market therefore provides the means whereby the Bank can influence short-term interest rates. Since August 1981 the procedure has been as follows. When cash is in short supply the Bank will invite the LDMA to sell eligible bills. If their selling price, and hence the associated discount (rate of interest), is acceptable to the Bank it will buy the bills and relieve the cash shortage. However, if the price is unacceptable, it will ask the LDMA to re-offer at a different price, thereby raising or lowering the interest rate as appropriate. The same procedure can be used if the Bank offers to sell eligible bills in order to mop up surplus cash.

If the Bank was, exceptionally, to refuse to buy bills at any price offered by the discount houses, then it would leave them with no option but to ask for a 'lender-of-last-resort' loan from the Bank, and the Bank would be able to charge any interest rate which it wished as a condition for making the cash available. The significance of this procedure is that the money markets cannot know for certain, in advance of the Bank's response to an offer to buy or sell eligible bills, what the Bank's views are about the appropriate level for short-term interest rates. The money markets are constantly nudging short-term interest rates up and down, but the Bank can signal its desire either to see these rate movements go beyond the limits set by the market, or the restoration of rates previously prevailing. By behaving in this way the Bank does not seek to dominate the markets on a continuous basis, as was the practice throughout most of the period prior to 1981, but rather to give clear guidance to the markets as and when it is considered to be appropriate.

As of June 1988 the Bank published a draft document which reassessed the decision made at the time when capital markets were deregulated ('Big Bang', October 1986) to allow other bodies to become members of the discount market. Whilst previously the discount houses had to be independently capitalised, it is now proposed that a gilt-edged market-maker will be able to incorporate a discount house within its other operations without separate capitalisation. However, its total operations will be limited to dealing in sterling debt, sterling money market instruments and related futures and options, and capital adequacy and other requirements will need to be met (see *Bank of England Quarterly Bulletin* (August 1988, pp. 391–402)). Prior to 1986 the discount market was kept adequately financed by making it a condition for 'eligibility' status that a bank keep at least 2.5 per cent of its eligible liabilities (ELs) with the LDMA, and at least 5 per cent of its ELs with the LDMA, money brokers and gilt-edged jobbers. It is hoped that the new proposals will guarantee sufficient capital adequacy for the really quite modest operations of the discount market to be expanded. In January 1989 it was revealed that two new intermediaries had applied to join the discount market, potentially increasing its capitalisation by only £25 mn to £375 mn, but only one joined in February. This poor response obviously reflected the post-Big Bang fallout (see **pp. 95–6**).

Non-bank financial intermediaries (NBFIs)

Taken in aggregate the NBFI currently hold a much more valuable portfolio of assets than the banks. In 1986 the largest group was the insurance companies with assets of £192 bn (up from £42 bn in 1977), followed by the pension funds (£190 bn, up from £30 bn); the building societies (£140 bn, up from £35 bn); the unit trusts (£30 bn, up from £3 bn); and the investment trusts (£20 bn, up from £6 bn). Pensions funds and unit trusts have grown very rapidly, with the other groups some way behind. The NBFI also include the National Savings Bank and the Finance Houses.

Building societies

The building societies began life as terminating societies, which lasted as long as it took to build houses for all of the members. Over time they became permanent, and came to monopolise a particular form of financial service. Modern societies are **mutual organisations**, which bring together the generally modest savings of large numbers of individuals and parcel them up into a much smaller number of mortgages. Savers' accounts are known as shares and deposits. Shareholders do not, however, share in a society's profits, but by virtue of being society members can vote at annual general meetings on such issues as conversion to banking status (see below). Interest rates are slightly lower on deposit accounts, which have the balancing advantage of priority in repayment if a society goes bankrupt. This is not generally thought to be much of a risk, so there are understandably many times as many shareholders as depositors.

During the 1970s the societies faced little competition from the banks, which thought mortgage lending too long-term; did not enjoy the composite tax rate arrangement which cheapened the cost of funds to societies; had, unlike the societies, to build a profit margin into the interest rate charged; and had their aggregate lending constrained by monetary controls. The societies chose to avoid competition amongst themselves by operating an **interest rate cartel**, and mortgage lending was heavily constrained by the inflow of retail funds in the absence of access to wholesale markets.

None of these considerations any longer apply. Building societies both compete amongst themselves for business, and are under attack not merely from the 'clearing' banks, but also from the foreign banks and the mortgage corporations which keep down costs by having no branch network. When funds were in short supply, large-scale borrowing attracted an interest rate penalty. These days the larger the loan the cheaper it tends to be, as funds from the wholesale markets appear to be almost limitless. Faced with bank encroachment upon their traditional business, the societies have responded by encroaching on the business of the banks.

Table 2.3 provides an interesting historical snapshot of the building society sector. The number of societies has dropped dramatically since 1960, and the process of merger is still continuing. Assets are now concentrated in the hands of a relatively small number of very large societies. However, the branch network has doubled over the past decade as High Street sites have been snapped up. The number of shareholders is a staggering 44 million, but this reflects the fact that many people have accounts at several societies. The number of borrowers has grown more steadily, but whilst the amount borrowed only rose by a factor of less than 5 during the highly inflationary 1970s, it trebled during the first half of this decade despite much tougher competition from other lenders, reflecting much sharper increases in house values than in prices generally, and an enormous influx of money into the mortgage market.

Not surprisingly, this was financed mainly from share and deposit account liabilities. These stood at £50 bn in 1980, and at the time this represented over 90 per cent of total liabilities. By 1988 deposit liabilities stood at £153 bn, but even so this represented only 80 per cent of the total.

Table 2.3   *Building society statistics, End-Year*

	1960	1970	1975	1980	1985	1987	1988
Number of societies	726	481	382	273	167	138	130
Number of branches	N/A	2 016	3 375	5 684	6 926	6 962	6 915
Number of shareholders (mn)	3.9	10.3	17.9	30.6	40.0	42.0	43.8
Number of depositors (mn)	0.6	0.6	0.7	0.9	2.1	3.6	4.3
Number of borrowers (mn)	2.4	3.7	4.4	5.4	6.7	7.2	7.4
Number of advances in year (mn)	0.4	0.6	0.8	0.9	1.7	1.9	2.0
Volume of advances in year (£bn)	0.6	2.0	4.9	9.5	26.5	36.0	46.9

Source: Housing Finance (formerly the BSA Bulletin) (July 1989).

This is accounted for by the fact that in 1979 wholesale borrowing from the money markets was non-existent, yet by 1988 a total of £20 bn was being borrowed, representing over 10 per cent of the total. In 1988 alone wholesale funding rose by £5 bn, and one can anticipate the continuance of this reduction in reliance upon retail deposits into the future.

The asset side of the balance sheet is dominated by mortgage lending (see **Figure 2.2**), the traditional business of the societies. In future years we are going to see the effects of the relaxed personal lending rules set out in the Building Society Act 1986. In recent years, however, there has been a different kind of portfolio adjustment. Over £1 bn of local authority investments have been sold off during the last two years, and after a significant build up of British government securities between 1980 and 1983, these have also been heavily depleted between 1986 and 1989.

The liquidity of the societies is hard to explain. The Chief Registrar of Friendly Societies used to require that cash plus investments be maintained at a minimum of 7.5 per cent of total assets. As the balance sheet shows, it is only rarely that the societies keep less than twice that amount. Historically, it was just about possible to argue that, if inflows dried up, commitments to mortgage lending could be maintained by running down these reserves, but with wholesale funding now freely available that hardly seems necessary any longer.

The Building Society Act 1986

As many deposits are effectively withdrawable upon demand, whilst mortgages are mostly granted for 25 years, the liquidity mismatch between assets and liabilities is very striking. However, the average life of a mortgage is in reality only seven years (which partly explains the belated enthusiasm for mortgage lending by the banking sector); there is a constant inflow of capital and interest repayments; very little bad debt; and almost all borrowing and lending is at floating

Figure 2.2   *Building societies, assets and liabilities, book-value, end-year*

	1988 £mn	1987 £mn	1988 %	1983 %	1979 %	1975 %
Assets						
Mortgage loans	155 195	131 518	81.2	78.4	80.2	77.5
Cash & bank balances	10 847	9 440	5.7	4.4	2.1	2.6
British government securities	8 956	8 396	4.7	11.2	8.7	7.8
Other investments[1]	10 668	7 100	5.6	1.6	1.1	1.9
Other assets[2]	4 808	2 993	2.5	1.7	1.9	1.4
Local authority investments	545	947	0.3	2.8	6.0	8.8
Total	191 019	160 394				
Liabilities						
Shares and deposits	152 875	131 971	80.0	90.1	92.8	93.2
Other borrowing[3]	19 898	14 992	10.4	2.3	0.0	0.0
Other liabilities & reserves	15 555	11 102	8.1	6.3	5.6	5.6
Accrued interest	2 691	2 329	1.5	1.3	1.5	1.2
Total	191 019	160 394				

Source: Housing Finance (July 1989)

interest rates, so there is always a margin between them to cover expenses and leave room for profit.

The Building Societies Act 1986 has operated since January 1987, and has subsequently been amended to relax its rules which, whilst allowing societies to move some way from their traditional business both in terms of methods of raising finance and of disposal of funds, are nevertheless regarded as overly restrictive. The societies began their frontal assault upon the business of banks when the Nationwide Anglia launched its interest-bearing Flex Account in May 1987, which is soon expected to attract its millionth customer, its approximate break-even figure. In March 1988 the Abbey National followed suit, combining this with a £100 cheque card, and the Halifax intends to follow suit in 1989. Now that the banks have also moved into interest-bearing current accounts, the societies will need to widen their range of services on offer.

The review of building society powers completed in June 1988 resulted in their being able to offer a wide range of banking and housing related services; to take up to a 100 per cent stake in life assurance companies and up to a 15 per cent stake in general insurance companies; to undertake fund management; and to take up to 100 per cent equity stakes in stockbrokers. With some societies anxious to expand their range of financial services even further, the issue inevitably arose as to whether any of them might wish to convert to banking status. The government adopted a neutral stance, and introduced draft rules governing conversion on 28 July 1988. The Abbey National, the second largest society, obtained the necessary majority to convert in April 1989, and was given the authorisation to proceed by the regulatory body set up by the 1986 Act, the Building Societies Commission. It became a plc in July 1989. Support for conversion by Abbey members was so high that other societies are almost certain to follow suit in 1990 but not including (for the time being) the Halifax.

The implementation of a single European market (see **pp. 172–5**) has so far made little progress with respect to the integration of housing finance systems in the EC. Levels of owner-occupancy vary from 43 per cent to 75 per cent in individual countries, and the legal procedures, institutions and financial instruments are often incompatible. As a result, there is unlikely ever to be a mortgage finance directive. Rather, the Second Banking Co-ordination Directive, published at the end of 1988, permits mortgage lenders to operate outside their home country in the same way as they operate at home.

In the meantime, the 'mutual recognition of techniques' is severely restricted, and only three UK institutions have made moves towards the European mortgage market. The Midland Bank already operates a subsidiary in France acquired in the late 1970s, as does the Abbey National in Spain acquired in 1988, whilst the Halifax is shortly expected to follow the Abbey National's example. Since UK building societies can currently operate elsewhere in the EC only through a subsidiary, the UK legislation will have to be amended before they can channel funds through their own branches.

Insurance companies and pension funds

The business of life insurance is often conducted by large composite insurers which also insure general risks such as damage to house and car. Our concern here is only with life insurance, which may also be provided by specialist insurance companies. The business of life insurance has little to do with liquidity. The commonest form of policy is where the individual makes regular monthly payments which entitle him to a lump sum at a specific future date (an endowment). If the endowment is 'with profits', then bonuses will be added in line with the profitability of the company. If the policyholder dies before the policy matures, then a lump-sum will be paid to the next-of-kin or specified beneficiary.

An endowment may alternatively be purchased via a single, large, lump-sum down-payment. Special forms of endowment are increasingly linked to mortgages, either 'low cost' endowments or mortgage protection policies which simply guarantee to repay the outstanding mortgage upon the death of the mortgagee (term insurance). Unit-linked endowments are also available, and indeed there is the now customary proliferation of new forms of life insurance in this exceptionally competitive market. Endowments can be cashed in before maturity, although this may result in a repayment of less than the total amount paid in since insurance brokers are frequently paid the first year's premium as a fee for arranging the endowment.

A pension cannot, however, be paid out to anyone other than the person in whose name the monthly payments are made, irrespective of who pays the premiums, nor in part to anyone other than his or her spouse or children upon the death of the pensioner. Most pension schemes involve payments both by the individual and the company he or she works for. Until recently, this has meant that if an individual changed jobs the pension in the old job would be frozen until retirement, and the individual would have to start up a new one with the new company. However, in certain circumstances pensions are now 'portable' between jobs. The self-employed must buy personal pensions, and it is possible for individuals to top up existing pension rights by buying additional personal pensions.

Pension, or superannuation, funds make (frequently inflation-adjusted) payments for as long as a pensioner lives after reaching pensionable age. Thus while life insurance is primarily a means of buying protection (for dependents) in the event of early death, a pension fund exists to cover the risk of living too long without an income. The popularity of life insurance and pension funds has traditionally been fostered by the existence of tax concessions both to individuals and companies. Tax relief on life insurance premiums has, however, been discontinued since the 1985 Budget. Many company pension funds are currently having a 'contributions holiday', since they already have more than sufficient income from investors to cover pension liabilities (they did very well from the bull market in equities during the 1980s).

Life insurance companies hold roughly half of their long-term assets in the form of UK and overseas equities, and the rest mostly comprises gilts and UK land, property and ground rents. Equities are even more prominent in the assets structure of pension funds, because fixed-yield assets would not keep pace with commitments to make payments based upon rapidly-rising incomes. These institutions clearly, therefore, play a dominant role in the equity and gilt-edged markets.

Unit trusts and investment trusts

Direct investment in equities has never been popular among individuals in the UK. This is partly because it is not possible to obtain a diversified portfolio of shares if there is only a modest amount of capital to invest. Unit trusts and investment trusts pool the savings of large numbers of individuals, and by giving them a share in a diversified portfolio of assets, reduce the risk element in equity-related saving. Nevertheless, as with any equity-linked portfolios, those of trusts can fall heavily in value when the Stock Exchange is depressed.

In the case of **unit trusts** there is a **legally binding trust deed**. A trustee, normally a large financial intermediary, holds the trust's assets on behalf of unitholders, and the trust is independently managed by another company within the terms of the trust deed. Units can only be bought and sold with the trust itself. New units are created as desired, and old ones eliminated when units are sold back to the trust. The trust repays such units by disposing of investments. There has recently been considerable dispute about the rules for calculating the purchase and sale price of units, and it is permissible for a unit trust to refuse to repurchase under specified circumstances.

Investment trusts operate differently. They are

Table 2.4 *Unit trusts, 1984–88.*

	No. of unit holdings (mn)	Total funds (£mn)
End 1984	2.20	15 099
1985	2.55	20 307
1986	3.41	32 131
1987	5.05	36 330
1988	4.89	41 574

public companies rather than legal trusts, and sell shares in the trust itself which are then invested in other equities and securities. Their shares are quoted on the Stock Exchange, and can be freely traded.

National Savings Bank (NSB)

The NSB, which had its origins in the need for wartime financing and which is now under the control of the Department of National Savings, is important primarily as a route for channeling private sector savings directly into the hands of the government. In this way the PSBR can be financed without the need to issue an equivalent amount of public sector debt. National Savings were unpopular in the decades prior to 1975, but it has subsequently been possible to widen their appeal by deliberately making them attractive compared to deposits at banks and building societies. This is done primarily either through index-linking, which guarantees that a specified real rate of interest, adjusted for inflation, is earned, or through a reduction in the tax burden to be borne by such savings. The great reduction in government borrowing in recent years has in turn much reduced the need for a National Savings movement.

Finance houses

The finance houses are no longer of much importance in the financial system because there has been a tendency for the largest houses to convert into banks, included statistically in the 'other British banks' category. Funds are raised in the wholesale markets and by issuing bills. They are used to provide loans to individuals (to be repaid in instalments) and to private companies, together with leasing finance whereby a finance house buys a machine or factory and leases it to a company. This type of business is also done by retail banks, but many finance houses have special relationships with large manufacturers and retail chains.

Money markets

A brief history

We have already referred, when discussing individual groups of financial intermediaries, to the existence of money markets, and it is now necessary to say something about these markets in general, and specifically about those of them not previously mentioned.

The movement of huge sums of short-term funds around the financial system is historically a relatively new phenomenon. Up until the early 1960s organisations acquired short-term funds either from the commercial banks in the form of overdrafts and loans or as trade credit from suppliers. The banks' ability to lend was itself determined largely by the value of retail deposits, and they did not compete amongst themselves as their interest rates were uniformly linked to the central Bank Rate. Furthermore, direct controls on lending were frequently imposed by the Bank of England.

However, commencing in the early 1960s, large amounts of dollars began to be deposited in London (see discussion of Eurocurrency markets below), and these deposits were totally independent of the existing banking system. They could, therefore, be handled by any institution willing to make a sufficiently attractive offer to depositors, and they could be handled flexibly because they did not fall within the compass of existing monetary controls. As a result, large numbers of foreign banks came to London, each intent on grabbing as big a share of the business as possible, and this in turn meant that competition for deposits was so intensive as to exclude the possibility of interest rate cartels. Once in the UK they also began to compete for sterling deposits, previously the exclusive preserve of the UK banks, which were obliged to match their interest rates.

The Bank of England acknowledged the desirability of competition on an equal footing between institutions when it introduced the Competition and Credit Control (CCC) document in 1971. This detached bank interest rates from Bank Rate, which was abolished, and allowed each bank to set its own **base rate**. The replacement of Bank Rate by the market-determined **Minimum Lending Rate**

(MLR) was, however, more apparent than real in practice, as the government found it increasingly difficult to forgo the use of the interest rate as a major instrument of monetary control. Furthermore, base rates have tended to fall back into line. However, this disguises the fact that whilst retail banking is still operated as a virtual cartel, wholesale banking is not. If one has a large sum of money to sell then it can be offered around to the highest bidder. One interesting consequence is that asset management whereby, as discussed above, financial intermediaries and especially banks must maintain part of their asset portfolio in liquid forms, becomes matched by liability management whereby liquidity can be supplemented via borrowing in the money markets. Precisely the same argument applies for governments and commercial organisations. Cash, which does not earn interest, can no longer be left lying idle, even overnight. It is hardly surprising, therefore, that retail banking, where small accounts are handled at considerable expense, is increasingly viewed as simply a means whereby a captive audience is acquired for the sale of profitable financial services, and the primary concerns of liquidity, risk and profitability are juggled in the money markets.

Types of money market

The primary money market is the **discount market**. This has already been discussed, and nothing further needs to be added at this juncture. In addition to the discount market there are currently five other significant sterling money markets known, collectively as the **'parallel' or secondary markets**. These are the inter-bank market; the certificate of deposit market; the local authority market; the finance house market; and the inter-company market. To these is likely soon to be added a building society market. They are called 'sterling markets' to distinguish them from the Eurocurrency markets discussed below.

The inter-bank market has also been mentioned previously. It is the largest parallel market and, as the name indicates, is the market in which **banks lend to one another**. Having started in 1955, the local authority market is the oldest of the five, and

is where local authorities issue their own debt instruments which are sold to banks and other investors. Loans are unsecured, so the reputation of the borrower is all-important. Until recently local authorities, with their right to levy rates, were regarded as low-risk borrowers, but the financial practices of certain authorities such as Liverpool have altered that somewhat. The inter-company market, which began in 1969, is where **large companies lend directly** to one another. It is a low-key affair because there are alternative ways to lend with security at much the same rate of interest. The finance house market is also fairly insignificant because of othe transfer of many of the largest houses to the banking sector. The sterling CD market, started in 1968, consists of a **primary** market in which new CDs are issued, and a **secondary** market in which they are subsequently bought and sold, thereby enhancing their liquidity and hence desirability. The market has grown rapidly, but it is totally dwarfed by the foreign currency CD market.

It is not always possible to distinguish to which market a particular transaction should be assigned, since many types of intermediary operate in several of them simultaneously. Supervision is accordingly exercised largely over participants' banking activities although, as discussed above, the Bank of England is involved in the discount market on a daily basis. In the parallel sterling markets supervision is light. Participants are expected to join the Sterling Brokers Association and to adhere to the Bank's issued code of practice. The Bank also checks on the various instruments issued to ensure that they are of the highest quality. This lightness of touch has provided a suitable environment for rapid growth, but the Bank must occasionally wonder why it fosters markets which make its monetary controls much harder to implement.

Financial futures and options

So far, we have been exclusively concerned with transactions involving a current payment in exchange for the current delivery of some kind of asset such as a share or bond. However, a large number of contracts involve either the delivery of an asset at some **future date** in exchange for a payment made **in the present**, or the purchase of the right to buy or sell (or to decline to buy or sell) an asset at some **future date** at a price **agreed when taking out the option**. The former are traded on the London International Financial Futures Exchange (LIFFE) and are known as **financial futures**, and might involve, for example, a contract to buy an amount of gilts in three months' time at a current price which reflects the expectations of the parties to the contract about the future trend of interest rates. Equities can also be traded in this way. The latter are known as **traded options** (as distinct from the similar but less-commonly purchased **traditional** options), and involve the outlay of a modest sum today for the rights to buy or sell in the future at an agreed price, known as 'calls' and 'puts' respectively. If the market price moves in such a way as, for example, to rise above the agreed price for a call option, then the option will be enforced by the buyer. Where the writer of the option (the seller) does not have the asset to hand it will have to be purchased in the market and immediately resold at a loss (which is partly offset because the seller has received the price of the option in cash). If, however, the market price has fallen below the price agreed at the time of buying the option (in other words, the asset can be bought more cheaply in the open market) then the option will be allowed to lapse, and the writer of the option gets to keep the money paid for the option *less* trading costs.

Financial futures and traded options clearly involve risks for both buyer and seller. Almost invariably one must gain at the expense of the other. However, there is a sound rationale behind this kind of behaviour. When a buyer agrees to buy an asset at some future date he runs the risk that he could have bought it more cheaply in the future compared to the present. On the other hand, he avoids the risk that he would have had to pay well above the agreed price. Traded options are thus a mechanism for financial leverage. In other words, for the downpayment of a modest sum a buyer of call options can guarantee himself the chance to make a profit by buying and instantly reselling a very expensive portfolio of assets which he could

not have afforded to pay for in full at the time of buying the option. Equally, the most he can lose is the total cost of the options should he decline to take them up, even if the price of the asset has fallen disastrously in the meantime.

Traded options also provide a hedge against share movements which would be disadvantageous to a shareholder. Thus, for example, a shareholder whose shares have risen sharply in value can protect at least part of his capital gain by taking out an option conferring the right to sell the shares at a price of his choosing. If this is the current share price then the maximum loss is the cost of taking out the options *plus* trading costs, irrespective of how much the shares subsequently fall in value.

Eurocurrency markets

The size of the Eurocurrency markets in the UK, as indicated in **Table 2.1**, is much larger than one might expect. At the present time the assets held in dollars alone amount to some $500 bn, to which should be added more than the equivalent of $200 bn in other currencies. Eurocurrency transactions are wholesale borrowing and lending in a currency other than that of the country in which the transactions take place. Thus Eurosterling can be transacted anywhere other than in the UK, and Eurodollars anywhere other than in the USA and so forth. The term 'Eurocurrency' is, therefore, something of a misnomer since it can involve non-European currencies and be transacted outside Europe. It arose because, as previously stated, the markets began with dollars deposited in Europe. At present London is the biggest Eurocurrency market, accounting for approximately 30 per cent of all transactions by value.

There is normally a lower limit of $1 mn set for each transaction, and also often an upper limit since loans are unsecured. Whilst much of the lending is very short term, sometimes for as little as a day, there are longer-term loans in the form of Euro-commercial paper (the total market for which rose from $4 bn in early 1986 to $45 bn in early 1988), and especially of Eurobonds which are largely fixed-interest securities or floating-rate notes

(FRNs) denominated in a Eurocurrency. FRNs are attached to LIBOR in the UK, and may be convertible to equity. They are issued by multi-national firms, foreign governments, local authorities and public corporations. There is also a great deal of inter-bank lending. Eurobonds are not usually traded on the stock Exchange, but rather certain international banks and security houses 'make a market'. There are sufficient market-makers to ensure that Eurobonds can be freely traded at competitive prices.

Origins

The central role of London in the Eurocurrency markets reflects the long-standing provision of finance for foreign trade combined with a large number of international banks and an efficient system of communications links throughout the world. New York was originally excluded by virtue of the fact that transactions were in dollars held **outside** the USA, but this inevitably begs the question as to why Americans (and subsequently everyone else) wished to hold their domestic currency somewhere other than in their own country.

The answer is particularly to be found by reference to **interest rates**. The sheer size of the sums transacted is itself important as it keeps costs per unit of currency transacted to an absolute minimum, but more importantly, because Eurocurrency does not constitute part of any individual country's money supply, it does not fall within the remit of any country's system of monetary control. Thus, for example, there are no reserve requirements as there are on dollars held in American banks or sterling held in UK banks. Reserve holdings do not earn interest, and the savings which accordingly arise if they are not applicable can be passed on to depositors in the form of higher interest rates. Furthermore, there have periodically been upper limits placed upon domestic interest rates. In the American case the Federal Reserve Board rule, known as Regulation Q, twice imposed upper limits on bank deposit interest rates during the 1960s, and as a result dollar deposits came to earn a higher rate of return outside the USA where Regulation Q could not be enforced.

Exchange controls have also played a major

role. Again, in the American case, large outflows of dollars resulted from the adverse balance of payments of the USA during the 1960s. Exchange controls were, therefore, introduced to stem the outflow, albeit somewhat ineffectively, but as the dollar was the most favoured currency for settlement of international trade transactions the demand for dollars did not disappear, but was simply turned aside into the Eurodollar market. This caused the rate of return on Eurodollars to rise, and most of the dollars received outside the USA were accordingly placed into the Eurodollar market, together with dollars transferred from the accounts of anyone in the USA whose status made their deposits exempt from the controls (including some central banks). As Eurodollar balances rapidly built up, it became clear to the US authorities that the controls were counter-productive (see also the discussion about disintermediation on **p. 323**), and they were abolished in the mid-1970s.

The growth of the Eurocurrency markets has also been affected by the behaviour of particular groups of countries. A significant part of the huge OPEC surpluses of the late 1970s found its way into the markets, and Eastern European countries, when buying American products, prefer to deal in the markets rather than hold dollars in the USA.

The abolition of exchange controls in the USA and elsewhere led to a significant readjustment of Eurocurrency holdings between financial centres. In the heyday of exchange controls many 'offshore' centres such as the Bahamas prospered by the simple expedient of offering an uncontrolled environment. However, once a much freer environment is created nearer to home, the desirability of such centres is bound to wane.

Consequences

The Eurocurrency markets have, as noted above, been an important source of funds for inter-bank lending. This has had the effect of bringing together banks throughout the world into an informal network, and there can be no doubt that international liquidity has been enhanced in the process. However, it is clear that there are dangers in moving around vast sums of money without there being any institution in overall control of proceedings. This can arise first with respect to individual banks. Eurocurrency tends to travel through a succession of banks on its route between ultimate lender and ultimate borrower. An individual bank cannot, therefore, know to what extent its lending may end up with any particular borrower, and therefore how vulnerable it is to that borrower's financial health (see **pp. 169–71** for a discussion of what can happen when it is lent to less-developed countries (LDCs)). Secondly, from the point of view of sovereign states, it is clear that domestic monetary policy may be rendered ineffectual by the Eurocurrency markets. The movement of 'hot money' has, for example, recently been of considerable concern to the UK government (see **p. 164**). It should be noted, in particular, that interest rate differentials between countries are critical in determining the direction of flow of hot money, and hence that no individual country can set its interest rate structure in isolation.

The loss of control implied by these developments is inevitably a considerable irritant to banks and governments alike, but attempts to regulate Eurocurrency markets would simply result in their replacement by other markets not subject to the new regulations. The steady growth of the Eurobond market has, perhaps fortunately in view of the above, faltered somewhat of late (although 1988 may turn out to be a record year for new issues). The removal of regulations has led to some of the funds returning to their country of origin, particularly dollars to the USA. The international debt problem, discussed below, has also made lenders wary of channelling funds to high-risk borrowers, and there are no longer any OPEC surpluses to be invested.

The analysis of the international debt problem is more appropriately left to Chapter 4 on international relations (see **pp. 168–71**), but we need to note in the present context that it has had a significant impact on banking practice. It was clear from the early 1980s that a good deal of the money lent to LDCs would never be repaid even if these countries did not officially renege on their outstanding debts. However, banks which had become heavily involved in this lending, possibly because of the fanciful idea that sovereign country debt is more secure than lending to households and

firms, but also because it gives a measure of status to a bank to be the banker to a sovereign state, were unwilling to write the debt off their balance sheets for fear that it would expose their inadequate capital structure. Initially, the common practice was to convert short-term loans into long-term loans, and to set aside some of the profits earned on other business into a reserve fund to cover international bad debts. Where possible the capital base of a bank was replenished by an additional issue of equity (see discussion of rights issues on **p. 94**), but the stock market was expected to take a very dim view of what was virtually a public confession that the capital base had been eroded by bad debt.

However, in 1987, the international banks, following the example set in America, decided to bite the bullet and write a significant part of the debt off their balance sheets (see **p. 169**). Rather interestingly, the Stock Market took a fairly positive view of this new sense of realism and bank share prices rose rather than fell. Nevertheless, it remained understandably difficult for banks to raise new capital in the markets, especially in the aftermath of the October 1987 Crash. The decision by Brazil to delay repayment of foreign debts in July 1989 raised the possibility either that further provisions for bad debts would have to be made or that the loans to those countries least likely to repay would be written off once and for all. The Midland and Lloyds both had outstanding loans of £4.2 bn in 1988, followed by National Westminster and Barclays at £2.5 bn, so the write-off alternative appeared to be more realistic in respect of the latter than of the former pair.

However, in late July 1989 Lloyds reported that 15 out of the 29 problem debtor countries which owed it money were in arrears with their repayments, and accordingly announced a massive £483 mn provision of which £183 mn was set against specific countries' debts. This caused the bank's net profits to slump to a loss of £88 mn for the first half of 1989, but as previously the share price rose sharply on the news. Lloyd's cover for problem country debts was accordingly raised to 47 per cent, well above that for the other three which stood at between 31 and 33 per cent in 1988, but with a potential total default on the

£547 mn owed by Argentina, Lloyds may yet need to make additional provisions. The other big three banks (and also Standard Chartered) have also raised their cover to much the same level as Lloyds even though it caused their profitability to fall dramatically.

ECU securities

Starting in 1987, a market developed for Eurobonds denominated in European Currency Units (ECUs) (see **pp. 176–7**). However, this peaked at an annual value of ECU 12.3 bn in 1985, and in 1988 only some 5 per cent of Eurobonds were priced in ECUs. Part of the reason for this small scale of business was the absence of any parallel market in short-term (up to six-month) ECU bills. It was, nevertheless, something of a surprise, bearing in mind the UK's reluctance to join the EMS and its positive antipathy to monetary union (see **pp. 179–81**), that the UK chose to launch ECU Treasury bills in August 1988, although it could be regarded as a pre-emptive measure to concentrate the ECU markets in London.

The Chancellor chose simultaneously to repay, at the earliest possible date, the $2.5 bn FRN issued in September 1985 at a time when the reserves were low, and to announce that there would be a series of Treasury bill tenders, beginning in October 1988 on a monthly basis, for amounts up to ECU 500 mn, building up to a total outstanding of between ECU 1 and 2 bn. Both subscriptions and repayments will be in ECU. At the end of the series of tenders the UK will be the largest international borrower in ECUs. The ECU bills are freely tradeable, and should prove popular given the creditworthiness of the UK government, although it will take some time to develop a yield curve comparable to that for other Eurosecurities. It is expected that the Bank of England, which typically keeps its assets and liabilities in a given currency in approximate balance, will accordingly acquire assets in the form of ECU Eurobonds.

In the event there was so much interest in the first tender that bills worth ECU 900 mn were put on offer, but these were still 3.5 times oversubscribed. By the completion of the fourth oversubscribed tender in January 1989, bills worth ECU 1.9 bn had been issued.

Capital markets

When companies need more medium- and long-term capital than is available from retained profits, and when the government cannot cover its expenditure from its tax revenue, they make up the shortfall by recourse to the capital markets. These thus encompass both the **institutions** which provide medium- and long-term finance, and the **forms of financial instrument** which are traded there.

There are two basic markets; the first, called the **new-issue or primary market**, is where new securities are offered to investors; the second, called the **secondary market**, is where existing securities are traded. The securities traded fall into two basic categories. Equities, or shares, are issued by companies and pay dividends, usually half-yearly, which are variable and linked to profitability. Most shares carry voting rights at the annual general meeting, although these are rarely exercised in practice. The value of a share is also variable, being determined by the forces of supply and demand, and a shareholder may, therefore, make either a capital gain or loss over time. Interest-bearing securities (stocks) come in a variety of forms. They are mostly issued by the government in the form of **gilts**. Those issued by companies are called **debentures**. There is also an active market in **Eurobonds** as outlined earlier. Stocks almost universally become redeemable at a specific future date, and yield a fixed rate of return. However, some are convertible into equity, and others are in the form of floating-rate notes, or are index-linked to guarantee their return in real rather than money terms. Stocks may also be subject to capital gains and losses as interest rates vary when sold before maturity.

The secondary market is essential if the primary market is to operate successfully. In other words, stocks and shares are regarded as liquid assets by investors although they are frequently held for long periods of time by the original purchaser, and it is essential that there is a mechanism for rapid trading (see the discussion of 'Big Bang' below). The International Stock Exchange, as it is now known, lies at the centre of the capital markets, but it is by no means necessary to use its services in order to raise longer-term capital. This is related to the role of financial intermediaries which hold the bulk of all stocks and shares in the UK. Whilst it is quite easy for individuals to deal in shares, personal portfolios are still, despite privatisation, very modest. In the UK most investors prefer to save with pension funds, insurance companies and unit trusts where there have normally been tax advantages whilst there are none for personal shareholdings (other than special concessions for privatisation issues).

In order to raise funds on the Stock Exchange a company must 'go public' and obtain a 'quotation'. This is an expensive affair, and a company is usually expected to show evidence of a respectable trading record over a period of years. Where a company is too new, operates in a very risky sector, or cannot afford the costs of a full listing, it will go either to the **Unlisted Securities Market** (USM) or the **Over the Counter** (OTC or 'third') market established in January 1987. Shares are, however, relatively difficult to trade in these markets. There are few market-makers and big differences in buy and sell prices in the USM, whilst in the OTC market a buy order has to be matched with a sell order and vice versa.

Where a full listing on the Stock Exchange is required, but the value of the new issue is modest, it is customary to opt for a 'public placing' whereby the issuing house (usually a merchant bank) places up to 75 per cent of the shares directly with institutional clients, the remainder being made available on the Exchange. Not surprisingly, shares issued in this way tend to end up concentrated in a very few hands. For major issues an Issue by Prospectus or an Offer for Sale is preferred, the difference being that in the latter case the issuing house first acquires the shares and then sells them to the public (favoured where the company is obscure but the issuing house is well known).

These methods are expensive because a prospectus has to be drawn up containing a full financial history of the company. The issue must be advertised nationally, and the issuing house and other advisors paid a commission. If oversubscribed a system of allocation will have to be chosen and implemented. In the great majority of cases the issue will be underwritten for a further fee as a precaution against an undersubscription, the underwriter then being obliged to purchase the outstanding shares. An Offer for Sale may be either at a fixed price, or less commonly by tender at (or above) a predetermined minimum price. The latter prevents the shares being seriously underpriced with attendant capital gains for 'stags' who immediately resell, but will almost certainly leave virtually all of the shares with the institutions.

Occasionally there are 'scrip' issues whereby, perhaps to make each share cheaper and hence more marketable, the number of shares may, for example, be doubled and their price halved. This does not raise any new capital as such, whilst 'rights' issue does. This is where existing shareholders are offered the right to buy additional shares. If they do not wish to acquire the extra shares then the rights can be sold on the Stock Exchange. Strictly speaking, the price of the old shares should fall to bring into line the higher total number of shares and the higher total capitalisation of the company. Rights issues are popular with companies themselves because all the company has to do is send a circular to existing shareholders, who benefit because there are no brokerage charges to pay, but who may find their shareholdings diluted if they cannot afford to take up their rights.

The International Stock Exchange in London is the world's third largest, but is totally dominated by those of New York and Tokyo. New issues of equities in the last full pre-Crash year of 1986 amounted to only £8 bn, whilst transactions in the secondary market were eight times as large. However, these in turn were dwarfed by transactions in gilts, and much more so by Eurobond issues.

The issue of gilts is the responsibility of the Bank of England, and the total value outstanding grew rapidly as a result of net borrowing by the government in the majority of postwar years. However, in the Autumn Statement of November 1988 Nigel Lawson declared that he would 'fully fund' the Public Sector Debt Repayment (PSDR), the actual effect of which was to withdraw £9 bn of gilts from the market during the financial year 1988–89. This not merely has the effect of altering considerably the shape of the yield curve which relates short-term to long-term yields, but causes problems for institutions such as pension funds which like to hold long-dated assets which match their long-dated liabilities. Indeed, given a shortage of alternative long-dated securities denominated in sterling offering an attractive rate of return, institutions are increasingly investing in foreign bonds, holdings of which rose by £5.5 bn during the first half of 1988. Nigel Lawson followed this up in December by announcing that, commencing in January 1989, the Bank of England would conduct reverse gilts auctions, concentrating on short-dated gilts. The first auction of £500 mn of gilts was 3.2 times oversubscribed.

'Big Bang' and its aftermath

The term 'Big Bang' is the colloquial name for the **deregulation of the Stock Exchange** in October 1986. A variety of circumstances conspired to bring it about at that particular point in time. Historically, there were two major groups of participants in the Exchange. The first, the **stockbrokers**, acted on behalf of clients, both personal and institutional, who paid a commission for stockbroking services. Brokers primarily traded equity, but also gave advice on portfolios. In order to obtain shares the brokers had to go to a **jobber** who acted as a **market-maker** – that is, he held a portfolio of shares which he bought and sold on his own account. His income came from the 'split' – the difference between the price at which he would buy and the price at which he would sell any given share. Since jobbers could not deal directly with the general public, they were independent of the brokers in a so-called 'single capacity' system. The Stock Exchange's own rules enforced the system, the main attractions of which were superficially that there were always jobbers willing to trade and that, since the brokers had nothing personally to gain by using one jobber rather than another, they would get the best deal they could for their clients.

However, the system had two particularly serious defects. In the first place, the scale of commissions paid to brokers was fixed by the Exchange. An institution buying shares worth £10 million had thus to pay virtually the same rate as a personal investor buying shares worth £1,000. Secondly, the Stock Exchange would not allow individual member firms to grow at the expense of others. Prior to 1970 no member firm could become a limited company, and only 10 per cent at most of the share capital could subsequently be held by anyone outside the Exchange. This was raised to 29.9 per cent in 1982, but did little to resolve the problem of undercapitalisation because the aggregate capital base could expand only if the internal shareholders were simultaneously adding to their investment. But as individual members of the Exchange were personally liable if their firms made losses, they understandably did not often want to add to their exposure by taking on too much additional business.

The single capacity system was out of line with normal practice in competing centres, and was causing considerable difficulties in the UK because, for example, of a shortage of jobbers in many stocks. This largely reflected the fact that with institutions trading huge parcels of shares, the jobbers had to hold large blocks on their own account, and they could raise the capital to do so only by merging, causing the number of jobbers to halve between 1968 and 1984. Furthermore, the New York stock market was already deregulated, and had expanded considerably as a consequence. Competition there kept commissions lower than in the UK, and most international shares were accordingly cheaper for institutions to buy and sell in New York than in London. New York trading was done electronically, so information was available more quickly and accurately than on the Stock Exchange floor in London. Whilst previously the cross-subsidy from institutions to personal clients implicit in the fixed commission rate had been justified by the quality of research done on behalf of the institutions, the lure of cheaper prices for heavily traded shares in New York was proving irresistible.

At the same time (1979) the new government was casting its eye over the Stock Exchange rule book, and not much liking what it saw. The Restrictive Practices Act 1976 was clearly being contravened, and the Stock Exchange was given an ultimatum – to bring its rule book into line with the Act or face an investigation in the Restrictive Practices Court (pencilled in for 1984). In 1983 the Stock Exchange agreed to **forgo fixed commissions and single capacity trading** as from 27 October 1986. Commencing in March 1986 any Stock Exchange firm could be **wholly taken over by outsiders**. This also held true in the gilt-edged market which had previously been dominated by only two firms of jobbers.

One obvious question which may be asked is why 'Big Bang' occurred in London rather than, say, in Frankfurt. There were already two very large exchanges in New York and Tokyo, but one shut well before the other opened so it was not possible to trade 24 hours around the clock. To connect them up a European exchange was needed. London had a long financial tradition, it was true, but in many respects the UK did not seem as ideal as Switzerland or West Germany. Probably a major factor in London's favour was the relatively light regulation of its financial markets. Also English (of a kind) was spoken there, making it an easy environment for Americans and English-speaking Japanese to work in, and London was regarded as a pleasant city with good educational facilities for children.

As Big Bang approached there was a mad rush to organise the new 'dual-capacity' market-making firms which stood ready to deal directly with investors, to trade on their own account, and to make markets in as many shares as they wished. Brokers and jobbers were taken over by UK and foreign banks, thereby **destroying the historic distinction between banking and security trading** in the UK. The number of trained personnel was understandably totally inadequate, and vast sums of money were offered to attract qualified staff.

One significant problem related to technology. Very few old-style jobbers had modern electronic dealing rooms, so there was also a mad scramble to obtain new premises and to get them wired up. The system for transmitting data throughout the Exchange known as SEAQ (Stock Exchange Automated Quotations), was only just about up and running in time for Big Bang. Once the electronics were in place, the Stock Exchange floor suffered a virtual mass desertion.

Some idea of the altered scale of operation post-Big Bang can be seen in the gilts market where the two main jobbers were replaced by 27 primary dealers licensed by the Bank of England. It was generally realised that not all could survive unless the volume of business rose dramatically, but all were individually confident that their expertise would win through. As predicted, commission rates for institutions fell, but for private clients they rose, and some brokers ceased to deal with such clients altogether because of the paperwork costs of executing small transactions.

For a year, all went very well. The stock market boomed and the volume of business rose to new heights. However, in October 1987 there was a market collapse which made even the Wall Street Crash of 1929 look insignificant. The authorities in the UK and elsewhere reacted positively on this occasion, making large amounts of liquidity available to prevent market-makers going to the wall, and in the event remarkably little damage was done. The real economy carried on working pretty much as before. The enormous cuts in the capitalisation of firms did not make any real difference because, at the end of the day, share prices simply reflect the use of capital which has already been invested. One thing that understandably was affected was the amount of new equity capital which could be raised, because that is not normally allowed to exceed a given proportion of the value of existing capital. The issue of 'rights' came to a grinding halt, and has only recently begun to recover.

Equally, on paper, investors have become less wealthy, which might have caused them to cut consumption and save more with consequent effects upon GDP. However, this has not discernably taken place. What has happened is that both personal and institutional investors have stayed out of the equity market, and the daily volume of shares traded has fallen well below 1987 levels. As a result, many market-makers and brokers are struggling to break even, and there have been extensive redundancies in the City. In the gilts market five firms had withdrawn by July 1988, although two Japanese firms had applied to join.

Personal investors have switched back to the building societies which have regained much of the mortgage market share previously lost to the banks, whilst the institutions have remained highly liquid by previous standards.

Investor protection

In the run up to Big Bang it became clear that deregulation on the intended scale could have highly adverse effects upon investors. The government therefore appointed Professor Gower to look into the issue of investor protection, and his Report was pulished in 1984. Gower raised a good many objections to existing practices, which were generally based upon the principle of letting the professionals look after their own because only they were competent to do so. With more and more cases of practices such as insider dealing coming to light, and wholly inconsequential punishments being meted out by the professionals, the government decided to build many of Gower's criticisms into a Financial Services Act which became law in 1986.

The Financial Services Act 1986

The Financial Services Act is intended as a **system of regulation covering the entire investment sector**, from the largest bank to the smallest investment advisor. It is intended to ensure that financial services are provided only by those who are fit and proper to do so; that legitimate complaints can be laid before the relevant authorities; and that compensation is available where appropriate. For the past two years the regulatory framework has been painfully pieced together. At its centre lies the Securities and Investments Board (SIB) whose powers are delegated to it by the Secretary of State for Trade and Industry. The SIB is a private company, financed by levies on its members, whose original Chairman was Sir Kenneth Berrill. The main responsibility of the SIB is to oversee the Self Regulatory Organisations (SROs) of which there are now five.

AFBD	Association of Futures Brokers and Dealers
FIMBRA	Financial Intermediaries, Managers and Brokers Regulatory Association
IMRO	Investment Management Regulatory Organisation
LAUTRO	Life Assurance and Unit Trust Regulatory Organisation
TSA	The Securities Association

The SIB's first task was to draw up its rule-book. Each SRO then had to draw up its own rule-book which had to be at least as rigorous as that of the SIB. All professional bodies have to register with the appropriate SRO. Failure to register is a criminal offence. The SIB can investigate any alleged malpractice, and apply sanctions as appropriate, and in certain circumstances bring legal proceedings.

The SROs were slow in putting their rules together, and were mostly hard pressed to get them agreed by the SIB before the deadline of February 1988. The deadline for professional bodies to register with the SRO was put back until April 1988, but even then there was a massive backlog of applications to be assessed, so 'interim authorisation' had to be granted to any firm which had applied in time.

The construction of rule-books created a good deal of controversy. In the case of the SIB it was argued that the rule-book was unnecessarily complicated, and as a consequence Berrill was replaced by David Walker as Chairman of the SIB in 1988. Several SROs disputed their rule-books with the SIB, and the protracted argument about how to price unit trusts was especially acrimonious. The key elements of all rule-books are that:

1. clients' money must be kept separate from that of professional bodies
2. written contracts must be provided to clients specifying agreed services
3. there must be 'polarisation' (see below)
4. investigations of clients' needs must be undertaken and the best possible advice given in the light of their findings
5. clients should be advised to go elsewhere if expertise is lacking

6. an established complaints procedure must be followed.

Polarisation requires all registered bodies to state clearly whether they are acting as a salesman or agent for the services of only one intermediary (such as one insurance company's endowments), or as independent advisors choosing the best services on offer. There is no middle ground. If a bank elects to be an independent advisor then it cannot recommend its own services (life insurance, endowments or whatever) although a client can expressly ask for them. Polarisation has caused particular controversy because of differences between the amount of information on commissions which has to be disclosed to clients by salesmen in each category.

The compensation scheme has operated since August 1988. It pays out a maximum of £48,000 to any investor who loses money when a registered firm goes into liquidation. Complaints must be taken up with the appropriate SRO as plans for an ombudsman have fallen through.

Interim authorisation has given much cause for concern. It was necessary to issue interim licences to many firms which had no real hope of ultimate acceptance. In July 1988 the SIB was forced to freeze the operations of DPR Futures Ltd whilst an investigation took place as a result of serious complaints about its business practices, and the Fraud Squad was simultaneously involved in an investigation. It was also made known that AFBD had another twenty cases waiting to be investigated.

These investigations may persuade the less circumspect suppliers of financial services that the full force of the regulatory regime will be brought to bear on them if they continue as before. However, there are likely to be a series of court cases, and doubtless lengthy appeals, before firms worry overmuch about the penalties for malpractice. From the viewpoint of David Walker, the crucial question is whether the degree of regulation is pitched about right. Fears have been expressed that, if other EC markets end up more lightly regulated, 1992 will see a good deal of business departing to more welcoming shores. On the other hand, there is just as much pressure to ensure that all early signs of abuse are stamped out.

A simplified set of conduct of business rules for the SIB have been incorporated in a new Companies Bill. The objectives of the regulations have been converted into guiding 'principles of conduct' which have the force of rules. The 93 principles for the SIB are expressed in plain English, but may subsequently need more detailed interpretation. Similar principles for other regulatory bodies are expected to follow.

Financial intermediation in the future

Let us turn, by way of summary, to pick out from the above discussion the most important themes which will determine how the financial system will evolve during the final decade of this century.

Deregulation and regulation

A particularly interesting issue is the balance between **deregulation** and **regulation**. Historically, the financial system in the UK was heavily regulated by the government acting through the Bank of England. In addition, specific kinds of financial assets and liabilities were favoured by tax concessions to lenders and/or borrowers. As a result, certain parts of the financial system grew rapidly whilst other parts stagnated. This imbalance was recognised in the UK when the present government came to power and, starting with the abolition of exchange controls in 1979, it set in train a process of freeing up the system. Most of the monetary controls were subsequently terminated or put into abeyance; public corporations were sold, partly to small shareholders; the Financial Services Act (1986) and Building Society Act (1986) became law; the Stock Exchange was reformed via Big Bang; portable pensions were introduced as were personal equity plans, and so on.

However, these processes have been incomplete, and the government has been forced to recognise that free-for-alls in financial markets are a recipe for widespread abuse, and hence deregulation has dragged regulation in its wake.

Whilst the Financial Services Act and Building Society Act, for example, have allowed NBFIs to provide services previously forbidden to them, they have also made it necessary to set up regulatory bodies to ensure that the new services are provided by fit-and-proper intermediaries, and that the new rules are obeyed to the letter. This in turn has caused many disputes about what kinds of regulatory bodies are needed, and how they should be financed. It must be recognised that financial markets always have been regulated in the sense that, for example, the Stock Exchange imposed a rule-book upon its members, but this kind of self-regulation is bound to be treated with considerable scepticism by outside parties who read about scandals, and their resolution behind closed doors. However, it is clear that other existing bodies such as the Bank of England and Monopolies and Mergers Commission do not have the resources to cope with the huge increase in regulatory work, and hence other bodies have had to be created.

Basle Capital Convergence Accord

In July 1988 the Governors of the Group of Ten central banks signed the **Basle Capital Convergence Accord**, thereby making banking the first industry to be regulated on a world-wide basis. The central purpose of the Accord is to force all international banks to comply with minimum capital requirements, and thereby to ensure fair competition between them. However, the Accord covers only **credit risk**, and, whilst it is true that non-repayment of international loans is currently the biggest risk faced by banks, other sources of risk such as those associated with exchange rate and interest rate variability will need to be added to the Accord at a later date.

The Accord essentially lays down a definition of 'capital' and a formula for working out **how much of it banks must have**, depending upon the riskiness of their assets. The definition was complicated by different practices in different countries, but needed to identify capital permanently available to meet losses. In the UK banks are financed with both equity and debt, but German banks have very little of the latter. Equally, US banks issue 'perpetual preferred stock' (PPS) which is neither one nor the other. In the event, a compromise was reached whereby at least 50 per cent of capital must be tier 1, comprising equity, disclosed reserves and PPS (but only if it is non-cumulative, meaning that failure to pay dividends in one year must not create an obligation to make them up in later years). Tier 2 includes long-term debt and other debt instruments.

The other complication concerned the **'risk weighting' of assets**. Risk assets are all bank assets, including off-balance sheet commitments, weighted according to their riskiness. The UK, as a full member of the OECD, is deemed to be a low-risk borrower, as are other OECD members (with the possible exception of Turkey) plus Saudi Arabia.

Bank lending to other countries is deemed to be at greater risk. All commercial lending is deemed to be at equal risk, irrespective of the size of the borrowing company, in order to avoid vast numbers of individual decisions about credit-worthiness.

Every bank has until 1992 to meet its minimum 'risk asset ratio', which may be imposed at a level higher than that of the Accord if individual countries so wish. The Accord itself requires that capital must be equivalent to **at least 8 per cent** of a bank's risk-weighted assets. UK banks will have little difficulty in meeting their ratios via retained earnings and, if necessary, modest rights issues. To pay for the maintenance of higher-than-normal capital backing, bank charges will need to rise. This should help to drag down credit spending, but may induce some banks to take even bigger risks to maintain profitability. In 1992, when the Accord will become law in the UK, the EC's own banking directives arising from the Single European Act will also require compliance. In December 1988, EC finance ministers adopted legislation governing capital adequacy which was almost identical to the Accord. The Bank of England had already announced, in November 1988, that UK banks would have to meet the Accord requirements by the end of 1989, well in advance of most other signatories. At the same time, the Bank of Scotland took advantage of the new rules to place £100 mn of preferred shares, the largest non-convertible preference issue ever made in the UK, and to have this approved as tier 1 capital by the Bank of England.

Innovation

At the present time these new regulatory systems are beginning to settle down, but it is far too early to form a judgement about their success or failure. It is reasonably to be expected that many amendments will be forthcoming in the years to come. Indeed, this is almost inevitable in the face of ever more rapid **innovation** in financial markets. Regulations can ultimately be applied only to cover existing practices, and it is clear that a rule-book set up to cover existing practices in 1980 would by now be looking totally out of date. Financial innovation is driven by a variety of forces, including most obviously changes in monetary control systems; the desire to avoid regulation; vast increases in the total sums being transacted; a wider variety of both lenders and borrowers; and increasing sophistication on the part of both in specifying their needs.

We have already referred to the rapid growth of Eurobonds and Eurocommercial paper. It is worth noting that, hand in hand with these, it is increasingly common to find transactions in the **swaps** market. According to the International Swap Dealers Association (ISDA) the nominal principal involved in interest rate and currency swaps has risen from $3 bn in 1983 to $225 bn in the first half of 1987. Despite their superficial complexity, at the heart of any swap lies simply an agreement between two institutions receiving or paying interest income to exchange payments or receipts. For example, if one bank has borrowed in dollars at a fixed rate, and a second bank has borrowed in yen at a floating rate, each then agrees to meet the interest payments of the other. Their decisions are influenced by different expectations concerning the future path of both the currencies and the interest rates in question. Whole sequences of swaps can be placed end-on-end in a single programme. However, most swaps currently involve simple swaps in dollars between fixed-rate and floating-rate notes. Currency swaps carry more risk than interest rate swaps because both exchange rates and interest rates may move adversely at the same time. Banks accordingly run a 'swaps book' in which swaps are matched up, thereby limiting their exposure to exchange rate or interest rate movements.

It is important to note that much innovative activity such as swaps is 'off-balance sheet'. In other words, the bank concerned in a transaction does not lend to the borrower funds which the bank has itself previously borrowed, which would cause both transactions to appear on its balance sheet, but rather acts as the agent organising a loan directly between ultimate lender and ultimate borrower. The process in which funds flow from lender to borrower other than via the banks is known as **disintermediation**, and has obvious consequences for monetary controls which are intended to operate via regulations imposed upon specified intermediaries (traditionally banks). It also involves the process known as *securitisation*, whereby conventional bank lending is replaced by other forms of financial instruments. A Eurobond, for example, is a 'securitised' debt, which means that it is sold by a borrowing institution to a lender without the money being either lent to, or by, a bank. The purchaser may subsequently resell the debt in the secondary Eurobond market, and the debt may be resold any number of times before maturity. The obvious consequence of securitisation is that the issuer of the security has no real idea who actually holds it as an asset at any given time. However, securitised debt is set to become increasingly popular as top quality borrowers such as 'blue chip' companies take advantage of the fact that they can actually borrow more cheaply in their own names than through the intermediation of a bank, the credit rating of which may have suffered as a result of underperforming LDC debt.

On the fact of it financial innovation should permit independent groups of intermediaries to carve out their own market niches, and indeed specialist intermediaries are often successful as niche operators. However, a successful niche operator with a limited capital base is sooner or later going to attract the attention of an intermediary in another part of the system which has spare capital and limited capacity to expand in its major lines of business. Historically, the process of merger and take-over between different kinds of intermediary was heavily restricted, but in a deregulated environment the key issue is simply whether the merged company will be a fit-and-proper operator in every market in which it wishes to operate. The process of merger and take-over may allow an intermediary to reduce the risk inherent in its exposure to a single or very small number of markets. It may provide a short cut, via merger with another intermediary overseas, to becoming an international as against a national operator. There are also going to be circumstances in which a company outside the financial system will want to merge with a financial intermediary, especially if it wants, for example, to provide credit facilities to its customers.

It is unclear where the adjustments implied by the above will end. It is certain that for many companies the process of merger will prove to be an unhappy and costly business, and parts of the merged organisations may subsequently need to be shut down or resold. It was clear at the time of Big Bang, for example, that there were too many players and too little talent in almost every part of the equity and bond markets. The Crash of October 1987 caused the process of readjustment to be speeded up, but it is by no means complete as yet. The link between economic efficiency and concentration in the financial markets cannot be determined by historical precedent. There is much evidence of a 'clash of cultures' when different kinds of intermediary are brought together. At the end of the day the authorities must also form a judgement both about their ability to oversee the system and also the compatibility of different kinds of financial system with the pursuit of their major objectives, and it is clear from recent disputes within the Cabinet that there is as yet no consensus about these matters.

Internationalisation

One of the trickier issues is raised by the **internationalisation** of the financial system. Predominantly national intermediaries still exist in the UK, particularly the building societies, but the process

of merger and take-over is increasingly international in scope. Big Bang specifically encouraged the inflow of foreign capital, but it would be wrong to suppose that this can be interpreted as a completely laissez-faire attitude on the part of the authorities. They have indicated that there are distinct limits beyond which internationalisation will not be permitted to go – the UK clearing banks, despite the rather modest level of their share capital, are not going to be allowed to fall into foreign hands (nor indeed into the dubious hands of non-financial companies in the UK if the abortive bid by Saatchi and Saatchi for the Midland Bank in 1988 is anything to go by).

New technology

To be a major international intermediary it must be possible for the head office to know what is going on in the farthest-flung outposts of the company. This has increasingly been made possible by the introduction of **new technology**, and especially of computers, which can communicate information instantaneously over vast distances. However, the introduction of computers has had much more widespread effects, because it has permitted an individual intermediary to handle an enormously increased range of data, and therefore made it possible for it to compete in many more markets than in previous periods when a lack of skilled manpower could not produce enough detailed information for rational decisions to be made. Dealing with a multiplicity of currencies is no longer more than a technicality, and the full spread of interest rates can be arranged on a screen at the touch of a button. Much of the software is marketed commercially, so it is not even necessary for organisations to develop their own software before joining in a new market. It should, however, be borne in mind that computers cannot think for themselves, so if information is mistakenly or fraudulently inserted, serious consequences can easily arise involving losses on a scale which would have been spotted much more quickly in less-sophsiticated systems.

Dealing in equities and gilts is so dependent upon modern technology that the Stock Exchange floor was deserted almost immediately after the

'Big Bang', and face-to-face transactions have become a virtual anachronism. Most readers will be familiar with modern dealing rooms through the media and especially such films as 'Wall Street', but this technology barely touches upon the everyday lives of individuals. However, automated teller machines (ATMs) are now in widespread usage, and the National Westminster Bank is, for example, spending £1 bn in order to create a computerised system which will allow it to deal with deposits, cash dispensing and account information at branches entirely through machines. The TSB has also experimented with an unmanned bank in Glasgow. It will not be long before EFTPOS (electronic funds transfer at point of sale) becomes equally familiar. EFTPOS is a system whereby, for example, a supermarket uses an individual's debit card to debit his or her purchases direct to a bank account, thereby rendering unnecessary the use both of cash and cheques. Other recent innovations are electronic gadgets which allow an individual sitting at home to access his bank account or a share dealing service via a telephone link, with the information shown on a home computer screen. This takes us one further step towards a cashless society, but as noted above there remains, and will remain for the foreseeable future, very large numbers of the 'unbanked'.

Conclusion

It is clear from this discussion that the circumstances of the financial markets post-Big Bang are somewhat different from those anticipated in 1986. There was an almost universal belief that the markets would be transformed by the quest for globalisation, and that in order to compete a financial supermarket would have to be created.

This would require the elimination of the weakest players from the markets, leaving the survivors with profitable businesses with significant shares of each market. The reality has been a fascinating illustration of the forces of competition, which in this case are dependent upon information flows. The quest for globalisation was based upon the assumption that the market players with the most sophisticated, and by implication most expensive, communications would have an advantage over the less-well capitalised players. Regrettably for those companies who spent vast sums of money following the path mapped out by this line of reasoning it proved possible for all the players, even those operating on a small scale and with relatively little capital, to access the necessary information on equal terms. Furthermore, the customer has found himself able to shop around at the touch of a button on a computer screen. He is largely indifferent from whom he buys, so he may simply opt continuously for the cheapest (and probably not very profitable) bargain such as is offered by a basic share dealing only service. Alternatively, he may be willing to pay a premium for high quality advice, but if this fails to meet expectations he can readily transfer his allegiance elsewhere.

Building up allegiance is largely a matter of personal relationships – hence the odd phenomenon of competitive bidding for personnel whose advice is valued highly even in an unprofitable market. In the end some kind of equilibrium will have to be reached, almost certainly with fewer players operating in smaller groups, either as independents or as semi-autonomous parts of larger organisations. Somewhat ironically, it may eventually prove to be the case that, in the marketing of financial services, small is beautiful.

3

Spending, Taxing & Borrowing *Peter Curwen*

Introduction

Our purpose in Chapter 3 is to describe the components of the UK fiscal system and to provide an up-to-date statistical analysis of government expenditure, taxes and borrowing. It does not seek to discuss the philosophy and mechanics of fiscal policy as such, which is left to the concluding Chapter 9, because it is unhelpful to discuss fiscal policy independently of monetary policy. Furthermore, it is impractical to discuss the use of policy instruments until all of the relevant policy objectives have been thoroughly reviewed, and their interrelationships assessed.

Our first task is to examine the available data on public spending. Whilst the government has shown some ambivalence about the presentation of its policy objectives since 1979, its public spending plans have always been an important element of its strategy. At the present time the government's stated objective is to hold the rate of growth of public spending below the growth of the economy as a whole, and thus to reduce public spending as a proportion of national income. This should then make it possible to ease the burden of taxation without any accompanying increase in the overall burden of the National Debt, and from this should flow the enterprise and efficiency which leads to growing output and employment. Once our discussion of public spending is complete we will move on to examine, first, the burden of taxation, and subsequently the government's borrowing requirements and their impact upon the National Debt.

Public expenditure

The growth of public expenditure

As shown in **Figure 3.1**, public expenditure has grown enormously during the twentieth century, a phenomenon common to all advanced industrial economies albeit to varying degees. As will be discussed subsequently, it is very difficult to reduce public expenditure once it has taken root, so it is of considerable interest briefly to review the origins of the growth of public expenditure in the UK.

At the microeconomic level it is first possible to argue that governments are constantly intervening in order to offset the undesirable side-effects of free markets. In the case of what are known as 'public goods' such as national defence and street lighting there is unlikely to be any provision in a private market since the provider would be unable to obtain payment from beneficiaries of his provision. Equally, in the case of merit goods, the provision in a private market of such things as health and education would be limited to those with the ability to pay. Since the benefit to society of the provision of merit goods exceeds the aggregate of the benefit to individuals – through, for example, the prevention of an epidemic created by the failure of an individual to afford the cost of treatment – there is a very strong case for communal provision. Once a health service is set up it also becomes subject to the 'problem' that if people remain healthy and live longer the costs of provision inevitably rise over time.

At the macroeconomic level the basic premise is that goods and services provided by the public sector have high income elasticities – that is, demand for them grows faster than the rate of growth of incomes. This sharp rise in demand manifests itself not only in the case of merit goods, including public housing, but also in the case of income support, including pensions, sickness pay and unemployment benefits. The 'displacement theory' put forward by Peacock and Wiseman suggested that the growth in public spending was not a broadly smooth and continuous process as previously thought, but rather was periodically jacked upwards on a permanent basis by events, of which the most prominent examples are world wars, which caused a radical reappraisal of the existing order. However, it is difficult to decide whether such upwards displacements in public expenditure are permanent or transitory, especially since they are divorced from the more general political influences that were referred to in the introductory chapter. What is evident is that if public expenditure is maintained in a recession – which is both standard Keynesian practice and a necessary consequence of needing to pay out much larger sums to the unemployed – the proportion of public spending in total national income is bound to rise, albeit temporarily. Logically, of course, as discussed later, the opposite argument holds during periods of rapid growth.

It is difficult to make out a case for the inevitability of continued growth in public spending, and there must therefore be a possibility of setting it on a downward path. Just how far along such a path it is possible to go is, however, equally difficult to assess, if only because there is no evidence from which to draw conclusions.

Public expenditure defined

There are different ways of defining public spending, and different aggregates are relevant for different purposes. The measure which is used for the formulation of macroeconomic policy and the Medium Term Financial Stategy (MTFS) is **general government expenditure**, consisting of the combined capital and current spending of central and local government including debt interest. This represents the amount which needs to be raised by taxation and borrowing. However, for the purposes of planning and control of programmes, the public expenditure cash planning total is the relevant figure since it is built up from the control totals for departmental programmes including public corporations. The comparable figures are shown in **Table 3.1**.

As can be seen from **Table 3.1**, the main difference between the two aggregates is currently debt interest. This is difficult to plan because interest rates are impossible to forecast accurately, and any repayment of debt such as occurred in 1987–88 and 1988–89 obviously reduces interest

Table 3.1 *Public expenditure totals (£ billion)*

	1985–86 Outturn	1986–87 Outturn	1987–88 Estimated outturn	1988–89 Plans[1]	1989–90 Plans	1990–91 Plans[2]
Central government	98.4	104.6	110.3	114.2	120.2	124.7
Local authorities	35.4	37.9	40.9	42.6	44.0	45.2
Public corporations	2.6	1.1	1.1	1.4	0.9	0.6
Reserve				3.5	7.0	10.5
Privatisation proceeds	− 2.7	− 4.4	− 5.0	− 5.0	− 5.0	− 5.0
PLANNING TOTAL	133.7	139.2	147.3[3]	156.8	167.1	176.1
Central government gross debt interest	17.7	17.6	17.8	18.0	18.0	18.0
Other national accounts adjustments	6.9	8.0	7.5	8.0	8.0	8.0
GENERAL GOVERNMENT EXPENDITURE	158.2	164.8	172.6[3]	183.9	193.2	202.1

Notes:
[1] The Autumn Statement of November 1988 anticipated an outturn of £153.6 bn for 1988–89, £3 bn less than planned (after adjusting for the using up of the £3.5 bn reserve to meet unforseen contingencies such as the nurses' pay award). The £3 bn 'saving' arose because of extra receipts from council house sales and privatisations, and lower spending on social security due to lower unemployment. The figure planned for 1989–90 remained unaffected. In the event, the readjusted privatisation proceeds of £6.1 bn had to be raised again to £6.9 bn because 800 million shares in British Petroleum had their final instalment paid early.
[2] The Autumn statement revised the 1990–91 planning total to £179.4 bn, and added a planning total of £191.6 bn for 1991–92. The equivalent figures for central government expenditure were £205 bn and £216 bn respectively.
[3] Revised to actual outturns of £145.7 bn and £171.5 bn respectively in the Autumn Statement. The latter has subsequently been raised to £171.8 bn.
Source: The Government's Expenditure Plans 1988–89 to 1990–91, vol. 1.

charges in all subsequent years. In all probability, therefore, the absolute figures for interest payments will tend to fall rather than remain stable as forecast, implying that debt interest will decline rapidly as a percentage of a rising GDP. Nevertheless, it should always be borne in mind that debt interest is the first claim on taxation.

Another significant feature has been the sharp rise in the unallocated reserve set aside to cover unforeseen requirements. It may be argued that once spending Ministries get to know of the reserve they are bound to think of justifiable ways to spend it, as illustrated by the financing of the nurses' pay award in the Spring of 1988, so

relatively little of it may end up covering truly 'unforeseen' circumstances.

It is important to strip out the effects of inflation, and also to assess how the above totals look in relation to the general trend over time. This can be done by reference to Figure 3.1.

The data used for **Figure 3.1** have been derived by taking the cash total adjusted to 1986–87 price levels through the GDP deflator. The totals for 1986–87 are, therefore, cash as well as real. In real terms, general government expenditure rose by about 3 per cent a year during the decade up to 1978–79, then by 2 per cent a year from 1978–79 to 1982–83, and by only 1 per cent a year from

Figure 3.1   *General government expenditure and planning total in real terms, 1963–64 to 1990–91*

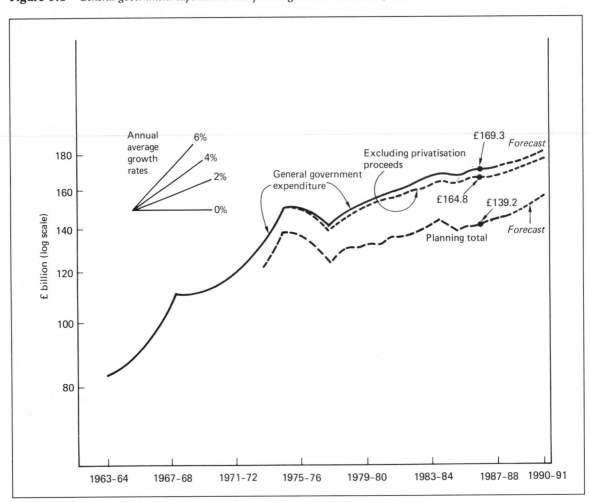

Source: The Government's Expenditure Plans 1988–89 to 1990–91, vol. 1

1982–83 to 1986–87. It is planned to rise at 1.25 per cent a year from 1986–87 to 1990–91. These growth rates are reduced between 1979 and 1987 by the inclusion of privatisation proceeds, and are 0.25 per cent a year higher when these proceeds are excluded.

Figures for expenditure in real terms (1987–88 = 100) have recently been published as a series of booklets (CM 601–621, HMSO, January 1989). These reveal that the 1987–88 planning total of £145.7 bn is expected to fall to £144.4 bn in 1988–89, as a prelude to re-establishing its normal upwards trend to £149.7, £155.4 and £161.1 bn respectively during the ensuing three years. General government expenditure is expected to follow suit, falling initially from £171.8 bn to £170.2 bn, then rising to £173.6, £177.5 and £181.6 bn respectively by 1991–92. A marked feature, despite the overall rise, is the projected fall in the real burden of debt interest from £17.8 bn in 1987–88 to £13.0 bn in 1991–92.

The approach to the calculation of public spending contained in this discussion dates back to the original surveys of public spending which were set up in accordance with the recommendations of the Plowden Committee (Cmnd 1432, 1961).

However, in a White Paper entitled *A New Public Expenditure Planning Total* (Cm 441, 1988), the government proposed a change in the coverage of the planning total, to take place when the new arrangements for local government financing come into operation in England and Wales in 1990 (see **pp. 122–3**). Under this proposal the planning total will include (1) spending on the government's own programmes; (2) grants, current and capital, paid to local authorities; (3) credit approvals issued by government for local authority borrowing for capital expenditure; (4) payments to the local authorities from the proceeds of the national non-domestic rate; (5) the external financing limits of public corporations; (6) privatisation proceeds; (7) a Reserve. Data collection in the appropriate form could not be integrated into the 1988 public expenditure survey because it was already in progress, but will commence with the 1989 survey.

The underlying purpose of this change is to distinguish that part of local authority spending which will be the responsibility of central government after 1990, from that part which local authorities will determine and finance for themselves. Public spending control will be enhanced in a number of ways, for example by including grants in the planning total for the first time. Furthermore, since this requires the grants to be planned for three years ahead, it will help the local authorities to plan their own expenditure more effectively.

It should be noted that this change will have no effect upon the total for general government expenditure. The effect, in accounting terms, will be to remove local authority self-financed expenditure from the planning total, and to place it, in terms of **Table 3.1**, together with debt interest and other adjustments. The revised presentation of **Table 3.1** is illustrated on p. 15 of the White Paper.

Public expenditure targets

As part of its MTFS the government sets targets for public spending, defined as general government expenditure excluding privatisation proceeds, as a percentage of GDP. The percentages for recent years are set out in **Table 3.2**.

Table 3.2 needs care in interpretation. On every occasion that the government produces figures for its expenditure these show a clear downward trend over time as a percentage of GDP. Initially the planned figures were consistently overoptimistic by a wide margin. By the mid-1980 the outturns were proving only modestly worse than the plans, whilst in recent years outturns have proved to be an improvement upon the planned figures. On the face of it, this seems to indicate that the government has got to grips with government expenditure, but as **Figure 3.1** indicates, this is not the case in reality: it is clear that the percentages have fallen of late not because the absolute amounts of real expenditure have fallen but because **GDP has risen sharply**.

It is also helpful to put the more recent percentages into their historic context, as shown in **Figure 3.2**. **Figure 3.2** includes both total general government expenditure and general government expenditure on goods and services as percentages of GDP.[1] The larger measure includes transfers, and shows the extent to which the government has to raise taxation and borrow on the financial markets to finance its activities. The narrower measure, which covers goods and services only, shows the extent to which the nation's resources are being directly absorbed by the government.

As noted above, measuring government expenditure as a percentage of GDP at a time when GDP is growing is bound to put a favourable gloss on the government's performance (an accusation about (ab)use of statistics which has been voiced in many other contexts, for example with respect to unemployment). Originally, in the 1980 White Paper, the government expressed the objective as a progressive reduction of its expenditure in real terms over the subsequent four years. When this failed to transpire in practice, the objective became to hold expenditure constant in real terms, but this was not achieved either, despite the best efforts of the 'star chamber' set up specifically for this purpose. The targeting of variables has never been the government's strong point, especially in the monetary area, so even the current formula may prove

Table 3.2   *General government expenditure, excluding privatisation proceeds, as a % of GDP: Plans and out-turns*

	1983–84	1984–85	1985–86	1986–87	1987–88	1988–89	1989–90	1990–91	1991–92
March 1984 FSBR[1]	46	45	44	43					
March 1985 FSBR[1]	46	46¼	45¾	44	43				
January 1986 White Paper	46¼	46¼	45	44	43	42¼			
January 1987 White Paper	46¼	46¼	44¾	44½	44	42¾	42¼		
January 1988 White Paper	46	46¼	44½	44	42½	42	41¾	41¼	
November 1988 Autumn statement	45¼	46¼	44½	43¾	41½	39¾	39¼	39	38¾

Notes:
Underlined figures are out-turns and estimated out-turns, those not underlined are plans.
[1] Financial Statement and Budget Report.
Source: The Government's Expenditure Plans 1988–89 to 1990–91, vol 1. *Autumn Statement* (November 1988).

elusive. Indeed, the recent buoyancy of tax revenue has reduced the pressure to achieve targets. However, the UK is most unlikely to return to the heights seen in the mid-1970s, which represented the culmination of an inexorable rise during the years of the Keynesian orthodoxy.

Much of the blame – if blame it is – for that rise can be laid at the door of the Plowden Committee since, first, planning came to be done on a volume basis which meant that spending Departments could expect their real spending to be maintained and, secondly, the volumes were adjusted upwards on the basis of forecast economic growth which never fully transpired in practice, with the result that real spending rose faster than real GDP.

In fact, the performance of the UK in this respect was by no means unusual. Data published by the OECD (1985) show that between 1960 and 1982 the mean ratio of government expenditure to GDP rose from 26 per cent to 47 per cent for OECD countries as a whole, with individual countries such as Sweden showing increases of over 100 per cent in their ratio. The difficulties faced by the UK economy in the mid-1970s did at least prevent that concensus from resulting in public expenditure growth permanently outstripping real GDP growth. Indeed, real expenditure actually fell for a while even though a Labour government was in power. Gradually expenditure was transformed onto a cash basis, a process completed in 1981, and this was accompanied by a more determined pursuit of value for money in public expenditure.

Functional analysis of expenditure

Figure 3.3 disaggregates public spending in terms of its main functions. During its first decade of office the government has executed a fairly significant redistribution between functions, and further

Figure 3.2 *General government expenditure as % of GDP, 1890–1986*

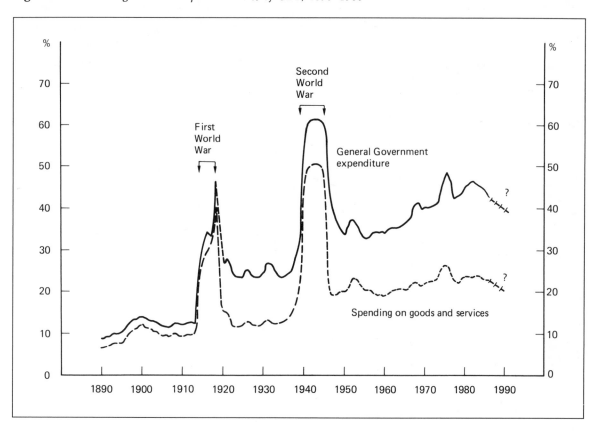

Source: *Economic Trends*, CSO (October 1987)

changes are implied by the plans for the next few years. Most obviously, there has been a major expansion in the share of the total taken by social security spending, reflecting in particular the growth in unemployment and in pensions. Of the other four functions accounting for over 10 per cent of the total in 1978–79, health and defence had become more prominent by 1986–87, whilst education and science and the catch-all 'other' (including environment services and overseas aid) had become less prominent. Among the lesser functions there was a notable increase in the share taken by law and order and employment and training, paralleled by a very sharp reduction in the share taken by housing and industry, trade and energy. These trends are mostly set to continue

into the future, although school rolls are beginning to rise again so education and science is set to regain some part of its lost share.

As these shares are of a growing total real expenditure, a minor reduction in share does not necessarily imply a reduction in absolute terms. To illustrate this Figure 3.3 also contains data on each function's percentage change in real terms between 1978–79 and 1987–88. As can be seen, the biggest increase was in employment and training followed by law and order, with significant improvements in defence, health and social security. Education and science also grew marginally despite its loss of share in the total, and agricultural spending grew quite rapidly although its small share was unaffected. The really big reductions were in industry,

Figure 3.3　*Public expenditure by function (excluding the Reserve and privatisation proceeds), % shares*

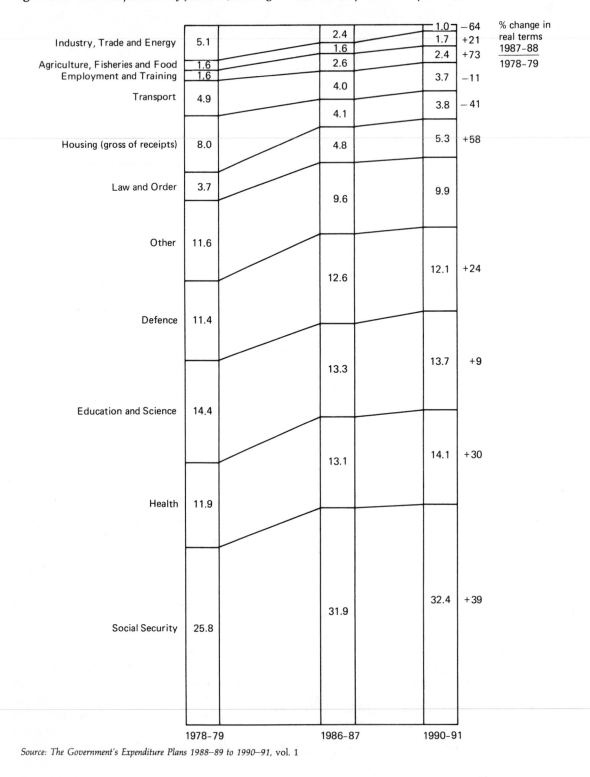

trade and energy and in housing.

These developments can also usefully be re-expressed in terms of capital (investment) versus current spending. In 1973, investment constituted 12 per cent of general government expenditure whilst in 1986 it constituted only 4.5 per cent. The reduction in the real level of fixed investment by roughly one half during the decade beginning in 1975 was particularly pronounced in housing. Public enterprise was also squeezed, as were investment grants to private sector organisations. It was also noticeable that subsidies were cut sharply, but although this tendency to make investment obey the rules of the market place sits comfortably within the philosophy of the present government, the reduction in investment was ironically much sharper under the Labour government in the late 1970s than under its Tory successor.[2]

By way of contrast, current spending on goods and services, especially in the categories of health, education and defence, remained very buoyant, and pensions and the dole grew rapidly. The problem which this has created is that the proportion of the total accounted for by the four largest functions has grown noticeably, as shown in Figure 3.3, and with law and order also a growth category there is now little left to squeeze in the other categories. By implication, any future curtailment of expenditure must take place in the largest categories, which is going to present considerable problems as the number of pensioners cannot be reduced; unemployment is likely to remain high; the numbers of school children are set to rise; and the NHS has proved impervious to cuts.

Measuring real spending

Many categories of public expenditure, such as health and education, are currently labour-intensive. This means that the public expenditure debate has been directed primarily towards **inputs** rather than **outputs**. The GDP deflator, which is used to express spending in real terms is, however, output-based and is therefore inappropriate for evaluating the **volume** of provision of labour-intensive services. This suggests that an own-cost deflator should be used in such circumstances, namely one

based upon the costs of inputs used in each spending category. A study by Levitt and Joyce (1987) has demonstrated what a difference this can make. In the case of health, real GDP-deflated spending rose by 25 per cent between 1979 and 1986, whilst own-cost deflated spending rose by only 9 per cent. Since population growth absorbed over half of this latter increase, and technological advances absorbed the rest, the actual volume of health care delivered *per capita* was effectively identical throughout the entire period. Thus, when the government claims to have increased real spending on the NHS, and the medical profession categorically denies that the resource base has improved, they are **both** in their respective ways telling the truth!

The obvious difficulty this creates is that, if real spending has to be constantly increased simply in order to deliver an unchanged volume of provision in crucial labour-intensive areas such as health, the only painless way to cut public spending as a percentage of GDP is to make GDP grow rapidly. One could alternatively, of course, move public spending into the private sector, so it is hardly surprising that educational loans rather than grants, and the tendering out of NHS services, are being actively promoted. However, these changes are very difficult to deliver politically even for a government with a big majority.

The demand for more resources in, for example, the NHS is inevitably couched in terms of **inputs** – too few nurses, hospital beds and so on. However, this tells us nothing about how efficiently these resources are going to be used, so the government has understandably tried to switch the emphasis of the public expenditure debate onto outputs and productivity. It introduced the Financial Management Initiative (FMI) in 1982; the programme of scrutinies of efficiency by the Cabinet Office under Lord Rayner in 1979; and the publication of performance indicators in the public expenditure White Paper. The drawback here is that one can, for example, show an increase in the number of in-patients treated per available bed by discharging patients more quickly than before! If, as a consequence, this means that many of them need to be readmitted, then they count as new patients and productivity remains high. There is also an inevi-

Figure 3.4 *The tax burden*

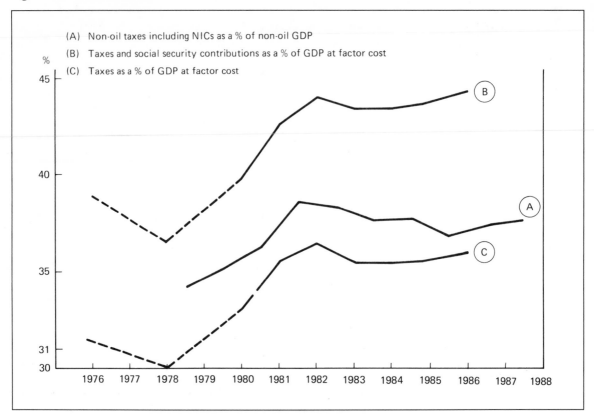

Sources: (A) *Financial Statement and Budget Report 1988–89*; (B), (C) *Economic Trends*, CSO (January 1989) p. 112

table tendency to use readily accessible measures of performance such as the size of GPs' lists, the pupil–teacher ratio in schools or the crime clean-up rate per police officer. However, there is no guarantee that reducing either of the first two will improve the quality of output, which would need to be measured by the ratio of cured patients per doctor or examination passes per teacher.

In conclusion, therefore, we appear to know a great deal about public expenditure, but it is perfectly fair to argue that what we know is inappropriate for the resolution of thorny issues such as the proper level of financing of the NHS. We also appear unable to keep public spending from rising unless we try very hard to reduce it. So long as the economy is growing rapidly, and tax revenue is buoyant, this does not seem to matter too much, but it is very difficult to predict how long this will hold true.

The overall tax burden

Between 1948 and 1985, in money terms, the gross receipts from taxation rose by 3200 per cent. Starting from 1948 it took 14 years to double tax revenue. It doubled again in eight years, and again in five. This acceleration was clearly associated with a sharp rise in the rate of inflation, and since 1975 the rate of increase has slowed down. However, prices rose by a total of only 1200 per cent during the equivalent period, which means that gross tax receipts more than doubled in real terms.

Figure 3.5   *Tax revenues as % of GDP, selected OECD countries, 1986*

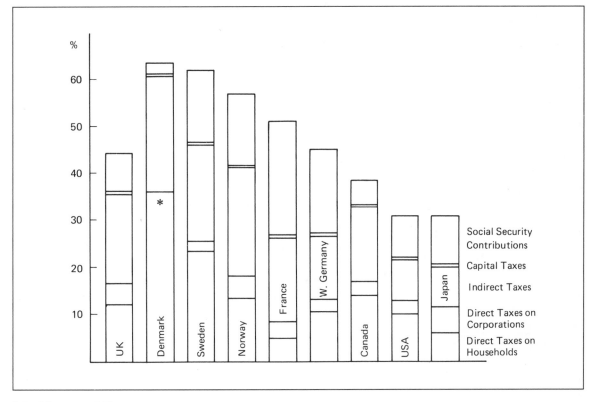

* Breakdown unavailable.
Source: Economic Trends, CSO (January 1989) p. 113

As the population has remained fairly constant the gross real burden of taxes *per capita* has also clearly more than doubled.

However, individuals are not simply interested in their total tax bill but also in the **proportion of their total earnings which is taxed away**. This makes it sensible to express the tax burden in the form of total taxation as a percentage of GDP. Interestingly, this has shown no long-term continuous tendency to rise. Taxation as a percentage of GDP fell from 1948 to 1960, admittedly from the high percentage required for postwar reconstruction. However, it was back to the 1948 level by 1970. Having fluctuated somewhat during the 1970s, it rose sharply after the election of the present government in 1979, as shown in Figure 3.4. More recently there has been a degree of stability, but the level remains persistently above

that ruling in the final years of the last Labour government!

International comparisons

The CSO calculates the tax burden for member countries on a uniform definition, as shown in **Figure 3.5**. This reveals the UK to be almost exactly half-way down the distribution of tax burden expressed as a percentage of GDP, well below Sweden, Norway and France, and equal to Germany. Clearly, therefore, the UK is not over-burdened by taxation relative to many other industrialised countries. However, there are contradictory conclusions to be drawn from this. For example, those favouring further public expenditure can reasonably claim that there is room for a

Table 3.3   *The structure of the UK tax system since 1948*

Ongoing Taxes	New Taxes	Repealed Taxes
Income tax	Selective employment tax (1967)	Profits tax (1965)
National insurance	Capital gains tax (1967) .	Purchase tax (1972)
Local authority rates	Corporation tax (1967)	Selective employment tax (1972)
Hydrocarbon oil duty	Value added tax (1974)	
Tobacco duty	Petroleum revenue tax (1978)	
Vehicle licences		
Wine and spirits duties		
Beer duty		
Customs and protective duties		
Stamp duty		

modest increase in the tax burden to finance it, whilst those who advocate the need to reduce the tax burden can cite the huge increase in real gross *per capita* tax payments. What is clear is that the present government has a long way to go before it can honestly claim to have reduced the tax burden during its terms of office.

Fiscal drag

It may come as something of a surprise, in view of the sharp reduction in the marginal rates of income and other taxes in recent years, that the burden of taxation has shown no consequent tendency to fall. This can primarily be explained by the phenomenon of **fiscal drag** which arises because, whilst the Rooker–Wise–Lawson amendments to the 1977 Finance Bill provided that tax allowances be raised in line with inflation unless the Budget specifically provided otherwise, the index used to adjust for inflation is for **prices** rather than **incomes**.

When the economy is growing strongly incomes tend, on average, to grow noticeably faster than prices. Hence, even if tax allowances are adjusted to compensate for rising prices, an increasingly larger proportion of total income is subjected to tax. In 1987–88 this caused tax revenue to be some £2 bn higher than forecast, and this was comfortably exceeded in 1988–89. In fact, despite the raising of allowances by more than the rate of price inflation in almost every recent Budget, and despite the reductions in the marginal

rate of tax, the tax burden has merely been stabilised – indicating that without these concessions it would have risen sharply. As a rule of thumb, each 1 per cent rise in real income increases the average personal tax rate by between 1.5 and 1.75 per cent. Though not technically fiscal drag, precisely the same effect will occur for corporate taxation when profits are rising much faster than GDP. Equally, spending tends to rise with real incomes, with the result that indirect tax receipts rise sharply.

The tax system

Introduction

The tax system in the UK is somewhat out of line with that typically found elsewhere in the OECD. Only in the UK, between 1955 and 1985, did the importance of income tax, measured as a percentage of GDP, fall rather than rise. However, the UK has been typical in its increased emphasis upon National Insurance (or its equivalent) which, though not technically a tax, has precisely the same effect as income tax upon disposable income.

The UK tax system has been developed in an **evolutionary** rather than a **revolutionary** manner since 1948. Whilst no Chancellor has chosen to institute a major programme of tax reform (unless, as some believe, Nigel Lawson is to be regarded as the exception in this respect), the long-term consequence of continuous small adjustments has been to alter the relative importance of different taxes quite dramatically. The preference for evolution is unsurprising from a political perspective since it has been calculated that, as a rule of thumb, tax reform is politically acceptable only if the beneficiaries outnumber the losers by a ratio of four to one. Furthermore, it is much easier to sweeten a reform which hurts the pockets of a large number of voters by giving them back bigger sums via tax cuts elsewhere in the system, and this can be done only if tax revenue is buoyant. In any event, the Inland Revenue are never keen on major administrative changes.

The structure of the tax system since 1948 is laid out in **Table 3.3**.

Taxes on income

Income tax

Income tax remains the most important element of the tax system, but its importance has declined since 1979. In general, income tax is charged on **all income which originates in the UK** (including, since 1987, the earnings of overseas entertainers and sportsmen), and on **all income arising abroad of people resident in the UK**.

However, every tax payer is entitled to a **personal allowance** to set against his or her gross taxable income (which is itself taken net of any pension fund contributions). There is currently a separate allowance for the single and for the married (but see discussion of personal allowances reform below). This is generally referred to as the **standard rate tax threshold**. It may also be supplemented by a whole variety of other allowances, of which the most common is tax relief on interest paid on mortgages. Currently this is almost always paid direct (at source) to the building society or bank acting as mortgagor by the Inland Revenue, with the mortgagee paying a net-of-tax relief monthly figure (the MIRAS system), so it does not normally affect an individual's tax code. Tax relief may also be given for such things as covenants, or for payments under the Business Expansion Scheme (BES). Once all allowances have been deducted the residual sum becomes the **taxable income**.

Historically, income tax was designed to be 'progressive' – that is, to take a higher proportion of income in tax as income rises. This was based upon the principle of 'ability to pay', and provided the main mechanism whereby the redistribution of spending power between households could be effected (see **p. 244**). Progressivity was thought to require a significant number of different tax rates, although in practice there is progressivity if there is a single tax threshold below which the tax rate is 0 per cent and above which it is positive. During the early postwar period the standard rate rose sharply, and was held at over 40 per cent throughout the period from 1948 to 1968, although until 1971 two-ninths of earned income was exempt from tax so that the effective rate was lower than the nominal rate.

The higher rates were raised to punitive levels, and predictable consequences followed. During the 1970s everyone in a position to do so earned 'income' in the form of legitimate tax-relieved 'perks', and taxable income fell to half the total income declared to the Inland Revenue. Furthermore, a good deal of income was undeclared (the black economy). But with the tax base shrinking in leaps and bounds, the only way to maintain total tax revenue was assumed at the time to be to raise tax rates even higher, setting off the vicious circle yet again.

The disincentive effects of high tax rates on hard work understandably did nothing for economic growth, and in recognition of this the standard rate had been brought down to 33 per cent by the beginning of the present government's term of office. The government declared its intention of bringing down the basic rate as part of the MTFS, and managed to reduce it steadily to 25 per cent by 1988/89. In so doing, it reduced the rewards of non-declaration relative to the drawback of a possible prison sentence, and the benefits of perks compared to cash. At the same time many perks were either abolished (for example, tax relief on life insurance premiums) or were held roughly constant in money terms thereby reducing their real value (for example, mortgage interest relief). As a result, taxable income rose to two-thirds of total income by 1987/88.

The possibility of moving to a 25 per cent standard rate, which the government had declared to be its ultimate goal but which was widely regarded at the time as little more than a pipe-dream, arose as a result of the immense fiscal drag in 1987/88. The Chancellor was very keen to emulate the USA which had already moved to a two-rate system of 15 per cent and 34.7 per cent (adjusted for local income tax), in the process abolishing a whole host of tax reliefs as a *quid pro quo*. The Chancellor had always been ambivalent about perks, inventing new ones such as the Business Expansion Scheme whilst abolishing existing ones. However, he found himself able in the Budget of 1988 not merely to fund higher levels of spending and to reduce the PSBR, but also to produce his own two-rate structure with the standard rate set at 25 per cent and the higher rate at 40 per cent (compared to the five higher rates ranging from 40 per cent to 60 per cent only the previous year). Furthermore, he did not need to eat heavily into perks.

Compared to other major industrialised countries the standard tax threshold in the UK still remains low (at £4,375 for a married couple in 1989/90), and the standard rate itself is almost the highest. However, the top rate is lower than all except that of the USA (although it bites at the very low threshold of £20,701). There is, therefore, still considerable scope for further rate reductions, and fiscal drag should continue to provide the means to achieve them. Indeed, in his 1988 Budget speech Nigel Lawson stated that the objective was to be a standard rate of 20p. Two issues do, however, need to be carefully noted. In the first place, the sharp reduction in the top rate of tax inevitably transferred huge sums of money to the highest income earners without offsetting reductions in perks, whilst the minor reduction in the standard rate made little difference to the bulk of the working population. This inevitably made the distribution of post-tax income less equal. Against this can be set the benefits of a simplified tax structure and the hoped-for incentive effect on work effort and entrepreneurial activity, but it is doubtful whether the balance between equity and efficiency can be pushed even further towards the latter by repeating the exercise. Secondly, the very high levels of consumer spending during 1988, and their alleged consequences for overheating and

inflation, made the Chancellor wary of anything which smacked of fiscal give-aways in his 1989 Budget.

Independent taxation for married couples

Recent changes in the structure of income tax have certainly altered it to a greater degree and at a faster rate than at any other time since 1945. Nevertheless, these changes still represent tinkering rather than true reform. There is little sign of the latter on the horizon, but one issue is worthy of mention, namely that of independent taxation for married couples. The present system of taxing husband and wives treats a married woman's income in law as if it belongs to her husband, a procedure dating back to the time when it was uncommon for wives to earn outside the home. This has given rise to dissatisfaction now that such a high proportion of married women are in employment outside the home. Furthermore, the married man's allowance, originally intended to compensate for the added burden of supporting non-earning members of a household, has become something of an anomaly in a world of two-income households where the working wife is given an additional single person's allowance in her own right. As a consequence, a household containing a married couple where both are working is in receipt of $2\frac{1}{2}$ times as much in allowances as a single-person household. Even more anomalous is the fact that if the wife alone is at work she is entitled to the full set of allowances, whilst if the husband alone is at work he is entitled only to the married man's allowance.

Green Papers, published in 1980 and 1981, considered how to eradicate these anomalies, and in his Budget speech in 1988 the Chancellor announced that, from 6 April 1990, husbands and wives will be taxed independently on their income and chargeable capital gains. This will mean that (**a**) husband and wife will become independent taxpayers, each with their own allowances to set against their own income from whatever source, and each responsible for dealings with the Inland Revenue; (**b**) every taxpayer will receive the single person's allowance; (**c**) in addition, a married couple will receive the difference between the current single allowance and married allowance, which will be set first against the husband's income but any unused amount may be transferred to the wife; (**d**) special arrangements will apply for those aged over 65; (**e**) no-one will be left worse off by these changes; (**f**) a husband and wife's capital gains will be taxed independently, with each entitled to a single person's exempt allowance; (**g**) the existing exemptions from capital gains tax and inheritance tax on transfers of capital between husband and wife will continue.

National Insurance Contribution (NICs)

An annual review of NICs is required by the provisions of the Social Security Act 1975. It is necessary to comment briefly on this because from the taxpayer's point of view both income tax and NICs have the same effect since they are deducted at source on Pay As You Earn (PAYE), which applies to all bar the self-employed in the UK. Whilst the income tax structure was simplified in the 1988 Budget, the structure of NICs retained the perverse principle that once a threshold was triggered the relevant rate was applied not only to income between thresholds but to all income, thereby generating very high marginal rates at the threshold points. Until 5 October 1989 those with weekly earnings between the lower thresholds of £43 and £75 per week will pay NICs of 5 per cent on **all** earnings; between £75 and £115 the rate rises to 7 per cent, and from £115 to £325 per week it rises again to 9 per cent on **all** earnings. Above £325 per week no further NICs are levied.

The reform of NICs introduced in the 1989 Budget will take effect in October 1989. This simplifies the system in that those with earnings below £43 per week will continue to pay nothing, whilst those with earnings at or above £43 per week will pay 2 per cent on the first £43 (86p) and 9 per cent on the rest up to the upper earnings limit of £325 per week.

Removal of all except a very modest NIC's liability on the first £43 of weekly earnings will undoubtedly benefit the low paid (and help to offset fiscal drag), but it will remain the case that the lower earnings limit is indeed very low (below that for income tax) and also that, once earnings rise above £325 per week, the combined rate of income tax plus NICs will fall back at the margin

from 34 per cent to 25 per cent. This can hardly be called a **progressive** structure, and it must also be borne in mind that it is only those whose incomes are high enough to provide spare cash who can afford to spend money in tax-deductible ways (by taking out a £30,000 mortgage, for example). Furthermore, employee benefits do not attract NICs. Despite the 1989 reform the employer will continue to pay NICs on **all** employee earnings, at the same rate as the employee up to £165 per week and at 10.45 per cent thereafter without limit.

Corporation tax

During the 1970s corporation tax, which is levied on company profits, had much in common with income tax. On the face of it the marginal rate was high, but deductible allowances were so extensive, particularly those concerned with capital investment, that large companies were able to adjust their balance sheets such as to incur little or no tax liability whatsoever.

As a result, the Chancellor reformed the tax in 1984 by phasing out many of the allowances and by simultaneously cutting the tax rate progressively from 52 per cent to 35 per cent. The matching rate for small companies earning profits below £100,000 per annum was initially set at 29 per cent (to match the existing income tax basic rate), and has been reduced to 25 per cent for their financial year 1988/89. By international standards company taxation in the UK is currently modest, although care must be taken to adjust for the phasing out of capital allowances.

The remaining allowances of any consequence are concerned with **depreciation provisions**. These exist in order to permit companies to build up a stock of money (often itself confusingly called 'capital') which can be used to replace their worn-out or obsolete physical capital stock. Since money set aside for this purpose is needed merely to keep the company in business as a going concern, it is clearly not 'profit' and should not be taxed as such. There are basically two ways of calculating how much money can be set aside each year without incurring a tax liability on the equivalent amount of gross profit. The first is the straight-line method whereby a given proportion of the original capital cost is set aside each year, for example 25 per cent each year for four years. Alternatively, the declining-balance method is used whereby a specified proportion of the original outlay is set against tax liability in Year 1, and the same proportion of the residual amount is written down in Year 2 and so on. This has the effect of setting aside the largest absolute amount of tax liability in Year 1, and successively smaller absolute amounts in successive years. It is up to the tax authorities to determine which depreciation method is to be applied. Historically, when inflation was unusually high, adjustments also needed to be made for the fact that the replacement cost of a unit of capital was much higher than the original cost, but this is no longer considered to be necessary.

Prior to 1984 it was customary to allow a very high proportion of all capital expenditure to be set against corporation tax liability in the year of purchase, but since 1986 these provisions have been made much less generous in view of the much lower rates of tax. Each year 25 per cent of the cost of plant and machinery can now be set against corporation tax liability on a declining-balance basis, whilst only 4 per cent of the cost of industrial or agricultural buildings and hotels can be written down on a straight-line basis each year (since buildings last much longer than machines). Short-life machinery and plant may be wholly written down over its lifetime. These provisions are universal because it would be far too difficult and expensive to deal with companies on an individual basis. However, it remains possible for the government to make exceptions, usually in the context of **regional policy**.

Corporation tax is levied on all profits, whether retained within the company or distributed to shareholders. However, if a company wishes to distribute profits in the form of dividends, then these are paid in a net-of-tax form. The company is obliged to pay the tax liability arising on the gross dividends at the standard rate of income tax on behalf of the shareholders. This is collected by the tax authorities at the time when dividends are paid out and is known as advance corporation tax (ACT). ACT currently represents one-third of the value of distributed profit (tax rate of 25 per cent: net dividend equals 75 per cent of gross dividend). The shareholder receives his dividend together

with a 'tax credit' which he can pass on to the Inland Revenue in order to show that the tax liability on his dividend has already been discharged (although he will have to pay extra tax if his marginal rate is 40 per cent). Any shareholders exempt from income tax can claim a refund.

The company then subtracts the ACT payment from the total corporation tax liability on its profits, and the outstanding sum is paid over at the end of the relevant financial year in the form of 'mainstream' corporation tax.

North Sea taxes

North Sea taxation consists of royalties, petroleum revenue tax (including advance payments) and corporation tax from North Sea oil and gas production (before advance corporation tax set off). In 1984/85 these amounted to £12 bn, but in 1986/87 there was a very sharp fall to £4.8 bn, and the current estimate of £3 bn for 1988/89, which is forecast to remain roughly constant in future years, indicates how unimportant this element of the tax system has become. Fortunately, as we have seen, this reduction in North Sea taxation has coincided with fiscal drag elsewhere in the system, and has therefore had far less impact than could reasonably have been predicted in the early 1980s.

Royalties are levied on the production of oil and gas fields on an individual basis. However, in order to induce oil companies to explore for oil and gas in less accessible – and hence more costly – tracts of the North Sea, the government first abolished royalties on newly-developed fields in the central and northern sectors in 1982, and in the 1988 Budget subsequently abolished royalties on post-1982 oil and gas fields in the Southern Basin and onshore areas. The latter development was primarily intended to stimulate gas production.

As a consequence North Sea taxation is now almost entirely dependent upon profit-related taxes. Petroleum revenue tax (PRT) is charged at a rate of 75 per cent on profits (net of royalties) from the production, as opposed to the refining, of oil and gas under licence in Britain and on its Continental Shelf. Various allowances can be set against PRT, in particular certain costs incurred in oil exploration. The 1988 Budget reduced the oil allowance from 250,000 tonnes to 100,000 tonnes for a chargeable period, thereby causing tax to become payable earlier than previously where profits are being earned. Corporation tax is payable on profits in the usual way, but is levied on profits net of royalties and PRT.

Taxes on wealth

For the most part, income has to be **earned**. By saving part of this income a pool of wealth can be accumulated. However, a very large proportion of the total pool of wealth currently results from capital gains (especially rising house values) and from inheritance, neither of which requires much effort to acquire. Thus, in principle, one would expect wealth to be taxed much more harshly than income on grounds of equity.

There are however, a number of practical difficulties. Much wealth is, for example, tied up in physical assets (houses, businesses, farms, etc.) and to pay a wealth tax in cash could require a part of these assets to be sold. This could be very damaging to efficiency (for example, farms could become progressively smaller). Equally, the incentive for an entrepreneur to build up a business would be much reduced were it to be necessary for the business to be sold off by his heirs in order to pay wealth taxes since it is reasonable to suppose that the entrepreneur is often driven by a desire to build up a business dynasty. Furthermore, it is inequitable and impractical to force widows to sell up their family homes upon the death of their husbands. As a result, wealth taxes have never accounted for more than a very small proportion of total tax revenue.

Inheritance tax

It is possible to value assets on an annual basis and to tax their value on an ongoing basis. Annual wealth taxes are levied elsewhere in Europe, but have never been implemented in the UK. Instead, wealth is liable to tax only upon its **transfer from one individual to another**, whether in the form of a gift during the donor's lifetime, or upon the donor's death. This is administratively convenient since estates must anyway be valued for probate purposes when a person dies.

Inheritance taxes have been levied in the UK since 1894. Until 1974 they were known as Estate Duty (or death duty) and applied only to transfers at death. The Labour government introduced Capital Transfer Tax (CTT) in 1974 in order to incorporate certain lifetime gifts. These were accumulated over time, with the tax rate being applied to each gift being determined by the cumulative total. However, transfers of property, between husbands and wives both during life and at death, were tax-exempt, together with gifts and bequests to charities. Tax-exempt thresholds also applied to transfers upon death, and to gifts both to individuals and in total during any one year.

In practice, CTT proved to be scarcely more punitive than its predecessor because of the widespread exemptions and the low rates levied on lifetime gifts. When elected in 1979 the Conservatives nevertheless set about 'drawing the teeth' of CTT by raising thresholds, lowering rates and reducing aggregation periods during which lifetime gifts were accumulated (those made previously being exempt). In 1986 CTT was renamed Inheritance Tax. The period of accumulation was reduced from 10 to seven years and the rate of tax was lowered. Anyone making a 'potentially exempt transfer', and living for a further seven years, could subsequently expunge that transfer from their cumulative lifetime total of taxable gifts. If that person lived on for between four and seven years, a proportion of the tax would become payable, ranging from 100 per cent for deaths occurring within three years of making a gift to 20 per cent in the seventh year.

Between 1979 and 1988 prices in general less than doubled. However, the tax threshold for inheritance tax (CTT) rose from £25,000 in 1979 to £110,000 in the Budget of 1988, representing a more than doubling in real terms. Furthermore, the multiple rate structure of previous years was abolished, and a single rate of 40 per cent introduced. The threshold and rate changes in 1988 had little effect upon modest estates, but reduced the tax bill on an estate of £1 million by £145,000 (and by even more where legitimate tax shelters had been used). The additional 50 per cent tax relief for family businesses means that they cannot be taxed at a rate in excess of 20 per cent.

In 1965 annual wealth taxes and capital transfer taxes accounted for 1.6 per cent of the total tax revenue of OECD countries, with the UK well above that figure. In 1985 the OECD average was down to 0.7 per cent with the UK below average at 0.5 per cent. It is therefore fair to conclude that, whilst becoming wealthy is problematic (although becoming progressively easier as houses are inherited), staying wealthy is no problem at all.

Capital gains tax (CGT)

This tax is levied on the difference between the purchase and sale price of any asset. This price difference might occur entirely because of inflation, and capital gains tax has accordingly been index-linked since 1982 so that only **real gains** are currently taxed. Were there no CGT it would pay those with spare income to invest it almost entirely in assets with potential for capital gains rather than in those which accrue interest or other forms of unearned income.

It has to be said that this tends to occur anyway because a large variety of assets are exempt from CGT, including principal private residences (but not second houses), agricultural property, winnings from the football pools and other forms of gambling, motor cars, National Savings instruments and so forth. Furthermore, there is a threshold below which gains are tax-exempt, and a provision to set losses against gains before tax liability is assessed.

Before April 1988 the tax threshold stood at £6,600, and the tax rate at 30 per cent. However, the tax was based on any assets acquired since 1965, and the high threshold existed partly to adjust for the fact that gains between 1965 and 1982 were not index-linked. In April 1988, the threshold was reduced to £5,000, and gains are currently taxed at the individual's highest income tax rate, either 25 or 40 per cent. However, any gains accruing prior to April 1982 are wholly tax-exempt.

The similar tax treatment of earned income and capital gains is at variance with the traditional view that earned income is morally superior to unearned income, and should accordingly be less-heavily taxed. However, the widespread exemptions allowed under CGT have made rather a mockery of this principle, and the government effectively wish it to be known that for tax purposes 'income' is henceforth simply income irrespective of source (it was never exactly clear whether a capital gain was wealth or unearned income although CGT has been listed here as a tax on wealth for convenience). This view is also consistent with the change made in 1987 for companies. Since 17 March 1987 companies' gains have been taxed at normal corporation tax rates (25 and 35 per cent) rather than 30 per cent. Gains of life assurance companies attributable to policy-holders remain taxable at 30 per cent, and the exemption of gains on business assets or on shares in family companies has been increased.

Stamp duty

Transfers or sales of property (other than of stocks and shares) above a value of £30,000, are subject to stamp duty of 1 per cent on the entire purchase price. Transfers of stocks and shares are subject to stamp duty of 0.5 per cent, regardless of the amount.

Taxes on expenditure

Value added tax (VAT)

VAT is the most wide-ranging tax on expenditure, and has been in force since the UK joined the EEC in 1973. It is levied in one instalment directly by the retailer upon the customer. The standard rate of VAT was raised sharply to 15 per cent in 1979 as part of the switch by the present government from direct to indirect taxation (initially with predictably inflationary consequences). This rate is not uniform throughout the EC, and is therefore one of the areas where harmonisation has yet to be achieved. However, this represents a highly elusive goal in practice because of the enormous problems which would need to be overcome if it became necessary in the UK case, for example, to switch some of the burden of taxation back on to income taxes.

VAT is collected at each stage in the production and distribution of goods and services by taxable persons (running a business with a turnover in excess of £22,100 per annum, or £7,500 per quarter, in fiscal year 1988/89). The burden of the tax is ultimately borne by the consumer as part of the final purchase price, but the tax is built up in stages. When a taxable person purchases taxable goods or services (say at £10), the supplier adds VAT to the supply price. This is called the taxable person's input tax (£1.5). When the taxable person subsequently adds value to the good or service, and sells it on to another taxable person, he adds VAT to the price charged (say at £20 which includes the input tax). This is known as the output tax (£3). Since the input tax has already been paid by the original supplier, it is necessary only for the taxable person to pay over to the Customs and Excise the difference between the output tax and the input tax, or in other words the tax on the **value which has been added to the good or service**. Since the final price in our example is £23, of which £3 is tax, the taxable person has added £10 to the supply price of £10 and paid a second instalment of £1.5 in tax.

There will normally be several such instalments before the final customer is reached, once account is taken of both wholesalers and retailers. VAT is further complicated by the fact that not all goods and services are taxable. This arises primarily because everyone pays 15p in tax on a taxable item costing £1.15 irrespective of income, so the tax bears down more severely on the low-paid who spend all of their income than on the high-paid who do not. In order to offset this there are two methods by which goods and services, especially those heavily consumed by the relatively poor, can be tax-relieved. The first method is where a taxable person does not charge any VAT to a customer and also reclaims any VAT paid to his supplier. In this case total VAT is zero. Zero rating applies, *inter alia*, to most food; reading matter; fuel other than for road use; construction of new buildings; exports; public transport fares; young childrens' clothing and footwear; prescription medicines; and caravans.

The second method is where a taxable person does not charge any output tax to a customer, but is not entitled to deduct or reclaim the input tax. In this case total VAT is not zero and the final good

or service is said to be VAT-exempt. Exemption applies, *inter alia*, to land (including rents); insurance; postal services; betting; finance; education; health; and burial and cremation.

Customs and Excise duties

Customs duties are charged on imported goods in accordance with the Common Customs Tariff of the European Community. This exempts community goods imported from other EC member states, and provides a uniform EC-wide tariff barrier against goods from elsewhere in the world. Special arrangements apply for agricultural products in accordance with the Common Agricultural Policy (CAP). As these duties are an EC rather than a purely national policy, their proceeds are transferred to Brussels to help finance the EC.

Excise duties, on the other hand, are not concerned with controlling trade flows but purely with raising revenue from goods and services which are either in inelastic demand (their consumption varies less than in proportion to price) or anti-social or both. They apply to oils used for road fuel (and for other uses at a reduced rate); to alcoholic drinks (taxed largely in accordance with alcoholic strength); to tobacco products (in accordance with number, price or weight); to betting, and to gaming machine and casino licences. Road usage is additionally taxed through vehicle licences.

These duties are very unpopular, but have the virtue (from the Chancellor's viewpoint) that consumers are really aware only of how much they are going up and not of how much has cumulatively been levied in the past. Each increase therefore causes great aggravation at the time, but very rapidly gets forgotten as consumers get used to the new levels of prices, which are anyway constantly adjusting for other reasons. Furthermore, as they are levied in incremental amounts expressed in pence, their incidence is very erratic, depending upon the Chancellor's whim at Budget time each year. VAT receipts automatically rise in money terms when product prices rise, but excise duties do not, and therefore can − and often do − fail to keep pace with inflation. Surprisingly, some products, such as whisky, are currently very cheap by historical standards once inflation is taken into account, partly as a result of a move to uniform taxation of alcohol content.

In recent years increasing attention has been paid to the wider social costs associated with the misuse of alcohol, tobacco and vehicles by individuals, but there has been no clear attempt to force a reduction in consumption via the price mechanism. This may partly reflect the desire to maintain revenue, since sharp increases in prices may, at least temporarily, cause demand (and hence revenue) to fall disproportionately. Perhaps more importantly, excise duties feed straight through to the rate of inflation, control of which is the primary macroeconomic objective.

One recent innovation, in the 1988 Budget, was the introduction of a reduced rate of duty on unleaded petrol which causes less pollution than its leaded equivalent.

Car tax

New cars, motor cycles, scooters, mopeds and some motor caravans, whether made in the UK or imported, are also chargeable with car tax at 10 per cent on the wholesale value. VAT is charged on the price including car tax.

Hybrid taxes

The Community Charge

The UK tax system has long been dependent upon taxes raised within the confines of a local authority rather than of the UK as a whole. These taxes were (and for the moment still are) traditionally based upon property — whether domestic or commercial (but excluding farms). The calculation of tax liability required that each property be given an imputed rental value, called a **rateable value**, in accordance with a complex formula devised by the responsible local authority to take into account location, size, amenities, provision of public services and so on. The local authority then levied a uniform rate per pound of rateable value, with a small rebate for domestic as against commercial property. A supplementary rate was then added to cover water, sewerage and environmental services.

The 'rates', as they were known, were a hybrid tax in the sense that whilst they were wholly divorced from a property occupier's income and clearly therefore not an income tax, they were not based directly upon the market value of a property and hence not exactly a wealth tax either. Obviously, house prices varied considerably over time, thereby making it necessary to revalue periodically in order to preserve equity between different properties. The sheer cost of the exercise militated against intervals of less than 10 years, but this in turn meant that some people would find their rateable values increased sharply, to their immense annoyance, whilst those who had seen their bills reduced thought this no more than their just desserts. The political ill-will engendered by the revaluation of 1973, coming as it did at the end of a period of sharply rising house prices, discouraged a repeat of the exercise in both 1978 and 1983. The Scottish revaluation of 1985 was blamed for the severe loss of Conservative electoral support in the subsequent General Election.

The failure to alter rateable values did not, however, imply a failure to raise rates. The ruling political party in a local authority could impose any rate poundage that it thought fit, although it would have to subject itself to periodic re-election. However, a number of local councils, especially in the larger towns and cities, had such large majorities that they could do virtually anything they liked and make their ratepayers, including local businesses (with no right to vote independent of the rights of their employees to vote as individual ratepayers if eligible), and also the government (which supplied over one-half of all local authority revenue via a rate support grant), foot the bill. The ability to charge high taxes, yet remain politically popular, reflected the high proportion of the total bill laid at the door of government and businesses (over 75 per cent by 1970 and higher still by 1980), and also the fact that domestic rates took no account of the number of individuals living in a property. Large, underoccupied, properties in expensive areas could be made to pay very high rates, whilst small, overoccupied, properties were frequently exempted from rates altogether because their main occupier was entitled to a rate rebate on account of his or her low income.

Not surprisingly, those who paid high rates wanted services to be cut and rates to be reduced, whilst those who paid little or no rates demanded more and more services regardless of expense. In the bigger towns the latter were often in a clear majority and elected a council committed to ever higher expenditure. When the Conservative government was elected in 1979 on a platform of reductions in public spending, their attention was inevitably drawn to the alleged profligacy of the local authorities. Since the highest spending local councils were almost all Labour controlled the issue inevitably became political as well as economic. The power of such councils, democratically elected though they were, had, in the government's view, to be subjugated to the constitutionally superior power of the democratically elected central government.

But how was this to be achieved? For several years the government sought desperately for a foolproof method of keeping local authority spending in check. However, the fatal flaws in most schemes were either that the local authorities could raise the rate poundage to substitute for reductions in revenue supplied by central government, or that, if prevented from so doing by rate capping, they could introduce increasingly innovative methods of raising finance such as sale and lease-back deals on local authority owned assets. The government's position was that all local voters had to be made to pay personally for increases in spending if that was what they wanted and voted for. The chosen solution was (a) to take the non-domestic rate away from the local authorities and transfer it to central government which then sets it nationally at a uniform rate. The revenue is then distributed to local authorities as a *per capita* grant; (b) to transfer the largest claim on local authority spending – namely, education – to central government; and (c) to introduce a Community Charge (often referred to as the 'poll tax' because it requires everyone above the minimum voting age of 18 to register with their local authority) to be paid by all voters either in full or in part (if eligible for a rebate) at a flat-rate. The contribution by central government to local authority spending is to be in the form of a fixed Block Grant, which is invariant to the level of local spending.

This solution is not without its drawbacks. It clearly implies a major redistribution of the burden of taxation, both from the single-adult household to the multiple-adult household, and from the well-off to those previously considered too poor to pay any rates at all. It is also going to be a problem to get all those who should be paying the Charge to register for that purpose, and to track them down if they refuse to do so. This does not necessarily imply that spending on the rump of services left in the hands of local authorities will fall, because voters can opt for as many such services as they wish to pay for, but the underlying assumption is that spending will indeed fall in order to keep the Charge as low as possible. However, it will still be the case that most spending by local authorities will be covered by the Block Grant and the apportioned non-domestic rate.

Perhaps the fundamental objection to the Community Charge is that its three central objectives – abolition of local control over non-domestic rates; elimination of 100 per cent domestic rate rebates; and any increases in spending to be met entirely by domestic ratepayers – can be met by amending rather than abolishing the present rating system (although regular revaluations are a precondition for this solution). However, the government is determined to proceed, and the Local Government Finance Act containing the Community Charge provisions will become operative in the spring of 1990.

The EC and tax harmonisation

The UK is obliged, as a member of the EC, to contribute tax revenue to cover EC expenditure in the areas of agriculture, social policy and regional policy. The EC Budget is financed by its 'own resources', comprising the proceeds of the common external tariff (*less* 10 per cent to cover national collection costs); the proceeds of agricultural import duties and levies (*less* 10 per cent); a share in national VAT proceeds and a share of GNP (see **pp. 187–8**). EC members have compiled a collection of goods and services known as the 'common assessment base'. The UK calculates the total value of sales of the base every year, applies VAT, and remits the EC's share to Brussels. This share was 1 per cent until 1984, and is currently 1.4

per cent. In practice, the UK has always argued that its contribution is excessive compared with that made by other EC members, and has had part of it returned each year (see **pp. 187–8**). It is also obviously the case that some of the money is returned in the form of EC expenditure.

Under the terms of the Single European Act 1985 (see **pp. 172–3**) there is supposed to be fiscal harmonisation in the EC. Initially, progress towards this objective achieved very little since, whilst VAT is levied in every country, each member state wished to impose its own preferred rates upon the others. The only progress of any note arose in that, since within the EC taxes are not supposed to favour domestic as against imported goods, the European Court of Justice felt obliged periodically to implement this principle in a piecemeal way by, for example, obliging the UK to reduce excise duties on wine (largely imported) relative to beer (largely domestic).

However, the debate about tax harmonisation became considerably more heated when, in September 1988, Nigel Lawson published his alternative plan to that put forward by the then European Commissioner, Lord Cockfield, on behalf of the EC in late 1987. In the Single European Act 1985 the internal market is defined as 'an area without internal frontiers'. What the Cockfield plan proposed was that all border controls within the EC should be abolished by 1992, and it concluded that this could not be achieved without first harmonising rates of VAT and excise duties within the EC. It thus proposed that the wide array of VAT rates (the 'standard' rate alone currently ranging from 12 per cent in Spain and Portugal to 22 per cent in Ireland), should be grouped into two 'bands', comprising a standard rate band at 14–20 per cent, and a reduced rate band at 4–9 per cent covering goods which member states wished to keep cheap for social reasons. All exports are technically zero-rated, with VAT being levied by the importer in his home market. Thus the abolition of frontier controls would mean that goods would have to cross frontiers VAT-inclusive, and that the importer would need to reclaim this VAT at a later date. The Cockfield plan therefore proposed that this procedure should be adopted, and that a clearing house should be set up for the settlement

of inter-country balances. The Cockfield plan also recommended a single EC-wide excise duty for alcohol, petrol and tobacco. This arises because VAT is levied on the price of goods inclusive of excise duty, and were excise duties to vary the proposed VAT bands would effectively be distorted. This is an important consideration because, like VAT, excise duties currently vary enormously within the EC, being very low in the south – where, for example, most wine is produced – and high in the north for health and environmental reasons.

In his response to the Cockfield plan Nigel Lawson firstly waxed enthusiastic about the retention of frontier controls, arguing that they were necessary to control the flow of drugs and firearms, and that since between 50 to 80 per cent of the cost of frontier controls could be trimmed by cutting back on frontier-post paperwork, the savings arising from total abolition would be quite small. As a concession, Lawson expressed his willingness to switch from the system of immediate payment of VAT on imports at the UK frontier to 'postponed accounting' whereby a truck driver collects a VAT stamp as he crosses into the UK and leaves his head office to sort out the paperwork later.

In reality, the implications of abolishing frontier controls are much less significant than the harmonisation of VAT and excise duties. It is clear that the Cockfield plan would have huge repercussions throughout the EC. On the one hand, if existing VAT rates are retained, but frontier controls are abolished, the citizens of high-VAT-rated countries will pour across their frontiers with lower-VAT-rated countries in order to shop in the latter, which is clearly unacceptable. On the other hand, harmonising tax rates will force prices up sharply in those countries where rates are currently low, whilst causing tax revenue to fall sharply in those countries where tax rates are currently very high, which is also unacceptable.

Nigel Lawson preferred to think in terms of an analogy with the USA where, despite differences in State taxes, freedom of movement and the federal system keep prices in neighbouring states from diverging significantly – a flawed analogy as it happens because all American States use the same currency which is not yet seriously on the agenda for the EC; State sales taxes are much less divergent than EC VAT rates; and VAT is levied in a quite different administrative manner. Cockfield's plan thus called for 'increasing scope for market forces to influence tax rates'. What this means is that whilst each EC member would be able to set its own rates for VAT, the phasing out of restrictions on cross-frontier shopping, and the eventual abolition of duty free allowances, would force countries to bring tax rates sufficiently into convergence as to discourage excessive flows between countries of citizens seeking cheaper goods. However, Nigel Lawson proposed that alcohol and tobacco should be treated separately because of the health implications of their consumption. In the Chancellor's view his plan was much more flexible than that of the European Commission, which was guaranteed to be unacceptable, but his, in its turn, smacked somewhat of special pleading because of the low rates of VAT in the UK.

What appears to be necessary is the establishment of **tax minima**, rather than tax maxima, and quite possible such minima need to be determined only in cases where abolition of frontier controls would otherwise result in a serious erosion of tax revenue though cross-frontier shopping. For this reason the European Commission now proposes a VAT floor for most goods and services together with a 0–9 per cent band for those items currently taxed either lightly or not at all. The alignment of excise taxes has for now been set aside, though new proposals may still appear. Cross-border tax evasion will be left to the internal control mechanisms of each country. Much of Nigel Lawson's plan may therefore become accepted in principle, but what the French will make of it in practice, given that their high savings tax will become easy to evade and given that they will start off in 1992 with a higher rate of VAT than their neighbours, is an interesting question.

Attempts to harmonise VAT are only a relatively modest step along the path towards tax harmonisation because, by virtue of the fact that VAT is payable only in the country of sale, there can be no biasing effect on the location of firms. This is not, however, the case if one considers taxes on unearned income. At the present time the

London stock market is much larger than all other EC stock markets added together. There are, however, drawbacks for foreign residents and institutions wishing to invest in UK companies in London. There is first the need to pay stamp duty, and secondly the widespread inability to set payments of advance corporation tax against dividends received in the manner described above which applies to UK residents. In certain cases part of ACT is currently refunded, but even so the unrefunded part may prove sufficient of a deterrent to would-be investors. In the absence of tax harmonisation the Chancellor is unlikely to make any concessions which would result in a reduction in total tax revenue, so there is at least a possibility that other financial centres may ultimately grow at London's expense.

It must also be recognised that differing corporation tax schedules do affect location decisions, although it is doubtful whether tax considerations often play a dominant role in commercial decisions. The European Commission originally proposed that there should be a uniform EC rate of between 45 and 55 per cent, but the rate in the UK is currently only 35 per cent and rates elsewhere are likely to fall rather than rise, so this will need to be amended. The issue of harmonisation is, as usual, bedevilled by the fact that firms in countries with special concessions are most reluctant to give them up in the cause of greater European harmony. So far, the European Commission has produced a preliminary draft on the subject of harmonising the calculation of taxable profits. This is unlikely to make speedy headway, so harmonisation of corporation tax rates is clearly some way from even reaching the agenda. What price harmonisation of personal taxation by 1992?

The Budget

The Budget is an annual event, in either March or April, which exists both to set out the government's proposals for changes in taxation and to provide an occasion for the annual review of economic policy. The proposals are announced to the House of Commons by the Chancellor of the Exchequer in the Budget Statement, and are published in the *Financial Statement and Budget Report* (FSBR).

The Budget statement is followed by the moving of a set of Ways and Means resolutions embodying the Budget proposals, and these form the foundations of the **Finance Bill** which goes forward for debate in Parliament. The Ways and Means resolutions exist so that taxes can be levied at the new levels set out in the Finance Bill pending its enactment. The Finance Bill, subject to any amendments volunteered by, or forced upon, the Chancellor during debate, is then passed as the **Finance Act**, usually in July.

Tax proposals are concerned primarily with changes in the rate or coverage of taxes, the introduction of new taxes and the abolition of existing ones, or changes in methods of administration. Most taxes are permanent, but in the case of income tax and corporation tax the Finance Act is needed every year to keep them in existence, which ties the Budget to the beginning of the fiscal year in April. It is, however, perfectly proper either to have a mini-Budget at any other time of year, which necessitates amendments to the Finance Act, or simply to operate the regulator which permits VAT to be varied by up to 25 per cent, and the main excise duties by up to 10 per cent between Budgets.

Budgetary changes are made both with a view to their effects upon **tax revenue** and also to their effects upon the **performance of the economy**. These are detailed in the FSBR which contains a review of recent developments in the economy; an economic forecast updating that contained in the Autumn statement; and an overview of the MTFS.

Figure 3.6 represents the breakdown of total

Figure 3.6   *Sources of revenue, 1989–90*

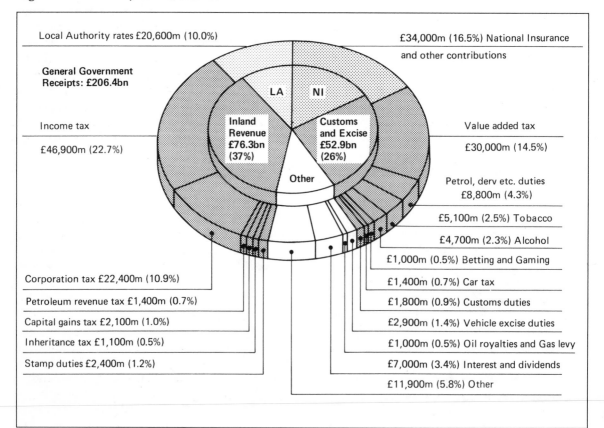

Source: The *Independent*, 15 March 1989

government revenue for 1989–90. As can be seen, 37 per cent of all revenue comes under the control of the Inland Revenue, whilst a further 26 per cent is handled by Customs and Excise. It is not generally appreciated how dependent tax revenue is upon a narrow range of taxes. NICs account for slightly more than VAT, which is itself exceeded only by income tax. Only a few years ago, in 1985, duty on petrol/derv plus petroleum revenue tax (PRT) were the next most important, followed by corporation tax, but the effects of the fall in the price of oil and of fiscal drag (both discussed below) have resulted in corporation tax currently yielding twice as much as the other two combined. No other taxes individually account for as much as 5 per cent of total revenue.

The Budget contains a vast array of changes to the tax system. It is clear, however, from the above discussion, that very few of these have other than marginal effects upon total revenue, whilst changes in income tax of an apparently modest kind (for example, a 1p reduction in the marginal rate) have quite dramatic effects (altering revenue by more than £1 bn).

The purpose of raising revenue is primarily to fund expenditure, so it is a little curious that the Budget was traditionally divorced from the two main discussions of public expenditure set out in the Autumn Statement and the Public Expenditure White Paper. The Treasury do not like making statements about revenue in the Autumn because tax receipts can alter sharply between November and April (perhaps due to fiscal drag). On the other hand, public expenditure needs to be planned well in advance and does not have to be financed solely through tax receipts. The drawback to the separation in time is that any increases in expenditure made in the Autumn have been largely forgotten by April, so any buoyancy in tax receipts immediately leads to demands for yet further spending.

Since 1980 it has been possible to see how revenue and expenditure are linked by recourse to the discussion of the MTFS in the FSBR, since this necessarily examines both the aggregates and the difference between them. However, it is this difference, the PSBR which tends to form the focus for discussion rather than the aggregates themselves.

The public sector borrowing requirement and public sector debt repayment

The public sector consists of central government, local government and the public corporations. The global figure for the PSBR does not, therefore, show flows between the three sectors, normally from central government to the other two and on a very large scale, but does include public corporations' borrowing from the money markets and overseas. The figures for the past two years, and projections for the next four are to be found in **Table 3.4**. These are in cash terms, and the PSBR is also expressed as a percentage of GDP.

The longer-term trend of the PSBR can be seen in **Figure 3.7**, again expressed as a percentage of GDP. During the oil crisis in the mid-1970s the percentage came close to reaching double figures and, despite some subsequent improvement, rose back to 5 per cent when the present government was elected.

It is important to note at this point the accounting convention used for privatisation proceeds. As shown earlier, in **Table 3.1**, these are recorded as **negative spending**. The government argues that, since the purchase price appears as public expenditure when assets are taken into public ownership, it is only logical to treat any monies arising when they are sold back to the private sector as negative spending. A more cynical view might be that the purpose of this exercise is to reduce the declared amount of public spending in order to reduce the difference between that total and total tax revenue – the PSBR. Certainly, it is undeniable that the government actually does spend the amount indicated before privatisation proceeds are subtracted, and it therefore seems to be more sensible to treat the PSBR as the excess of gross public expenditure over total tax revenue, and to treat privatisation proceeds as a means of **financing the shortfall**. Were this alternative convention to be adopted then the PSBR data in **Table 3.4** and **Figure 3.2** would obviously look markedly worse than they do.

During the major part of the present government's period in office the PSBR remained stub-

Table 3.4 *Debt repayments of central government (CGDR) and public sector (PSDR)*

	£billion, cash					
	1987–88	*1988–89*	*1989–90*	*1990–91*	*1991–92*	*1992–93*
General government expenditure	172	179	194	205	216	224
General government receipts	174	191	206	214	225	233
Fiscal adjustment from previous years	—	—	—	—	1	3
Annual fiscal adjustment	—	—	—	1	2	3
CGDR	2.0	12	12	8	6	3
Public corporations' market and overseas debt repayment	1.5	2	2	2	0	0
PSDR	3.5	14	14	10	6	3
Money GDP at market prices	426	472	509	539	571	603
PSDR as % of GDP	$\frac{3}{4}$	3	$2\frac{3}{4}$	$1\frac{3}{4}$	1	$\frac{1}{2}$

Source: Financial Statement and Budget Report 1989–90.

bornly higher than forecast, for reasons familiar from our previous discussion. In five of the seven years since 1981/82 public expenditure exceeded its forecast value, and bettered the forecast only in 1983/84. Four of the five overshoots were serious, exceeding £4 bn. On the other hand, tax revenue exceeded its forecast value on four occasions, falling short only in 1986/87 because of a sharp drop in North Sea taxes. However, these overshoots were generally more modest than those for spending, and the PSBR consequently did no better than hit its target value for the six consecutive years beginning in 1981/82.

Public sector debt repayment

The dramatic turnaround came in 1987/88 when tax revenue overshot the forecast by an astonishing £7.5 bn, with the result that, despite a serious £4 bn overshoot in spending, the PSBR became negative for the first time since 1971. It is now the custom to refer to the PSDR – public sector **debt repayment** – although the Chancellor still prefers to talk in terms of an eventual PSBR of zero. It could be argued that he has been overtaken by events, since he formally advocated the desirability of a balanced budget only in the Budget of 1988, and did so then only on the grounds that 'it provides a clear and simple rule, with a good historical pedigree'. The reality is, however, rather different, and the 1988 Autumn Statement itself forecast a PSDR of £10 bn for both 1988/89 and 1989/90, the former of which was exceeded by over £4 bn.

This makes the UK unique amongst the seven major industrialised nations, but it is nevertheless likely to be a lasting feature of the UK economy. This is because the first claim on tax revenue is interest on the National Debt, which fell below £200 bn during 1988. As the Debt is repaid (it will disappear altogether within 20 years at present

Figure 3.7 *PSBR as % of GDP*

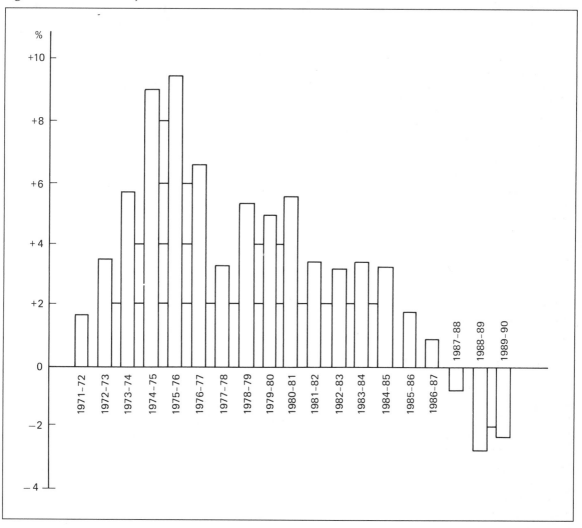

Source: Financial Statement and Budget Report 1988–89 and 1989–90

rates of repayment), so other forms of expenditure can be increased to replace the reduced burden of interest charges without raising the aggregate spending figure. Thus, so long as tax revenue remains buoyant, extra spending on, for example, the NHS, will be perfectly compatible with running a sizeable PSDR.

Certain consequences obviously follow from this. In the first place, the use of the term 'lax' when applied to fiscal policy will come to mean running 'only' a modest PSDR, whereas in the mid-1970s fiscal policy was considered 'tight' when the PSBR was 'only' £10 bn. Secondly, there will be no need to issue new gilts to cover borrowing, but only to neutralise foreign currency inflows. This in turn means that the implications of the PSBR for the money supply – an issue at the centre of the policy debate in the late 1970s – will become a total irrelevance in the 1990s. Indeed, a PSDR implies that the fiscal stance of the government is reducing the money supply. Unhappily, as we will also discover (on **pp. 323–6**) this is a far cry from implying that the money supply is under control.

Notes

1. The figures for general government expenditure back to 1950 and general government expenditure as a percentage of GDP back to 1890 are contained in an article entitled 'Long term trends in public expenditure', published in *Economic Trends* (October 1987).

2. The November 1988 Autumn Statement predicted that capital spending would rise by £2.25 bn in 1989–90, the first real increase for five years, mainly to pay for better prisons and roads.

References

1. Cm 441(1988) *A New Public Expenditure Planning Total* (HMSO) (July).
2. Cmnd 1432 (1961) *Control of Public Spending* (HMSO).
3. Levitt, M. and Joyce, M. (1987) *The Growth and Efficiency of Public Spending* (NIESR).
4. OECD (1985) *Economic Studies* (Spring).

4

External Transactions

Peter Curwen

Introduction

There are enormous differences in the extent to which individual nations are dependent upon transactions with the outside world. The UK has always been an 'open' economy, both importing and exporting on a massive scale. Superficially this may simply be seen to reflect the difficulties which any nation the size of the UK must inevitably face in trying to be self-sufficient across the whole range of goods and services, but it is important to note both that the UK's degree of openness has been increasing steadily over the past several decades (as has also been true elsewhere in the EC), and that external transactions increasingly involve one-way flows of capital which are unrelated to the immediate consumption requirements of UK residents. In recent years the value of both imports and exports has grown to exceed 30 per cent of the UK's GDP, and it is obvious that these trade flows impact significantly upon the UK's industrial structure, the level of employment, the standard of living of UK nationals and so on. In other words, the **internal and external sectors are inextricably linked**, and it is impossible to control internal macroeconomic objectives such as the level of employment and the rate of inflation without taking into account their links with the external sector. Indeed, as we shall see, much of the postwar history of UK macroeconomic policy can be viewed in terms of a struggle to find **acceptable trade-offs between the internal and external objectives of policy.**

Economic policy is frequently focussed upon the **balance of payments**, and our first task is, therefore, to set out the accounting system used to measure it, and to explain how policy objectives are expressed in relation to these accounts. The

131

other central task is to examine the primary instrument used to achieve this objective, namely the **exchange rate**. However, as we will discover, these apparently straightforward tasks are in practice greatly complicated by the need to take account of other related policy objectives and instruments; of the behaviour of other countries insofar as it impinges upon the UK; of international institutions; and of the whole plethora of arrangements which govern the conduct of the world economy.

The system of balance of payments accounts

The balance of payments (BoP) may be defined as a systematic record, over a given period of time, of **all transactions between residents and non-residents of the UK**. The term 'resident' covers both individuals living permanently in the UK, and corporate bodies located therein, but not their overseas branches and subsidiaries. It also includes government agencies and military forces located abroad. 'Permanent' residence is determined by the intention to remain in the UK for at least one full year.

The object of the accounting system is to record these transactions in a way which is suitable for analysing the economic relations between the UK economy and the rest of the world. The transactions may represent **resources** provided by or to UK residents (imports and exports of goods and services, and the use of investments); **changes** in the UK's **foreign assets or liabilities**; or **transfer payments**.

In principle, transactions are recorded when the ownership of goods or assets changes and when services are rendered. In practice, however, trade flows are recorded on a **shipments basis**, and the payments which match these shipments are not only almost invariably delayed, but the length of this delay is quite erratic from one period to another. In the longer term all the shipments and monetary flows can be matched up, but the short-term picture is almost inevitably quite heavily distorted. This is important because, first, both foreign exchange markets – and indeed sometimes the government – respond in a volatile way to monthly or quarterly BoP statistics and, secondly, because the annual accounts are constantly being adjusted retrospectively to a degree that can turn surpluses into deficits, or vice versa. In other words, the short-term picture can conflict with the longer-term perspective, yet by the time the latter is visible it is too late to take appropriate action.

A further element of ambiguity is introduced by the need to **convert currencies**. The general rule in international trade is that the exporter dictates the form in which payment is made – which, in the case of a developed nation like the UK, is mostly in its own currency. A much smaller proportion of UK imports will also be paid for in sterling. All non-sterling payments must then be converted into sterling at the ruling exchange rates, but these may fluctuate enormously during the course of a financial year, with the result that the valuation of imports and exports can be influenced by the precise timing of currency conversion.

Double-entry accounting

The BoP accounts are, like any accounting system, constructed according to the double-entry principle. Every transaction involves equal credit and debit entries but, instead of arranging these in separate columns, all BoP entries are arranged in a single column, and given different signs so that they sum to zero. It is therefore the case that the BoP accounts must balance by definition. (This should not be confused with the concept of **equilibrium**, which is discussed below.) This method accommodates account items which are generally recorded only on a net basis.

Under the conventions of the accounts all credit items are entered with a **plus (+) sign**. The credit relates to the **flow of currency** and not to the flow of resources. If resources are provided in the form of exports of goods or services, then the payment in currency thus **flows into the UK** and is recorded with a plus sign in the accounts. Where resources are provided to UK residents – for example, as imports of goods or services – payment **flows out of the UK** and is recorded with a **minus (−) sign** in the accounts.

Every positive entry must, as indicated, have its matching negative entry, but this may appear in a variety of forms. For example, an export of goods may be matched by either (**a**) an increase in the foreign assets owned by UK residents (where the export receipts are, for example, deposited in a bank outside the UK); (**b**) a reduction in non-residents' holdings of sterling in the UK (which are transferred to the exporter's bank account); or (**c**) a direct exchange for imports of equal value (barter trade). It is undoubtedly rather confusing at first to regard an increase in foreign assets as a negative item in the accounts, but it makes sense in terms of identifying **where the currency goes**. The above example works exactly in reverse where one starts with a negative entry for an import of goods.

To make things somewhat easier to follow, the BoP accounts are currently divided into two halves. This division is relatively recent, and whilst the accounts have been recalculated in this format going back as far as is necessary for the purpose of this book, it should be recognised that variants of the accounts published before 1987 are in the original format which is difficult to match up with the new and should, therefore, no longer be used. The upper half of the accounts is called the **current account**. In this are to be found transactions covering exports and imports of goods and services, investment income, and transfers. The lower half of the accounts is called **transactions in UK external assets and liabilities**. In this are to be found inward and outward investment; external transactions by banks in the UK; borrowing and lending overseas by other UK residents; drawings on and additions to the official reserves; and other capital transactions. For simplicity this will be referred to as the **capital account**.

As previously mentioned, where there is a positive entry in the current account – arising, for example, from the export of goods – the corresponding negative entry is normally to be found in the capital account as in (a) to (b) above (there are no monetary flows generated by (c)). However, it must also be noted that corresponding plus and minus entries may both appear in the capital account, as would be the case if a UK resident borrowed from a bank in France in order to buy shares in a French company.

It is also necessary to remind ourselves about the difficulties of estimation with respect to items in the BoP accounts because, as previously noted, the accounts must balance as a matter of definition (for every plus a corresponding minus). The two entries made in respect of each transaction are generally derived from separate sources, and the methods of estimation are neither complete nor precisely accurate. Hence the two entries either may not match precisely, and/or may fall within different recording periods. It is also possible that two entries, both in the same foreign currency, have been converted at different exchange rates. Hence, when all the entries in the accounts are added together, they never actually do sum to zero, and in order to make them do so the **balancing item** has to be added at the foot of the accounts.

The balancing item

The balancing item is a very volatile item in the accounts. Some part of it will be permanent insofar as, for example, the data collection system consistently fails to record certain transactions. Other parts will be erratic and arise because, for example, the data collection system either becomes able to record transactions in the capital account which could not previously be attributed to any of its headings, and therefore had to be lumped into the balancing item, or ceases to be able to do so, with the reverse effect. Large balancing items (whether plus or minus) have been a feature of the 1980s in the accounts. This is partly because, since 1982, a substantial proportion of trade credit between unrelated companies, required to bridge the gap between the time goods are shipped and the settlement of the invoice, has been switched from the capital account to the balancing item. Furthermore, in 1986, the high level of capital flows during the period leading up to and following 'Big Bang', created difficulties of attribution to appropriate headings in the capital account.

Hopes that the balancing item would settle down, as it did temporarily in 1987 when the accounts for that year were first published, have unfortunately been confounded. This is more important than it seems because, if the balancing item is large, and if it is not known whether it is created by under- or over-recording in the current account and/or capital account, it is difficult to know how seriously to take the recorded data. What is worse is that, taking the world as a whole, whilst as a matter of simple definition total world exports must equal total world imports, they actually fall short by a wide margin ($45 bn in 1987 but higher in previous years). It therefore follows that in many parts of the world exports are significantly under-recorded, and it is reasonable to suppose that this must be the case in the UK as it is one of the major trading nations. According to Phillips and Drew, after adjusting for the relative accuracy of UK statistics compared with elsewhere, the UK's BoP accounts were understated by £2 bn in 1987. One can thus make out a case in support of the proposition that, since part of the balancing item when it is positive (as in recent years) represents under-recording of exports, and since exports may anyway be under-recorded as explained above, no-one – and that includes the Chancellor and the exchange rate dealers – has any real idea how much exports are really worth in any single quarter, let alone any single month, which suggests that it is unwise to pay so much attention to month-to-month movements in the figures. In all fairness it should, however, be pointed out that according to the CSO's version of events the data on visible exports is highly reliable, but on invisibles is highly unreliable; the balancing item consists primarily of under-recorded capital inflows; and the missing world exports do not originate at all from the UK[1].

The structure of the accounts

The current account

The full set of accounts is set out for the period 1983 to 1988 in **Figure 4.1**. The first part of the accounts covers exports and imports of goods, and the net figure is called the **visible** balance. Note that both exports and imports are entered as positive amounts, but the net figure is plus or

minus as appropriate. The next entry relates to credits and debits generated by trade in services, which are again entered as positive amounts with the net figure, called the **invisibles** balance, signed as appropriate. This net balance is then broken down into its three component parts – namely, services (primarily sea transport, civil aviation, tourism and financial); interest, profits and dividends; and transfers (primarily central government grants to overseas countries and contributions to the EC Budget and to international organisations, and private transfers of assets by migrants). The sum of the visible and invisibles balance, signed as appropriate, is called the **current balance**. Adjustments to the current balance usually occur as a result of changes in national income both at home and abroad; the proportion of it which is spent; and the proportion of that spending which goes on domestic as against overseas goods and services. A sharp deterioration in the current balance is usually taken to indicate an upturn in consumption (either private or public) which has spilled over into imports, but an alternative, and more beneficial, interpretation is that it indicates the importation of capital goods for investment by UK companies to improve their productive capacity. Unfortunately, it is very difficult for analytical purposes to distinguish at the time between these interpretations.

The capital account

The rest of the accounts can be distinguished by virtue of the fact that no goods and services flow in the opposite direction to the flows of currency. What are being acquired are foreign assets such as shares and securities. When such flows of currency are recorded they can be attributed to a number of basic influences. The first – of critical importance over the past year or so – is the **structure of interest rates** in the UK compared to that overseas. If interest rates are higher in the UK than elsewhere, after adjusting for any risk of default, currency will tend to flow into the UK in very large amounts. For the most part, such currency flows will be short-term (colloquially called 'hot money'). The second is the **rate of return on investment**. If a UK company takes over a foreign

Figure 4.1 *UK balance of payments accounts, 1983–88*

	1983	1984	1985	1986	1987	1988
CURRENT ACCOUNT	£m	£m	£m	£m	£m	£m
Visible trade						
Exports (fob)	60 698	70 263	77 988	72 656	79 421	80 602
Imports (fob)	62 207	75 432	81 120	82 020	90 350	101 428
Visible balance	− 1 509	− 5 169	− 3 132	− 9 364	− 10 929	− 20 826
Invisibles						
Credits	65 887	77 665	80 583	77 421	80 037	87 233
Debits	60 619	70 611	74 248	67 991	72 779	81 024
Invisible balance	5 267	7 054	6 335	430	7 258	6 209
of which:						
Services balance	3 995	4 339	6 606	6 247	5 682	4 165
Interest, profits and dividends balance	2 857	4 449	2 763	5 364	4 987	5 619
Transfers balance	− 1 585	− 1 734	− 3 034	− 2 181	− 3 411	− 3 575
Current balance	3 758	1 885	3 203	66	− 3 671	− 14 617
TRANSACTIONS IN EXTERNAL ASSETS AND LIABILITIES						
Investment overseas by UK residents						
Direct	− 5 417	− 6 033	− 8 799	− 11 304	− 18 615	− 15 219
Portfolio	− 7 194	− 9 870	− 19 435	− 23 068	2 702	− 9 718
Total UK investment overseas	− 12 612	− 15 903	− 28 234	− 34 373	− 15 913	− 24 937
Investment in the United Kingdom by overseas residents						
Direct	3 386	− 181	3 784	4 846	8 108	7 346
Portfolio	1 888	1 419	7 121	8 135	10 440	4 639
Total overseas investment in the United Kingdom	5 274	1 238	10 905	12 981	18 548	11 985
Foreign currency lending abroad by UK banks	− 16 162	− 9 439	− 20 200	− 47 885	− 45 684	− 14 692
Foreign currency borrowing abroad by UK banks	17 192	18 648	25 306	58 361	44 283	20 300
Net foreign currency transactions of UK banks	1 030	9 209	5 106	10 476	− 1 401	5 608
Sterling lending abroad by UK banks	− 232	− 4 933	− 1 635	− 5 955	− 4 638	− 4 569
Sterling borrowing and deposit liabilities abroad of UK banks	3 945	6 149	4 155	5 605	8 547	13 556
Net sterling transactions of UK banks	1 713	1 216	2 520	− 350	3 909	8 987
Deposits with and lending to banks abroad by UK non-bank private sector	863	− 3 239	− 1 253	− 2 782	− 5 311	− 3 035
Borrowing from banks abroad by:						
UK non-bank private sector	73	− 2 176	2 598	3 735	2 069	3 830
Public corporations	− 35	− 47	64	− 31	− 166	− 253
General government	78	49	87	100	104	− 10
Official reserves (additions to −, drawings on +)	607	908	− 1 758	− 2 891	− 12 012	− 2 761
Other external assets of:						
UK non-bank private sector and public corporations	− 161	1 281	533	1 933	433	812
General government	− 478	− 743	− 730	− 509	− 796	− 891
Other external liabilities of:						
UK non-bank private sector and public corporations	− 55	517	728	539	1 402	2 089
General government	− 661	− 89	− 64	78	1 466	912
Net transactions in assets and liabilities	− 4 366	− 7 780	− 9 497	− 11 091	− 7 667	2 334
Balancing item	608	5 895	6 294	11 025	11 338	12 283

Source: CSO, 'Pink Book', 1989;

company, it does so in the belief that the investment will yield a higher rate of return than would result from the take-over of another UK company. Equally, private investors in the UK will buy shares in foreign companies if they believe that the dividend yield and/or the prospect of capital gains is better than that to be achieved in the UK. These currency flows are mostly long-term. If interest rates and rates of return are relatively low in the UK, the above discussion will operate in the reverse direction.

The third influence is the **exchange rate**. All capital flows must take place in a particular currency, the value of which can vary quite considerably over time. Whilst long-term investment is not much affected by this influence, given that exchange rate movements in the longer term are impossible to predict and that the investor can anyway hedge against changes in currency value within reason, hot money flows are a different matter. Even where the interest rate on offer is higher than in other financial centres, a financial asset denominated in a currency the value of which is expected to fall sharply will be unpopular, whilst that denominated in a currency the value of which is expected to rise sharply will prove popular, even if its yield is very poor, as this will be more than compensated by the prospect of a capital gain on the asset. Apropos the UK situation in 1988 it is worth noting that, where both interest rates and rates of return are high, and the currency is appreciating, it follows that the inflow of hot money is going to be of monumental proportions until such time as the exchange rate has risen to the point at which the majority opinion is that it will subsequently begin to fall again.

Direct investment primarily comprises net investment by overseas companies in their UK affiliates, including the re-investment of retained profits, and by UK companies in their overseas branches, subsidiaries and associates. Portfolio investment by UK residents comprises net purchases and sales of overseas government, municipal and company securities, whilst portfolio investment in the UK primarily comprises net purchases and sales of UK company securities and government stocks. These flows clearly affect the net asset/liability position of the UK relative to the

rest of the world. In principle, one simply adds or subtracts the net annual change to the existing cumulative net value of assets, but in addition there may be capital gains and losses arising from, for example, changes in share prices which cannot show up in the BoP accounts until such time as the asset is sold. The recent scale of financial asset acquisition by UK residents has resulted in the UK becoming one of the world's four largest net creditor nations as shown in **Table 4.1** expressed in dollars. This is obviously balanced by growing net indebtedness elsewhere, and although it is hard to accept, the USA does appear to have become a net debtor, although this is probably the case only if capital gains are excluded (see *Bank of England Quarterly Bulletin*, November 1989).

Net foreign currency transactions of UK banks consist of changes in deposits of foreign currencies made with UK resident banks by non-residents, and loans by the banks in those currencies to non-residents. **Net sterling transactions** of UK banks consist of sterling advances and overdrafts (net of repayments) provided to overseas residents (including banks abroad) by UK banks, sterling commercial bills discounted, acceptances, and sterling borrowing and deposit liabilities abroad.

Deposits with, and lending to, banks abroad by UK non-bank private sector consist of UK residents' deposits with banks in the Bank for International Settlements (BIS) reporting area *plus* assets held in the custody of banks in the USA. **Borrowing from banks abroad** covers predominantly borrowing from commercial banks in the BIS reporting area, the European Investment Bank and the United States Export–Import Bank.

The sterling balances

The above items are all concerned with what are called generically the 'sterling balances'. These take the form of overseas residents' holdings of sterling bank balances, UK money market instruments denominated in sterling, and Treasury bills and gilts. All except for the latter are short-term. Their total value in mid-1988 was roughly £55 bn, of which one-fifth was held by overseas monetary

Table 4.1 *International comparisons of external net assets*[1,2]

End-years	1981	1982	1983	1984	1985	1986	1987	1988
United States								
$ billions	130	126	78	−8	−122	−280	−379	−544
Per cent of GNP	4	4	2	0	−3	−7	−8	−11
Per cent of exports[3]	44	47	30	−3	−43	−97	−114	−126
Japan								
$ billions	10	24	36	74	129	179	240	291
Per cent of GNP	1	2	3	6	8	9	8	10
Per cent of exports[3]	5	13	19	37	50	65	66	76
West Germany								
$ billions	24	26	27	36	46	87	160	199
Per cent of GNP	3	4	4	6	6	9	12	17
Per cent of exports[3]	11	12	14	19	17	26	39	52
United Kingdom								
$ billions	53	59	72	87	110	161	160	162
Per cent of GNP	11	13	16	23	21	28	20	19
Per cent of exports[3]	41	50	61	81	74	110	79	83

Notes:
[1] Excluding gold holdings.
[2] The data underlying this table are taken from national sources which may use disparate methodology.
[3] Gross exports of goods and services
Source: Bank of England Quarterly Bulletin (November 1989).

institutions, and four-fifths in private hands. Prior to 1945 sterling was the major reserve currency for governments, and widely used for international transactions between private individuals and companies. Many countries, mostly in the British Commonwealth and known generically as the overseas sterling area (OSA), tied their exchange rate to sterling and kept their reserves primarily in that currency. During the Second World War these countries supplied the UK with raw materials and in return were credited with the materials' sterling value, with the attached right to withdraw the money at any time in the form of gold or foreign currency held as reserves in the UK.

The total amount of these balances remained roughly stable for 20 years after 1945, although their owners tended to fluctuate somewhat. However, two associated problems had come increasingly to the fore. In the first place, the number of countries willing to tie their exchange rates to sterling was on the decline, and with it their willingness to trade with one another only in sterling. Secondly, the steady depletion of UK gold and foreign currency reserves which resulted from recurring BoP deficits meant that they were no longer sufficient to meet the outstanding claims of holders of sterling balances. As a result, these holders understandably began to run their balances down by drawing on the reserves, thereby depleting them further and helping to precipitate the devaluation of sterling in 1967. In 1966 the BIS and other central banks created a facility to allow the UK to acquire foreign currency reserves, and steps were taken to guarantee the value in dollars of part of the sterling balances held by the OSA. Subsequent to the 1967 devaluation the trade situation improved sufficiently to render these arrangements unnecessary, and the OSA faded away by 1972 without the need for any further crisis measures. Since the mid-1970s the sterling balances have been significantly linked to OPEC oil surpluses and North Sea oil, but this is more appropriately discussed below where we review the recent history of the UK balance of payments.

Returning briefly to complete our review of the accounts we come next to changes in the official reserves, which are also analysed in more detail below. Other external assets include identified trade credit between unrelated companies, inter-government loans by the UK and subscriptions to international lending bodies, whilst other external liabilities include broadly the same items. The balancing item has already been discussed above, but attention is once again drawn to its size relative to other aggregates in the accounts.

The accounts in retrospect

In taking a retrospective view of the BoP accounts it is clearly not practicable to operate at the detailed disaggregated level presented in **Figure 4.1** except insofar as it is needed to shed light on the peculiarities of recent policy *vis-à-vis* the external sector. **Table 4.4** below, which covers the period prior to the present government's election and its full period in office, accordingly treats transactions in external assets and liabilities only in the aggregate. This accords with the customary presentation of the accounts in the media, but does have the drawback that it fails to distinguish between short-term and long-term capital flows.

The meaning of equilibrium

Before proceeding we need to consider the meaning of the term 'equilibrium' in the context of the accounts. As we have explained, the accounts as a whole must balance by definition, but to achieve that it is not necessary for any individual component of the accounts, for example the current balance, to have a zero value. The main issue is how to express the objective of policy concerning the balance of payments. The messages sent out

about the state of the economy by the current and capital accounts are rather different, and the focus of concern about the accounts has always been upon the current balance. It is, therefore, often argued that this should be in equilibrium in the sense that it should have a value of zero.

Since, however, the UK historically has been predominantly a manufacturing nation, it is sometimes argued that attention should be focussed more narrowly upon the visible balance, and that this should be kept in equilibrium with a value of zero. The first important lesson is, therefore, that when the word 'equilibrium' is encountered, it requires one to look carefully to see to which part of the accounts it is being applied.

In the second place, there is clearly a time dimension to the issue. The current balance might sum to zero over a period of years, and hence yield an equilibrium, albeit possibly more by chance than by design. This may be preferable to the requirement that it be in equilibrium over a period of months, or in any given year, since it will allow for cyclical adjustments and the problems of data collection discussed above. But unless a government is prepared to state in advance that it is pursuing a set of policies intended to achieve equilibrium within a specified period, the fact that it can retrospectively identify such an equilibrium cannot be said to prove anything one way or another about its policies.

In any event, the whole issue is clouded by the choice of a particular exchange rate regime. Without discussing this in detail here as it is covered below, the essential point is that it is possible to choose a regime which will, other than in the very short term, keep the accounts as a whole in equilibrium. However, it will not keep the individual components of the accounts in equilibrium, and there are also likely to be conflicts with other objectives of policy which rule out this approach to the achievement of equilibrium. It is finally worth reminding ourselves that it is current practice to isolate the balancing item from both the current and capital account balances. But if, as has generally been the case, the balancing item is large, and if it is unclear how it should be divided between current and capital accounts, one may reasonably enquire how on earth one is supposed to know whether either account is anywhere near, let alone specifically at, its equilibrium value, whether in the short or the longer term.

Index numbers of UK visible trade

It must be recognised that when one has become used to regarding a current account deficit of £10 bn as giving cause for concern, there is a tendency to be dismissive of historic deficits of a 'mere' £1 bn, let alone those of £100 mn. Yet these figures, in their historic context, were regarded with equal dismay because of their size in relation to the then value of GDP. The escalation in the numbers partly reflects the effects of economic growth, but primarily those of continuous – and in many individual years very rapid – inflation. It is possible to give a general impression of the relative effects of growth and inflation by the use of index numbers, as in **Table 4.2**.

The volume index for visible exports roughly

Table 4.2 *Index numbers, UK visible trade (1980 = 100)*

	Volume indices[1]					Unit value index[2]		Terms of trade ((a)/(b))
	Exports			Imports		(a) Exports	(b) Imports	
	Manu-factures	Share of world exports of manufactures	Total	Total	% Total Final Expenditure			
1968			52.7	65.4		23.5	23.0	102.2
1969			58.5	66.5		24.3	23.7	102.5
1970			60.0	69.7		25.9	24.8	104.4
1971			65.2	73.3		27.4	26.0	105.4
1972			66.5	80.6		28.9	27.2	106.3
1973			75.6	91.1		32.6	34.8	93.7
1974			81.0	92.7		41.5	50.9	81.5
1975			77.8	84.7		50.9	58.0	87.6
1976			85.4	89.7		60.8	70.9	85.7
1977			92.1	91.3		72.0	82.1	87.7
1978	100	111	94.5	95.5	11.4	79.1	85.2	92.7
1979	99	105	99.1	105.7	11.8	87.6	90.9	96.4
1980	100	100	100.0	100.0	10.8	100.0	100.0	100.0
1981	94	92	99.1	96.0	10.2	108.9	108.4	100.5
1982	96	95	101.8	101.4	10.8	116.4	117.0	99.5
1983	96	92	104.2	110.1	11.9	125.9	127.7	98.6
1984	105	92	112.9	122.4	12.8	136.2	139.7	97.5
1985	111	93	119.1	126.4	12.9	143.8	145.5	98.8
1986	114	95	123.3	134.6	13.1	136.8	134.3	101.8
1987	124	99	130.4	144.6	13.5	142.0	138.1	102.8
1988	128	95	130.8[3]	163.4[3]	14.4	144.4	138.8	104.0

Notes:
[1] Seasonally adjusted.
[2] Unadjusted.
[3] Export volume is forecast to rise by 7 per cent in 1989.
Import volume is forecast to rise by 5 per cent in 1989.
Sources: Annual Abstract of Statistics. CSO 'Pink Book' 1989.

doubled between 1968 and 1980, a markedly better performance than for the volume of imports. However, since 1982 the volume of imports has easily outstripped that of exports. Over the period 1968 to 1980 the value of both visible exports and imports roughly quadrupled, indicating that prices of traded visibles more than doubled during this period. Whilst volumes initially stagnated during the recession after 1980, prices continued to rise sharply, but have remained almost static since 1984.

If the unit value of visible exports is divided by the unit value of visible imports we get a measure of the 'terms of trade'. As can be seen, these worsened sharply between 1971 and 1974, but subsequently improved more steadily until 1981. There has been relatively little change in recent years. The terms of trade must be treated with care. On the face of it, an improvement, resulting perhaps from relatively high inflation in the UK, enables the same volume of imports to be bought in exchange for a lesser volume of exports than before. However, much depends upon the price elasticity of demand for exports and imports. If demand for UK visible exports is elastic, as is generally the case, an increase in price results in a reduction in revenue. Equally, if demand for visible imports is inelastic, as is generally the case, a reduction in price results in an increase in payments. Thus, overall, the 'balance of trade' (visible exports less visible imports) will worsen rather than the reverse. In other words, a dose of domestic inflation in the UK is likely to cause serious damage to the visible trade balance, and is also likely to damage invisible trade in an increasingly competitive world. The, albeit modest, improvement in recent years has not, therefore, been beneficial to the UK.

Visible trade in retrospect

Prior to 1967 the UK managed to keep the current balance in surplus but, with the exception of 1956 and 1958 when the visible balance was positive, the pattern of a negative visible balance more than compensated by a positive invisible balance was already well-established. As mentioned above, there was considerable volatility with respect to short-term capital flows during the dying years of the overseas sterling area, but long-term capital flows were mostly outflows, and hence negative in the accounts. In looking at the current situation one might be tempted to believe that nothing much has changed since the 1960s. However, as we shall see, this is not the case because of differences in the exchange rate regime in operation; in the UK's reserve position; and in the contribution of North Sea oil.

The steady deterioration in the UK's share of world trade in manufactures, exacerbated by an uncompetitive fixed exchange rate, and combined with a tendency for hot money to pour out of the UK whenever a crisis loomed, thereby draining the inadequate reserves, was an unsustainable situation. The BoP accounts gave every appearance of being in 'fundamental disequilibrium' and only a reduction in the value of the pound could remedy the situation. This duly took place in November 1967, and a programme of domestic deflation was set in hand. The combination proved successful, albeit not immediately and not soon enough to prevent a change of government. Starting from a balance of $-£286$ mn in 1968, the current account moved to $+£460$ mn in 1971. Whilst long-term capital continued to flood out of the UK, an even larger amount began to flood in after 1969, and this was paralleled by net inflows of hot money sustained by the belief that the UK was making a determined attempt to restore sound finance. It was true that the domestic deflation was taking its toll in terms, for example, of rising unemployment, but this was of less concern at the time than the symbolic value of the deflationary measures.

From this point on fundamental disequilibrium never reappeared in the same guise as before. One major factor was the abandonment of the fixed exchange rate regime in 1972, which subsequently permitted the exchange rate to be used more positively to regulate the current balance. A second factor, which was initially of much less help, was the sharp increase in the price of North Sea oil. The subsequent picture is spelt out by **Table 4.4**. From 1975 to 1979 the visible balance remained heavily in deficit. The invisibles largely offset the damage, although the negative transfer component (including contributions to the EC) grew too rapidly to prevent the offset being total other than in 1978 at the end of a long period of oil price stability. The exceptionally high rate of inflation, partly triggered by the first oil price rise (see **pp. 57–8**) was ultimately the key problem, because although long-term capital was flowing in to finance the development of the North Sea oilfields, international confidence in the UK's ability to deal with its domestic problems caused a massive outflow of hot money. This caused the then Labour government both to deplete the reserves and to borrow from the IMF (agreeing in return to deflate the economy along 'monetarist' lines), as shown in **Table 4.3**.

With confidence restored by the IMF intervention, the reserve position took a dramatic turn for the better, and although the reserves remained fairly volatile they never again fell to a level which suggested further recourse to the IMF would be needed.

Visible trade in the 1980s

With North Sea oil coming on stream, the visible balance actually returned to surplus from 1980 to 1982, and the oil surplus itself grew steadily from £0.3 bn in 1980 to £8.1 bn in 1985. Under the circumstances it seems extraordinary that the visible balance should have returned to deficit, but whilst non-oil visibles were £1 bn in surplus in 1980, they had collapsed to show a deficit of £11 bn by 1984 as depicted in Figure 4.3. The decimation of the UK manufacturing sector when the present government first took office, resulting

Table 4.3   *UK official reserves, 1973–87, end-year values*[1] *($mn)*

	Gold	SDRs	Reserve position at IMF	Convertible currencies	TOTAL
1973	887	724	140	4 725	6 476
1974	888	830	248	4 823	6 789
1975	888	840	366	3 335	5 429
1976	888	728	—	2 513	4 129
1977	938	604	—	19 015	20 557.
1978	964	500	—	14 230	15 694
1979	3 259	1 245	—	18 034	22 538
1980	6 987	560	1 308	18 621	27 476
1981	7 334	1 043	1 513	13 457	23 347
1982	4 562	1 233	1 568	9 634	16 997
1983	5 914	695	2 168	9 040	17 817
1984	5 476	531	2 110	7 577	15 694
1985	4 310	996	1 751	8 486	15 543
1986	4 897	1 425	1 820	13 781	21 923
1987	5 792	1 229	1 579	35 726	44 326
1988	6 466	1 341	1 694	42 184	51 685

Note:
[1] The level of the reserves is affected by changes in the dollar valuation of gold, SDRs and convertible currencies as well as by transactions. Expressed in terms of sterling, at end-period middle market rates of exchange, the reserves rose from £14.8 bn in 1986 to £23.5 bn in 1987. This increase incorporated an upwards adjustment of £1.8 bn due to the annual revaluation exercise. The reserves rose by a further £5.1 bn in 1988 to stand at £28.6 bn. The increase incorporated an upwards adjustment of £1.5 bn due to the annual revaluation exercise. A further annual revaluation reduced the book value of the reserves from $50.46 bn to $46.93 bn in March 1989. At the end of June 1989 the reserves stood at $43.7 bn after the largest ever monthly reduction of $2.24 bn in June as a result of intervention to support the pound.
Source: Bank of England Quarterly Bulletin.

Table 4.4 Balance of payments of the UK, 1975–88 (£ million)

	1975	1976	1977	1978	1979	1980	1981	1982	1983	1984	1985	1986	1987	1988
CURRENT ACCOUNT[1]														
Visible Balance	−3 333	−3 929	−2 324	−1 593	−3 344	1 355	3 250	1 908	−1 509	−5 169	−3 132	−9 364	−10 929	−20 826
Invisibles:														
Services	1 336	2 245	3 037	3 514	3 799	3 653	3 715	2 971	3 995	4 339	6 606	6 247	5 682	4 165
Interest, profits and dividends	890	1 576	265	806	1 205	−204	1 210	1 449	2 857	4 449	2 763	5 364	4 987	5 619
Transfers	−475	−786	−1 128	−1 791	−2 210	−1 984	−1 547	−1 741	−1 585	−1 734	−3 034	−2 181	−3 411	−3 575
Invisibles Balance	1 751	3 035	2 174	2 529	2 794	1 465	3 378	2 679	5 267	7 054	6 335	9 430	7 258	6 209
CURRENT BALANCE	−1 582	−894	−150	936	−550	2 820	6 628	4 587	3 758	1 885	3 203	66	−3 671	−14 617
TRANSACTIONS IN EXTERNAL ASSETS AND LIABILITIES[2]														
Net Transactions[3]	1 599	586	−3 892	−2 871	−742	−3 873	−7 370	−2 353	−4 366	−7 780	−9 497	−11 091	−7 667	−2 334
Allocation of SDRs[3]	0	0	0	0	195	180	158	0	0	0	0	0	0	0
Balancing Item	−17	−308	4 042	1 935	1 097	873	584	−2 234	608	5 895	6 294	11 025	11 338	12 283

Notes:
[1] Seasonally adjusted.
[2] Assets: increase −/decrease +. Liabilities: increase +/decrease −. Not seasonally adjusted.
[3] Special Drawing Rights.
Sources: Financial Statistics, Table A1.
CSO '*Pink Book*' 1989, Table 11.

from a combination of a deliberate policy of domestic deflation, the UK's relatively high rate of inflation and the high value of the effective exchange rate (see **pp. 328, 54**, and **157** respectively) was largely to blame, since the damage done at that time has never been fully rectified. Whilst the effective exchange rate fell to an historic low by 1986, and the rump of the manufacturing sector performed very creditably in export markets, the growth in the UK economy sucked in vast amounts of foreign manufactures, many of which could no longer be produced at all in the UK (see **Table 4.7**). Individual events such as the coal-miners' strike in 1984–85 added to the difficulties, and it is possible to argue that although many UK products were highly competitive on price alone, they fell down with respect to non-price factors such as quality and speed of delivery.

It is also necessary, in looking at the visible balance, to appreciate a peculiarity of the way in which exchange rates work. In practice many products, and especially raw materials including oil, are priced in dollars. Thus if the pound rises in value against the dollar these become cheaper in sterling and vice versa. However, exports to the EC are affected by the rate at which the pound is exchanged for EC currencies. If the pound rises against these currencies then UK exports become expensive and vice versa. The worst combination for the UK is, therefore, for the pound to fall against the dollar, making raw material imports expensive, and to rise simultaneously against EC currencies, making exports expensive. From 1979 to 1985 this combination broadly held true (see **p. 000**) and the visible balance was salvaged only by North Sea oil coming on stream.

From 1980 to 1985 the invisibles balance remained very healthy. The balance on private services was a major contributory factor. Equally, whilst interest payments needed to be made on outstanding government borrowings from abroad, the long-term capital outflows in the 1970s mentioned above resulted in a sharp upturn in private sector interest, profits and dividends (appearing, note, in the **current** rather than the capital account).

Because of its diversity the capital account is much more difficult to interpret. Account must be

taken of the lifting of exchange controls in October 1979, which resulted in a sharp upturn in investment overseas by UK residents (rising from £12.6 bn in 1983 to £34.4 bn in 1986 as shown in **Figure 4.1**). These were offset by large amounts of foreign currency borrowing by UK banks and, as already mentioned, short-term inflows were heavily influenced by sterling's new status as a petro-currency and the government's determined attack upon inflation via its 'monetarist' policies, including of late high interest rates. Over the past two years UK companies have continued to perform creditably in export markets. However, **Table 4.2** indicates the scale of the problem. From 1985 to 1987 the volume of visible exports rose by roughly 10 per cent, but the volume of imports rose by 15 per cent, and the gap has continued to widen subsequently. If the comparison is linked only to manufactured goods, then the margin of difference is considerably wider. The consequences, taken in conjunction with the collapse in the price of North Sea oil, show up clearly in the visible balance which worsened sharply in 1986 to record a deficit of £9.4 bn. This would have been worse had the £ not risen against the dollar, thereby cheapening raw material imports, and fallen against EC currencies, thereby cheapening UK exports. The invisibles balance, on the other hand, improved sharply in 1986, and just matched the visible balance overall. However, the extraordinary behaviour of the balancing item, which was larger than both visible and invisibles balances, inevitably leaves a question mark over the value of these statistics.

Recent history

In 1987 the visible balance deteriorated further to show a deficit of £10.9 bn. At first the invisibles balance was recorded at + £7.1 bn, but this was revised upwards to + £7.9 bn in March 1988 before being brought down to + £7.6 bn in the 1988 'Pink Book'. However, it was down again to + £7.3 bn in the 1989 'Pink Book' (a not untypical example of how variable the statistics are), resulting in a current account deficit of £3.7 bn for the year, the first major deficit since 1979. 1987 also seemed at first to be exceptional in relation to earlier years in the decade in that net transactions were recorded in the 1988 'Pink Book' as being only marginally negative, a turnaround of £13 bn in one year. This was widely thought to be due to the appreciation of sterling which lowered the sterling value of assets priced in other currencies, and also because UK residents ran down their overseas investments, mainly after the stock market crash in October. The attraction of the UK as a haven for hot money grew even stronger because of the combination of fiscal rectitude (the only major industrial country to repay debt rather than to borrow) and high nominal interest rates. The year was accordingly also unusual in that the balancing item appeared to fall sharply. However, the revisions published in the 1989 'Pink Book' now suggest a balancing item for 1987 very similar to that of 1986 (no wonder the government set in hand a major overhaul of the statistical service!).

In 1988 these trends have for the most part continued. The (subject to revision) current balance recorded a deficit of £14.6 bn for the full year (compared to the forecast of £13 bn in the 1988 Autumn Statement). One factor, apart from the general surge in imports of all kinds, was a sharp decline in the oil surplus as domestic industry increased its oil consumption and the Piper Alpha platform disaster affected supplies. This may herald the end of an era for North Sea oil and gas insofar as it affects the balance of payments, and the full sequence of events is reviewed in the next section.

So far in 1989 the news is largely bad. Most commentators are predicting a current account deficit of record proportions, including a visible trade deficit approaching £20 bn. They may well prove to be correct, since the first quarter's deficit was £5.9 bn whilst that of the second quarter was £5.8 bn. The invisibles surplus was £2.2 bn for the six month period yielding a current account deficit of £9.5 bn for the half year.

Balance of payments effects of North Sea oil

The BoP effects of the North Sea show up in four ways. The first two are current account items,

appearing mainly in the visible balance. First, there is the balance of trade in oil and gas. This, as discussed above, was heavily in deficit during the 1970s, but showed a healthy surplus during the 1980s until the more than halving of the price of oil in early 1986. Events in 1988 suggest that this surplus may no longer be of sufficient size to warrant the level of attention accorded to the oil balance over the past decade. The second item relates to the net purchase of goods and services required to discover and extract the oil and gas. This was a significant deficit item in the early 1970s, but is no longer of any consequence. One of the other two effects appears in the capital account, namely capital inflows to finance the discovery and extraction activities. These basically can be set against the cost of purchasing goods and services, and like them have been inconsequential for a good many years. However, in the usual way, these inflows of capital generate the final effect, namely a requirement to pay interest, profits and dividends at a later date, which have accordingly been a negative item in the invisibles during the 1980s.

If this is added to the worsening in the balance of trade in oil and gas, it is clear that net revenue from the North Sea is unlikely to be able to offset any further deterioration which may occur in trade in manufactures. It is possible to speculate that this offset will continue because the price of oil will rise a good deal in the future, but this is less than probable. It is equally possible to argue that output of oil and gas will rise rapidly, and the change in the tax regime mentioned on **p. 000** should assist in this respect, but even if true this is likely to hold down prices and it has adverse fiscal effects in the short term. Indeed, the North Sea sector in general is clearly going to provide less tax revenue than of late, but that, at least, is something the government is not unduly short of for the present. If the BoP benefits of North Sea oil and gas have now largely come to an end, but the non-oil variables are showing even higher deficits, it is certainly possible to argue that the existence of North Sea resources has simply been used as an excuse for not tackling some of the most deep-rooted problems of the economy.

Furthermore, it is possible to argue that the UK's net trading position with respect to manufactures has been permanently damaged by the effects of North Sea oil on the exchange rate. As noted elsewhere, the willingness of the government to let the exchange rate appreciate rapidly at the beginning of the 1980s in response to both the current account benefits of oil and the boost to foreign confidence in the UK which accompanied it made it very difficult for many firms to sell in export markets. The subsequent decline in the oil balance was not, however, accompanied by a parallel resurgence in manufactured exports.

Competitiveness

Measuring competitiveness

It is appropriate to refer, at this point in our discussion of trade performance, to the 'competitiveness' of the UK. 'Competitiveness' is impossible to measure in any absolute sense, so it must be judged by compiling indices of **relative performance** compared to other relevant countries. Even this is fraught with data collection difficulties, because we need to take some relevant characteristic of the UK economy, measure it over time as an index, and compare that index with the corresponding indices for other countries. Since no single index can be expected to tell the whole story, we need to provide as wide a variety as possible. However, whilst some of these should incorporate non-price characteristics, these cannot realistically be measured, so indices must concentrate upon **cost and price competitiveness**, on the assumption that price and non-price factors are interdependent.

Many goods are in practice sold almost entirely on the home market, so the indices need to incorporate only those goods which are internationally traded on a major scale. As manufactured goods comprise the largest element in both UK imports and exports, they are used exclusively for the indices. Additionally, because competitiveness is affected by the exchange rate, all the costs and prices need to be converted into a common currency, in this case dollars, at the ruling spot rate. With every country's index valued in a common currency, the ratio expressing one relative to another can then be measured as an absolute number.

Figure 4.2 illustrates the most important measures of competitiveness on a quarterly basis for the past ten years. These measures represent changes in the degree of competitiveness over time. The ratios are compiled as follows:

- **Import price competitiveness**: UK wholesale price index for home market sales of manufactures (other than food, drink and tobacco) divided by the unit value index of imports of finished manufactures (SITC sections 7–8, Revision 2).
- **Relative normal unit labour costs**: index of normal labour costs per unit of output in the UK divided by a weighted geometric average of competitors' normal unit labour costs adjusted for exchange rate changes.
- **Relative producer prices**: UK wholesale price index for home sales of manufactures (including food, drink and tobacco) divided by a weighted average of the indices of competitors' wholesale prices.
- **Relative profitability of exports**: ratio of the UK export unit value index for manufactured goods (SITC sections 5–8, Revision 2) to the UK wholesale price index for home market sales of the products of manufacturing industries (other than food, drink and tobacco).
- **Relative export prices**: unit value index of UK exports of manufactured goods divided by a weighted average of competitors' export price indices for manufactures.

All of these indices are subject to data measurement problems (see *Economic Trends*, No. 304 (February 1979) and No. 319 (May 1980) for details). However, the various measures of competitiveness do appear to follow the same pattern, so the overall picture can be taken as acceptably accurate.

The historical pattern

During the 1970s, as shown in **Figure 4.3**, sterling's effective exchange rate (EER) fell steadily,

Figure 4.2   *Measures of UK trade competitiveness, 1980 = 100*

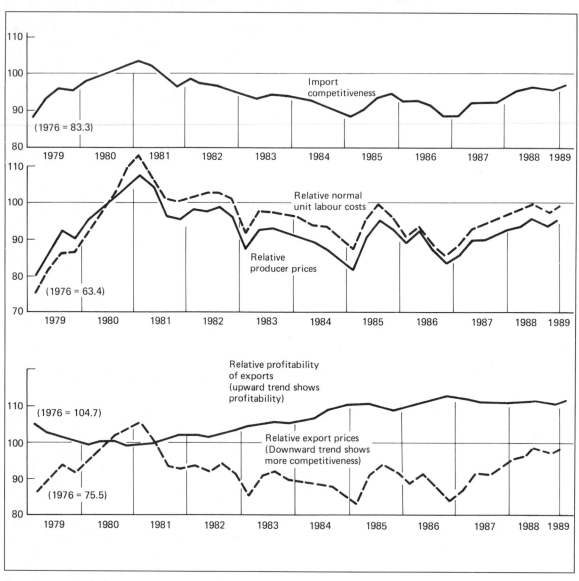

Source: Economic Trends, CSO

thereby cheapening exports and making imports more expensive. Unfortunately, this did not, as we have seen, prevent the trade balance from remaining firmly in deficit. The reason can partly be seen in the data for relative normal unit labour costs, where the index, standing at 63.4 in 1976, rose sharply to 100.0 in 1980, and actually peaked at over 110.0 in the first quarter of 1981. Irrespective of non-price factors, which in any event were unfavourable for the UK, it is understandable that the UK's relatively high costs caused relative export prices to move unfavourably despite the advantage of a falling exchange rate. Equally, even though this caused import prices to rise, domestic prices also rose steadily, albeit less dramatically, relative to import prices. The only positive feature was that the steady rise in relative export prices maintained the relative profitability of exports on an even keel, although it was showing clear signs of sagging at the end of the decade.

A generally similar picture is shown in **Table 4.2**. The UK's share of world exports of manufactures had been falling throughout the postwar period. This, of itself, was only to be expected since the initially very high share held by the UK reflected the early date of industrialisation, and progressive entry into her markets by newly industrialising countries, using more modern technology, was bound to have a profound impact. The disturbing aspect was, however, that the total volume of world trade in manufactures was itself rising very rapidly, commonly at over 10 per cent per annum, so there was plenty of room for new entrants without the need to eat heavily into the market share of existing producers, and indeed the UK was unique amongst the established industrial nations in suffering more than a marginal loss in market share.

The increased share of imports in Total Final Expenditure (TFE) was also to be expected as industrialised nations increasingly traded manufactured goods with one another, and indeed was characteristic of all such nations. Again, however, the disturbing aspect was the relatively rapid pace at which this occurred in the UK, reflecting in part the UK's relatively high income elasticity of demand for imports.

The overall picture during the period from 1981 to 1984 was a generally much happier one. As shown in **Table 4.2**, the UK's share of world exports of manufactures appeared to have reached an equilibrium situation. **Figure 4.2** shows that relative normal unit labour costs declined steadily, and with the effective exchange rate moving sharply downwards, relative export prices became significantly more competitive, and the relative profitability of exports rose slowly but steadily. Despite the rise in import prices, the competitiveness of imports also improved, albeit understandably more slowly, and the visible balance showed several years of surplus. The major problem was, however, the fact that imports as a share of TFE

had bottomed out in 1981, and by 1984 was up 2.6 percentage points. The visible balance in 1984 was accordingly back in substantial deficit.

During 1985 competitiveness suddenly deteriorated, in particular because of a sharp rise in relative normal unit labour costs and in the EER, and although the following year witnessed a recovery, it was clear that the first quarter of 1985 was going to prove difficult to emulate, let alone improve on. The recent picture has, as discussed elsewhere, been very gloomy. Relative normal unit labour costs have resumed their upward climb, and both relative export prices and import competitiveness have followed suit. Imports as a percentage of TFE have risen yet further, but the one modest saving grace has been an increase in the UK's share of world exports of manufactures and the resilience of relative export profitability. With the EER being prevented from falling much as a matter of policy (see **pp. 163–4**), and wage demands showing signs of escalating, it is reasonable to suppose that competitiveness will continue to deteriorate for the foreseeable future.

Area composition of UK visible trade

During the nineteenth century circumstances conspired to create a pattern of trade in the UK consisting essentially of the importation of raw materials and the exportation of finished goods. This arose in the first place because the UK was the earliest country to industrialise, and in the second place because most of the trade was conducted with former or existing colonies. The latter was to a considerable extent a consequence of the former, since other newly-industrialising countries erected barriers against imports from the UK in order to protect their infant industries, but in any event the existence of a common language facilitated trade even with ex-colonies such as the USA.

Trading links with Europe developed gradually during the twentieth century, but as **Tables 4.5** and **4.6** indicate, Europe accounted for only one-quarter of UK imports and a slightly higher proportion of her exports even in 1955. At that time the LDCs accounted for roughly 40 per cent of

Table 4.5   *Area composition of UK exports, f.o.b., 1955–88 (% total value)*

	1955	1965	1970	1975	1980	1985	1986	1987	1988
EC	15.0	26.3	28.9	32.2	45.4	48.6	47.8	49.1	50.6
Rest of Western Europe	13.9	15.5	17.1	15.9	12.1	9.7	9.9	9.8	9.2
TOTAL EUROPEAN	28.9	41.8	46.0	48.1	57.5	58.3	57.7	58.9	59.8
North America	12.0	14.8	15.0	11.8	11.2	17.0	16.7	16.4	15.7
Other developed[1]	20.5	14.8	12.0	9.5	5.6	4.9	5.0	5.1	5.6
TOTAL DEVELOPED	61.4	71.4	73.0	69.4	74.3	80.2	79.4	80.4	81.1
Oil exporting	5.1	5.6	5.8	11.6	10.2	7.6	7.6	6.5	6.1
Other developing	31.8	20.1	17.5	15.7	12.5	9.8	10.6	10.7	10.4
TOTAL LESS DEVELOPED	36.9	25.7	23.9	27.3	22.7	17.4	18.2	17.2	16.5
Centrally planned	1.7	2.9	3.7	3.3	3.0	2.4	2.4	2.4	2.4

Note:
[1] Japan, Australia, New Zealand, South Africa.
Source: Annual Abstract of Statistics, CSO, various issues.

Table 4.6   *Area composition of UK imports, c.i.f., 1955–88 (% total value)*

	1955	1965	1970	1975	1980	1985	1986	1987	1988
EC	12.6	23.6	28.3	36.5	45.1	50.0	53.1	53.6	53.5
Rest of Western Europe	13.1	12.2	14.9	14.9	13.0	14.3	14.0	13.8	13.2
TOTAL EUROPEAN	25.7	35.8	43.2	51.4	58.1	64.3	67.1	67.4	66.7
North America	19.5	19.6	20.9	13.3	14.9	13.5	11.5	11.3	12.0
Other developed[1]	14.2	11.9	10.1	7.7	6.2	7.3	7.8	7.7	7.9
TOTAL DEVELOPED	59.4	67.3	74.0	72.4	79.2	85.1	86.4	86.4	86.6
Oil exporting	9.2	9.8	7.2	13.5	8.4	3.2	2.0	1.8	1.8
Other developing	28.7	18.4	14.7	11.4	10.0	9.5	9.4	9.2	9.0
TOTAL LESS DEVELOPED	37.9	28.2	21.9	24.9	18.4	12.7	11.4	11.0	10.8
Centrally planned	2.7	4.5	3.9	2.7	2.4	2.2	2.2	2.6	2.6

Note:
[1] Japan, Australia, New Zealand, South Africa.
Source: Annual Abstract of Statistics, CSO, various issues.

both UK imports and exports, of which very little was contributed by the Eastern bloc countries. Over the past three decades the UK has come to trade increasingly with other developed countries. In the case of exports the share has risen to approximately 80 per cent, although there was a marked temporary dip in the mid-1970s due to the oil-price effect discussed below. In the case of imports the growth in the share taken by the developed countries has been much steadier, with no comparable mid-1970s effect, and the current figure of over 85 per cent is, as a consequence, even higher than that for exports. It is clear that this rate of growth cannot continue for much longer if the UK is to maintain any meaningful trade links with the LDCs, and **Tables 4.5** and **4.6** give some reason to believe that the ultimate equilibrium between developed and less-developed countries has just about been reached.

The increased share of both imports and exports taken by developed countries has not, however, been evenly distributed. The UK joined the EC in 1972 at a time when trade links with Western Europe were already significantly outweighing those with developed countries outside Europe. Exports to America were still fairly buoyant, whilst imports had only very recently begun to decline, but a marked reduction in trade with other English-speaking ex-colonies had by then become evident.

Prior to 1972 the switch from non-EC to EC countries was already quite marked, but the sharp increase in the share of UK imports from the EC between 1970 and 1975, and the even bigger increase in the share of UK exports taken by EC countries between 1975 and 1980, can reasonably be attributed to UK membership. Recent figures suggest that the UK is likely to become increasingly dependent upon the EC for her imports, but whilst the rest of Western Europe is currently a more significant source of UK imports than it was in 1955, it has been in decline as an export market ever since the UK joined the EC. The quadrupling of the share of UK imports originating from the EC has undoubtedly been the most dramatic adjustment to UK trade patterns over the past three decades, and it is hardly surprising that the UK economy has been reorientated geographically, swinging around from north-west (feeding trade

with America) to south-east (feeding trade with Europe).

As previously mentioned, the oil price has affected the pattern of UK trade with the LDCs. The effect of the sharp increase in the oil price in 1974 was to transfer huge sums to OPEC countries, and as **Table 4.5** shows this resulted in a doubling of the share of UK exports to oil exporting countries in 1975. Imports did not follow suit on the same scale because only one product was involved, but in the short term the low price elasticity of UK demand for oil did result in a marked increase in the value of oil imports. The oil price rose sharply again in 1980, but by then the UK was becoming self-sufficient. Subsequently, imports from OPEC have virtually disappeared, although exports remain high compared to the 1960s because the OPEC countries have much greater spending power.

The reasons behind some of the changes described above are fairly obvious, but the heavy dependence upon imports from other developed countries is less so, given that they must consist primarily of finished manufactures which traditionally formed the bulk of UK exports. However, it is increasingly a phenomenon of advanced industrial countries that they simultaneously import and export the same types of product such as cars and electronic apparatus, and there has also been a marked reduction in the dependence of the UK economy upon the exportation of finished manufactures.

Commodity composition of UK visible trade

As indicated above the UK was traditionally an importer of raw materials and an exporter of manufactured goods. Even in 1955, as shown in **Tables 4.7** and **4.8**, raw materials constituted some 75 per cent of UK imports, whilst over 80 per cent of UK exports consisted of semi-manufactured or finished manufactured goods. However, the switch towards European markets documented above went hand-in-hand with a sharp change in the nature of imports during the 1970s, such that raw materials currently constitute only one-third

Table 4.7   *Commodity analysis of imports (% total value)*

	1955	1965	1970	1975	1980	1985	1986	1987	1988
Food, beverages and tobacco	36.9	29.7	22.6	18.0	12.2	10.6	11.4	10.5	9.8
Basic materials	29.0	19.3	13.7	8.4	7.4	6.0	5.4	5.8	5.4
Fuels	10.6	10.6	8.3	17.5	14.2	12.8	7.3	6.4	4.6
Total	76.5	59.6	44.6	43.9	33.8	29.4	24.1	22.7	19.8
Semi-manufactured	17.9	23.8	29.2	23.9	27.3	24.8	26.5	26.9	27.5
Finished manufactured	5.3	15.4	24.6	29.9	36.6	44.0	47.3	48.9	50.9
Total	23.2	39.2	53.8	53.8	63.9	68.8	73.8	75.8	78.4
Unclassified	0.3	1.2	1.6	2.7	2.3	1.8	2.1	1.5	1.8

Source: Annual Abstract of Statistics, CSO, various issues.

Table 4.8   *Commodity analysis of exports (% total value)*

	1955	1965	1970	1975	1980	1985	1986	1987	1988
Food, beverages and tobacco	6.0	6.6	6.2	7.1	6.8	6.3	7.5	7.0	6.8
Basic materials	3.9	4.0	3.2	2.7	3.1	2.7	2.8	2.8	2.6
Fuels[1]	4.9	2.7	2.2	4.2	13.6	21.5	11.9	11.0	7.8
Total	14.8	13.3	11.6	14.0	23.5	30.5	22.2	20.8	17.2
Semi-manufactured	36.9	34.6	34.4	31.2	29.6	25.6	28.8	28.2	29.9
Finished manufactured	43.5	49.0	50.2	51.0	44.0	41.2	46.0	48.1	50.4
Total	80.4	83.6	84.6	82.2	79.6	66.8	74.8	76.3	80.3
Unclassified	4.8	3.1	3.8	3.8	2.9	2.7	3.0	2.9	2.5

Note:
[1] Roughly 95 per cent oil.
Source: Annual Abstract of Statistics, CSO, various issues.

of the share of total imports which they represented in 1955. As can be seen in **Table 4.7**, the steady decline in this share disguised some volatile behaviour among the sub-aggregates. In particular, fuel imports shot up as a result of OPEC during the mid-1970s, only to decline sharply thereafter as the UK became self-sufficient in oil.

The share of semi-manufactured imports has also been rather volatile, whilst that of finished manufactured imports has shown a steady rise. As a result, the two parts of **Table 4.7** currently stand in approximately the inverse ratio to that of 1955. The shares are of a total value which has grown steadily in money terms throughout the period examined, but it is difficult to assess whether the current position is near to its ultimate equilibrium because sharp changes in sub-aggregates – such as the virtual halving of fuel imports in money terms during 1986 – have introduced an element of instability which may prove either to be an aberration or the beginning of a new long-term trend. Readers may perhaps wonder whether the relative self-sufficiency in agriculture implied by the figures is strictly necessary given a low probability of invasion, or at least whether the cost of achieving it has been worth paying.

The situation with respect to exports has generally been much more stable until relatively recently. However, from 1980 to 1985 the share of exports taken by manufactured goods of all kinds declined quite sharply. This was not altogether surprising given the effects of the recession brought on by the MTFS combined with an overvalued exchange rate, and it reflected in part the sharp increase in the share taken by fuels. The improvement in 1986 is somewhat deceptive since, exceptionally, the money value of exports fell during the year as a direct consequence of a halving of the value of exports of oil from £16 bn to £8 bn. However, although fuel exports remained the same in 1987, the total value of exports rose to a record high with manufactured goods gaining ground, helped by rising productivity and an acceptable exchange rate in relation to the EC. Further modest progress was made in 1988 although oil exports fell away to £6 bn.

The aggregates also disguise some significant switches between industrial sectors. Amongst the semi-manufactured exports the share taken by chemicals rose steadily throughout the period from 1955 whilst that of metals fell by almost one-half and that of textiles by three-quarters. Although engineering products constituted roughly one-third of all exports in both 1955 and 1985, the peak share was 10 per cent higher in 1970. There has thus in fact been a steady decline over the past decade and a half, of which the great bulk took place in the road motor vehicles classification.

It is also of interest to look at the visible balance for each of the aggregates as depicted in **Figure 4.3**. Throughout the period 1967–88 imports of food, beverages and tobacco consistently exceeded exports although the size of the deficit in money terms has remained much the same for the past decade. This has also been the case for basic materials, so the deficits in both cases have clearly improved substantially in real terms. The oil aggregate fell to a record deficit of £4 bn in 1976, but moved into surplus by 1980. The record surplus of £8 bn in 1985 therefore represented a turnaround of £12 bn over a 10-year period but the surplus remained at half that value for the next two years and fell sharply again in 1988. Semi-manufactured goods remained in surplus until 1983, but recorded deficits thereafter, and the problem has become significantly worse since 1985.

However, this is insignificant compared to the situation with respect to finished manufactured goods which also remained in surplus until 1982, before moving sharply into deficit thereafter. The surplus of £4 bn in 1980 was transformed into a £6 bn deficit in 1987, a somewhat smaller turnaround than for oil (though larger if the oil figure for 1987 is taken) but accomplished in half the time. In 1988 the deficit soared to £11 bn. Not surprisingly, much of the policy debate over the past year or two has focussed on this phenomenon.

Exchange rates

Introduction

An 'exchange rate' is the **price of one currency**, for our purposes £ (pounds) sterling, **in terms of another currency or set of currencies**. As such it

Figure 4.3   *Visible trade balance, current prices*

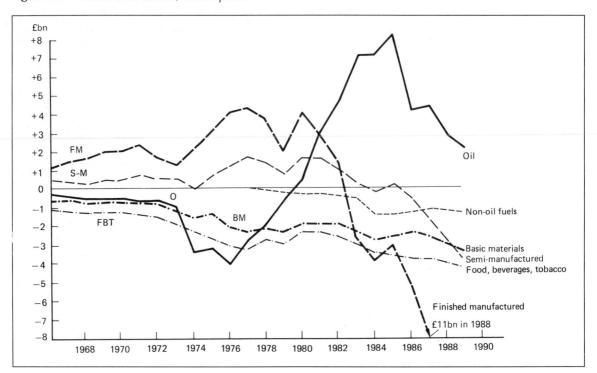

Source: *Annual Abstract of Statistics,* CSO

is in principle determined in the market place for currencies, and moves up or down in accordance with the relative forces of demand and supply. In this case the market place is no longer physical, since currency transactions are these days conducted on electronic screens, and this in turn means that anyone can deal in currencies at any time of the day or night anywhere in the world. Not surprisingly, exchange rates are as a consequence constantly on the move as dealers try to make money by taking advantage of very small movements in rates. Most transactions are for immediate delivery at the current price on the 'spot' market, but it is possible to transact in the 'forward' market where a price is agreed today for delivery **at some future date**. Buying or selling forward is valuable for firms engaging in trade, since it guarantees for them the amount of £ sterling which they will have to pay for imports or receive for exports.

However, although currency transactions are open to all, there are huge discrepancies between the market power of different participants. In particular, governments, especially of industrial nations, have powers derived from being the ultimate suppliers of currencies which are widely traded, and they are therefore in a position to influence strongly the way the currency markets behave. At the one extreme they may be happy to allow the markets to trade freely, neither deliberately adding to, nor subtracting from, the amount of their own currencies in circulation which arise from imbalances in their balance of payments accounts. At the other extreme they may set out to prevent the exchange rate from varying at all, by buying and selling their own currencies on whatever scale is necessary to neutralise exactly any buying or selling in the market place. Between these extremes there are a host of variants which reflect gradations in the extent to which governments seek to prevent the market working freely. Nevertheless, it must be borne in mind that non-governmental traders are **in aggregate** also very powerful, and it is not altogether clear in principle whether they, or governments, will be the dominant influence on exchange rates. A reasonable view might be that whilst traders in aggregate can dominate **individual** governments (the average *daily* gross trading in the foreign exchange markets in London, New York and Tokyo amounted to $431 bn in 1988), they cannot dominate the major industrial nations **acting in concert** over extended periods of time. Since in practice, as we will see below, this latter eventuality is very uncommon, it is fair to say that in the long term exchange rates are broadly determined by market forces irrespective of which exchange rate system is nominally in operation.

When the forces of the market are dominant, and the exchange rate is constantly on the move in response either to excess demand or supply, an upwards movement is called an 'appreciation' and a downwards movement is called a 'depreciation'. Where, however, the government engineers a unilateral change in the rate from one value to another, an upwards adjustment is called a 'revaluation' and a downwards adjustment is called a 'devaluation'. The action of the government may, however, not be intended to alter the rate, but rather to halt its upward or downward movement. When it intervenes in the foreign exchange market in order to prevent sterling from rising, it is obliged, via the Bank of England, to sell sterling and to buy foreign currency in exchange. This is then mostly deposited in the official reserves. When, however, the government wishes to prevent sterling from falling, it is obliged to buy sterling and in exchange to sell foreign currency which is withdrawn from the official reserves.

As suggested above, the government may, or may not, be successful in its endeavours. To some extent this is conditioned by whether or not the government has openly declared the value of the £ at which it wishes it to be stabilised since this is bound to affect market expectations. Even if there is no official upper or lower limit to the value of the £, the currency markets can work out the unofficial policy by retrospective inspection of changes in the reserves. Clearly, if there has been, for example, a rise of $1 billion in the monthly reserves figure, it

follows that the Bank of England must have been intervening heavily in order to prevent the value of the £ from rising against the $ (by selling £s and buying $s).

It is reasonable to suppose that, officially or unofficially, the government will usually have a clear view about the appropriate level for the exchange rate because of its effects upon the balance of payments. This is not invariably the case as recent events testify (see discussion on **pp. 179–80**), but in any event it must be recognised that the currency markets are not interested in the official position other than as a pointer as to whether to buy or sell a currency at a particular point in time. They do not necessarily agree with the government about the consequences of its economic policy, and having formulated their own view about the probable direction of change of the £, will be looking for signals from the Bank of England in order to determine whether they will be allowed to push the rate to where they believe it should be, or whether – and to what extent – they are likely to be thwarted by intervention.

The view about the exchange rate, whether governmental or market, will be influenced by a whole host of factors, of which the following are the most important: the rate of inflation compared that of major competitors; the structure of interest rates compared with that of major competitors; and the balance of payments on current account. In addition the market view will, as indicated, be influenced by its forecast of how the government will respond to these factors. Clearly, in order to form an opinion about these matters their underlying causes will themselves have to be studied with care – including, for example, the rate of growth in the economy; capacity constraints; unit labour costs; the fiscal and monetary aggregates and so on. Under the circumstances it is hardly surprising that there should be disagreement about the 'proper' value for the exchange rate.

The theory of purchasing power parity (PPP)

This theory, which dates back to the 1920s, has traditionally been used to explain long-term trends in the exchange rate. PPP states that the exchange rate between two currencies depends upon the **purchasing power of each currency in its country of origin**. If both the UK and USA can produce a set of identical products, in the former case for £100 and in the latter for $100, PPP dictates an exchange rate of £1 = $1. If, however, the set of products in the UK rises in price to £200, but the price of the set in the USA stays unchanged, then PPP dictates an exchange rate of £2 = $1.

The change in the exchange rate comes about through adjustments to trade flows. In the above example, at the original exchange rate, it would pay UK residents to buy US exports for £100 in preference to identical domestic products at any higher price, and that would continue to be the case until the £/$ exchange rate had fallen in value (by one-half if UK prices had doubled). Unfortunately, this is an oversimplified view of the real world in which sets of identical products are difficult to identify, and are certainly less than comprehensive. In addition, allowance must be made for **trading costs** including transportation costs when comparing prices in domestic and foreign markets. In any event, these matters relate only to **visible trade flows**, and the exchange rate is likely to be affected by capital flows which fall outside the confines of the theory.

A looser – and hence by implication a more accurate but at the same time less analytically helpful – definition of PPP is that the currency of a country which has a **higher inflation rate** than its main trading partners will **depreciate**, and vice versa. Such testing of the theory as has been undertaken (and even that has to be treated with care because of problems with respect both to the measurement of the price level and of the exchange rate and to the choice of countries) indicates that, starting at any particular year, the exchange rate eventually reaches an equilibrium level compatible with PPP, but that in the intervening period it may deviate significantly from it in either – and probably both – directions. It follows, therefore, that PPP is of little value of itself, but it does have the virtue of focussing attention on the reasons why deviations of the exchange rate from PPP actually occurred.

Interest rates

We have already remarked upon the fact that hot money is attracted to countries which, after allowing for risk, offer the highest short-term rate of interest. This is also true, but on a much lesser scale, where non-residents wish to hold longer-term interest-bearing securities. If UK interest rates exceed those in the USA, West Germany and Japan there is going to be a high demand for £s to invest in the UK, and hence upwards pressure upon the exchange rate. The sums involved can best be thought of in terms of billions rather than millions, but there is fortunately a limiting device in operation.

This arises because, when a non-resident buys sterling at the current or 'spot' exchange rate in order to acquire an interest-bearing asset, he or she may wish to protect against a capital loss, should interest rates rise further, by arranging to sell the asset 'forward' at an agreed price. Buying in the present pushes the spot rate up, whilst selling in the future pushes the forward rate down. The greater the volume of sterling being bought and sold, the greater the difference between purchase and sale prices. Hence, beyond a certain point, the extra interest earned by investing in the UK is in principle entirely offset by the loss resulting from the need to sell at an exchange rate lower than that at the time of purchase. The **interest rate parity theory** argues that the difference between spot and forward rates will automatically adjust to neutralise differences in short-term interest rates between countries, thereby greatly limiting flows of hot money. However, this argument may be defeated by the sheer volume of hot money, since it follows that a flood of hot money will drive up the exchange rate even higher, and hence even though forward rates are below the matching spot rates at any point in time, they will be rising above the spot rates which ruled in the preceding period. If sterling becomes a 'one-way bet' to continue rising, there is thus no necessity to accept a forward rate until it has risen above the spot rate at the time of purchase, or even perhaps to trade forward at all, since the spot rate at the time of sale will almost certainly be higher than any forward rate contracted previously.

In practice, the above effect is frequently stronger than any influence which the current account surplus or deficit may have upon the exchange rate. This is not to argue that the latter cannot be significant, but it follows logically that if the exchange rate is driven by the current account, then the current balance should be perpetually close to, or at, equilibrium. Since this has rarely been the case for the UK it follows that, particularly in the short term, the exchange rate is more responsive to capital flows. The obvious exceptions are where the current account deficits become so large that even after adjusting for offsetting capital inflows the reserves will run out unless the exchange rate is devalued. Where this is not at issue, it is quite possible that even a massive current account deficit will have less influence upon the exchange rate than hot money responding to rising interest rates, and hence that the **exchange rate will itself continue to rise**.

Measuring the exchange rate

It is such a commonplace to read about movements in 'the' exchange rate that few non-economists ever bother to question whether it is always the **same exchange rate** which is moving. In fact it isn't, so we must consider below the appropriate ways to measure exchange rate movements.

It is clear, to begin with, that there is an exchange rate linking sterling to every other currency belonging to a country with which the UK conducts trade. Naturally, some of these are much more important than others, either in terms of the pattern of UK trade or because of their significance for world affairs. For both these reasons it is customary to place most attention, in terms of individual exchange rates, upon the dollar, and it is indeed the £/$ rate which is most often quoted in the media. However, as shown in the section on the area composition of trade, the UK now trades increasingly with the EC, and within the EC the W. German currency, the Deutsch Mark (DM), plays a central role, so there are often good reasons to concentrate upon the £/DM rate. Whilst Japan is also very important from the point of view of its

share of total world trade, the yen has less significance than the $ or DM specifically in terms of UK trade patterns. Nevertheless, it must be recognised that if the $/yen rate alters sharply, then this is bound to have some repercussions for the £/$ rate as well.

Measuring exchange rates in terms of individual currencies does, however, have drawbacks. In the first place, such rates can be very volatile, as the discussion of recent history below will demonstrate. But this volatility is much greater in certain cases, such as the $, compared to others such as the DM, and individual rates may not simply move in the same direction, but at **different speeds** and in **opposite directions**. Clearly, to concentrate exclusively on the $ when it is rising against the £, at a time when the DM is simultaneously falling against the £, may prove highly misleading in terms of consequences for the UK economy.

In order to adjust for this, the sensible procedure is to measure the exchange rate in terms of a **basket of currencies** which includes all those of any significance in terms of UK and, by implication, of world trade. One could simply take the arithmetic average of all the rates included in such a basket, but it also seems sensible to make adjustments for the **relative importance of different countries in terms of UK trade** through a system of **weights**. Such a weighted average is in use, and is called the **effective** exchange rate (EER), where the weights used represent the share of total UK world trade conducted with each country whose currency is included in the basket. It follows that, if a volatile currency is highly weighted, as is true of the $, then the EER will itself show a tendency to be volatile, albeit on a much reduced scale. However, a low-weighted currency will have little effect upon the EER, no matter how volatile it is.

Unfortunately, because the EER measures the £ in relation to other currencies, it may be a poor guide to changes in the competitiveness of UK goods and services. For this reason, it is preferable for certain purposes to use a **real** exchange rate (RER), which measures the price of UK goods (and hence of UK exports) relative to the average price of foreign goods (and hence of UK imports). Since the latter need to be converted into sterling, the average price of foreign goods is multiplied by the EER for this purpose, and the RER is given by UK price index ÷ overseas average price index × EER. If the RER **falls** then UK competitiveness **improves** because, converted to sterling, imports have become more expensive relative to exports. One obvious drawback to the RER is that not all UK and foreign goods are traded, so the formula is something of an approximation as a measure of competitiveness in the traded goods sector, but it provides a useful supplement to other exchange rate measures.

Table 4.9 sets out the data for the three most important bilateral exchange rates, and for the EER, since 1972 when the £ first began to float. During this period the DM and the yen were the world's strongest currencies, and as can clearly be seen the £ depreciated steadily against both currencies other than during 1980 and 1981 and more recently, against the DM in 1988. However, the £/$ rate was much more volatile, with peaks in 1972, 1980 and 1988, and troughs in 1977 and 1985. As these are annual averages they obviously understate the daily high and low values for each year, some of which are also referred to in the following sections. Again, it is important to remember in the wider context that, even if the £ is falling against the DM whilst simultaneously rising against the $, the DM is not necessarily also rising against the $, and so forth.

Table 4.9   *Selected sterling exchange rates and effective exchange rate index (ERI), 1972–89*

	US$	DM	Yen	Ecu	Sterling effective exchange rate index[1]	
		Exchange value of sterling in			*(1975 = 100)*	*(1985 = 100)*
1972	2.502	7.975	752.3		123.3	
1973	2.453	6.540	664.6		111.8	
1974	2.340	6.049	682.7		108.3	
1975	2.220	5.447	658.1		100.0	
1976	1.805	4.552	535.3		85.7	
1977	1.746	4.050	467.6		81.2	
1978	1.920	3.851	402.6		81.5	
1979	2.123	3.888	465.6		87.3	
1980	2.328	4.227	525.6	1.674	96.1	
1981	2.025	4.556	444.6	1.811	94.9	
1982	1.749	4.243	435.2	1.785	90.5	
1983	1.516	3.870	359.9	1.704	83.2	
1984	1.336	3.791	316.8	1.693	78.6	100.6
1985	1.298	3.784	307.1	1.700	78.3	100.0
1986	1.467	3.183	246.8	1.495	72.8	91.5
1987	1.639	2.941	236.5	1.420	72.6	90.1
1988	1.780	3.124	228.0	1.506	76.5	95.5
1989 (Sept)	1.581	3.067	229.2	1.447	.	91.1

Note:
[1] The weights used for the ERI used to be calculated by the IMF using its Multilateral Exchange Rate Model (MERM). However, as from January 1989, the index is that published in the IMF *International Financial Statistics*, where the weights reflect the relative importance of other countries as competitors to the UK in both domestic and overseas markets. The base year is 1985. The weight of the $US in the new ERI has fallen from 24.6 per cent to 20.4 per cent compared to the old ERI, whilst the DM has risen from 14.1 per cent to 20 per cent (see *Bank of England Quarterly Bulletin* (November 1988) pp. 528–9).
Source: Bank of England Quarterly Bulletin, various issues.

The EER is also plotted graphically, on a quarterly basis, in **Figure 4.4** since the annual averages are a little misleading. As can be seen, the EER stood at 100 in mid-1975 in the midst of a massive depreciation lasting from early 1972 to the end of 1976, with only one temporary abatement in 1974/75. From early 1977 to early 1981 it subsequently appreciated steadily to stand once again at a value of 100, only to collapse back to a value of 72 at the end of 1984. On an annualised basis the EER continued to fall until the end of 1987, but as the graph in **Figure 4.4** shows, the quarterly pattern was actually quite volatile, and showed a rising tendency from 1986 to 1988 before falling sharply again in 1989. It is worth noting that the UK's EER has in general shown considerably less volatility than that of other major countries, especially Japan and the USA. Hence a quite different

perspective is gained in the longer term when comparing volatility in the EER with volatility in, say, the £/$ rate. In the short term the EER shows little volatility, even though bilateral rates may be highly volatile, which might be taken as a lesson for financial markets that what you see depends upon where you look.

The RER is rarely mentioned in the media, so detailed figures are not given here. By and large the RER is affected mostly by the EER in the short term, and mostly by relative inflation rates in the longer term, much as one would expect. Since the UK has almost continuously suffered more inflation than her main competitors since 1972, this has exerted constant upwards pressure upon the RER and led to a corresponding loss of competitiveness. During those periods in which the EER has risen sharply, for example in 1979/80, this has combined

Figure 4.4   *'Old' sterling ERI, 1972–88, quarterly averages, 1975 = 100; inset graph: 'Old' and 'New' ERI, quarterly averages, 1985 = 100*

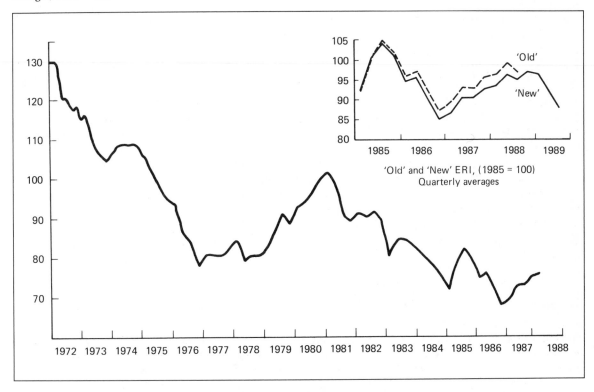

with the relative price effect to produce a disastrous loss of competitiveness. The same combination, albeit on a lesser scale, was also evident in 1988. At other times, however, the decline in the EER has more than outweighed the relative price effect, and the RER has fallen (as in 1986/87). It is finally worth noting that a country which is undergoing a strong currency appreciation need not necessarily become uncompetitive. As the Japanese have shown in recent times, the RER can still be induced to fall provided domestic prices can be kept down relative to world prices.

Exchange rate regimes

Gold standard

Although there is no realistic prospect of an equivalent exchange rate regime being restored, it is of some importance to explain briefly the workings of the old **gold standard** which involved strict rules, but which did not require any international co-operation since each country could apply the rules independently of the others. The gold standard operated in the UK from 1821 to 1914, and from 1925 to 1931. During these periods the UK money supply was determined by the gold reserves, and gold was the medium used to settle international indebtedness. Each country's currency was fixed in value in terms of gold, which in turn meant that the value of each currency was absolutely fixed in terms of all other currencies. If a country ran a BoP deficit, it would have to transfer gold to the country in surplus. This in turn would lower the money supply in the former and raise it in the latter, with prices subsequently following suit. This movement in relative prices would then boost the exports of the deficit country, and reduce those of the surplus country, until equilibrium was restored.

At the time, the fact that the gold standard left no leeway for discretionary behaviour on the part of individual governments, whilst restoring BoP equilibrium and bringing prices into line, was seen as a great virtue. In practice, the adjustment mechanism was far from smooth since, for example, prices tended to be insufficiently flexible. The attempt to go back to the gold standard in the

UK in 1925 was fairly disastrous because the conversion rate of sterling into gold was set at too high a level, and after the 1929 Crash the worldwide rush to convert currencies into gold forced the UK, whose gold reserves were limited, to suspend convertibility and to float the £ in 1931.

From a more modern perspective, a gold standard type of mechanism is sometimes advocated because it provides a strong brake upon inflation. However, against this has to be set the fact that an individual country cannot **choose** its rate of inflation; it cannot use money supply control as an instrument of demand management; and it cannot vary the exchange rate to deal with BoP problems arising either because of differences in national inflation rates, or because of unforeseen external shocks. The fact that it might no longer be possible to use gold to underpin the mechanism because it is unavailable in sufficient quantities does not rule out the use of the mechanism as such. Something else which is available can quite easily be used instead. This could either be an existing currency such as the $, or an artificial currency linked to a basket of existing currencies.

Bretton Woods 1944–71

At the end of the Second World War a new set of rules was introduced for controlling the world's monetary system. These included a fixed exchange rate mechanism harking back in many respects, but in a less rigid manner, to the gold standard. All members of the IMF had to peg their currencies to the $, which was in turn pegged to gold at a rate of $35 per ounce. However, this peg was not immovable, but 'adjustable'. Any individual currency could freely move up or down by up to 1 per cent in relation to its $ par value, but beyond that point the relevant central bank would have to intervene, and to use its reserves in order to keep within the permitted variance about the par value. In addition, any country could, without seeking the permission of the IMF, unilaterally lower (devalue) or raise (revalue) its currency by up to 10 per cent. If a larger alteration was thought to be necessary, then the permission of the IMF had to be sought, but this was certain to be forthcoming provided the country could demonstrate that its BoP was in 'fundamental disequilibrium'. Since no specific definition of this term existed, it was hard to see how the IMF could refuse a country which claimed that such a condition was indeed in force.

For the most part the adjustable peg worked quite well until the later 1960s. It was a period of generally sustained growth, and the gold reserves of the USA were sufficient to settle trade imbalances in the few cases where dollars, effectively as good as gold, were unacceptable. Compared to the gold standard, inflation control was weakened because currencies could be realigned, but the widespread adoption of fiscal policy as an instrument of demand management overcame a serious deficiency of the gold standard in that it had no instruments for demand management.

However, the Bretton Woods system came under increasing pressure, primarily because (1) countries arguably in fundamental disequilibrium, such as the UK in the 1960s, were afraid to admit it and to devalue, since their governments feared the political consequences of being seen as unable to manage their economies. Whilst devaluations did occur, as in the UK in 1967, these were always by too little and too late. (2) Since such countries preferred instead to deflate their economies by fiscal means, their growth – and hence that of the world economy – was held back. (3) Countries in surplus generally refused to revalue, arguing that this would stimulate spending on cheap imports and impart an inflationary bias to their economies. (4) But this in turn meant that speculators could be fairly certain that a fundamental disequilibrium would be resolved by a devaluation, effectively yielding a one-way bet which in turn put further pressure on deficit countries' reserves. (5) The dollars needed to maintain international liquidity, and to allow for BoP deficits to be paid for, had to come as a result of the USA running a BoP deficit and paying its debts in its own currency (which no other country could do). Eventually these dollar holdings outside the USA grew larger than the value of the gold reserves held in the USA to which they were fixed, and the whole system became overdependent upon US macroeconomic policy. Confidence in this policy could not be restored, and as a result, attempts were made to convert dollars into gold at the fixed parity, and the USA was forced to suspend convertibility in

August 1971. This signalled the end of the era during which gold played an important role in international trade.

In an attempt to salvage the adjustable peg, agreement was reached at the Smithsonian Conference in December 1971 to increase the permitted fluctuation around par values from ±1 per cent to ±2.25 per cent; to revalue certain strong currencies; and to raise the $ price of gold (which was worth far more in the free market than when held in reserves). However, the situation could not be salvaged, and in the particular case of the UK the BoP problems of the early 1970s forced the government to float the £ in June 1972. One year later, floating exchange rates were the norm rather than the exception.

Managed floating

The floating exchange rate system adopted after 1973 was 'dirty' rather than 'clean'. Even so, it was considered that a number of advantages would follow compared with the adjustable peg, many of which were compatible with the newly popular monetarist doctrines. In this latter respect it was argued that the adjustable peg had necessitated the use of monetary instruments to manage demand, with a view to keeping the BoP in equilibrium. Once the exchange rate was floated, equilibrium would automatically be restored by appreciation or depreciation of the currency, and as a result monetary instruments could be transferred to their proper use, namely control of inflation. Strictly speaking, this required the float to be clean if it was to work properly, but even a dirty float would free up the hands of the authorities to some extent.

In principle, any country experiencing relatively rapid inflation should not suffer a permanent competitive disadvantage. As prices rise faster than in competing countries, so the exchange rate should depreciate to offset this. The nominal exchange rate thus adjusts to keep the real exchange rate constant. But this should not create unemployment in uncompetitive countries. As their currencies depreciate, the price of imports – and hence retail prices in general – will begin to rise. Provided nominal wages stay more or less unchanged, real wages will therefore fall, and bear the brunt of the adjustment rather than the number of jobs on offer.

Furthermore, there should be much reduced scope for destabilising speculation compared with the adjustable peg. By their trading operations, speculators actually move the currency towards its equilibrium value, and hence reduce the opportunities for further speculation.

Unhappily, the era of managed floating has not been an unqualified success, and a number of serious drawbacks have manifested themselves in practice. Most importantly, (1) certain currencies have remained overvalued in relation to the current account, which has accordingly remained heavily in deficit, with this current account deficit financed by capital inflows. (2) Monetary policy has often not succeeded in controlling domestic inflation because, for example, of the problems of defining the monetary aggregates for this purpose, and so the exchange rate has needed to be depreciated further, once again driving up import prices. Where domestic wage rises have been demanded by way of compensation, further damaging effects upon inflation and employment have ensued. (3) Exchange rates have been much more volatile than can be accounted for by differences in inflation rates, leading to large fluctuations in real exchange rates which have had damaging effects upon world trade flows. (4) Speculation has at times been very heavy. Whilst it is clear that if one party gains £1 another party must have lost £1, it does not necessarily follow that winners and losers come from the same group. Professional speculators may gain continuously at the expense of the ill-informed.

In essence, acknowledgement of these difficulties has led to two distinct developments. Firstly, the EC countries have introduced the European Monetary System (EMS), discussed in detail in Chapter 5, which harks back to the adjustable peg in that it requires much the same degree of co-operation between participants, but in the context of a somewhat less rigid set of rules. Secondly, the USA under President Reagan has attempted to move away from unco-ordinated floating towards a system, essentially centred upon the dollar, the yen and the Deutsch Mark (and hence linking in to the EMS), requiring progressively more co-operation and the adherence to progressively more specific rules. Before discussing this, it is worth noting that the UK has been party to both these developments, either as a member of the EC or as a member of the Group of 5 (G5) or 7 (G7) major industrial countries, but has largely remained on the sidelines pursuing a policy of an essentially ad hoc nature.

There have been a large number of minor milestones along the road which may perhaps best be labelled 'informal' management of the world's major three currencies. However, the more notable ones were the Plaza Agreement of September 1985, the Louvre Accord of February 1987 and the Group of Seven Statement of December 1987 (issued in the absence of a formal meeting).

In March 1985 the $ stood at Y260 and DM3.4, a rise of roughly one-half in its RER since 1980. This was viewed in the USA as a virtue insofar as it reflected the strength of the US economy, and simultaneously as a vice insofar as it produced huge BoP deficits and stirred up strong protectionist sentiments. The $ then began to fall of its own accord, but only temporarily, and the Plaza Agreement (between the members of G5 including the UK) was designed to talk it down a further 10 per cent or so, essentially by stating that it was too high. The sum of $18 bn was made available for supportive intervention, 30 per cent contributed by the USA, 30 per cent by Japan and 40 per cent by European countries. By October the $ had fallen to its desired level, but it continued to fall sharply, thereby raising fears in Japan and Germany that it was not going to achieve a 'soft landing' – with consequent undesirable effects upon their competitiveness. Eventually this led to the Louvre Accord in early 1987, which agreed 'reference rates' for the $ of Y153.50 and DM1.825. A 2.5 per cent fluctuation on either side could be ignored, but if it increased to 5 per cent then there would need to be obligatory consultations. These consultations should be distinguished from an obligation to intervene, and implied only a modest increase both in co-operation and in the establishment of rules compared with the Plaza Agreement.

However, a substantial amount of buying intervention to stabilise the $ did take place, roughly of the order of $100 bn, and with considerable initial success. But the G7 summit in Venice in June, which reaffirmed the Louvre Accord, failed to instil confidence in the financial markets that the USA was determined to deal with its twin Budget and BoP deficits. This was the trigger for the stock market Crash in October 1987, subsequent to which the $ fell sharply. The G7 Statement in December sought to re-emphasise that the Louvre Accord was alive and well, and in order to demonstrate that there was a clear intent to keep the $ at a reference level of around Y125 the authorities intervened heavily to punish speculators who were attempting to drive down the $.

All this did not bode particularly well for international co-operation. The Japanese were very keen to prevent the $ falling sharply against the yen until they realised, in early 1988, that their exporters had learned to live with a high yen value. As a result, active intervention is no longer high on the agenda. The West Germans never showed much interest in reference ranges in the first place, and have always been unhappy at being attacked by the USA for not expanding their economy in order to increase imports, and hence raise the DM/ $ rate, arguing that this would be inflationary and that the USA was, after all, the source of the problem. The oddest aspect of all this is, perhaps, that the USA is the country least able to keep its promises about exchange rate co-operation, because the US Treasury Secretary controls neither fiscal policy nor monetary policy, respectively the responsibilities of Congress and the Federal Reserve.

As previously stated, the UK is not actively locked into the above manoeuvres insofar as there is no official reference range for sterling against the $, yen or DM. However, it is clear that, after a period of floating wherever the Chancellor saw fit, sterling has recently veered more towards an adjustable peg in the sense that attempts have been made to keep the £ broadly constant in terms of DM, thereby effectively shadowing the EMS without making this an explicit objective.

Exchange rate issues

It is helpful at this stage to summarise some of the threads which run through the preceding discus-

sion. We may note, for example, that each exchange rate system can be designated according, first, to the rigidity of its rules, and secondly to the degree of co-operation required of participants.

The postwar years have witnessed a considerable diversity of systems, all quite distinct from the prewar gold standard. This, as explained above, required currencies to be fixed in terms of gold, with no discretion to alter the rate and with each country able to fix its rate wholly independently of other countries. Subsequently, countries have periodically reimposed either fairly rigid rules or adopted an independent stance, but never both together. The Bretton Woods 'adjustable peg' allowed for some variation around par values, and also for periodic realignment of currencies, so it was less rigid than the gold standard, but it differed from the latter primarily insofar as it could only operate successfully through co-operative behaviour. However, the willingness to set supranational interests above national interests was distinctly limited, and indeed the system ultimately faltered because of a general unwillingness to adopt co-operative solutions.

The EMS, discussed in detail in Chapter 5, is essentially a more flexible version of the adjustable peg, but like that system it allows participants to behave in somewhat different ways. The country at the centre of the system, West Germany, has thus more room for manoeuvre than any of the others. Those participants which peg themselves to the Deutsch Mark, such as Holland, are relatively rule-bound compared with those, such as France, which are willing to realign their currencies. Italy has even more discretion than these because of its wider permitted variation around its par value.

The UK, since 1979, has largely done its own thing. It has avoided becoming rule-bound by pegging sterling neither to the EMS nor to any other currency, but has periodically shown some enthusiasm for shadowing the Deutsch Mark as a possible prelude to eventual EMS membership, as in 1988. For much of the earlier period the dollar was also managed very independently, but the recent agreements such as the Louvre Accord indicate a growing preference for more co-operation combined with adherence to some loosely defined rules which require the G7 central banks to limit the volatility of the major currencies.

In the second place, it has already been noted that the exchange rate is currently one of the major instruments of macroeconomic policy. Hence countries which are eager to grow more quickly will tend to prefer an undervalued exchange rate, since this keeps down export prices. Equally, if control of inflation is the primary concern, then an overvalued exchange becomes more desirable, since it keeps down import prices. It is difficult to prove that exchange rates are deliberately managed in order to pursue national interests (at the expense of other countries), since governments are overtly dedicated to better co-operation. But insofar as it does occur, it prevents rather than enhances the move towards equilibrium in international trade. Some, indeed, would go so far as to categorise recent behaviour as 'mis-managed' floating.

This returns us, finally, to the issue of credibility underlying our remarks in the introduction to this chapter. We noted there that whilst governments, acting in concert, have considerable leverage over their exchange rates, they cannot defeat the forces of the market once these are pushing uniformly in one direction. The implication is that if the international capital markets believe, for example, that the G7 countries have no clear-sighted long-term strategy, then they will continue to drive rates up and down in search of a speculative profit. Clearly, the UK government can limit this by declaring, either openly or by 'coded' messages, what its exchange rate target is against the DM and/or the $, and by intervening heavily to hold the declared rate constant. Equally, G7 countries can seek, as they have done recently, to persuade the markets that they do indeed have a clear view on the appropriate level for the $ and DM by sudden interventions on a massive scale which inflict heavy losses on speculators. The issue for the markets is then to decide whether the rate is being held at the 'right' level. But this is difficult to define. In general it may be interpreted as the rate which is neither so high as to make UK exports uncompetitive, nor so low as to raise the rate of inflation via rising import prices. But in which direction is it better to err?

The recent experiences of West Germany and Japan are quite illuminating in this respect. Historically, both countries grew steadily, kept demand management tight to control inflation and generated large BoP surpluses via a buoyant export sector. This combination resulted in both the DM and yen rising sharply against the $ from 1985 to 1987. The most commonly held view at the time was that this would scythe down the Japanese BoP current account surplus. In fact it did not, basically because Japanese businessmen accepted that the rate had moved against them, and would continue to do so, and responded by closing plants and shedding labour, and by improving their products and moving into new markets with higher added value. Wages fell because they were partly tied to profits which were initially depressed. This combined with higher productivity to result in lower unit wage costs, and the Japanese carried on as successfully as before despite the higher exchange rate. Their West German counterparts, on the other hand, asked for subsidies and for protectionism, and cut back on investment. They failed to shed much labour, partly because of legal obstacles, and continued to pay lavish social security to those who became unemployed. Workers accordingly continued to demand higher wages and/or shorter working hours, productivity stagnated, and unit wage costs rose sharply. Between mid-1987 and mid-1988 industrial production in West Germany languished, whilst in Japan it rose by 12 per cent, three times as fast as in the UK.

A relatively high nominal exchange rate does not therefore, of itself, make industry uncompetitive, and indeed may be viewed as a positive force because it should stimulate a drive to reduce unit wage costs. A relatively low nominal exchange rate is less desirable because of its inflationary consequences. In choosing, and intervening to protect, a target zone, for example for the £ against the DM, this consideration should be clearly adhered to. Of course this does not directly address the question of what is 'high' and 'low', but in current circumstances (September 1989) a figure around 2.90 DM to the £ appears to be high enough to provide a stimulus to improved competitiveness without feeding inflation. Whether competitiveness does respond is something which we will have to reflect upon in the next edition.

Is there a balance of payments crisis?

We have noted above that the current account deficit for 1988 is estimated, subject to revision, to be £15 bn. The cumulative deficit to end-July 1989 was £8 bn, equivalent to 3 per cent of GDP. The July figure was itself equivalent to 5.5 per cent of GDP, a ratio last seen during the rebuilding of industry after 1945. In 1987 the USA ran a current account deficit equivalent to 3.5 per cent of its GDP, and that was treated as a 'crisis', so it is necessary to address the question as to whether the current situation in the UK is a 'crisis', and what, if anything, should be done about it. Certainly, one thing is immediately clear. If indeed there is a 'crisis', then a much lower exchange rate, at least in relation to surplus currencies such as the DM, will be needed to deter imports irrespective of the inflationary consequences.

The first issue to address is just how bad the situation is. As we have indicated above, the current account is always understated, first because of the UK's share of unattributed world exports, and secondly because of unattributed entries in the balancing item. Unofficial estimates of the former in 1987 range from roughly £2 bn to £4 bn (although the CSO considers them to be negligible). The latter is very uncertain, partly because the balancing item has itself fluctuated sharply during recent years. However, a figure of £2 bn is unlikely to be excessive, so the combined understatement of the current account may be approximated at £4–5 bn for 1987. Since the recorded deficit was only £2.5 bn, it follows that, even on a conservative estimate, there was probably a small surplus rather than a deficit. The situation in 1988 was undoubtedly much worse. The extent of under-recording of exports is difficult to assess, but is very unlikely to be less than that for 1987 (when both sources of under-recording were lower than in 1986). A reasonable guess is, therefore, that the understatement represented one-third of the

recorded deficit, which in reality, therefore, was approximately £9–10 bn.

This is a sizeable deficit, especially if it is viewed as the first in a series. But whether it implies a crisis obviously depends on why it has arisen. The approach taken by the government can best be addressed in the form of representative responses (**R**) to accusations (**A**) that it is turning a blind eye to a serious problem.

(**A**) Between September 1987 and September 1988 imports rose in volume terms by over 10 per cent. There is no sign of a slowing down in this rate of growth, and it will lead to a current account deficit of unsustainable proportions in 1989 and subsequent years.

(**R**) But the 1988 Budget predicted a growth rate of 10 per cent. It is only to be expected in the light of the exceptionally rapid growth of the UK economy.

(**A**) Nevertheless, the most rapid growth in imports has been of finished manufactures, and in particular of vehicles and other consumer goods. The importation of capital goods for investment purposes has lagged behind. This combination will produce a crisis situation sooner or later.

(**R**) But this takes no account of the fact that capital goods comprise a much bigger share of imports than vehicles, so the former account for a bigger share of the increase in import volume than the latter even though the latter have risen more rapidly.

(**A**) But what about other consumer goods?

(**R**) It must be remembered that the current balance started turning down in 1982. If the first half of 1982 is compared with the first half of 1988 then the aggregate increase in capital goods' imports has accounted for a much bigger proportion of the total growth in import volumes than the aggregate increase in imports of consumer goods, including vehicles.

(A) Nevertheless, capital goods have accounted for much less of the total growth in import volumes than imports of semi-manufactures, raw materials and fuels.

(R) Whilst that is correct, the latter clearly need to be imported if the UK is to expand production of finished manufactures. Strictly speaking, only imports of consumer goods cause long-term damage to the economy.

(A) Even so, these finished manufactures are not being exported in sufficient quantities, nor indeed is anything else. The 1988 Budget predicted growth in the volume of exports of goods and services to be 4.5 per cent higher in the first half of 1988 compared with the first half of 1987. In the event the growth rate was slightly negative, at a time when the world economy was very buoyant. Exports to the USA were particularly hard-hit.

(R) What this indicates is that exports are uncompetitive because the exchange rate is overvalued, at least in terms of the dollar. However, before rushing out to lower the £/$ rate, thereby stimulating an increase in inflation, it is appropriate to consider which sector is overspending. There is clear evidence that, over the medium term, the private sector runs a financial surplus which is partly converted into foreign assets. In 1966 these amounted to £1.5 bn, whereas by 1986 they had grown to £114 bn. It is quite possible that the private sector is temporarily overconsuming and eating into its wealth, including its foreign assets. But as it does so it will become steadily poorer, and will respond by cutting its consumption, thereby reducing imports. Until there is clear evidence that this overconsumption is permanent, there is every reason to assume otherwise. In recent history the sector which has been overconsuming has, after all, been the government sector with its persistent Budget deficits. Rather interestingly, however, the government sector is currently in surplus and looks like remaining that way. Once private consumption begins to falter, probably in the face of higher interest rates, imports will

fall, and exports will turn up again as growth continues in the world economy and firms find it more difficult to sell on the home market.

(A) There still seems to be a reasonable case for reducing the value of the £.

(R) This may ultimately prove to be necessary. However, it is not the government's intention to let it happen unnecessarily. There are also, bear in mind, $50 bn in the official reserves. Indeed, there is a positive aspect in that if it was not for the fact that excess domestic demand was spilling over into imports, it would be forcing up domestic prices in the face of an inadequate domestic supply. Furthermore, the risk that higher interest rates designed to control domestic demand will attract so much hot money that the exchange rate will be pushed up to a hopelessly uncompetitive level will be much reduced by the downwards pressure exerted on the exchange rate by the current account deficit.

(A) This all has some internal logic, but it does not imply that the current account deficit is a matter of indifference. In the first place, high interest rates have an adverse effect upon investment, and hence output and employment. Secondly, if high rates of growth result in deficits then equilibrium can be compatible only with lower rates of growth. If steps are not taken to deal with the causes of the problem the UK will never be able to achieve a higher growth rate compatible with external equilibrium.

The international monetary system

International liquidity

As has become clear from our previous discussion, it is impossible to isolate an individual country such as the UK from the economic forces which affect the rest of the world. The UK is, hence, not merely linked into these forces via the institutions which try to control them, but through the flows of international liquidity which are the physical manifestation of these forces.

International liquidity is the stock of assets which is held by the appropriate body in each country, on behalf of its government, in order to settle BoP deficits and to defend its exchange rate. The assets in question must obviously be acceptable throughout the non-Eastern bloc world, and at any point in time the great bulk of them are to be found in the official reserves of the major industrialised countries. However, since few individual countries are either able – or, indeed, wish – to hold sufficient reserves to cover every eventuality, existing reserves need to be supplemented by a variety of sources, whether money markets or international institutions, from which additional liquidity can be obtained as required.

International liquidity is no different from domestic money in terms of its functions, such as acting as a medium of exchange or unit of account, but is much more restrictive in its physical forms. A greatly expanded volume of trade has caused a dramatic escalation in the need for such liquidity since the 1970s. This is to be expected, because it is obviously a precondition for international liquidity that it is acceptable not merely within an individual country, but well beyond its boundaries.

International liquidity takes three basic forms – namely, gold; the domestic currencies of individual countries which are acceptable as 'reserve' currencies; and non-domestic currencies created by international bodies such as the IMF. The holdings of gold and reserve currencies are largely to be found in the reserves of individual countries, but substantial quantities are also held by the IMF quite independent of its own 'artificial' currency.

Until fairly recent times gold was the most favoured form of international liquidity, since it has always been universally desired for its intrinsic qualities. Given that its value has always greatly exceeded its production costs, those countries which mine it – mainly the USSR and South Africa, and hence not the most popular of sources – have profited enormously from its supply, but the main economic issue is that its supply is inflexible even in the face of a rapid increase in its price. Hence the enormous increase in the demand for international liquidity after 1945 could not be met by an increase in the supply of gold at its existing price. Whilst it would have been possible to raise the value of the existing stocks to the required level, this would have seriously affected the world economy because of the very unequal distribution of gold stocks between countries. Thus, so long as gold was fixed in terms of dollars, as was the case until 1972, the increasing demand for international liquidity had to be met in other ways, although gold still constitutes a very significant proportion of the value of reserves held by industrialised nations.

The use of domestic currencies as 'reserve' currencies has many advantages. Paper money is cheap to produce and to store; it can be supplied on any scale that can conceivably be required; and there is widespread familiarity with its use. It is also worth noting that reserves do not have to be held in the form of currency as such. Rather, the currency can be placed on deposit and hence earn interest, or be converted into financial instruments denominated in the relevant currency.

Most international liquidity has been held in the form of reserve currencies since 1945. The obvious drawback is that no-one wishes to hold reserves in the form of a currency which is subject to capital losses. Until 1972 the US $ was pegged to gold, and hence was a universally popular reserve currency (unlike the £ which was devalued in 1949 and 1967). Since 1972 the volatile behaviour of the $ has considerably undermined its desirability, and the yen and the Deutsch Mark (and more recently the £) have tended to displace the $. However, the vast $ reserves built up over the years (issued to settle US balance of payments deficits with the rest of the world), mean that international liquidity will remain dominated by the $ for the foreseeable future. There are clear advantages accruing to a country whose currency is used for reserve purposes, not least of which is its ability to settle its debts in its own currency (which it can print at virtually no cost to itself). The main drawback is that if there is a severe loss of confidence in the currency – arising perhaps as a result of large and ongoing BoP deficits – attempts by foreigners to switch into other, stronger, currencies may have severe implications for the domestic economy. When there is a run on a currency it is unlikely that the country whose currency it is will by itself have the resources to stem the tide. Hence international co-operation between the central banks of industrial nations is a prerequisite for stability in the international monetary system.

Special Drawing Rights (SDRs)

The shortage of gold, and the increasing overdependence upon the dollar, stimulated moves towards the creation oif an 'artificial' form of currency (that is, one controlled not by the monetary authorities of an individual country but by an international body). As part of the Bretton Woods agreement discussed above, the IMF had been set up to oversee the adjustable peg mechanism and to help countries in BoP difficulties to set their houses in order. In order to do this it received funds from member countries, varying according to their ability to pay. Originally, these funds were paid as a quota, of which 75 per cent constituted the domestic currency of the contributor and 25 per cent constituted gold. The funds were then lent in the same form by way of temporary loans to countries in difficulties, in the expectation that they would be repaid within three to five years once the difficulties had been resolved (following guidelines determined by the IMF).

In 1969 the IMF managed to obtain international agreement for the introduction of an international currency called Special Drawing Rights (SDRs), and these first began to circulate in 1970 following an amendment to the IMF's Articles of Agreement. The SDRs are not put into circulation in the form of banknotes, but rather exist as **credits in ledgers to be drawn on as required in relation to members' quotas**, as explained below.

The creation of SDRs was certainly a major improvement on preceding arrangements because it offered a permanent solution to the shortage of international liquidity which existed at the time, rather than the kind of ad hoc arrangement previously adopted. In particular, the General Agreements to Borrow (GAB) had been brought into being in 1962 whereby members of the Group of Ten (major industrial countries) agreed to increase allocations of their domestic currencies to the IMF

if other members of the group needed to withdraw larger amounts than the IMF had in stock. The UK was itself able to utilise GAB during its periodic BoP crises in the 1970s, and especially in 1976. Over the years, the sums allocated to GAB have been periodically revised, with Switzerland joining the other ten members in 1984, and the possibility of access to GAB being extended beyond its immediate membership.

Like GAB, SDRs are available only temporarily (the World Bank being the appropriate body to approach for more permanent financing). Each country paying over its quota to the IMF is guaranteed a borrowing facility related to the size of that quota, which is measured in terms of SDRs. Furthermore, this facility rises in value over time as the size of the quotas is periodically raised.

A country seeking to borrow from the IMF obviously desires reserve currencies and/or gold. It purchases these with its SDRs, acquired either in return for its quota payments or as a loan from the IMF, thereby transferring the SDRs to the country supplying the currency which is being borrowed.

The IMF expects to influence a borrowing country's macroeconomic policy in order to ensure that the borrower creates the capacity to repay. However, no conditions are imposed where the borrower seeks a loan no greater than 25 per cent of its quota. This is called its 'reserve' tranche and is contained in the figure for the borrower's official reserves (denoted 'reserve position at IMF' in **Table 4.3**). Conditions begin to be imposed when a loan exceeds this figure, and are made increasingly stringent as the size of the loan increases. Loans in excess of the reserve tranche are available in four equal instalments, each amounting to 25 per cent of a country's quota. These 'credit' tranches can thus bring total borrowings up to a maximum of 125 per cent of a country's quota, but unlike the reserve tranche they are recorded, where relevant, in the BoP accounts as 'allocation of Special Drawing Rights'.

The conditions placed upon credit tranches are understandably somewhat unpopular in the borrowing country. When the UK was forced to borrow in 1976, the IMF demanded that public spending be sharply reduced and that the growth of the money supply be curtailed, neither policy being likely to appeal to the Keynesian Labour government of the time. Inevitably, borrowers are wont to place the blame for austerity measures at the IMF's door, since this avoids explaining why the problems arose in the first place, so the IMF has something of an image problem. It also has something of a credibility problem, because it is dealing in an artificial currency on a scale which is deliberately restricted by the major industrial countries wielding large blocks of votes on its Governing Board.

The size of quotas is subject to five-yearly reviews, but the initial intention steadily to replace reserves held in other forms by SDRs has never found favour with the major industrial countries, which are understandably wary of handing over control over monetary matters to a supranational body. Certainly, some attempts were made over the years to bring the SDR into increasing prominence, including the partial or full payment of increases in quotas in the form of SDRs rather than gold, and the payment of attractive rates of interest to countries receiving SDRs in exchange for their currencies, but a major consideration has been the ready availability of dollars arising from the huge US BoP deficits of the mid-1970s and 1980s. SDRs thus currently account for only some 5 per cent of world reserves.

Throughout the 1980s the UK reserve position has been relatively sound, and the need to borrow from the IMF has become a non-issue. Whilst, therefore, the SDR is of some relevance insofar as it constitutes a small part of total UK reserves, and also insofar as the £ is one of the five currencies on which the value of the SDR is based (as a weighted average), it has to be recognised that the UK is currently far more affected by the remarkable rise in international currency reserves which has occurred since 1985.

Recent trends in international liquidity

As can be seen from **Table 4.3** above, the UK's reserves rose from $15.5 bn in 1985 to $44 bn in 1987 (and to $50.6 bn in September 1988). Virtually the entire increase consisted of convertible currencies, with SDRs and reserves at the IMF

remaining static. In 1987 the reserves of Japan, West Germany and Taiwan rose in absolute terms by even more than those of the UK, but in proportionate terms the UK's rise was outstanding. In 1987 the LDCs' reserves changed only marginally, while those of the USA fell by $3 bn. Reserves held at the IMF actually fell by $5 bn because there was a net repayment of outstanding debts.

On the face of it there was, therefore, a major imbalance between the net gains and the vastly smaller net losses in 1987. This is accounted for largely by the huge US BoP deficit of $160 bn. Above $130 bn of the increase of $206 bn in world reserves (to a total value of $758 bn) in 1987 resulted from the buying of dollar-denominated securities. Perhaps $50 bn of securities were purchased officially by governments, including that of the UK, in order to bolster the value of the $. However, almost twice as much was spent 'unofficially', in the sense that central banks bought securities through private sector intermediaries or via the Eurodollar markets. Obviously, since the US was exporting dollars, its reserves were largely unaffected. During 1988 the pattern was somewhat different because central banks were periodically selling dollars in order to prevent the value of the $ from rising, and global reserves rose by only $12 bn as a consequence, but as noted above the UK's reserves nevertheless again rose sharply. Where the central banks have drawn back the private sector has stepped into the breach, so sales of dollar-denominated securities remain at a level sufficient to finance the ongoing US deficit. The role of Taiwan has been most notable, since virtually all of its huge BoP surpluses have been channelled into US Treasury bonds.

As can be seen in Figure **4.5**, the situation is beginning to look like a repeat of two decades ago. Attempts by America to finance the Vietnam war by exporting dollars in return for imports rather than by raising taxes was widely believed at the time to have been responsible for the beginning of the era of stagflation. It is, therefore, unsurprising that inflation has once again returned to the centre of the political arena after a period of several years during which fears of recession were paramount.

It is clear from this discussion that the world is

Figure 4.5 *International reserves[1], % change on previous year.*

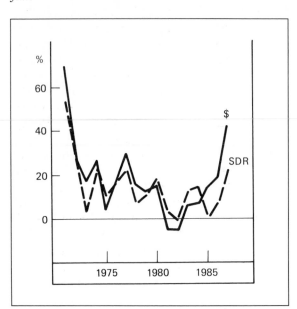

Note:
[1] Excluding gold.
Source: IMF, UBS, Phillips and Drew

currently afloat on a sea of international liquidity, defined narrowly in terms of reserves let alone more widely to allow for access to money markets. The consequences of a shortage of international liquidity are therefore irrelevant for the world as a whole, although, as discussed below, there may nevertheless still be a severe shortage of liquidity amongst particular groups of countries. The current preoccupation relates to the consequences of all of this liquidity for **inflation**. Here the prognosis is not altogether bad, even assuming the belief that there is a direct link between rising international liquidity and subsequently rising inflation. This is first because most of the recent increase in liquidity has accrued to the large developed countries rather than the LDCs. Whilst the latter can reasonably be expected to spend any additional liquidity, there is very little tendency to do so on the part of, for example, Japan and West Germany, where fears of inflation have long underpinned their macroeconomic strategy. The typical behaviour of the central banks of developed countries has recently been to 'sterilise' inflows of

liquidity by issuing gilts or their equivalent. There is a ready market for such securities, but it does have to be said that, as in the case of the UK, the sheer scale of the inflows has caused some disarray in policy-making circles over the appropriate course for monetary policy. Overall, the prevailing view for the moment is that with real growth mopping up some of the extra liquidity, and with sterilisation taking care of much of the rest, inflation is much more likely to inch upwards than to surge. It is to be hoped, however, that the newly elected American government (1989) will keep a tight rein on the size of the US BoP deficit.

The international debt crisis

Origins of the crisis

During the period prior to the early 1970s, the volume of world trade was growing rapidly, to the mutual benefit of both developed and less-developed countries. Lending to the LDCs, whether via the banks or bodies such as the IMF, was not considered to be at widespread risk of default since these countries were, with occasional exceptions, generating sufficient national income to service the interest payments on their debts. However, the sudden sharp rise in the price of oil engineered by OPEC in 1974 severely affected not merely the non-oil LDCs but some of the more developed countries as well, and so reduced their national income as to prevent full payment of outstanding debt interest. The second oil price rise in 1979 worsened their situation yet further – partly via increased costs of production, and partly via the resultant recession amongst their industrialised customers.

During the 1970s the IMF provided very limited assistance. The largest sum lent in any one year was $3 bn, and that included loans to the developed countries in difficulties. The burden of lending accordingly fell upon the commercial banks in industrialised countries which, rather foolishly in retrospect, were happy to offer short-term loans tied to floating interest rates. At the time, such behaviour did not appear to be quite so foolish. In the first place, the borrowers were sovereign states which, unlike industrial concerns, were not thought to be in any danger of bankruptcy. Secondly, the recycled OPEC surpluses were swilling around the banking system looking for a profitable home, and with industrial profitability falling sharply in domestic markets, the number of customers wishing to borrow expensive money was on the decline.

With interest rates floating upwards rather than down, it gradually became clear that sooner or later a major default on interest payments was going to occur, and that this could have a disastrous impact if such a default threatened to bankrupt commercial banks, which would then call in other loans to LDCs, and so on. In 1982 the three largest debtors, Mexico, Brazil and Argentina, between them owed $220 bn in debt, with an annual interest bill of $13 bn. Since it was clear that countries such as these literally – for the time being, at least – lacked the capacity to repay, some kind of debt rescheduling operation was clearly required. Between them, the IMF and the banks devised a way to proceed. The IMF stood prepared to make further loans available, albeit on a relatively modest scale, through a variety of programmes such as the extended fund facility (EFF); the supplementary financing facility (SFF); the compensatory financing facility (CFF); and the enlarged access policy (EAP). Most of the loans were not merely made 'conditional' upon changes in the macroeconomic policies of the debtor nations, itself not a new idea, but also conditional upon the creditor banks accepting a **restructuring of those debts** and, if necessary, further increases in their lending. In other words, the banks needed the reassurance of an IMF-imposed austerity programme, whilst the IMF needed the banks' co-operation in order to induce the debtor countries to accept such a programme. It has to be said that the debtor countries were somewhat ungrateful, arguing that their sovereignty was being undermined (which, in truth, it had to be), whilst the creditor banks complained about the throwing of good money after bad (which again was a calculated risk in order to avoid an immediate default, and possibly to create an ability to repay both the old and new borrowing at some future date).

Recent developments

During 1983 and 1984 the IMF lent some $20 bn to 70 countries, although the effect was multiplied many times by the debt rescheduling which accompanied this lending, and the feared collapse among the banks whose balance sheets contained what, on any definition, were 'bad' debts in excess of their issued capital, was headed off. However, that is not the same thing as saying that the underlying problem went away, which it did not. The drop in the oil price provided some relief for the non-oil LDCs, although it also served to create problems for oil-producers such as Mexico and Nigeria, and the general upsurge in economic growth amongst the industrialised nations helped to boost world trade. Nevertheless, the scale of the problem remained severe, as shown in **Table 4.10** which sets out debt owed to the main creditors by the most important debtors at the end of 1985.

Between 1982 and mid-1987 the 'Paris Club' creditor governments rescheduled $48 bn of debt for 39 countries, of which the UK share was $4.5 bn. The problem for the banks, as indicated above, was their high exposure to 'non-performing' debt in relation to their capital base. They have, therefore, continued to strengthen their balance sheets. Between 1982 and 1986 the UK banks managed to reduce loans to problem debtors as a proportion of their total assets from 9.3 to 6.9 per cent. They simultaneously increased their capital as a proportion of problem loans from below 100 per cent to roughly 140 per cent. With the encouragement of the Bank of England the banks improved their provisions against the risk of bad debts.

In June 1987 the National Westminster Bank increased provisions by £0.5 bn, followed by the Midland with an increase of just under £1 bn (see also **p. 79**). These various developments mean that further lending need not be undertaken solely to try to protect existing loans, but rather can be judged on normal commercial criteria. As such lending often fails to meet these criteria, many banks have been trying to avoid being drawn into concerted lending packages. The difficulty here is the free-rider problem which arises because a bank which refuses to lend fresh money is still entitled

Table 4.10 *Selected external indebtedness, 1985 ($ billion)*

| | Multilateral agencies | IMF | OECD countries | | | | |
			Banks	Export credits	Official aid	Other	Total
15 middle income debtors[1]	32	17	308	52	10	30	449
Sub-Saharan Africa[2]	16	6	13	19	8	11	73

Notes:

[1] These are Argentina, Bolivia, Brazil, Chile, Colombia, Ecuador, Ivory Coast, Mexico, Morocco, Peru, the Philippines, Uruguay, Venezuela and Yugoslavia.

[2] All African countries south of the Sahara other than Nigeria and South Africa.

Source: External Debt Statistics, OECD, Paris 1987.

to the repayment of interest on old lending which it finances, which is unpopular with those banks putting up new loans. This is, however, affected by the secondary market in debt discussed below.

Unfortunately, little parallel progress was made to reduce the indebtedness of the problem debtors where the ratio of debt to export earnings continued to rise. At meetings of the IMF and World Bank in April 1987 Nigel Lawson restated the UK's policy on international debt, the core of which was that in the long-term debtors must restore their creditworthiness so that they could once again borrow on world capital markets. This necessitates policy reform in debtor countries and new finance should be conditional upon such reform. The weakening of conditions which Nigel Lawson detected should be reversed, and rescheduling held back until it was certain that new policies were operational.

One rather embarrassing aspect of the debt problem at the end of 1988 was the acknowledgement by the IMF that instead of the IMF financing the debtor nations, the debtor nations were financing the IMF. During the three years to April 1988 net repayments to the IMF totalled SDRs 7 bn as a result of repayments of loans made in the early 1980s even though the debt burden of countries making repayments was simultaneously rising. The IMF intends to return to being a net lender, but it is an irony of the nature of short-term lending that periods of heavy lending must inevitably be followed by periods of heavy repayments.

In early 1989 the debt problem was suddenly pushed back into prominence by rioting in Venezuela triggered by price rises introduced to qualify for new IMF loans. The US Treasury Secretary, Nicholas Brady, hastily cobbled together a plan, apparently without first consulting the President or Federal Reserve, which proposed that commercial banks forgive a part of their loans to Latin America, with the rest of the outstanding debt guaranteed by the World Bank and the IMF (in other words, by the nations contributing funds to these organisations).

In effect, the debtor nations demanded that resolution of their problems should be divorced from internal reform. This stirred up a storm of protest which centred around the argument that debtor countries should privatise their astonishingly inefficient state enterprises (as had been done in Chile), crack down on corruption and introduce market forces, in the absence of which residents of debtor countries had hidden away hard currency equal, in many cases, to a debtor's total external debts.

The refusal by debtor nations to implement structural reforms had previously caused the demise of the Baker plan, and the softer line contained in the Brady plan understandably resulted in a more positive reaction by debtor nations. However, no-one seemed anxious to come forward with new money or to offer to take the losses on existing loans. Whatever the outcome of short-term palliatives, the only long-term solution is to **speed up the rate of growth in debtor nations** so that they acquire the capacity to repay debts without eroding the existing standard of living of their inhabitants. There is clearly a strong case to be made out for requesting the industrialised nations to open up their markets, especially to agricultural products, and for the debtor countries to become more export-oriented. The debtor nations may well have a comparative advantage in food production, but world prices have long been poor because of protectionism in America, the EC and Japan. The discussion of the agricultural problem in Chapter 5 does not, however, hold out much hope in this respect.

In the meantime, the main hope is to proceed with the development of financial innovations, including a secondary market in debt. It is now possible to trade debt at some percentage of its face value (for example, Brazilian and Mexican debt currently sells at between 40 and 50 per cent of its face value). By selling all of its outstanding debt a bank can clean up its balance sheet – but only by taking an actual rather than a theoretical loss. For the most part, debt is bought by other banks which raise loans to pay for it. In 1987, some $10 to $15 bn of debt was swapped between banks. Brazil and Argentina also offer 'exit bonds' which if taken up relieve a bank of the obligation to supply new money. Some debtors permit debt to be converted into equity, and others run auctions at which banks bid to swap their customers' foreign debt for local currency which they need for projects in those countries.

The debt problems of Latin America have played such a dominant part in discussions that little attention has been paid to the parallel problems in Eastern Europe. Eastern European debt rose from $70 bn in 1985 to $99 bn in 1987 – small beer by Latin American standards, but no-one in the West has any intention of being sucked into a repeat of the Latin American situation. Probably some kind of approach similar to that applicable in Latin America will be offered, and at least there is a much improved commitment to the introduction of market forces. The fact is, however, that the Brady plan is a long way from being universally accepted, and it looks as though the immediate future will offer little more than the exercises in papering over cracks so familiar from previous failed attempts to resolve debt issues.

Note

1. For an alternative version of why the CSO's claims should be viewed with some scepticism see S. Brittan, *Financial Times*, 23 November 1989, p. 28.

5

External Relations
Peter Curwen

Introduction

The distinction between external transactions and external relations is necessarily a rather fine one, and there are clearly other ways to manage the division of material. Essentially, there seemed to be advantages in assembling together most of the material which impinges upon the role of the UK as a member of the EC, and Chapter 5 is broadly given over to this topic. This means that the issues pertaining to exchange rate relationships within the EC are also contained within Chapter 5, even though the more general discussion of exchange rates appears in Chapter 4. However, it is difficult to disentangle issues concerning the EMS, the EMU and the single European market, and these are accordingly dealt with in sequence at the begin-

ning of the chapter. Chapter 5 then goes on to examine relationships between the EC and the rest of the world, treating the UK in its capacity of EC member, and finally looks in detail at the agricultural problem which is sumultaneously an issue in terms of the UK's relationship with the EC and also in terms of the EC's relationship with other agricultural trading blocs.

The single European market

During 1989 the issue of how best to create a single European market, in accordance with the Single European Act (SEA) 1985, has shot to prominence as the comparative immediacy of the implementation of the Act on 31 December 1992

172

has begun to permeate the consciousness of policy-makers. This reflects, in part, the efforts of the incumbent President of the European Commission, Jacques Delors, who was reappointed in June 1988 to a second four-year term in office beginning in January 1989. When he was first appointed in 1984, M. Delors considered carefully the areas in which to concentrate his attention. His first priority was to create an economic and monetary union within the EC, but neither the UK nor West Germany showed sufficient enthusiasm for that idea. He accordingly turned next to matters of foreign policy, but again found no takers for a policy of increased co-ordination. His third choice proved more inspired. Noting the movement towards deregulation and liberalisation in economic affairs, he advocated **freedom of movement for goods and services, people and financial flows throughout the EC**, now enshrined in article 8A of the SEA 1985.

At the present time a number of developments are working their way through the complicated and time-consuming process of ratification by all EC members. Most decisions are subject to qualified (weighted by size of country) majority voting, but some significant ones – such as those concerned with taxation – require unanimous approval. The qualified majority is 54 votes out of a total of 76 (of which the UK has 10). Roughly 300 directives have been proposed by the European Commission, of which 5 per cent have been withdrawn (leaving 279 in July 1989) and 80 per cent tabled. The Council of Ministers awaits the remaining 15 per cent, and of those tabled has so far fully adopted 39 per cent or well over 100. One still under consideration, on the matter of fiscal harmonisation, has necessarily already been discussed in Chapter 3. At this juncture we need to take a more general look at the single European market, concentrating in particular upon those aspects which affect trade flows between member states.

It has to be borne in mind that every step towards a single market implies a loss of national sovereignty on the part of member states. By a stroke of historic irony, the original impetus towards a Europe of nation-states came from de Gaulle in France, but when the French attempted to expand their way to prosperity in the early 1980s,

their failure caused them to become the arch-advocates of the single market. The fact that M. Delors has maintained close links with the French Socialist Party has thus created a suspicion in other countries that he is over-keen on the French version of the single market. When he recently claimed that 80 per cent of economic legislation, and perhaps tax and social legislation, would be decided in Brussels within 10 years, he was rapidly brought to earth by Mrs Thatcher, who pointed out that she did not expect the loss of national sovereignty on such a scale to take place during her lifetime.[1]

The evolution of the UK's attitude to European matters is discussed in the appropriate sections of the book (and see also the *Economist*'s Survey of Europe's Internal Market on 8 July 1989). The UK has played a leading role in resolving disputes about the CAP and the EC Budget (see **pp. 187–8**), and has accepted the need for intervention in matters such as state aid and competition policy (see **pp. 282–3**). It stands prepared to move in gradual stages (see, for example, the discussion of the Bank of England's role in fostering the use of the ECU for international finance on **p. 93**), but not in leaps and bounds. This, understandably, sometimes gives the impression that the UK has severe reservations about the whole idea of European co-operation, but it is fair to say that most other members support the UK's gradualist approach.

1992 and EC trade

If all goes according to plan, all border restrictions on trade between member countries of the EC will be discarded at the end of 1992. Goods and services, labour and capital, will flow freely across national borders. In principle, there is already free movement between member countries, and there is already a common external tariff. However, this is not exactly the case in practice. There are, *inter alia*, a host of protectionist agreements involving individual EC members and non-EC countries. There is, for example, a quota regulating the importation of Japanese cars into the UK. Furthermore, article 115 of the EC prevents prospective importers from obtaining goods subject to restricted entry in their own country by routeing them via another EC country where they are imported freely. 1992 necessarily spells the abolition of article 115, and the erection of truly common external trade barriers. Some EC members want these to be as high as possible in order to keep the internal market as a near-exclusive preserve for members, whilst others, including the UK, consider that the net effect should be to reduce protectionism for the sake of the world economy.

From the viewpoint of consumers there is a clear gain where the common external tariff after 1992 is lower than that ruling prior to that time, since prices on the domestic market will be lower. On the other hand, the reverse will be true where the new common external tariff provides a higher degree of protection than before. For the moment, in the absence of any clear directive on this issue from the EC Commission which, in its usual way, is postponing making a decision which cannot please all EC members simultaneously, there is nothing further to add. However, the issue of subsidies is probably more critical anyway, especially if countries which are unhappy with a lowering of trade barriers, should it transpire, respond by introducing a substitute protectionism in the form of subsidies.

Subsidies

As **Figure 5.1** shows clearly, subsidies play a very minor role in the USA and Japan, but are quite significant in the case of certain EC members (albeit typically less so than in Norway and Sweden). In most cases the degree of subsidisation is on the increase, although it is diminishing in the UK which is currently the least-subsidised EC member other than France – at least according to official statistics. Governments are understandably somewhat reticent about publishing their efforts to

Figure 5.1   *National subsidies as % of domestic income**

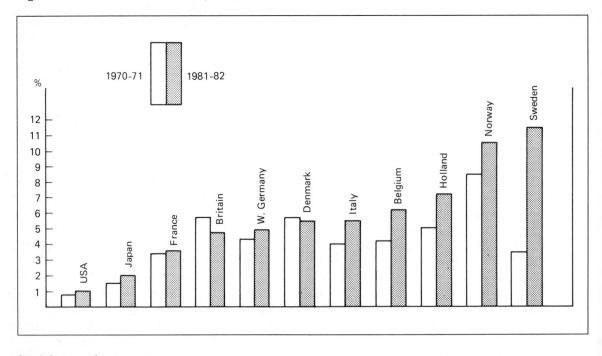

* Excluding general government.
Source: Kiel Institute

distort trade flows in their favour. **Figure 5.1** in fact refers only to direct subsidies and capital grants, and excludes tax relief and cheap loans which are commonplace in, for example, West Germany.

In recent years the European Commission has toughened up its stance on subsidies which distort trade flows between member states, but here again there is, as yet, no clear-cut directive about policy after 1992. It is feared that unless the Commission comes down heavily against the use of subsidies, their introduction by any one member state will set off competitive retaliation.

The free movement of capital

This is of particular concern to the UK. The directive removing controls from all capital movements within the EC was adopted on 24 June 1988. It will apply to most countries from 1 July 1990, although Spain, Ireland, Greece and Portugal have until the end of 1992 to achieve full compliance, and perhaps even until 1995 in the case of the latter two countries. The current position is that the UK, where exchange controls were abolished in 1979, West Germany, the Netherlands, Belgium and Luxembourg are free from restrictions on capital movements. Denmark and Italy are close to reaching that objective, whilst France still has some way to go. It is the newer, less developed members which present real difficulties, and the 1988 directive allows for the temporary reimposition of controls after 1992 where a member's macroeconomic strategy has been blown off course.

It is intended that controls on capital movements with non-members will ultimately also be lifted. This is already largely the case for the UK, but there should still be opportunities to profit from the increased volume of business which should arise in a less-tightly regulated world. One major hurdle which has now largely been overcome through the Basle Agreement is the need to agree standards on issues such as capital adequacy so that a UK bank can, for example, acquire a 'passport' to do business throughout the EC on the basis that it has been authorised by a single member state, but subject also to community-wide minimum standards to be applied by regulators in each country. In recognition of the fact that freeing up capital movements may cause BoP difficulties for member states, the EC has combined its two existing facilitis for medium-term financial assistance into a provision worth up to ECU 16 bn which is available to members with such difficulties.

The European Monetary System (EMS)

In the Treaty of Rome, which originally set up the EEC in 1957, a target of 12 years was set by which time all tariffs and quotas were to be removed between EEC members. This proved to be more than a little unrealistic, since it became clear that individual countries were in no rush to give up their national sovreignty. However, an attempt was made to take a major step forward with the publication of the Werner Report in 1970, which proposed the setting up of a European Monetary Union (EMU). Initially, this took the form of a narrowly constrained adjustable peg mechanism linked to the existing adjustable peg based on the dollar.

The widening of the dollar-based peg in 1971 resulted in the EMU taking the form of the 'snake in the tunnel', whereby each EMU member's currency was allowed to fluctuate only narrowly around its own par value, thereby restricting the gap between the strongest and the weakest currency to no more than 2.25 per cent, whilst the EMU currencies taken as a whole were permitted to fluctuate against the dollar within a 4.5 per cent band.

The EMU, operated by the original six EEC members from the beginning of 1972, and also by the UK for one month in May 1972, quickly fell apart at the seams. In part this reflected the continuing precedence of national interests over monetary union, but the EMU also, by chance, coincided historically with the demise of the adjustable peg system (the UK dropping out of both when it floated in June 1972). Other EMU members either withdrew permanently, or moved in and out of the system, and by the mid-1970s it was regarded as terminated in practice even if not in principle.

The idea of monetary union was resurrected at the Bremen Summit in July 1978, which resulted in the setting up of the EMS in March 1979. The idea behind the EMS, apart from the longer-term objective of an economic and monetary union within the EC (a still elusive goal, as discussed below), was firstly to promote economic convergence in the EC by inducing member governments to adopt the sorts of policies being implemented by its most successful member, West Germany, and in particular to bring inflation down to the West German level, and secondly to create a 'zone of monetary stability' which would facilitate trade between EC members whilst providing insulation against the erratic behaviour of the dollar.

The European Currency Unit

The major innovation of the EMS was the introduction in 1979 of a new European currency, the European Currency Unit (ECU). This is a weighted average of the EMS currencies (and therefore has to be recalculated when new members join, as with the Greek drachma in September 1984), where the weights are calculated according to the relative importance of the individual currencies in terms of key indicators such as national output and the volume of trade with other members. The contribution of different currencies to the ECU is shown, in October 1988, in **Table 5.1**. It should be noted that there are now eleven contributing currencies as Belgium and Luxembourg are treated as a single entity, and the UK, whilst never a member of the EMS, does contribute to the ECU. As can be seen, the Deutsch Mark dominates the ECU, with the Franc also a significant contributor, whilst the Greek and Irish currencies are almost irrelevant. In respect of the above the 'official' ECU performs the function of unit of account to the exchange rate mechanism described below, and also provides a currency which can circulate between central banks

Table 5.1   *The composition of an ECU*

	Amount of each currency in basket[1]	Market value of ECU in national currency (central rate)[2]	Current weight % of currency in basket[3]	Weight as from September 1989
Deutsch Mark	0.6242	2.07364	34.7	30.1
Sterling	0.08784	0.657398	13.4	13.0
French franc	1.332	7.06251	18.5	19.0
Italian lira	151.8	1545.62	9.1	10.15
Dutch guilder	0.2198	2.33765	11.0	9.4
Belgian franc	3.301	43.4556	8.5	7.6
Luxembourg franc	0.130	43.4556	0.3	0.3
Danish krone	0.1976	7.97707	2.7	2.45
Irish punt	0.008552	0.773584	1.1	1.1
Greek drachma	1.440	168.531	0.7	0.8
Spanish peseta	6.885	n/a	n/a	5.3
Portuguese escudo	1.393	n/a	n/a	0.8

Notes:
[1] Fixed for a five year period on 20 September 1989.
[2] Based on market value at 6 October 1988.
[3] The currency amounts in the ECU must be reviewed every five years, or on request if the weight of any currency has changed more than 25 per cent since the last revision.
Source: Eurostat.

throughout the EC. In recent years there has also developed a separate private market for securities denominated in ECU, but, as noted previously, this has yet to form more than a marginal part of the total Eurocurrency markets.

The most recent five-yearly recomposition of the ECU took place in September 1989. The European Commission decided in June 1989 that the currencies of members admitted since 1984, namely Spain and Portugal, should be included in the make-up of the ECU, the weight which was to be assigned to them and from which other currencies to transfer it (as shown in Table 5.1). Clearly this was as much a matter of political infighting as straightforward assessment of relative economic strength. The 1984 recomposition gave rather too much weight to the Deutsch Mark and Guilder, and rather too little to the Lira, in relation to their relative economic strength at the time, and the weight of the DM should in principle have been reduced to roughly 24 per cent in order to make way for the new currencies and also to adjust for recent slow growth in the West German economy. This unsurprisingly proved objectionable to the West Germans, so the readjustment was in practice rather more modest. It is also the case that since bonds issued in each ECU contributor's own currency yield different interest rates, altering the balance of the ECU necessarily also affects the yield of bonds denominated in ECU. Considerable instability in the ECU bond market will, therefore, result from a major restructuring of the ECU, and this is always likely to operate to keep any restructuring within modest bounds.

The exchange rate mechanism

The second element of the EMS is the exchange rate mechanism (ERM). This is, in fact, a dual mechanism similar to, but more complex than, the old-style adjustable peg. In the first place, each country (but not the UK, Portugal or Greece which are not members) has a 'parity grid' which permits each currency to move against any other EMS currency by no more than 2.25 per cent in either direction (6 per cent in the case of Italy and Spain – see **Figure 5.2**). Once this limit is reached the

Figure 5.2   *EMS exchange rate constraints*[1]

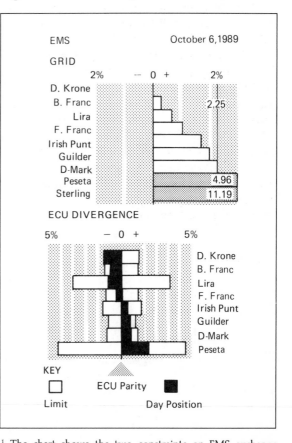

[1] The chart shows the two constraints on EMS exchange rates. The upper grid, based on the weakest currency in the system on that day, defines the cross-rates from which no currency (except the lira and peseta) may move by more than 2.5 per cent. The lower chart gives each currency's divergence from the 'central rate' against the European Currency Unit (ECU), itself derived from a basket of European currencies.

Source: Financial Times

two countries in question must intervene to keep their currencies within the predetermined limits. This involves sales of the strong currency and purchases of the weak currency. The second element consists of an ECU 'divergence indicator' as shown in **Figure 5.2**. Each EMS member is assigned a central rate against the ECU, as in **Table 5.1** and when it 'diverges' from that rate by more than a predetermined amount it is treated as an early warning device, which it is anticipated will set in motion a change in the way in which the country in question is conducting its economic policy. Where the divergence is below the central rate a suitable response might be a tightening of interest rates, and where it is above the central rate it might be a relaxation of fiscal policy. It may be noted from **Figure 5.2** that the permitted divergences are all different. This is because, when a currency's central rate moves, it also alters the value of the ECU. Hence, for example, the heavily weighted DM can only move by less than 1.5 per cent before the gap between it and some other currency becomes excessive. The formula determining the limit to divergence is ± 2.25 $(1 - \text{weight})$ per cent. However, the Lira merits exceptional treatment and sterling does not count.

If the early warning system is effective it should prevent the currency running up against its upper or lower limit on the parity grid, although the speed of response to signs of excessive divergence has in practice been too slow to achieve much in this respect. Hence, there have been a number of occasions when currencies have run up against the limits of the parity grid without either adjustment of domestic policies or intervention by central banks proving sufficient to prevent these limits being breached. As a consequence, both devaluations and revaluations have occurred, as set out in **Table 5.2**.

Given that remedial action was expected to be taken at two prior stages, a currency realignment was intended to be very much a last resort operation, and a total of eleven realignments does, therefore, appear superficially to represent a rather

excessive use of this ultimate remedy. However, as **Table 5.2** shows clearly, realignments mostly took place in the early days of the EMS when it was moving towards a longer-term equilibrium, and the system has been much more settled since 1983. As explained above, it was a characteristic of the adjustable peg that currencies were almost always devalued rather than revalued, whereas there have been more revaluations than devaluations under the EMS. This has reflected, in particular, a general tendency for the Deutsch Mark to rise, mirrored by the Guilder, and for the French Franc and the Lira to decline.

European Monetary Co-operation Fund

The third major component of the EMS is the European Monetary Co-operation Fund (EMCF), the purpose of which is to provide funds to assist with the stabilisation of exchange rates. At the inception of the EMS, members were required to deposit 20 per cent of their gold and dollar reserves with the EMCF (which the UK does also), in return of which they received a credit in ECUs which they could then use to settle indebtness with other members or for intervention purposes. It was originally anticipated that this would evolve into a fully fledged European Monetary Fund as a major step on the path to monetary union, but this never developed as intended. The EMCF uses funds deposited with it to offer a range of credit facilities, responding to requests by individual countries rather than to policy adjustments jointly agreed by

Table 5.2   *Central parity realignments[1] within the EMS (%)*

	September 1979	November 1979	March 1981	October 1981	February 1982	June 1982	March 1983	July 1985	April 1986	August 1986	January 1987
Deutsch Mark	+2.0			+5.5		+4.25	+5.5	+2.0	+3.0		+3.0
French franc				-3.0		-5.75	-2.5	+2.0	-3.0		
Guilder				+5.5		+4.25	+3.5	+2.0	+3.0		+3.0
Lira			-6.0	-3.0		-2.75	-2.5	-6.0			
Belgian/ Lux. franc					-8.5		+1.5	+2.0	+1.0		+2.0
Krone	-3.0	-5.0			-3.0		+2.5	+2.0	+1.0		
Irish £							-3.5	+2.0		-8.0	

[1] + indicates a revaluation, − indicates a devaluation.

Source: European Commission.

all members. Virtually unlimited funds are available on a very-short-term basis, but only modest amounts, measured in ECUs, can be provided on either a short-term (up to nine months) or medium-term (two to four years) basis. Were the UK to join the EMS these credit facilities would virtually be an irrelevance, in the first place because the UK has not borrowed from an international institution since 1977, and in the second place because it already has much larger credit facilities lying untouched at the IMF.

As indicated above, there clearly are similarities between the adjustable peg and the EMS. It is argued, however, that the latter has improved upon the former because more frequent, but smaller scale, realignments have allowed the system to operate much more smoothly. Equally, if one compares the Deutsch Mark and French Franc with sterling in terms of ECUs, the former have pursued a remarkably smooth path compared to the latter. One other obvious virtue of the EMS compared to the adjustable peg is that it has not put all the pressure to realign upon the deficit countries. It is fair to conclude, therefore, that the EMS has represented a distinct forward step in the creation of a zone of monetary stability. On the issue of economic convergence the evidence is less clear-cut, since whilst it is true that inflation rates have tended to fall into line amongst EMS members, this has also broadly been true for non-members amongst the industrialised nations.[2]. Unfortunately, this means that there is little 'proof' either way as to whether the UK should join the EMS, and the issue has become bound up with where in the political firmament the ultimate decision will lie, and with those providing the advice.

The debate over joining the EMS

The re-emergence of Sir Alan Walters as Mrs Thatcher's economic 'guru' in mid-1988 was notable, primarily because of his outright opposition to joining the EMS. He puts forward three main arguments to support his position. He claims, in the first place, that no matter how 'right' the exchange rate is at the time of joining the EMS, it can only be a matter of time before the need for a realignment arises. Since inflation in the UK is more rapid than in West Germany, the financial markets will have reason to anticipate a devaluation of sterling. Hence, as the likely date for a realignment approaches, speculators will sell sterling to the point at which the value of sterling can be shored up only by a huge rise in interest rates. Realignment will, however, still take place because of the inflation rate differential, and subsequently speculators will switch back into sterling, causing interest rates to be lowered again in the UK to keep sterling from rising too far.

Both interest rates and exchange rates will, therefore, be highly volatile. However, the switching of funds from one currency to another between realignments will, Walters argues, also act to equalise interest rates in member countries. Funds will flow out of a low-inflation, low-interest-rate-country such as West Germany, causing interest rates there to rise, and into a high-inflation, high-interest-rate country such as the UK, causing interest rates there to fall. But the addition of such funds will stimulate further inflationary pressures in the UK, whilst their loss will deflate the West German economy even further, so exchange rates will soon come under further pressure to realign.

Finally, Walters argues that the 'right' exchange rates have not typically been adopted. Hence, he alleges, France has had to live with a permanent overvaluation of the Franc which has held back the growth potential of the French economy.

Proponents of the EMS have responded to these arguments largely by falling back on the lessons of experience. They claim first that, according to data compiled by the Bank of England, the EMS has reduced the volatility of both exchange rates and interest rates, a factor which the Bank ascribes to the enhanced credibility of the exchange-rate policies of the member countries. There is, according to this view, no reason to expect a rapid adjustment away from the initial exchange rate set were the UK to join the EMS. This is partly because relative rates of inflation are not a good guide to competitiveness in the traded goods sector. Rapid productivity growth has helped keep down costs of finished manufactures in the UK, so export prices are unlikely to suffer, especially in the short term, compared to those of, for example, West

Germany. In any event, a high-interest-rate country attracts capital flows which themselves serve to bolster the exchange rate, so there are contradictory forces acting upon the exchange rate which may ultimately balance out so as to keep the exchange rate above its equilibrium level. Speculating that a devaluation will occur is not, therefore, a 'one-way bet'.

Furthermore, add the proponents of the EMS, there is an alternative to the use of interest rates to control the macroeconomy. The government could try tightening fiscal policy when appropriate – or, in the West German case, loosening it. Finally, even if the exchange rates fixed upon entry to the EMS were incorrect, although EMS proponents cannot see any very good reason why that should be the case, industry will still obtain clear benefits from stabilising the exchange rate. According to the Confederation of British Industry (CBI), exchange-rate stability, even if it requires relatively volatile interest rates to maintain it, has the great virtue of providing an anchor for inflationary expectations. Experience of the EMS has clearly shown that it operates so as to bring members' rates of inflation down to the level of the lowest rather than the reverse. The possibility of profitability being stripped away by an adverse movement of exchange rates will, they argue, also be much reduced.

The major dilemma posed by the EMS in the months to come is how to strike an acceptable balance between **inflation** and **growth**. By tying their currencies to the Deutsch Mark, the other EMS members have subjugated their monetary policies to that of West Germany, and have reaped the reward in the form of inflation rates falling towards that of West Germany. However, most members remain keen to increase their growth rates, especially France which learned to its cost, when its Socialist government was first elected, that an independent dash for growth simply generates massive BoP deficits and is ccordingly unsustainable. But West Germany has always put inflation control as its first priority, and remains insistent that any sign of inflationary pressure should be met by restrictive policies such as higher interest rates. Unlike the UK, West Germany has made modest progress in introducing supply-side

economics; its labour market is accordingly inflexible and industry is excessively subsidised. As a result, growth in recent years has generally been below the EC average (although recent estimates suggest a distinct improvement in 1988), and this in turn means that tax revenues are far from buoyant and that the Budget deficit is forecast to rise to 3 per cent of GDP in 1988. The West German government intend to counter this by raising consumer taxes in 1989, concentrating on bringing demand down into line with supply rather than raising supply into line with demand, so growth will inevitably remain depressed.

This approach is turning the EMS into something of a strait-jacket for other members, which cannot grow significantly faster than West Germany without running into BoP difficulties. One solution might be for certain members such as France to devalue their currencies, but the new French government understandably finds that option extremely unattractive, and argues that in the light of its huge BoP surplus West Germany can afford to pursue a more expansionary set of policies. This issue is particularly contentious because this surplus has largely been generated via trade with other EC members, and has been instrumental in driving the French and Italian (and UK) current accounts further into deficit.

The next step: EMU or not EMU?

Whilst the EMS is generally held to have been a success, it is seen in many quarters as simply a necessary step on the road to a 'United States of Europe', incorporating a single European currency in an EMU structure. The Single European Act to which the UK is committed as a member of the EC refers to EMU as '*cooperation* in economic and monetary policy', and talks about EMU's 'progressive realisation'. These are sentiments with which Mrs Thatcher is happy to comply, but an attempt was made at the Madrid Summit at the end of June 1989 to set a rigid timetable for the full implementation of EMU as envisaged in the Report prepared by Jacques Delors and a group of central bankers. The Report recommended a single currency regulated by an autonomous group of central bankers, a concept little short of anathema to Mrs Thatcher because of the implied loss of national sovereignty. But although the Delors Report was widely supported, especially by the French, Mrs Thatcher managed to turn the tables by offering to join the EMS (on the face of it a major concession given the prior discussion) at such time as the rest of the EC fulfilled its obligations for 'the removal of all exchange controls, the full implementation of a free market in financial services and strengthening of competition policy'.

This apparently innocuous statement effectively postpones the introduction of EMU for quite a long time because, although all EC countries are committed in principle to the abolition of exchange controls, this may itself run a team of horses through the EMS (see, for example, the discussion in *The Economist* on 24 June 1989). As already noted, the success of the EMS relies largely on the tough anti-inflationary stance taken by the West Germans, whose central bank, the Bundesbank, is like the American Federal Reserve largely independent of the government. By tying a currency to the DM any attempt to create inflationary forces through, for example, excessive reflation, causes the offender's currency to fall in value and to reach the outer limit of the permitted range in the EMS, beyond which point either the reflation must stop or the currency must be devalued (which is bad for a government's authority).

Capital controls, either in the form of exchange controls used in France, Italy and elsewhere in the EC, or in the form of restrictions on the investment abroad by financial institutions such as pension funds, play a role in this process because whereas a country whose currency was under pressure due to inflation would expect to see a massive outflow of capital unless it raised its interest rates significantly, this need take place on a much reduced scale if the capital is prevented from flowing out in the first place. A country with high interest rates somewhat oddly needs to prevent too much capital flowing in since this would drive the currency up against its upper limit and force a revaluation – the position faced by Spain at the time of entry to the EC.

The UK actually faced this dilemma when Nigel Lawson chose to shadow the DM early in 1988 since, in the absence of exchange controls, the high UK interest rates induced a huge inflow of hot money which Nigel Lawson tried to stem by reducing interest rates. The consumer spending boom which this action triggered eventually forced a major reversal of policy which is still working its way through the system, and it is hard to see other EC members rushing to repeat the UK experience by abolishing wholesale their capital controls. If the EMS is to remain as steady as before without capital controls in place then other members will have to keep their borrowing to finance personal consumption down to German levels and become less strike-prone in the pursuit of higher wages. This is going to be a difficult trick for the UK to pull off. However, the other members of the EC may not be rushing to meet Mrs Thatcher's conditions and she may be able to justify her reluctance to join the EMS, let alone the EMU, by reference to, for example, the refusal by other EC members to let their financial intermediaries face open competition with the very competitive – and hence cheap – services available in the UK.

Protectionism

Forms of protectionism

Protectionism has recently become a matter of controversy because of the difficulties which the US government has had in reducing its enormous BoP deficit by more acceptable means. All countries, including, as we have noted above, the UK, operate some protectionist policies, but it is fair to say that the UK has been one of the less protectionist-minded of the industrial countries throughout the 1980s. However, protectionism is something of a negative-sum game, in that once the process is set in motion in one country its main trading partners usually respond with offsetting measures of their own, thereby causing all of them to lose out. It is, therefore, possible that the UK will be drawn into protectionism if it is instigated elsewhere on a sufficiently large scale.

Until fairly recently the commonest form of protectionism was the **tariff**, which is a tax imposed on imports either as a lump sum or as a percentage of their value. This drives up domestic prices, which is not particularly desirable, but the government obtains an additional source of revenue to fund its expenditure and the illusion is given that the foreign exporter is suffering most because he is virtually forced to pay the tax.

Tariffs have been restricted because major industrial countries have agreed to abide by the GATT rules (see below) which greatly limit their use, but in any event their inflationary consequences are undesirable and can apparently be avoided by resort to other non-tariff barriers. Of these the commonest are **quotas**, which serve to limit the access of overseas producers to the domestic market. The quotas are generally fixed in terms of the number or value of imports to be permitted. Inflationary consequences might still arise if the importer takes advantage of the artificial shortage of the product to put up its price, in which case it is the private sector, rather than the government, which gets the extra revenue, but the government could obtain extra revenue by auctioning import licences. In recent years many countries have preferred to avoid overt confrontation by 'requesting' foreign governments to limit their exports of particular products. In the case of cars, for example, both the UK and USA have agreed import quotas with Japan during the 1980s (although it is argued in the UK case that this makes little difference to trade flows since Japanese cars are simply replaced by imports from the EC which cannot be quota restricted). Underlying such voluntary export restraints (VERs) is an unspoken threat of 'official' quotas if compliance if not adhered to. It is alleged that the Japanese impose unofficial quotas by requiring foreign products such as cars to meet specifications, for safety or other reasons, which they cannot meet without expensive modifications. The Japanese counter-argument is, naturally, that products of 'inferior' quality simply do not sell on their domestic market.

Occasionally certain imports and/or exports are embargoed (given a **zero quota**). This is usually to 'punish' a country, such as South Africa, which is pursuing domestic policies unacceptable to the wider political community. The present UK government has never favoured such methods of dealing with errant regimes, but irrespective of the moral issues it has to be said that embargoes are constantly being broken, perhaps because certain products are difficult to obtain from elsewhere.

A rather more subtle procedure is to **subsidise exports**. This obviously costs the government a good deal of money, but protects jobs and hence, indirectly, the **tax base of the domestic economy**. An industry which is subsidised almost everywhere is the shipbuilding industry, which has long suffered from chronic world overcapacity. These subsidies are more subtle in the sense that they can be disguised as regional development grants or 'infant industry' support. The UK also operates **export credit guarantees** which insure exporters against default by overseas buyers.

Finally, there is the possibility of introducing various forms of **exchange control**. Exchange controls operated in the UK until 1979. Such controls were philosophically incompatible with the free-market beliefs of the new Conservative government, and their abolition was the first major step along the path to widespread deregulation. However, there was also an underlying economic rationale to abolition. At the time, the balance of payments on current account was about to improve markedly as a result of North Sea oil coming on stream. This was bound to exert strong upward pressure on the exchange rate, and whilst the government did not wish to intervene to keep the rate down, it was realised that the abolition of exchange controls would result in a huge outflow of capital, mostly for long-term investment, and that this would help to limit the appreciation of sterling. Furthermore, there would be a net inflow of interest and dividends in later years.

Other major countries have followed the UK example, but there is still pressure in certain circles to reinstate exchange controls on the grounds that the capital being exported could be better used within the UK. Such controls could be reimposed in a variety of forms. In the past there have been controls both on capital inflows, for example by suspending the convertibility of foreign currency into sterling, and upon capital outflows, for example by routeing requests to obtain foreign currency via the central bank which has the right to refuse authorisation, or by refusing permission for private individuals to export capital other than in small amounts.

It is worth observing, by way of conclusion, that most of the forms of protection discussed above were developed during the era of fixed exchange rates. Obviously, if exports are uncompetitive, the simplest ways to deal with the problem in recent years have been to allow the currency to depreciate or to intervene to force down the exchange rate. This is much less likely to invite retaliation, although competitive depreciation is by no means unknown, but it has to be said that this policy can help only industries which are close to being competitive at the higher exchange rate. Where an industry, such as shipbuilding, is regularly being undercut by up to 50 per cent, selective assistance, whatever its merits, is the only solution if it is to survive.

Effects of protectionism

In a major review the OECD (1985) concluded that non-inflationary growth was being impeded by protectionism. The simple Keynesian model indicates that if one country refuses to buy the exports of another country, then the latter will suffer a reduction in its national income and hence reduce its own imports. The original country thus protects jobs in its industries previously losing out to import substitution, but suffers job losses in industries dependent upon exporting. One might have thought that this lesson was learned in the 1930s following the US Smoot–Hawley Tariff of 1930, but regrettably this is not the case. In the first place, the jobs saved by protectionism are more immediate and more visible than the jobs lost as exports subsequently suffer. Secondly, politicians are elected to represent specific areas, and are obliged to speak out strongly in favour of measures to protect jobs there in order to ensure their re-election. They are supported by local businessmen and trades unions, and form an effective political lobby, whereas consumers who would benefit from lower prices in unrestricted markets are poorly organised.

The GATT regulations on trade barriers are based upon 'reciprocity'. **First-difference recipro-**

city aims to reduce trade barriers through the requirement that a country provides a tariff reduction comparable in value to that introduced by a trading partner. In the USA, however, there has recently been a movement towards the principle of **full reciprocity** which requires equal access, which is measured by the balance of trade both overall and/or in specific sectors. A trade deficit is taken to be evidence of unequal access and to justify retaliation. The worst offender is, as usual, claimed to be Japan, and the UK government has also recently had cause to make representations about reciprocal access to financial markets in Japan. If this approach becomes more prevalent, the movement towards a more protectionist environment may become an unstoppable force. It is, perhaps, naive to point out that bilateral trade balances are rarely in equilibrium in the normal course of events, because even if the UK is in overall equilibrium it will almost certainly be in surplus with, for example, the USA whilst simultaneously in deficit with, for example, Japan. Indeed, the principle of comparative advantage should bring about precisely such an outcome. When all is said and done, the empirical economic evidence shows incontrovertibly that protectionism yields much greater costs than benefits, both in the short and long term.

This may not, however, be sufficient to prevent the reappearance of protectionism for the reasons cited above, as has indeed been confirmed in 1989 by the ongoing dispute over growth hormones in meat. Hormones are used in livestock production in most non-EC meat producing countries, including the USA, but were banned in the EC in December 1985. Fedesa, the association representing the veterinary pharmaceutical industry in Europe, claimed that the ban was based on dubious scientific evidence and did not originally relate to hormones used in the USA, and the European Commission accepted privately that this was indeed the case. However, they claimed in public that it was an issue of consumer concern, and that the ban was applied in a non-discriminatory way in much the same way as the USA unilaterally introduced rigorous emission standards for cars.

The USA, in its turn claimed that the ban on hormones in meat (introduced on 1 January 1988 but one year later in the case of American meat) represented an unfair barrier to trade. Hence, although the ban affected only $120 mn of US exports, it responded by imposing a 100 per cent duty on an equal value on food imports from the EC (see *Financial Times*, 20 December 1988 for details). The EC immediately threatened counter-retaliation of equal value, but held back temporarily from its implementation. With a total US/EC trade of $160 bn at stake it is clearly not the value of the disputed products which is at issue, but whether the issue of principle can quickly be resolved is by no means clear. If it is not, then protectionism may quickly escalate to other traded products.

Reciprocity

At the present time the European Commission is not intent upon demanding full reciprocity, but rather a guarantee of similar – or at least non-discriminatory – opportunities for EC companies to operate in foreign markets on the same basis as local companies.

Reciprocity in financial services

The issue of what precisely is meant by 'reciprocal access' to foreign markets has recently arisen in the specific area of financial services. During early 1988 the UK government prevented the Japanese from becoming gilt-edged dealers in order to pressurise Japan into granting Stock Exchange membership to UK firms which had been excluded for over a year. In July the UK authorised the Japanese without obtaining a reciprocal concession, but this may be regarded as a muscle-flexing exercise before the real reciprocity debate got going within the EC.

The EC proposes shortly to legislate proposals contained in the directives on banking and investment services, which make it a condition for access to EC markets by non-EC banks and security houses that their home markets be opened up on a reciprocal basis to EC institutions. Somewhat oddly, in the light of the dispute with Japan cited above, the UK is demanding that these reciprocity

provisions be removed from the directives before it is willing to approve them. The government's position is that these provisions are protectionist – and, more importantly, since reciprocity will have to be administered centrally from Brussels, domestic control over London's financial markets will be seriously eroded. The UK's concern arises from the fact that, with some 400 foreign banks and 120 foreign securities houses based in London, any reciprocity dispute within the EC will sooner or later spill over into London, even if no UK institutions are directly involved.

The UK's financial services legislation contains reciprocity provisions such as those used to lean on the Japanese, and there is clearly some benefit to be gained were the EC to use reciprocity provisions as a bargaining lever in trade discussions at GATT. Furthermore, it is hard to see how there can ever be a single European market unless it is administered centrally in Brussels, since it will otherwise prove possible for a non-EC bank, prevented by an unresolved reciprocity dispute from access to the EC by setting itself up in Denmark, from accessing the EC via relocation to the UK. Since it happens to be the case that most foreign banks and securities houses are already established in the EC, the Commission has decided that exceptionally, in the specific case of banking, the reciprocity provision should be applied only to a limited number of newcomers, with already established foreign banks having the same access rights as EC banks. However, this leaves unresolved the question as to how to deal with an EC-based foreign company which decides to enter banking for the first time. These quibbles may ultimately prove to be less important, given the almost certain continuation of London's dominant role in providing financial services in the EC, than the Bank of England's attitude to the potential take-over of UK banks. In a single European market any EC institution will have the right to bid for a UK bank. Such a move would currently be vetoed by the Bank, and it is clearly in no rush to make any pronouncements on this matter.

Whether the Commission will require retrospective reciprocity in non-banking fields is as yet undecided, but there seems little doubt that reciprocity provisions will be included in all directives, the UK's reluctance notwithstanding. However, one likely path through this minefield will involve allowing EC members to vary the terms of reciprocity on an individual basis, and for certain LDCs to be exempt from reciprocity as Brussels sees fit.

General Agreement on Tariffs and Trade (GATT)

GATT was originally signed in 1947 by 23 countries (currently 100) determined to avoid a repetition of the worst consequences of protectionism evidenced during the 1930s. Its aims were to reduce existing barriers to free trade (but excluding agriculture and services, which are not covered); to eliminate trade discrimination; and to curb the reintroduction of protectionist measures by requiring member countries to consult together prior to such action. A critical principle was the **'most-favoured-nation' clause**, whereby any member country offering a tariff reduction to another country was obliged to offer the same reduction to all other member countries.

It may be argued that the oddest thing about GATT was the need for anyone to join. Given that members already accepted the principle that more trade was better than less trade, it had to be in their mutual self-interest to lower tariff barriers. The necessity to treat a tariff reduction as a concession requiring reciprocity would seem to be redundant when self-interest dictates that tariff reductions should anyway be pursued, since bilateral tariff reductions should be taking place in the absence of reciprocity conditions. However, as discussed above, the economic virtues of free trade are not always self-evident to interest groups when domestic industries are being 'destroyed' by imports, so governments needed to counteract this by reference to their obligations to maintain GATT rules. In any event, governments have always been afraid of appearing to be weak when allowing competitors free access to their markets in the absence of publically-stated reciprocity. In this respect the attitude of the present UK government is interesting, since it continues to play the reciprocity game even though, according to its economic philosophy, reciprocity cannot be a precondition for trade.

GATT therefore exists as a precaution against the facile adoption of the 'imports are bad, exports are good' creed, a creed which is intuitively appealing to the proverbial man-in-the-street. A virtue of the most-favoured-nation clause in this respect is that if a tariff is raised against one competitor it has to be raised against them all, thereby greatly increasing the risk of retaliation – an argument which the government can fall back on when pressed to protect a specific bilateral trade. This is bolstered by the principle of reciprocity, since it becomes possible to counter the argument that tariff reductions will damage domestic industries with the claim that benefits of equal value will accrue to exporting industries.

GATT and protectionism

The move towards protectionism discussed above obviously threatens the foundations on which GATT is built. For several years now many countried have been busy negotiating bilateral agreements to the detriment of excluded countries. The Uraguay Round of trade talks, initiated at the end of 1986, has done little to stem the tide, with 23 new non-tariff barriers coming into force in the six months subsequent to the start of the latest round of discussions in late 1987. One obvious difficulty is that the GATT secretariat has no resources to dispose to support its powers of persuasion, nor indeed any real functions other than adverse publicity, so it is obliged to fall back upon its stature as a body which exists to foster free trade without favour to any individual country. The trouble then, however, is that too-overt criticism of countries which are abusing the rules is likely to send their representatives scuttling home claiming unfair discrimination.

The trickiest question currently being addressed concerns bilateral agreements which are advocated on the grounds that they promote free trade between the signatories. A recent example is the agreement signed between the USA and Canada in 1988. The outcome is likely to be that the USA will buy certain products from Canada which were previously acquired from more expensive domestic sources. However, there is no most-favoured-nation clause which requires the treatment accorded to the most favoured trading partner to be made available to others, and it therefore follows that other products will be bought from Canada rather than, say, the UK, since they will now be cheaper from the former source on a tariff-free basis. This simply serves to divert trade rather than to create it, and indeed may result in the purchase of tariff-free products from an inefficient source being substituted for tariff-bearing products from a more efficient source.

The US–Canada trade zone is, fortunately, not dissimilar in its effects to the EC which has served more to create trade than to divert it, and it keeps to most of the GATT rules insofar as it covers 'substantially all trade' and does not result in the raising of tariff barriers against other countries.

At the end of the day, it all comes down to whether or not the US–Canada agreement is to be regarded as a special case, given that there is a clear benefit to Canada (though somewhat less to the USA). If the USA were to extend this type of agreement to other parts of the world, which it clearly has the economic muscle to do, then trade-diverting agreements may become the norm, with the destruction of GATT an almost certain consequence. The outgoing US administration promised not to do so – but its successor may hold other views.

Where the UK does fall into line with the USA is in feeling that GATT has gone too far along the road of permitting LDCs to be exempted from reciprocity in their trade relations with the industrialised nations. On the face of it, it is understandable that concessions were originally made, since free access to the markets of the developed countries without the need for reciprocity appeared to guarantee an improvement in the balance of payments of the LDCs. However, it is unclear whether the LDCs actually benefit from their ability to produce goods domestically at much higher prices than they could have been obtained from elsewhere in the absence of tariffs, and it has left their export industries very vulnerable to the possibility that the industrialised nations will lose patience and impose reciprocal tariffs. In return for their compliance, the LDCs should be entitled to demand concessions on discriminatory non-tariff barriers such as the Multifibre Arrangement.

Anti-dumping suits

Faced with breaking GATT rules if they are overtly protectionist, both the EC and the USA have increasingly resorted to a subtler, but no less effective, means of curbing Japanese and South Korean imports. The method is to threaten to take the exporters to court in an **anti-dumping suit.** It is true that the number of such cases actually investigated by the EC fell from 82 in 1984 to 62 in 1987, but the value of the products subjected to anti-dumping duties has risen dramatically. In 1988 such duties have been imposed on Japanese photo-copiers, Japanese printers and Japanese and South Korean video-cassette recorders. Under GATT's anti-dumping code 'dumping' is held to occur when a good is sold abroad at a price lower than that charged by the exporter for the same good in his home market, and it is permissible to impose penalties where deliberate underpricing is causing or threatening to cause 'material injury' to producers in the importing countries. When in August 1988 the European Commission imposed duties on imported video-cassette recorders, its justification was that unless Europe could remain conversant with the technology it would lose the ability to develop new high-tech products. Whilst this may be a legitimate aim of industrial policy, one can understand why the Japanese promptly complained to GATT's anti-dumping committee that it could be regarded as evidence of dumping only by stretching GATT rules well beyond breaking point. Much the same could be said about duties levied in April 1988 on typewriters and scales actually assembled in Europe by Japanese companies, which the European Commission claimed was simply a device to dodge the duties.

The Japanese, since joining GATT in 1955, have never yet taken a case to arbitration, but if the EC follow up typewriters with similar duties on other products, they may be forced to proceed. Meanwhile, the EC is keeping one move ahead by introducing additional penalties where anti-dumping duties are not added to the price of the goods in question, and looking into the possibility of extending duties to services.

Unless the Japanese, or some other country, try to force the issue of dumping out into the open, the inherent ambiguity of the GATT code will allow virtually any action to be deemed 'justification' by that code. It is generally accepted that a duty can be levied where an import is sold at less than its price in the country of manufacture – called 'fair value' in the code. Where, however, a country such as South Korea deliberately holds down the value of its currency, its exports are bound to seem cheap in Europe, and this is not the same thing as dumping. Equally the GATT code contains no provisions about assembly operations abroad.

The US omnibus trade bill, originally vetoed by President Reagan in May 1988, but receiving his signature in a virtually unchanged form in August as the Omnibus Trade and Competitiveness Act 1988, is not merely directed at trade with the Far East but with any countries persistently in surplus with the USA, which puts the EC second on the list. The Act cites a whole range of circumstances which will automatically trigger US sanctions. Whether, however, the EC is itself going to be penalised for dumping goods in the USA has yet to be seen.

The image of 'Fortress Europe' created by US–EC quarrelling does, however, tend to distract attention away from the fact that, if Fortress Europe is indeed to be created, its ramparts will be much higher on the side facing East than on that facing West (see B. Hindley, *Financial Times*, 6 January 1989, p. 9). The EC denies that this either is, or will be, the case, citing the fact that whereas more than 390 anti-dumping investigations have been opened since 1980, only 27 concerned Japan and in only 4 cases were significant duties imposed (ball-bearings, electronic typewriters, photocopiers and printers). Furthermore, in three other cases (titanium, microwave ovens and cellular mobile radio telephones) no action was taken (see letters, *Financial Times*, 19 January 1989). However, it is widely believed that in circumstances such as dealing with products with high distribution costs, EC rules contain a structural bias towards finding dumping. This is not an issue of interpretation

since the European Court of Justice has recently confirmed that the rules are being correctly applied, and indeed the legislation has itself been clarified. Unfortunately, the issues are much too technical to permit the debate to involve the public at large so the EC is unlikely to be persuaded to change its stance on the matter.

UK/EC budgetary relationships

The EC Budget relies, apart from periodic intergovernmental agreements (IGAs), upon its 'own resources' (see **p. 123**). Until recently these comprised duties and levies on imports from non-members of the EC (net of a 10 per cent contribution to cover collection and administrations costs), together with a gross share of each member's VAT proceeds (raised from 1 per cent to 1.4 per cent in January 1986). These are itemised as UK debits in **Table 5.3.** In return for these each country receives credits, primarily from the European Agricultural Guarantee and Guidance Fund (EAGGF), the Social Fund and the Regional Development Fund. The difference between debits and credits constitutes the UK's net contribution to the EC Budget.

However, as can be seen from **Table 5.3**, if this difference is expressed gross of any refunds and abatements then it is extremely large in the case of the UK (approximately £3 bn in 1987). This arises both because duties and levies are boosted by the UK's relatively heavy dependence on non-EC imports, and also because the UK's relatively efficient agricultural sector attracts only modest levels of support. In 1979 debits were 2.5 times as large as credits, and the net contribution amounted to almost £1 bn. As a consequence the UK government sought, and obtained, agreement for a series of annual refunds, based upon the UK's excess net contributions to EC Budgets in earlier years. In addition, certain relatively modest adjustments were made with respect to previous years' gross contributions. These amounted to ECU 1 bn (£583 mn) in 1985, a figure agreed at the June 1984 Fontainebleau Summit. The agreed rule governing the calculation of this figure was that the refund should equal two-thirds of the difference

Table 5.3   *General government transactions with the institutions of the European Community (£mn)*[1]

	1977	1978	1979	1980	1981	1982	1983	1984	1985	1986	1987	1988
EUROPEAN COMMUNITY BUDGET												
UK CREDITS												
Services	78	94	115	112	122	150	148	186	157	157	127	86
Transfers												
EAGGF	181	329	371	550	683	791	1 082	1 353	1 203	1 385	1 344	1 379
Social Fund	48	63	87	95	107	152	128	283	256	335	428	277
Regional Development Fund	60	35	71	173	145	111	139	184	274	298	404	370
Negotiated refunds[2]	—	—	—	98	693	1 019	807	528	61	—	—	—
Other	1	5	14	34	27	36	24	11	16	41	32	75
TOTAL	368	526	658	1 062	1 777	2 259	2 328	2 545	1 967	2 216	2 335	2 187
UK DEBITS												
Transfers												
Agriculture and sugar levies	154	242	246	260	218	307	232	260	189	244	354	226
Customs protective duties	613	714	868	861	861	1 001	1 075	1 276	1 291	1 244	1 417	1 521
GNP financial contribution	—	596	—	—	—	—	—	—	—	—	—	—
Budget adjustments[3]	− 30	− 204	− 352	− 95	—	—	—	—	—	—	—	—
VAT-gross before abatement/ adjustments	—	—	844	728	960	1 497	1 712	1 720	1 945	2 742	3 347	2 886[4]
Abatement[2]	—	—	—	—	—	—	—	—	− 166	− 1 701	− 1 153	− 1 595
Adjustments[3]	—	—	—	13	135	57	− 43	− 55	145	263	84	− 127
Inter-governmental agreements	—	—	—	—	—	—	—	—	370	—	—	613
TOTAL	737	1 348	1 606	1 767	2 174	2 862	2 976	3 201	3 774	2 792	4 049	3 525
BALANCE	− 369	− 822	− 948	− 705	− 397	− 603	− 648	− 656	− 1 807	− 576	− 1 714	− 1 338

Notes:
[1] For all years sterling figures reflect actual payments made during the year, not payments in respect of particular Budgets.
[2] Refunds and abatements received in respect of the UK's excess net contributions to EC Budgets in earlier years.
[3] Adjustments reflecting reassessments of the gross contributions required for the EC Budgets for the previous years.
[4] Including VAT adjustment.
Source: CSO, 'Pink Book' 1989.

between UK VAT receipts passed over to the EC and EC payments to the UK. The rule has recently ben amended, but in such a way as to yield the same refund were the old rule to be applied. UK refunds are contributed by all other EC members in equal proportion to their share in EC GNP (but West Germany pays only two-thirds of the relevant figure). These refunds are no longer accounted for as a credit, but, as shown in Table 5.3, are entered as an **abatement on the debit side of the accounts**.

Agriculture

Whilst agriculture is a domestic industry, and could therefore be discussed in the context of Chapter 8, most of the issues which it raises are concerned with relationships both within the EC and between the EC and other trading blocs. It raises issues of protectionism and involves GATT, and this section has, therefore, been placed in its entirety alongside the sections which deal with the latter topics.

The markets for agricultural products operate poorly in the absence of intervention. Demand tends to grow slowly over time, both because population growth in developed countries is very low, and because as incomes rise the extra money does not get spent on agricultural produce. Supply, however, grows rapidly as a consequence of mechanisation, improved crop strains and the intensive use of fertilisers. In a free market these forces would anyway tend to drive down prices — and hence also farmers' incomes — but the situation is further compounded by the unpredictable effects of climate conditions and the small size of individual farms in relation to total supply, which conspire to leave farmers with very little control over the prices of their products.

Rationale for intervention

In practice, the governments of developed countries have, with few exceptions, been unwilling to let agricultural prices be determined by the forces of the free market during the postwar period. The rationale for intervention has taken a variety of forms, including the contribution of the sector to employment and to the balance of payments; the need for security of food supply in the event of external aggression; the need to protect the rural way of life; and the need to ensure delivery of the rural vote. Whilst many of these justifications currently have an archaic ring about them it must be recognised that, once a pressure group has been built up to keep them in the public eye, it becomes very difficult to persuade the public that they are no longer relevant.

Broadly speaking, farmers in any single domestic market, such as the UK, can be protected against the forces of the free market either by paying them subsidies, or by erecting a wall around the domestic market through which imports cannot pass at prices which undercut domestic suppliers. Given

that the UK had traditional obligations towards the Commonwealth, which included the freedom for Commonwealth countries to export to the UK, the widespread use of tariff barriers or quotas was considered to be inappropriate, and those UK farmers who could not match import prices were therefore paid a subsidy known as a **deficiency payment**. The burden of financing such a payment fell upon the taxpayer, and not upon the consumer who paid a shop price based upon the costs of the cheapest world suppliers. As agricultural productivity rose, and world prices accordingly fell, the deficiency payments scheme became increasingly burdensome, and the government began to toy with the use of tariffs and quotas.

The supremacy of the latter form of protection came with the devising of the Common Agricultural Policy (CAP) in 1958 by the original six members of the EEC. At the time UK agriculture was considerably more efficient than its continental counterparts, in good part because the system of inheritance whereby land had been handed down to the eldest son rather than dispersed among all male children, as was the custom in, for example, France, had kept land holdings intact. Furthermore, UK farmers were used to competing in the open market unprotected by tariffs. As a consequence, a much smaller proportion of the UK population was employed in agriculture in 1960 than in continental Europe.

The objectives set out for the CAP under article 39 of the Treaty of Rome were not, of themselves, incompatible with the objectives of UK agricultural policy. They were (1) to increase agricultural productivity by promoting technical progress, and by ensuring the rational development of agricultural production and the optimum utilisation of the factors of production, in particular labour. (2) To ensure a fair standard of living for the agricultural community, in particular by increasing the individual earnings of persons engaged in agriculture. (3) To stabilise markets. (4) To guarantee the availability of supplies. (5) To ensure reasonable consumer prices. However, their implementation over the ensuing decade did create certain incompatibilities with UK practice, in particular the much greater emphasis upon import controls and, as a consequence, the payment by the consumer in the shop of a price sufficient to cover the full costs of operating the CAP.

It should be borne in mind that at the time of its inception the CAP was not expected to generate huge surpluses with their attendant difficulties. The reason for the rather dreadful mess in which it currently finds itself is that the EC sought to respond to the developing crisis of overproduction in a piecemeal way. It never sat down and tried to rethink the CAP from first principles in the light of the changes which had occurred in agricultural markets during the 1970s and 1980s. Hence reform has always been too little, too late.

Since 1958 the EC has acquired a further six members, amongst them the UK. Not surprisingly, the history of agriculture in the UK has created major disparities between the UK and other members, especially the most recent who have not as yet enjoyed even the limited attempts at restructuring directed at the original six. This can be seen from **Table 5.4** which gives data for six representative members; all 12 current members; and the 10 who were the members until 1989. Of the six members noted, only West Germany has an agricultural sector as insignificant in relation to its GDP as the UK. Nevertheless, it is twice as important in employment terms as that of the UK. The UK's total Utilised Agricultural Area (UAA) is reasonably large, but the number of farms in relation to that UAA is exceptionally low (less than 3 per cent of total EC farms, but covering 14 per cent of its UAA). This means that the typical UK farm is five times as large as the EC average, and over twice as large as that of any individual EC member.

Price support

The system of price support has two distinct strands, one applicable to EC products and the other to imports. At the apex of the price pyramid for EC products sits the **target** price, which is in theory the ideal farm-gate price negotiated annually by the Council of Agricultural Ministers. For certain products the terms 'guide', 'norm' or 'basic' price are also used. In practice, a product price will rise to its target level only at a time of great shortage, so target prices have little operational meaning. Of greater importance is the **intervention** price, which is the lowest level to which product prices are permitted to fall before the relevant intervention agency is obliged to buy in all surplus supply. This price is fixed annually as a percentage of the target price by the Council of Ministers on an individual product basis. Payments are delayed to discourage selling into intervention.

Table 5.4   *Comparative agricultural data in the EC*

	EUR 10	EUR 12	UK	FGR	FR	DK	IT	S
UAA[1] (m.ha) (1985)	100.8	132.5	18.6	12.0	31.3	2.8	17.5	27.3
% Agriculture GDP (1984)	3.7	3.9	2.2	2.0	4.0	5.5	6.1	5.7
% Employment (1985)	7.2	8.6	2.6	5.6	7.6	7.1	11.2	16.9
No. of farms (000) (1983)	6 516	9 103	262	768	1 130	99	2 832	2 213
UAA per holding (ha) (1983)	13.6	12.7	64.4	15.5	24.5	28.8	5.6	12.9

Note:
[1] Utilised Agricultural Area.
Source: Eurostat.

Should producers be willing to export they are paid a subsidy, equal to the difference between the world price and the EC market price, in the form of an **export restitution**. The total cost of these subsidies is approximately twice that of storing products bought into intervention.

The position for imports is that, almost without exception, they must be sold in the EC at a **threshold** price which is equivalent to the target price. The minimum price at which non-EC products can be imported into the EC is known as the **reference** or **sluice-gate** price, and to this is added a **variable levy** in order to bring the actual import price (which may exceed the reference price) up to the threshold price. All proceeds from the variable levy are paid into the EAGGF, (often identified by its equivalent French initials as FEOGA) which uses roughly 95 per cent of the proceeds in order to fund intervention buying and export restitution payments (guarantees). The remaining 5 per cent is spent on guidance, largely to finance structural improvements. Guidance spending is discretionary, and EC funds usually have to be matched by recipient countries.

Since the inception of the CAP, the proportion of agricultural produce which has attracted some degree of price support has risen inexorably, and currently stands at roughly 90 per cent. However, it is significant that over 50 per cent of all price support expenditure goes upon milk, cereals and beef and veal, and that sugar and oils each attract just under 10 per cent each. This arises because all of these products are automatically bought into intervention. They represent almost 50 per cent of all output. The other 50 per cent attracts only 25 per cent of support spending, among which certain products – for example, table wine – attract support in some form or another, whilst other products – particularly fruit and vegetables, eggs and poultry and flowers – are assisted only by the existence of the variable levy. Direct income support is used only at a modest level for small farmers producing specified products.

It can be seen that intervention buying applies predominantly to products originating in northern Europe, and whilst guidance expenditure is directed largely to the more southerly members, the disparity between the guarantee and guidance funds represents a strong bias in favour of northern members.

Green money and MCAs

At the inception of the CAP it was intended that agricultural products should have a **common price throughout the EC**. In a world of fixed exchange rates and zero inflation it is clearly possible to fix the price of, for example, wheat in several currencies, and to keep those prices constant for evermore. However, where exchange rates are subject to adjustment, and where different countries suffer different rates of inflation, common prices can be maintained only through the introduction of a complicated adjustment mechanism.

Agricultural products in the EC are priced in **ECUs**. These are converted into a number of units of a national currency at the prevailing exchange rate between that currency and the ECU, and the farmer then receives as payment the appropriate amount of his domestic currency. But if that currency is devalued against the ECU, then the farmer ends up with more of his domestic currency than before (less in the case of a revaluation) even though the price in ECUs has not altered. It was in order to avoid this outcome that 'green' money was introduced.

Suppose, for illustrative purposes, that 1 ECU = 5 Francs = 0.50p. A product priced at 10 ECU per tonne would be worth 50 Francs and £5 respectively. But were the £ to be revalued to 1 ECU = 40p, then the UK farmer would end up with £4 per tonne, £1 per tonne less than before. In order to maintain his income at the previous level he has to be paid at 1 ECU = 0.50p, but this is no longer the market rate but an artificial 'green' rate, introduced specifically in order to prevent farmers' incomes becoming subject to undesirable volatility.

Unfortunately, this is not the end of the adjustment process, because the French farmer will realise that, at the green exchange rate, he can sell his tonne of wheat in the UK for £5, which he can subsequently convert back into Francs at the rate of 40p = 5 Francs in the open market. He thus ends up with 62.5 Francs per tonne, a windfall profit of

25 per cent. The UK farmer, on the other hand, were he to sell in France, would obtain 50 Francs per tonne which, converted into sterling at the market exchange rate, is worth only £4, 20 per cent less than he can obtain on the domestic market.

Assuming that the £ alone had revalued, every other EC member's farmers would obviously rush to sell everything they produced either on the UK market or into intervention in the UK. In order to prevent this **Monetary Compensatory Amounts** (MCAs) are employed in order either to tax products moving from a low-price to a high-price market, or to subsidise products moving in the opposite direction. In our example, a tax of 25 Francs per tonne would be applied to French exports to the UK, and a subsidy of £1 paid on UK exports to France. MCAs are normally adjusted during the annual price review, but any adjustment requires unanimous support.

This messy adjustment is further complicated by the fact that in order to differentiate between products there are five green rates. Whilst the ultimate objective of stabilising prices for farmers in different countries may approximately be achieved, the need for reform is pressing. It is impractical to foresee green rates diverging from market rates by ever-increasing amounts. Furthermore, there is a good deal of cross-border smuggling in order to avoid MCA taxes. The critical issue is, however, that the concept of a single European market is incompatible with market exchange rates operating in certain sectors of the economy at a time when artificial ones operate in other sectors such as agriculture. The European Commission is intent upon abolishing green rates and MCAs by 1992, but has as yet made little progress in this respect. This is hardly surprising since, by implication, abolition would make price fixing a market rather than a politically administered process, and would result in potentially sharp fluctuations in retail food prices.

Mountains and lakes

In the UK, between 1975 and 1985, disposable incomes, prices in general and processed prices in

particular rose at an almost identical rate. However, starting in 1978, farm-gate prices began to lag behind. This meant that the only way for farmers to maintain their incomes was to raise their output, which in turn meant more-intensive use of fertilisers. However, the latter rose in price much faster than end-products, partly because of their oil-based content, and the ratio of producer prices to input prices fell sharply, both in the UK and in the EC as a whole, as depicted in **Table 5.5**.

Table 5.5   *'Cost–price squeeze', ratio of producer prices to input prices*[1]

	1973	1981	1982	1983	1984	1985
UK	119.8	101.4	100.3	97.5	95.5	92.4
EUR 10	116.7	97.9	98.6	96.6	94.4	94.6

Note:
[1] This is calculated by dividing changes in the deflated index prices of the value of final agricultural production by changes in the deflated index prices of the value of inputs.
Source: Eurostat.

This has had a number of consequences. In the first place, farmers' incomes, as officially recorded, have failed to keep pace with incomes in other sectors. However, it is important to note in this respect that very few studies have ever been done on agricultural incomes, so there is great uncertainty about the validity of income comparisons; that those studies which exist indicate that farmers' incomes (though not those of their labourers) were on average well above the average for the whole economy before 1980 (although a large part of these incomes is a return on the ownership of land rather than on the farming of the land), and that the cost-price squeeze has served merely to reduce this differential somewhat; that the indiscriminate nature of price support means that large-scale farmers never have been, nor are likely to be, near the breadline. On average, the wealthiest 2.5 per cent of farmers receive $9,000 per year in subsidies from the CAP, whilst the other 75 per cent average only $1,000 per year; and that whilst small-scale farmers may earn only modest incomes from their farms, they generally have other sources of income, and in many cases farming is a secondary rather than a primary occupation. Whilst this should not be taken to imply that there is no such thing as a poor farmer, it is clear that no-one really knows how to identify which farmers genuinely need help and which could survive quite happily with a reduced level of price support, or even with none at all.

In the second place, there is the problem of vast overproduction, and this in turn creates a major problem of storage. In early 1987, for example, EC butter stocks exceeded 1.3 mn tonnes, and those of skimmed milk powder just under 1 mn tonnes. In practice, these stocks can be disposed of only at prices well below those paid to buy them into intervention, and this difference is an immense strain upon the EC Budget. In response to the 'butter mountain', the EC was obliged to sell over 500,000 tonnes to non-EC markets, 400,000 tonnes to the animal feed industry and 50,000 tonnes to be turned ito concentrated butter. A further disposal of 100,000 tonnes to the USSR is also underway. As a result of these operations, and similar ones for skimmed milk, there is currently 'only' 300,000 tonnes of butter and 40,000 tonnes of skimmed milk in storage. However, the exercise cost ECU 3.2 bn (£2.1 bn), to be paid back in equal instalments out of the EC own resources between 1989 and 1993, and that excludes the latest sale to the USSR.

Unfortunately, it has not been possible to reduce stocks of all products in this way. Whilst EC cereal stocks, already relatively low because of the poor harvest in 1987, are bound to benefit further from the recent severe drought in the USA, stocks of beef and wine are still building up. Between June 1987 and June 1988 beef stocks rose from 637,000 to 760,000 tonnes, which is likely to lead to a forced sale of 200,000 tonnes to the USSR at another huge loss, but meanwhile beef keeps pouring into intervention. The level of beef stocks is hardly surprising since the introduction of milk quotas resulted in a wide-scale slaughter of cows no longer required for their milk. However, there is at least a fairly ready market for cheap beef, which is more than can be said for undrinkable wine. Between 1983 and 1988 the EC paid out ECU 2 bn in order to turn unwanted wine into industrial alcohol. The resultant 750 mn litre lake of alcohol now sits awaiting customers, but to generate these the EC has had to budget ECU 660 mn for sales promotion by the end of 1989.

Finally, it should be noted that attempts to raise crop yields have also done a great deal of damage to the environment. Excessive use of chemical fertilisers has long been a particular cause for concern, and the need to enlarge farms in order to permit mechanisation has produced a major change in the face of the countryside, which few outside farming circles regard as an improvement.

Quotas

The need to reform the CAP was evident even prior to the entry of the UK. As long ago as 1969 incentive payments were being offered for cows to be reared for beef rather than for milk. Sugar quotas were introduced in 1976, and in 1977 milk production was subjected to a co-responsibility levy which taxed production in excess of quotas in order to help pay for its disposal.

An approach which particularly affected UK farmers was the introduction of **quotas on milk production** in 1984. At the time 30 per cent of EAGGF guarantee spending was on milk products. What was really needed was a price reduction of over 10 per cent to discourage output, but as usual the solution was to tackle the symptoms via a quota rather than effect a cure via a price reduction. Quotas work inefficiently because, for example, farmers with expensive machinery cannot afford to leave it lying idle, and therefore seek to buy quotas from other farmers. Whilst this helps to unfreeze arbitrary market shares, which ironically are largest for those farmers who started with the largest surpluses, it often results in a farmer's milk quotas becoming more valuable than the land which he farms. Furthermore, cows no longer wanted for their milk will be slaughtered for beef, thereby adding to the beef mountain. The 1984 quotas, in practice, achieved very little, but a tougher set introduced in December 1986, combined with harsher penalties on overproduction, effected a noticeable improvrment, with farmers willing to pay up to 50p per litre for unused quotas in order to avoid the penalties. Nevertheless, the combined costs of subsidising surplus production, of subsidising exports and of paying for the disposal of surpluses, remain very large.

Recent EC Budget negotiations

The 1988 EC Budget negotiations were, as usual, conducted in an atmosphere of impending crisis. On this occasion, however, there was clear evidence that previous measures to reduce both the degree of price support, and also surplus production, had failed to rein back expenditure on the CAP. In 1975 the EC Budget amounted to ECU 6.5 bn, of which ECU 4.5 bn went to the EAGGF. By 1980 the respective figures were ECU 16.3 bn and ECU 11.3 bn, subsequently rising to ECU 28 bn and ECU 19.7 bn respectively in 1985. In each case the percentage allocated to the EAGGF was 70 per cent. By 1987 the EAGGF allocation had risen to ECU 22.8 bn, but this represented only 63.5 per cent of the total Budget of ECU 36 bn, with an enlarged share of 18.3 per cent allocated to the Regional and Social Fund.

In the course of the 1988 negotiations, concern was expressed that the Budget should continue to be readjusted towards regional and social spending, and within the EAGGF towards structural support. These aims will be quite difficult to implement in practice given that, first, allocations to the CAP are the only obligatory element in the EC Budget, and secondly that the Council of Agricultural Ministers, backed by the business interests dependent upon agriculture, have a strong vested interest in maintaining the status quo. Nevertheless, the package put forward by M. Delors included a proposal to double the Regional and Social Fund by 1992. The other significant proposals were (1) to substitute a percentage of each member's GNP for a percentage of its VAT, thereby ensuring that economic growth would deliver increased revenue. (2) To restrict EAGGF growth to a maximum of 75 per cent of the Budget growth, thereby reducing its share of the total to 50 per cent by 1992 (ECU 26 bn out of a total Budget of ECU 52.1 bn). (3) To limit the full intervention price for cereals to a total output of 155 million tonnes, which if exceeded would trigger a price reduction of 3 per cent in 1989 (a policy known as a budget 'stabiliser'). (4) To exempt small farmers from co-responsibility levies.

A Summit was called in February 1988 to discuss these proposals, and for once Mrs Thatcher was obliged to make significant concessions. It was agreed, with retrospective effect as from 1 January 1988, that the EAGGF growth rate would be limited to 74 per cent of the annual growth of EC GNP in volume terms; 'that the Budget should absorb no more than 1.2 per cent of the EC GNP; that the VAT base of each member would be capped at 55 per cent of it GNP, with the continuation of the ceiling of 1.4 per cent of VAT proceeds to be given over; that a fourth source of revenue should be introduced based on shares in GNP, the rate levied to be that which is required, given all other revenue, to balance the Budget;[3] that a production levy of 3 per cent would be placed on cereal production, at the beginning of each year up to 1992, which would be reimbursed only if total output fell below a ceiling of 160 million tonnes (with small farmers exempted), and that if this figure was exceeded the price in the following year would be reduced by 3 per cent; that a similar scheme would be applied to oil seeds; and that farmers agreeing to take land out of production for five years would receive set-aside payments of between ECU 100–600 per hectare by way of compensation, provided at least 20 per cent of arable land was set aside and also not reutilised as grazing.

ECU 600 mn was allocated for set-aside payments up to 1992, enough to fund 2 million hectares, representing only 1.5 per cent of the total UAA. The EAGGF was also to be rebalanced, with 50 per cent of the funds being used for structural purposes by 1992, and with a greater proportion directed towards the less developed members of the EC.

These developments are unlikely to achieve all that much in practice. The set-aside scheme is too modest to have any real impact, and may be neutralised by more intensive use of the remaining UAA. If so, the production levy will become a permanent feature of life, since it will take a very poor cereals harvest to keep below the levy threshold, and this will exert downwards pressure upon farmers' incomes. This, in turn, is likely to lead to pressure to adjust green rates which, as in the case of the UK, are seriously out of line with market rates. By devaluing the green pound a product priced in ECUs becomes worth more when converted to £ for payment to the farmer. However, all this juggling with prices is supposed to stop by 1992, by which time a coherent set of policies for meeting the objectives of the CAP is supposed to be in place. It is a brave man who is willing to bet on such an outcome.

Indeed, it may well turn out to be the case that the situation is further clouded by the use of **direct income support**. Direct income support has always been favoured by M. Delors on the grounds that it provides extra money for farmers without triggering overproduction. The UK position, on the other hand, has always been that this is simply another name for a social security scheme for farmers. Nevertheless, in January 1989, EC agriculture ministers agreed that member states should have the option to provide cash payments to farmers, and the West Germans are almost certain to take advantage of this provision. Since the UK Treasury must provide the bulk of the national contribution of up to £1,050 per farmer annually it is unlikely to want to follow suit, and UK farmers themselves may well reject such payments on the grounds that they do not want to be seen to receive even larger subsidies from UK taxpayers at this particular point in time.

There are those who believe that additional payouts to farmers can be made without increasing the burden to the taxpayer at all, which would resolve many of these difficulties. According to the EC Court of Auditors hundreds of millions of pounds, perhaps even in excess of £1 bn per annum, go to thieves and embezzlers rather than honest farmers. This arises because, for example, member states do not keep proper checks on whether traders actually export the quantity and quality of food for which they claim export subsidies, imports are incorrectly labelled in order to avoid import duties, and stocktaking at intervention stores is at best inadequate. Whilst the UK is by no means the worst offender in these respects, much could be done to save money both in the UK

and elsewhere in the EC by implementing proper control procedures.

The 1989 proposals, as yet unratified, appear to take a tough line in reining back agricultural support in the face of rising real farm incomes in the EC (but not in the UK). This looks to be less problematic than usual because of relatively buoyant world prices, caused in part by the 1988 drought. A target budget saving of ECU 31 mn is projected for 1989 through a package which reduces the period in the year during which purchases of cereals, oilseeds and protein products are guaranteed to four months by 1990/91; a price reduction of 5 per cent for sugar; a reduction in the minimum price of beans; unchanged prices for animal products including milk; and lower prices for citrus fruits withdrawn from the market.

Costs and benefits of agricultural reform

During 1988 several attempts were made to evalute the costs and benefits of world-wide agricultural reform. Of these, the report by the UK National Consumer Council (1988) made only a modest impact. However, that of the Canberra Centre for International Economics (1988), caused a considerable stir by virtue of the huge sums which it claimed could be saved by abolishing subsidies in developed countries. It was suggested that this would result in an annual windfall gain to LDCs of $26 bn, in addition to an annual reduction of $40 bn in the US budget deficit and of $42 bn in the US trade deficit. The effect in the EC would be to create around 3 million new jobs. Furthermore, in its latest report on agriculture the OECD (1988) calculated that, between 1979–81 and 1984–86, the overall cost of subsidising the agricultural sectors of OECD members had doubled to roughly ECU 200 bn (£132 bn), a sum vastly in excess of the same countries' aid to LDCs. The OECD also produced data on the total value of assistance to producers as a percentage of their total incomes, as shown in **Figure 5.3**. As can be seen the level of Producer Subsidy Equivalents (PSEs) is very close to the average at present, although previously the

Figure 5.3 *Producer subsidy equivalents[1], 1979–81 and 1984–86, %*

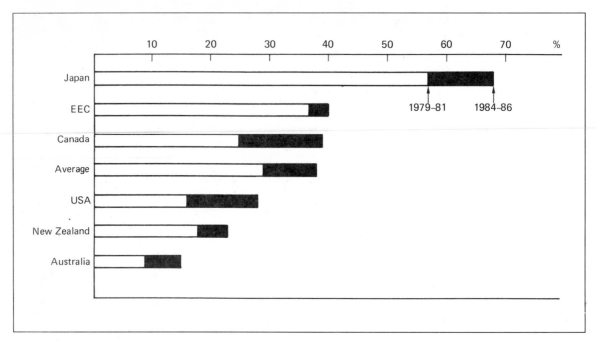

Note:

[1] A Producer Subsidy Equivalent (PSE) is defined by the OECD as 'the payment that would be required to compensate farmers for the loss of income resulting from the removal of a given policy measure. Expressed as a percentage, it represents that part of the value of output accounted for by assistance of various kinds'. A PSE cannot, however, incorporate intervention in the form of, for example, quotas which have no budgetary cost.

Source: OECD.

gap was much wider. It is also illuminating to examine the effects in individual product markets, about which a good deal is now known through, for example, *The World Development Report 1986*. In the case of cereals much the worst offender is Japan, where rice producers are paid over eight times the world price (see **Figure 5.4a**), whilst even that is dwarfed by the ratio of 14 times with respect to Japanese sugar (see **Figure 5.4b**). In addition, US farmers receive roughly three times the world price for sugar and butter, and EC farmers up to three times the world price for wheat, barley, butter and sugar. The EC subsidy from consumers and taxpayers to dairy farmers is currently around $400 per cow, yet this represents only just under half the equivalent figure in the USA.

Even a cursory glance at **Figures 5.4a** and **5.4b**

indicates that the situation has shown an underlying tendency to worsen during the 1980s, and this has led to increasingly urgent calls for the resolution of world-wide agricultural problems in a recognised international forum.

Reform through international co-operation

It was always clear that the withdrawal of agricultural subsidies would have to take place on a co-operative basis, but no forum existed for discussing how this was to be done. GATT, in particular, had rarely considered trade matters other than those pertaining to manufactured goods, but at its September 1986 meeting in Punte del Este in Uraguay, GATT members showed a new willingness to discuss the removal of subsidies which they were

Figure 5.4a *Price adjustment gap: cereals*[1]*;* **b** *Price adjustment gap: sugar*

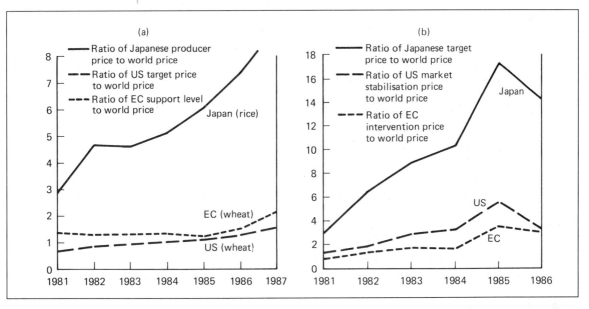

Note:

[1] These charts provide a rough measure of the potential 'adjustment gap' faced by producers, should their internal prices be reduced to world prices. Technical difficulties in calculation mean the 'gaps' are approximate.

Source: Department of Primary Industry, Australia, reproduced from *Economic Progress Report* (February 1988).

finding increasingly difficult to finance, and they also proved willing, in principle, to negotiate reductions in tariffs on foodstuffs. As a result, negotiations were set in hand to establish 'strengthened and more operationally effective GATT rules and disciplines' to cover 'all measures affecting import access and export competition'.

Subsequently, in May 1987, OECD ministers agreed a set of principles to guide reform, and these were endorsed by the Venice Economic Summit of G7 in June. The main points agreed (see *Economic Progress Report*, February 1988) were:

1. to allow market signals to influence agricultural production through a progressive and concerted reduction of agricultural support
2. the immediate need to prevent yet greater market imbalances, by reducing guaranteed prices and other production incentives
3. any production restrictions or other interventions in markets should be implemented in ways that allow markets to work better

4. low income farmers would best be helped through direct income support rather than price guarantees or output-related assistance
5. to promote the earliest possible progress in the GATT negotiations.

During 1987, in accordance with these objectives, both the two largest trading blocs, the USA and the EC, and also in particular a group of 13 major food-exporting countries called the Cairns Group (which includes Australia, Canada, Brazil and Argentina) submitted proposals for reform.

Unfortunately, those of the USA and the EC were not, and currently still are not, compatible. The USA opted for the 'zero solution' whereby, within 10 years, all subsidies and trade barriers were to be abolished other than those concerned with food aid to developing countries. The USA also advocated the introduction of 'production neutral' income compensation for farmers. The EC, however, opted for a more gradual approach with no specified targets either for the timetable or the extent of reform. Instead, the EC proposal highlighted the need for short-term reform of specified product markets such as cereals and sugar, but this was rejected outright by the USA until such time as the EC agreed a timetable for their zero solution. The Cairns Group attempted to float a compromise solution, but as yet neither the USA nor the EC has paid any attention. There are many reasons to explain their intransigence in the short term, including the view prevalent in the EC that the reforms so far achieved are not thought by the USA to have involved any real sacrifice.

At the present juncture there is little prospect for anything close to a full agreement between the USA and the EC, let alone one which is acceptable to other interested parties. However, the US 'discussion paper' on tariffication, published in July 1989 may provide a longer-term solution. **Tariffication** represents the conversion of all restrictions on agricultural imports, such as the EC levy, into fixed tariffs. The central proposition is that import quotas, variable levies, voluntary restraint agreements and the like can all be converted into a tariff equal to the difference in value between the free market price and the domestic price of a product. This difference is then expressed as a percentage of the world price.

By adjusting the method of conversion to take account of different systems such as the use of threshold prices rather than domestic prices in the EC, all countries can be made to start off with an equal degree of protection in their home markets which they are then committed to reduce progressively. Provided all participating countries can reach agreement that they are all starting with the same degree of protection (a major proviso!) this approach may provide a solution to the problems raised by import barriers. However, it does not even begin to address the equally thorny problem of export subsidies.

All in all, agriculture is in a considerable mess. Advanced countries pay huge subsidies, mainly to already well-off farmers, for production of commodities no-one wants to buy. These subsidies become a burden on their taxpayers who must pay unnecessarily high prices for their food. Meanwhile, heavily indebted LDCs cannot extricate themselves by selling their cheap produce in the advanced countries' markets. The positive aspect is that there is now universal agreement that this situation must be taken in hand and that concessions will have to be made by all parties. The negative aspect is that no trading group is keen to be the first to make concessions for fear of the political fallout at home.

Notes

1. In Bruges, attending the European Summit of September 1988, Mrs Thatcher caused something of a stir by stating 'We have not successfully rolled back the frontiers of the state in Britain only to see them reimposed at a European level ... The Treaty of Rome was intended as a charter for economic liberty ... Our aim should not be more and more detailed regulation from the centre: it should be to deregulate, to remove the constraints on trade and to open up'. She added that 'To try to suppress nationhood and concentrate power at the centre of a European conglomerate would be highly damaging'. Such opinions do not altogether project the image of the good European in the style of Edward Heath. On the other hand, Mrs Thatcher expresses reservations which other European leaders are afraid to voice in public because they are reliant upon coalition support to remain in power, which she is not.
2. A recent, very sceptical view of the value of the EMS for economic convergence is to be found in Bolongia (1988) pp. 19–29.
3. See Annex to *Statement on the 1989 Community Budget*, Cm 680, HMSO (April 1989).

References

Bolongia, M. (1988) 'Prospects for International Policy Coordination: Some Lessons From the EMS', *Federal Reserve Bank of St Louis Review* (July–August).

Canberra Centre for International Economics (1988) *Macroeconomic Consequences of Farm Support Policies* (CIE).

National Consumer Council (1985) *Consumers and the CAP* (HMSO).

OECD (1985) *Costs and Benefits of Protection*.

OECD (1986) *The World Development Report* (Oxford University Press).

OECD (1988) *Agricultural Policies, Markets and Trade, Monitoring and Outlook, 1988*.

6

The Labour Market

Brian McCormick

Introduction

The Conservative government which came into office in 1979 envisaged a long period, some 10 years, over which the reforms of the British economy would be undertaken. The reforms embraced fiscal stability; deregulation of the economy; privatisation of the nationalised industries; and the reduction of trade union powers. The first three of these issues are dealt with in detail elsewhere in this book, but all have a bearing upon the efficiency of the labour market. The pursuit of fiscal stability has, for example, led to a reduction of aggregate demand with repercussions on the demand for labour, whilst the pursuit of tax cuts has

had implications for incentives and the supply of labour. Deregulation has led to a modification of the operation of minimum wage legislation and to a reconsideration of policies which had been designed to eliminate casual labour in the ports. Privatisation has meant the intrusion of commercial criteria into the operations of some industries and the abandonment of nationalisation as a means of income redistribution and stabilisation. Finally, the reduction of trade union power raises questions as to the future role of trade unions; are they to be merely friendly societies or are they to be replaced by company unions (along the lines of Japanese unions) or works councils (which are common in West Germany)? In a wider context the role of trade unions has implications for the financial support of the Labour Party and the effectiveness of parliamentary democracy.

The implementation of Conservative policy has invited two forms of comparison. In the first place, it has invited a comparison with the behaviour of the labour market policy under previous administrations during the postwar period, and secondly, it has led to a reconsideration of the Liberal reforms of 1906–13. The last decades of the nineteenth century saw a sharp check to the rise in real wages, in conjunction with an adverse movement in the terms of trade between manufactures and raw materials and increasing competition in manufactures. The rise in the prices of raw materials and foodstuffs implied a fall in real wages and led to trade union resistance which resulted in a squeeze on profits, a check to investment and a rise in unemployment.

Many of these features were replicated in the 1970s. The 1906 solution was to improve the status of trade unions as ameliorators of workers' hardships by granting them immunities from damages incurred in contemplation or furtherance of trade disputes; to introduce minimum wage legislation; to legislate for unemployment benefits; and to reform local government. These measures constituted an attempt to amend the 1834 solution of recourse to the new Poor Law, and they, in their turn, were amplified and extended through the introduction of the Welfare State between 1945 and 1951 in the course of which universal, as opposed to selective, benefits, were introduced. The 1980s solution has been to curtail heavily the scope of the 1906–13 and 1945–51 reforms. In other words, instead of a collective solution there has been an attempt to place greater emphasis upon the **responsibility of the individual**. In the labour market, legislation has been passed to weaken the powers of trade unions and to give the employee a set of statutory rights against employers. However, as will be argued below, statutory rights are insufficient if market forces are strong. Hence there is the need to improve the education and training of workers, which may require collective action.

Membership of the EC has also complicated the attempts of UK governments to manage the labour market. The UK joined the EC in order to revive a flagging economy, but membership has brought obligations and created tensions between the UK, with its newly found emphasis upon individualism, and its European partners with their greater stress upon collective responsibility and their provision of positive **rights** (as opposed to **immunities**) for trade unions.

In the sections which follow we shall attempt to disentangle the complex forces which have shaped the labour market, commencing with a description and commentary upon the changes in the legal framework in terms of health and safety, the contract of employment for the individual, the power of trade unions and the education and training of workers. To begin with, however, it is necessary to introduce trade unions into the framework since they will be playing a major role in the whole of the subsequent discussion.

Trade unions: introduction

Workplace organisation

Many of the problems of workplace organisation originate in matters pertaining to teamwork. Consider, for example, the case of two men lifting boxes into a truck. The productivity of each man depends both upon his own efforts and also upon those of his colleague. If both are paid on a common rate then each has an incentive to shirk in the hope that the other man will work harder in order to compensate for this. However, the probability is that if either shirks then total output will fall. A potential solution to this problem is the introduction of a monitor who oversees the performance of each worker and who derives his wage from the difference between the output in his absence and the output in his presence. However, the supervisor might then himself attempt to exaggerate the effects of his presence. The solution to this issue can potentially lie in competition between supervisors, in their presence on the shopfloor, in the emergence of trade unions and in the development of non-economic influences such as trust relationships.

We can distinguish between two methods of

determining pay within a firm. One method consists in the combination of managers and trade unions which constitute the main elements in an **adversarial climate** such as that which has characterised British collective bargaining. The second, the **trust method**, may be said to characterise the Japanese system.

The British system may be said to have emerged out of a workshop organisation in which there was an elaborate division of labour in which workers were employed on specific tasks and in which the performance of each worker and the co-ordination of all the tasks was the responsibility of a supervisor. The high degree of division of labour meant that there was a problem of determining the contribution of the supervisor and therefore there emerged the trade union as a monitor. Attempts by supervisors to introduce personal incentive schemes (piece rates) instead of time rates provoked a response from trade unions which led to the decline of piece rates in the 1950s. But with the decline of unions in the 1980s and with the shift from manufacturing to the service trades there has been a movement towards introducing personal incentive schemes.

Four features which characterise the Japanese firm are: (1) job rotation; (2) the *ringi* system of bottom-up consultation; (3) profit sharing; and (4) the greater presence of managers on the shopfloor. Job rotation increases a worker's involvement in the firm and develops trust relationships which are reinforced by the *ringi* system and by profit sharing. The presence of managers on the shopfloor means that workers are more aware of the managers' contributions. The success of Japanese firms and the presence of many Japanese firms in Britain has led to experiments with Japanese styles of work organisation.

Trade unions and wages

Trade unions may influence wages either by behaving as monopolists and leaving productivity unchanged but restricting output or by exerting an influence upon methods of work so that output (and also possibly employment) is increased. There now exist a considerable number of studies which suggest that trade unions do raise wages, although the union differential appears to vary with the level at which collective bargaining is conducted and whether a post-entry closed shop exists. The effect of national collective bargaining is to create a small differential (which may in fact be zero). This is unsurprising given that minimum wage legislation has tended to keep the wages of unorganised workers in line with those of unionised unskilled workers. Where plant bargaining occurs the differential has tended to be, on average, 10 per cent. Such high differentials may, of course, reflect some form of productivity bargaining or the greater monopoly power which can be exerted at a single plant. Here again the available evidence suggests that productivity has tended to be lower and employment losses greater in unionised plants than in comparable non-unionised plants.

Trade union membership

As indicated in **Table 6.1**, trade union membership reached its peak of 13.3 million members in 1979, at which point it represented roughly one-half of the working population. It subsequently fell quite sharply until 1983, since when it has shown a more gradual, but continuous decline. It is currently back at the level it was at some 30 years ago.

At the end of 1986 there were 335 unions still in existence, a figure which can be compared with the total of 519 in 1973. In fact the number of unions has been in decline for some 70 years. Much of this reduction can be explained by an ongoing process of mergers and transfers. In 1986, for example, 30 local and craft unions transferred to national unions. However, new unions also constantly appear on a modest scale – three in 1986. Despite mergers and transfers, just over one-half of all unions consist of less than 1,000 members. By way of contrast the 24 unions with in excess of 100,000 members accounted for over 80 per cent of total membership, and the largest eight unions for over 50 per cent (*Department of Employment Gazette*, May 1988).

The causes of the fall in membership lie in the recession of 1980–81, trade union legislation and the changing nature of the firm and the industry. In

Table 6.1   *Trade unions: numbers and membership in the UK*

	Number	Membership (millions)	% of working population[1]
1975	470	12.0	47.2
1976	473	12.4	48.5
1977	481	12.8	50.1
1978	462	13.1	50.7
1979	453	13.3	51.1
1980	438	12.9	49.5
1981	414	12.1	46.6
1982	408	11.6	44.8
1983	394	11.2	41.6
1984	375	11.0	39.9
1985	370	10.8	38.1
1986	335	10.5	36.4

Note:
[1] Author's calculations
Source: Department of Employment Gazette (Feb 1987 and May 1988).

boom periods real incomes rise, and if unionism is a normal good then more trade unionism will be demanded. Furthermore, in boom periods the cost of joining unions falls as labour scarcity weakens employers' resistance to unions. Conversely, as real incomes fall and employers' resistance increases during recessions, less unionism will be demanded. In recent decades the cycle effects have been reinforced as a result of anti-union legislation. Finally, the changing nature of the firm (with an increasing emphasis upon the use of temporary and part-time labour) and the changing nature of the industry (with the shift from manufacturing to services and the consequent relocation of jobs) has led to a persistent fall in union membership despite the economic recovery since 1983.

The legal framework

The legal framework for the labour market can be considered under four headings: health and safety; the individual worker and his employer; trade unions and collective bargaining; and education and training. Throughout the postwar period there has been a tendency to substitute statute law for common law, but in the 1970s and 1980s there has been a noticeable shift away from the use of collective bargaining to determine the contents of a worker's contract, and towards the assertion of statutory rights for the individual.

Health and safety

There has been a long history of factory legislation devoted to health and safety throughout the nineteenth and twentieth centuries. It represented the first serious amendment of the common law contract of employment by accepting that the common law assumption of bargaining between equals might not apply to women and young persons, and that the employer's defence of acceptance of risks by workers might not apply when a worker was ignorant of the risks and had no control over the hiring of his fellow workers.

The main achievement of the postwar period has been the Health and Safety at Work Act 1974, which was a product of the deliberations of the Robens Committee on Health and Safety. The Act consolidated previous legislation and also introduced some new ideas, such as workers' safety representatives, in order to involve workers and their unions in accident prevention. There was, however, a noticeable difference between the Robens Report and the subsequent legislation. The Committee was conscious of the public unease at the legal remedies available to the thalidomide victims, and recommended an investigation into the desirability of introducing a no-fault compensation scheme for the common law system of damages.

The common law system of accident compensation can be regarded as an application of market principles. Workers in risky trades should receive higher wages than those in relatively safe trades and thereby achieve an equalisation of net advantages. But not all risks are foreseeable or can be compensated in advance. Hence, employers may be liable for damages and may attempt to reduce their liabilities by taking out insurance. The payment of insurance premiums is then supposed to make employers safety conscious, to induce insurance companies to carry out factory inspections and to provide for compensation to injured workers.

However, the common law system has been subjected to a great deal of criticism. The amount paid out in compensation bears little relationship to the amounts paid in premiums, with the bulk of the premiums being absorbed in litigation fees. It is also argued that the recovery of workers tends to be hindered by the prospects of substantial damages – the **moral hazard** argument. Workers could also spend their compensation rashly and then fall back upon the State. Insurance companies might fail to carry out surveillances and assume that the State's factory inspectors are sufficient. Finally, with the noticeable exception of unions such as the National Union of Miners (NUM), most trade unions appear to take little interest in accident prevention – hence the pressure (replicated in other areas such as car accidents and medical negligence) to introduce a no-fault system along the lines pioneered in New Zealand and some Canadian provinces where, irrespective of blame, an injured worker would receive an income from the State and the costs of administering such a scheme would be about 1 per cent of the premiums. However, the Pearson Committee on Personal Injuries failed to recommend such a scheme – although the issue is still widely canvassed.

The workings of the Health and Safety at Work Act have not been subject to investigation but the following points should be noted. In the first place, the Act was heavily influenced by experiences in manufacturing, and with the decline of activity in manufacturing and the expansion of the service trades there may have been a fall in accidents. Secondly, the increase in the number of small firms has led to conflicting tendencies. On the one hand, large firms tend to have higher accident rates because of the greater interaction of workers with each other and with their environment and, possibly, because they keep records. On the other hand, the expansion of sub-contracting, part-time employment and temporary work have resulted in problems of supervising and co-ordinating accident prevention measures and, possibly, poorer record keeping. Thirdly, there has been a reduction in the number of factory inspectors and this may have led to an increase in the number of unrecorded accidents. Fourthly, the decline of trade unions may have reduced the effectiveness of the system of workers' safety representatives. Fifthly, some establishments lie outside the scope of the prevention measures and inside the orbit of government departments which are ill-equipped to implement safety measures, for example oil rigs. Finally, the proposals to allow women and young persons to do night work and to work down coal mines would reverse the historic basis of factory legislation which had sought, through the Factory Act 1833 and the Mines Act 1842, to restrict the hours of those groups on the grounds that they could not fend for themselves. Conservative revisionism now sees those Acts as attempts to restrict the use of labour and to restrict the opportunities open to women.

The individual worker and his employer

Prior to 1963 employment law relating to the individual rested upon common law. It was implicitly assumed that it was a contract between equals in which the worker allowed the employer to direct his activities in return for a wage. It was, in effect, a command disguised as a contract, although economists might assume that in competitive conditions the workers hired the employer and the employer hired the worker. In practice the common law was seldom invoked due to the lack of adequate remedies for breach of contract by the employer. Workers had thus to rely upon trade unions for remedial action.

The Contract of Employment Act 1963 was passed largely as a result of two influences. The first of these was the attempts by unions to extend the seniority principle (last in, first out) in order to protect shop stewards against victimisation. The second influence arose as a result of the problems raised by mass redundancies in the car industry which threatened to sweep away even the last vestiges of protection afforded by the seniority principle. The Act introduced rules on periods of notice, required an employer to give an employee a written statement of the terms of employment and provided statutory rules on 'continuity of employment'. In 1965 the Redundancy Payments Act provided for payments to be made in the event of involuntary termination of employment by the worker. The Industrial Relations Act 1971 introduced the concept of 'unfair dismissal'. Subsequently, the employment law was amended to exclude workers in small firms in the first few years of their formation. The effectiveness of the legislation on dismissals has been the subject of much debate. On the one hand, it has given workers a means of redress of grievances and the lawyers considerable income from the resulting litigation. On the other hand, it has possibly resulted in a greater readiness to permit dismissals rather than attempt reconciliation.

In 1908 minimum wage legislation was introduced to cover workers in those trades in which it was felt that wages were **unduly low**. In 1918 the legislation was extended to trades where collective bargaining was weak, and in 1943 and 1945 it was extended to the catering and retail trades in an effort to prevent a possible collapse of wages in a postwar slump in those trades pulling down wages in organised trades. In the 1950s and 1960s minimum wage legislation covered about 3.5 million workers. In the subsequent years there was some removal of the protection of minimum wage legislation from trades where it was felt that their voluntary collective bargaining machinery had taken root. However, the major changes took place in the 1980s when the wage councils for the various retail trades were amalgamated and a single wage rate was introduced. In 1986 young workers were removed from the scope of the legislation, despite the fact that the empirical evidence did not support the assertion that minimum wage legislation was responsible for increased unemployment. Thus, a study by Lund *et al.* (1985) of the workings of the Agricultural Wages Board between 1960 and 1981 revealed that the increase in wage rates tended to be a catching-up on what was being paid in bonuses. A study of the effects of minimum wage legislation in the clothing industry by Morgan *et al.* (1985) suggested that, for the period 1950–81, a 10 per cent increase in wages reduced employment by between 0.28 and 0.12 per cent. But the most significant feature of the study was that the effects of changes in social security contributions were

three times greater than the effects of minimum wage changes.

The Wages Councils Act 1986 also limited the powers of the councils to setting a single minimum rate (of £1.96 – £2.38 per hour) and a single overtime rate for workers over 21. It was anticipated that this would limit their role considerably, but the government came to the view that they were overactive and inhibiting pay flexibility by increasing rates by a uniform percentage; that the clustering of pay on or close to the minimum indicated that councils set pay above market rates; and that social security and welfare provisions had improved sufficiently to render minimum wage legislation unnecessary. A document setting out these issues was published in December 1988 (Wage Councils: 1988 Consultation Document) and responses were requested by February 1989, so it is possible that abolition will follow later in 1989. It is interesting to note that this would leave the UK as the only EC country without minimum wage legislation.

Trade unions and collective bargaining

The most extensive changes in employment law have centred around the position of trade unions in the labour market. Indeed, prior to the Employment Act 1980 labour law was primarily **trade union law** – the rights of workers were protected by trade unions. In the 1980s trade union law underwent a transformation which involved four issues: (1) trade union government (the relationship between a member and his officials); (2) the closed shop, which determined the relationship between unionists and non-unionists; (3) the relationship between unions and political parties; and (4) strike activity.

The problems of trade union government have centred around the rights of the individual member against his officials and the potential for union officials to control their members and to prevent unofficial strikes. These issues have been complicated by disputes over the interpretation of the role of trade unions in capitalist societies and over the nature of the labour markets in which unions operate. By way of illustration of the former point the allegation that trade unions are undemocratic could be countered by the argument that democracy is a political concept applicable to nation-states, and hence inapplicable to unions which lack the coercive power of the State and which cannot afford the luxury of an official opposition when confronted by a powerful capitalist class.

In respect of the nature of labour markets a distinction is drawn between **closed** and **open** unions. Closed unions organise skilled workers who have served some form of apprenticeship, who have a commitment to their occupations and who show a high degree of participation in their unions. In contrast, open unions organise unskilled workers who have a high turnover and whose unions tend to be dominated by full-time officials. Nevertheless, despite these factors, open unions exhibit a variety of countervailing pressures such as a tendency to be involved in unofficial strikes. During the 1960s the membership of open unions seemed to be stabilising to an extent which permitted of the devolution of power. However, the 'Winter of Discontent' of 1979 brought home the realisation that union officials lacked any real control over their members, and this led to the view that unofficial strikes should be suppressed and that union officials should be made more accountable to their members. Hence the Employment Acts of the 1980s have sought to resolve the problems of trade union government by stipulating that union leaders should be subject to periodic elections and that strikes can be called only after a ballot of members.

The closed shop

The justification for the closed shop is that it provides a solution to the free-rider problem – non-unionists should not get the same wages as those for which union members have struggled. However, unions can be tolerant of less than 100 per cent membership. In the coal industry, for example, development work has often been carried out by contractors who employ non-union labour. Elsewhere, in manufacturing industry, pockets of non-unionism exist. Some of the anomalies can be explained in terms of non-competing groups:

workers in small firms or catering workers in engineering firms may not be union members. The viability of pockets of non-unionism, and the absence of a threat to union members, might also be explained in terms of the latter's awareness that an employer might be unable to hire sufficient non-union workers.

There exist two types of closed shop, namely the **pre-entry** closed shop which requires a worker to be a member of a union before he is hired, and the **post-entry** closed shop which permits a worker to be hired but makes it a condition of his continuing employment that he joins a union. During the 1960s the closed shop became more widespread as unionism expanded and plant level bargaining became more important, and the numbers employed in closed shops is estimated to have reached a peak of over 5 million in 1978. The 1984 Workplace Industrial Relations Survey estimated that the pre-entry closed shop covered only about half a million workers out of the then much reduced total of 3.6 million, indicating that the post-entry closed shop was the prevalent form.

However, research carried out for the Green Paper on ending closed shops (*Removing Barriers to Employment: Proposals For the Further Reform of Industrial Relations and Trade Union Law*, 1989) indicated that of the 2.6 million workers in closed shops in early 1989 one-half were working in pre-entry shops which were most common in the nationalised industries. The Green Paper noted that making the pre-entry closed shop unlawful was an inappropriate way to proceed since employers had shown no great desire to get rid of it. As the law currently stands, any dismissal or discriminatory action against an individual short of dismissal, on the grounds of non-membership of a union, is unlawful. The problem for the government is that it remains legal for employers to discriminate against non-members by not employing them. The Green Paper therefore proposes that individuals should be given the right not to be refused a post on the ground of non-membership, and if they believe that to be the case then they should have the right to put their case before a tribunal. If the tribunal accepts a worker's version of events then it will be empowered to ask the employer to take on the worker in question, and if he refuses to do so, to order him to pay compensation.

The trend towards the curbing of the closed shop is not purely a UK phenomenon. The European Court, for example, found that a group of railway workers who had been dismissed because they had refused to join a union were unfairly dismissed. There are those who believe that the Green Paper has ducked the issue, and there is pressure for an outright ban on closed shops in the UK. The eventual outcome is, therefore, at least slightly uncertain.

Trade unions and political levies

The third area of contention has been the union support of political parties. Trade union support for, and sponsorship of, a political party began to emerge around the turn of the century and arose because of incidents such as the Taff Vale decision which threatened trade union funds when damages arose out of a dispute; because it reflected a feeling that acting as a pressure group upon the Conservative and Liberal Parties was no longer tenable; and because the new unions of semi-skilled and unskilled workers saw parliamentary intervention as the only method of raising living standards. Later, trade union support of the Labour Party came to be regarded as the only means of ensuring democracy in a two-party system. However, those arguments came to be challenged in the 1970s and 1980s. The working class vote, it has been argued, has been dwindling and working class support for the Labour Party has been falling. More seriously, there have been allegations that the unions' use of the bloc vote has tended to obscure differences of opinion within individual unions. Finally, it has been suggested that trade union members should be allowed to 'contract-in' to the payment of the political levy and not be asked to 'contract-out' if they do not wish to pay it. Hence, attempts have been made to control the conduct of union ballots on the payment of the political levy. But when union members have been balloted they have affirmed their intention to continue with political funds. Furthermore, attempts to substitute 'con-

tracting-in' for 'contracting-out' would require a similar principle being applied to the payment of monies to the Conservative Party by companies.

Strikes and collective bargaining

Finally, there is the issue of collective bargaining and the use of the strike weapon. The British system of collective bargaining was established at the turn of the century and underwent only minor modifications in subsequent decades. Unionism had been legalised in 1872, but union funds were not protected until the passing of the Industrial Disputes Act 1906, which rendered their funds immune from damages incurred in contemplation or furtherance of a trade dispute. Subsequently, this immunity was extended to damages resulting from secondary picketing by the case of *Crofter Handwoven Harris Tweed* v. *Veitch* (1943) which involved a union attempting to put pressure on an employer by getting its members in the transport industry to black the movement of goods.

At the turn of the century the predominant form of collective bargaining was the district agreement, supplemented by minimum wage legislation in some trades and by the existence of arbitration, conciliation and courts of enquiry. Subsequently, the shift to plant level bargaining was assisted by the 1906 Act and by two world wars. The wars also promoted a movement towards industry-wide or national collective bargaining, although that was to prove less significant in the long run. After the Second World War the movement towards plant level bargaining was assisted by the desire of some employers, notably in the car industry, to break away from national agreements and offer high wages in order to get more labour.

Whilst it was always possible to control some aspects of collective bargaining through the common law remedies for intimidation, mass picketing and conspiracy, there was a shift to increased statutory control over strike ballots, picketing and the removal of some union immunities during the 1980s. The context of these legal changes was the feeling that unions were monopolies and that their actions constituted public disorder as, for example, in the strikes of local authority and health workers in the 1978–79 'Winter of Discontent' and of the miners in 1984–85.

Strikes must currently be confined to economic matters and relate wholly or mainly to economic issues. Campaigns to protest against privatisation are thus considered to be outside the scope of the legal immunities. Whereas secondary picketing is now tightly controlled under the Employment Act 1980, the parallel form of secondary lock-out is not. In the case of *Dimbleby and Sons Ltd* v. *NUJ* (1984) an employer was permitted to transfer work from one plant to another and the union was prevented from picketing the second plant.

What the trade union reforms of the1980s have sought is to promote a different distribution of bargaining strength in the labour market and to create a form of **co-operative unionism**. This can be illustrated with respect to secondary picketing. Under the Employment Act 1980 secondary action is lawful if the workers are employed by a customer and supplier of the company in dispute; if the company has a contract with the employer in dispute; if the principal aim of the secondary action is to disrupt supplies to or from the employer in dispute and the action is likely to achieve that purpose. This is a complicated issue and the Green Paper (CM 665, 1989) seeks to simplify the position. It accordingly proposes that it should be unlawful for a union to induce workers to take secondary action other than by picketing. Given that the existing legislation outlaws picketing other than at a worker's place of work this will effectively restrict secondary action to the turning away by pickets of suppliers seeking to gain entry to the workplace at the centre of a dispute. The underlying rationale is that no company which is not party to a dispute should find itself involuntarily involved in industrial action.

The government clearly has in mind the circumstances surrounding the eventual refusal of the Ford Motor Co to set up an electronic components plant in Dundee in 1988 because it wanted a single union agreement and other unions threatened to black the plant. In addition, the Green Paper proposes to tighten up the rules governing pre-strike ballots which, whilst compulsory, apply only where workers would be breaking their contracts of employment. The Green Paper proposes that such ballots should also be compulsory where the workers are subject to 'contracts of service'.

Education and training

Living standards depend upon the productivity of labour which is related to skills and capital equipment. In the nineteenth century unskilled labour was plentiful, and many labour markets were casual. The deregulation of labour markets and the introduction of labour-saving technologies as well as increased foreign competition could lead to a return to casual markets. Hence, the interest in whether the privatisation of education and training can provide adequate programmes of instruction and prove attractive to potential buyers.

Education

We begin by distinguishing between **compulsory** and **voluntary** education. Up to the age of 16 education is compulsory, and although conceived of as non-vocational it can provide the interest and springboard for further education. The standard criticisms of existing compulsory education are that it is mainly provided by the public sector, is too short in duration and is too specialised and unresponsive to society's needs. Some two-thirds of young people leave shool at 16, as compared with the two-thirds who stay on at school after the age of 16 in Japan and the tendency for most Americans not to seek full-time jobs until they are 21. The period of nine years from 5 to 16 has been considered to be too short to provide young people with the interests and skills to fill productive jobs in an advanced society. It is also argued that the content of the compulsory curriculum is too specialised. Many pupils do not continue to study science subjects in the fourth and fifth years of secondary schools and, in 1986, only 65 per cent of school leavers had attempted O level (ordinary) or CSE (Certificate of Secondary Education) in one or more main science subjects – physics, chemistry or biology. Weaknesses in mathematics and sciences have been complemented by deficiencies in the use of English. Some of these criticisms are well taken, although it has to be noted that even the experts disagree about the content of an English course. Nevertheless, there are now serious attempts being made to press forward with a national curriculum which attempts to provide a broad-based education for young people.

Beyond the age of 16 further and higher education are voluntary. Potential school leavers have a choice: they can opt for more education or seek a job. The important determinants of the choice appear to be parental education, state grants and the future earnings of school leavers relative to those who stay on in further and higher education. Given the absence of a market for educational loans or a system of working one's way through further education, parental income may dictate whether young people stay in education. Hence, an increase in parental incomes may be expected to lead to an increase in the numbers seeking further and higher education. The cost of staying on can be measured by the lifetime earnings stream of 16 year olds. A rise in the future earnings of 16 year olds may be expected to reduce the demand for further education; the decision to pay the adult wage at 18 (instead of 21) seems to have reduced the demand for further education by 9 per cent.

A further factor which can influence the decision to stay on is **unemployment**. Unemployment depresses earnings and tends to exert its greatest influence upon the earnings of the unskilled. Thus, in 1981 the unemployment rate of the unskilled was double that of people possessing 'A' levels and four times that of those possessing degrees despite the fact that wage differentials narrowed between 1977 and 1981.

Since 1950 there have been variations in the pattern of post-compulsory enrolment rates for boys and girls. During the 1950s and 1960s the enrolment rates of boys and girls rose rapidly – by 5 per cent for boys and by 4 per cent for girls between 1951 and 1961, and by 7 per cent for both sexes between 1961 and 1968. There was subsequently a slowing down between 1969 and 1972, and in 1972 they were affected by the raising of the school-leaving age (which also had the effect of creating a scarcity of labour and of raising the wages of young workers). After 1979 enrolment rates started to rise again. A marked feature of the period since the 1950s has been the greater rise in

the enrolment rates in colleges as compared to schools.

Some 90 per cent of the variation in enrolment rates in further education can be explained in terms of parental incomes, relative earnings and unemployment rates. A rise of 1 per cent in real disposable incomes of households seems to be associated with a 1.6 per cent rise in the enrolment rate of boys and a 1.7 per cent enrolment rate increase for girls. The slowing down of enrolment rates between 1969 and 1972 can be linked to a slowing down of real household income and the narrowing of wage differentials. After 1979 unemployment rose but real household incomes also rose, although since 1982 enrolment rates have been influenced by the Youth Training Scheme (YTS).

As a result of the Robbins Report on higher education with its suggestion that students should be admitted to polytechnics and universities if they had the requisite 'A' level grades, ability and academic attainment have been more important than income in determining the demand for places. However, the situation could now change as a result of the government's decision to make students express more commitment to higher education, and to make universities and polytechnics more consumer-oriented by replacing most of the grant system with loans. What effect such a change will have upon the demand for places in higher education and upon the types of courses demanded remains to be seen. The government favours an expansion of the sciences, but market forces in the form of relative earnings are suggesting that many students will choose accountancy, business studies and law.

The decision to move in the direction of a greater use of the market in determining places in higher education stems from three issues: (**1**) specialisation; (**2**) misallocation of resources; and (**3**) methods of financing. Only one-third of school leavers have tended to stay on into higher education. Those who do so tend to receive a highly specialised education which concentrates upon three subjects at 'A' level. As we have noted, specialisation can begin even before 16. One noticeable effect of this is that the British labour market tends to be less responsive to changes in demand than, say, the American education system and labour market. A system of persistent shortages and gluts can be created. For example, a university medical education takes about $5\frac{1}{2}$ years and builds upon two years of specialisation in further education and possibly two years of specialisation before the age of 16, with the result that a change in the demand for doctors may result in a lag of 10 years before there is a corresponding change in supply.

A second effect is that the education system results in a misallocation of resources. The popular view is that it turns out too few scientists and engineers, but this is an argument that is difficult to sustain in the light of the relative movements of the earnings of science and non-science graduates. A more pertinent criticism is that resources have been misallocated between further and higher education with the result that the UK does not train enough technicians. The evidence does suggest that the rate of return on degrees tends to be lower than on investment in shorter training programmes, but there may be additional non-monetary rewards from possessing a degree. If there were a serious shortage of technicians relative to graduates than we should have expected the relative rewards to adjust until the demand was met. Perhaps the problem lies in the uses to which technicians are put by managers.

This brings us to the third criticism — namely, that the education system is too elitist, dominated by the public sector and unresponsive to the national interest. The education system is strongly influenced by the universities, whose leverage determines the scope and content of further education with the result that the demands of some 5 per cent of the population determines what is provided for the other 95 per cent. It is unresponsive to the national interest because it receives State finance and, as a result, does not take into account consumers' needs. Some of these points do merit attention and reflect an inability to create a mass education system.

Training

This brings us to developments in industrial training. State intervention in high level training of scientists and engineers began at the turn of the century, and the provincial universities represented a response to foreign competition. The science lobby continued to exert an influence on government spending on research and development during two world wars and after 1945. In contrast, the bulk of industrial training was on-the-job training. For craftsmen it was imparted through the apprenticeship system supplemented by City and Guilds examinations, and for the semi-skilled it was obtained through informal on-the-job training.

The first serious State intervention in industrial training came with the Industrial Training Act 1964. It represented, in part, an attempt to cope with the bulge in school leavers about to enter the labour market (the other response being the expansion of higher education). The Act created training boards which were to be financed partly by State funds and mainly by levies on firms. The boards were administered by representatives of employers, trade unions and civil servants. The reactions to the boards were mixed. In theory the boards were designed to cope with skill shortages arising through poaching; it was alleged that some firms did not train labour but poached workers from firms which did.

Many employers resented paying the levy. The existence of poaching was disputed and a distinction was drawn between general and specific skills. General skills were those which could be used in a variety of firms or industries whilst specific skills were those which could be used in only one firm. Because workers could not be bought and sold like slaves, employers would be unwilling to invest in the provision of general skills if they feared that, once trained, workers would leave their employ. If, however, skills were specific then employers might be willing to pay for training, hence poaching could not exist. If there were a shortage of skilled labour then it must be due to a lack of appropriate market signals, such as the wage differential for the acquisition of skills, or an inability of young people to finance their training — in which case they should have received grants like university students. If there was a shortage of skilled labour then it might also be due to unions restricting the openings for young workers. By permitting unions to sit on training boards, governments may have allowed unions to extend their controls. What may have been required, therefore, was the removal of the controls by, for example, productivity agreements. Such a policy was attempted in the late 1960s but, unfortunately, ran into the intense inflation which rendered impossible any proposal to trade off wage increases for the removal of restrictions. In 1973 an attempt was made to meet some of these criticisms by distinguishing between statutory training boards (for example, that for engineering) and voluntary boards. However, a 1987 survey of the voluntary boards showed that the workings of many of them were unsatisfactory.

The establishment of statutory and non-statutory boards in the early 1970s was part of an ambitious attempt to create a national training programme under the aegis of the Manpower Services Commission (MSC) – a semi-autonomous body set up separately from the Department of Employment. In the face of rising youth unemployment a Recruitment Subsidy for School Leavers (RSSL) was introduced in 1975 which offered an employer £5 per week for six months if he recruited a school leaver who had been unemployed during the summer. In 1976 a Youth Employment Subsidy (YES) replaced RSSL, and offered £10 per week to employers for every recruit who had been unemployed for less than six months. But neither RSSL nor YES were satisfactory because they gave rise to deadweight and substitution effects. A deadweight loss occurs when an employer receives a subsidy even though he would have recruited a worker without the subsidy, whilst a substitution effect can result from the tendency to dismiss existing workers and to replace them with young unemployed people for whom firms receive the subsidy.

The Youth Opportunity Programme (YOP) was introduced in 1978. Each participant was given six months' job experience and an allowance of £25 per week. Initially, some 70 per cent of unemployed school leavers were placed on various schemes and obtained jobs, but as unemployment rose the percentage fell to 41 per cent. Its credibility was eroded as few trainees got jobs, and the subsidy tended to be concentrated on low-paid, non-union jobs. However, YOP did provide an induction period for some inexperienced school leavers, and may have improved the employment prospects of those with modest educational qualifications.

In 1982 the government made a more serious attempt to deal with problems of young workers through the introduction of the Youth Training Scheme (YTS), and in 1986 the Scheme was extended to provide a two-year structured period of training and work experience for 16 year old school leavers and a one year period for 17 year old school leavers. It was intended to provide all school leavers with training and, in effect, to eliminate the youth labour market. A preliminary study of the effects of YTS in 1986 suggested that the deadweight and substitution effects tended to decrease with the size of the establishment, and that the deadweight effect was highest in the construction industry where employers used the YTS as a first year of apprenticeship and would have recruited many of the apprentices even if they had received no subsidy. But net output and employment effects were also recorded, especially in the motor vehicle repair, retail distribution and personal services where the value of output was above the (then) YTS rate of pay of £27.30 per week. The YTS also encouraged firms to accelerate the recruitment of young workers by lowering hiring costs, and by encouraging firms to take on YTS trainees in addition to their normal recruitment. There was, however, a disturbingly high accident rate among YTS trainees. In 1988 the accident rate per 100,000 trainees was 20 per cent higher than in 1987, and 130 per cent higher than in 1985.

In 1986 the government introduced the Restart Programme which was aimed at the long-term unemployed. At first anyone unemployed for one year or longer was invited to an interview at a Job Centre and offered opportunities designed to help him or her back to employment. In 1987 coverage was extended to anyone unemployed for six months or longer. The opportunities on offer included an interview for a job; a place on a government scheme, mainly the new Job Training Scheme; a place on a Restart Course; a Jobstart allowance; or a place in a Jobclub, of which there were 1,230 at the end of 1988.

In September 1988 the government introduced Employment Training (ET) with the slogan 'Training the workers without jobs to do the jobs without workers', the main aim being to bring together all the former government training programmes into a single training scheme for the longer-term unemployed (details of programmes can be found in the public expenditure White Paper booklet which covers the Department of Employment). In particular, it replaced the Community Programme, the New Job Training Scheme, the old Job Training Scheme, the Voluntary Projects Programme and the Wider Opportunities Training Programme. It was intended to provide training for some 550,000 people. The objectives of ET are first, to give the long-term unemployed the skills they need to get and keep jobs and, secondly, to guarantee a training opportunity for all those aged 18 to 24 who have been unemployed for between six and 12 months and for all those aged 18 to 50 who have been unemployed for more than two years. The unemployed are allocated to training agents (who may be employers or employers' organisations) and whilst on the Scheme continue to receive benefits as though they were unemployed plus a training allowance and, if eligible, Income Support and travelling expenses. In addition, training managers are allowed to make a number of discretionary payments without affecting benefits or liabilities for tax. Such topping-up allowances may comprise free or subsidised meals or additional payments for special clothing.

Figure 6.1 *Employment and training measures, numbers of people supported (000), Great Britain, three-month averages*

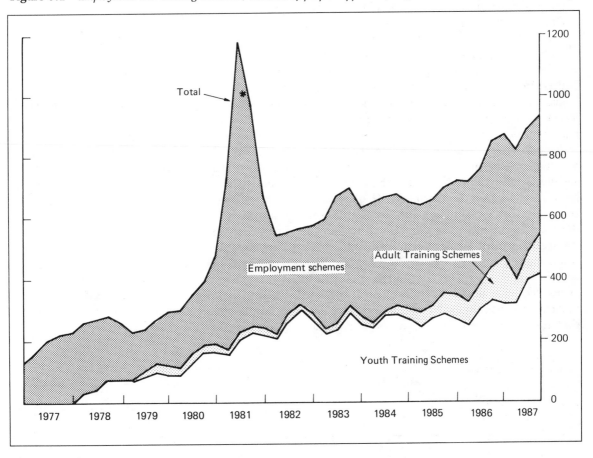

Note:
* This reflects the Temporary Short-Time Working Compensation Scheme.
Source: Employment Department Training Agency; Department of Employment, reproduced from *Social Trends*, 19 (1989 edn).

In the White Paper on training (*Employment For the 1990s*, Cmnd 540, 1988) the government went a stage further by proposing to restructure training through the establishment of 80 locally-based, employer-led Training and Enterprise Councils (TECs) in England and Wales, together with 20 local councils in Scotland. The Department of Employment will invite local groups of employers to submit proposals for setting up the councils which will then draw up local training strategies, arrange for the delivery of appropriate training programmes and concentrate upon the support of training in small businesses.

The TECs will sign a contract with the Training Agency[1] once the groundwork is laid to provide programmes for young people, the unemployed, workers made redundant and those changing jobs. They will also promote training within companies and establish close links with the education service.

The Conservative government came to power in 1979 with the objective of rolling back the State and freeing markets. However, it has ended up with direct responsibility for training just as it began, if not more so. **Figure 6.1** gives some indication of the breadth of coverage of government schemes.

At first youth training was expected to keep young people off the streets. There was an attempt to bypass local authorities and to bridge the gap between education and training. There was an attempt to change cultural values by emphasising the need for an enterprise culture, and to deregulate labour markets whilst stressing work discipline and personal transferable skills. There has also been an attempt to cope with the shift to the service trades. The overall effect of these policies was to centralise training. In 1987 an attempt was made to shift the focus of attention through the introduc-

tion of a New Training Initiative. The unions objected to the underfunding of the Initiative and voted to boycott the scheme, with the result that the Minister of Employment decided, as from December 1988, to absorb the Training Commission (previously the Manpower Services Commission) under the umbrella of a new Training Agency and to exclude the unions. Subsequently the unions relented, although it is too soon to say what role the unions might have in a system which gives greater emphasis to employers' involvement in the design and operation of training schemes, and which attempts to replicate the German system of local employment committees.

Employment

The working population

The legal and political measures which have been described interact with broader socio-economic forces which may be summarised under the headings of supply and demand or employment and unemployment. The starting point is movements in the size of the population, as shown in **Table 6.2**. From the total population can be extracted a summary statistic known as the **population of working age**, which by convention embraces males aged 16 to 64 and females aged 16 to 60. The population of working age comprises all those who might work and excludes those at school or in retirement. However, part of the population of working age are economically inactive. Some are engaged in further and higher education and some in raising children; some are physically unable to work; and some may continue to work beyond the

Table 6.2   *UK population (millions)*

1951	1961	1971	1981	1984	1985	1986	1987	1991	2001
50.3	52.8	55.9	56.4	56.5	56.6	56.8	56.9	57.5*	59.0*

Note:
* Estimate.
Source: Social Trends, 19 (1989 edn) CSO.

age of retirement. By adjusting for these factors a further summary statistic is arrived at called the **labour force** (or the **civilian labour force** if those in the armed forces are excluded) which comprises those willing and able to work.

In 1986 the population was 56.8 million of whom 33.9 million were in the working population and 26.7 million were in the labour force. The ratio of the labour force to the working population is known as the 'activity rate' or 'participation rate'. This stood at 49.2 per cent in 1986. Between 1961 and 1986 the labour force grew by 2.4 million. However, this growth concealed considerable fluctuations stemming from demographic factors and changes in activity rates. Thus, between 1976 and 1986 the population of working age grew by 2 million as a result of a low birth rate during the First World War (eventually giving rise to fewer retirements) and also of high birth rates in the 1960s giving rise to an inflow into the labour market in the late 1970s and early 1980s. In the depressed circumstances of the early 1980s a youth unemployment problem accordingly emerged and there were problems for redundant workers in acquiring new jobs.

Figure 6.2 indicates the trend in the civilian labour force of working age and the population of working age by sex in Great Britain (rather than the UK) from 1971 onwards. As shown in Figure 6.2 the population of working age increased continuously throughout the period with both sexes growing by over 1 million. However, the civilian labour force grew more rapidly, and 87 per cent of the growth consisted of women. Overall, the civilian labour force reached a peak of 26.2 million in 1980 at the end of a surge in the number of women entrants, subsequently fell by 300,000 between 1980 and 1981 and then resumed the upward trend to reach a total of 26.7 million in 1986. The figure also contains projections up to 1992.

In the early 1980s some workers dropped out of the labour force and the Labour Force Survey estimated that some 340,000 workers had become discouraged. The notion of discouragement should, however, be treated with caution because discouraged workers may have jobs in the black (unofficial) economy. It is difficult to establish

Figure 6.2 *Civilian labour force of working age and population of working age by sex, Great Britain*

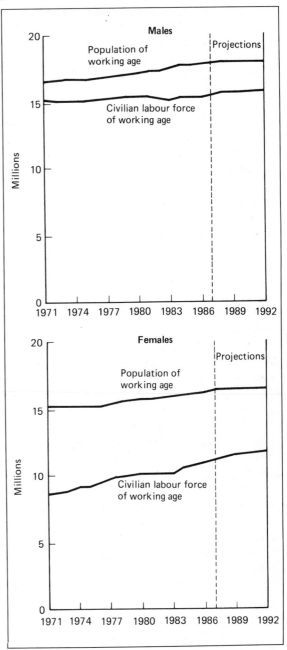

Source: Social Trends, 19 (1989 edn) Chart 4.4; Department of Employment Gazette.

whether the output generated in the black economy comes from workers who are not employed in the official (market) economy, since it could come from the efforts of those with more than one job.

Thus, in the Spring of 1987 males worked some 3.9 million hours in second jobs and females worked about 2.2 million hours in second jobs. Furthermore, the attempt to estimate the numbers of people working in the black economy by counting the number of bogus claimants for unemployment insurance suggests that the number of fraudulant claimants is about 10,000 or less than 1 per cent of the unemployed, and this figure must be set against the number entitled to benefit but who do not claim.

Activity rates

Activity rates for men and women show considerable variation. In the case of men the activity rate has been falling since the 1930s. In part, this has been due to an increase in the numbers staying on in further and higher education, although that factor was probably more important in the 1960s. More recently, the decline in the male activity rate has been due to earlier retirements, stemming from improved pensions, and the discouraged worker effect, resulting from the difficulties older workers have had in obtaining jobs during the recession.

In contrast to the decline in the male activity rate, there has been an increase for females. In 1971 the female activity rate was 43.9 per cent as compared with the male rate of 80.5 per cent, whilst in 1986 the male rate had fallen to 73.3 per cent and the female rate had risen to 49.9 per cent. However, a distinction should be made between married and non-married females. The participation rates of young non-married females have been falling whilst those for older married women have been rising. The lower rates for non-married females may have been due to more girls staying on in further and higher education and to the increase in the number of single-parent families.

The rise in the activity rates of married women has been the subject of much research and debate. The decline in the average number of children per family and the introduction of household labour-saving devices may have released more women for work outside the household. Changing social attitudes in relation to married women working may also have become important. In addition, there have been significant changes in the structure of industry. The shift to the service trades, and away from manufacturing, may have enabled women to compete against men for jobs. There has also been a noticeable increase in temporary and part-time jobs which have enabled women to combine work within and outside the household and the shift to part-time work may have been assisted by the increase in National Insurance contributions.

Supply elasticities

It is important to consider whether economists have anything to say about how the supply of labour responds to monetary rewards. Such rewards may take the form of wage increases or decreases, or they may take the form of changes in tax rates. A central tenet of the government since 1979 has been that tax rates are too high and have a disincentive effect upon work effort. The effect of changes in monetary rewards cannot, however, be predicted in advance, but must depend upon the relative strengths of the substitution and income effects, and these may vary for different individuals and households. A wage rise (or cut in income tax) will thus induce people to work longer and to reduce their hours of leisure because one hour's work is now worth more at the margin – this is the **substitution effect of the change in reward**. However, the change in the wage rate, or tax cut, could enable an individual to obtain the same total income for a reduced number of hours at work, or enable him to reach a higher standard of living in terms of being able to obtain a greater money income with which to buy more goods. This **income effect** can result in an individual working either more or less, and the overall outcome depends upon the relative strengths of the two effects.

The available evidence suggests that the response of males to changes in their own wages is low whilst that of married women is high. Some part of the explanation of the differences may lie in the fact that hours of work may not be so easily variable for males whilst married women may find it relatively easier to find jobs which permit greater flexibility in terms of part-time and temporary work. In manufacturing industries the hours of work may be demand determined or technologically determined, and to increase hours of work may necessitate a change of jobs. In contrast, the self-employed and professional classes may find it much easier to increase their effort. Attempts to measure the impact of recent tax cuts run into the difficulty that they have been accompanied by a rise in economic activity with the result that incomes would probably have gone up in the absence of the tax cuts.

Hours of work: primary and secondary labour forces

Nominal hours of work (those which form the basis for overtime rates) held steady at 40 per week between 1965 and 1980, but have subsequently fallen to 39. This minor fall disguises the true situation since, in the first place, the number of paid holidays has risen from roughly 3 weeks in 1970 to $4\frac{1}{2}$ weeks in 1989, and secondly the amount of overtime and part-time working has been subject to considerable variability. In the case of overtime there was an understandable dip during the 1981–83 recession, but it has subsequently risen sharply in the face of the high fixed costs of hiring labour. At bottom, it is cheaper to pay an existing employee to work a few extra hours than to recruit a new worker who must be trained and who incurs additional NICs and other overheads (and who may need to be laid off again if orders fall away). For this reason actual hours worked have risen despite the fall in the nominal working week.

At the same time there has been an enormous increase in the numbers of part-time and temporary workers, which has given rise to a distinction between two, and possibly three labour forces, namely (1) the permanent staff or core who be required to work overtime to meet emergencies

and whose overtime conditions are now being made more flexible by attempts to calculate overtime on an annual rather than on a weekly basis; (2) the part-time and temporary workers who may be dismissed easily and who form a buffer with which to cope with short-run fluctuations in demand; and (3) outside the firm, the sub-contractors who can be called upon to deal with emergencies. According to a 1986 Labour Force Survey one-third of the labour force was in the flexible labour force comprising part-time, temporary and self-employed workers. About one-quarter of all men and one-half of all women in the labour force were in the flexible labour force, with the main concentration being in the service sector in such occupations as catering, cleaning, hairdressing and other personal service occupations.

The government is intent upon increasing the potential flexibility of the workforce yet further. In the Employment Bill of December 1988 it proposed, for example, to abolish all restrictions on the hours of work for young people aged between 16 and 18, many of which date back to the 1920 Employment of Women, Young Persons and Children's Act, although all legislation governing the employment of children of school age will be retained. Furthermore, the Bill provides for a series of restrictions on the employment and vocational training of women to be over-ridden by the Sex Discrimination Act 1975 and repeals restrictions on women working in mines and quarries.

The enormous surge in part-time working during the 1980s is by no means a phenomenon limited to the UK. The increase has, however, been quite marked in the UK given that it already had one of the highest proportions of part-time workers among industrialised countries in 1979 (it has now overtaken the USA). During the five years to March 1988 the number of part-time jobs increased by 1.4 million (28.2 per cent) whilst the number of full-time jobs increased by 0.8 million (4.3 per cent). One difficulty is, however, the definition of 'part-time work' itself. Officially the dividing line is drawn at 30 hours per week, but 20 per cent of men who work fewer hours still describe themselves as full-time employees, although this is far less common amongst women.

During the same period the numbers in self-employment rose by 505,000 men and 241,000 women, again indicating the increasing flexibility of the workforce. One final point should, however, be carefully borne in mind. If one compares the typical working week between countries one discovers, for example, that the Japanese work much longer hours than in the UK, whilst the equivalent figure is significantly higher in the USA and West Germany and slightly higher in France. These differences partly reflect the relatively high female activity rate and the higher proportion of part-time work in the UK. One consequence is, interestingly, that UK workers actually do more work during working hours than their Japanese and American equivalents. In other words, whilst it is true that Japanese industrial workers are more productive than their UK counterparts, the rest of the Japanese economy would appear to be remarkably inflexible and unproductive by UK standards.

Table 6.3   *Employees in employment, by industry, UK (000)*[1]

	1971	1979	1981	1986	1988		
					Males	*Females*	*Total*
Manufacturing							
Extraction of minerals and ores other than fuels, manufacture of metal, mineral products, and chemicals	1 282	1 147	939	778	592	179	771
Metal goods, engineering, and vehicle industries	3 709	3 374	2 923	2 334	1 751	468	2 219
Other	3 074	2 732	2 360	2 125	1 214	893	2 108
Total manufacturing	8 065	7 253	6 222	5 236	3 557	1 541	5 097
Services							
Distribution, hotels, catering, and repairs	3 686	4 257	4 172	4 403	2 043	2 509	4 551
Transport and communication	1 556	1 479	1 425	1 340	1 080	293	1 372
Banking, finance, insurance, business services, and leasing	1 336	1 647	1 739	2 202	1 239	1 229	2 468
Other	5 049	6 197	6 132	6 541	2 509	4 311	6 820
Total services	11 627	13 580	13 468	14 486	6 870	8 342	15 212
Agriculture, forestry, and fishing	450	380	363	329	230	83	313
Energy and water supply industries	798	722	710	539	387	72	459
Construction	1198	1239	1130	991	901	121	1022
All industries and services	22 139	23 173	21 892	21 581	11 946	10 158	22 104

Note:
[1] As at June each year.
Source: Social Trends, 19 (1989 edn), CSO, Table 4.10.

Figure 6.3 *Workforce and workforce in employment, UK, millions, seasonally adjusted*

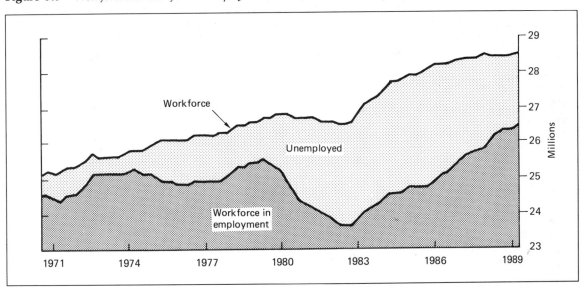

Source: Social Trends, 19 (1989 edn) Chart 4.1; Department of Employment Gazette.

The demand for labour

Although demand factors intruded into the previous sections, we concentrated primarily upon **supply**. Now we shall examine changes in **demand**. The most noticeable feature of the 1970s and 1980s has been the decline in manufacturing, with the fall in the demand for labour being associated with a reduction in output and, probably, a rise in the wage relative to the prices of other factors. Some fall in manufacturing output may have been expected from the exploitation of North Sea oil and gas and from the rise in energy prices. The rise in energy prices might have been expected to have caused a shift away from energy-intensive industries, and the exploitation of North Sea oil and gas could have enabled them to be traded for imports of manufactures and also permitted an expansion of the domestic non-traded (services) sector. The process was, however, intensified by the tight monetary and fiscal measures pursued between 1979 and 1981. The change in the **industrial structure** of the economy has also been accompanied by a shift in the **occupational structure** of the economy.

These factors can be clearly identified in **Table 6.3**. It is interesting to note that in 1988 there were almost exactly the same number of employees in employment as in 1971. However, the manufacturing sector has shrunk by 3 million over this period whilst the service sector has grown by 3.5 million, the difference being accounted for by a modest reduction in absolute terms – but large proportionately – in agriculture, energy and construction. Not all of the services have grown despite the overall effect. The most notable growth has occurred in financial and business services followed by the unspecified 'others', whilst the transport and communication sector has shown a decline. However, the losses in manufacturing are widespread and fairly evenly distributed.

Unemployment[2]

Problems of measurement

The most important measure of the demand for labour is unemployment. Regrettably, it is also one of the most ambiguous. The official picture is

Table 6.4   *Measures of unemployment, all workers, UK, 1971–88 (%)*

	Labour Force Surveys	OECD	Department of Employment (old)	Department of Employment (new)[1]
1971		4.0	2.8	2.6
1972		4.2	3.1	2.9
1973		3.2	2.1	2.0
1974		3.1	2.1	2.0
1975		4.7	3.3	3.1
1976		6.1	4.5	4.2
1977	5.1	3.7	4.8	4.4
1978		6.4	4.7	4.3
1979		5.7	4.3	4.0
1980		7.3	5.4	5.1
1981	9.7	12.4	8.5	8.1
1982		13.1	9.8	9.5
1983		12.5	10.8	10.5
1984	11.0	11.7	11.1	10.7
1985	11.0	11.3	11.3	10.9
1986	11.0	11.5	11.5	11.1
1987		10.3	10.6	10.0
1988				8.0
1989 (June)				6.3

Note:

[1] Seasonally adjusted annual average.

Sources: Labour Force Surveys: OECD Monthly Main Indicators; Department of Employment Gazette; Department of Employment, press release (November 1988); Annual Abstract of Statistics.

contained in **Figure 6.3**, where the 'workforce in employment' consists of employees in employment as measured by employer enquiries, self-employed, HM Forces and participants on work-related government training schemes, and the 'workforce' consists of the workforce in employment plus people claiming benefit at Unemployment Benefit offices.

As can be seen, the official version has just under 2 million people out of work, but this figure is subject to considerable dispute. It relies, for example, upon a count of claimants for unemployment insurance benefits. However, not all of those seeking jobs are eligible for benefits; for example, married women may claim social security benefits on the basis of their husband's premiums, and part-time and temporary workers do not pay unemployment insurance premiums unless their earnings reach a particular level. An alternative definition, which is used in the Labour Force Survey, counts the unemployed as those seeking work in the last

week and who have not done any work whatsoever in the last week before the Survey. A somewhat less stringent approach is used by the OECD, adopting the methodology of the International Labour Office, which counts those seeking work in the last four weeks and who have not done any work during that period. Some idea of how the various definitions in common usage yield different estimates for unemployment expressed as a percentage can be seen in **Table 6.4**.

In recent years the various definitions have produced fairly similar estimates, although this was not previously the case and it has resulted in part from the many adjustments set out in **Table 6.5** which have been made to the official figures. It is worth noting that these estimates satisfy neither those on the political far right nor those on the political far left. The far right argue that the unemployed should exclude all those who could be in education or training; all those who could have retired early; all women, or at least all who are

Table 6.5 *Changes in the methods of recording unemployment statistics, 1979–88*

October 1979	Fortnightly payment of benefits	+ 20 000
November 1981	Men over 60 offered higher supplementary benefit to leave the working population	− 37 000
October 1982	Registration at Job Centres made voluntary Computer count of benefit claimants substituted for clerical count of registrants	− 190 000
March 1983	Men 60 and over given national insurance credits or higher supplementary benefit without claiming unemployment benefit	− 162 000
July 1985	Discrepancies in Northern Ireland count corrected	− 5 000
March 1986	Two-week delay in compilation of figures to reduce over-recording	− 50 000
July 1986	Inclusion of self-employed and HM Forces in denominator of unemployment percentage	− 1.4%
September 1988	Removal of all under 18s who have left school and not found a job but guaranteed a YTS place	− 50 000

Sources: Department of Employment Gazette (October 1986; October 1988); Unemployment Unit Briefing, *Statistical Supplement* (June 1988); Department of Employment, press release (November 1988).

married; and all those who have been unemployed for less than six months. The far left, on the other hand, believe that many people do not choose to register as available to work, and that there is a conspiracy on the part of the government deliberately to massage down the real figures.

This latter view is understandable since it is clear from **Table 6.5** that in virtually every case redefining the meaning of 'unemployment' has caused the percentage to fall. Certainly, each change can be defended on the grounds of greater accuracy or practicality, but it is slightly curious that those not claiming benefit, but who are counted as unemployed in the Labour Force Survey, are ignored in official figures which would be rendered more accurate by their inclusion. However, it is also fair to point out that a certain number of those officially counted as unemployed are economically active in the black economy.

As shown in **Table 6.5** about 190,000 people were removed from the count in 1982 for two reasons. The first was that the old system of registering at an unemployment centre for both benefits and for another job was abolished. Under the old system an unemployed worker would receive benefits and might be offered a choice of three jobs from which to pick one. If he refused the job offers and could not find alternative work then he might forfeit benefits. The system therefore contained an incentive to find work and not to stay unemployed for long. What the new system did was to split the payment of benefits (which was handed over to the DHSS) from the problem of finding a job. The argument for the change was that it would improve efficiency by enabling the staff at Job Centres to concentrate on trying to fit workers to suitable jobs. But the split meant that there was no compulsion to register at the Centres and the effect was to decrease unemployment. In 1983 another significant change was introduced when it was decided to offer men over 60 National Insurance credits or higher supplementary benefit without claiming unemployment benefit, on the ground that older workers might find it impossible to obtain jobs during the recession. In 1988 the removal of all young workers from the unemployment registers reduced the unemployment figures by 50,000. Changes in the percentage of workers unemployed are affected by the definition of unemployment (that is, the numerator); they are also influenced by changes in the denominator (for example, whether the armed forces are included in the labour force). In addition to the factors set out in **Table 6.5** there are immeasurable influences, some of which may be the result of government policy. The numbers unemployed can thus be affected by the tenacity with which people seek jobs. If they are discouraged, then they may drop out of the labour force altogether and thereby reduce the numbers unemployed.

Stocks and flows

It is important to remember that even if the number of unemployed people remains entirely static, this does not mean that the same people are continuously unemployed. In the course of a year a very large number of people move in and out of employment, and the total will remain unchanged if the inflow exactly matches the outflow. **Figure 6.4** plots the inflow and outflow, both male and female, in the course of the year commencing April 1988. This was a period during which the total number unemployed fell, so the outflow mostly exceeds the inflow in any one month. It can be seen that the numbers involved are very large in relation to the total number unemployed of roughly 2 million.

What **Figure 6.4** cannot tell us is anything specific about the **duration of unemployment** since it might either be the case that the outflow during the period comprised almost entirely those flowing in, in which case those unemployed at the beginning of the period would still be unemployed at the end, or the case that those flowing out comprised almost entirely those unemployed at the beginning of the period, in which case the average duration of unemployment would fall rather than rise.

Unemployment by age, duration and sex

The overall position as of April 1989, when there were 1.9 million officially unemployed in the UK,

Figure 6.4   *UK employment flows, April 1988–April 1989 (000)*[1]

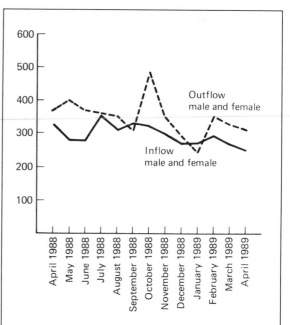

Note:
[1] Not seasonally adjusted, standardised to 4⅓ week months.
Source: Department of Employment Gazette (June 1989).

and as of April 1987 when there were officially 3.1 million unemployed, is shown in **Figure 6.5**. In each case the unemployed are broken down into three age groups, namely 18–24, 25–49 and over 50 respectively, and also according to the duration of unemployment, namely up to 26 weeks, 26–52 weeks and over 52 weeks respectively. Each subcategory represents a combination of a specific age group and duration, and is also divided up into its male and female components.

The discussion below concentrates upon the current (June 1989) position, but the April 1987 figures are also included in order to show how the situation has changed compared to a recent year during which unemployment was at a much higher level. In practice, it is interesting to note that the relationship between age and duration has been little affected by the sharp drop in unemployment. For example, the 18–24 age group comprised 30.5 per cent of the unemployed in 1987 and 28.2 per cent in 1989; the 25–49 age group comprised 48.5

Figure 6.5   *Unemployment by age, duration and sex, April 1987 and April 1989*

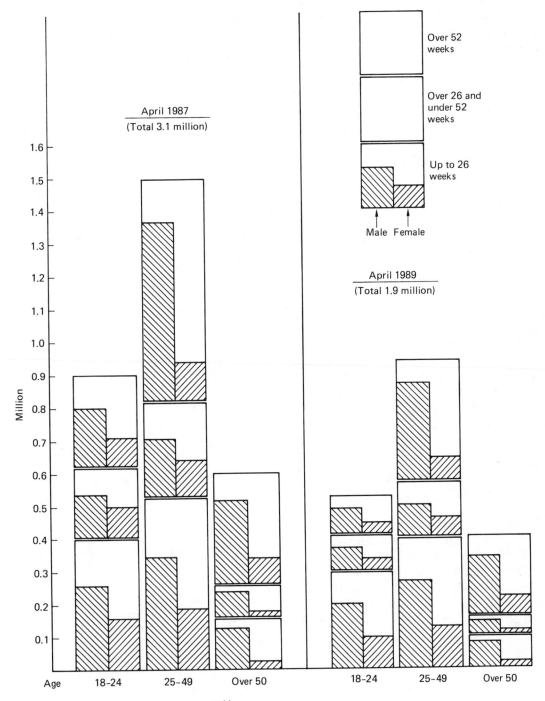

Source: Department of Employment Gazette (June 1989) Table 2.5.

per cent in 1987 and 50.2 per cent in 1989; and the over 50 age group rose from 21 per cent to 21.5 per cent.

On the whole, this accords with a reasonable expectation that continuing economic growth will absorb increasing numbers of those with a potentially long working life ahead of them. In terms of duration, whereas 38 per cent of the unemployed were unemployed for up to 26 weeks in 1987, this was true of 42 per cent in 1989 (with balancing reductions in the two longer-term unemployed categories from 20 to 18 per cent and 42 to 40 per cent respectively), indicating the **increasingly transient nature of unemployment** as economic growth has continued apace. Nevertheless, the high proportion of long-term unemployed (over one year) has remained a notable feature.

Looking at the position in 1989, it appears to be an approximate rule of thumb that there are 2 unemployed males for every 1 female for unemployment durations of up to one year, but beyond that period the ratio rises to 7:3. This 2:1 ratio also holds approximately true for the 18–24 age group irrespective of duration, but in the 25–49 age group the male–female ratio for those unemployed in excess of 52 weeks is 80:20. However, for those aged over 50 the ratio is approximately 75:25 irrespective of duration. The most notable conclusions are thus that young males are twice as likely to be unemployed as young females, and older males three times as likely to be unemployed as older females no matter how long they have been unemployed. However, long-term unemployment amongst the middle age-group is very much a male phenomenon.

It is finally worth noting that the frequency of long-term unemployment is not of itself a necessary condition of the labour market. Data on the USA show, for example, that the percentage of the unemployed who have been out of work for over 26 weeks is virtually never in excess of 20 per cent. However, not merely is the UK figure currently around 60 per cent, but it has virtually never fallen below 30 per cent. Clearly, there are impediments to the outflow of the unemployed in the UK which are not replicated elsewhere.

International comparisons of unemployment

It is possible to make a more general comparison of unemployment rates across countries using both national (and generally incompatible) definitions and on the basis of the standardised measures used by the OECD. Such a comparison is set out in **Figure 6.6** which gives the rate in 1988 and also measures the change in the rate from 1983 to 1988 on national definitions.

It is not that well appreciated that the UK is far from the top of the unemployment table. By the standards of the USA and Japan the UK has little to be proud of, but the picture, at least currently, looks much better if comparisons are limited to Europe. Even West Germany currently has much the same rate as the UK, and indeed the German

Figure 6.6 *International comparisons of unemployment, %*[1]

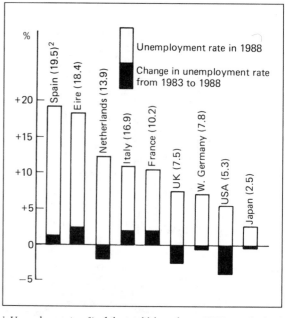

[1] Unemployment as % of the total labour force, OECD standardised rates.

[2] National definitions, seasonally adjusted.

Source: OECD; *Department of Employment Gazette.*

rate is not falling on a comparable basis. Clearly, countries such as Germany which unlike the UK did not engineer a massive recession at the turn of the decade, enjoyed initially a much lower level of unemployment. In the longer term, however, the restructuring of the UK economy has eroded that differential and at least the rate in the UK is on a generally downward path.

Regional dispersion of unemployment

Figure 6.7 illustrates the changing pattern of the regional dispersion of unemployment since 1984. By the standards of many other EC countries such as Italy the regional disparities in the UK have never been particularly severe, and it is reasonable to treat Northern Ireland as something of a special case, permanently marooned at the top of the unemployed pile. As an approximation, excluding Northern Ireland, the region with the highest rate of unemployment has since 1979 suffered twice as much unemployment as the region with the lowest rate irrespective of the stage in the trade cycle. Prior to 1979 the gap had closed somewhat due to regional policy, but this has largely been allowed to wither away under the present government (see **pp. 295–6**).

In general, the same regions appear consistently at the top and bottom of the distribution. In 1979 and 1989 the same regions appear above and below the UK average – with one exception of particular note. In 1979 the West Midlands was still very prosperous, but the 1980–81 recession caused it to suffer a disproportionate rise in unemployment (up from 5 per cent in 1979 to 12.5 per cent in 1984). However, it has improved markedly since 1986 and is currently once again very close to the UK average, and should fall below it by the end of 1989. Interestingly, East Anglia (with its small working population) has for the past two years had less unemployment even than the South East, partly as a result of improved communications. Northern Ireland excepted, it is clear that the improvement in the employment situation has been fairly evenly dispersed and that the gap

between East Anglia and the North is exactly the same as in 1984, albeit at a lower level. In the first half of 1989 the sharpest downward movements appear in respect of Scotland and Wales.

The consistency of the pecking order in terms of regional unemployment is a feature common to EC countries and Japan (with the UK exhibiting the most consistent order of all – see *The Economist*, 29 July 1989, p. 73) but not to the USA. This suggests that it has its roots in **labour immobility**, and hence that it will remain a feature of the UK economy until such time as local wage bargaining becomes widespread and/or regional house price differentials narrow considerably. Since these matters are not directly the concern of regional policy measures, it is understandable that attention has recently been focussed upon specific unemployment blackspots such as towns where the main industry has gone into terminal decline and the inner areas of large cities.

Skill shortages

Despite widespread unemployment, one of the most prominent features of the current labour market is the shortage of certain skills. According to the CBI the proportion of companies expecting shortages of skilled labour to constrain their output has risen from roughly 2.5 per cent in 1982 to roughly 20 per cent in 1988. Whilst this figure has been exceeded in past booms, the rate of increase is exceptionally rapid so past peaks may yet be exceeded. In specific locations such as the Thames Valley the great majority of all companies are affected. The problem is felt most acutely where companies wish to introduce new technology. The most frequent response has been either to increase overtime working, to use temporary and contract staff and to introduce increased rates of pay. However, these are no more than short-term palliatives, and longer-term solutions are needed. Some companies have accordingly formed compacts with schools to ease recruitment of school leavers, whilst others have introduced schemes to train the long-term unemployed.

Figure 6.7   *Regional unemployment rates, %*[1]

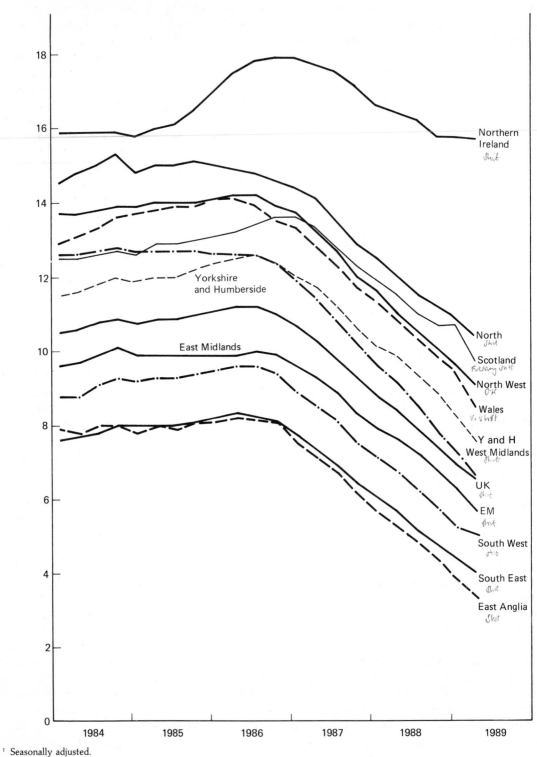

[1] Seasonally adjusted.

Source: Economic Trends, CSO, Table 22.

Causes of unemployment

Unemployment may be caused by a variety of factors, and these are usually grouped under the headings of **frictional**, **seasonal**, **cyclical** and **structural**. In turn, these headings may be reduced to factors stemming from the **demand side** or the **supply side** of the labour market. Throughout the postwar period attention tended to be concentrated upon demand management on the assumption that it was changes in aggregate money demand which were the main cause of unemployment. In the 1970s and 1980s interest shifted to the supply-side explanations of unemployment. It was recognised that the rise in energy prices in 1973 and 1979 had increased costs of production and, in the face of workers' resistance to reductions in their real wage, that this had led to a squeeze on profits with a resultant fall in investment and in the demand for labour. Reductions in aggregate demand certainly occurred after the 1979 rise in energy prices, but there were also significant changes on the supply side.

The discovery and exploitation of North Sea oil led to a shift away from energy-using industries such as manufacturing and towards labour intensive service trades. This shift was emphasised by the fact that the exploitation of North Sea oil caused a rise in the exchange rate and led to exports of oil being in effect offered in exchange for imports of manufactures. The movement of the exchange rate was accentuated by the severe fiscal and monetary policies pursued after 1979, but it was noticeable that the level of imports was such as to suggest that there was demand within the economy which could have been absorbed if domestic prices had been lower. These forces had implications for the relationship between wage changes and unemployment. **Figure 6.8** reveals the nature of the relationship between increases in money earnings and the level of unemployment since the first oil shock.

What **Figure 6.8** shows is that from 1973 to 1975 the rate of increase of money earnings accelerated despite rising unemployment. This was the period known as 'stagflation' — the condition in which inflation and unemployment co-existed as workers sought to protect their incomes against rising prices. The rate of increase of earnings then fell between 1975 and 1977 only to resume its acceleration between 1977 and 1980. The most surprising feature of **Figure 6.8** is, however, that over the 1980s earnings remained at levels higher than those experienced during the 1960s in spite of a sharp increase in the level of unemployment.

What this appeared to demonstrate was that there was **no longer any trade-off between inflation and unemployment** — the underlying premise of the Phillips Curve relationship which had been in vogue during the 1970s. Hence much attention has been directed during the 1980s to the idea of a '**natural**' rate of unemployment. This represents that part of the labour force which will remain unemployed even when the supply of and demand for labour are in equilibrium at a given real wage. The unemployment which remains may be termed frictional and structural, but these terms are not themselves of great significance. The key point is that, at the natural rate, employment is 'full' in the sense that anyone who wishes to work at the prevailing real wage rate can find employment. The natural rate is a flexible concept since any movement in either the demand curve for labour or resulting from the introduction of supply-side policies will cause it to alter over time. Indeed, this is the rationale for supply-side economics as discussed in Chapter 1. Unfortunately, whilst much of the discussion of unemployment is currently couched in terms of the natural rate, its measurement has remained too imprecise to be particularly helpful. Layard and Nickell (1985) and Nickell (1987) offer the best estimates so far which reveal that the natural rate (which is also known as the NRU, or the non-accelerating inflation rate of unemployment — NAIRU) was less than 3 per cent for male employees during the 1960s; that it rose steadily during the 1970s, with a temporary fall at the end of the decade; and that it rose again to a peak in 1983 at roughly 13.7 per cent. Thereafter it has almost certainly been in continuous decline.

The importance of this estimate lies in the fact that if actual unemployment lies above the natural rate then the gap can be bridged by expanding demand without setting off an inflationary spiral, whilst if there is no gap the only solution is first to lower the natural rate through expanding supply.

Figure 6.8   *Annual rate of change of weekly earnings of all workers*

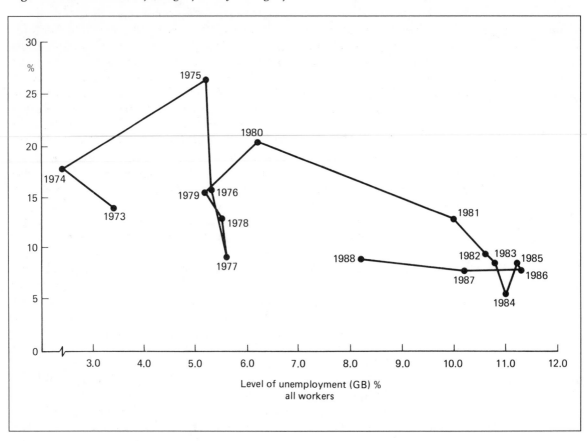

Source: Department of Employment Gazette

In examining the causes of unemployment it is possible to relate many of these to the natural rate. Such potential causes would include excessive pay awards, too high a level of unemployment benefit relative to wage levels and any other factors causing the labour market to malfunction. The more orthodox Keynesian view remains that of placing the blame upon a deficiency in aggregate demand. There are also those who place major responsibility at the door of technical progress as a destroyer of jobs, and those who emphasise the role of an overvalued exchange rate or of North Sea oil.

It is beyond our scope to analyse all these factors in detail, although it is reasonably certain that all of them have had something to do with the rise in unemployment. One factor which can, however, be substantially played down is that of **technologically induced unemployment**. In past decades there has been little evidence of this phenomenon, and it is evident that the greater the number of computers the greater the output of information and the greater the need for people to do something with all of the data. In any event, it can hardly have thrown a million workers onto the dole. What it probably has done is to shift people from manufacturing to service employment with some temporary structural unemployment created in the process.

There is also little support for the role of excessive unemployment benefits although it is strongly advocated by Minford (1983). Here again the sheer scale of the problem militates against such an explanation, and there would have had to have been a marked rise in the replacement ratio, which is difficult to discern at the end of the 1970s, to justify a massive preference for living off unemployment benefits.

The Keynesian approach, which sees the problem as one of demand deficiency, must cope with the difficulty that the onset of North Sea oil at the end of the 1970s offset the deflationary impact of the sharp rise in the oil price, which manifestly did not happen after the first OPEC-induced rise in 1973. It is argued that the economy was actually already in recession by 1979 but that this was temporarily disguised by the high level of consumer demand resulting from buoyant real wages. Once, however, the government set about deflating the economy after 1979, net-of-tax incomes fell and savings rose in line with higher interest rates thereby creating a severe shortfall in demand which was exacerbated by the over-valued exchange rate.

The government have tended to place great emphasis upon excessive real wages as the reason for unemployment. However, as noted in the discussion concerning inflation in Chapter 1, earnings have until recently done little more than keep pace with productivity, and the earlier discussion of the decline in trade union membership is such as to suggest that trade union power is on the wane rather than the contrary. Hence, it is reasonable to conclude that the correlation between earnings and unemployment is extremely weak.

One of the recurrent themes in recent studies emphasises the supply side of the economy. It is argued, in line with previous comments, that the 1970s were a period characterised by an oil price shock, a decline in productivity and a consequent fall in profitability. In response to these factors firms had either to cut real wages or to shed workers. Given trade union resistance to real wage cuts the brunt of the adjustment fell upon the number of jobs. Taxation, and especially increases in such non-wage costs as National Insurance contributions, served to accelerate this process.

One final factor worthy of mention is that of **labour market imperfections**. The trend mentioned previously with respect to long-term unemployment suggests that it has become more difficult to match job-seekers and vacancies. This is unlikely to be attributable to excessive choosiness about jobs by those out of work, but may have something to do with imperfections in the housing market. With differences in house prices at historic highs between different regions it is understandable that many potential workers cannot afford to move to the high-priced areas where jobs are available. Equally, the system for allocating council houses makes it very difficult for a council tenant to move to a prosperous area with a housing waiting list.

The reduction of unemployment

The problem of unemployment is complex and there can therefore be no simple nostrum to make it go away. There are a variety of possible approaches to ameliorate the situation,[2] the most significant of which are discussed below.

Job Centres

Unemployment may be reduced through the provision and dissemination of information about the availability of jobs. Job Centres (previously called labour exchanges) were introduced into Britain in 1911 and complemented the means by which unemployment benefits were paid. An unemployed worker was obliged to register at a labour exchange for his unemployment benefits. As a test of his willingness to work he would be offered a choice of three jobs from a register, and if he refused all of the jobs and failed to provide one for himself then his benefit might be stopped. During the 1970s, as we saw above, the provision of information about jobs was divorced from the payment of benefits. Job information came to be provided by the Job Centres which were responsible to the MSC, and the payment of benefits was handed over to the DHSS. The result was an increase in unemployment. In 1987, however, there was a tightening up of the procedures for claiming benefits through the introduction of the Job Restart Scheme for the long-term unemployed.

However, questions concerning the importance and efficiency of Job Centres came to the fore in 1986 when the government was faced with rising unemployment and the pressure to cut spending. At the time the MSC judged the efficiency of the Job Centres by the speed with which jobs were filled. At the time some 40 per cent of vacancies were filled within one day and 68 per cent were filled within two weeks. But given that there were more unemployed than vacancies, and given that employers notified only those jobs which they thought could be filled by Job Centres, it was hardly surprising that jobs were filled quickly.

Some light was thrown upon the methods by which workers got jobs through the 1983 General Household Survey which enquired as to the source from which employees first learned about their present job, although it has to be noted that workers may use Job Centres without taking a job on offer. Despite reservations, the 1983 Survey is the best available information, and what the data suggested was that about one in three workers got their jobs through the help of friends and relatives and one in four as a result of direct approaches to, and from, employers. The importance of specialist agencies was slight since they served specialist markets such as those for part-time clerical staffs and some managerial grades. Proportionately more women than men got their jobs as a result of reading advertisements but the influence of advertising declined in the 1980s as the recession deepened. In the case of married women returning to work, the most successfully used routes were to scan a newspaper, consult friends or relatives or approach employers directly. The importance of Job Centres increased when full-time work was sought, although the preponderance of jobs in recent years has been for married women who were prepared to work part-time. Finally, we may note that the market share of Job Centres increased between 1973 and 1983.

It therefore appears that most workers tend to get their jobs through friends and relatives and direct approaches to, and from, employers. There is an informal network of information in the labour market and Job Centres tend to act as information agencies of last resort whose importance increases in severe recessions. They are used most frequently

by the unskilled, which suggests that what the State does is to provide a subsidised information service for the low income groups. But throughout the 1970s and 1980s Job Centres were ill-equipped to cope with the problems of the unemployed. One reason for their failure was the divorce of information transmission from both the provision of training and unemployment benefits. In an ideal system these three functions would be brought together in an effort to assist the unemployed because the three functions address four issues – namely, the matching of an unemployed person with a vacancy; the length of time that a job is likely to last; the savings to the community of an unemployed person being placed in a job or on a training programme; and the costs to the community of a person being permanently unemployed. Unfortunately, the issues became separated in the 1970s when the payment of unemployment benefit was handed over to the DHSS and there was no compulsion on the unemployed to use Job Centres. Moreover, when attempts were made to improve the efficiency of Job Centres by cutting costs, the Centres reacted by reducing the amount of assistance to the long-term unemployed, and as a result many of the costs of unemployment were transferred to the DHSS. In 1987 an attempt was made to improve the efficiency of Job Centres by linking advice and assistance throuh the Job Restart Scheme which was introduced to do something for the long-time unemployed.

Unemployment benefits

Unemployment might be reduced by cutting unemployment benefits and by imposing more stringest tests for qualifying for benefits. The subject is controversial and the evidence not clear-cut. **Table 6.6** suggests that the 'replacement ratio' (which measures the percentage of wages for which benefits are a substitute) has been falling throughout the 1980s and, although the government has introduced the Restart Scheme as a means of dealing with the long-term unemployed, there is not much evidence to support the view that interviewed people have found jobs. Indeed, the main effects of the Scheme may be to force some people to despair and withdraw from the labour force.

Job subsidies, training and factory legislation

Jobs can also be increased by introducing subsidies. The problem is, as we saw earlier, to avoid paying subsidies on workers who would have been employed in any case. Jobs can also be increased through profit sharing and the government has introduced tax incentives to encourage profit sharing.

The real problem concerns the amount of subsidy required to induce employers to train workers in high grade skills and the kinds of non-wage reductions which may have to be removed in order to allow young people to enter highly skilled jobs. It has been suggested that young people are prevented from entering high wage jobs because of the impact of factory legislation which prevents them from working at night. Some of these restrictions are now being removed. The problem of the optimum subsidy stems from the fact that the wage differential between young and adult workers in Britain is much smaller than in Germany and Japan, and the grants offered by governments have been too little to persuade firms to train workers. Such incentive as has existed has tended to perpetuate the main weaknesses of the existing system. Employers have been persuaded or cajoled into offering jobs which dealt with their short-term needs rather than the long-term requirements of the community. In the depressed areas MSC tended to approve any scheme from any source and to maintain low skill training. The new training programmes which leave decisions to employers may perpetuate past practices.

Issues in pay determination

Pay differentials

The size distribution of male manual workers' earnings has tended to exhibit a high degree of stability for over a century. However, the 1980s has shown there can be short-run variations in the distribution of wages. The widening of differentials which has taken place has been the result of market forces as well as of political intervention. Comparable data for women manual workers and for non-manual workers does not exist, but the short-run statistics also exhibit widening in the earnings distribution.

The distribution of higher incomes is presumed to reflect the fact that salaries are paid **according to rank**. Thus managers are paid more than foremen and foremen are paid more than shopfloor workers. The differentials between the occupations tend to be multiples of the productivities of the groups each person supervises. A foreman in charge of eight men will thus receive a salary which will reflect the difference between output with and without his presence. The widening of differentials can also be observed in the movement of the salary differentials of non-manual workers, occupational differentials and the relative position of low-paid workers covered by wages councils. It is worth noting that in order to effect a widening of differentials there has had to be a tremendous change in the demand for labour, which at one point in the 1980s resulted in 3 million workers being unemployed.

Table 6.6 *Ratio of unemployment benefits[1] to average earnings net of tax (%)*

1970	1971	1972	1973	1974	1975	1976	1977	1978	1979	1980	1981	1982	1983	1984	1985
68.7	63.3	66.7	65.0	65.2	65.6	64.7	67.5	64.2	59.1	55.9	52.2	40.7	40.6	40.0	39.0

Note:
[1] Including earnings-related benefits
Source: National Economic Development Office, *The British Labour Market and Unemployment* (NEDC, 1987).

Narrowing of differentials: equal pay, equal value

The pay of women has been an exception to the general widening of differentials, as shown in **Table 6.7**, and has been ascribed to a variety of factors. In the first place, there was the impact of incomes policies in the early 1970s which tended to favour the low paid. Secondly, there have been the changes in the industrial distribution of jobs. Heavy manufacturing industries, which were predominantly male preserves, contracted in the 1980s, and there was a shift to increased employment in the service trades.

The Equal Pay Act 1975 interpreted 'equal pay' as meaning that women should be doing similar work to men. In 1983 the European Court found that the UK was in contravention of EC legislation which defined equal pay in terms of equal value. In 1983 the Equal Pay (Amendment) Regulations were passed to bring the UK into line with member States. But what 'equal value' means is still open to interpretation by the Courts. In the case of *Hayward* v. *Cammell Laird Shipbuilders* a cook claimed equal pay with a joiner and other males in diverse occupations. The company countered by pointing to the monetary value of perks given to the cook but not available to the men. However, the House of Lords took equal pay to mean equal money wages and chose to ignore the value of other aspects of the employment contract. Furthermore, the Regulations must be set in the context of the deregulation of many state activities by the government. The law thus applies not only to individual employers but to groups of employers who negotiate collectively, and to obtain exemp-

tion employers must be able to show that their wage structures have been subject to acceptable job evaluation exercises.

In 1987 the National Joint Council for Local Authorities' Services, which is a joint body representing employers and trade unions in local government, sought to avoid claims and counter-claims (leap-frogging) by instituting a **job evaluation scheme**. A wage structure based on a job evaluation scheme conducted in 1969 was in existence, and although it had been modified in 1975 by the introduction of equal pay and in 1986 by the merger of the three lowest grades, it was obsolete and subject to questioning for three reasons. In the first place, most women were employed in part-time jobs (which may have been due to choice, but also reflected the opportunities available to them under the pay structure). Secondly, most women were employed on jobs which paid low wage rates. Thirdly, male earnings tended to be boosted by piecework, overtime and shift working.

Youth unemployment and pay

Age cohorts of young people have described cycles around a declining birth rate trend. In the 1930s the birth rate was low with the result that young workers entering the labour market in the 1940s and 1950s encountered relatively good job prospects which were accentuated by the boom and conscription. The baby boom of the late 1940s and 1950s was the outcome of lags in family formation during the Second World War, together with the relatively high wages in the postwar

Table 6.7   *Women's hourly earnings relative to those of men, in April of each year, 1970–88*[1]

1970	63.1	1978	73.9	1982	73.9	1986	74.3
1975	72.1	1979	73.0	1983	74.2	1987	73.6
1976	75.1	1980	73.5	1984	73.5	1988	75.1
1977	75.5	1981	74.8	1985	74.1		

Note:

[1] Average gross hourly earnings, excluding overtime, of full-time employees aged 18 and over whose pay was not affected by absence.
Source: New Earnings Surveys, Annual.

boom. The baby boom led to an influx of young workers into the labour market in the 1960s, and their wage and employment prospects were rendered favourable by the continuance of the boom and by the expansion of higher education. However, the school leavers of the late 1970s – the result of a high birth rate during the 1960s – encountered depressed demand conditions.

Common sense suggests that if there is an excess supply then the price of the factor of production should fall until the market is cleared. However, if we plot the ratio of the labour costs of young workers to the labour costs of adult workers against their relative employment, then no simple demand curves can be detected. In 1980 the Department of Employment came to the view that young workers were not being priced out of good jobs, but the rather limited evidence of more recent periods suggest the contrary to be the case, and the government has accordingly taken the steps described earlier to try and ensure that there are no impediments to the free working of the labour market.

Insiders and outsiders

Youth unemployment has been one component of unemployment, but youth unemployment tends to follow the general pattern of unemployment, albeit at much higher levels during recessions when young workers are hard hit by their lack of skills. During the recessionary periods of the 1970s and 1980s many school leavers were unable to get a job, and this suggests that queueing occurs in labour markets and also that employment may be related to rules which transcend simple economics, but which are no less effective in determining wages and which might explain why wages have risen despite massive unemployment.

Suppose that trade unions are not simple economic agencies which operate as monopoly sellers of labour. Suppose they are political agencies operating in an economic environment. That they may be political agencies follows from the fact that it is not possible to buy and sell union membership rights. Consequently, decisions within unions tend to be governed by political considerations. Faced

with a fall in demand, older members will thus resist wage cuts because that will redistribute income to new members. Alternatively, faced with an increase in demand, they will press for wage increases rather than expand the membership because the latter policy would redistribute income to new recruits. So, given that unions prefer to dismiss members rather than retain them, a distinction is drawn between 'insiders' and 'outsiders'. Outsiders may not be able to get jobs because insiders may resist their employment. Outsiders may be content to queue for jobs and not be tempted to look for jobs if unemployment benefits are high. Employers may be reluctant to hire unemployed workers because they fear that they possess outmoded skills and attitudes. They may also fear the reactions of existing workers.

An objection to the 'senior voter' argument is that it suggests that a worker will be prepared to acquiesce in such a policy even though it may mean that he will eventually become the worker on the margin of employment. Furthermore, the policy may make sense only if the lay-offs are slight, and when there are mass redundancies the seniority principle may break down. We thus need to consider the possibility that unions may agree to contracts which allow for no dismissals or contracts which permit wage flexibility.

Wage, salaried and profit-sharing contracts

The seniority model, as has been noted, is subject to a major weakness. Why, after all, should a worker agree to a policy which may make him the marginal worker – the one who is most likely to be dismissed if demand falls further?

In order to overcome this problem it is postulated that workers will be more responsive in their wage demands to changes in unemployment but not to the level of unemployment. However, the type of contract accepted by a worker or offered by an employer will depend upon the following factors:

1. the degree of risk-averseness of employers and workers

2. the ease of access to information of both employers and workers
3. the work–leisure preferences of workers
4. the effects of unemployment benefits
5. the methods and costs of enforcing contracts
6. the costs associated with hiring, training and dismissing workers.

Wage contracts

If workers are more risk-averse than employers, and if employers can spread their risks through the capital market by adopting limited liability methods of raising finance, then employers may offer a guaranteed income but no guarantee of employment. They will also be willing to offer such contracts if they can hire workers easily and if the costs of training workers are low. Workers may be willing to accept such contracts if they can offset the loss of wages through the receipt of unemployment benefits. Unions may prefer such contracts when faced with uncertainty as to future levels of demand if it is possible to introduce a seniority rule which copes with the problems of those who have incurred the greatest or longest periods of investment in human capital and, additionally, if they are preoccupied with wage differentials between different groups of members, some of whose wages may be threatened with reductions and some of whose wages may be rising.

Salaried contracts

If workers are more risk-averse than employers, and if employers find it difficult to hire and train workers, then employers may offer workers a guarantee of both income and employment. Such conditions are those in which a union may be able to obtain an all-or-nothing contract – that is, a contract which stipulates both the **wage** and the **numbers to be employed**.

Profit-sharing contracts

If workers are no more risk-averse than employers, and have equal access to information, then they may accept contracts which guarantee them employment but which do not guarantee their income. In practice, the distribution of **profit-sharing contracts** reveals a concentration in the financial sector and in some of the service trades where many workers are, in effect, self-employed.

Strikes

Strikes are one method of resolving differences of opinion concerning appropriate employment contracts. They are not, however, the only method and their occurrence has been ascribed to accidents arising from differences in the information available to employers and trade unions. Such divergencies in the information available are likely to occur during periods of rapid economic change, and the prolongation of a dispute can result from the length of time it takes union leaders or managers to conduct internal negotiations with their members or employers. Strike activity has, therefore, been linked to changes in the cost of living, unemployment, productivity and profitability.

Table 6.8 sheds some light upon the movement of strike activity since 1970. There was a rise in strikes (in both frequency and severity) in the early 1970s which was associated with the rapid inflation at the time and with the attempts to control wages through incomes policies. Strike activity subsequently moderated between the two oil shocks of 1973 and 1979, although the latter year was notable for a peak of 29 million working days lost, mainly as a consequence of the 'Winter of Discontent'. The severe deflation of 1979–80 then caused strike activity to fall away until it experienced a sudden peak of activity in 1984. Many of the strikes of the 1980s were in protest against redundancies and anti-union policies. There are currently signs of a resurgence in strike activity, primarily undertaken in order to pursue wage claims at a time of rising inflation.

Arbitration: automatic and third party

We have distinguished contracts which permit income flexibility and those which do not. We have also commented upon the use of strikes to enforce or alter contracts. Contracts which permit flexibility rely upon an automatic response to the random movements of the markets for goods and services: **if profits fall, then incomes fall**. In the past automatic mechanisms were built into some wage contracts, but these have fallen into disuse in recent decades. For example, wages were some-

Table 6.8 *Stoppages[1] in progress, UK, 1967–88*

Year	Number of recorded stoppages in progress	Workers involved in period (000)	Working days lost (000)	Working days lost per 1,000 employees[2]
1967	2 133	734	2 787	122
1968	2 390	2 258	4 690	207
1969	3 146	1 665	6 846	303
1970	3 943	1 801	10 980	489
1971	2 263	1 178	13 551	612
1972	2 530	1 734	23 909	1 080
1973	2 902	1 528	7 197	317
1974	2 946	1 626	14 750	647
1975	2 332	809	6 012	265
1976	2 034	668	3 284	146
1977	2 737	1 166	10 142	448
1978	2 498	1 041	9 405	413
1979	2 125	4 608	29 474	1 273
1980	1 348	834	11 964	521
1981	1 344	1 513	4 266	195
1982	1 538	2 103	5 313	248
1983	1 364	574	3 754	178
1984	1 221	1 464	27 135	1 278
1985	903	791	6 402	298
1986	1 074	720	1 920	89
1987	1 016	887	3 546	166
1988	781	790	3 702	168

Notes:

[1] The statistics relate to stoppages of work in the UK due to industrial disputes between employers and workers, or between workers and other workers, connected with terms and conditions of employment. Work to rules and go-slows are not included nor are stoppages involving fewer than ten workers or lasting less than one day unless the total number of workers' days lost in the dispute exceeds 100. The statistics include lock-outs and unlawful strikes (see *Employment Gazette* (July 1989) p. 359).

[2] Based on the latest available mid-year (June) estimate of employees in employment.

Source: Department of Employment Gazette.

times linked to the selling prices of products, but if the demand for the goods was price-inelastic then both wages and prices might have to fall greatly – a circumstance which workers were to reject in favour of a minimum wage. Wages have also been linked to the prices of consumer goods, but the procedure suffered from two defects. In the first place, the prices of consumer goods could be outside the control of employers; there might be no expedient which would allow employers to bargain about wages in real terms. Secondly, if governments agreed to compensate workers for rises in prices then there might be no end to inflation. An alternative to these forms of automa-

tic arbitration is **third party intervention**. Third party intervention comprises conciliation, mediation and arbitration. The function of the conciliator is passive – he or she merely brings the disputants together and allows them to find their own solution. The mediator suggests possible solutions which both parties may have overlooked. Arbitration may be voluntary or compulsory and the arbitrator makes an award which is binding on both sides.

Third party intervention may enable one side to make a concession without appearing to be weak. A union leader may have threatened a strike without assessing the consequences. A long period of industrial peace may be terminated abruptly by the emergence of inexperienced negotiators. In such circumstances an arbitrator may be used as a fall-guy: that is, he or she may be blamed for a result which was inevitable although one side may be reluctant to accept it.

All of this raises the question of whether an arbitrator can or should be independent. Arbitrators cannot be independent if they wish to keep the peace, since any award that fails to satisfy either side will be rejected. Arbitrators must be guided by opportunism and expediency rather than attempt to carry out a government's economic policy. Once having drawn such a conclusion we must address ourselves to the concept of **pendulum arbitration** (or final offer arbitration), which has been canvassed recently, and to the apparent decline in arbitration because the government is less concerned with industrial peace and more preoccupied with economic efficiency. The objection to expediency and opportunism is that it lends itself to the suggestion that all arbitrators do is 'split the difference'. Hence, the desire to impose some control over the awards. However, not all awards amount to splitting the difference nor do all the final offers lend themselves to easy interpretation. In many cases they are capable of improvement, especially if the offer is a complex package of proposals. Therefore, a policy of imposing the final offer may be too simple and inefficient.

Conciliation and arbitration boards have a long history in British industrial relations, and were prominent in the nineteenth century in the textiles and coal mining industry. At the turn of the century the State became actively involved through the creation of arbitrators and conciliators and courts of enquiry, and these channels of intervention have been organised under the aegis of ACAS (Arbitration, Conciliation and Advisory Service) since 1975. Hoever, two things should be noted about the use of third party intervention. In the first place, it has tended to operate at the periphery of industrial relations, and it has not always been invoked when there have been major disputes. Secondly, the use of third party intervention has been declining since the mid-1970s. The fall in usage has been due, in part, to the decline in employment and economic activity and to the

verdicts reached in the major disputes of the 1980s. A further reason for the decline has been the refusal of Ministers to submit disputes in the public sector to third parties.

Conclusion

During the 1980s the labour market has been subjected to a number of severe shocks. Deflation, the exploitation of North Sea oil and the shift of economic activity to the South have been accompanied by a sharp and persistent rise in unemployment and by the introduction of legislation designed to reduce the power of trade unions and to create a floor of rights for the individual worker. The result has been a fall in union membership in the private sector to about 5 million; a lowering of the minimum income level through reduced unemployment and earning-related benefits; a shrinkage of the male manual labour force and the manufacturing sector and an increase in the number of women in the labour force. Methods of wage payment have also been changing and there has been an increased interest in the use of personal incentive schemes. The income redistribution effects which were built into the public sector have been reduced as a result of denationalisation, privatisation and tendering. The distribution of wages has therefore widened.

However, wages still keep rising despite the persistence of high levels of unemployment, which suggests that whatever else may be pushing up wages, it is not trade unionism. Wages are rising partly under the influence of the increase in aggregate money demand brought about by tax changes and by company policies which emphasise productivity. There is also a growing awareness that in the 1990s the flow of young people on to the labour market will be much less than in the 1980s. All of this means that in a labour market increasingly characterised by individualism and an absence of recognisable institutional restraints on wage movement, the only method of curbing inflation will be monetary policy and the only method of reducing unemployment will be more State intervention in the labour market.

Notes

1. The Department of Employment is currently made up of a number of component parts known collectively as the Employment Department Group. The main parts are:
   - The **Training Agency**, formed in September 1988, with responsibility for training programmes
   - The **Employment Service**, formed in 1987, which brings together unemployment benefit, Job Centre and other services centred on the unemployed
   - **ACAS**
   - The **Health and Safety Commission** and the **Health and Safety Executive**.

2. The definition of such terms as 'unemployed', 'workforce', 'employees in employment' and so forth can be ambiguous. If their meaning is insufficiently clear in the text a list of official definitions is to be found in *Employment Gazette* (October 1989) p.567.

3. This discussion does not cover the more general issue of the use of demand management techniques which are the subject matter of Chapter 9, nor is there any replication of the supply-side discussion in Chapter 1.

References

Cm 665 (1989) *Removing Barriers to Employment:.Proposals For the Further Reform of Industrial Relations and Trade Union Law* (HMSO) (March).

Cmnd 540 (1988) *Employment for the 1990s* (HMSO) (December).

Layard, R. and Nickell, S. (1985) 'The Causes of British Unemployment', *NIER* (February).

Lund, P.J. *et al.*, (1985) *Wages and Employment in Agriculture: England and Wales 1960–1981*, Government Economic Working Paper, 52, Ministry of Agriculture.

Minford, P. (1983) *Unemployment: Cause and Cure* (Martin Robertson).

Morgan, P. *et al.* (1985) *Wage Floors in the Clothing Industry 1950–1981*, Research Paper, 54, Department of Employment.

Nickell, S. (1987) 'Why is Wage Inflation So High?, *Oxford Bulletin of Economics and Statistics* (February).

7

Welfare: Inequality & Poverty · *Paul Marshall*

Inequality and income distribution

Even at the crudest level no assessment of the well-being of a society can have much credibility unless it takes some account of the distribution of income as well as its aggregate total (Morris and Preston, 1986).

This quotation is from a study of income distribution over time. Even for a simple economy, measuring the distribution of economic gain is very difficult; for a large, developed, mixed economy, in which both public and private sectors exert their influences on income distribution, the complications of measuring distribution patterns are endless. The study from which the quotation is taken is of income distribution in the UK and covers a period during which there were major structural changes to the economy, several exogenous shocks (including the oil price hike of the early 1970s) and major social and political upheavals, including three changes of government. Nevertheless, as the quotation underlines, if we are interested in measuring economic welfare, and its tendency to change over time, we must take account of the **distribution of the gains from economic processes** no matter how complicated or dynamic they may be.

In the case of a mixed economy like the UK the role of government is a crucial influence upon the distribution of income and wealth and this will be emphasised in the course of Chapter 7, particularly in relation to government's objective of reducing inequality. Within the government spending section of the national accounts are many items which relate to programmes aimed at improvements in individual welfare. The range of such programmes is considerable, spanning subsidies to both production (for example, farm income support programmes) and consumption (for example, household income maintenance programmes). Indeed, such is the range that any overview must be selective. For present purposes the selection concentrates on issues which lie at the heart of government aims to reduce inequalities in the distribution of income and wealth, issues which are often subsumed under the heading of 'social policy'. **Why** governments need to finance and/or provide such programmes and to **what extent** they should do so are extremely difficult questions to answer and Chapter 7 can do no more than shed some light on the policy debate.

So far as economists are concerned the issues to be discussed concern individual 'welfare' – whether welfare is maximised for everyone through the market system or whether market determined incomes require alteration by State action and, if so, how the alteration is to be achieved. Clearly, the welfare of individuals depends upon a multitude of things and not simply on the acquisition of material goods and services: it is the search for an understanding of the characteristics of, and the influences exerted by, this multitude that forms the basis of enquiry in social science. Within social science it is Economics which has concentrated on the material aspects of well-being, but it is difficult to maintain a strict divorce between Economics and other disciplines when trying to analyse the causes of the distribution of material consumption.

The efficiency/equity trade-off

As an analytical concept, and as an aim of government policy, **efficiency** holds centre stage throughout this book, reflecting the main preoccupation of economists. But questions of welfare relate often to **equity** as well as to efficiency, and here lies a problem for both the analyst and the policy-maker: **it is rare for an efficiency objective to be achieved without an inequality being created**. Indeed, to recognise the reality of the problem of managing a mixed economy is to see it as a search for acceptable **trade-offs** between equity and efficiency. What the trade-offs look like

is a major question for research into the evaluation of government expenditure programmes. What the trade-offs **should** look like is part of a normative debate which manifests itself in the varying policies advanced from different political standpoints. Thus, for some observers, the question of equity should be at the forefront of political debate and should be the primary consideration in the formation of government expenditure plans. This argument may stem from altruism but it may also be based on pragmatism – if 'the system' creates too much inequality it may invite violent political upheaval, or revolution! On the other hand, some observers argue that efficiency should be always the main criterion for judging public expenditure programmes since only if the economy is efficient in every respect can the income available for redistribution be maximised – in other words reducing inequality depends on reducing inefficiency! The issue of the trade-off will recur throughout Chapter 7 and is often illustrated by the characteristics of the social policies implemented by different governments.

The concept of inequality

Using the term 'inequality' in the present context is intended as a comment upon the extent to which the rewards of the market place, supplemented and modified by government tax/transfer programmes, are distributed equally throughout the population. To measure inequality in this way is very difficult for reasons of practical computation and for reasons of principle. Practical difficulties loom large when choosing appropriate data from which to analyse distributions. In the UK, for example, official estimates of income distribution are often derived from Inland Revenue returns whereby the definition of 'income' is that used for the purposes of income taxation. Since income defined for tax purposes may exclude some important sources of income (for example capital gains, imputed income from home production and property ownership, fringe benefits and certain government transfers), measures of distribution based on this definition may be inaccurate.

But even if comprehensive measures of income

were available and distributions were to be computed accurately, there remains a difficult issue of principle – namely, how to **judge** distributions as 'equal' or 'unequal'. Certainly, we know what an equal distribution of incomes looks like – one in which **every income unit** (individual or household) has the **same income as any other unit**. We might be tempted to say, therefore, that any distribution in which at least one income unit has more or less than each of the other units is unequal. But this is not very helpful when looking at a world of many distributions in which the **degree** of inequality differs; it is this very question of degree which makes the measurement problem so difficult to resolve. If we are interested in comparing distributions at a point in time, or assessing changes in inequality over time, the problem becomes acute.

The crux of the problem lies in the fact that while it is possible always to describe different patterns of income distribution, it is not possible often to describe different patterns of **inequality** without invoking a value judgement. Suppose, for example, that a change in government policy makes the top 10 per cent of income recipients slightly better off, the next 80 per cent much better off and the bottom 10 per cent slightly worse off. Has the policy change effected a more equal distribution of income? How is the small loss suffered by the bottom 10 per cent of income recipients to be weighed against the large gain to the majority of the population? What comment can we make about a change which has made the bottom 10 per cent of income recipients worse off while raising the incomes received by the top 10 per cent?

Clearly, for an observer to describe one pattern of income distribution as more or less equal than another, reference must be made to an accepted concept of **social justice**, a rule by which any pattern of shares may be judged. Later on we shall concentrate on **poverty** as an important manifestation of inequality, and this issue of social justice takes on more obvious relevance when we try to make judgements about government measures to improve the relative positions of individuals or households at the bottom of the income distribution. But we must not lose sight of the fact that to

compare distributions may involve comparisons of gains and losses – that is altered distributional positions for different percentile groupings – in which case judgements about which is more equal or even, perhaps, 'preferred' cannot be made on any objective criteria. The history of 'Welfare Economics' has been written in terms of a search for an objective criterion by which to judge the outcome of economic processes but the question of social justice does not reside exclusively within the domain of academic reasoning. Indeed, the very question of a trade-off between equity and efficiency, discussed earlier and to be returned to later, lies (again) at the heart of real-world government decisions affecting the distribution of income. Both government expenditures and methods of raising revenue affect income distribution; a government implementing policies to promote efficiency at the expense of equity will be more likely to create inequalities than a government opting to sacrifice efficiency gains for equity goals.

The measurement of inequality

The problem of trying to judge between alternative distributions is illustrated clearly by the statistical summary measures most favoured by both private researchers and government reports: the **Lorenz curve** and the **Gini coefficient**. The Lorenz curve offers a pictorial representation of inequality. The Gini coefficient, which is the measure favoured by statisticians and often used in government reports, provides a numerical summary measure of inequality

The Lorenz curve is used for **comparative** analysis – for example comparing income distributions between countries at some point in time or between different points in time in a given country. The curve shows cumulative percentage income shares: the bottom 10 per cent of the population (income units) receive x per cent of income, the bottom 20 per cent receive y per cent, where y is greater than x, and so on. When there is perfect equality – when every n per cent of the population receives n per cent of total income – the Lorenz curve is a 45° line or **line of income equality**. Such a line thus operates as a yardstick by which to gauge the inequality in any given distribution. If there is inequality the Lorenz curve lies below the 45° line, and the more unequal the distribution the further away from the 45° line lies the Lorenz curve. **Figure 7.1(a)** shows two hypothetical Lorenz curves with the distribution in year *t* represented as more equal than that in year *t* + 50.

It is possible to draw unambiguous conclusions from **Figure 7.1(a)** because one Lorenz curve lies completely outside the other. But let us examine **Figure 7.1(b)** where the two Lorenz curves cross. Are we still able to judge which of the two distributions is most equal? The Lorenz curves show that for all percentile groups up to the bottom 40 per cent their share in total income was higher in year *t* + 50 than in year *t*, but above this point shares were higher in year *t*. A measure of inequality which gives a greater weight to improvements in the share of total income enjoyed by the lower income groups would register *t* + 50 as the year of greater equality; a measure of inequality which gives a greater weight to improvements in upper income group shares would yield a preference for year *t*.

The same problem arises when using the Gini coefficient. This numerical measure of inequality is based on the relationship between the Lorenz curve and the line of income equality; it measures the ratio of the area between the Lorenz curve and the diagonal (the line of income equality) to the total area beneath the diagonal. In **Figure 7.2** the Gini coefficient is measured as the ratio $A/(A + B)$.

It can be seen from **Figure 7.2** that when the Lorenz curve follows the diagonal, when incomes are equally distributed, the Gini coefficient has a value of $0(A = 0)$. At the other extreme, when all income is held by one individual ($B = 0$), the Gini coefficient has a value of 1. Thus for purposes of comparison, the nearer the Gini coefficient is to 0 the more equal the distribution may be considered to be. However, when two Lorenz curves cross how can we draw an unambiguous conclusion regarding relative inequalities? Consider **Figure 7.1(b)** again: the Gini coefficient suggests that incomes are more equally distributed in year *t* but this obscures the fact that from the viewpoint of the bottom four deciles year *t* + 50 is more equal.

It would seem, than, that when measuring the

Figure 7.1 *Hypothetical Lorenz curves and the measurement of inequality*

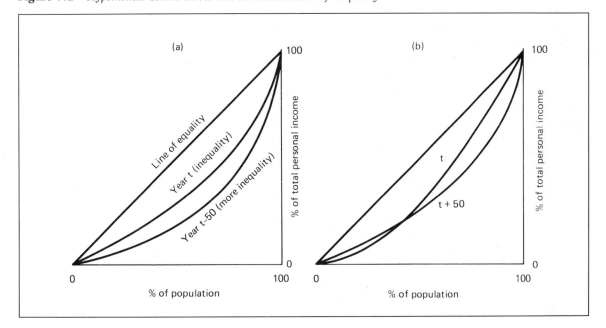

Figure 7.2 *Measuring the Gini coefficient from the Lorenz curve*

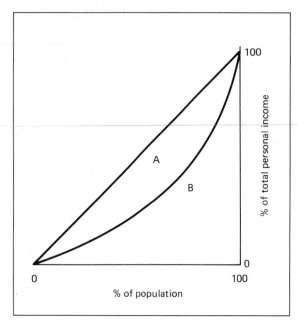

The distribution of pre-tax incomes in the UK

The official estimates of the distribution of personal incomes in the UK are published by the Central Statistical Office and illustrate the problems referred to so far. Note that the estimates are of the **size** distribution of **personal** incomes. In the modern economy the distinctions between factors of production are rather blurred, and although analysing the distribution of incomes among capitalists, labourers and rentiers still has its uses, it tends to be inferior to the size distribution as a summary measure of inequality. Consider the estimates shown in **Table 7.1**. Those estimates are from the annual 'Blue Book', *National Income and Expenditure*, and, as such, are based mainly on the Survey of Personal Incomes undertaken by the Inland Revenue.

So what do the data suggest? If the period since the Second World War has been one of rising prosperity for the UK how has this prosperity been shared out among the populations? The data show clearly that pre-tax income has not been shared equally at any point in time. Insofar as pre-tax incomes reflect a market determined set of rewards, this is to be expected. But what about shares over time – have pre-tax incomes become more or less equally shared?

The data suggest that we cannot draw unambiguous conclusions about changes in the degree of inequality over time, the main reason being that the percentile groupings at different points in the distribution have fared differently over time. We

degree of inequality in income distribution we cannot avoid introducing value judgements about the 'desired' state of distribution. Any two observers with different views on the weight which should be given by society to improvements in the position of the lower income groups could place two different interpretations on any decrease in the value of the Gini coefficient between two points in time. Only if the Gini coefficient is used in conjuction with the original data on percentile shares is an adequate comparative picture likely to emerge.

Table 7.1 *Cumulative distribution of personal income before tax, UK, 1949–85 (selected years)*

Quantile groups	1949 %	1959 %	1967 %	1975–76 %	1984–85 %
Top 1%	11.2	8.4	7.4	5.7	6.4
Top 10%	33.2	29.4	28.0	26.2	29.4
Top 50%	76.3	76.9	76.0	76.2	77.7
Bottom 50%	23.7	23.1	24.0	23.8	22.3

Sources: Diamond Commission, Report no. 1, Table 15.
CSO, *Social Trends*, 19 (1989 edn) Table 5.14.

must bear in mind that the individual tax units also differ within each percentile grouping at different points in time: for example, the tax units comprising the top 10 per cent group in 1985 are not the same units as those in the same percentile group in 1955. In other words, the data do not tell us anything about upward mobility within the distribution. However, if we do accept that inequality is reflected in the shares enjoyed by different percentile groupings, looking at these shares over time suggests that the degree of inequality has been subjected to opposing forces, at least until the 1980s. Over the 30-year period, from the end of the 1940s to the end of the 1970s, the share of pre-tax income enjoyed by the top percentiles of income recipients fell — the share of the top 1 per cent fell from just over 11 per cent to just over 5 per cent, while the share of the top 10 per cent fell from just over 33 per cent to just over 26 per cent. This suggests that incomes were becoming more equally distributed. However, during the same period the share enjoyed by the bottom percentiles also fell, with recovery in the 1960s and early/mid-1970s proving insufficient to regain the share enjoyed at the end of the 1940s, suggesting that incomes became more unequally distributed over the period. How are we to weigh these opposing forces?. It would appear that the Lorenz curves at different points of time are crossed and we cannot make a clear judgement about overall inequality without reference to a specific concept of social justice — the very problem discussed earlier. The only firm conclusion which might be drawn from the data is that whatever redistribution of pre-tax incomes has taken place, it has done so from the top to the middle.

Similar difficulties face us when trying to assess the changing degree of inequality throughout the 1980s — that is, some percentile groupings have fared better (or worse) than others in the overall distribution. However, it **is** possible to say that there is little evidence from CSO data to suggest that the degree of inequality in the distribution of pre-tax incomes has been reduced. Over the decade the share enjoyed by the top half of the distribution has increased while the share of the bottom half has decreased.

Trends in factor incomes

To explain the causes of the observed changes in the distribution of pre-tax incomes over the period in question requires an understanding of highly complicated and interrelated forces. Not all of these forces are economic, although for present purposes we shall look in more detail at the distribution of factor market incomes. Social and demographic factors play their part in altering income shares over time. In the 1970s the Royal Commission on the Distribution of Income and Wealth (the Diamond Commission) identified four major forces: changes in the age structure of the population; changes in the activity rates of various sectors of the population; changes in marital patterns; and changes in education patterns. Not surprisingly, the Commission concluded that alterations to the pattern of income distribution were often attributable to some combination of these separately identified factors (Diamond Commission, 1975). For present purposes we shall let the observation rest there, although we shall return to the age factor when we consider the incidence of poverty and the problem of intergenerational finance of social security arrangements. Several relevant observations on activity rates (for example, labour force participation of married women) are also made in Chapter 6 (see **pp. 213–14**).

So far as economic forces are concerned, we can usefully begin with a closer look at factor market patterns. When a mixed economy allocates resources it determines rewards to factors of production in both private and public sectors, while the State's tax-transfer mechanism provides income maintenance for those who are eligible. We shall leave the distribution of State transfers until later and concentrate first on factor incomes as an indication of how rewards are shared out on the supply side of the economy, the many determinants of this distribution being discussed in every other chapter of this book.

The distribution of factor rewards

Whatever the nature of social and demographic changes, the distribution of rewards in a market-oriented economy must reflect the nature of markets. Thus, there are at least two important questions to address: how are the total rewards from economic processess shared out among the various factors of production and, if one type of reward dominates, what forces help to determine **its** distribution? The answer to the first question offers a guide to answering the second. To understand the forces which determine the distribution of incomes we need to know the dominant source of income; an increase in the share going to capital is likely to have an impact on overall size distribution which is different from that resulting from an increase in the share enjoyed by labour. Furthermore, if one component of income accounts for, say, more than half the rewards in an economy, then any change in the dispersion of that component will result in a change in the overall dispersion of incomes. **Table 7.2** shows the relative shares of the main components of total personal/(household) income in the UK for the period 1967–87.

As can be seen from **Table 7.2** the largest component of personal incomes in the UK is **income from employment**. Researchers into the distribution of incomes have seen the changes in this large component as indicators of both the overall state of the economy and the prevailing degree of inequality. Lydall, for example, discerned a trend towards equality in the distribution of

incomes, from the immediate postwar years until the later 1950s, and argued that this trend owed much to postwar economic expansion and the improving fortunes of labour (Lydall, 1959). According to Lydall, the sustained high level of employment during the period meant that earned income rose faster than any other form of personal income, and that such a trend would be a major force towards equality. However, as calculated by Nicholson, this pattern changed during the period 1957–63 with the rate of growth of employment income slowing down relative to that of self-employment (and, within employment income, the rate of growth of wages slowed down relative to that of salaries). During this period rent, dividends and interest became the most rapidly growing sector of personal income. The result, according to Nicholson, was a slowing down in any trend towards equality (Nicholson, 1967).

According to official estimates the downward slide in the share of labour income continued into the 1970s, when it steadied before resuming its downward trend, at an accelerated pace, during the 1980s – from 73 per cent in 1978 to 69 per cent by 1985. Nevertheless, the trend over the long run remains in labour's favour, namely a rising share in total income relative to the share enjoyed by capital. By itself this long-term trend reduces inequality if the gains are equally distributed among labour units. However, over time such redistribution has not been equal. Earnings (wages and salaries) constitute the largest proportion of factor incomes, yet there are forces at work to

Table 7.2   *% shares of main components in total personal income, UK, 1967–87*[1]

	1967	1972	1977	1982	1987
Wages and salaries	70	69	67	62	61
Income from self-employment	8	10	9	8	8
Rent, interest and dividends	11	9	5	6	7
Private pensions, annuities, etc.	—	5	5	7	8
Social security benefits	9	9	11	14	13
Other current transfers		2	2	2	3

[1] Figures to nearest whole numbers.
Sources: Diamond Commission, Report no. 4, Table 3.
CSO, *Social Trends*, 19 (1989 edn) Table 5.2.

prevent an equal distribution of earnings among earners.

Between the sexes there is considerable inequality. **Figure 7.3** plots the weekly earnings enjoyed by the extremes of the earnings distribution for each sex over the decade 1977–87. The observed pattern is one of persistent inequality.

There are two main conclusions to be drawn from **Figure 7.3**. In the first place, the top male earners consistently earn more than the top female earners. Secondly, the difference between the highest female earnings and the lowest male earnings is consistently less than that between highest and lowest female earnings. It should be noted that a similar pattern emerges in the case of hourly earnings and that differences in earnings performance are equally marked for the other percentile groupings in the distributions (of both weekly and hourly earnings) For example, in 1987 the weekly earnings figure for the highest female decile (full-time) was only about 15 per cent higher than the median for men (full-time), while the median for women was only some 70 per cent of that for men. Such inequalities have persisted despite the flurry of legislation on equal pay and sex discrimination documented in Chapter 6. Another significant inequality persists between manual and non-manual earners (regardless of sex), with non-manual earnings consistently outstripping manual earnings in all deciles within the two distributions.

The share of personal income going to rents, dividends and interest behaved more erratically during the period from 1960. Throughout the 1960s this share fell steadily before 'hitting bottom' in the early 1970s, since when it has climbed again, particularly during the 1980s (although the ramifications of the 1987 stock market crash and the subsequent recovery have yet to show up in the official data).

Looking at the shares accruing to the major components of personal income cannot 'explain' changes in inequality. There is much more to the story than this. However, the broad categories which we have considered do give some strong indications of what is happening to the degree of inequality associated with the overall distribution of personal incomes. In particular, it is difficult to avoid the conclusion that during the first two

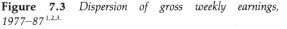

Figure 7.3 *Dispersion of gross weekly earnings, 1977–87* [1,2,3].

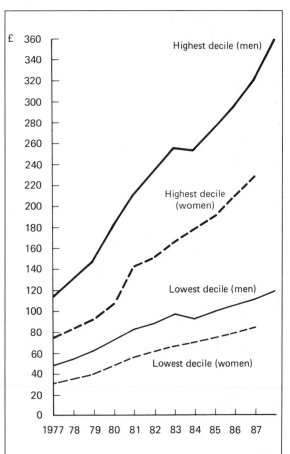

Notes:
[1] Of full-time adults whose pay was not affected by absence.
[2] From 1977 to 1983 adult rates on the basis of males aged 21 and over and females aged 18 and over.
[3] From 1984 onwards on the basis of all on adult rates.
Source: New Earnings Survey 1987, Table 30.

terms of the present government the increased share in pre-tax income enjoyed by the highest percentiles in the distribution resulted, in part, from an increased concentration of earned income due to a rise in the proportions of the population who were unemployed or retired.

The distributional impact of taxes and transfers

Income tax

When considering how UK governments have influenced the pattern of personal income distribution over the period since 1945 we must concentrate on two things: the effect of progressive income taxation and the effect of Welfare State transfers. A progressive tax structure smooths out the dispersion of incomes after tax and works towards a more equal distribution. Welfare State benefits, in principle, are transfers of income both in cash and in kind to the poorest percentiles in the distribution and, hence, a force towards reducing inequality.

In practice, the evidence suggests that it is only the benefits side of the tax/transfer mechanism which has worked to reduce inequality. Consider first the distribution of post-tax income as shown in **Table 7.3**.

Taking first the period from the end of the 1940s up to the end of the 1970s, two observations can be made. First, income tax does indeed reduce the income dispersion at any point in time. Second, over time the post-tax dispersion of income alters in roughly the same directions as the pre-tax dispersion. In other words the redistribution of post-tax income has been from the top of the distribution towards the middle rather than towards the bottom. It would thus appear to be the case that, for the period in question, income tax was progressive and a force for equality but that its progressivity altered little over time.

What about the period since 1979? The most obvious point to make is that for the first time since the Second World War the share of post-tax income enjoyed by the top 10 per cent of the distribution has begun to rise. The share of the top 50 per cent of the distribution has also risen steadily during the period since 1979. For the most part, these trends are a reflection of the same patterns emerging in the distribution of pre-tax incomes. However, an additional factor is that, successive governments since 1979 have set out to reduce the burden of direct taxation, either by raising tax thresholds or by reducing the tax rates. Since 1979 both these changes have been implemented on several occasions, the most dramatic being the reduction in the standard rate of income tax from 33 per cent to 25 per cent by the end of 1988. Raising the tax threshold takes some income earners out of the income tax net, but it does nothing positive to improve the relative positions of those whose earned incomes are initially too low to be liable for income tax. Reducing the standard rate of income tax affects only taxpayers, and cannot be considered a force to reduce inequality in post-tax income distribution. It must be noted also that the 1980s have seen a massive reduction in higher rates of income tax – from 83 per cent to 40 per cent on earned income.

Other direct taxes plus welfare benefits

Income taxation is by no means the only method by which governments can influence the dispersion of income and consumption. Government expenditures confer benefits (with unequal effects upon the community, often in disproportionate amounts) and other forms of taxation, including social secur-

Table 7.3 *Cumulative distribution of personal income after income tax, UK, 1949–85 (selected years)*

Quantile groups	1949 %	1959 %	1967 %	1975–76 %	1984–85 %
Top 1%	6.4	5.3	4.9	3.9	4.9
Top 10%	27.1	25.9	24.3	23.1	26.5
Top 50%	73.5	74.8	73.2	73.4	75.1
Bottom 50%	26.5	25.2	26.8	26.6	24.9

Sources: Diamond Commission, Report no. 1, Table 15.
CSO, *Social Trends*, 19 (1989 edn) Table 5.14.

ity 'contributions', can alter significantly the dispersion of disposable income. The CSO attempts to gauge the fuller impact of government activity on the distribution of incomes by estimating differences between 'original' and 'final' income. Using data collected by the Family Expenditure Survey, the CSO publishes estimates of the distribution of **household** income, including distributions modified by taxes and social security benefits. **Table 7.4** gives the items included in the various income categories.

Since the CSO figures are based on a sample of households and upon an assumed incidence of taxes and benefits, they provide estimates rather than hard facts about income redistribution through State action. What do the estmates suggest? **Table 7.5** gives a summary of CSO findings for the period 1976 to 1986.

On the basis of the CSO estimates we can make two important observations. In the first place, throughout the whole of the period covered by the estimates, the combined impact of taxes and benefits has been to reduce inequality at any point in time. Secondly, the combined influence of taxes and benefits has not prevented a widening of the gap between the very top and the very bottom of the distribution.

The first observation stems from the fact that while the distribution of original income in **Table 7.5** shows a pattern very similar to that of the distribution of pre-tax incomes in **Table 7.1**, the dispersion in the shares of disposable and final incomes are much less marked at any point in time.

Table 7.4 *Household definitions used by CSO in estimates of income distribution as modified by state tax/transfer programmes, 1989*

Income concept	Definition
Original income	Earnings plus Occupational pensions *plus* Annuities, *plus* Investment income *plus* Other income
Disposable income	Original income *plus* Cash benefits *minus* Income tax *minus* National insurance contributions
Final income	Disposable income *minus* Indirect taxes *plus* Benefits in kind (Education, National Health Service, Travel subsidies, Housing subsidy and Welfare foods)

In 1986, for example, the top fifth enjoyed 50.7 per cent of original income but only 42.2 per cent of disposable income and 41.7 per cent of final income, while the negligible share of the bottom fifth in original income rose to 5.9 per cent of disposable income and final income. The second observation is based on the wider dispersions in disposable and final incomes in 1986 as compared

Table 7.5 *Cumulative distribution of original, disposable and final household income, UK, 1976–86*

Quantile group	Original income			Disposable income			Final income		
	1976	1981	1986	1976	1981	1986	1976	1981	1986
Top 20%	44.4	46.4	50.7	38.1	39.4	42.2	37.9	38.6	41.7
Top 40%	71.0	73.3	77.6	62.2	63.5	66.3	61.9	62.6	65.6
Top 60%	89.8	91.3	94.0	80.4	81.2	83.2	79.9	80.5	82.6
Bottom 40%	10.2	8.7	6.0	19.6	18.8	16.9	20.1	19.5	17.3
Bottom 20%	0.8	0.6	0.3	7.0	6.7	5.9	7.4	7.1	5.9

Source: CSO, *Social Trends* 19 (1989 edn).

with 1976. In terms of percentage points, in 1976 the gap in shares of original income between the bottom and top fifths was 43.6, for disposable income it was 31.1 and for final income it was 30.5; whereas in 1986 the respective gaps were 50.4, 36.3 and 35.8.

Thus, over the decade in question, so far as the extremes of the distribution were concerned, there was a trend towards greater inequality not only in the distribution of original income but also in the distribution of incomes after adjustments for taxes paid and benefits received. This conclusion is endorsed by the more detailed study of the longer period, from 1968–83, undertaken by Morris and Preston using the raw data of the Family Expenditure Survey rather than the published group data. The results are calculated using the Institute for Fiscal Studies' tax and benefit model, which adopts income definitions similar to those used by the CSO. The authors found that both the Lorenz curve and the Gini coefficient give reliable results for the period studied, concluding that their calculations show 'an unambiguous outward movement taking the curve completely beyond that of 1968 and *creating a clear-cut rise in inequality over the 1968–83 period*' (present author's italics). **Figure 7.4** gives a summary of the Morris and Preston findings.

That governments' tax/transfer arrangements have softened the trend towards more inequality is also borne out by the Morris and Preston findings, although they emphasise that it is the benefit side of the picture which takes the credit.

Morris and Preston's findings suggest also that the inequality of original income rose by more than inequality of final income over the course of the period and, hence, that the redistributive impact of taxes and benefits was increasing. They attribute this to the fact that although more is paid in direct taxes in the UK than is received in cash benefits, benefits are the more important redistributive element because they are so much more unequally allocated. Indeed, they calculate that over the period from 1968 to 1983 taxes became substantially less unequal in their allocation while benefits became slightly more unequally allocated. We shall return to this issue of the intensification of the redistributive effects of benefits when considering

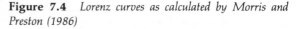

Figure 7.4   *Lorenz curves as calculated by Morris and Preston (1986)*

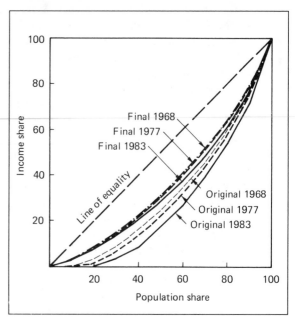

Source: Fiscal Studies (1987).

poverty as a separate problem but, for now, we should note that, despite the redistributive impact of Welfare State arrangements over the period 1968–83, the Gini coefficient for the distribution of final income increased, as did the gap between the shares in final income enjoyed by the top and bottom fifths of the distribution.

The concentration of wealth

In the view of many observers the distribution of wealth shares within a society gives a more accurate picture of the degree of inequality, because the full extent of individuals' economic power is determined ultimately by their potential command over available resources and this must reflect ownership of assets as well as current income. It is thus held that any society concerned with social justice will be concerned about both wealth and income shares. Unfortunately, when it comes to measuring wealth shares, obstacles are met which are even bigger than those encountered in the estimation of income distributions. This is true even though wealth and income are but different dimensions of a common set of means by which individuals satisfy their wants. **Wealth** refers to the **stock** of means available, while **income** refers to the **flow** of means from the given stock. Another term for wealth is 'net worth' which, perhaps, underlines better the fact that wealth relates to a **net stock** – the difference between a set of assets and a set of liabilities.

The definition and measurement of wealth

Given that any stock of means is measured by the total (capitalised) value of the various items within the stock, the essential preliminary step in empirical work is to determine which assets are to be included in the definition of the wealth stock. Some researchers see the crux of the problem in the relationship between 'value' and 'ownership', the key concept being that of 'marketability'. An individual may own the right to an income flow from a given asset yet he or she may not be able to realise the market value of that asset, because it is **non-transferable**. A prime example of this is the State pension – the asset has a value to its owner because it bestows income, but the pension right cannot be traded in the market-place. Should such rights be included in the calculation of a comprehensive wealth stock? Less difficult to handle in empirical work are those assets which confer income benefits upon their owner and are disposable at an **exchange price** – cash, bank deposits, company shares, government bonds, dwellings and so forth. Clearly, such assets must be included in any definition of personal wealth.

Official measures of wealth distribution in the UK represent **estimates** of wealth holdings since the Inland Revenue does not undertake a regular survey of such holdings in the way that it does for personal incomes. This is because the UK fiscal system does not include a comprehensive wealth tax; it does include capital taxes but those relate to disposals or transfers of assets rather than holdings (see **pp. 119–20**). This means that estimates of

holdings are made from too narrow a definition of wealth since transfers of 'capital', as defined for tax purposes, exclude some forms of wealth. Prior to the 1960s no official estimates of wealth distribution appeared in government statistical publications, but since then such estimates have been published annually. From 1962 to 1978 the Inland Revenue published annual estimates of both total wealth holdings and the distribution of those holdings based on the 'estate multiplier' method, whereby the estates of persons who die in a given year are used as the sample base for estimating the wealth of the living in that year. From the mid-1970s the CSO published their estimates of wealth holdings based on calculations of the aggregates of assets *minus* liabilities owned by individuals – the so-called 'balance-sheet' approach. From 1978 the Inland Revenue combined these two approaches to produce a new annual series which is also published by the CSO in *Social Trends*.

Needless to say, the methods adopted by government statisticians are disputed by other researchers, and a comprehensive survey must include these alternative estimates. For present purposes we shall confine ourselves to official estimates. For estimates of wealth distribution prior to the 1960s we shall refer to the calculations of Professor Jack Revell who pioneered the balance-sheet approach, later taken up by the CSO. This was the line taken by the Diamond Commission in the mid-1970s and, following the Commission, we can present the trends in wealth concentration in two distinct periods with 1960 as the watershed. **Table 7.6** overleaf presents the various estimates of the distribution of **marketable wealth** – that is, excluding pension rights (both State and occupational).

Table 7.6 suggests that over the course of this century there has been a considerable levelling down of shares in marketable wealth from the very top of the distribution but, overall, the majority of wealth-holdings have remained concentrated in the hands of a minority of wealth-holders. The share of the top 10 per cent of the population fell, from over 90 per cent around 1911 to less than 55 per cent by 1985. However, in 1985, over 90 per cent of wealth was still owned by the wealthiest 50 per cent of the population. Measured in terms of the

Table 7.6   *The distribution of wealth in Great Britain, 1911–60 and the UK, 1966–85*[1]

Quantile group	% Share of wealth, GB			% Share of wealth, UK		
	1911–13	*1936–8*	*1960*	*1966*[2]	*1976*	*1985*
Top 1%	69	56	42	33	24	20
Top 5%	87	78	75	56	45	40
Top 10%	92	88	83	69	60	54
Top 25%				87	84	76
Top 50%				97	95	93

Note:
[1]Figures to nearest whole number.
[2]Using 'estate multiplier' method.
Sources: Diamond Commission, Report no. 1, Table 41 for figures for Great Britain only; CSO, *Social Trends*, 10 for 1966 figure; CSO, *Social Trends*, 19 (1989 edn) for estimate for 1976 and 1985.

rate of decline in wealth shares at the **top** of the distribution, any movement towards equality quickened pace between 1960 and 1980 but slowed down considerably between 1980 and 1985. Since 1960 the Gini coefficient for wealth has been falling but the fall in shares around the middle of the distribution has been sluggish.

If we take account of pension rights the distribution pattern becomes more equal in terms of reducing the shares enjoyed by the top percentiles. **Figure 7.5** shows the changes brought about by including both occupational and State pension rights.

As **Figure 7.5** shows, the share enjoyed by the top 1 per cent fell very sharply between 1971 and 1985, while that of the top 10 per cent also fell heavily over the same period. But note that the fall in share of the top 10 per cent was less dramatic than that of the top 1 per cent – the redistribution was taking place among the wealthiest precentiles. Note also that in 1985 over 80 per cent of wealth, even when defined to include pension rights, was held by the wealthiest 50 per cent of the population.

The growth and spread of pension rights has been very much a feature of the pattern of wealth ownership over the time period since the Second World War, following the introduction of the State retirement pension under the National Insurance Scheme and the later growth in occupational pen-

sions. We shall consider this feature again in the later discussion of poverty. Other important changes have taken place during the same period in the ownership of property (dwellings) and of financial assets, and we shall discuss these presently. But it must be appreciated that over the longer period the break-up of wealth concentration tends to be slow because the interplay of social,

Figure 7.5   *Distribution of wealth, UK, 1976–88, selected years*

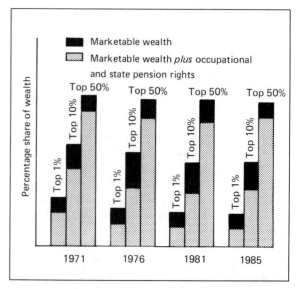

Source: *Social Trends*, 19 (1989 edn).

demographic and economic influences upon such concentrations is a long process. Observers of this interplay have concentrated on three important features: the forces of accumulation, the patterns of mating and fertility and the mode of inheritance.

Accumulation patterns

Analysis of the determinants of accumulation is complex and difficult; it includes exploration of **savings functions** – the relative propensities to save out of income in different property regimes, the relative influences of earnings and profit, and so on. This is not the place to attempt such analysis, but it must be borne in mind. What we can note, however, is that, other things remaining unchanged, an increase in the spread of ownership of property will break down any concentration in property incomes. Part of the explanation of the break-up of wealth concentration in the top half of the distribution in the UK lies in the increased share of the value of dwellings in the composition of net wealth. **Figure 7.6** plots the main patterns in wealth composition between 1971 and 1987.

In 1971 the net value of dwellings made up just over one-fifth of total net wealth in the UK but only sixteen years later this proportion had increased to one-third. The increase was most noticeable during the 1970s following the very sharp rise in house prices during the early years of that decade. Another very sharp rise in house prices during 1987–88 will no doubt have a significant impact on the final picture for the 1980s. But an increase in the proportional value of dwellings does not reduce inequality in wealth-holdings unless accompanied by an increased spread of ownership. Over the period since the Second World War the UK has increasingly become a 'property-owning democracy' – over the quarter of a century after 1960 the number of owner-occupied dwellings in the UK housing stock actually doubled and, currently, about 63 per cent of households are owner-occupied.

The direction of influence of other major components of net wealth is less certain and there are likely to have been forces pulling in opposite directions. For example, while the proportion of wealth accounted for by building society shares increased steadily between 1971 and 1986, that of

Figure 7.6 *Composition of net wealth of personal sector, UK, 1971–87*

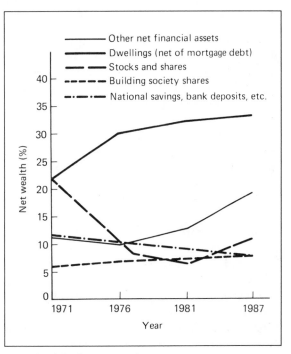

Source: *Social Trends*, 19 (1989 edn).

national savings and bank deposits fell markedly. The combined effect of these movements on the overall concentration of wealth will depend upon the extent to which they represent switching among 'popular' assets compared with changes in relative patterns of ownership.

Nor do the trends exhibited by stocks and shares suggest an obvious influence on concentration. The proportion of wealth held in this form fell considerably after the stock market collapse of the early 1970s (the fall in share prices in 1974 was 42 per cent – much greater than in any of the previous 14 years). Between 1971 and 1976 the proportional value of wealth held in the form of stocks and shares fell from 21.7 per cent to 8.2 per cent and by 1981 the proportion was down to 7.0 per cent. However, during the early to mid-1980s this trend changed direction as the proportional value of stocks and shares rose to 10.3 per cent by 1987. During the same period stocks and shares became a more popular form of wealth-holding as the pro-

protion of the adult population owning shares increased from 6 per cent in 1984 to over 20 per cent by the beginning of 1988. Much impetus to this increase in share ownership was given by the privatisation of state-owned enterprises such as British Telecom in 1984, and the Trustee Savings Bank and British Gas in 1986. Clearly stocks and shares became a more popular form of asset during the 1980s but this trend does not tell us anything about **relative values of individual share holdings**. What has happened to such values and how they were affected by the impact of the stock market Crash of Autumn 1987 will leave a firm mark on the overall pattern of inequality for the 1980s.

Socio-demographic patterns

Strong influences on the long-term distribution of wealth are exerted by the extent to which the rich marry the rich and the poor marry the poor and by differential fertility – if the rich have fewer children than the poor then concentration increases and vice versa. These are very important considerations, but we do not have the space here to discuss them further. However, one socio-demographic factor which we must look at more closely is that of inheritance patterns. One custom which works strongly against the dispersion of wealth is that of **primogeniture**, strictly the passing on of wealth to the first-born child (although, historically, this has been interpreted as the first-born son). If inheritance were not an important determinant of the degree of wealth concentration then such a custom would assume less importance. However, available evidence suggests that inheritance is a major factor in the self-perpetuating cycle of wealth determination.

Much of the evidence collected for the United Kingdom is found in the important work of C.D Harbury and his collaborators. In 1962, Harbury published the results of an attempt to quantify the effect of inheritance on the distribution of wealth (Harbury, 1962). The attempt was based largely on an examination of the relationship between estates left by top wealth-holders and the estates left by their fathers, using a sample of large estates left in the years 1956 and 1957. Among other things, the study found that around two thirds of rich sons (estates over £100,000) had fathers who were in

the top 0.25 per cent of wealth-holders, and that the 'self-made man' was in a small minority. In comparing Harbury's study with an earlier one undertaken by Wedgwood for the years 1924–6, Atkinson found that, in spite of social upheavals, inflation, estate duty and so on, there was no clear decline in the importance of inheritance during the first half of the twentieth century (Atkinson, 1972). Later empirical work by Harbury suggested that this view should be qualified somewhat, because inheritance had declined in importance since the earlier studies, but nevertheless the basic argument remains that inheritance is a prime factor in determining wealth. Thus Harbury and McMahon found that over 50 per cent of sons leaving over £100,000 had fathers who had done the same, (Harbury and McMahon, 1973) while Harbury and Hitchens found that some 58 per cent of those who died wealthy had themselves inherited large fortunes. (Harbury and Hitchens, 1976).

It must be said, of course, that as far as the future is concerned this inheritance factor will work in conjunction with the 'property-owning democracy' to spread inheritances across more of the population. The impact of this on the degree of inequality in the distribution of wealth will depend upon how unequal is the initial distribution of property. A report published in late 1988 calculated that around 200,000 families each year inherit a property (dwelling) with an average value of £50,000. This figure was based on the 'reasoned' assumption that 80 per cent of homeowners bequeath their property to descendants.

Wealth taxation: inheritance and concentration

If inheritance is such an important determinant of wealth concentration, and if government had a serious commitment to reducing inequality, one might expect that the fiscal system would be used to discourage the concentration of inheritances. So far in the UK, however, this has not been the case.

Until 1974 Estate Duty was the main tax on wealth in the UK. Unfortunately, estate duty was not a noteable success in reducing inequalities, partly because it was never applied properly to discretionary trusts, and partly because the rules permitted exemption of gifts *inter vivos* unless such transfers took place within seven years prior to the donor's death. Perhaps, though, the greatest fault of estate duty as a means of reducing wealth inequality lay in the principle of taxing the value of an estate rather than the value of an inheritance. It is not large estates *per se* which perpetuate inequalities, but the fact that they are passed on as large inheritances and the most efficient way to promote equility to taxing wealth is to tax inherited receipts. Furthermore, if its rates structure is progressive, an inheritance tax offers an incentive to donors to disperse their wealth more widely than they would in the face of an estates tax. In 1974 the Estate Duty was replaced by the Capital Transfer Tax. This represented an improvement in that the new tax was levied on a cumulative basis, not just on wealth at death but also on gifts and bequests *inter vivos*. However, the Capital Transfer Tax was still based on the estates principle and not levied on receipts of transfer, and thus did not provide the additional incentive to disperse wealth that is offered by an inheritance tax.

The Finance Act of 1986 brought in yet another change, with Capital Transfer Tax being replaced by the Inheritance Tax. As in the cases of Estate Duty and Capital Transfer Tax, the new levy was hedged by a long list of wealth exemptions. Further, although the tax is cumulative, no tax is payable on the first part of the cumulative total, an exemption which is increased in April of each year, in line with the rise in the Retail Prices Index. Finally, once again (despite its name) the Inheritance Tax is levied on the value of a gift or an estate and not the amount received or inherited; the main charge under the tax arises on transfers made by an individual on death, or within seven years of death. As with its predecessors, there is no incentive provided under this tax for a wider dispersal of inheritances.

Poverty and income maintenance

'Absolute' versus 'relative' definitions

While the discussion of distribution and inequality referred mainly to a summary index, the Gini coefficient, important occasional use was made of the comparison between extremes in a distribution. We turn now to this question of extremes in more detail as we consider poverty as a manifestation of inequality. However, while 'poverty' is indeed a reflection of 'inequality', the two concepts are quite separate and have different meanings. It is a tautology to state that where incomes are unequally distributed the poorest members of the population will be found at the bottom of the distribution. But it may be that these poor individuals are rich indeed when compared with those in the bottom percentile (or even the top percentile) or the income distribution in some other population. In other words, we might judge, say, the bottom 20 per cent of any population to be 'poor' but this may be true in only a relative sense, rather than an absolute one.

The question of relative versus absolute makes it difficult to identify the poor in an empirical sense. If we could rely on an absolute (an objective) measure we could estimate poverty simply by counting the individuals (or the households) who do not possess the means of achieving the absolute minimum standard of living. An absolute yardstick can also be applied over time and, hence, offers the means of checking whether or not the incidence of poverty is changing. So why not rely on an absolute measure of poverty? To answer this question we must consider carefully what is meant by an 'absolute standard of poverty'. Such a measure would attempt to define a minimum level of subsistence for the chosen income unit (individual or household) and to determine the level of income necessary to guarantee that such a minimum can be enjoyed. Thus, 'the poor' would be those units with incomes short of the minimum level. It should be easy to appreciate that defining absolute subsistence is difficult and not very helpful in the formulation of social policy.

One obvious criticism of absolute measures is that any population is likely to be heterogeneous in terms of minimum requirements. Compare, for example, the basic food and clothing requirements of an 18-year old male who is tall and heavy and whose occupation is felling trees, with those of a retired female schoolteacher who is small and light. But a more fundamental criticism is that 'poverty' can be defined only in relation to prevailing social conventions and available 'life-styles', that is by comparing the differing living standards enjoyed by different units in the population. But this, in turn, causes further difficulties for empirical measurement. What is the minimum living standard for a UK household in 1989? For example, should every household be expected to own a television set? Many social observers have wrestled with the problems of defining minimum relative living standards (and, hence, standards of 'relative deprivation') but none has yet derived a definition which has proved universally acceptable.

Poverty estimates

Given the problems associated with defining minimum standards, most researchers into the incidence of poverty rely on the definition accepted for determining levels of income maintenance under State tax/transfer programmes. This is not to say that State minima are 'correct', but they do provide a benchmark against which successive government programmes might be assessed, at least so long as the minima remain constant in real terms. When the minima themselves are shifting over time, appropriate adjustments must be made if the incidence of poverty is to be tracked across time. For example Abel-Smith and Townsend have estimated that 1.2 per cent of the population were living below National Assistance level in 1953, while official estimates for 1983 suggest that 5.3 per cent were then living in families with incomes below the Supplementary Benefit levels (Abel-Smith and Townsend, 1965). Does this mean that over that 30-year period there was a more than a fourfold increase in poverty, despite the impressive improvements in living standards for the bulk of the population during the same period? One obvious reason why poverty may not have increased on this sort of scale over the period is that the 'poverty line' was itself raised by successive governments, and the more generous the poverty line the more people become classified as 'poor'.

Another problem to be faced when trying to trace the extent and incidence of poverty over time is that researchers have not used a consistent data base, nor have they maintained a consistent definition of the income unit. For example, Abel-Smith and Townsend, in their comparative study of 1953 and 1960, used the Family Expenditure Survey (FES) and based their findings on expenditure data for 1953 and income data for 1960. Since 1972 the DHSS has also used the FES for its own estimates of the numbers in poverty. However, while Abel-Smith and Townsend based their analysis on the 'household' as the income of expenditure unit, later studies by the DHSS adopt the 'family' which usually means 'tax unit' or 'budget unit' and, therefore, constitutes a narrower income/expenditure unit. Since broader units, like households, offer greater access to shared resources than do narrower units like the family and the tax unit, it is not surprising that the extent of poverty is relatively greater when measured across the narrower units.

The two difficulties emphasised are but examples of many differences in the way researchers have tried to estimate the extent of poverty. Some studies have used the General Household Survey as their data base; studies differ in their definition of disposable income and the items to be offset against gross income; studies differ in their treatment of 'necessary' expenditure on children's welfare; and so on. Thus, taking account of the many different approaches, it is not surprising that estimates of, say, individuals in poverty can vary from 1.2 per cent to 12.3 per cent for 1953/54 and between 2.3 per cent and 11.3 per cent for 1975 (Hemming, 1984). One way to achieve a consistent measure of the extent of poverty has been suggested by Piachaud who uses a poverty line which remains constant relative to prevailing living standards (Piachaud, 1988). Piachaud's guideline is the level of personal disposable income *per capita* which includes all forms of money income and is not directly affected by changes in the composition of households. Thus, if the poverty line keeps pace with this guideline, then the relative poverty level can be said to have remained constant. Using this index Piachaud is able to adjust both the findings of Abel-Smith and Townsend and the later estimates of the DHSS to make them directly comparable. His findings suggest a four-fold increase in poverty over the 30-year period from 1953 to 1983, insofar as they identify 6.2 per cent of households in 1953 and 23.3 per cent of families in 1983. If we use Piachaud's findings for families only, covering the decade 1973–83, the increase in poverty is very much smaller over the shorter period – from 19.4 per cent to 23.3 per cent.

But while there is no agreement among empirical observers on the magnitude of changes in the extent of poverty in the UK, there is unanimity on the observation that poverty has remained a stubbornly persistent feature of UK society. This feature was justly highlighted by the sociologists Abel-Smith and Townsend, and came as a major surprise to a society which had undergone significant restructuring of its public sector, including its system of income maintenance, shortly after the Second World War, and which had enjoyed, in the aggregate, the fruits of considerable economic growth over the first two postwar decades. The Abel-Smith and Townsend findings were to inspire the many further efforts to monitor the scale and incidence of poverty over the next 20 years and more as the extent of poverty became once again a major concern of social policy.

The origins of the present system

For most of the period since the Second World War anti-poverty legislation in the UK has built on the foundations laid down in the Beveridge Report of 1942, subject to occasional modification (Cmd. 6404, 1942). There was no attempt at a comprehensive overhaul of the Beveridge system until the Conservative government's White Paper in 1985 and the subsequent reforms embodied in the 1986 Social Security Act (implemented fully only in 1988). The primary aim of the Beveridge Plan was to eradicate all want by concentrating on its causes: loss of work through unemployment or sickness, cessation of work through retirement and the drain on household resources created by large numbers of dependents. The main instrument of the system was a comprehensive programme of social (or 'national') insurance, offering flat-rate benefits to the unemployed and the sick and flat-rate retirement pensions, financed mainly by weekly contributions from those covered by the scheme. This programme was supported by Family

Allowances (later to become Child Benefits) payable on behalf of all children except the first born. As a minimum income guarantee the programme included National Assistance (later Supplementary Benefit and the Income Supplement) for those whose needs could not be met by the insurance scheme. The insurance benefits were intended to be sufficient to satisfy subsistence needs, and the role of National Assistance was anticipated to be minimal.

The optimism underlying the anticipation of such a minimal role for National Assistance was founded on an assumption that full employment would prevail. This optimism was reflected also in the fact that Family Allowance was not to be payable for the first child in a family since the family wage in a fully employed economy would be sufficient to support one child. It must be remembered that the Beveridge scheme was introduced at a time when government believed that management of aggregate demand would in future ensure that the evil of mass unemployment did not return. This new found faith in demand management was to be enshrined in the famous White Paper of 1944 (UK, 1944, Cmd. 6527). It is worth remembering also that the years 1945–50 witnessed the introduction of other 'social welfare' programmes to complete a massive frontal attack on the main causes of deprivation; in particular the Education Act 1944 and the National Health Service Act 1946 were meant to add significant firepower to the State's armoury. **Table 7.7** overleaf summarises the flurry of State activity in the 1940s which provided the foundations to what came to be known as the 'Welfare State'.

Socio-economic changes and the incidence of poverty

Although not intended by Beveridge, the social security system in the UK grew steadily over the decades following the Second World War until, by the mid-1980s, it was accounting for almost one-third of all public expenditure. Over this same period the importance of social security benefits as a component of personal incomes grew dramati-

Table 7.7   *The 1940's foundations of the Welfare State in the UK*

Social Security	Beveridge Report (1942)
	Social Insurance White Paper (1944) – accepted most of Beveridge's recommendations
	Family Allowance Act 1945
	National Insurance Act 1946 – based on 1944 White Paper
	National Insurance (Industrial Injuries) Act 1946
	National Assistance Act 1948
Employment	Employment Policy White Paper (1944) – Committed government to maintaining a high (and stable) level of employment through deficit spending when necessary
Health	National Health Service White Paper (1944) – set plans for comprehensive health care for all, free of direct user charge and financed out of general taxation
	National Health Service Act 1946 – based on 1944 White Paper
Education	Educational Reconstruction White Paper (1943) – set out plans for comprehensive national system of primary, secondary and further education, primary and secondary education to be free of direct user charge and financed out of general taxation
	Education Act 1946 – based on 1943 White Paper

cally, from less than 10 pr cent in the mid-1950s to over 20 per cent by the mid-1980s. According to its critics, this relative growth of the social security system is further testimony to its failure, brought about by its intrinsic nature and by the fact that its basic philosophy has been interpreted differently by successive governments. So large a scheme, covering so many categories of want through State discretion, is likely to be slow to adapt to changes in the social and economic structure. The period after the Second World War has seen many demographic changes. In particular it has seen proportional increases in the dependent sectors of the population, as well as changes in the scale and incidence of unemployment and changes in the occupational wage structure. One result of the many changes unforseen by Beveridge has been the heavy dependency upon the role of the so-called 'safety net' of National Assistance/Supplementary Benefit/Income Supplement. The Beveridge intention that the safety net would play a minimal role has not been realised, a problem compounded by government's refusals to guarantee that National Insurance benefits at least be equal to subsistence requirements.

In terms of demographic and structural changes, the three most significant ones have been in the number of aged people, family composition, and the level and incidence of unemployment.

Poverty and old age

The population of the UK like that of the rest of Europe and other parts of the developed world, has been getting older and is expected to continue doing so well into the forseeable future. In the UK at the beginning o the 1950s the proportion of the population aged 65 and over was just under 11 per cent, but by the middle of the 1980s it had risen to just under 15 per cent. Projections published by the OECD, and reproduced in Table 7.8, suggest that by the middle of the next century the elderly populations of the UK and several other developed countries will have doubled their proportional sizes.

The projections in **Table 7.8** suggest severe implications for future income maintenance arrangements (and for the health care of the elderly) in the light of its performance in the face of the

Table 7.8 *Projections of the elderly population, UK and selected countries (percentage of population aged 65 and over)*

	UK	US	Japan	Canada	France	W. Germany	Italy
1980[1]	14.9	11.3	9.1	9.5	14.0	15.5	13.5
1985[1]	15.1	11.9	10.2	10.4	13.0	14.8	12.9
2000	14.5	12.1	15.2	12.8	15.3	17.1	15.3
2020	18.7	17.2	22.9	20.0	21.2	23.5	20.7
2040	26.4	25.3	29.2	29.2	29.7	34.1	29.1
2050	28.7	29.0	33.1	33.0	34.0	36.2	31.0

Note:
[1] Actual.
Source: Financial Times, 6 July 1988 (using OECD Demographic Data Files).

ageing of the population to date. One vivid representation of the burden placed on the system so far is that around 16 per cent of the social security budget in the mid-1980s would not have been required if the benefit then had been payable to the number of pensioners alive in the early 1950s. (Dilnot, Kay and Morris, 1984). This is not to say that the burden of the elderly had been completely unanticipated by Beveridge. Indeed the Report envisaged that over the 'transitional period' up to 1965, social security costs would rise by some 25 per cent due to the increasing burden of retirement pensions. However, over the course of the transitional period the cost of retirement pensions, in real terms, was twice as high as Beveridge had envisaged.

Poverty among old people is not a new feature of society, but it has been a notorious contributor to total domestic poverty over the course of the twentieth century. The famous surveys of poverty in York undertaken by Rowntree found that old age was the major cause of poverty in under 5 per cent of poor households in 1899 whereas in 1951 old age was estimated to be the cause of poverty in two-thirds of poor households. Rowntree's explanation of this trend included the increase in the relative size of the aged population and the increase tendency for the aged to live alone rather than with their families. As we have seen, the proportion of old people in the population has increased markedly since Rowntree's last survey.

Income sources for the aged are based less on market earnings than is the case with younger age groups. Labour market activity rates for pensioner households have fallen dramatically since the beginning of the twentieth century, and retirement pensions, both State and private, have become the main source of income for such households. Some indication of how this reliance on pension income affects living standards for old people can be taken from a comprehensive survey of poverty in the early 1970s which found a 17 per cent risk of poverty for the elderly compared with only 2.5 per cent of other adults (the risk for old people living alone was calculated to be as high as 30 per cent) and that, in total, elderly households accounted for approximately 42 per cent of the poverty among the sample (Fiegehen, Lansley and Smith, 1977).

While the risk factor remains high for old people, recent government estimates suggest that old age has diminished as a factor in poverty since the beginning of the 1970s. New legislation to combat poverty introduced in the mid-1980s gave more emphasis to the burden of pensions on taxpayers than to the burden of poverty on pensioners, against the background of a fall in the proportion of pensioners in the poorest fifth of the population from 35 per cent to 19 per cent between 1971 and 1982. Nevertheless, such an estimate still suggests that roughly one in five of the poorest fifth were pensioners at the start of the 1980s.

Family poverty

The other major component of the dependency sector of the population is children. Various surveys of poverty in the years before the Second World War had identified the number of children in a family as a major determinant of family poverty. In recent years concern has arisen again over this issue. Despite a fall in the proportion of households with dependent children from 39 per cent to 32 per cent over the period 1971–85, the proportion of couples with children, together with single parents, rose from 48 per cent to 58 per cent among the poorest fifth of the population over roughly the same period (1971–82). One estimate has claimed that between £1.5 bn and £2 bn of social security expenditure in the mid-1980s was due to trends in the number of children wholly or partly within the social security system's responsibility (Berthoud 1985). The increase in the number of single parents has been a particular cause for concern. According to official estimates the rise in divorces, the increasing incidence of illegitimate births and fewer illegitimate children being put forward for adoption, all contributed to the proportion of people living in one-parent families with children doubling from 2.5 per cent in 1961 to 5 per cent by 1985. It must be said that the one-parent family was a problem identified by Beveridge, but its increase on such a scale was not anticipated.

Low earnings and unemployment

The Beveridge Report paid a lot of attention to the problems created by unemployment, taking account of the history of the labour market and, in particular, the 1930s. However, in this one respect, the experience of the first three decades after Beveridge seemed to suggest that full employment was now the norm and unemployment was, indeed, a contingency. The reality after 1970 was to shatter this illusion as unemployment rose to over 13 per cent by 1984, including a dramatic increase in the numbers of long-term unemployed which swelled the numbers in receipt of Supplementary Benefit following the exhaustion of rights to Unemployment Benefit.

However, unemployment has not been the sole economic cause of poverty among families. Another problem which Beveridge failed to antici-

pate was the high incidence of low earnings among households in poverty after the Second World War. Beveridge virtually took it for granted that earnings in a fully employed labour market would be sufficient to support a dependent spouse and one child – this was the main reason why Family Allowance was to be for the second and any further children in a family.

However, the general increase in living standards which has pushed up the poverty line has left behind certain groups in low-paid employment. In 1986 there were 290,000 families (680,000 persons including children) with incomes below Supplementary Benefit level despite the family head being in full-time employment.

The response from the system

Poverty among the aged

How well has the system coped with these social and economic pressures? Given the numbers remaining in poverty, particularly in specific groups of dependents, the UK's social security programme has been found wanting. Some observers have blamed successive governments for failing to implement fully the Beveridge proposals, while others have emphasised that the cause of the problem lies in the nature of social insurance programmes. One important principle of the Beveridge scheme which has not been adhered to consistently is that National Insurance benefits should be at least equal to the basic poverty standard. On this principle was based the expectation that National Assistance (now Income Support) would be a genuine 'safety net'. Yet for long periods throughout the post-Beveridge years this principle was not adhered to in the categories of pensioners and children. Many pensioner households have had to rely on a flat-rate State retirement pension which has not been maintained at all times at a level above the State minimum. Hence those pensioner households totally dependent on the State retirement pension have required supplementation to their flat-rate benefit and even in the early 1980s more than a fifth of pensioners were supported by Supplementary Benefit. Until Child

Benefits were introduced in 1977, direct State income support for children was founded on Family Allowances, where the rate payable to the first eligible child was raised only twice between 1945 and 1975. Indeed, over the period 1948–67 the real value of Family Allowances declined by 22 per cent.

The most important determinant of the system's response to changes in the socio-economic structure has been the fact that benefit levels and eligibility conditions have been at the discretion of government. Social security budgeting has had to take its place in the ranking of expenditure priorities, set against available government revenues. Recall that the Beveridge perception of social security was one of insurance against contingencies like unemployment and sickness, and against loss of earnings on retirement, with earmarked benefits for children and all supported by National Assistance for those not catered for within the insurance scheme. The Beveridge programme of income maintenance was thus founded on a relationship between the principles of 'contribution' (the insurance part) and 'eligibility' (or means-testing, for the assistance part). This has given rise to two difficulties for governments. In the first place, social insurance is not very flexible; because its benefits depend on past contributions it reacts slowly to socio-economic change. Secondly, the relationship between contribution record and means testing for supplementation is very difficult to maintain.

To try and resolve the first difficulty, successive UK governments added on several new measures to the fundamental, Beveridge-based, social security programme. Inevitably, this increased the scheme's complexity. Significant steps were taken to modify provision in the three main areas outlined earlier: retirement, family size and low earnings. The increase in the number of pensioners was to put pressure on the social security system in terms of both the increasing costs of providing Beveridge-style retirement pensions and the need to make adequate provision for pensioners as living standards rose for the population as a whole. The year 1961 saw the introduction of a graduated pension, financed by a graduated contribution (a scheme which was extended to earnings-related

supplements to unemployment benefit, sickness benefit and maternity allowances in 1966). Those employees with occupational pension rights considered by the authorities to be 'adequate' were permitted to 'contract out' of the graduated pensions scheme, another significant factor leading, by the end of the 1960s, to a situation wherein the cost of benefits had risen significantly in relation to the size of the potential 'tax base'. From 1969 onwards graduated contributions financed more and more of the flat-rate benefits.

However, the major change in State pension arrangements was to come in the Social Security Pensions Act 1975 and its implementation in April 1978. This legislation introduced the State Earnings Related Pension Scheme (SERPS) under which retirement pensions were to comprise an earnings-related addition to the basic flat-rate benefit (once again provision was made for adequate occupational pension schemes to be 'contracted out' of SERPS). Early fears about the full cost of SERPS led to a proposal for its abandonment in a government Green Paper published only seven years after its introduction. However, the ensuing White Paper of 1986 retained SERPS with modifications designed to reduce its long-term cost – the 1986 White Paper will be considered in more detail later.

Insurance or 'pay as you go'

On the question of pensions, the second difficulty referred to earlier links closely with the first since the problem of the ever increasing costs of pensions has arisen mainly because public preoccupation has been with the income maintenance aspect of pensions rather than the principle of insurance. It is difficult to see how this could be otherwise in a State-provided scheme. To try and appreciate this point it might help to rehearse the arguments for State involvement in provisions for retirement.

Microeconomic theory depicts the individual as maximising the satisfaction which he or she derives from consuming goods (including leisure) and services, according to taste and subject to various constraints. Since the rational individual is interested in lifetime utility, he or she will attach relative weights to present and future consumption levels according to his or her time-preference pattern of consumption, and attempt to maximise satisfaction subject to both present and expected future constraints. Given that individuals do behave in this way, a State programme of compulsory provision for old age may distort the individual's 'optimal' (from the point of view of his or her own time-preference pattern) allocation of consumption between time periods. The individual with positive time preference is forced to increase future consumption at the expense of the present, and even the individual who places a greater weight upon future consumption is satisfied only if the level of State provision accords with his or her own expectations and desires.

The counter-argument is that the time preferences of most individuals are such that they make inadequate provision for old age for two main reasons, namely widespread myopia, intensified by the difficulties of decision-making which takes account of the distant future, and a lack of means by which to plan a consumption pattern over more than one time period. Even if the State could mitigate the latter part of the problem by providing those without means with a margin of saving over current consumption, this would be fruitful only if the first part of the problem could be solved. Thus, given that individuals are improvident, or find the calculus of optimisation concerning future income streams, investment yields, family circumstances, likelihood of employment and so on beyond their mental powers, the State assumes a paternalistic role via the compulsory purchase of annuities so as to protect the individual. If the individual does not want this protection – for example, if he or she has a very strong positive time preference for consumption – the State justifies its interference on the grounds of social costs. While concern for others might lead society to help the myopic and improvident, it does not prevent society from taking steps to ensure that the need for such aid is minimised. Furthermore, it is reasonable to expect that the working population at any point in time might wish to minimise the likelihood of their children having to support the retired population at some future date and demand that individuals be compelled to make proper provision for their retirement needs.

It must be admitted that even if a case exists for compulsory insurance, itself debatable, it is by no means obvious that this requires the compulsory purchase of State annuities. But assuming that this method of protection is adopted, should a State scheme be organised, as far as possible, on an insurance basis? The pension problem is an intergenerational one. If we accept that the sole rationale for intervention is to protect a future generation of tax-payers (the assumption we made above), then the State has a duty to organise its scheme on a funded basis, that is to ensure its actuarial soundness. To protect current policy-holders against the possibility of receipts being less than adequate to cover benefit payments at some future date, a reserve fund would be accumulated on behalf of all insured persons. To create such a reserve, premiums would be set at a sufficiently high level; if the individual wants the promise of a higher level of benefit, or more comprehensive coverage than is allowed by the original contract, he or she must be prepared to pay a higher premium. In this way, then, a reserve is accumulated for each individual, and it follows that an increase in the number of people insured must mean an increase in total reserves.

However, if we modify the rationale of intervention to one of protecting all generations, including current taxpayers, then the State has no need to organise its scheme on a funded basis (even assuming it could do so), but can make use of its coercive powers to establish the programme on a 'pay-as-you-go' basis, whereby current beneficiaries are supported by current contributions. In other words, an 'acceptable' tax/transfer plan can be devised. This argument is based on two assumptions – namely, that the scheme is financed by compulsory contributions and that future governments maintain the compulsion. Given these conditions, we can view social 'insurance' as a form of social contract whereby the young are prepared to support the old on the guarantee that a future generation of taxpayers will do the same for them when they grow old.

But what happens if the age structure of the

population changes? In particular, what happens if the proportion of the retired population increases significantly? In order to maintain the same level of pension per head of the retired population the contributory costs on the active population must rise. If this situation persists, and these costs continue to rise, the contract is very much weakened and is likely to be modified by government action. This problem appears even with real incomes growing over time if pension levels are to be determined relative to current living stanards. In other words, the insurance system collapses into the government's general tax/transfer programme.

The consequences of accepting the provision of income maintenance for retired people as part of a State tax/transfer mechanism are many. One important feature at the time of inception is that 'pensions' can be paid immediately – that is, contributions do not have to grow on a funded basis before an individual enjoys the fruits of entitlement. But the most important, if obvious, consequence is that pension arrangements as part of a wider tax/transfer mechanism, are decided by government and become the subject of political as well as financial constraints. One area where this can raise difficult problems is on the question of inequality again – what should be the 'reasonable' level for State pension benefits given the benefits enjoyed by those in receipt of occupational pensions? And how should State retirement transfers compare with, say, transfers to the temporarily sick or unemployed?

These very questions have been discussed constantly in the debate over pensions in the UK. At the same time eligibility for retirement pension has been, and continues to be, based on contribution records. From the very start the post-Beveridge scheme of national insurance was not funded on an actuarial basis. Even in its early years current contributions from employees and employers comprised a very large proportion of the total current receipts of the National Insurance Fund, and by the middle of the 1960s this proportion has risen to 80 per cent with contributions from interest income and exchequer grants having fallen dramatically.

Clearly the social security system has moved a long way from the insurance principles recom-

mended in the Beveridge Report. As one research report puts it 'in introducing full-rate pensions straight away, the Government acknowledged a funding deficiency to be met from general taxation. When the time came to pay the subsidy on any substantial scale, the pledge was abandoned and a 'pay as you go' basis adopted. The National Insurance Fund was reduced to meaningless accounting and the actuarial link between contribution and benefits abandoned' (Dilnot, Kay and Morris, 1984). Yet, as the same report points out, 'contribution records' are still the basis of eligibility (at substantial administrative cost). Whether or not this is because governments still believe (as Beveridge did) that individuals are more willing to pay 'contributions' than 'taxes' is debatable. Of course if governments do believe this to be so they might also believe that their capacity for raising revenue without generating too much political 'heat' is enhanced.

Poverty among families with children

In the area of family poverty too there have been major changes. We have mentioned the long-term decline in the real value of Family Allowances. In 1957 child tax allowances were reintroduced (first introduced in 1909 but removed when the Family Allowance was introduced) whereby deductions could be allowed from income for tax purposes at rates varying according to the age of the child. While such allowances offered indirect help to families with children, their distributional consequences differed from those of direct benefits. To see this more clearly consider the situation after 1968 when Family Allowances became classified as taxable income and recouped by the Inland Revenue (the 'claw-back' principle). This clawing-back meant that the real value of the Family Allowance rose as family income fell. Tax allowances, on the other hand, increased in value as family income rose because of the rate structure of income tax. This meant that families with incomes so low as to be unaffected by income tax did not receive any real benefit from the tax allowances, and the benefits enjoyed by tax-paying families favoured the higher income groups. Both tax allowances and Family Allowance were merged in the Child Benefit Act 1975 which introduced a flat-rate benefit on behalf of each child in a family and paid at a higher rate for one-parent families, the latter in recognition of the growth in single parenthood. Child Benefit, like the Family Allowance, is a 'universal' benefit – that is, payable to every family unit with children irrespective of the income of that family unit. As such it remains a contentious issue and we shall return to it shortly when considering the vexed question of how to make social security more efficient.

The other main cause of family poverty discussed earlier was that of earnings too low to support a spouse and child, contrary to the anticipation of the Beveridge Report. This problem was brought to governments' attention on several occasions by various lobbies, in particular by the Child Poverty Action Group. A response was offered by the Conservative government of 1971 when it introduced Family Income Supplement (FIS), a means-tested benefit specifically aimed at those families where the family head was in full-time employment but whose earnings were below the 'prescribed amount'. FIS was welcomed with great optimism, but its effects were disappointing and it was replaced in 1988 by Family Credits.

There were many other modifications and additions to social security over the post-Beveridge period. We cannot enter into the details of the main 'piecemeal' changes, but we should note here that help with housing costs was another major source of help offered to low-income families. Rate rebates were introduced in 1968, and a national scheme of rent rebates and allowances was introduced in 1972 following years of development in local authority schemes in the 1950s and 1960s. In 1983 Housing Benefit was introduced to replace these earlier arrangements. The other major change to note is the extension of the principle of earnings-related income maintenance, not only from the supplement offered under the 1961 graduated pension scheme to the later pension arrangements already discussed, but also to other national insurance benefits in 1966 and 1975. By 1985 the social security system offered a complex array of 30 separate benfits with differing structures and ratio-

nales and costing over £2 bn annually to administer.

The problem of 'take-up'

We turn now to a question which has so far only been hinted at. While the pressures on the social security system go some of the way to explain why so many individuals have had to rely on the safety net of benefit supplementations, they do not explain why so many have fallen **below** the poverty line. The main reason why so many fall below this line is because they are not in receipt of full income supplementations **even when entitled to them**. This is the infamous problem of low 'take-up' thought, by most commentators, to be due to two causes: the complexity of the social security system and the stigma which attaches to receipt of means-tested benefits. The complexity of the system was underlined earlier. Not only is there a plethora of benefits for claimants to consider, but there is also a detailed and, for many claimants, difficult application procedure. Part of the difficulty lies in the detail required in order to assess the means and needs of claimants but this very enquiry is also considered to be degrading by many potential claimants. As a consequence, many eligible individuals refrain from claiming means-tested benefits.

A government inquiry in 1965 found that one-third of pensioners were ignorant of the availability of National Assistance, while 30 per cent of married couples and 20 per cent of single men and women indicated that pride prevented them from applying for supplementary help. Family Income Supplement at the end of the 1970s was being taken up by only 50 per cent out of those eligible while, at the same time, the take-up rate for Supplementary Benefit was around 74 per cent and that for Rent and Rates Rebates in the region of 70 per cent, all according to government estimates. In 1987 Fry and Stark published a comparison of their own estimates of Supplementary Benefit take-up and those of the DHSS for a period covering the end of the 1950s to the middle of the 1980s (Fry and Stark, 1987). Their findings, reproduced in **Table 7.9** underline the fact that take-up of the

Table 7.9 *Estimates of supplementary benefit take-up*

Study	Year	Take-up rate		
		Pensioners	Non-pensioners	All
DHSS	1977	0.72	0.79	—
DHSS	1979	0.65	0.78	0.70
DHSS	1981	0.67	0.75	0.71
Fry and Stark	1984	0.87	0.81	0.83
Fry and Stark[1]	1984	0.66	0.78	0.74

Note:
[1] Estimates on 'DHSS basis'.
Source: Fry and Stark (1986).

'bottom line' income support for the period in question was well short of 100 per cent.

Low take-up of means-tested benefits creates two serious problems for income maintenance programmes. An obvious, but important consequence of low take-up among means-tested households is that income support is not being given to many of the households most in need of it. A second consequence, creating a problem for the longer run, is that low take-up rates affect the accuracy of policy planning because they influence the outcome of benefit expenditure by the government. For example, a reduction in universal benefits and an increase in selective or 'targeted' (means-tested) benefits should, in principle, result in a more equal distribution of final incomes, but, if the former type of benefit has a high take-up rate and the latter a low one, the move towards equality is lessened. This is a problem we shall return to later.

The social security 'traps'

Another reason advanced to explain high numbers remaining in poverty, even during a time of economic growth for the country as a whole, relates to the implicit taxation of earned income in a social security system which relies on means-tested benefits, for basic income support. This implicit taxation arises from the interaction among means-tested benefits and between them and the income tax system. As the number of means-tested benefits rose over the decades following the Bever-idge Report this was to become an increasing problem.

The various means-tested benefits and the social security programme are, in fact, examples of the principle of 'negative (income) taxation' in the sense that principles governing the receipt of benefit include elements of tax as well as welfare payment. These separable elements emerge from both the direction of the **total** resource flow involved and the nature of the impact at the **margin** of economic activity. Taking the case of a family unit of given size, we can demonstrate this point by assuming eligibility for weekly benefit to be determined by the amount of weekly income earned by the unit from other sources, say from earned income. Thus, at the margin, the net flow of resources is from the private sector to the government. In other words, the family unit is being taxed on **additional earnings**. However, the total flow of resources remains in the opposite direction to that of a tax since the net overall effect of the scheme is a supplement to the income of the family unit.

We may also note at this stage that the structure of means-tested benefits, as in this example, usually bears the other hallmarks of a taxation scheme. Benefit is paid to, or withheld from, a defined tax unit (say, head of household plus dependants); is determined by reference to a defined base (say, earned income); and the benefit payable in any period depends on income received by the tax unit from the base source during that same period. There is, however, one feature of means-tested social security benefits which does set them apart from usual tax conventions: the marginal rate of tax applied to low levels of income is often very high because State supplements to income are a substitute for a lack of income from other sources within the tax base. Hence, as other income rises, the supplement is withdrawn. The rationale for this may lie in the philosophy behind the system (only those who have a genuine need for State help can receive it) and/or a lack of resources in society to permit a more generous redistribution of resources towards the lower income groups.

The prepensity for claimants to incur high marginal tax rates, is, of course, increased by interaction between the benefits system and the income tax. The so-called 'poverty trap' operates usually when an increase in earnings offers only a small increase in final income because of simultaneous lower benefit receipt and higher taxes and National Insurance contributions; in its most extreme form it has affected families in work so as to make them **worse off** by earning an extra £1 of income. While the withdrawal of means-tested benefits has placed claimants on high marginal rates of (implicit) tax throughout the post-Beveridge period, the piece-meal additions to the benefit system served to intensify the problem. In particular, the introduction of FIS and its resulting interaction with housing subsidies was to become the main reason for poor households facing marginal rates of tax in excess of 100 per cent: the numbers of families in this severe form of the poverty trap was estimated by the Treasury and Civil Service Committee in 1982 to have increased from 15,000 in early 1974 to 105,600 by the end of 1981.

The 'unemployment trap' operates when low-earning households find that they are either financially better off depending on State benefits than in paid employment, or that the difference in living standards offered by the two choices are so small that the incentive to find paid work is very small. This particular problem was considered to be severe by the 1970s in the case of the short-term unemployed. It has been estimated that in 1978 about 21 per cent of the heads of working families would have received more than 90 per cent of their weekly income if, instead, they had been unemployed for a short time (Dilnot, Kay and Morris, 1984). This was probably due to the availability of

earnings-related benefit supplements and the fact that tax rebates were received during unemployment of short duration. In 1982, Unemployment Benefit was made taxable and earnings-related benefit supplement were abolished earlier in the same year. It has been estimated that only 2.9 per cent of people would have been able to enjoy more than 90 per cent of that income in work during a short spell of unemployment (Dilnot, Kay and Morris, 1984).

Fairness, incentives and 'supply-side' effects

High marginal rates of tax on the earnings of poor individuals or households are considered to be undesirable for reasons of equity as well as efficiency. When a tax system, like that of the UK, is based on a principle of 'ability to pay' supported by a progressive rates structure, it is absurd as well as unfair for the tax system to combine with the social security programme and impose higher marginal rates of tax on low income groups than on higher income groups. While most observers agree about the inequity of the system's regressive rates structure, there is less agreement on the extent to which means-testing creates genuine disincentives to effort. Government preoccupation with the question of work disincentives has been a constant feature of social security in the UK, although this concern has been dressed up in different language from time to time. Hence, 'less eligibility' was the principle behind the nineteenth-century Poor Law condition that State aid to the unemployed should be less than the lowest earnings rate; the same principle supported the 'wages stop' of the post-Beveridge Unemployment Benefit programme; the need to minimise the 'disincentive to effort' became an essential ingredient of government policies on 'supply-side economics' during the 1970s and 1980s.

The increasing government preoccupation with 'supply-side economics' has encouraged several investigations by economists into household reactions to changes in the relative costs of work and leisure. These have concentrated more on changes in the marginal rate of taxation, and less on the average rate which affects disposable incomes and is more significant when considering Keynesian demand-side policy. If marginal tax rates are reduced, households are faced with an increase in the monetary reward for extra time at work. But microeconomic theory suggests that the resulting change in labour supply will depend upon the directions and relative strengths of **income and substitution effects**; the former is an inducement to substitute work for the now relatively more expensive leisure, while the latter may encourage the household to work less hours and enjoy some of its increase in real income in the form of leisure. Thus, if the substitution effect dominates, households will supply more work, but if the income effect dominates more leisure might be consumed. The likely outcome to a change in marginal rates of tax is clearly an empirical question, but one which has proved difficult to answer, and research into labour supply reactions have unearthed evidence of both incentives and disincentives arising from alterations in the marginal net income of households. However, so far as the poverty trap is concerned, since the effective marginal tax rates can be so high it is difficult to assume that disincentives to effort do not exist in and around the trap, and government concern has accordingly centred on how many individuals are actively caught in the trap.

In looking at the unemployment trap, empirical work has tended to concentrate on the estimation of the **replacement rate** – that is, the ratio of net income out of work to net income in work, for various household categories. Our earlier reference to relative returns from working and living on State benefit before and after 1978 took account of replacement rates. The estimate quoted there of the proportions affected by high replacement rates was but one of several attempts to measure the 'supply-side' disincentives of the benefit system before and after the 1978 changes. As with the poverty trap, estimation of the impact of the unemployment trap have proved difficult, and there is by no means a consensus on the issue of whether or not the benefit system has induced unemployment. A correlation of the benefit–income rates to unemployment for the period up to the end of the 1970s has

been calculated by Hemming which suggests that, on the whole, both increased from 1948 to the end of the period. In particular, a large increase in the benefit-income ratio after the introduction of the earnings-related supplement in 1966 is worthy of note (Hemming, 1984).

The Conservative reforms of the 1980s

As part of its comprehensive reappraisal of the relative roles of public and private sector in the mixed economy, and in its determination to ensure that government spending is 'efficient' the Conservative Government turned its attentions to issues of social security in the mid-1980s. A Green Paper in June 1985 outlined the main points at issue and was followed by a White Paper later the same year containing detailed proposals for major reforms of the social security system. The resulting parliamentary debate led to the Social Security Act 1986, which introduced several major changes to the benefit side of social security arrangements, and full implementation of these reforms took place in April 1988. What we see in both the debate and the subsequent reforms is clear recognition of the list of problems discussed so far in this chapter, with added emphasis to the efficiency-equity trade-off referred to at the outset. The main defects of the system, as identified by the 1985 White Paper, were deemed to be: its complexity, its failure to give proper support to those most in need, the problems created by the poverty and unemployment 'traps' and the burden of costs on future generations of taxpayers. In addition, the White Paper emphasised the government's concern about the restrictions on individual choice on the matter of pensions.

The response to the problems identified in the White Paper was set out in the 1986 Act, and centred on changes to the income-related benefits. The Green Paper had, in fact, proposed the abolition of SERPS, but this met with stiff opposition and the Act, instead, set out modifications aimed at reducing its cost on future generations. Supplementary Benefit was replaced by Income Support; Family Income Support was replaced by Family Credit; and a new Housing Benefit replaced the previous two-part scheme (one for recipients of Supplementary Benefit and one for all others on low incomes). But these changes were not in name only. The new system rationalised the relationship between these three main income-related benefits and established their entitlements on the same basis for the first time. At the same time, the changes represented a shift in resources towards Income Support and Family Credit and away from Housing Benefit which, in effect meant a shift of emphasis in the system towards families with children and away from pensioners. Income Support could continue to be the main benefit for those not in full-time work, offering a benefit of a personal allowance plus increases for dependents. Under the new benefit there would be no additions for specific needs whether 'one-off' or longer-term. Instead, such needs would be met out of a new Social Fund. Like its predecessor, Family Credit is designed to offer supplements to low-income families in full-time work and with children to support; it is designed also to be more extensive in its coverage than was FIS.

The issue as to whether or not the provisions in the 1986 Act are likely to achieve the objectives of the earlier White Paper has provoked a mixed response. It is true that the social system has been simplified, but it has not been made simple. This may lead to problems particularly since the reforms offered no structural alterations which might improve take-up – even the White Paper's optimism was limited to an assumed take-up rate of 60 per cent for Family Credit. In the respect to helping those most in need, estimates suggest that the majority of couples with children and single parents will be made better off by the reforms, while about three-quarters of pensioners will either be unaffected or be worse off. Finally, on the question of the social security traps, the position is ambiguous. The unemployment trap should be eased and the extreme form of the poverty trap has been virtually eliminated (no more marginal tax rates of 100 per cent or greater). However, the extension of cover offered under the Family Credit arrangements has faced many more individuals than previously with marginal tax rates around 80 per cent (Dilnot and Webb, 1988).

Recent debate and the future of social security

Given the doubts still remaining it is not surprising, perhaps, to find that the issue of 'universal' versus 'selective' benefits remains at the centre of debate on social security. The government has placed **efficiency** at the forefront of economic objectives, and increasingly blurred the distinctions between economic and social issues. Since universal benefits are made available to all, regardless of means, they are deemed to be a less efficient means of income redistribution than selective benefits which, by definition, are targeted on those recipients most in need. This issue underpinned the 1986 reforms but the argument has continued. Nowhere has the debate been more intense than over the issue of Child Benefit. When Mr John Moore announced to the House of Commons in October 1988 that Child Benefit was to be frozen for the second year running, the howls of protest were confined mainly to the Opposition benches only because the proposed freeze was to be part of a package of anti-poverty measures to be available **only to those who were most in need of Child Benefit**. In other words, poor families with children were to be given special benefit rises (of up to 9.3 per cent) but they were to be targeted (means-tested).

This proposal for a resource switch, and consequent denial of the fundamental Beveridge principle of providing a flat-rate benefit for all families with children, represented a significant denial of 'universality' as a cornerstone of the social security system. The door was now opened wider to make possible further 'selective' arrangements. It could be argued, for example, that future tax/transfer support of the aged will be modified along similar lines. Bearing in mind the burden on future generations of working taxpayers of providing income support to a proportionally growing retired population, many of whom will be enjoying the fruits of their occupational pension schemes, the demand by voters for more selective measures to concentrate transfers on the 'genuinely needy' within the retired population is likely to grow. Increased awareness that the UK State pension scheme has not been 'as of right' but 'pay as you go' is likely to fuel such demands.

The debate over selectivity in the social security system brings us back, full circle, to the efficiency/equity trade-off. On the one hand is a concern for efficiency and the removal of disincentives in tax/transfer programmes while, on the other, is a concern for the welfare of the poor. A problem for the party image-makers in the 1980s was how to present the government as a 'caring' administration as well as one which promoted efficiency and increased incentives. The solution to the problem for the future lies in persuading the electorate that 'targeting' is 'cost-effective caring'.

So to persuade the electorate is conditional on achieving two related objectives, namely finding a way to much simpler means-testing and improving markedly the take-up of available benefits. One way to reach these goals which has received a lot of attention from economists and which enjoys a degree of consensus among political opinions, is to introduce some form of **truly comprehensive negative income tax** which would follow the principles outlined earlier but would combine social security benefits and income tax payments in a single system of redistribution, centrally administered. To date no government has gone that far in its legislation (although a variant was proposed in a Green Paper published by the Heath-led Conservative Government of 1972) and Mr Fowler's overhaul of the mid-1980s fell a long way short of such radicalism.

References

Abel-Smith, B. and Townsend, P. (1965) *The Poor and the Poorest* (Bell & Sons).

Atkinson, A.B. (1972) *Unequal Shares* (Allen Lane, The Penguin Press).

Berthoud, R. (1985) 'Mr Fowler's Examination', *Catalyst* (Autumn).

Cmd. 6404 (1942) *Social Insurance and Allied Services* (The Beveridge Report), (HMSO).

Cmd., 6527 (1944) *Employment Policy* (HMSO).

Diamond Commission (Royal Commission on the Distribution of Income and Wealth), Report No. 1 (1975) Cmnd 6171 (HMSO; Report No. 4 (1976) Cmnd 6626 (HMSO).

Dilnot, A.W., Kay, J.A. and Morris, C.N. (1984) *The Reform of Social Security* (Oxford, Clarendon Press, for the Institute of Fiscal Studies, London).

Dilnot, A.W. and Webb, S. (1988) 'The 1988 Social Security Reforms', *Fiscal Studies* (August).

Fiegehen, G.C., Lansley P.S. and Smith, A.D. (1977) *Poverty and Progress in Britain, 1953–73* (Cambridge University Press).

Fry, V. and Stark, G. (1986) 'The Take-Up of Supplementary Benefit: Gaps in the "Safety Net"?', *Fiscal Studies* (November).

Harbury, C.D. (1962) 'Inheritance in the Distribution of Personal Wealth', *Economic Journal* (December).

Harbury, C.D. and Hitchens, D.M. (1976) 'The Inheritance of Top Wealth Leavers', *Economic Journal* (vol. 86).

Harbury, C.D. and McMahon, P.C. (1973) 'Inheritance and the Distribution of Personal Wealth in Britain', *Economic Journal* (vol. 83).

Hemming, R. (1984) *Poverty and Incentives* (Oxford University Press).

Lydall, H.F. (1959) 'The Long Term Trend in the Size Distribution of Income', *Journal of the Royal Statistical Society* (Series A, 122, Part 1).

Morris, N. and Preston, I. (1986) 'Taxes, Benefits and the Distribution of Income 1968–83', *Fiscal Studies* (November).

Nicholson, R.J. (1967) 'The Distribution of Personal Income', *Lloyds Bank Review* (January).

Piachaud, D. (1988) 'Poverty in Britain 1899 to 1983', *Journal of Social Policy* (vol. 17, no. 3).

8

Industry and Policy
Keith Hartley and Nick Hooper

Introduction: the policy issues

Industrial policy has been the victim of various definitions reflecting different views about the role, extent and appropriate form of state intervention in the economy. At the one extreme, interventionists favour an active role with governments intervening throughout the economy at the industry and, ultimately, the firm level. The other extreme takes a laissez-faire approach leaving everything to market forces. In the UK, these alternative views about industrial policy have been reflected in continuing controversy between the major political parties.

During the 1970s and 1980s controversy has raged over policy towards manufacturing industry and over the size of the public sector, reflecting concern about crowding-out, deindustrialisation and the decline of the UK's manufacturing industrial base. Aspects of this controversy were apparent in debates about State rescue operations for companies such as British Leyland (now Rover), Chrysler, Rolls Royce 1971 and the Westland helicopter company. In the 1980s the debate focused on the decision to sell off valuable national assets such as British Aerospace, British Telecom, British Steel and the Royal Ordnance Factories; the sale of public utilities such as gas, electricity and water; and whether major government defence contracts should be used to support British industry (Nimrod AEW, tanks). On such issues the major political parties have differed in their views on the extent and appropriate form of State intervention.

The Labour Government of the 1970s (1974–79) favoured interventionist policies in the form of an industrial strategy. This strategy was supported by an interventionist State agency (the National Enterprise Board; state ownership; planning agreements; industrial democracy; a policy of 'selecting the winners'; and an extensive system of financial subsidies to firms, industries and regions. In contrast, the Conservative Government of the 1980s has relied on market forces as its preferred industrial policy. Its emphasis has been on supply-side policies with a smaller public sector and reduced state intervention reflected in privatisation; contracting-out; deregulation; the withdrawal of industrial and regional subsidies; and more emphasis on competition policy and support for small firms. This policy aims to replace a 'culture of dependency' with an 'enterprise culture' based on profitability and lower personal taxation, offering greater incentives for managers, workers, shareholders and new businesses.

Whilst governments have differed in their policies towards UK industry, their performance can be assessed against some broad indicators of the trends in manufacturing, its productivity and its export and import record. A starting point is the changing role of manufacturing in the economy. The overall picture is of a continuing shift away from an economy dominated by industry to one based on services. As shown in **Table 8.1**, the manufacturing share of gross domestic product has fallen from a third in 1969 to under a quarter in

1987. Over this period activity shifted towards services, with private services rising from 38 per cent to 48 per cent and public services from 12 per cent to 15 per cent of GDP. Inevitably, concern has been expressed about the contraction in manufacturing industry reflected in deindustrialisation and its possible adverse effects upon the economy's investment and export performance. Various explanations have been advanced, ranging from rising government spending 'crowding-out' private sector investment to the long-run decline in the competitiveness of UK industry (as in Blackaby, 1979).

The falling share of manufacturing is reflected in steadily declining industrial employment. In 1988 manufacturing employment was 63 per cent of its 1969 level, while total employment had recovered from a slump to show a 2 per cent increase over the period. Part of the fall in manufacturing employment over this period was due to productivity gains. Labour productivity in manufacturing grew faster than in the whole economy, so that by 1988 output per person employed in manufacturing stood at nearly twice the level of 1969, while the economy as a whole achieved a more modest 46 per cent gain as shown in **Table 8.2** overleaf. Indeed, the substantial UK productivity gains in the 1980s raise questions as to whether the Conservative Governments have succeeded since 1979 in reversing permanently the UK's relative economic decline.

The decline in the role of manufacturing in the UK economy is reflected internationally in the pattern of trade (see Chapter 4). The manufacturing share of UK exports fell from 85 per cent in 1969

Table 8.1 *Contribution to GDP by sector (%)*

	1969	1975	1980	1985	1987
Manufacturing	34.10	28.07	25.38	22.62	22.81
Agriculture	3.12	2.62	2.03	1.73	1.57
Energy	4.90	4.88	9.28	10.06	6.45
Construction	7.04	6.86	5.78	5.62	5.74
Private services	38.53	41.21	41.96	45.22	48.35
Public services	12.31	16.36	15.57	14.76	15.08
	100.00	100.00	100.00	100.00	100.00

Source: UK National Accounts 'Blue Book', CSO, various years.

Table 8.2 *Employment and productivity (1980 = 100)*

	1969	1975	1980	1985	1988
Employment					
Manufacturing	121.8	109.6	100.0	79.5	76.6
Total labour force	98.6	99.4	100.0	96.9	101.0
Productivity					
Manufacturing	84.6	95.9	100.0	134.6	162.6
Whole economy	85.5	92.4	100.0	114.2	124.5

Source: Monthly Digest of Statistics.

to 76 per cent in 1987. At the same time the proportion of sales going to exports rose from 17 per cent to some 30 per cent. By 1987 finished and semi-manufactured goods accounted for three-quarters of all imports, up from one-half in 1969. The proportion of imports to home demand doubled over this period, from 17 per cent to 34 per cent. Such stylised facts raise questions about the performance of UK manufacturing industry and whether public policy can improve performance.

The contribution which economists can make to this debate about industrial policy is to subject myths and special pleading to economic analysis and critical appraisal, and to confront the arguments with the available evidence. Some of the major issues are now apparent, and we must ask whether economic theory offers any guidelines for a public policy towards industry. What, for example, are the implications of the analysis for the size, structure, location, ownership and performance of UK industries? In particular, how can economic theory be used to evaluate specific industrial policies such as policy towards competition, subsidies, privatisation and the role of government purchasing?

Theory and industrial policy

Introduction

Questions about the proper role of government in the economy dominate policy debates. In relation to industry, it has to be asked whether there are any economic arguments for government interven-

tion, and if so, to what extent should the State intervene, and in what form? For example, should the State favour British manufacturing industry? Should policy be applied to all firms or to a selected group (selected by industry or region)? Should intervention be in the form of subsidies (to firms, capital, labour or R & D); import controls; a buy-British government purchasing policy; competition and merger policy; nationalisation; or privatisation with State regulation? These are the general issues behind such specific examples as the UK Ministry of Defence decision to buy US Boeing AWACS aircraft and to cancel the British Nimrod AEW project; to bring Rolls Royce into public ownership in 1971 rather than to bail out the privately-owned company through subsidies; and to replace publicly-owned enterprises such as British Telecom and British Gas with privately-owned companies subject to State regulation.

The methodology of economic policy provides a framework for analysing industrial policy issues. The approach requires economists to seek answers to three questions:

1. What is the policy problem and what are governments seeking to achieve? Usually, the underlying problem worrying policy-makers can be deduced from the government's stated objectives (and vice versa). For example, in the 1970s, the Labour Government's industrial strategy was concerned with the relative decline of UK manufacturing industry (deindustrialisation), and the need to reverse this decline and to improve UK industry's international competitiveness. Such aims also need to be

operationalised and performance indicators (for example, the UK's share of world exports) are required to evaluate the success or otherwise of industrial policy.

2. Why is there a problem? Economists use their theories to explain the causes of problems which are worrying governments. For example, British industry's declining international competitiveness might result from a structure of too many small firms unable to undertake the necessary R & D and obtain the scale economies required to compete in world markets. Alternatively, it might be due to general inefficiency reflecting the motivation and attitudes of managers and workers, or it could reflect interest rate and exchange rate policy. The choice between these alternative theories depends on which best explains the facts.

3. What can be done to solve the problem? Usually, there are alternative policy solutions. To improve the performance of UK manufacturing industry might require an industrial strategy, the creation of labour-managed firms or a competition policy. Private monopolies could be controlled through nationalisation, through encouragement of competition or by State regulation of prices or profits. Governments might promote technical progress through subsidising R & D, by training more scientists or through placing contracts with UK firms for advanced technology equipment (such as computers, Concorde, nuclear power stations and space satellites). Theories can be used to predict the likely effects of alternative policy solutions, with governments having to choose between the alternatives. Such choices will reflect the governing party's values and ideology, its possible interest in maximising the welfare of the community and its immediate concern with votes and re-election.

Economic theory approaches industrial policy issues from the starting point of Paretian welfare economics. It is assumed that society aims to maximise welfare by achieving an **optimum allocation of resources** (that is, a Pareto optimum occurs where it is impossible to make one person better off without making someone else worse off).

In a private enterprise economy, the Paretian model suggests that properly-functioning competitive markets are socially desirable since perfectly competitive markets result in a Pareto optimum allocation of resources. On this basis, market forces determine the optimum size of the manufacturing sector. The model provides some broad guidelines for industrial policy. State intervention is required whenever markets are failing to work properly (that is, where there are substantial departures from the competitive ideal). This approach suggests that industrial policy is a means of correcting for major market failures. The obvious focus is on the operation of product markets, although it has to be recognised that failures can occur in markets for capital, labour, money and foreign exchange.

There are two general sources of market failure — (**a**) imperfections in the form of monopoly, oligopoly, restrictive practices and entry barriers, and (**b**) beneficial or harmful externalities, including public goods (for example, defence). Externalities mean that, left to themselves, private competitive markets might provide too little of some socially desirable activities such as information and basic R & D and too much of some socially undesirable products such as pollution, noise and traffic congestion. Here, however, economists have to be careful in distinguishing between the technical issues concerned with the causes of market failure and the policy issues concerned with the choice of the most appropriate solution. For example, even if imperfections are identified as the main source of market failure, governments have to choose between such alternative policies as increased competition, reduced tariff barriers and the State regulation of monopoly prices and profits. Similarly, externalities might be corrected through taxes and subsidies or public ownership, or by legislative changes in property rights allowing the courts to determine compensation for the victims of spillovers. Care must also be taken to distinguish between efficiency issues concerned with market failure, and equity issues where the outcomes are unacceptable. Finally, a Pareto optimum allocation of resources can be achieved through either a perfectly competitive private enterprise economy or by direct controls and commands in a centrally-planned economy.

The structure–conduct–performance paradigm

In examining the causes of market failure and the range of policy solutions, we also need to be aware of the standard tool kit of industrial economists, namely, the structure–conduct–performance framework. This states that industrial performance depends ultimately upon industry structure where the variables in the model are structure, conduct and performance.

Structure

Structure comprises the number and size distribution of firms in an industry and the conditions governing the entry of new firms. There are two extremes – **perfect competition** and **monopoly** – with the intermediate and often typical cases of **monopolistic competition** and **oligopoly**. With this approach industry concentration is determined by economies of scale, the size of the market (the number of firms of optimal scale it will support) and entry barriers. Perfectly competitive markets are characterised by free entry, with large numbers of relatively small firms each operating at optimal scale.

Conduct

Conduct embraces the pricing, advertising, marketing, R & D and product differentiation aspects of firm behaviour (in other words, price and non-price competition), as well as the possibilities for collusion and restrictive agreements.

Performance

Performance is measured by technical and allocative efficiency. In this context, a concern with a Pareto optimum allocation of resources requires that prices equal marginal cost throughout the economy. Applied to a private enterprise competitive economy, the result would be firms which are technically efficient so that X-inefficiency (organisational slack) is absent and, in the long run, normal profits would be earned. On this basis, the efficiency of an economy's industries might be measured by such performance indicators as profitability, and by inter-firm and international comparisons of labour productivity and total factor productivity. However, the Pareto approach is static, and a society interested in growth will be concerned with the dynamic aspects of industrial performance as reflected in innovation and technical progress (see the taxonomy in **Table 8.3**).

The model in **Table 8.3** runs from industry structure to conduct to performance with the relationships depending on the assumptions about firm behaviour (that is, its objectives). The standard assumption is that firms are **profit maximisers**. On this basis, the neo-classical model shows that, for given demand and cost conditions, monopoly leads to a higher price and to a lower output than perfect competition. Also, since monopoly prices exceed marginal costs, Paretian welfare economics concludes that there will be a misallocation of resources and hence a market failure: monopoly is regarded as socially undesirable (see **Figure 8.1**). Estimates of the losses of consumer benefit due to monopoly have ranged from extremely small to up to 7 per cent of gross corporate product in the UK and up to 13 per cent of gross corporate output in the USA. However, the analysis can be modified to allow for a trade-off between the cost savings from mergers and economies of scale and the loss of consumer benefits due to monopoly. Alternative approaches have also emerged involving contestability, transaction costs and the Austrian critique all of which are discussed in the sections which follow. Moreover, the theory of second-best shows the limited applicability of the Paretian model.

Trade-offs

Let us consider a competitive industry and ask whether such an industry should be monopolised through mergers? If we assume that a merger leads to economies of scale which would not otherwise be available to a competitive industry, then a merger to monopolise a competitive industry will result in cost savings. There will thus be a trade-off between the cost savings from scale economies and the loss of consumer benefit (surplus) due to the monopolisation of the competitive industry. Logically, the merger should be allowed to proceed if the additions to producer profits (surplus) exceed the loss of consumer benefits (surplus) as shown in **Figure 8.1**.

Table 8.3 *A taxonomy of industrial policy*

Industry features	Main characteristics	Examples of industrial policy options
1. **Structure**	Number of firms Size of firms Entry conditions	Monopoly, mergers and restrictive practices policies in UK and EEC Tariff policy; government contracts
2. **Conduct**	Pricing Advertising Marketing Product differentiation Research and development Collusion and restrictive agreements	Monopoly and restrictive practices policy Regulation of prices and advertising Consumer protection policy Regulation of new products and standards Restrictive practices policy
3. **Location**	Regional Towns Inner cities Rural areas	Subsidies to firms and labour Location of industry policy Local authority planning controls Tourism policy; subsidies to rural industry and to agriculture

4. **Ownership**	Firm behaviour
	– profit maximisation
	– non-profit objectives
		Nationalisation of firms and industries
		Privatisation with or without:
		   a. competition
		   b. regulation

5. **Performance**	Efficiency – technical – allocative Profitability Growth	Monopoly, merger and competition policy State regulation of profits Industrial strategy; R & D and technology policy

Figure 8.1 *Mergers, scale economies and competition*

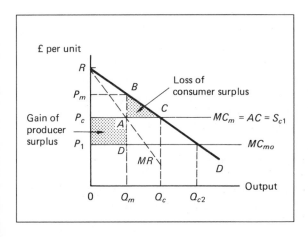

This trade-off analysis is not, however, without its critics. It uses a modified form of Paretian welfare function which allows a comparison of gains and losses, but distributional issues cannot be ignored so that we must ask whether the same or different weights should be attached to changes in producer and consumer benefits. Moreover, after the merger has taken place, a profit-maximising monopolist will expand output (beyond OQ_m in **Figure 8.1**) so raising producer profits and reducing the loss of consumer surplus, resulting in an even stronger case for the merger. Nevertheless, the merger will continue to be associated with a misallocation of resources, with price greater than the new marginal costs. In the circumstances, consumers could in principle bribe the monopolist to produce at the new competitive price and output (Q_{c2} at P_1 in **Figure 8.1**): the monopoly would be no worse off since it would be compensated for its lost profits and consumers would be substantially better off. Such socially desirable compensation does not occur because substantial transaction costs make it too costly to negotiate such a solution between the consumers and the monopolist. Finally, once the merger has occurred, competitive pressures will be absent, allowing the firm to become technically inefficient which results in a departure from cost-minimising behaviour.

Contestable markets

The concept of contestable markets represents a further modification to the standard structure–performance paradigm. A contestable market is one where there is the possibility and threat of entry by domestic and foreign firms, and therefore the **threat** of rivalry. A perfectly contestable market is one which has no entry barriers, where entry and exit are easy and costless, and which may or may not be characterised by economies of scale or economies of scope (that is, economies which result from the range or scope of a multi-product firm's activities). In contestable markets, potential entrants are attracted by opportunities for profits. 'Hit-and-run behaviour' is evident since new entrants are not at a cost disadvantage compared with established suppliers, and the absence of sunk (irrevocable) costs means that exit is costless. One of the major features and policy implications of this approach is that a contestable market need not be populated by a large number of firms (as in perfect competition). In fact, a contestable market may contain only one or a small number of firms. Thus, with contestable markets, economists no longer have to assume that efficient outcomes occur only where there are large numbers of firms as in perfect competition. Contestability, rather than structure, determines performance.

Transaction costs

Economic activity and exchange is a transaction process in a world of imperfect information and knowledge. Producers do not have complete knowledge of production possibilities and market opportunities. Similarly, individuals as consumers lack information on the price and quality of goods and services on offer, and as workers they will have only limited information on the wages, employment conditions and career prospects available in the labour market. Further costs are incurred in completing a transaction or doing business. For instance, after searching the market for a new car, costs are incurred in negotiating a price, and then policing, monitoring and enforcing a contract. After all, if producers and consumers were perfectly informed, and there were no transaction costs, then markets would not fail since all opportunities for mutually advantageous trade and exchange would be fully exploited.

Transaction costs have been defined as the costs of running the economic system, and include all the costs involved in planning, bargaining, modifying, monitoring and enforcing an implicit or explicit contract (Williamson, 1981, p. 1544). On this approach, the modern corporation and other economic institutions reflect efforts to economise on transaction costs rather than to pursue anti-competitive practices and create monopolies. Two assumptions are central to transaction costs: bounded rationality and opportunism. Bounded rationality recognises that economic agents have a limited capacity to handle information and to solve complex problems. Opportunism recognises that individuals will affect transactions through pursuing self-interest by hoarding valuable information, distorting data and sending misleading messages.

Transaction cost economics offers some distinctive explanations and interpretations of economic organisations:

1. Transactions will be organised in markets unless market exchange creates substantial transaction cost penalties
2. It explains decisions by firms to undertake activities in-house or to buy-in, as reflected in the extent of integration
3. It explains the internal organisation of firms in the form of hierarchies, internal government and divisions. An example is the multi-divisional, or *M*-form, organisation which resembles a mini-capital market compared with the centralised, unitary or *U*-form structure. The success

of the *M*-form was due to its ability to econo-mise further on transaction costs

4. It explains non-standard and unfamiliar forms of economic organisation such as conglomer-ates, multi-nationals and franchising.

This approach accepts that whilst firms seek to economise on transaction costs, they might also aim to become monopolists. However, the transac-tions school believes that monopolising behaviour is the exception. In advocating transaction cost economics, it has been suggested that it is the only hypothesis that is able to provide a discriminating rationale for the succession of organisational inno-vations that have occurred over the past 150 years and out of which the modern corporation has emerged (Williamson, 1981, p. 1564). But critics claim that transaction costs are so general that they can be used to rationalise almost anything, and that the approach does not offer any testable and refutable predictions. However, the notions of imperfect information and contestability are ele-ments in the Austrian critique.

The Austrian critique

The Austrian economists (such as Hayek, Schum-peter and Kirzner) are critical of the structure–conduct–performance paradigm, with its underly-ing emphasis on perfect competition and equi-librium. They assert that actual economies consist-ing of real world firms and industries are never in equilibrium (that is, never at a state of rest). Instead, economies are characterised by ignorance and uncertainty, which leads to continuous change and continuous market disequilibrium. Ignorance and uncertainty create opportunities for profits and it is the entrepreneur's task to discover these profitable opportunities. To the Austrians, compe-tition means continuous rivalry (contestability) with entrepreneurs searching for opportunities to make money before anyone else – all of which occurs in a world of ignorance and uncertainty where there is no such thing as perfect information and knowledge. To the Austrians, trial and error price adjustments, and trial and error advertising and product variations are simply a **search and discovery process** – they are methods of trying to obtain market information in situations where

knowledge is imperfect and costly to acquire. But conventional theory regards these actions by a businessman as evidence that he possesses some monopoly power. In other words, the competitive process which we witness in the high street seems alien to our model of a perfectly competitive equilibrium. In the high street, the trial and error price cuts made by businessmen are simply ex-amples of the way they try to gain information on their profit-maximising price (they are searching for profits).

The public policy implications of the Austrian approach concern two major issues in particular. In the first place, they concern the role of **profits**. At any given moment, profits may seem to be mono-polistic resulting from output restrictions – the monopoly problem. Austrians, however, regard high profits as temporary since rival entrepreneurs will be attracted into the relatively profitable activity. Austrians suggest that monopoly control regulations should involve an assessment of profits over the **long run** (whatever that might be). They believe that any public policy which minimises the rewards of entrepreneurship will **reduce** future entrepreneurial effort with adverse effects on the competitive process.

Secondly, they concern **industrial organisa-tion**. Austrians believe that policy-makers should avoid making statements either about the most efficient form of industrial organisation or about the wastes of advertising, product differentiation and duplication. Austrians claim that no one has sufficient knowledge and competence to judge which form of market structure is the most efficient for meeting **tomorrow's** consumer needs (given that some of today's sunrise industries will almost certainly prove to be tomorrow's dinosaurs and smokestack industries). Entrepreneurs do not have perfect foresight, but they do have a greater motivation than politicians and bureaucrats to meet new and unexpected consumer demands – namely, their desire to seek out profitable opportu-nities.

The theory of second best

There is a further problem in using the Paretian model. It requires that all the conditions for an optimum are satisfied simultaneously throughout the whole of the economy. For example, optimality requires that all markets be perfectly competitive throughout the economy. However, consider the case where perfect competition exists in only a limited section of the economy, but not everywhere. Assume also that there is a constraint in the form of at least one private market which is monopolistic and which can **never** be made perfectly competitive. In these circumstances, it does not follow that policy efforts to introduce perfect competition into some, but not all, of the private markets will necessarily move the economy towards an optimum position. It might, but it might also either leave welfare or efficiency unchanged or affect it adversely. Thus, given a constraint such that the rules for optimum resource allocation cannot be satisfied throughout the economy, it becomes necessary to resort to a next-best or second-best solution, in which efforts are made to make the best of the existing situation. A second-best solution is likely to involve a complete departure from the conditions required for optimum resource allocation. In the example given above, the second-best policy rule might require the departure from perfect competition in those markets where it already exists. Similar examples apply to other Paretian-type, piecemeal policy recommendations involving proposals for more marginal cost pricing or more centralisation or more free trade.

Given the importance of constraints preventing the achievement of a first-best or Pareto optimum, questions arise about their nature. Constraints can be policy-created, such as a government's support for domestic monopoly defence contractors or its desire to protect newly-privatised State industries from competition. But such policy-created constraints can always be removed by changing public policy! Presumably, therefore, governments are reluctant to change policy because of the likely effects on their popularity. If so, an alternative theory of industrial policy is required which embraces voters and political parties, and which recognises the role of the political market place.

A public choice approach

Traditionally, State intervention in an economy was rationalised on grounds of market failure, and governments and bureaucracies were assumed to formulate policies to correct such failures. Government was regarded as a black box and was not analysed using the same self-interest, maximising and exchange concepts which had been applied extensively to households, firms and markets in capitalist economies. Instead, elected politicians and bureaucracies were assumed, somewhat simplistically, to pursue the public interest and to implement the will of the people. By way of contrast, public choice analysis is concerned with collective non-market decision-making. It applies neo-classical concepts of exchange and self-interest to the political market place of voters, political parties, governments, bureaucracies and interest groups.

Voters are assumed to act like consumers and to maximise their expected benefit or utility from the policies offered by rival politicians and political parties. Similarly, political parties resemble firms and seek to maximise votes. Parties compete in market structures ranging from small to large numbers of rivals, where new parties can enter or threaten to enter the market. The majority party forms the government and obtains the entire market. Its policies will be implemented through bureaucracies which are monopoly suppliers of information and services, aiming to maximise their budgets. In the UK, the Department of Trade and Industry has a central role in policy towards industry, including aerospace, shipbuilding and steel manufacture, together with support for regions, inner cities and industrial innovation. Other Departments with an involvement in industrial policy include Defence (R & D and equipment procurement); Employment (enterprise schemes, small firms, tourism and health and safety at work); Energy (coal and nuclear R & D); Environment (environmental protection); the Home Office (fraud); Transport (civil aviation and bus and rail services); the local authorities (for example industrial estates) and the State regulatory agencies (for example, Office of Fair Trading (OFT), the Office of Gas Supply (OFGAS) and the Office of Tele-communications (OFTEL)).

In the course of formulating and implementing policies, governments and bureaucracies are lobbied by pressure groups pursuing their own self-interest by trying to influence policy in their favour. With the intention of safeguarding or improving their incomes, producer groups of management, professional associations and trade unions lobby governments for contracts (to buy British), subsidies, laws to license and restrict entry and for protection from foreign competition. Producer groups are willing to allocate resources in their efforts to persuade governments to create or protect monopoly rights – sometimes referred to as rent seeking and rent protection. For example, producers in a competitive industry will seek to obtain monopoly profits by persuading the government to introduce economic regulation of their industry, perhaps by pointing to the wastes and duplication of competition and to the fragmented nature of competitive industries. Presumably they would be willing to invest resources in order to capture monopoly profits. At the limit, they would spend $P_m B A P_c$ in **Figure 8.1**, so that the social cost of monopoly is the sizeable area $P_m B C P_c$. It happens that not all lobbying costs are wasted. Politicians and officials may receive payments in kind in the form of expenses-paid trips or free meals. In some cases the market may be provided with valuable information. Nevertheless, the producer group and rent-seeking approach to government explains public policies in terms of wealth transfers. Government is a mechanism for promoting exchanges of wealth or rents, the aim being to take wealth from some groups and to transfer it to other groups. On this view, industrial policy is about which firms, industries and regions gain from policy and about who loses and who has to pay. Such wealth transfers and rent seeking occurs in a political market place where the rules and constraints on behaviour are determined by the Constitution, which is itself the result of exchanges within the political market.

When the various agents in the political market place are recognised, it is perhaps not surprising that governments often seem to ignore obvious opportunities for making people better off. Many economists are fond of advocating public policies which expand the opportunities for consumer choice by promoting competition and mutually advantageous trade and exchange both within and between nations. But if such policies are socially desirable, why do governments frequently ignore them? Why the use of tariffs to protect British industry, regulations to prevent entry and preference to buy defence equipment from higher cost domestic firms? Changes and policies which appear so attractive to economists often fail to recognise the influence of the different agents in the political market place and their impact on policy formulation. **Figure 8.2** overleaf presents a framework for identifying and mapping the various linkages within the political market. It takes the example of government policy towards cigarette smoking and shows the agents which will try to influence and modify government policy in their favour.

The economics of politics and bureaucracies provides predictions which are relevant to explaining UK industrial policy (Downs, 1957 and Niskanen, 1971):

1. In a two-party democracy, both parties agree on any issues which are strongly favoured by a majority of voters. As a result, party policies will be more vague, more similar to those of the other party (consensus politics) and less directly linked to an ideology than in a multi-party system.

2. Political parties will attempt to differentiate their policies, but movements towards the political extremes of total laissez-faire or complete collectivism are likely to be constrained by the potential losses of moderate voters.

3. Government is more attentive to producers than consumers when it formulates policies. Producer groups dominate, both because they can afford to invest in the specialised information needed to influence government and also because they have the most to gain from influencing public policy in their favour. As a result, government policies tend to favour producers more than consumers.

4. Bureaucracies aiming to maximise their budgets

Figure 8.2   *Linkages[1] in the political market: the example of smoking*

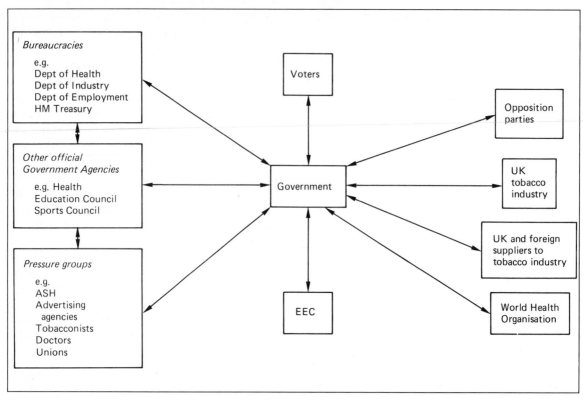

Note:
[1] For simplicity, most of the linkages shown by the arrows focus on the government. Other inter-relationships are possible.

will be inefficient in supplying a given output and will overspend. Their budgets are likely to be too large as they exaggerate the demand for their services and underestimate the costs of their preferred activities. This affects the way in which information is presented to politicians. In bidding for a larger budget, a bureaucracy can stress how the funds will contribute to social benefits in the form of, say, jobs, high technology and exports.

The public choice approach shows that the form and extent of state intervention as reflected in industrial policy cannot be divorced from the motives and behaviour of politicians, bureaucracies and interest groups. The traditional market failure analysis suggested that state intervention was needed to correct market failure and to improve the operation of markets. By way of contrast, the public choice approach recognises that governments and state intervention can also fail!

These approaches to analysing aspects of industrial policy will now be applied to a set of issues which dominate current debates. We will address the issue as to whether governments should regulate the economy and whether competition policy is an effective regulatory instrument. We will also consider whether policy should focus on ownership, choosing between private or public, and whether firm behaviour and performance can be sufficiently influenced by subsidies. We must bear in mind that governments can affect industrial performance directly through their public purchasing policies. In some cases, the absence of a policy, or doing nothing, is a conscious policy decision! The rest of Chapter 8 will show how economists can contribute to these debates, all of which involve public policy towards UK industry.

The economics of regulation and regulatory policy

The issues

Since 1960 there have been numerous examples of regulation. They have included employment legislation embracing contracts: employment protection; equal opportunities; health and safety at work and training and redundancy. At various times there have been controls on prices, wages and profits in such forms as minimum wages; equal pay; rent control; price regulation schemes (for example NHS drugs); profit rules on government contracts; and price freezes for the nationalised industries. The structure, conduct and performance of industry has been regulated by monopolies, mergers and restrictive practices policy. Regulation has also taken the form of government licensing of entry as with patents; public houses; taxis; television companies; road and air transport; and new pharmaceutical products. Finally, output is regulated through such forms as pollution controls and safety standards, as in the case of food products and passenger transport (for example, speed restrictions).

The 1980s have been characterised by a mix of both regulation and deregulation, which can be linked to a broad interpretation of privatisation (see **Table 8.7, p. 292**). The actual or impending privatisation of public monopolies such as British Telecom, gas, electricity and water has resulted in the creation of industry-specific regulatory agencies (for example OFTEL). At the same time, the government has *deregulated* some markets such as bus transport and financial services. All of this raises general issues concerning the rationale for regulation, the likely response of firms to regulatory constraints on their behaviour and the calculation of the costs and benefits of regulation. In addressing such issues it is useful to start with a classification system.

The forms of regulation

Regulation takes various forms, and a distinction can be made between voluntary self-regulation and government regulation via laws and regulatory agencies. The professions and the Stock Exchange, together with codes of conduct for advertisers (such as cigarette companies) and the media are examples of voluntary self-regulation. In contrast, government regulations can be general or specific. General regulations such as competition policy affect all firms in the economy, whilst specific regulations can be specific to a sector such as telecommunications or gas and/or relate to specific aspects of firm behaviour such as advertising, prices or profits. For example, the Review Board for Government Contracts regulates profit rates on all non-competitive government contracts, whilst the Medicines Act 1968 regulates the introduction of new pharmaceutical products into the UK market. In these various forms regulations affect aspects of structure through entry conditions, as well as conduct (advertising, R & D) and performance (prices, profits). Whatever its form, the central issue is why regulation is needed.

The rationale for regulation

Economic theory suggests that regulation is a means of correcting for market failure, thereby improving the operation of markets. State regulation might, for example, be a means of controlling private monopoly power or, alternatively, a means of controlling harmful externalities. An alternative public choice view suggests that government regulation benefits producers rather than consumers. Firms will devote resources to lobbying governments to introduce favourable policies, such as regulating entry, on the pretext of protecting consumers from cowboy operators and from cheap, inferior and unsafe foreign products. Regulators will have only limited information about producers. The possibility arises of new or existing regulatory agencies being captured by the industry and persuaded to act in favour of producers rather than consumers. Senior officials in the regulatory agency might seek employment in their regulated industry (for example defence). Firms also have an incentive to persuade the regulatory agency that its required standards can be met voluntarily, claiming that excessively high standards will lead to bankruptcy with implications for plant closures, unemployment and a government's popularity. Alternatively, firms might accept the costs of government regulations in return for more beneficial policies elsewhere such as restrictions on new entry. Certainly, firms are unlikely to be passive-mechanistic agents, but will seek to change regulations and to adapt to them. This in turn requires an explanation of to how firms are likely to respond to different regulatory rules.

The response of firms

Regulation can take various forms such as licence requirements; certification; entry fees; inspection systems and fines for breaching regulations; the auctioning of rights; and controls on prices and profits. In choosing between these alternatives policy-makers need to know what they are trying to achieve, and how firms are likely to respond to different regulatory instruments.

At the outset, it has to be recognised that regulators do not have perfect information about producers in the regulated industry. For example, a regulator trying to enforce cost-based prices incorporating an average profit rate does not know whether a firm's costs reflect efficient behaviour or X-inefficiency. In these circumstances regulators have to formulate incentives which will change firm behaviour in certain desirable directions, but some incentives can give unexpected and undesirable results. A State-determined limit on profits might, for example, induce a firm to pursue objectives other than maximum profits, so substituting expenditure on staff or other discretionary items for profits. Alternatively, if the profit controls take the form of a maximum rate of return earned on capital, the regulated firm may use more capital-intensive production methods. Regulatory controls on advertising may encourage a firm to expand its

unregulated marketing inputs – for example, by employing more salesmen or introducing new sponsorship schemes (as with sports sponsorship). In other words, firms may respond to regulatory constraints by seeking alternative ways of making money, thereby raising questions about the effectiveness of regulation.

The desirability of regulation

Some governments, politicians and civil servants are fond of proposing regulation – they seem to believe that all regulation is good and that more is desirable regardless of cost. However, regulation is not costless, so it is necessary to examine the likely costs and benefits, and to assess any evidence, particularly on costs and benefits at the **margin**, in order to enable a choice to be made about the optimal amount of regulation.

Regulation involves substantial transaction costs in negotiating, monitoring and enforcing regulatory rules. Staff are needed by the regulatory agency and costs are imposed on producers in responding to the regulator's requirements. For example, a monopoly inquiry involves substantial inputs by members of the inquiry team and corresponding inputs by the monopolist. Specialist witnesses will also be hired by both parties, and the monopolist might devote resources to a public relations campaign and to lobbying politicians. There are also possible indirect costs which need to be included in the analysis. For example, regulatory requirements for the introduction of new drugs into the NHS might lead to longer development periods, so delaying the introduction of new pharmaceutical products. There might also be adverse effects on innovation with fewer new drugs being marketed, and firms might shift their R & D activities to foreign locations where there are fewer regulatory restrictions. In the meantime, delays in the introduction of new drugs can have harmful effects on patients in the form of prolonged suffering and death which might have been avoided by the earlier use of the new product. Questions then arise as to whether the delays are beneficial by protecting consumers from the unforeseen and possibly harmful side effects of new drugs: a classic trade-off situation!

A cost–benefit analysis of regulation must also take account of its potential benefits. Regulatory agencies which aim to remove market failures will introduce policies to correct for externalities or to change the structure, conduct or performance of markets with the ultimate objective of improving consumer welfare. But can society assess the output or performance of a regulatory agency? Various performance indicators have been suggested, not all of which can be easily related to consumer satisfaction. For example, agencies are likely to emphasise the number of inquiries and reports; the number of licences issued, the number of inspections; the number of prosecutions; and the size of the regulatory authority. The Director-General of Fair Trading will refer to the number of monopoly inquiries; the number of merger investigations; reports issued; and the number of cases brought before the Restrictive Practices Court. Similarly, in regulating the introduction of new drugs, the Medicines Division of the Department of Health will eagerly report the number of licences awarded; the time taken to process applications; the introduction of any new testing requirements; inspection and enforcement activities; and the number of statutory orders.

The various performance indicators **appear** impressive, indicating a lively, active and vigorous regulatory authority. However, many of the indicators measure inputs or intermediate output rather than **final** output: they do not indicate the effects on consumers and how highly consumers might value such effects. Supporters of regulation will obviously claim that it results in substantial social benefits. However, a regulatory agency aiming to maximise its size or budget will exaggerate the social benefits of its activities (such as improved product safety) and underestimate or ignore the costs of regulation. A regulatory agency will also favour independent fund-raising powers in the form of, say, licence fees which enable it to finance inefficiency, labour hoarding and discretionary activities such as luxury headquarters and offices. Some of these arguments about regula-

tion will now be applied to UK competition policy which is a classic example of a general form of regulatory policy.

Competition policy

The economic rationale

Competition policy is a classic example of general regulatory arrangements applying to all firms in the UK economy. It embraces policy towards monopolies, mergers and restrictive practices. In this context, standard economic theory offers some clear policy guidelines suggesting that monopoly and other imperfections result in market failure and hence are socially undesirable (see **Figure 8.1, p. 271**). Theory defines monopoly as a single seller of a product with no close substitutes. This model indicates that policy-makers need to focus on structural characteristics, the resulting performance reflected in the relationship between price and marginal cost and whether excessive profits are earned in the long run. However, theory also recognises that small numbers of firms constituting an oligopoly can have market power, and that groups of firms acting together through collective agreements can behave like a monopolist. As a result, policy needs to focus on mergers creating oligopoly or monopoly situations; on the conduct of firms in relation to entry barriers (for example advertising); and on collective agreements which restrict competition in an industry. How far have such guidelines from economic theory influenced UK competition policy?

UK practice

UK competition policy is based on various pieces of legislation dating from 1948, concerned with monopolies, mergers, restrictive practices, resale price maintenance (RPM) and consumer protection (see **Table 8.4**). Monopolies and mergers may be referred for investigation by the Monopolies and Mergers Commission (MMC) whilst restrictive practices including RPM are the subject of legal

Table 8.4   *Major competition policy measures*

Legislation	Agencies	Features
Monopolies and Restrictive Practices Act 1948	Monopolies Commission	Monopoly = one-third or more of a market
Restrictive Trade Practices Act 1956	Registrar and Restrictive Practices Court	Restrictive agreements illegal but exemptions (gateways); if agreement passes through a gateway it still has to satisfy a public interest criterion
Resale Prices Act 1964	Restrictive Practices Court	RPM declared illegal subject to exemptions (gateways) and ultimate public interest test
Monopolies and Mergers Act 1965	Board of Trade mergers panel Monopolies Commission	Mergers to be investigated involving one-third or more market share, or where value of assets taken over exceeded £5 mn
Restrictive Trade Practices Act 1968	Registrar and Restrictive Practices Court	Amendment of 1956 Act to incorporate information agreements
Fair Trading Act 1973	Director-General of Fair Trading Monopolies and Mergers Commission Consumer Protection Advisory Committee	Replaced 1948 and 1965 Acts Monopoly = 25 per cent or more of a local or national market. Mergers to be investigated involving one-quarter or more market share or value of assets taken over exceeded £15 mn (increased to £30 mn in 1984) Public interest defined to include competition Reference to consumer protection
Restrictive Trade Practices Act 1976	Director-General of Fair Trading Restrictive Practices Court	Consolidated previous legislation (1956, 1968) with an extension to services Agreements registered with Director-General of Fair Trading
Resale Prices Act 1976	Director-General of Fair Trading Restrictive Practices Court	Consolidated previous legislation (1964), banning RPM
Competition Act 1980	Director-General of Fair Trading Monopolies and Mergers Commission	Deals with anti-competitive practices and extended monopoly control to public sector bodies and nationalised industries

Table 8.4 *Cont.*

Legislation	Agencies	Features
EC articles 85 and 86 of Treaty of Rome	Directorate General for Competition (European Commission) European Court of Justice	Only applies where trade between member states is affected Article 85 deals with restrictive practices and allows exemptions Article 86 originally applied to monopolies; but extended to prohibit mergers

procedures in the Restrictive Practices Court. Specific reference to consumer protection was first incorporated in the Fair Trading Act 1973.

Current policy towards monopolies and mergers is based on Acts passed in 1973 and 1980. The Fair Trading Act 1973 created an Office of Fair Trading with a Director-General and with cases selected for investigation referred to the MMC. Where a monopoly situation appears to exist, both the Director-General of Fair Trading and the Secretary of State for Trade and Industry can refer cases to the MMC. A monopoly is defined as one firm or a group of firms acting together (called a complex monopoly) accounting for at least 25 per cent of the relevant local or national market. Selected mergers are referred to the MMC by the Secretary of State for Trade and Industry. Mergers may be investigated where they involve a 25 per cent or more market share or where at least £30mn worth of assets are taken over. These definitions are interesting. The market share criterion contrasts with the economist's definition of monopoly as a single seller. Whilst the policy definition embraces oligopoly, it also implies that as the number of similar-sized firms declines from five to four a market changes from competition to a monopoly situation constituting a policy-relevant imperfection. Moreover, the value of assets taken over figure for mergers introduces an absolute size of firm criterion into the policy definition of monopoly. This contrasts with the economists' emphasis on market share. However, an absolute size criterion allows vertical and conglomerate mergers to be investigated. It might also reflect a public choice

perspective, whereby large size can create dominant producer groups capable of influencing government purchasing and regulatory policies: hence, large firms might be undesirable.

In its investigations the MMC has to determine whether a monopoly or proposed merger either operates, or is likely to operate, **against the public interest**. In the case of both monopolies and mergers which are contrary to the public interest the MMC can recommend appropriate action to be taken, but cannot itself enforce a remedy. Only the relevant Secretary of State can enforce remedies against monopolies and can choose to prohibit a merger or to allow it to proceed either unconditionally or subject to conditions. For the first time, the 1973 Act defined the 'public interest' to include the desirability of maintaining and promoting **competition**. However, the public interest definition is wide-ranging. It includes a concern with consumer interests in relation to price, quality and variety; encouraging cost reductions, technical progress and new entry; a consideration of the international competitive position of UK producers; and promoting a balanced distribution of industry and employment. It is not at all obvious that some of these elements such as a balanced distribution of industry — itself an ambiguous term — are the proper concern of competition policy. Moreover, the MMC retains substantial discretion since it is allowed to take into account any factors which it deems to be relevant in determining the public interest! This is, in fact, a distinctive feature of UK policy towards monopolies and mergers.

Whilst standard economic theory suggests that

competition is socially desirable, UK policy has not condemned monopolies and mergers as undesirable. A discretionary cost–benefit approach is adopted, with each case examined on its merits. Policy recognises that monopolies and mergers involve a trade-off between the costs of reduced competition, including X-inefficiency, and the potential benefits through scale economies and technical progress. Moreover, existing UK monopolies and mergers policy might be rationalised on second-best grounds. The standard welfare economics case for competition has to be modified where governments accept as policy-created constraints the continued existence of monopolies in parts of the economy. Alternatively, a public choice approach would explain current policy, with its wide-ranging public interest criterion and a reluctance to act against monopolies, as reflecting the influence of producer groups.

UK policy towards restrictive practices and RPM has taken a different approach. The Restrictive Practices Act 1976 and the Resale Prices Act 1976 consolidated the prior legislation of 1956, 1964 and 1968. Restrictive practices legislation applies to the supply of both goods and services. It is concerned with agreements which restrict prices, conditions of sale and quantities to be supplied, and which lead firms to exchange information on prices and costs. Restrictive agreements have to be registered, and are presumed to be illegal and against the public interest unless the parties can establish a case for exemption before the Restrictive Practices Court. To be exempted, an agreement has to pass through one or more of eight **gateways**. For example, it has to be shown that an agreement protects the public against injury; that it provides substantial benefits to the public as purchasers, consumers or users; that it acts as a countervailing power against the anti-competitive practices of third parties; or that its removal would result in serious and persistent local unemployment or a substantial reduction in exports. Once again, some of these gateways (such as the concern with employment and exports) are rather odd aims for competition policy. However, even if an agreement passes through the gateways, it still has to satisfy the 'tailpiece' or public interest test. The Court has to determine whether, both currently and in the future, on balance the benefits to the public outweigh the detriments or costs.

The Resale Prices Act 1976 controls RPM in the same way as restrictive agreements. There is a general presumption that RPM is contrary to the public interest, unless a supplier can gain exemption through one or more of five gateways. RPM might be allowed if its abolition would substantially reduce the quality and variety of goods for sale; if there would be a substantial reduction in the number of retail outlets; if there is likely to be a long-run increase in retail prices; or where there might be dangers to health or a substantial reduction in necessary sales or after-sales services. Once through a gateway, it is still necessary to satisfy the tailpiece where the Court has to consider the balance of benefits and detriments.

The Competition Act 1980 complemented existing legislation and takes a different approach from that of the 1976 Acts. It is concerned with the anti-competitive practices of individual firms supplying goods or services which have the effect of restricting, distorting or preventing competition. Examples include price discrimination, predatory pricing, exclusive supply and rental-only contracts, all of which are aspects of firms' **conduct**. The 1980 Act also extended monopoly control to include the nationalised industries and other public sector bodies (for example the bus companies, and water authorities). The 1980 procedure requires the Director-General of Fair Trading to investigate alleged anti-competitive practices. Where such a practice exists, the Director-General can require the firm to cease the practice, or it can be referred to the MMC which will apply the 1973 public interest test.

As a member of the EC, the UK is also subject to European competition law, reflected in articles 85 and 86 of the Treaty of Rome which are enforced by the European Commission. Article 85 prohibits restrictive agreements and practices which prevent, restrict or distort competition within the EC and which affect trade between member states. Examples include price-fixing, market-sharing and limitations of production, technical progress and investment. As in the UK, agreements may be exempted where they improve production, distribution or technical progress, subject to the requirement that these benefits must not be outweighed by other detriments associated with reduced competition. The European Commission has the power to impose heavy fines on the guilty parties to a restrictive agreement.

Article 86 originally applied to monopolies but has since been extended to mergers. It deals with situations where trade between member states might be affected by one or more enterprises taking 'improper advantage of a dominant position'. Examples of improper practices include the imposition of inequitable purchase or selling prices, or limiting production, markets or technical developments. However, questions arise as to what constitutes a firm with a dominant position. In the case of mergers, the position is clearer. The European Commission can prohibit mergers which hinder competition between member states and where the combined turnover of the companies exceeds ECU 200 mn or where they share 25 per cent or more of a national market. Firms and member states can appeal to the European Court of Justice against decisions of the European Commission. Clearly, European competition policy and its relationship with national policy will become a more important issue with the creation of the Single European Market in 1992.

Three issues are likely to dominate the evolution of an EC competition policy required for achieving a genuinely free internal market from 1992 onwards. In the first place, the development of an EC merger policy enabling the European Commission to investigate large cross-border mergers with an EC dimension. As indicated this involves potential conflicts with national merger policy as in the case where the European Commission required British Airways to sell some of the routes acquired from its purchase of British Caledonian – a takeover previously approved by the MMC. Secondly, the European Commission has become increasingly concerned about the competition implications of state subsidies and other forms of government protectionism. An example was the European Commission's requirement that the UK government reduce the amount of state aid offered as part of the British Aerospace acquisition of the Rover Group. Thirdly, the European Commission is likely to become more actively involved in policy tow-

ards cartels and restrictive practices, particularly in the services sector and in markets dominated by state-owned industries.

In respect of merger policy it is now expected that the unanimous agreement of the 12 member states will be forthcoming by the end of 1989. The key provisions of the policy, which are currently still subject to amendment, are that it will apply to cross-border takeovers where (a) the combined world turnover of the companies involved exceeds ECU 5 bn per annum until the end of 1992 (equivalent to £3.35 bn at the current conversion rate) and subsequently where it exceeds ECU 2 bn; (b) the smaller company has an EC-wide turnover of more than ECU 100 mn; and (c) less than two-thirds of the combined turnover originates in one member state. It will be necessary for companies involved to inform the European Commission of their intentions in advance, and the Commission will be given one month to decide whether there are obvious problems and four more to determine whether competition will be harmed. The Commission will be empowered to block any proposals or to ask for them to be amended, but the bidder will retain the right to appeal against either eventuality in the European Court of Justice.

The outstanding difficulty is that whilst the Commission will not wish to interfere with takeovers which fall outside the new terms of reference, it will still be possible for parties involved in take-overs to appeal to the Court of Justice citing other EC Treaty provisions.

The results of competition policy

Any evaluation of UK competition policy needs to focus on final output indicators in terms of the effects of policy on market structure, conduct and, ultimately, performance. Such an appraisal requires a model of structure, conduct and performance which holds constant all other relevant influences and identifies the contribution of competition policy. Other influences such as newly-industrialising nations, international trade, membership of the EC, technical progress, oil price shocks and the general level of aggregate demand and expectations in the UK economy cannot be ignored.

Competition policy can be evaluated against the general evidence on trends in the size of firms and industry structure in the UK economy. **Table 8.5** shows data on aggregate concentration in the form of the share of the 100 largest enterprises in manufacturing output. Aggregate concentration rose significantly from a pre-1939 figure of some 25 per cent to about 40 per cent by the late 1960s. However, since 1970, aggregate concentration has remained relatively stable – a feature which shows the uncertainties involved in predicting future trends. Interestingly, in 1987, about 10 per cent of the top 100 enterprises were the leading alcohol and tobacco companies such as BAT Industries, Grand-Metropolitan, Hanson Trust (Imperial), Allied Lyons, Gallaher, Bass and Guinness.

The extent of competition in a single market is usually shown by a five-firm concentration ratio which measures the proportion of industry output accounted for by the five largest firms in the industry. Evidence on concentration ratios is shown in **Table 8.5**. Following a small rise in the early 1970s, industry concentration declined up to the mid-1980s. Indeed, once the ratios are adjusted for foreign trade, industry concentration actually declined between 1970 and 1984. Interestingly, even after allowing for foreign trade, a number of UK manufacturing industries remain highly concentrated, with five-firm concentration ratios

exceeding 75 per cent in 1984. Examples include asbestos; biscuits; cement; fertilisers; glass; locomotives; margarine; ordnance and tobacco. Inevitably, such data raise questions about the role and effects of monopoly policy.

By 1987, the MMC had issued some 50 reports on UK monopoly situations. Examples included the supply of beer (tied houses); cigarettes; soap and detergents; postal franking machines; animal waste; greyhound track management services; cross channel ferries and travel agency services for tour operators. There have also been investigations of professional services (for example of architects, surveyors and solicitors) and such public sector activities as British Rail commuter services, some water authorities and the National Coal Board. Various monopoly situations and practices have been found to be against the public interest. In 1986, for example, the MMC found monopolies which were against the public interest in postal franking machines; white salt; greyhound track management and travel agency services. In its judgements the MMC assesses monopolies in terms of their policies and their effects on prices; advertising; marketing; new entrants and, ultimately, profitability. For example, the 1986 Report on postal franking machines found that a monopoly in the supply, maintenance and repair of equipment existed in favour of Pitney Bowes and

Table 8.5   *Firm size and market structures*

	1970	1974	1979	1979	1980	1984
100 largest enterprises share in manufacturing output (%)	39.3	42.1	n.a.	n.a.	40.5[1]	38.7
Unadjusted 5-firm CR[2,3] (%)	49.0	50.9	48.5	51.4	n.a.	49.1
Adjusted 5-firm CR[3] (%)	41.3	40.9	36.5	39.3	n.a.	33.8
Mergers[4]						
Number of companies acquired	793	504	534	—	469	568
Expenditure on acquisitions (£ bn at 1986 prices)	5.9	1.7	2.8	—	2.1	5.9

Notes:
[1] Change in defintion after 1980.
[2] 5-firm concentration ratios (CR) based on a sample of 93 comparable industries 1970–9 and a sample of 195 comparable industries 1979–84.
[3] Unadjusted 5-firm CR is unadjusted for foreign trade while the adjusted CR allows for foreign trade.
[4] Mergers refer to acquisitions and mergers by UK industrial and commercial companies.
Source: DTI, 1988.

Roneo Alcatel and that the companies' pricing policies and some other practices operated against the public interest. Similarly, the 1969 report on the supply of beer concluded that the tied house system operated against the public interest. The restrictions on competition involved in the tied house system operated by the brewers were 'detrimental to efficiency in brewing, wholesaling and retailing, to the interests of independent suppliers (including potential new entrants) and to the interests of consumers' (Cmnd 216, 1969, p. 119; see also Cmnd 651, 1989).

The concern of UK monopoly policy with prices, entry, profitability and consumers has a possible economic basis in models of perfect competition and contestable markets. But such models do not provide operational guidelines for determining when prices are too high and profits become excessive. Are prices too high if they result in abnormal profits, and, if so, how is it possible to distinguish abnormal from normal profits? Austrian economists would adopt a different approach suggesting that market power is usually transitory and that so-called monopoly profits are the temporary reward of successful entrepreneurship. To the Austrians, an innovating monopolist generates a **social gain** represented by the firm's profits and the resulting consumer surplus: without the innovation a new product such as a micro-computer would never have been produced, so there is no question of a deadweight loss due to a departure from the perfectly competitive output. Such contrasting interpretations of monopoly makes life extremely difficult and complicated for governments who have to determine a monopoly policy!

Critics of UK monopoly policy claim that it is slow and ineffective. Typically, a MMC enquiry may take 2–3 years. Few reports are issued in any one year and, to date, the total number of monopoly investigations represents only a small part of the UK's monopoly and oligopoly industries. Moreover, governments are often reluctant to take effective remedial action against monopolies, preferring to rely on informal undertakings which may reflect pressure from producer groups and the possibility that the regulatory agency has been captured by producers. The result is that UK monopoly policy has not achieved any major changes in either the structure or the conduct of monopoly industries which have been investigated. Unfortunately, the issues are not diminishing. The government's initiatives on privatisation, deregulation, contracting-out and public purchasing policy are likely to create new demands on the UK's competition agencies. Also, mergers are contributing to major structural changes in the UK economy with substantial numbers of mergers being of the horizontal and conglomerate types.

Between 1964 and 1985 the annual rate of mergers within the UK varied between 315 and some 1,200 per annum, with a similar variation in annual expenditure on acquisitions of between £0.8 bn and almost £15 bn at 1986 prices, as shown in **Table 8.5**. Peaks of merger activity in terms of numbers and expenditure occurred in 1965, 1972–73 and 1986–87. Despite the high level of activity, relatively few qualifying mergers, typically well under 5 per cent, are actually referred to the MMC. Of those referred, not all are found to be contrary to the public interest. For example, between 1984 and 1986 there were 13 merger reports from the MMC, of which only four references were declared to be against the public interest. However, by the mid-1980s concern was expressed over the continued merger boom, especially the size of some acquisitions and their controversial nature (for example GEC–Plessey and Nestlé–Rowntree). As a result, the government reviewed its merger policy and published the results in 1988 (DTI, 1988).

The 1988 government review of merger policy examined two performance indicators – namely, trends in concentration ratios and post-merger performance. Whilst evidence showed a substantial increase in industry concentration in the 1950s and 1960s, it seems that between 1970 and 1984 concentration ratios adjusted for foreign trade actually declined, as shown in **Table 8.5**. The 1988 review also confirmed the earlier findings of poor, disappointing or inconclusive post-merger performance (for example with respect to profitability). Such evidence has been used to suggest that mergers were failing to provide economic benefits. Nevertheless, the government review reaffirmed its policy of leaving most merger decisions to the market: 'the vast majority of mergers raise no competition or other objections, and are rightly left free to be decided by the market' (DTI, 1988, p. 7). The review also confirmed that the main, though not the only, factor in determining whether a merger should be referred to the MMC should be its **potential effects on competition in the UK market**. However, to allow for a few exceptional cases (such as foreign ownership of UK companies), it is planned to retain an open-ended public interest criterion in the legislation. Finally, the 1988 review proposed two legislative changes to improve the speed and flexibility of merger policy. In the first place, a procedure for voluntary prenotification is designed to obtain faster clearance of mergers involving no major public interest issues. Secondly, the merging parties can give statutory undertakings as a possible alternative to a full MMC reference. Under this proposal it would be possible for the merger parties to make a legally-binding agreement to remove any obvious anti-competitive effects of a merger (for example, an agreement on divestments or post-merger conduct).

Restrictive practices legislation has been extremely effective in removing certain restrictive agreements which were the basis for the widespread cartelisation of UK industry in the 1950s. By 1988 some 6,650 agreements had been registered, over 70 per cent of which were goods agreements. A substantial number of agreements have been abandoned, and many have been modified to remove any anti-competitive effects. Interestingly, it is possible that restrictive practices legislation, originally introduced in 1956, might have contributed to the high rate of merger activity in the 1960s. Nevertheless, evidence shows that the legislation resulted in new entry, increased competition, lower prices and generally contributed to its main objective of improving industrial efficiency (Cmnd 331, 1988). Similarly, legislation was effective against resale price maintenance. In 1960 RPM applied to about 20–25 per cent of consumer expenditure; by 1979 it was restricted to net books and medicines, representing under 2 per cent of consumer expenditure. The result was improved efficiency in retailing and lower prices, although the effects were smaller than expected

and some groups such as small independent retailers and their customers had to bear the costs of the change. Nevertheless, the Resale Prices Act has made a major contribution to increased competition in retailing to the general benefit of consumers.

By the late 1980s there were serious doubts about the effectiveness of restrictive practices legislation in tackling cartels. A government Review suggested that 'the Act must now appear a relatively weak piece of legislation' (Cmnd 331, 1988, p. 29). It is criticised because potential colluders are unlikely to be detected; penalties for ignoring the law are not sufficiently heavy to act as a deterrent; it catches trivia by including agreements which do not restrict competition; there are too many exemptions, and the whole registration process is costly and a waste of resources. Instead, it is proposed that the registration system be abolished and **any agreement with anti-competitive effects will be prohibited (illegal)**. Examples of anti-competitive agreements include the price fixing of goods and services, collusive tendering, market sharing, restrictions on advertising and collective refusals to supply. Exemptions will be allowed using a broad test similar to article 85(3) of the Treaty of Rome. The new policy will be administered by a competition authority, which will be part of the Office of Fair Trading. The authority will have to determine whether an agreement is anti-competitive and, if so, whether it qualifies for an exemption. It is proposed that fines be imposed by the authority, up to 10 per cent of a firm's turnover. Appeals on prohibitions and exemptions can be made to the Restrictive Practices Court, which will also have the power to impose fines above the competition authority's maximum limit (Cmnd 331, 1988).

The Single European Market

In addition to competition policy within the UK market, a major change is planned which will affect competition and contestability within the EC. Whilst there are no tariffs between member states of the EC, there remain a number of substantial and costly non-tariff barriers. Physical, technical and fiscal barriers mean that the EC consists of 12 fragmented national markets, separated by frontier controls, public procurement practices and different product and technical standards, all of which hinder trade in goods and services between member states. The EC aims to remove these various barriers and to create a single internal market by 1992.

It is estimated that the single European market will result in potential gains of over ECU 200 bn, equivalent to 5.3 per cent of EC GDP in 1988 (Cecchini, 1988, p. 84). Such gains will result from lower costs due to the aboliton of frontier barriers, removing the barriers to entry into national markets (for example, for public procurement), exploiting scale economies and a general increase in competitive pressures in both goods and services markets. Currently, for example, cross-frontier trade is hindered by administrative formalities and border controls (red tape and delays); public procurement protects national industries from foreign competition; and divergent technical regulations, standards and certification procedures means costly market fragmentation (as in the case of financial services and telecommunications). However, the estimated benefits from abolishing non-tariff barriers will not be achieved immediately in 1992: it will take time for economies to adjust and adapt to the new market conditions.

Critics claim that the likely benefits have been exaggerated, that they are based on a simple perfectly competitive model which will never be achieved and that most of the worthwhile economies of scale have been exploited. Moreover, efforts to exploit any potential scale economies within the EC will probably require mergers, leading to possible conflicts with competition policy: the price of efficient scale might be monopoly which will benefit producer groups rather that consumers. Similar worries about the potential gainers and the potential losers from policy changes have dominated the debate about UK privatisation policy. Indeed, privatisation involves issues of ownership, monopoly, regulation and market competition. We must, therefore, turn to examine the relative merits of public versus private ownership and the role of ownership.

Ownership

The nationalised industries

The UK economy consists of a mix of publicly and privately-owned firms and industries. Within the public sector public corporations, including nationalised industries, are state-owned bodies accountable to government but with a substantial degree of independence, and whose activities in the case of nationalised industries are financed largely by the consumers of their goods and services rather than by the taxpayer. These industries have been the focal point of continuing debate between the political parties, with Labour Governments traditionally preferring state ownership of the means of production. Since 1945 UK industries such as aerospace, airlines, coal, gas, electricity, rail, shipbuilding, steel and telecommunications have at various times been state-owned, as too have individual firms such as British Leyland, British Petroleum, Rolls Royce and Royal Ordnance. However, since 1979, a substantial number of nationalised industries and state-owned companies have been privatised, raising debates about whether ownership is an important determinant of enterprise performance.

Various economic arguments have been used to explain and justify nationalisation. After 1945 much emphasis was placed on the need to control private monopoly power, to plan and control the commanding heights of the economy, to include social costs and benefits into decision-making, and to improve industrial relations by removing the traditional conflict between labour and capital. In the 1970s state ownership of firms such as British Leyland and Rolls Royce was justified as a rescue operation to save strategically and economically important companies and to prevent substantial job losses. Nationalisation, however, is not without its problems. Objectives have to be specified, pricing, investment and financial rules are required and performace has to be monitored. Problems have often arisen because of the lack of clearly specified objectives or because of changing and conflicting aims, resulting from the need to balance a concern with economic efficiency, technical efficiency, anti-inflationary pricing policies, social objectives and financial targets (Curwen, 1986).

Economists seeking economically efficient solutions are fond of proposing marginal cost pricing rules for nationalised industries, requiring them to set price equal to long-run marginal cost. However, 'marginal cost' has to be defined and measured, and difficulties arise where state industries are monopolies not subject to competitive pressures. In such circumstances the lack of contestability is likely to be associated with organisational slack and X-inefficiency: marginal cost is whatever the Chairman of the nationalised industry says it is! Moreover, in decreasing cost industries, marginal cost pricing will be associated with losses. In such circumstances, losses are consistent with an economically-efficient solution and are not an indication of inefficiency. However, marginal cost pricing is further criticised on second-best grounds. Where prices do not equal marginal cost throughout the economy, the appropriate second-best pricing rule for a nationalised industry is likely to require a departure from strict marginal cost pricing.

Actual pricing policies for the UK nationalised industries have varied from a requirement to break even (that is, average cost pricing) to marginal cost pricing to a requirement to act commercially. Marginal cost pricing was introduced following a 1967 White Paper. In a 1978 White Paper a further element was introduced requiring nationalised industries to aim at a real rate of return on their new investment programmes of 5 per cent. The required rate of return is reviewed periodically and is related to the return achieved by private companies, thereby ensuring that the nationalised industries do not divert resources away from more valuable alternatives. Also, since 1976, the nationalised industries and most other public corporations have been subject to external financing limits (EFLs) which control the amount of finance, whether grants or borrowing, which an industry may raise during the financial year to supplement its income from normal trading.

Since 1979 the government has been concerned about the efficiency and losses incurred by the nationalised industries and has sought to reduce the size of this sector through denationalisation or privatisation. By 1989 the government's major aim for the nationalised industries was to 'ensure their effectiveness and efficiency as commercial concerns and to strengthen them to the point where they can be transferred to the private sector or, where necessary, remain as successful businesses within the public sector' (Cmnd 621, 1989, p. 62). As successful public sector businesses they are expected to minimise the burden on the taxpayer (via subsidies), earn an economic return on their assets and improve their commercial performance. In other words, the remaining nationalised industries are to act commercially. If such an objective is interpreted as profit maximisation it will promote technical efficiency but, in the absence of competition, it will not produce allocative efficiency.

Since 1979 a substantial number of nationalised industries have been privatised. In 1979 the nationalised industries accounted for some 9 per cent of GDP and employed over 1.8 million people; by 1988, the corresponding figures were about 5 per cent and some 750,000 employees. During this period the productivity of the nationalised industries increased substantially, reflecting efficiency improvements, reductions in overmanning and the incentive of possible privatisation. Between 1978–79 and 1987–88 average annual productivity growth of the nationalised industries was 4.1 per cent, exceeding that for both manufacturing (3.7 per cent) and the economy as a whole (2.2 per cent). By 1990, if all goes according to plan in the case of electricity and water, the remaining UK nationalised industries will be British Coal, British Rail, British Waterways, the Civil Aviation Authority, London Regional Transport and the Post Office, together with such public corporations as the BBC, the Commonwealth Development Corporation and the Urban Development Corporations. In the 1980s the policy emphasis has been on denationalisation.

Privatisation: a classification system

Privatisation has been a central feature of the successive Conservative Governments elected since 1979. The policy has embraced denationalisation or selling-off of State assets, deregulation (liberalisation) and competitive tendering. Public sector assets have been sold to the private sector in the form of both share issues and private sales. Examples include British Aerospace, British Airways, British Gas, British Steel, British Telecom, Cable and Wireless, the National Freight Corporation, Rolls Royce, and the Royal Ordnance Factories (see **Table 8.6**). In 1989 further sales are planned involving electricity and water. A number of markets have been deregulated thereby reducing or removing restrictions on new entrants. Examples include short and long-distance bus services (Transport Acts 1980 and 1985), the Stock Exchange, opticians, building societies offering banking services, together with the emergence of Mercury as a rival supplier of telecommunications services. Finally, a range of services provided by central and local government and by the NHS have been exposed to rivalry through competitive tendering and contracting-out. Examples include catering, cleaning and laundry services, refuse collection and the maintenance of grounds and vehicles (Bishop and Kay, 1988).

The distinction between government (public) and private finance and provision can be used to classify the different forms of UK privatisation policy. Such a classification system is shown in **Figure 8.3** which provides a useful starting point for analysis and also allows the rival advocates of private and state ownership to comtemplate horizontal, vertical and diagonal movements between the boxes. Inevitably, **Figure 8.3** is only a broad classification system. For instance, state-owned enterprises selling products to private markets may also receive subsidies (British Coal and British Rail) and there are privately-owned schools and hospitals. In addition, monopolies transferred from the public to the private sector are subject to regulatory constraints. In the case of airports, gas and telecommunications, the regulatory agencies impose a pricing rule known as RPI-X, where RPI is the retail price index and X is a percentage figure. This rule imposes a ceiling on the annual increase

Figure 8.3 *Classifying privatisation*

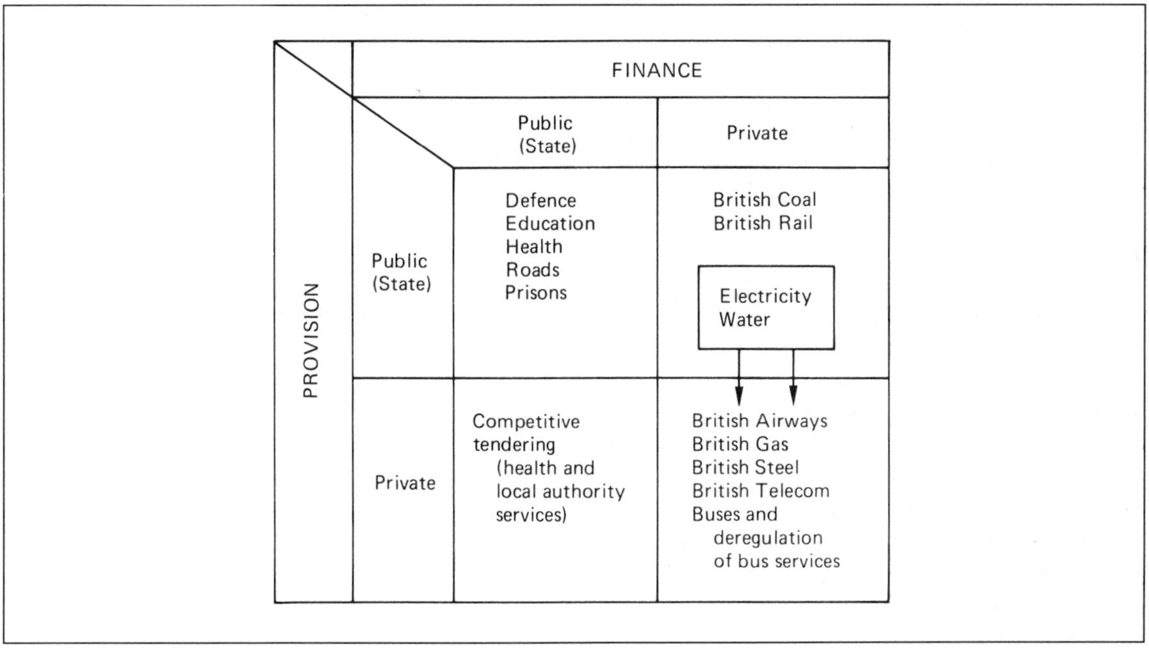

Table 8.6   *UK privatisations*

Year	Type of sale	% sold	Proceeds[3] £ billion (1987–88 prices)
1979			0.7
British Petroleum (phase 1)	S[1]	17.0	
ICL	P[2]		
1980			0.6
Fairey Engineering	P		
Ferranti	P		
1981			0.7
British Aerospace (phase 1)	S	51.0	
British Petroleum (phase 2)	S	5.0	
Cable & Wireless (phase 1)	S	49.0	
1982			0.6
Amersham International	S	100.0	
Britoil (phase 1)	S	51.0	
National Freight Corporation	P		
1983			1.4
Associated British Ports (phase 1)	S	51.5	
British Petroleum (phase 3)	S	7.0	
BR Hotels	P		
Cable & Wireless (phase 2)	S	22.0	
International Aeradio	P		
1984			2.5
Associated British Ports (phase 2)	S	48.5	
British Telecom	S	50.2	
Enterprise Oil	P	100.0	
Inmos	P		
Jaguar	S	99.0	
Scott Lithgow	P		
Sealink	P		
Wytch Farm	P		
1985			2.9
British Aerospace (phase 2)	S	49.0	
Britoil (phase 2)	S	48.0	
Cable & Wireless (phase 3)	S	31.0	
Vosper Thorneycroft	P		
Yarrow Shipbuilders	P		
1986			4.7
BA Helicopters	P		
British Gas	S	97.0	
Hall Russell	P		
National Bus Company	P		
Royal Ordnance (phase 1)	P		
Swan Hunter	P		
Vickers Shipbuilding	P		
1987			5.1
British Airports Authority	S	100.0	
British Airways	S	100.0	
British Petroleum (phase 4)	S	36.8	

Table 8.6 *Cont.*

Year	Type of sale	% sold	Proceeds[3] £ billion (1987–8 prices)
DAB	P		
Istel	P		
Leyland Bus Company	P		
Rolls Royce	S	100.0	
Royal Ordnance (phase 2)	P		
Unipart	P		
1988			5.7
British Steel	S	100.0	
Rover Group	P		

Notes:

[1] S = privatisation by share issue: those sold in phases reflect flotation of government holdings in the private companies.

[2] P = private sale of company – for example National Freight was sold to its employees; Royal Ordnance and Rover were sold to British Aerospace. In all cases the entire company was disposed of.

[3] Proceeds are based on financial years – for example, 1979 is 1979–80.

Source: Cmnd 621, 1989.

in a firm's prices which will always be X per cent below the general inflation rate.

Objectives of privatisation policy

Current privatisation policy has been associated with various objectives, some of which are in conflict. Consumers are expected to benefit from rivalry, more choice, greater efficiency and innovation. The policy is also aimed at reducing the size of the public sector through denationalisation and reducing public sector borrowing. Furthermore, it has been associated with a desire for wider share ownership. Suggestions have also been made that the real purpose of the policy is to reduce the monopoly power of trade unions. There are conflicts between some of these objectives. For example, reducing the size of the public sector and maximising Treasury income from selling public assets can be achieved by transferring monopoly power from the public to the private sector without increasing rivalry. It is, of course, likely that the actual extent and form of privatisation policy will reflect the influence of agents in the political market place – namely, governments seeking votes and established interest groups trying to protect their positions, especially their income and on-the-job leisure.

The debate about privatisation in its wider aspects raises the general question of whether ownership is an important determinant of economic performance. The current government has claimed that, following privatisation, productivity and profitability in the newly-privatised companies have increased dramatically (as in the case, for example, of British Aerospace, Jaguar and the National Freight Consortium). The official explanation offered is that 'the overwhelming majority of employees have become shareholders in the newly privatised companies. They want their companies to succeed. Their companies have been released from the detailed controls of Whitehall and given more freedom to manage their own affairs. And they have been exposed to the full commercial disciplines of the customer. Even former monopolies now face increased competition (Conservative Manifesto, 1987, p. 36). This suggests a model in which improvements in economic performance depend not only upon ownership, but also on competition and managerial freedom (for example, in respect of internal organisation and employment contracts). Others would add the external environment as a further variable in the model in the form

Table 8.7   *Ownership and market structure: a taxonomy*

	Monopoly	Competition
	A	*B*
Public Ownership	1. Absence of competition induces technical inefficiency 2. No fear of going bankrupt 3. Government intervention distorts decision-making 4. Potential for allocative efficiency $(P=MC)$	1. Market forces promote greater technical efficiency 2. Still no fear of bankruptcy 3. Government intervention still distorts decision-making 4. Potential for allocative efficiency
	C	*D*
Private Ownership	1. Fear of bankruptcy 2. No government intervention 3. Pressure exerted by shareholders 4. Allocative efficiency unlikely	1. Competition induces technical efficiency 2. Fear of bankruptcy 3. No government intervention 4. Pressure exerted by shareholders 5. Allocative efficiency

of, for example, the Thatcher effect via Rayner scrutinies, Financial Management Initiatives and the withdrawal of subsidies providing a shock effect throughout the public and private sectors (Dunsire *et al.*, 1988). Some of these complex and sometimes interdependent issues can be simplified into a two variable model showing the impact of ownership and market structure on efficiency. A framework is shown in **Table 8.7** where the following hypotheses on enterprise performance or efficiency can be formulated:

1. *D* is superior to *A*, where *D* represents private ownership and a competitive product market
2. *D* is superior to *C* – neo-classical economics favours competition
3. *D* is equal to, or superior to, *B* – does ownership matter? One review of the evidence suggests that under competition, private firms are likely to be superior (Kay *et al.*, 1986, p. 16)
4. *B* is superior to *A*, reflecting the role of competition
5. *C* is superior to *A*, reflecting the policing role of private capital markets
6. *B* could be superior, inferior or equal to *C* (inconclusive) depending on the relative strengths of competition and ownership.

Testing hypotheses about the effects of ownership and market structure on enterprise performance and efficiency is not without its problems.

Indicators are required to measure enterprise performance and, ultimately, economic efficiency. Some crude performance indicators are readily available such as profitability, labour productivity and international competitiveness, and tests can be undertaken to determine whether performance improves following a change from public to private ownership, *ceteris paribus*. It should be borne in mind that an increase in profitability might reflect the exercise of market power by a newly-privitised monopolist, and higher labour productivity could reflect investment in new equipment. Moreover, empirical tests of performance before and after an ownership change need to allow for what would have happened without the change, and the distinct possibility that a transfer of ownership will result in the pursuit of different objectives. There are, however, alternative policies for influencing enterprise performance, with subsidies as an obvious option.

Subsidy policy

A classification system

At their simplest, subsidies are payments by government to producers which are designed to reduce prices. Such a definition can be modified to allow for payments to firms and industries to ensure their survival or to prevent contraction. More generally, subsidies are a means of affecting the allocation and use of resources in the economy, thereby interfering in the operation of markets. The issue is, however, whether such interference is desirable.

Over time British governments have offered various subsidies to firms, industries, regions and to factors of production. Examples have included private firms such as British Leyland and Chrysler, private and state industries such as aerospace, computers, cotton, steel and shipbuilding, as well as high unemployment regions, namely development areas. Subsidies have been used to achieve specific policy objectives such as maintaining or increasing employment, assisting the balance of payments through export promotion and import saving and encouraging growth through supporting high technology. At times the range of industrial subsidies has been bewildering, and so extensive that questions have arisen as to whether there are any economic activities in the UK which should not qualify for a subsidy!

As a starting point in analysing subsidies a classification system is required. Subsidies can be classified in at least three related ways:

General and specific types

General schemes offer subsidies to all firms satisfying certain conditions which might relate to investment, location, employment, size of firm or type of activity (for example agriculture, manufacturing or tourism). General schemes have been the traditional method of subsidising UK industry. They are automatic and aim to influence industry decisions and hence the operation of markets without involving substantial transaction costs. In contrast, specific or discretionary schemes are designed for an individual firm or project with subsidies being used to prevent bankruptcy and plant closure or to promote reorganisation, re-equipment and restructuring. Or specific subsidies might be offered for the development of a new high technology project such as a supersonic airliner or a new generation of computer. In principle, specific schemes aim at fine tuning by setting the subsidy at the minimum level required to influence a firm's decisions. However, this approach involves substantial transaction costs. It requires detailed information about a

firm's costs and its efficiency, and it assumes that civil servants will be motivated to negotiate the minimum subsidy. Further costs will be incurred in bargaining, monitoring and policing. Critics claim that public servants may be influenced in their decisions by the prospect of employment in industry or that specific subsidies result in an undesirable cosiness between civil servants and the firms with which they negotiate.

The production function approach.

A distinction can be made between subsidies for outputs and for factor inputs. Farmers, for example, receive output subsidies. Factor inputs can also be subsidised, the aim being to encourage and increase the use of relatively cheaper (subsidised) factors. Input subsidies embrace capital, labour and technology. Examples include incentives to invest in new plant and machinery, to substitute labour for capital and to increase research and development.

The geographic or location dimension

Subsidies in their general and specific forms, for inputs and outputs, can be 'tied' to specially designated areas of the country embracing development areas, intermediate areas, enterprise zones, free ports and inner cities.

During the 1960s and 1970s UK expenditure on subsidies increased substantially, from under 2 per cent of GDP at market prices and around 4 per cent of government expenditure in 1965 to corresponding figures of almost 4 per cent and around 7–8 per cent respectively in 1975. The government since 1979 has taken a different attitude towards a general and massive subsidy policy. Indeed, **Table 8.8** shows the declining trends in public sector subsidies between 1979 and 1992 and the impact upon the nationalised industries, regional support, and on aerospace, shipbuilding, steel and vehicle manufacture. At the same time, as a further indication of the government's industrial policy, the annual level of real spending by the Department of Trade and Industry will have declined substantially between 1979 and 1992, whilst privatisation proceeds will have increased considerably. In view of the major contrasts between the 1970s and 1980s, questions have to be asked about the economic logic of UK subsidy policy.

Table 8.8   *DTI and government subsidies*[1]

DTI expenditure	1979–80	1986–87	1991–92 (plans)
Total expenditure (£ bn at 1987–88 prices)	3.5	2.5	1.0
Privatisation proceeds (£ bn at 1987–88 prices)	−0.7	−4.7	−4.2
Expenditure on major programmes (£ mn at current prices)			
Regional and general industrial support	462	424	410
Support for aerospace, shipbuilding, steel and vehicle manufacture	338	847	20
Support for industry, including general R & D and R & D in aerospace industry	142	360	400
Public corporations and nationalised industries external finance	1 178	173	−70
Government subsidies (£ mn at current prices)			
Central government	4 151	2 725	2 890
Local authorities	766	1 145	970
Nationalised industries	1 081	1 719	840
Other public corporations	123	371	390
Total public sector subsidies	6 121	5 810	5 090
GDP deflator (1978–88 = 100)	57.0	95.0	118.9
Public sector subsidies as % of public expenditure	7.95	4.17	2.66
Public sector subsidies as % of GDP	2.9	1.5	0.9

Note:

[1] Subsidies are current expenditures by the public sector excluding capital grants.

Sources: HM Treasury, *The Government's Expenditure Plans*, HMSO, 1985, 1988, 1989.

Economic theory and subsidies

A market failure approach suggests that subsidies are required whenever there are substantial and beneficial externalities or social benefits. Alternatively, subsidies might be required to cover the losses associated with marginal cost pricing applied to a decreasing cost industry. Whilst a number of UK firms and nationalised industries have received subsidies to reduce losses and to prevent closure, usually these have not been associated with marginal cost pricing and decreasing costs. Instead, subsidies have more often been justified on grounds of social benefits. The argument is that private markets, if left to themselves, will provide too little of some socially desirable activities and that subsidies are required to correct this market failure. Typically, governments have used the social benefits argument to justify subsi-

dies to protect jobs, to promote high technology and to support the balance of payments, all of which are deemed to be in the national or public interest. Economists need to assess these arguments critically, subjecting them to economic analysis and empirical evidence.

The methodology of economic policy can be applied to subsidy policy, although critics might claim that it is a counsel of perfection. The objectives of policy have to be clearly stated. The causes of the policy problem have to be identified, and it needs to be shown that subsidies are the most appropriate and efficient solution from the available alternatives. For example, with regional policy, the aim might be to increase employment in the high unemployment areas of the country. However, this might conflict with the objective of promoting a reallocation of resources from declining to expanding regions and encouraging firms to locate in their most efficient areas. Questions then arise about the causes of local unemployment. Is it, for example, due to high wages failing to reflect local labour scarcities; do firms elsewhere lack information about local labour supplies; are there infrastructure deficiencies which raise the costs to firms locating in the area; is the housing market impairing labour mobility; or is the capital market failing to finance worthwhile human investments in mobility and training? From this analysis of causes, it does not follow that subsidies to firms in high unemployment areas are the most appropriate and efficient solution. Questions have to be asked about the effectiveness of policy: has it achieved its objectives? If so, at what cost? Regional policy which offers a variety of incentives and subsidies to firms located in high unemployment areas is an obvious candidate for evaluation.

Regional policy

Markets are changing continuously and the results of change are reflected in the expansion and decline of different regions in the UK. High unemployment areas in northern England, Scotland, Wales and Northern Ireland are associated with the decline of the UK's traditional smokestack industries such as coal, shipbuilding, steel and textiles. Sunrise industries such as electronics have developed elsewhere. The regional policy problem arises because markets do not adjust instantly, and because private markets do not consider the social costs and benefits of their activities (externalities). Successive UK governments have intervened to correct regional imbalances by seeking to reduce the regional differentials in unemployment rates; however, problems have arisen because the objectives of regional policy are often social and political rather than economic. Budget-conscious government departments can offer schemes to solve regional unemployment which will be supported by producers likely to benefit and by governments attracted by the likely favourable effects on votes.

A new UK regional policy was introduced in

1984. This was a result of substantial economic changes which had occurred in the 1970s, with UK membership of the EC, the oil crisis and higher national unemployment. It was estimated that, between 1972 and 1983, the previous regional policy created some 500,000 more jobs in the assisted areas at an Exchequer expenditure of £35,000 per job (at 1982 prices). Nevertheless, it was felt that the 1970s regional policy was not cost-effective; was not sufficiently selective; discriminated against services; favoured capital-intensive projects and often resulted in a transfer of jobs and a failure to emphasise job creation.

Under the current policy introduced in 1984 there are two types of regions – development areas and intermediate areas – together with two types of grants – regional development grants (RDGs) and regional selective assistance (RSA). Firms in development areas qualify for both RDGs and RSA. RDGs are automatic and paid at 15 per cent of eligible capital expenditure subject to a cost ceiling per job or, where higher, at £3,000 for each new full-time job created (at 1989 prices). In 1988–89 it was estimated that RDGs led to some 56,000 jobs for an Exchequer outlay of £220 mn. Expenditure on RDGs will decline following the phasing-out of the scheme announced in 1988. In future, RSA will be the main form of regional industrial assistance. RSA grants are discretionary and are available to firms in both development and intermediate areas. They are provided for projects which maintain employment or create additional jobs, the aim being to provide the minimum assistance needed for the project to proceed in an assisted area. In 1988–89 RSA was reputed to have created over 32,000 new jobs and safeguarded almost 9,000 jobs for an Exchequer outlay of £93 mn. In addition, UK government support is available for inner cities, enterprise zones and free ports. Furthermore, some forms of government expenditure, such as the decision to relocate civil servants in the North of England, represent implicit regional policy.

Critics of current UK regional policy claim that it represents a move towards a free market approach, with reductions in special support for the regions and an emphasis on improving the operation of product and factor (including labour) markets throughout the economy. They claim that there will be too little government assistance and financial support to solve the regional problem, and they also assert that there is a need for more policy instruments. In particular, supporters of an interventionist policy favour Industrial Development Certificates (IDCs) as a means of controlling new factor buildings and extensions, thereby influencing the location decisions of firms. Originally, IDCs were used to reduce congestion in London and the South-East and to promote activity in the assisted areas, but they were no longer used after 1982. Nonetheless, whether an interventionist or laissez-faire approach is preferred, there remain some outstanding issues for regional policy. Questions arise about the aims of policy and the potential conflicts between efficiency and social objectives, about whether policy is simply transferring jobs between different parts of the country and ultimately about the beneficiaries from the policy.

Regional policy also operates as part of the EC's so-called 'structural funds' which in 1989 amount to ECU 9 bn and which are expected to build up rapidly to ECU 14.5 bn in 1993. Traditionally, EC regional policy served only to shift resources from rich to poor areas of the EC, but henceforth aid is to be directed at 'less developed' regions; areas of industrial decline (which encompass the bulk of the UK north of Cambridge); declining rural areas; and areas with long-term and youth unemployment. Whereas each member state used to get a set share of available funds, the approach is to be more flexible in future and should result in the UK receiving around 40 per cent of the funds allocated to declining industrial areas. However, the funds will be available only for projects approved by the European Commission. The main difficulty stems from the concept of '**additionality**'. In future EC funds must be additional to funds already committed by national governments. The UK interprets this to mean that it can replace its own funds with those from the EC provided it spends an additional sum of equal value in order to benefit the region in question, but the EC may insist that the UK honours its regional aid commitments in their original form.

Technology policy

Government support for science, technology and R & D is designed to improve the efficiency, competitiveness and innovative capacity of the UK (Cmnd 621, 1989, p. 25). But why is State intervention required? Here, the argument is that R & D is risky, that it may take a long time to produce marketable results and that the benefits are likely to extend far beyond a single innovating firm. On this basis it is argued that, if left to themselves, private markets will fail to provide the socially desirable amount of R & D and will encourage the hoarding of valuable ideas, so resulting in too little innovation and its dissemination with adverse effects on economic growth. Such market failure reflects at least three factors. In the first place, a belief that capital markets will fail to finance large-scale, risky and long-term projects. Secondly, it might reflect the costs of establishing property rights in valuable ideas. Thirdly, the pursuit of profits might lead to the hoarding of valuable ideas and a failure to generate the socially desirable transfer of knowledge throughout the economy.

Persuasive though these arguments appear, they are often long on emotion and short on economic analysis, critical content and empirical evidence. For example, what might appear to be market failures in research and scientific activity might simply reflect the diversity of solutions adopted by firms to economise on transaction costs. Similarly, it is not sufficiently convincing evidence of a capital market failure to claim that it failed to provide funds for such high technology projects as Airbus and Concorde. In such cases, the capital market might be working properly and judging that the projects are likely to be unprofitable. After all, the UK capital market has funded large-scale, long-term and risky projects such as the Channel Tunnel and the North Sea oil fields. Nor does it follow that State intervention will take an impartial long-term view, independently of the political market including a government's need to be re-elected. In fact, public choice analysis predicts that governments can also fail.

Once governments decide to intervene in research and scientific markets they are faced with a complex choice set. Decisions are needed on support for basic or applied research and technology transfer, on training the appropriate number and mix of different types of scientists and engineers and on whether to offer support in the form of cash incentives (such as subsidies), tariff protection, patent legislation or public procurement. Further choices are required on whether to support key high technology industries such as aerospace, electronics and telecommunications and, if so, whether to favour small or large firms and a competitive, oligopolistic or monopoly industry structure. Here, the evidence suggests that an industry with many moderate-to-large firms of relatively similar size will be the most technically progressive, and that a market structure intermediate between monopoly and perfect competition would promote the highest rate of inventive activity (Kamien and Schwartz, 1982, p. 3).

Some of the results of UK government choices on science and technology policy are shown in **Table 8.9**. Defence is the largest programme, followed by Education and Science (including the universities), DTI, Energy (including atomic energy) and Agriculture. Within defence R & D some 60 per cent of expenditure is allocated to the aerospace and electronics industries. Moreover, the large share of defence in government spending on science and technology has led to fears that defence R & D may crowd-out valuable investment in the civil sector, so impairing industry's ability to compete in international markets for civil high technology products.

The DTI has a major programme of assistance for industrial innovation. In recent years policy has changed from support for near-market R & D to support for long-term research collaboration and technology transfer. The DTI has encouraged collaborative programmes involving European firms (Eureka), as well as collaboration between government, industry and higher education. It has also promoted technology transfer where the market may be slow to adapt (Cmnd 605, 1989, p. 7). In addition, the DTI has provided further support for specific sectors, namely aircraft, aeroengine and civil space research programmes together with launch aid for civil aerospace projects. Interestingly, both the defence and DTI R & D programmes offer substantial public sector support to the UK aerospace industry. In evaluating government support for civil aircraft programmes, one study concluded that between 1945 and 1975 'the net effect of aerospace launching aid has been a net loss of national welfare' (Gardner, 1976, p. 149).

Table 8.9 *Government spending on science and technology*

Department[1]	1982–83	1985–86	1988–89	1991–92 plans
Defence	1 765	2 341	2 354	2 550
Education & Science	1 135	1 324	1 580	1 800
DTI[2]	327	458	503	390
Energy	250	227	211	160
Agriculture, Fisheries & Food	150	159	167	160
Total[3]	3 839	4 754	5 126	5 390
Of which: Civil science and technology	2 074	2 413	2 772	2 840
% civil	54	51	54	53

Notes:
[1] Only najor spending Departments are shown.
[2] The DTI figures include launch aid.
[3] Excluding R & D by nationalised industries.
Source: Cmnd 621, 1989.

European collaboration

The trend towards the rising costs of some advanced technology projects means that the minimum entry costs are so high that it is necessary for a number of large firms or even nations to combine. Even before the completion of the single internal market in the EC, there have been some notable examples of European government involvement in collaborative programmes. These include Airbus, Concorde, the European Centre for Nuclear Research, ESPRIT (an information technology programme), the European Space Agency and a series of joint defence ventures mainly involving military aircraft, helicopters and missiles such as the three-nation Tornado and the four-nation European Fighter Aircraft. For these projects European collaboration reflects the fact that independence based on small national markets is too costly.

Europe's high technology industries such as aerospace, defence, electronics and telecommunications are frequently criticised for the wasteful duplication of costly R & D and for the relatively short production runs resulting from a dependence on a small domestic market. International collaboration is often presented as the appropriate solution leading, so it is claimed, to the eventual creation of European-wide high technology industries capable of competing with Japan and the USA in world markets. Supporters of European collaboration in high technology claim a variety of benefits as indicated below:

1. Cost savings for both R & D and production
2. The sharing of risks and costs allows projects to be undertaken which would be too costly on an independent national basis (for example space satellites and supersonic airliners)
3. The creation of a European industry able to compete in world markets for high technology products, so avoiding Europe becoming a nation of metal bashers
4. A set of general economic and political benefits in the form of domestic jobs, the balance of payments, rivalry in ideas and the creation of a united Europe through reducing national barriers and prejudice.

The simple economics of collaboration are shown in **Figure 8.4**. Consider the case of a two nation collaborative military aerospace project based on equal sharing of R & D costs and a pooling of national orders. In the ideal case, each nation bears only 50 per cent of the development costs compared with an independent national venture and gains from the doubling of output which, through learning economies, will reduce unit production costs by about 10 per cent. However, collaboration has some disadvantages and costs leading to departures from the ideal model. Where governments are involved, substantial transaction costs arise as each partner nation seeks to establish property rights in the joint programme. Bargaining between partner governments, their bureaucracies and customers (such as the armed forces), together with lobbying from producer groups of scientists and contractors, can lead to substantial inefficiencies. Work might be shared on political, equity and bargaining criteria and not on the basis of efficiency and competition. Each partner will demand its fair share of high technology work. Also, there might be substantial administrative costs in the form of duplicate organisations, frequent committee meetings, delays in decision-making and excessive government involvement in monitoring and policing international contracts. As a result, collaborative programmes involving governments might involve higher costs and take longer to develop than a national project. Government involvement in collaboration also raises wider issues of public purchasing, and we must accordingly turn to consider the likely effects of government purchasing on industrial performance.

Public purchasing

Scope of government procurement

Government purchasing is big business. In 1988–89 central and local government purchases of assets, goods and services was almost £39 bn, representing about 25 per cent of public expenditure. Government purchases range from standard items such as clothing, paper clips, furniture, motor cars, office equipment and accommodation, to

Figure 8.4 *The economics of collaboration: (a) R & D costs, (b) Unit production costs*

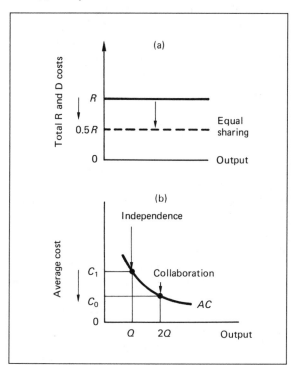

pursuit of such wider ends makes it difficult for Parliament and independent analysts to determine whether public procurement is giving good value for money. However, privatisation results in the transfer of purchasing from the public to the private sector where commercial criteria rather than wider public interest considerations dominate procurement choices.

The range and complexity of public procurement choices can be illustrated by considering two limiting models. At one extreme the government as the buyer knows what it wants, the products exist and they are being traded in competitive-type markets. In these circumstances the State acts as a competitive buyer, specifies its requirements, invites competitive tenders and awards a fixed price contract to the lowest bidder. Problems arise at the other extreme where the government is the only buyer, it is uncertain about its requirements, and the product does not yet exist (as is often the case for high technology products such as defence equipment and telecommunications). Moreover, the domestic market might contain only one or relatively few actual or potential suppliers. The government as the major, or only, buyer might have to select a contractor and to write a contract for a project which either does not exist, might involve a major jump in the state of the art and where the contractor requires a cost-based contract with a substantial proportion of the risks borne by the State. Contracts for such advanced technology projects are often associated with cost overruns, time slippages and major modifications and sometimes with cancellations (for example the Nimrod AEW project) leading to allegations of waste, incompetence and contractor inefficiency.

Where a government Department is a major buyer, as with defence equipment, the NHS, electricity generating stations (pre-privatisation) and railway equipment, its procurement choices and contracting policies can have a decisive effect on an industry's size, structure, entry and exit, technical progress, efficiency, prices and profitability. For example, non-competitive government contracts, as with some defence equipment and pharmaceuticals for the NHS, are subject to state regulatory constraints. A Review Board for Non-Competitive Government Contracts and a Pharmaceutical Profit

more complex products such as computers, space satellites, nuclear power stations and Trident submarines. Such purchases have the potential for influencing industrial performance. Defence and Health are the major spending Departments, purchasing from industries such as aerospace, electronics, ordnance, shipbuilding, pharmaceuticals and medical equipment.

Government purchasing from private and state-owned enterprises involves choices about a product, a contractor and a contract. Decisions are required on the type of goods and services to be purchased, the selection of a contractor and the choice of a contract. Often such choices provide scope for governments to pursue wider economic and social objectives and not simply the acquisition of goods and services. Considerations of the national interest might lead a government to purchase from higher-cost domestic suppliers so as to protect a nation's key strategic industries, its technology, jobs and the balance of payments. The

Regulation Scheme are designed to ensure that government contractors receive a reasonable rate of return on capital, where 'reasonable' usually means a profit rate similar to the average return earned by British industry. However, firms respond and adapt to regulatory constraints. The possibility of post-costing and renegotiation of excessive profits provides firms with an inducement to sacrifice profits for expenditures which give satisfaction (utility) to the company's managers such as company cars, luxury offices and the hoarding of scientists.

For many years there have been continued debates about whether co-ordinated government purchasing might improve industrial performance through, for example, exploiting the economies of scale associated with combining and standardising orders from different state agencies. Since 1979 the emphasis has been on achieving better value for money from public purchasing. Government Departments have been subject to Rayner scrutinies, budgets have been cash limited, civil service manpower has been reduced and functions traditionally undertaken in-house have been contracted-out to private firms. Also, in 1984, an official review concluded that government procurement was costing the taxpayer too much, mainly due to administration costs and because the prices paid were often higher than necessary. At the same time, defence has been the focus of a major initiative in the form of its competitive procurement policy which was launched officially in 1984.

Evidence suggests that there is substantial scope for improving the efficiency of public procurement, not only in the UK but throughout the EC. As the only or major buyer governments will be lobbied to buy British, thereby preventing foreign firms bidding for UK government contracts. In fact, protectionism and support for domestic industries characterises public procurement throughout the EC. The creation of a single market in 1992 will enable public procurement to benefit from increased competition, free trade and economies of scale. It has been estimated that open public procurement throughout the EC would result in aggregate savings for the twelve EC nations equivalent to some 0.6 per cent of 1986 Community GDP (Cecchini, 1988, p. 17). For the UK, ending

protectionism and introducing open competition into public procurement at the national and local levels would produce price savings of 25 per cent in coal and 40 per cent in pharmaceuticals. (Cecchini, 1988, pp. 19–20). The UK's experience with competitive tendering further illustrates the potential gains from a more competitive public procurement policy.

Competitive tendering

Competitive tendering and contracting-out is potentially a vast area covering the possible use of private contractors for a whole range of public sector services. Contracting-out is one element of the current government's privatisation policy. It is concerned with the central or local government financing of services which could be supplied by private contractors (see **Figure 8.3**). By the late 1980s it was the focus of the major policy initiatives in local government, the NHS, defence and other parts of central government. Cleaning, catering, laundry, refuse collection, maintenance and security services are popular examples (**Table 8.10**). With its emphasis on better value for money, government policy aims to extend the use of private contractors by public bodies where this will increase their 'economy, efficiency and effectiveness'.

Contracting-out can be viewed as an aspect of public procurement policy since it involves the public sector purchasing goods and services from private firms. As such, the debate about contracting-out is not new. For example, within the NHS there is a tradition of buying pharmaceutical products, high technology medical equipment and buildings from private firms. Similarly, within defence there is a long tradition of buying weapons and equipment from private firms.

Consideration now needs to be given to the basic policy problem, which is the means by which public bodies such as NHS hospitals can assess the efficiency of their direct labour departments and in-house services. The starting point is that direct labour departments are usually monopoly suppliers of services protected from possible public and private sector rivals. In the absence of compe-

Table 8.10 *Contracting-out: progress and potential*

Local Authorities

---

1. Since legislation in 1980, direct labour organisations are required to compete with private firms for most of their construction and maintenance work.
2. The Local Government Act 1988 extended compulsory tendering to refuse collection, catering, cleaning streets and buildings, the maintenance of grounds and vehicles and the management of local authority sport and leisure facilities.
3. Other possibilities for contracting-out might include accountancy, architectural services, careers advice, computer and data processing services, housing sales and fire protection.

NHS

---

1. Currently there is a major DHSS policy initiative to introduce competitive tendering for hospital catering, cleaning and laundry services (domestic services).
2. Other possibilities could include ambulance and transport services, the contracting-out of major surgery and patient care to private hospitals, together with hospital management, and care for the elderly, disabled and mentally handicapped.

Ministry of Defence

Current examples include catering and cleaning at defence establishments, the refitting of warships (traditionally undertaken in the Royal Dockyards), some limited aircraft servicing and vehicle repair, air transport and the management of stores.

---

tition from rival departments and from private contractors, there are no alternative sources of information and no alternative cost yardsticks to assess the efficiency of a public agency. Here, efficiency is defined to embrace two aspects. In the first place, it is concerned with the lowest-cost method of supplying a **given** quantity and quality of service. Secondly, it is also concerned with the lowest-cost method of supplying **different** levels of service. This second aspect of efficiency enables a local authority or hospital to determine whether its existing level of service is worthwhile. For example, a lower level of service might be so much cheaper that the extra cost of the existing provision is deemed not to be worthwhile.

Contracting-out is offered as a solution to the problem of public sector monopolies which are criticised as inefficient bureaucracies responding to the wishes of producer groups rather than consumers. To its supporters, competitive tendering, or even the threat of rivalry, means improved efficiency and cost savings. It allows public procurement agents to recontract with different suppliers and for different levels of service. Competition between rival suppliers leads to the introduction of new ideas, the latest management techniques and modern equipment, thereby resulting in major changes in established and traditional methods of working. New equipment might replace labour; manning levels can be reassessed; and part-time workers might replace full-timers. Successful firms in a competition are also subject to the incentives and penalties of a fixed price contract so that there is not the open-ended financial commitment which can arise with in-house units.

The opponents of contracting-out claim that it leads to a poor quality and unreliable service. Examples are given of dirty streets, schools and hospital wards, and of penalty clauses being imposed on contractors. Proposals for privately-managed prisons have been condemned because of fears of lower standards and conditions in prisons, with discipline determined by profit-conscious managers. Private contractors are also believed to be less reliable than in-house units: it is suggested that they are less able to respond to emergencies; they are liable to default and bankruptcy; and that the award of a contract to a private firm leads to

Table 8.11 *Contracting-out: the arguments*

The case for contracting-out	The case against contracting-out
1. Public sector in-house monopolies are inefficient bureaucracies	1. Private contractors offer a poor quality and unreliable service
2. Competition allows regular recontracting by public procurement agents	2. Private contractors are liable to default, bankruptcy, and are less able to respond to emergencies
3. Competition leads to new ideas, modern equipment and changes in traditional methods of working	3. Contractors use low bids to but into attractive contracts and eliminate the in-house capacity so that public authority becomes dependent on a private monopoly
4. Successful firms in a competition are subject to the incentives and penalties of a fixed price contract	4. Private contractors achieve cost savings by cutting jobs, reducing wages and worsening working conditions

industrial relations problems and strikes. On the issue of cost savings, critics claim that these are short-lived. Low bids can be used to buy into an attractive new contract and eliminate the in-house capacity, so that the public authority loses its bargaining power. As a result, it becomes dependent on a private monopoly which, in the long run, means higher prices, a lack of dynamism and a poor quality service. Competitive tendering also involves substantial transaction costs which are often ignored by the supporters of contracting-out. Moreover, critics claim that any cost savings from contracting-out are achieved at the expense of the poorly paid members of society, so that the policy cannot avoid equity issues and debates about the distribution of income. The various arguments are summarised in **Table 8.11**.

The arguments for and against contracting-out provide extensive opportunities for critical analysis and evaluation. Some of the arguments obviously represent special pleading by those interest groups most likely to gain or lose from the policy. However, many of the arguments for and against contracting-out can be resolved by empirical testing. UK studies suggest, for a given level of service, annual cost savings of some 25 per cent over a range of hospital and local authority activities and 20 per cent for refuse collection (Domberger, *et al.*, 1986; Hartley and Huby, 1985).

If society wants improved efficiency, then privatisation and contracting-out are not sufficient: **competition** is also required. However, competitive tendering is likely to be associated with contractors lobbying for public sector business and for entry barriers to protect their existing markets and profits. Inevitably, there will be opposition from established interest groups likely to lose from the policy. Opponents of the policy can impose delays by insisting upon discussions with all interested parties; the timing of any change can be inappropriate; administrative time might be unavailable to prepare the tender documents and to undertake the necessary comparative studies, especially in an era of manpower cuts; and an authority might be reluctant to face a confrontation with the trade unions leading to major industrial relations problems. There is a more fundamental worry. With competitive tendering, choices about the quantity and quality of service provision are ultimately made by elected representatives whose preferences are unlikely to reflect the diversity of preferences of large numbers of individual consumers in properly functioning markets. The government's commitment to better value for money in public purchasing has also been reflected in its new competitive procurement policy for defence equipment.

A competitive procurement policy: the case of defence

The Ministry of Defence (MoD) is the largest single customer for the products of British industry with its purchases ranging from simple items such as batteries, cars and furniture to highly complex equipment such as missiles, submarines and advanced combat aircraft. For 1988–89 expenditure on defence equipment totalled £8.2 bn, with a further £3.4 bn spent on other items such as works, buildings and stores. About 75 per cent of the MoD's defence equipment is purchased directly from UK industry, a further 15 per cent benefits domestic industry through its participation in collaborative programmes and the remaining 10 per cent is imported. Within the UK the MoD purchases about 60 per cent of the output of the ordnance industry, 50 per cent of the output of the aerospace industry, 40 per cent of shipbuilding output and 20 per cent of electronics output. In 1986–87 the leading UK defence equipment contractors which were each paid over £250 mn by the MoD were British Aerospace (including Royal Ordnance), GEC, Plessey, Rolls Royce and Vickers.

R & D also forms a substantial part of the defence equipment programme through which it can have a major impact on technical progress in specific sectors of the UK economy, particularly aerospace, electronics and shipbuilding. Also, it is often claimed that there are additional economic benefits associated with **spin-off and technology transfer** from defence to the civil sector of the economy. Government defence R & D spending in 1986 was almost 50 per cent of all government R & D expenditure and was equivalent to 0.6 per cent of GDP. However, the government has announced that necessary investment in defence R & D may crowd-out valuable investment in the civil sector and that restraints on government-funded defence R & D spending were required to free resources for civil work (Cmnd 101-1, 1987, p. 48). Nevertheless, such a proposition needs to be carefully assessed, particularly the evidence on crowding-out and whether the UK's commitment to defence R & D has adversely affected its international competitiveness. Furthermore, where

there is evidence of these adverse effects, it is necessary to discover whether they have arisen because, in the past, cost-plus defence contracts have tended to reduce a firm's innovative drive, and whether the situation will change now that the MoD operates a competitive procurement policy. Issues also arise as to what happens to the resources released from defence R & D – are they used in civil technology or elsewhere in the civil sector in the UK, do they remain unemployed or do they emigrate? It is evident that, in the long run, reduced defence R & D sends out clear signals to the labour market about future employment prospects in military technology work.

Traditionally, MoD procurement policy was characterised by support for UK industry, by non-competitive cost-plus or cost-based contracts and by contractors bearing none of the risks of the project. Defence contractors were often criticised for cost escalation, delays, 'gold plating', labour hoarding, inefficiency and project failures. In 1983 the MoD introduced a new competitive procurement policy in an effort to change the traditional dependency relationship in which defence business was regarded as 'lucrative, not very competitive and a cosy relationship' (HCP 392, 1988, p. xxvi). The MoD became a more demanding customer, introducing and extending competition and encouraging new entrants, especially small firms. Risks are being shifted from the MoD to industry, with a greater use of firm or fixed price contracts rather than cost-plus contracting. In 1988 a further extension of competition occurred when the MoD announced that it was more willing to purchase equipment from overseas sources where they are likely to offer 'greater value for money'.

The published results of the new competition policy are impressive. In 1979–80, 30 per cent of MoD contracts by value were awarded on a competitive basis and 22 per cent were cost plus a percentage fee contracts; by 1986–87 the corresponding figures were 53 per cent and 7 per cent respectively. At the outset of the new policy a target was announced for achieving cost savings of 10 per cent on the total equipment budget. Some of the actual results of competition have been impressive, with cost savings ranging from 10 per cent to 70 per cent, all of which might be taken as

Table 8.12   *Savings from competition*

Project	% Savings
Harrier GR5 airframe fatigue testing	70
Watchman airfield radar	66
Missile pallets	50
Tucano trainer simulator	40
RAF trainer aircraft	35
Sample quoted in SDE 1984	30+
Armoured repair and recovery vehicles	20
Combat vehicle MCV 80	12
Minehunter vessels	10

Source; Cmnd 344, 1988, vol. 1, p. 37.

indicators of monopoly pricing and/or inefficiency in UK defence industries. In 1987–88, for example, the median cost saving on a group of 13 equipment projects was 40 per cent, giving total savings of over £100 mn. Similarly, there are examples where competition resulted in savings of over £400 mn from 10 projects originally expected to cost £2.4 bn. Some examples are shown in **Table 8.12**.

Competition policy as implemented by the MoD is not without its problems and it is subject to both constraints and conflicts. A potential constraint arises if the MoD or the government is unwilling to impose the ultimate sanction on poor performance by a major contractor – namely, bankruptcy. Until 1988 there was a further constraint in that domestic monopolies dominate the high technology and costly equipment programmes. These comprise British Aerospace (aircraft, missiles, ordnance and small arms), Rolls Royce (aero-engines), Westland (helicopters), GEC (torpedoes), Vickers Shipbuilding (nuclear-powered submarines) and Vickers (tanks). However, the 1988 announcement that the MoD is willing to buy from overseas means that the threat of competition is likely to increase the contestability of those UK defence markets dominated by domestic monopolies. But conflicts arise between competition policy leading to foreign purchases and support for the UK defence industrial base which appears to offer attractive wider economic and social benefits in the form of security, independence, jobs, technology and an improved balance of payments. Such conflicts also involve different government Departments such as the MoD, the DTI and the Monopolies and Mergers Commission.

The UK defence industrial base

The debate in 1985–86 over the future of the Westland helicopter company was a classic example of the arguments about the need for a defence industrial base (DIB). It was claimed that the UK needed a strong DIB for strategic objectives and for national economic benefits. The strategic benefits included security of supply in times of tension and war (an insurance policy), the need for equipment designed specially for national requirements and the capability to respond to emergencies (such as the Falklands crisis). There are also claimed to be national economic benefits in the form of employment, foreign exchange savings and earnings and the development of high technology, including spin-offs to the civil sector. Certainly, defence sales are a major source of industrial employment, accounting for over 600,000 jobs in 1986. The result is a significant pressure group which will seek to persuade governments to spend more on defence equipment and to buy British. Large producers with domestic monopolies will use their political influence and lobbying to oppose foreign purchases (of, for example, Boeing AWACS and tanks). Stress will be placed on job losses, possibly in marginal constituencies, the loss of a vital defence capability and the dangers of depending on foreigners. Economists have the task of subjecting such claims to independent analysis, critical scrutiny and confronting the arguments with the available evidence.

Many of the arguments for a DIB are vague and emotive and are used to rationalise and justify the *status quo*. Costs are ignored. Informed public choices on the appropriate or optimal size and composition of the UK's DIB need answers to three questions. In the first place, what is meant by 'DIB' and why is it needed? Secondly, what is the minimum size and composition of the DIB? For example, should it comprise only a R & D capability in certain key technologies (which?) and what would be the costs and benefits if the current DIB were reduced by, say, 10 per cent or 20 per cent? Thirdly, how much are the Armed Forces willing to pay for retaining key UK industrial capabilities for military objectives? Any wider economic benefits such as jobs and advanced technology should be charged to other government Departments (for example Employment and Trade and Industry). Indeed, the point has to be made that there are usually alternative ways of achieving employment, technology and balance of payments objectives.

Buying British is not costless. It can mean paying more for equipment, perhaps an extra 25 per cent or more, and waiting longer for delivery (as was the case for the Nimrod AEW and torpedoes). The result is smaller defence forces and less protection. Ultimately, it is necessary to ask what the defence budget is buying: protection for UK citizens or protection for UK defence industries? Each option involves different sets of costs and benefits and, once again, choices cannot be avoided.

Conclusion

Economics is the study of choices and industrial policy is a classic example of choices under uncertainty. Economists contribute to policy debates by focusing on policy objectives, by applying their theories and by identifying alternative policy solutions. They are also concerned about the economic welfare implications of alternative policies. Increasingly, though, it is recognised that this ideal approach to policy issues cannot be divorced from the realities of the political market. Moreover, many of the traditional certainties in industrial economics are being challenged. New models of the supply side are being developed and applied, all of which makes it more difficult for economists to be confident about the advice which can be offered to policy-makers.

References

Bishop, M. and Kay, J. (1988) *Does Privatization Work?* (London Business School.

Blackaby, F. (ed.) (1979) *De-industrialisation* (Heinemann).

Cecchini, P. (1988) *The European Challenge 1992* (Wildwood House).

Cmnd 216 (1969) *Report on the Supply of Beer* (Monopolies Commission, HMSO).

Cmnd 101 (1987) *Statement on the Defence Estimates 1987*, I (HMSO).

Cmnd 331 (1988) *Review of Restrictive Trade Practices Policy*, Department of Trade and Industry (HMSO) (March).

Cmnd 344 (1988) *Statement on the Defence Estimates 1988*, I (HMSO).

Cmnd 605, 621, 629 (1989) *The Government's Expenditure Plans 1989–90 to 1991–92* (HMSO).

Cmnd 651 (1989) *The Supply of Beer*, Monopolies and Mergers Commission (HMSO).

Conservative Party (1987) *The Next Moves Forward* (Conservative Political Centre).

Curwen, P.J. (1986) *Public Enterprise* (Wheatsheaf).

Department of Trade and Industry (DTI) (1988) *Mergers Policy* (HMSO).

Domberger, S., Meadowcroft, D. and Thompson, D. (1986) 'Competitive tendering and efficiency: the case of refuse collection', *Fiscal Studies* (vol. 7) pp. 69–87.

Downs, A. (1957) *An Economic Theory of Democracy* (Harper & Row).

Dunsire, A., Hartley, K., Parker, D. and Dimitriou, B. (1988) 'Organizational status and performance', *Public Administration* (Winter) pp. 343–58.

Gardner, N. (1976) 'Economics of launching aid', in A. Whiting (ed.), *The Economics of Industrial Subsidies* (HMSO).

Hartley, K. and Huby, M. (1985) 'Contracting-out in health and local authorities', *Public Money* (September) pp. 23–6.

HCP 392 (1988) Defence Committee, *Business Appointments* (HMSO) (March).

Kamien, M.I. and Schwartz, N.L. (1982) *Market Structure and Innovation* (Cambridge University Press).

Kay, J. and Thompson, D. (1986) *Privatization and Regulation: the UK Experience* (Clarendon Press).

Niskanen, W.A. (1971) *Bureaucracy and Representative Government* (Aldine Atherton).

Williamson, O.E. (1981) 'The modern corporation: origins, evolution, attributes', *Journal of Economic Literature* (December) pp. 1537–68.

9

Macroeconomic Policy *David Gowland and Stephen James*

Introduction

In the course of this chapter many of the threads which run through earlier chapters will be pulled together with a view to explaining the evolution of macroeconomic policy in the UK. The purpose is both to examine the theoretical models which at various times have been adhered to with varying degrees of conviction by UK governments, and also at the empirical assessment of the outcomes from their use. This chapter necessarily contains a more wide-ranging historical perspective than most others, but in common with them it concentrates upon the evolution of theory and practice over the past two decades. In setting this discussion at the end of the book, rather than at the beginning as is commonly the case in other texts, the problem of introducing many matters as yet unfamiliar to some readers, such as the exchange rate, is avoided. To retain the continuity of the narrative it is assumed that the reader has indeed read the previous chapters, but where necessary he or she is referred back to the discussion earlier in the book. Thus there is, for example, no attempt to replicate the discussion of supply-side economics in Chapter 1, but models such as New Classical macroeconomics, which were mentioned only briefly in the Introduction, are spelled out in some detail.

Virtually everything mentioned in this chapter is in some way controversial. Some controversies are concerned with matters of theory such as the debate about expectations, and some with the interpretation of the statistical data. **These controversies are ongoing**, and it is not the purpose of this chapter to do other than to spell out the key issues and to form a reasoned judgement to guide the reader through the debate. As in certain other chapters, this one ends by addressing specific controversies which are currently at the forefront of the policy debate in the UK – in particular, whether credit controls have any useful role to play as an alternative to interest rates, and whether the government is justified in running a continuing Budget surplus.

Macroeconomic policy

The phrase **macroeconomic policy** is used to describe the actions of governments when they seek to manipulate the economy so as to influence the level of inflation and unemployment. Sometimes macroeconomic policy is used to try to stimulate the level of economic activity so as to increase the level of output and employment and so reduce unemployment. These policies are usually referred to as **expansionary**, or **reflationary**. However, critics of such policies point out that they sometimes lead to inflation and so term them 'inflationary policies'. On other occasions governments seek to reduce the level of economic activity in an attempt to reduce inflation. These policies are referred to as **deflationary** (or occasionally disinflationary). In the United Kingdom the government first started to pursue active macroeconomic policies in 1941. As the date suggests this was part of their effort to manage the economy so as to win the Second World War in the most efficient and equitable manner. For most of the period since

1941 governments have frequently referred to macroeconomic policy as **stabilisation** policy. This presumed that the level of economic activity was likely to fluctuate. Hence the role of macroeconomic policy was to be to minimise the fluctuations of output around its long-run trend level.

Logically, the term macroeconomic policy could be used to refer either to policies which sought to influence aggregate supply or to policies which sought to influence aggregate demand. In practice, however, the term was traditionally used to refer only to **demand management policies**, although in recent years there has been a revival of supply-side policies. The underlying objective of governments in formulating macroeconomic policy is to achieve the best available (that is, the **optimal**) combination of output, inflation, employment and other desirable objectives (such as the distribution of income, or, more generally, equity). These are also known alternatively as the goals or final targets of economic policy.

In Chapter 1 we considered the role of instruments, intermediate targets and objectives in our macroeconomic model (see **pp. 20–2**). Tinbergen's law states that a government can achieve as many objectives as it has independent instruments: with five instruments a government can achieve five objectives, **but no more**. In practice, however, due to uncertainty, it is much harder to make economic policy than Tinbergen's law suggests. Attempts to modify this approach to incorporate uncertainty and other real world complexities are called **optimal control**. A number of economists have worked on this for several years, but with little result so far.

There are various ways in which instruments can influence objectives. It is useful to group these into three forms of economic policy – direct controls; Keynesian policy (fiscal policy is the best known form of this); and financial policy (monetary policy is one form of financial policy).

Direct controls

Direct, or one-stage, controls are so named because they operate **directly upon objectives**. For example, a government seeking to control inflation might issue an ordinance setting out maximum prices and Draconian penalties for charging in excess of them (the penalty in Stalin's Russia was death). Such policies are easy to understand because it is clear to the general public how they are intended to work. However, economists believe they are generally ineffective because of the problem of *black markets* – the control creates an incentive to set up an unofficial market in which mutually beneficial exchanges can be made in violation of the control. In the UK the only direct control used in the last twenty years has been incomes policy. The general form of an incomes policy consisted of a direct attempt by the government to reduce the level of wage settlement. It thereby hoped, through various mechanisms, to reduce not only the level of wages but also the level of prices and to increase the level of output. The present government immediately abandoned incomes policy when it came into power in 1979. However, its critics feel that this was a mistake, and the issue of incomes policy still forms one of the major issues dividing Thatcherite opinion from its opponents.

Keynesian policy

Keynesian policy consists of using instruments in the **goods market**: the government operates so as to change demand in the goods market. Keynesian policy thus involves two stages: the instrument is used to influence the goods market which, in turn, is used to influence the objective variable. For example, if the government sought to reduce inflation it would use its instruments to reduce demand in the goods market (the 'real sector') and would hope that lower demand would reduce the price level (below the level at which it would otherwise have been). Hence Keynesian policy can fail if either:

(a) the government's instruments do not influence demand in the predicted fashion, or

(b) the reduction in demand does not influence price (or output) as intended, for example because (aggregate) supply shifts.

Financial policy

Financial policy is the most indirect of the three forms of economic policy, involving three stages, hence Milton Friedman's famous aphorism that monetary policy would operate only with a long and variable lag. The three stages are, respectively:

1. The monetary authorities (an umbrella term to describe all branches of government including the Bank of England) **do something**. This disturbs the financial system in a way which can be analysed using supply and demand curves. This disturbance is often called a 'shock' because it disturbs equilibrium. This stage involves the use of an instrument of policy. In the case of monetary policy, narrowly defined, this is called a **technique of monetary control**.

2. The purpose of stage 1 is to change either **price** or **quantity in financial markets**. The quantity might be the quantity of money or of credit (see below). The price might be the price of borrowing (the rate of interest) or the price of foreign currency (the exchange rate). This variable is called the **intermediate target**. The arguments for the money supply being the most appropriate intermediate target are examined below.

3. The purpose of stage 2 is to influence the **real sector**, the goods or labour market. In this way a government hopes to achieve its ultimate objective.

Because three stages are involved, the possibility of error is much greater than with direct or Keynesian policy. This does not mean that financial policy is necessarily less effective or less important – indeed the contrary may be the case. It does, however, mean that greater care in its use is essential. The crucial feature of the analysis of financial policy is to examine the means by which changes in financial markets influence developments in the real sector – how stage 2 leads on to stage 3. This is usually called the **transmission mechanism** of monetary policy – the means by which developments in financial markets are passed on to (transmitted to) the real sector.

It is important to distinguish between *direct* and *indirect* transmission mechanisms since the core of the monetarist position is a belief in a direct transmission mechanism whereas Keynesians believe in an indirect one. This means that they accept that money influences income but only through its effect on **some other variable**. Young Keynesians believe that this variable is the exchange rate, whereas older Keynesians believe it is the rate of interest. All Keynesians believe that government policy should focus on these variables. Monetarists, on the other hand, believe that money has a direct impact on income and hence that monetary policy should be used.

Financial, monetary and credit policy

It is important to distinguish financial policy in general from monetary policy. Narrowly used, the phrase **monetary policy** refers to control of the **money supply**. Financial policy encompasses not only monetary policy but also credit policy, interest rate policy and exchange rate policy. The latter two terms are quite straightforward. Exchange rate policy occurs when a government seeks to control the exchange rate. This policy has both micro- and macroeconomic aspects, some of which were analysed in Chapter 4. Interest rate policy is mainly concerned with influencing the level and structure of interest rates, and thereby influencing the rate of interest which firms and persons pay when they borrow to finance expenditure.

Credit policy, however, is more complicated and more controversial. The distinction between money and credit is straightforward. **Money** is an asset which a person owns, whereas **credit** is a liability which a person owes. It is not hard to tell the difference! Monetarists believe that a person's actions are largely influenced by the amount of money which he has – that, as the proverb puts it, 'money burns a hole in one's pocket'. Keynesians, on the other hand, emphasise the importance of credit. Keynesians believe that consumers' expenditure is very likely to be influenced by the cost and availability of credit to the personal sector. If the cost of borrowing falls then Keynesians expect expenditure to rise. Moreover, if individuals are allowed to borrow more, then their expenditure will rise. Such a general increase in borrowing possibilities occurred in the UK in the 1980s due to

financial innovation. Keynesians believe that credit-availability is critically important in economic analysis because they believe that individuals are rarely able to borrow as much as they would wish to. Consequently, any relaxation in credit limits is likely to lead to increased spending. Monetarists, on the other hand, usually believe that this would have litte effect in itself.

In seeking to clarify the relationship between instruments and objectives many economists and most governments believe that it is useful to introduce a further concept, the **intermediate target**. The idea is that a government should use its instruments to control the intermediate target, and rely upon the effect of the intermediate target in attaining its objectives. Economists tend to have some of their fiercest debates about the question as to which is the most appropriate intermediate target. Monetarism is defined by most authors as being belief in a monetarist target – in other words that the money supply should be the intermediate target. It is consequently important to distinguish between a belief in the use of financial or even monetary policy and monetarism itself. Monetarism is a belief that the best intermediate target is the *money supply*, and that a government should sacrifice other variables such as government spending, tax rates, interest rates and exchange rates to as to ensure that the money supply performs this function.

Monetary policy is one of the means by which governments can seek to manipulate the economy so as to influence inflation and unemployment. In 1960 it was unfashionable in the UK, and regarded as of little importance. Thereafter, its importance grew steadily until 1981, especially after the adoption of monetary targets (defined below) in June 1976. Since 1981, the Conservative government has de-emphasised the role of monetary policy, particularly after Mr Lawson became Chancellor of the Exchequer. Similar developments have occurred in other countries, but the extent of the controversy has been much greater in the UK. Some critics believe that the government was wrong to abandon monetary targets. In their view the price for this mistake could be seen in 1988 with rising inflation, soaring house prices and an enormous and growing balance of payments deficit. Their view was put eloquently by Sir Alan Walters, a close associate of Mrs Thatcher (Walters, 1986). In this view, the need to increase interest rates nine times (by 5 per cent in all) in the second half of 1988 was a belated attempt to correct for the error, although perhaps too late. At the least, the need for such strong medicine showed to monetarists the extent of the error in abandoning their nostrum.

Other critics argued that the government had been wrong to put as much emphasis on money as it had. Instead it should have sought to manage – and indeed stabilise – the exchange rate. Many such critics believed that the attempt to control the money supply in 1978–81 led to an excessively high exchange rate and so to deindustrialisation. Some argued that membership of the EMS was the best form of exchange rate policy – keen supporters of the Common Market believed that it was inevitable anyway, so the sooner the UK joined the better.

A framework of analysis

The same macroeconimic instrument may have both a direct (Keynesian) impact on the goods market, and also an indirect one through its effect on financial markets. For example, in increase of £100 mn in government expenditure on currently produced goods and services can be regarded as a Keynesian policy designed to raise the level of planned injections (exports plus investment plus government spending) at each level of income, and so to raise the equilibrium level of income. However, *ceteris paribus*, such a policy also increases the money supply permanently by £100 mn – that is by the exact amount of the spending – and is therefore also an instrument of monetary policy. In whichever way the instrument is regarded, its effect is nevertheless to **raise income**. However, the amount and duration of the change in income may depend crucially on how it is viewed. The **interdependence of policy instruments**, as it is usually called, is thus essential to understanding macroeconomic policy. It is the source of both theoretical and practical controversies in economics, because it means that it is usually impos-

sible for a government to achieve all of its intermediate targets simultaneously. If one target variable is too high (for example, the money supply) and one too low (for example, a measure of fiscal policy) then the use of an instrument which will bring the first back on course (lower government spending) will tend to depress the other (fiscal) target still more and so cause it to move even further away from its desired value.

The supply-side counterpart equation

It is therefore necessary to have some sort of conceptual framework both in order to elucidate this interrelationship between variables and also to analyse their impact. The most useful such framework is the flow-of-funds or supply-side counterpart equation. This uses the orthodox definition of the change in (Δ) the money supply as:

Δ Money Supply = Δ Currency held by the non-bank private sector

+

Δ Bank Deposits

This is a very general definition of money. In practice, a number of definitions of money are consistent with it; UK policy makers currently use 6, US ones over 40. Until the end of July 1989 the UK definitions were M_0; non-interest bearing M_1 (nib M_1); M_1; M_2; M_3; M_{3c}; M_4; and M_5. M_1, M_3 and M_{3c} are no longer in use but there is now a M_{4c}. The reason for this multiplicity of definitions is that it is not clear in practice which institutions are banks (see **p. 312**). Given that a building society is similar, but not identical, to a clearing bank, it is treated as a bank for some definitions but not for others. The Abbey National Building Society's conversion to a bank on 12 July 1989 triggered an alteration in definitions of money because it caused a huge switch of assets from the buildng society to the banking sector.

There are similar difficulties over the definition of a deposit. As a concept it is an 'almost perfectly liquid' claim on a bank. However, it is unclear whether a 7-day account is 'almost perfectly liquid', or indeed whether such a term can be applied to funds which can be obtained instantly, but subject only to the payment of a penalty. Different answers to these issues produce different definitions of money. It is preferable to examine a range of definitions rather than to risk being misled by a single one. The full range, both current and recent, is set out in **Figure 9.1**.

The basic definition of money in **Figure 9.1**

Figure 9.1 *Relationships among monetary aggregates and their components*[1]

	Notes and coins in circulation with the public		Notes and coins in circulation outside the Bank of England
plus	Private sector non-interest-bearing sterling sight bank deposits	*plus*	Bankers' operational balances with the Bank of England
		equals	M_0
equals	Non-interest bearing M_1		
plus	Private sector interest-bearing sight bank deposits	*plus*	Private sector interest-bearing retail sterling deposits with banks and building societies and National Savings Bank ordinary accounts
equals	M_1		
		equals	M_2
plus	Private sector sterling time bank deposits Private sector holdings of sterling bank certificates of deposit		
equals	M_3		
plus	Private sector holdings of building society shares and deposits and sterling certificates of deposit	*plus*	Private sector foreign currency bank deposits
		equals	M_{3c}
less	Building society holdings of bank deposits and bank certificates of deposit, and notes and coin		
equals	M_4		
plus	Holdings by the private sector (excluding building societies) of money-market instruments (bank bills, Treasury bills, local authority deposits) certificates of tax deposit and National Savings instruments (excluding certificates, SAYE and other long-term deposits)	*plus*	Private sector foreign currency bank and building society deposits
		equals	M_{4c}
equals	M_5		

(deposits plus currency) is often used by economists to analyse financial developments, and is referred to as **demand-side analysis**. However, supply-side analysis is more common. The supply-side counterpart equation is derived by two substitutions into the definition of money:

(a) **the bank balance sheet equation**: bank assets are equal to liabilities so loans (assets) can be substituted for deposits (liabilities)

(b) **the government finance equation**: bank loans to the government are replaced by a rearrangement of the government finance equation:

PSBR = Δ Bank loans to the government

+

Δ Non-bank private sector loans to the government

+

Δ Non-bank private sector holdings of currency

These substitutions are merely rearrangements of accounting identities. When the government runs a surplus called a Public Sector Debt Repayment the relationship still holds: (− PSDR) replaces PSBR. The purpose is to derive a useful and economically meaningful relationship, which now takes the form:

Δ Money Supply = Public Sector Borrowing Requirement

+

Bank loans to the non-bank private sector

−

Non-bank private sector loans to the public sector (government)

+

Overseas effect

The supply-side counterpart is thus the key to the analysis of macroeconomic policy-making in the UK.

Intermediate targets

Many of the rival candidates for the role of intermediate targets can be identified from this equation. They are respectively

(a) **Money supply**: this, the preferred target of monetarists such as Milton Friedman, is the sum of the four supply-side counterparts.

(b) **Domestic Credit Expansion (DCE)**: this is the domestic component of money creation, that is the first three of the supply-side counterparts.

---

[1] The Abbey National Building Society was authorised under the Banking Act 1987 as from the date of its conversion to a public limited company on 12 July 1989. From the end of July onwards its assets were transferred into the category of retail banks and ceased to be included in the building societies category. The amount of assets transferred (£32 bn) were such as to cause a major discontinuity in the series which included bank deposits but excluded building society deposits (namely M_1, M_3 and M_{3c}) and these were accordingly terminated as of June 1989. In aggregate M_2, M_4 and M_5 were unaffected as there were equal and offsetting changes in the bank and building society contribution to each aggregate. There was a small but easy to adjust for statistical break in M_0 due to the appearance of bankers' deposits at the Bank of England placed by the Abbey National, and an insignificant break in nib M_1. The disappearance of M_{3c} was compensated by the creation of a new definition M_{4c} which has yet to be specifically defined but which will include certain deposits in currencies other than sterling placed with UK banks *and* building societies by the rest of the UK private sector.

The term 'non-bank private sector' is used throughout this text to refer to the sector comprising UK residents other than the public sector and banks. The increasingly blurred distinction between banks and building societies will result in the increased use of the term 'M_4 private sector' to indicate that both banks and building societies are excluded. In addition, the definition of M_5 will be re-examined in due course, and possibly also that of M_2 and nib M_1, in order to make them more compatible with M_4 in the light of the Abbey National conversion, new financial instruments and new regulations governing the money markets announced in the 1989 Budget.
Source: Bank of England

(c) Public Sector Borrowing Requirement: Mr Lawson had a variety of targets for the PSBR. From 1985–88 his target was a PSBR equal to 1 per cent of GDP. Thereafter his target was for a substantial surplus. Mr Lawson indicated that in the long run he might revert to a balanced budget (Mr Major's decision now).

(d) Measures of fiscal policy: the PSBR is equal to:
- Government spending (a Keynesian injection)

  −
- taxation (a Keynesian withdrawal)

  −
- asset sales by the public sector

  +
- public sector loans to the rest of the economy

By an accounting quirk the last category includes nationalised industries' profits and losses. Losses appear as loans by the National Loans Funds to the industry concerned; a profit as a notional repayment.

Keynesian measures of fiscal policy could be weighted averages of the first, second and fourth of these. For example, 'fiscal leverage' might be government spending − 0.7 taxation + 0.5 public sector loans (Musgrave's values for 1967). Moreover, Keynesians might disaggregate some components further − government spending might be divided into expenditure on goods and services and on transfers, with a higher weight given to the former.

(e) Credit: credit, the preferred target of both Ben Friedman and other Keynesians, is measured by the second supply-side counterpart: bank lending to the non-bank private sector.

(f) Interest rates: the level of interest rates influences both bank lending and non-bank private sector purchases of public sector securities (National Savings and gilt-edged). Higher rates reduce the demand for bank loans and increase the demand for public sector debt. Hence the level and structure of interest rates are critical determinants of these supply-side counterparts.

(g) Exchange rate: the overseas influence on the money supply, the fourth of the supply-side counterparts, is closely related to the balance of payments surplus − hence exchange rate policy will be reflected in monetary developments and vice versa.

This framework can be used to analyse a large number, indeed virtually all, issues in UK macroeconomic policy. More importantly, perhaps, it has been used by policy-makers in formulating their policy. Hence the use of flow-of-funds analysis is crucial to an understanding of the origins and objectives of economic policy. For example, the Conservative government used it to devise the Medium Term Financial Strategy in 1979. The government purported to commit itself to setting the key values of economic policy for a period of four years in advance; the purpose was to give the private sector information about macroeconomic policy and to increase the credibility of economic policy. It did this by announcing its target values for the key flow-of-funds variables − especially money supply and PSBR. However, the values included in the MTFS bore no relationship to the actual outturn as shown in **Table 9.3 pp. 324–5**. Hence they were useless both as forecasts and as targets. Thus, while the government has continued to publish the MTFS in order to avoid losing face, neither it nor its critics have regarded it as of any importance.

Methods of monetary control

The most useful and fruitful use of supply-side counterpart or flow-of-funds analysis is in analysing the methods of monetary control used in the UK. In presenting the range of options open to the monetary authorities textbooks frequently emphasise the reserve ratio/reserve base system whereby a change in either the quantity of reserve assets or the reserve ratio leads to a corresponding change in the money supply. It does this by either forcing banks to lend less or making it possible for them to lend more through the workings of the credit multiplier. Such a system has never been used in the UK, though the government might have chosen to introduce it and did consider doing so in 1979–80. There have been various reserve ratios in the UK but they were neither designed to – nor did they – work in the textbook fashion. In the reserve ratio method of monetary control a bank lends whenever, **but only when**, it has the necessary reserve assets. In other words, the direction of causality runs from reserves to loans. In the UK there has been no attempt to control the volume of reserves and the direction of causality has run from loans to reserves – in other words banks lent because they wanted to (usually because it was profitable) and then acquired the necessary reserves. This meant that the various ratios were partly prudential (to reduce the risk of bank failure) and partly devices to increase the authorities' control of short-term interest rates – an intention made clear in *Competition and Credit Control* in 1971 and repeated in *Monetary Control* (Cmnd 7858) in 1980. However, as was also made clear in the latter, these devices did not work very well. Hence neither the introduction of a 12.5 per cent minimum liquid assets ratio in 1971 nor its abolition (in stages) in 1980–81 was of much importance.

Competition and Credit Control

Instead of relying on a reserve base system the authorities sought to control the money supply through the various items of the flow-of-funds equation. The five crucial flow-of-funds variables are bank deposits (from the demand side) and the four supply-side variables: PSBR, bank lending, non-bank lending to the public sector and overseas effect. The PSBR can be influenced in a variety of ways, such as via changes in government spending, tax rates and asset sales (privatisation). The remaining variables can be influenced by either quantity controls or price devices. The latter work by seeking to induce economic agents to change their behaviour – in other words, to move along a

demand curve. Quantity controls, in contrast, seek to override demand by official fiat.

Prior to 1971 monetary policy was in effect credit policy since the principal tool of monetary policy was a number of quantity controls on bank lending and other forms of credit, notably hire purchase (instalment credit). The quantity control on bank lending took the form of 'ceilings' whereby the Bank of England set a maximum level of lending (the 'ceiling') for each bank. The ceiling took two forms – **quantitative** in the form of a ceiling on overall lending, and **qualitative** in the form of restrictions on lending to certain categories of borrower, especially personal customers and property companies. Any form of rationing or quantity control will create an incentive to evade it – the familiar 'black market' argument of elementary microeconomics. Financial markets are no exception; new institutions, notably secondary banks, grew up whose main purpose was to evade the controls. The extent of evasion is still unclear but this is not very important. What is relevant is that the authorities were convinced that their ceilings were no longer effective, and this regime of monetary control, the 'old approach', was abandoned in 1971.

Its replacement was known as either the 'new approach' (1971–73) or 'Competition and Credit Control'. Its principal feature was a decision to seek to control bank lending solely by means of **interest rates**. If the money supply grew too quickly then interest rates would be raised so as to reduce the demand for bank loans and thus the money supply. In December 1973 Monetary policy seemed to be a shambles – for example, £M$_3$ had grown by over 60 per cent in 27 months. The effects of this explosion were clearly seen in accelerating inflation, a massive balance of payments deficit and massive growth in house prices. Monetary policy had failed. However, it is still not clear why. To some extent the new approach was flawed technically, since the authorities had less control over bank base rates than they had anticipated. Largely, however, the problem was a lack of political will by Mr Heath and his Chancellor, Mr Barber: they were unwilling to change interest rates often enough, or by a large enough amount.

It fell to the incoming Labour government to

devise a new regime of monetary control early in 1974. It had three instruments of control: a ceiling on interest-bearing eligible liabilities (IBELs), an aggressive debt management policy and manipulation of the PSBR for monetary purposes. The latter was accomplished by a combination of tax increases, public expenditure cuts and, after 1977, asset sales – mainly of BP shares and government holdings of private sector loans. Such policies were continued after 1979 by the incoming Conservative government and were largely successful as macroeconomic tools. Debt management policy was similarly successful, especially through selling National Savings Securities to the private sector. The controversial element of the package was the ceiling on IBELs (a legal term for bank deposits), often called the 'corset'. This ceiling was reinforced by a system of penalties whereby a bank whose deposits grew faster than permitted had to deposit a proportion of the excess interest-free with the Bank of England. This interest-free deposit was termed a 'supplementary special deposit'. Initially the ceiling held, but it was later evaded on a massive scale; in other words the black market problem was once more evident.

Policy after 1979

Monetary policy was reasonably successful under the 1974–79 Labour government but the breakdown of the IBELs ceiling, and the election of a new Conservative government in 1979 headed by Mrs Thatcher, led to a reappraisal of monetary policy. The PSBR and debt management instruments of monetary policy remained, although the latter was abandoned in November 1985. However, the IBELs ceiling was dropped in June 1980 and replaced by a plethora of new instruments:

(a) A reiteration of the **interest rate weapon** as a tool to control bank lending, as in the 'new approach'.
(b) Use of the **exchange rate** to influence overseas flows, especially in 1979. Later the exchange rate was an intermediate target rather than an instrument of monetary policy. The idea was that a high exchange rate made foreign assets cheaper. UK citizens and finan-

cial institutions would buy them and the resultant capital account deficit would reduce the money supply. This mechanism was the centrepiece of criticism of the government by moderate left and 'young Keynesians' who argued that the consequent high level of the exchange rate was a major cause of deindustrialisation.

(c) The **abolition of exchange controls** in November 1979. This mechanism was similar to (b) in that a balance of payments deficit on capital account would reduce monetary growth. The Labour party made this the centrepiece of their criticism of the government. £100 bn of capital was exported during 1979–86 which, they argued, reduced domestic investment and hence caused unemployment to rise.

In addition the government made a number of technical changes in monetary policy in 1980–81. The most important was the replacement of minimum lending rate (MLR) by the much more flexible 'intervention rate'. In all western countries the banking system normally borrows from the central bank. The central bank uses variations in the cost and terms of such borrowing as a means of controlling the short-term rate of interest. The Bank of England has made a number of changes in this system since 1971. Their goal has been a system in which the rate at which the banking system borrowed could be changed frequently – if necessary several times a day. They wished such changes to be viewed as normal, minor technical acts of policy rather than as major changes. In some countries, as in the UK prior to 1971, publicity is sought for such changes so as to reinforce their impact through changing expectations. At the present time the Bank prefers the flexibility of frequent unobtrusive changes.

The 1950s and 1960s: The age of demand management

The development phase

This period constituted the high years of demand management in the UK. In retrospect, at least from

Table 9.1   *GDP, inflation and unemployment, 1950–79, selected years (%)*

	1950–69	1950–59	1960–69	1970–79	1970–73	1974–79
Real GDP growth (annual average)	2.7	2.4	3.1	1.8	2.9	0.5
Inflation (annual average)	3.1	2.7	3.5	12.6	8.0	15.7
Unemployment (% of employed labour force)	1.7	1.5	1.9	4.1	3.1	4.8

Source: Economic Trends, Annual Supplements.

the standpoint of the recession of the early 1980s, these years seemed to be a time when economic principles were successfully applied so as to achieve high employment, moderate growth and reasonably stable prices. Granted, the growth rate was moderate by comparison with other European countries and it gave rise to increasing concern as time wore on. Periodic balance of payments and sterling crises and inflationary spurts required the application of the economic brakes to the extent that the booms and slumps of earlier periods became the policy-induced stop–go cycle. Nevertheless, it was a period in which unemployment never rose above 2.4 per cent, GDP grew at an average rate of 2.7 per cent per annum, and inflation – at least until the late 1960s – fluctuated in the range of 1 to 5 per cent per annum. **Table 9.1** gives a summary of the economic performance.

The consensus view that it was the responsibility of the government to regulate demand grew out of the inter-war experience and the development of Keynesian macroeconomics. The policy can be characterised as the short-term management of the level of demand through the use of fiscal and monetary policies in order to iron out fluctuations in the level of economic activity, thereby maintaining the economy at or near its full employment level. In the extreme the policy becomes one of 'fine tuning' whereby frequent adjustments are made to keep the economy on course. The principal instrument was to be fiscal policy, and in particular the adjustment of **tax rates**. Public expenditure was regarded as less flexible in the short term and in any case was determined by long-term factors. Monetary policy played a sub-

sidiary and supportive role, mainly through the use of direct controls on credit. Interest rates were primarily deployed in defending the exchange rate. The economy fluctuated in a fairly regular pattern, with a cycle of around four to five years duration, that is from peak to peak or trough to trough. Policy was adjusted in a **counter-cyclical fashion**, becoming contractionary in times of current account deficit and rising inflation, and expansionary when unemployment rose.

It was not until the boom associated with the Korean War in 1951 that this form of demand management became the major preoccupation of economic policy. Then commodity price rises and defence spending commitments resulted in severe inflationary pressure to the extent that in both 1951 and 1952 retail price rises were in excess of 9 per cent, and the current balance moved into serious deficit – £307 mn in 1951. The first Bank Rate rise since 1939 and the introduction of hire-purchase (HP) controls for the first time constituted the main acts of demand management, along with the introduction of import controls. As the economy slowed expansionary measures followed; in 1953 there were reductions in direct and indirect taxes and HP controls were removed in 1954.

1955 saw the first major piece of economic mismanagement (or misjudgement). In his Spring Budget, shortly before an election, R. A. Butler lowered tax rates, instituting, at the same time, a restrictive monetary policy to hold back demand. Inflation accelerated and the current account moved into deficit shortly afterwards. Following an election in May, the Chancellor was forced into taking supplementary restrictive measures in the

Autumn. Whether Mr Butler was politically unscrupulous or economically naive about the potency of monetary policy (or possibly both), this episode discredited monetary policy for nearly twenty years.

Fiscal policy in the ascendant

Demand management was in future operated primarily through **fiscal policy**, with interest rates directed towards influencing the capital account of the balance of payments. This latter policy became apparent in 1956, and more so in 1957 when the Bank Rate was raised to 7 per cent in the face of heavy speculation against the currency. It was to become a regular feature in the 1960s.

In terms of the flow-of-funds equation the authorities relied during the period 1951–55 on the manipulation of the bank lending term, but from 1955 they relied primarily on adjustment of the PSBR term through tax changes. The failure to look at economic policy as a whole – that is, at all four parts of the equation simultaneously – handicapped policy considerably.

The 'stop' period of the mid-1950s cycle lasted from 1956 to 1958, as Budgets remained relatively neutral or mildly contractionary in demand management terms, until the Budgets of 1958 and 1959 reversed the policy and once again expanded demand. The result was the familiar, repeated pattern: accelerating real GDP growth – 4.6 per cent and 5.3 per cent in 1959 and 1960 respectively – combined with declining unemployment and ending in overexpansion with a current account deficit in 1960, rising inflation and contractionary Budget measures. In prospect was another sterling cirsis, and the neutral Budget of Spring 1961 had to be followed by a July package aimed primarily at the balance of payments and at defending the value of sterling. As well as fiscal contraction and a rise in the Bank Rate to 7 per cent, there was a public sector incomes policy – a 'pay pause' and, for the first time, a call for special deposits.

By the beginning of the 1960s it had become apparent that the management of demand alone was not sufficient to achieve all macroeconomic objectives simultaneously, and the authorities began to look for alternatives to supplement their fiscal instruments. On the one hand, there was an experiment with supply-side policies with a shift to planning, first with the establishment of the National Economic Development Council (NEDC) and later with Labour's Department of Economic Affairs and its National Plan. Attempts were made to control inflationary pressure through various prices and incomes policies, monitored from 1964–70 by the National Board for Prices and Incomes (NBPI). Overall, the period 1964 to 1970 was, however, mostly dominated by the balance of payments and the attempt to maintain the exchange rate (Blackaby, 1978).

The first Wilson government

On its accession to office Harold Wilson's first government faced what appeared at the time to be a major current account deficit (but one which subsequently has been shown not to have been so bad) and initiated deflationary measures. Further restrictive action was taken in response to the three successive sterling crises (November 1964, July 1965 and July 1966) that ultimately led to the 1967 devaluation. The packages comprised the conventional adjustments: rises in the Bank Rate and intervention in the currency markets to protect sterling, and on the domestic side the tightening of controls on HP and bank lending and the raising of tax rates via the 'Regulator', a device to raise indirect taxes without a separate Finance Act.

When in November 1967 **devaluation** finally came it was accompanied by, and followed soon after by, further deflation as the current account failed to respond in the way the government had expected and as set out in the Letter of Intent to the IMF in November 1967. Moreover, speculative pressures on sterling continued. 1968 witnessed the most deflationary Budget since the War, which included significant cuts in public spending.

It was backed up with additional monetary tightening throughout the year. This was mainly achieved by 'import deposits' – a requirement to lodge 50 per cent of the cost of imports with the Bank of England for six months as a condition of importing goods into the UK. This acted as a fixed loan to the government. The government was now acting on three of the flow-of-funds items – PSBR via budgetary policy, bank lending via ceilings and private lending to the government via import deposits. Compared to the 1950s and earlier 1960s the use of policy instruments was more co-ordinated and hence more successful.

The restrictive policy stance continued into 1969 when the current account finally responded and moved into surplus. The costs of the balance of payments improvement were, however, in terms of rising unemployment (2.4 per cent in 1969) and the slowing down in the growth of output to 2 per cent in 1969 and 1.7 per cent in 1970. It is evident that by the end of the period the focus of demand management policies had shifted from maintaining internal to external balance although, by comparison with previous years, unemployment, at over 500,000, was high. However, the authorities had been successful in achieving their objective after the half-hearted drift of the 1960s, largely because of their improved co-ordination of economic policy.

The 1970s

The 1970s were a time of major and repeated crises in the UK economy. During this period macroeconomic policy lurched from overexpansion to crisis management as the governments of Heath, Wilson and Callaghan attempted to cope with major developments, both within the UK and in the world economy. In common with the latter part of the 1960s demand management alone proved insufficient, and during much of the period governments attempted to control wage inflationary pressures by the use of income policies, either as voluntary agreements or imposed by statute. Furthermore, in the desire to release economic policy from the constraint of maintaining the value of sterling, it was allowed to float from 1972 although this owed much to the developments in international monetary relations (see **pp. 158–60**).

The period can be usefully divided into a number of sub-periods, although the division is somewhat arbitrary:

- **1970–71:** A short-lived market experiment, with no active demand management policy
- **1971– early 1974:** An initial period of overexpansion ending in the chaos of a wage–price spiral, a major external shock to the economy and 'stagflation' (often referred to as Barberism after the then Chancellor)
- **early 1974– mid-1975:** A time without major policy initiatives during a major crisis as the new Labour government consolidated on re-election
- **mid-1975–77:** Labour's deflationist period
- **1977–79:** A time of misjudgement on major policy issues.

The Heath government

Table 9.1 provides a summary of the economic performance over the decade. In the first year of the 1970–74 Conservative government there were no major policy initiatives in managing the economy: policy was primarily aimed at reducing the involvement of government in economic life. This followed the 'Selsdon' philosophy announced by Edward Heath during the Conservatives' last months in opposition. On the other hand, subsequent action would seem to imply that the government had by no means given up its commitment to maintaining high employment. As output stagnated and unemployment rose towards the 1 million mark, the government's policy shifted from neutral to expansionary, culminating in the infamous Barber Budget in the spring of 1972 and the Barber boom that followed.

The 1972 Budget was designed to raise the annual rate of growth of output to 5 per cent over the ensuing 18 months, and its main measures were significant tax reductions (achieved by raising allowances and cutting purchase tax) since they were faster acting than increases in public expenditure. They were also more in line with the government's philosophy. In addition, the Chancellor announced that monetary growth was to be allowed to accelerate in order to accommodate this expansion, and that an unrealistic exchange rate would not be maintained if it meant unacceptable distortion to the domestic economy. This was the first public indication that the government might permit the exchange rate to fall if the current account of the balance of payments constrained the growth of the economy.

This Budget has often been presented as a U-turn in policy: it is probably truer to say that the U-turn best describes the shift in the government's attitude to intervention at the microeconomic level – notably that of supporting lame ducks. It also marks the embarkation on a prices and incomes policy as a solution to the growing inflation problem.

This 'dash for growth' Budget was almost certainly misconceived. Not only had fiscal policy become steadily reflationary from mid-1971, but output had begun to rise, unemployment was expected to stabilise by the end of the year and significant underlying inflationary pressure was building up in the economy. In 1970 the inflation rate had been 6.3 per cent but by the end of 1971 it had accelerated to 9.4 per cent. More importantly, monetary policy had become expansionary from the early summer of 1971. The abolition of direct controls on bank lending under the new monetary control framework ('Competition and Credit Control') had led to a surge in bank lending, partly the result of reintermediation – that is, the re-entry into the banking system of lending that had been forced out of the officially regulated banking sector by the operation of credit ceilings – and partly as a result of the fact that banks were now able to satisfy previously frustrated demand for credit. The latter added directly to demand, which was stoked further by the lowering of interest rates and the ending of the agreement by which banks collectively fixed interest rates on deposits which restricted their ability to bid competitively for funds in order to finance lending.

Credit was made even more attractive by the reintroduction of the relief on loan interest in the 1972 Budget. In the event, the money supply expanded wildly out of control, growing by 60 per cent in 1972 and 1973 and by 80 per cent from 1971 to 1973.

The effects of such monetary laxity soon became apparent in the inflation figures. One of the major routes for the transmission of the inflationary effects came through the **property market** where there was an enormous speculative bubble. Between 1970 and 1973, commercial property prices almost tripled and house prices rose by an annual average of 34 per cent in 1972 and 1973. There are numerous channels through which house price inflation may be linked to more general inflation, including the wealth effects on consumption or the cost and wage inflation impact of higher property prices (Gowland, 1984, pp. 127–31). For a monetarist the experience of the period provided an almost perfect fit for the proposition that an excessive expansion in the money supply would result in accelerating inflation after a lag of about 18 months to two years.

Further inflationary twists were added by a world-wide commodity price boom and the depreciation of sterling after it had been floated in 1972. Indeed, as in previous reflations there followed the characteristic sterling crises (in June 1972 and March 1973) and a marked worsening of the current account which went into deficit in 1973 and even more so in 1974. As if these developments were not sufficient, the 1973/74 oil crisis administered a severe supply-side shock to an already fragile economy. Whatever interpretation is put on the period – whether monetarist or Keynesian – such developments made the appearance of stagflation almost inevitable.

The authorities' response was slow in coming and may be seen as a classic case of 'too little too late' and of a misalignment of instruments and objectives. Attempts were made to hold back wage pressure by the use of a statutory prices and incomes policy (in three stages) whilst demand was kept at a level sufficient to reduce unemployment. By the end of 1973 interest rates had been raised significantly, and in December of that year 'Competition and Credit Control' was abandoned, being replaced by a new form of direct control on bank liabilities called supplementary special deposits (the 'corset'). Monetary growth did indeed fall as bank lending was reduced under the new regime, but the growth in demand was enough to raise output by 5.2 per cent in 1973 and to cut unemployment to 2.6 per cent – at the cost of raising inflation to 10 per cent at an annual rate by the end of the year. In early 1974 the government, now facing a rapidly deteriorating economic climate, with a three-day week and a second miners' strike, panicked, called an early election and got thrown out of office for its pains.

Labour back in power

Mindful perhaps of its tenuous position and the rapidly contracting economy during the year, the subsequent minority Labour government took no major deflationary measure in 1974 despite four Budgets. Indeed, public spending rose by 28.3 per cent in 1974 and by 31.4 per cent in 1975: in cash terms it was out of control. The PSBR also soared to over £10 bn in 1975 (11 per cent of GDP) although its effect on monetary growth was offset by falling bank lending and a large negative overseas impact – the result of the sizeable balance of payments deficit. The £M$_3$ measure of the money supply rose by only 10.4 per cent in 1974 and by 6.8 per cent in 1975.

In mid-1975 the government finally produced a coherent policy reponse to the economic crisis, and this date marks a watershed in postwar macroeconomic management. There are a number of main strands to consider. In the first place, **inflation** became the primary policy objective. As a consequence, the commitment to full employment, to be achieved by manipulating aggregate demand, was dropped. This is best summed up in the Prime Minister's (James Callaghan) famous speech to the Labour Party Conference in 1976 when he said:

> We used to think that you could just spend your way out of a recession, and increase employment, by cutting taxes and boosting government spending. I tell you in all candour that that option no longer exists, and that in so far as it ever did exist, it worked by injecting inflation into the economy.

Secondly, the principal instrument of policy was **incomes restraint** in the form of a notionally voluntary agreement with the trades unions – the Social Contract. Thirdly, a major role in the attack on inflation was assigned to **financial policy**, specifically controlling and targetting the money

supply and manipulating the PSBR to this end.

Even if the adoption of a money supply policy did not represent a conversion to monetarism as such, it did indicate a recognition of the importance of the money supply in the inflationary process, possibly as a way of validating inflationary pressure. There are alternative justifications for the adoption of money supply targets. One is that, **ceteris paribus**, a money supply target implied a given PSBR and thus a given stance on public spending and taxation. Public expenditure, as a consequence, became easier to control. Another is that such targets were required to convince 'monetarist' financial markets of the government's resolve to combat inflation. A final possibility is that the targets were foisted on the UK by the IMF in 1976 after the collapse of sterling. This third explanation can be rejected as the government had shifted towards targetting before IMF involvement in the economy whereas to other two might well have been accepted by the authorities (Gowland, 1984, pp. 154–6). Moreover the IMF put the emphasis upon DCE rather than money.

Another important factor at that time which requires emphasis concerns the use of the PSBR as a means of controlling the money supply. This meant that fiscal and monetary policy became inextricably linked as part of the government's financial policy, and was a major change from the earlier demand management approach of the 1950s and 1960s when fiscal and monetary policy were seen as independent instruments with the former as the senior partner. Indeed, it was something of a role reversal. The authorities now used the flow-of-funds approach to guide policy with instruments aimed at each component. Macroeconomic or monetary policy had thus changed over twenty years from a naive Keynesian analysis of injections and withdrawals to a financial analysis of flow of funds and an emphasis upon the money supply as a summary indicator of this.

The deflationist period

The first positive deflationary action was taken in the April Budget of 1975. There followed a pay freeze under a renegotiated Social Contract and

Table 9.2 *Monetary targets and outcomes, 1976–79*

Target set	Period covered	Aggregate	Target range %	Out-turn %
December 1976	Financial year 1976/77	£M₃	9–13	7.7
March 1977	Financial Year 1977/78	£M₃	9–13	15.5
April 1978	Financial Year 1978/79	£M₃	8–12	10.8
November 1978	12 Months to October 1979	£M₃	8–12	13.1

Source: Bank of England.

further rounds of public expenditure cuts throughout 1976. In addition, cash limits were introduced to control the growth of public spending. On the monetary side, the first official money supply target was announced (July 1975) and there was a tightening of monetary policy, with rises in the MLR and the re-introduction of the supplementary special deposits scheme, particularly during 1976 as sterling began to slide in the foreign exchange markets. Following the fall in sterling to an all-time low against the dollar in October 1976 – a crisis that resulted from a mismanaged attempt to float the currency down to a more competitive level – and negotiations with the IMF for a loan, the Chancellor announced a further package of spending cuts along with targets for both £M₃ and DCE.

There can be little doubt that these policies achieved their objectives, at least over the short term. £M₃ growth was well within its target range for 1976/77 as shown in **Table 9.2** and DCE was some 45 per cent below its target level in the same period. Public spending growth fell to 5.8 per cent in 1977 and the PSBR was reduced to 4.7 per cent of GDP in the same year, the latter being significantly less than its forecast levels in the financial years 1976/77 and 1977/78. By mid-1978 inflation had fallen to 8 per cent at an annual rate, although unemployment remained intractably high despite the moderate growth of GDP in 1976 and 1977.

However, from late 1977 policy had become markedly more expansionary as monetary policy eased and public spending and the PSBR rose. This was largely a paradoxical by-product of the IMF agreement. The government, equipped with the

IMF seal of approval, was less constrained and indeed was pressed by the IMF to reflate. £M₃ also overshot its target range. This combination of circumstances produced a mini pre-election boom in 1978, but this was accompanied by consequent pressure on the housing market, inflation and the government's incomes policy. Indeed, it occurred just as the government was tightening that incomes policy, setting a 5 per cent guideline for settlements in the 1978/79 pay round. This was rather like trying to hold the lid on a saucepan whilst turning up the heat, albeit accidentally. Not only did the lid come off wages, which rose rapidly after the notorious 17 per cent Ford settlement in November 1978, but the government also got embroiled in the 'Winter of Discontent' which preceded its electoral defeat in May 1979. As in 1971–73, monetary expansion led to a house price explosion, a balance of payments problem and finally to rapid inflation.

One final aspect of policy of some importance at this time was the approach to the exchange rate, that is the means of influencing the fourth flow-of-funds item. At first, in 1972, the exchange rate was floated in the hope tht this would reduce the balance of payments constraint on expansion, but it subsequently became an **instrument** of demand management policy. As has been noted (Allsop and Mayes, 1985), it was argued by some economists, notably Kaldor, that the exchange rate could be depreciated in a controlled way, inducing expansion from the export sector and from import substitution. This is the well known 'export-led growth' policy. There would, therefore, be no need to compromise on the tight stance of domestic policy required to combat inflation. The experiment with this policy effectively came to an end with the sterling crisis in 1976: a managed depreciation was not quite so easy to accomplish in practice. Moreover, it was increasingly realised that the cost inflationary impact of a lower exchange rate would be faster working and more than outweigh the trade benefits of a lower exchange rate.

The 1980s: the Thatcher years

During the years since 1979 discussion of economic policy in Britain has been dominated by 'Thatcherism', an economic doctrine that is wider in scope than the macroeconomy but which has particular relevance to it. Whilst demand management is consistent with either more or less government involvement in economic life, and hence was acceptable to both Labour and Conservative governments of the 1950s and 1960s, Thatcherism is consistent only with less involvement. Indeed, the reduction of government activity – or, more graphically, 'rolling back the frontiers of the state' – is one of the central tenets of this economic outlook.

It should be recognised that the **ultimate** objectives of government policy in the 1980s have not changed: that is, the aim of achieving a high growth in living standards combined with stable prices. What is distinctive are the methods by which these are to be achieved and the costs the government, and implicitly the British electorate, are prepared to accept in their pursuit.

The principal features of the approach can be identified as follows:

1. **The necessity of eradicating inflation** is of fundamental importance, not only for its own sake but because of its effects on the level of **unemployment**. In contrast to the more pragmatic policies of Denis Healey, who saw the abandonment of demand-managed full employment, and the need for higher unemployment, as a requirement for bringing inflation under control, the major proposition of Thatcherism

is that inflation has to be reduced as it is a major **cause** of rising unemployment. Thus, instead of a conventional Phillips Curve trade-off, or even a monetarist vertical long-run Phillips Curve, the government believes in an **upward sloping one**. Traditional demand management is rejected since it can have no beneficial long-term effect on the economy.

2. The emphasis of macroeconomic policy is to provide a **stable non-inflationary framework** within which the private sector of the economy can flourish. The means to this end is to exercise control over the growth in the money supply – the government, at least in its early years, was self-proclaimed monetarist. Furthermore, the policy is to be operated over the medium and long term. This ties in closely with the view, accepted by the government, that manipulation of policy for short-term stabilisation will have unpredictable and possibly destabilising effects on the economy.

3. **Free market supply-side policies** constitute the main weapons for tackling unemployment and raising the rate of growth of output. These include tax cuts to boost incentives, privatisation and deregulation to extract the State and its agencies from the economy, and especially a series of reforms in the labour market which have removed a number of trade union privileges (see Chapter 1). The aim of the last was both political and economic, the economic aim being to increase labour market flexibility. It is also interesting to note that the government is at pains to stress that the unions can not only be held responsible for a significant part of the high unemployment – the 'pricing themselves out of a job' view – but also can increase the unemployment costs of the adjustment to a low inflation rate. Encouraging labour market flexibility is preferred to direct intervention via an incomes policy on two grounds. In the first place, such policies interfere with market forces. Secondly, it is maintained tht the relaxation of the policy usually resulted in a 'catching-up' period, undoing any benefits that might have been produced during the time income restraint was in operation.

The Medium-Term Financial Strategy (MTFS)

The specific details of the government's macroeconomic policy intentions were enshrined in the MTFS, first published with the 1980 Budget and detailed in **Table 9.3**. The strategy set out a declining target for $£M_3$ over the subsequent four years as the principal mechanism for reducing inflation.

The importance of the declining target lay not only in the government's attachment to a monetarist view of the inflation process but also for the supposed effects of such targets on inflation expectations. It was believed that by committing the government to the creation of a stable environment over the medium term, **wage and price expectations could be reduced**. The prime benefit was that the unemployment costs of the transition to a low inflation economy could be cut significantly.

Monetary policy was thus the dominant weapon in the government's array of macroeconomic policy instruments. Particular reliance was placed on the use of interest rates, the PSBR and debt sales to contain monetary growth. Direct controls were rejected on the grounds of their distortionary impact on the banking sector; they reduced the efficiency of the financial institutions and produced disintermediation (see **p. 100**).

The use of the PSBR as an instrument of monetary control continued the subordination of fiscal to monetary policy. The government aimed to decrease the PSBR because of its direct impact on the growth of $£M_3$ and also because of the effect of financing a high PSBR on interest rates – the so-called 'crowding out' effect. As a result the MTFS and other government policy statements emphasised the need for consistency between the PSBR and monetary targets, and a series of projections (not targets) for the PSBR was announced in 1980 as shown in **Table 9.3**. It is worth emphasising that the achievement of a stable financial policy, summarised in the $£M_3$ target, required a reduction in the PSBR if interest rates were to be prevented from rising to an excessive level because of the need to finance the deficit from debt sales.

This is evident from the flow-of-funds money supply counterpart equation.

For all the faults in its operation, the benefits of the principles of such an approach should be clear: it does attempt to produce harmonisation of the stance of macroeconomic policy which can be contrasted with the tight monetary but loose fiscal policy stance of the Reagan era in the USA. In practice however, the UK experience was the converse, combining a loose monetary with a tight fiscal policy. Another important feature of the government's policy as initially conceived was the eschewal of an exchange rate policy and the commitment to a market-determined, floating exchange rate. In the early years, at least, it was fortuitous that the commitment came at a time of a rising £; it was to provide the main mechanism through which monetary policy deflated the economy in 1979–81 and set the conditions for falling inflation rates. As the exchange rate environment changed so did the government's policy, shifting increasingly towards a managed exchange rate by the mid-1980s. Indeed, such was Mrs Thatcher's committment to this that she became an adamant opponent of membership of the EMS. She wished to retain the freedom to depreciate if unemployment rose or to appreciate in order to combat inflation. Broadly speaking, such were the intentions of policy – to provide a non-inflationary environment in which an increasing market economy would flourish. However, as is the case with all grand economic policy designs, the principles are more clear-cut than their application. The practice of the policy has, in fact, been laced with a good deal of pragmatism, if not some degree of opportunism as the government has had to respond to changing circumstances and failure, in many cases, to meet the intermediate policy targets that had been set as shown in **Table 9.3**. Such flexibility should not necessarily be held against the government: in an ever-changing world economic policy clearly must adapt and targets set at one time may not be relevant at another. Examples of shifts in emphasis in policy include the move from a single money supply target to multiple targets, and their subsequent abandonment. Another is the adoption of an exchange rate target which later had to be revised upwards as domestic

Table 9.3   Medium Term Financial Strategy: target ranges[1] and outcomes (%)

	1979/80	1980/81	1981/82	1982/83	1983/84	1984/85	1985/86	1986/87	1987/1988	1988/89	1989/90	1990/91	1991/92	1992/93
Money Supply: M_0 (% change)														
March 1984	*	*	*	*	*	4–8	3–7[6]	2–6[6]	1–5[6]	0–4[6]	*	*	*	*
March 1985	*	*	*	*	*	*	3–7	2–6	1–5[6]	0–4[6]	*	*	*	*
March 1986	*	*	*	*	*	*	*	2–6	2–6	1–5[6]	1–5[6]	*	*	*
March 1987	*	*	*	*	*	*	*	*	2–6	1–5	1–5	0–4	*	*
March 1988	*	*	*	*	*	*	*	*	*	1–5	1–5	0–4	0–4	*
March 1989	*	*	*	*	*	*	*	*	*	*	1–5	0–4	0–4	–3–3
Outcome[5]	10	6½	0	3½	6¼	5½	3½	4	5	7	*	*	*	*
Money Supply: M_1 (% change)														
March 1982	*	*	*	8–12	7–11	*	*	*	*	*	*	*	*	*
March 1983	*	*	*	*	7–11	*	*	*	*	*	*	*	*	*
Outcome	*	*	*	11	11	*	*	*	*	*	*	*	*	*
Money Supply: £M_3														
June 1979[2]	7–11	*	*	*	*	*	*	*	*	*	*	*	*	*
March 1980	*	7–11	6–10	5–9	4–8	*	*	*	*	*	*	*	*	*
March 1981	*	*	6–10	5–9[6]	4–8[6]	*	*	*	*	*	*	*	*	*
March 1982	*	*	*	8–12	7–11	6–10	*	*	*	*	*	*	*	*
March 1983	*	*	*	*	7–11	6–10	5–9	*	*	*	*	*	*	*
March 1984	*	*	*	*	*	6–10	5–9[6]	4–8[6]	*	*	*	*	*	*
March 1985[3]	*	*	*	*	*	*	5–9	4–8[6]	3–7[6]	2–6[6]	*	*	*	*
March 1986	*	*	*	*	*	*	*	11–15	3–7[6]	2–6[6]	*	*	*	*
Outcome[5]	16¼	19½	12¾	10	9¾	9½	14¾	*	*	*	*	*	*	*
Money Supply: PSL_2 (% change)														
March 1982	*	*	*	8–12	7–11	*	*	*	*	*	*	*	*	*
March 1983	*	*	*	*	7–11	*	*	*	*	*	*	*	*	*
Outcome	*	*	*	9	12¼	*	*	*	*	*	*	*	*	*

PSBR (% of GDP)														
June 1979	4½	*	*	*	*	*	*	*	*	*	*	*	*	*
March 1980	4¾	3¾	3	2¼	1½	*	*	*	*	*	*	*	*	*
March 1981	5	6	4¼	3¼	2	*	*	*	*	*	*	*	*	*
March 1982	*	5¾	4¼	3½	2¾	2	*	*	*	*	*	*	*	*
March 1983	*	*	3½	2¾	2¾	2½	2	*	*	*	*	*	*	*
March 1984	*	*	*	3⅓	3¼	2¼	2	2	1¾	1¾	*	*	*	*
March 1985	*	*	*	*	3¼	3¼	2	2	1¾	1¾	*	*	*	*
March 1986	*	*	*	*	*	3	2	1¾	1¾	1½	1½	*	*	*
March 1987	*	*	*	*	*	*	1½	1	1	1	1	1	*	*
March 1988	*	*	*	*	*	*	*	1	−¾	−¾	0	0	*	*
March 1989	*	*	*	*	*	*	*	*	−¾	−3	−2¾	−1¾	−1	−½
Outcome	4¾	5½	3½	3¼	3¼	3	1½	1	−¾	−3	*	*	*	*
Money GDP (% change)														
March 1985	*	*	*	*	7¾	6¾ (8¼)[4]	8½ (7)[4]	6¾	5¾	5	*	*	*	*
March 1986	*	*	*	*	*	*	9½ (8¼)[4]	6¾	6½	6	5½	*	*	*
March 1987	*	*	*	*	*	*	*	6	7½	6½	6	*	*	*
March 1988	*	*	*	*	*	*	*	*	*	7½	6½	6	5½	*
March 1989	*	*	*	*	*	*	*	*	*	11	7¾	6	6	5½

Notes:
[1] Targets are set for a 14 month period commencing in February.
[2] Old definition including public sector deposits.
[3] New definition excluding public sector deposits.
[4] Adjusted for coal strike.
[5] Data taken from source cited. Slightly different figures are cited elsewhere. Outcomes relate to a 12-month period commencing in February.
[6] 'Illustrative range'.
Source: *Financial Statement and Budget Report*, 'Red Book', for each year, of which the most recent is that for 1989–90 HC 235 (March 1989).

and external pressures clashed. A further one is the use of asset sales as a means of enabling the government simultaneously to reduce the PSBR and to cut personal tax rates.

Despite these changes the following quotation from the ex-Chancellor signifies that the broad thrust of the government's policy has remained remarkably similar over a decade. Thus:

> The Government's job, in short, is to deal with the *financial* framework, which it *can* influence, rather than the activities of businesses and individuals within that framework ... I would maintain that provided the overall fiscal, monetary and exchange rate framework is sound, and markets are working effectively, the results of the private sector's economic activity should not normally be something in which it is sensible for Government to interfere (Lawson, 1988, p. 16).

The policy in action

The first Budget

The operation of policy and the fortunes of the economy can be divided for convenience into a number of phases:

- **1979–81:** **A policy-induced recession** as the government set up its anti-inflation strategy
- **1982–85:** A period during which the authorities **abandoned a single monetary target** and experimented with multiple ones; as the inflation rate fell the policy stance eased, and the economy recovered slowly but steadily
- **November 1985– Summer 1988:** A time when the focus of monetary policy switched to the **exchange rate**; policy was relaxed and the boom in the economy intensified
- **Summer 1988 onwards:** A **tightening of policy** as the government attempted to deal with the effects of the boom.

Table 9.4 summarises the performance of the economy at this time.

Table 9.4 *The performance of the economy, 1979–88*

	1979–88	1979–83	1984–88
Real GDP growth (average % p.a.)	2.3	1	3.5
Inflation (average % p.a.)	8	11.2	4.7
Unemployment (average % of labour force)	9.3	8.4	10.3

Source: Economic Trends, Annual Supplement 1989.

Committed to an anti-inflationary strategy from the outset, the government began to tighten both fiscal and monetary policy almost immediately after taking office. The first Budget, in June 1979, saw the announcement of some £1.5 bn cuts in public expenditure and a planned fall in the PSBR from £9.2 bn to £8.2 bn over the year, reducing it from 5.5 per cent to 4.5 per cent of GDP. On the monetary side the MLR was raised by 2 per cent to 14 per cent and the £M_3 target range of 8–10 per cent was adjusted to 7–11 per cent, although this was for the 10-month period to April 1980. For the time being the direct controls on the banking system remained in place. More controversially, there was a major switch in **taxation policy**: income tax rates were reduced (the basic rate from 33 to 30 per cent and the top rate from 86 to 60 per cent) and VAT rates were raised to a uniform 15 per cent. At a time when inflation was rising, from 8.1 per cent in the fourth quarter in 1978 to 10.6 per cent by the second quarter of 1979, the policy can be seen as perverse since it added to the RPI, and thus to inflationary expectations. Some writers have dismissed such a view as confusing a once-and-for-all rise in prices with a persistent increase in the general price level. In the event inflation continued to accelerate, reaching a peak of almost 22 per cent by mid-1980. This was aided by the government's commitment to meeting in full the Clegg Committee pay awards, established in the closing months of the Labour government. The removal of subsidies to, and of price controls on, the nationalised industries was pursued vigorously. Nationalised industry prices rose by 25 per cent in 1980, by 19 per cent in 1981 and by 58 per cent between 1980 and 1982. This increased cost inflation but reduced demand inflation.

Further tightening occurred during 1979 with the MLR being raised to 17 per cent as the government attempted to cope with a policy that seemed to be going awry. By the end of the third quarter £M$_3$ was growing at an annual rate of 14 per cent, well outside its target range, and the PSBR appeared to be on course for a major overshoot. It was only the abolition of exchange controls in July which prevented the money supply from rising completely out of control: the external impact in the third quarter of 1979 was £1.7 bn alone.

Introducing the MTFS

The introduction of the MTFS in the Budget of 1980 saw the reaffirmation of the government's principal objective of attacking inflation by reducing the rate of growth of £M$_3$. A declining target range for this broad money aggregate was announced (**Table 9.3**). The tightening of fiscal policy was reflected in a projected PSBR of £8.5 bn to be achieved through planned cuts in public spending and increases in taxation – the raising of excise duties and the abolition of the reduced income tax band of 25 per cent. There was also a projected decrease in the PSBR as a percentage of GDP over the next four years to 1.5 per cent of GDP (**Table 9.3**). The apparent monetary squeeze continued.

The MLR was maintained at an historically high level in nominal terms (although it was nevertheless negative in real terms) and by the end of 1980 stood at 14 per cent, having been reduced to 16 per cent in July and to 14 per cent in November. The general trend of interest rates can be seen in **Figure 9.2**. The exchange rate appreciated sharply and M$_1$, a narrow money aggregate, slowed.

During 1980 it became clear that the economy had moved into a major downturn as output contracted rapidly and unemployment began to mount, rising to 1.7 million by the end of the year. It was to be the severest recession of the postwar period, reaching its depth in output terms sometime in the second quarter of 1981 with GDP 7.5 per cent below its previous peak two years earlier. Manufacturing output contracted by nearly 9 per cent in 1980 alone.

The most cogent explanation of the severity of the recession is that it was the effect of the extremely tight monetary policy on the exchange rate that produced such an intense squeeze on UK industry. Not only did sterling rise to over $2.40 in 1980, but the Exchange Rate Index in the second quarter of 1981 was also over 17 per cent above the level it had been two years before. (see **p. 000**). Coupled with the surge in domestic prices and costs, the real exchange rate was even higher. Domestic producers were caught between rising costs and interest rates at home and a major loss of competitiveness abroad. Exports held up surprisingly well; it was the **import-competing sector** that bore the brunt of the adjustment.

Other explanations of the contraction include the impact of oil on the exchange rate and the effect of the second oil price shock with the ensuing world-wide downturn in economic activity. Whilst these added to the UK's problems, some estimates suggest that North Sea oil contributed 8–12 per cent of the real appreciation whilst others suggest much less. As regards the international recession, the slowdown occurred rather later, in 1980/81, than the downturn in activity in the UK.

It was against such a background that the government tightened its fiscal policy further in the 1981 Budget. This was achieved primarily through significant rises in taxation, principally increases in excise duty and the non-indexation of income tax allowances. The objective was clearly to bring the PSBR and money supply closer into line with the MTFS plans after they had increased beyond their anticipated levels and target ranges respectively in 1980/81. The PSBR overshot by about £5 bn and £M$_3$ grew at 19 per cent. It was surprising to most commentators, however, that the government was apparently ignoring the

Figure 9.2   *Bank base rates, 1977–89*

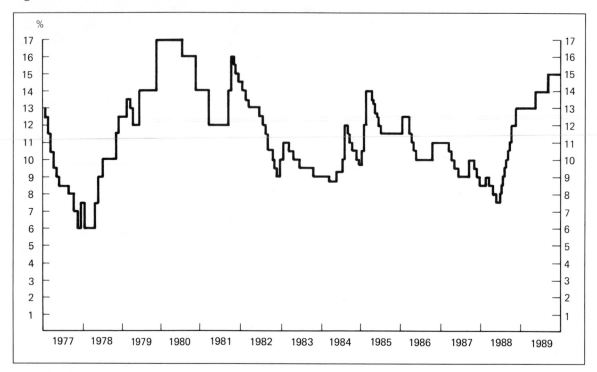

Source: Barclays Economic Review

increasing evidence of the stringency of policy. In the first place, there was the fact that the PSBR would be expected to rise as the economy moved into recession. Secondly, there was the obvious unreliability of £M$_3$, following the ending of the Corset, the 'distress' borrowing by UK businesses and the high interest rates encouraging a shift from non-interest to interest-bearing accounts. The reason why the government chose to maintain such a policy stance can perhaps best be explained by the desire to retain the credibility of its anti-inflation commitment. Undoubtedly the 1981 Budget was an act of considerable political and economic courage, and almost certainly it paved the way for the successes of subsequent years.

Towards the end of 1981 economic activity reached a lower turning point and there were some signs of an incipient recovery in output despite the fact that unemployment was rising inexorably to over 2.5 million by the end of the year. The anti-inflationary policy was also beginning to show its first fruits as the annual rate fell to 12 per cent.

From this time a number of changes in policy became apparent. One was the beginning of the disillusionment with £M$_3$ as the proximate target for economic policy. In the 1982 Budget target ranges were set for M$_1$ and a broader aggregate PSL$_2$ (now M$_5$). There was also an indication that some account would be taken of the exchange rate in the operation of monetary policy. Another change was a switch in emphasis to nominal (money) GDP as the target for economic policy, with projections set for four years ahead as part of the MTFS. The basis of the GDP target was that if inflation showed signs of reaccelerating it would not be accommodated: policy would be adjusted to keep money GDP in the target range, and output would decline until price inflation fell.

Emerging from recession

A further development was that the general stance of policy was eased slightly and progressively

Table 9.5 The Lawson boom – selected indicators, 1985–88

	Real GDP growth % pa[1]	Inflation (% pa)	Average earnings (%) pa	Real consumers' expenditure (%)	Consumer credit (%)	M_3 (% pa)	Current balance £ mn
1986 I	2.0	5.0	8.3	4.5	43.0	16.9	763
II	2.4	2.9	8.1	6.6	50.0	18.9	138
III	3.5	2.7	7.4	5.2	43.1	19.1	−856
IV	3.8	3.5	7.9	5.2	36.9	19.1	−898
1987 I	4.3	3.8	7.0	4.5	12.4	19.7	−872
II	4.4	4.2	7.5	4.2	20.1	19.8	−388
III	5.1	4.2	7.7	5.4	21.2	20.2	−1205
IV	5.1	3.8	8.4	6.4	29.2	22.8	−1968
1988 I	5.7	3.4	8.9	6.8	30.4	21.0	−2835
II	5.0	4.3	8.2	5.4	25.0	20.1	−2661
III	4.3*	5.6	8.7	6.0*	27.9	22.5	−3724
IV	3.8*	6.5	—	5.5*	18.4	20.3	−5051

Notes:
*Estimates.
[1] All % changes are year on year.
Source: Economic Trends, Annual Supplement 1989; Bank of England Quarterly Bulletin (February 1989); National Institute Economic Review, various issues.

over the next two years. The emphasis on reducing the PSBR continued as it repeatedly overshot its original target level set in 1980, but fiscal policy did ease a little. In the 1983 Budget income tax thresholds were raised by 14 per cent, well above the 5.5 per cent inflation rate and the National Insurance surcharge was cut. These measures were seen as mildly reflationary in some quarters, although the Chancellor of the time, Sir Geoffrey Howe, reemphasised that such cuts were not part of a scheme of demand management. The cynic, however, might point to the election that was called in June of that year and the additional spending cuts introduced in the Autumn. On the other hand, most indicators of the fiscal stance show that it was still tight; the cyclically adjusted public sector balance suggested that there was a real structural budget surplus (Dornbusch and Layard, 1987, p. 37).

The main easing came through the monetary side, the money supply targets notwithstanding. By the Autumn of 1982 interest rates, as measured by short-term money market rates, had fallen to 9 per cent (**Figure 9.2**) and despite a sharp increase in the Winter of 1982/83 to prevent too fast a fall in the exchange rate, interest rates remained in the 8–9 per cent range until June 1984. It was this monetary relaxation, and the corresponding fall in the exchange rate, as interest rates rose abroad, which provided some of the stimulus to growth. But the main impetus came from consumers' expenditure. This was boosted by the rise in real incomes as earnings grew faster than prices, a credit boom inspired by deregulation and the effects of falling inflation on the saving ratio via a wealth effect. At the end of 1983 the inflation rate had fallen to 4.5 per cent per annum, and GDP grew by 1.9 per cent in 1982 and 3.7 per cent in 1983.

Under a new Chancellor, Mr Lawson (1983), the monetariest strategy, though not the other elements of Thatcherism, was finally abandoned. The official date is November 1985 when it was announced that £M$_3$ was to be downgraded from a target variable to a monitored one. Since 1987, M$_0$ has been the only targeted monetary aggregate. Monetary policy reverted to influencing the exchange rate; this had been evident for some time

before the official abandonment of monetary targets. In June 1984, for example, the Bank of England signalled a rise in interest rates, which persisted until the Autumn, as sterling fell to 76 per cent of its 1980 level. More dramatic were the events of January 1985. At a time of increasing uncertainty over oil prices, the UK's balance of payments and the government's resolve to maintain its anti-inflation policy – inflation had begun to accelerate during 1984 and the government had shown increasing concern over the serious unemployment problem – sterling fell sharply. At one time it went below the $1.10 level. The government responded by reintroducing the MLR at 12 per cent for a short period and interest rates remained high for most of 1985 (**Figure 9.2**).

The reasons for the shift in monetary policy towards the exchange rate lay in an increasing concern that exchange rate volatility affected adversely the trade performance of UK industry, and an acceptance of the view that exchange rate depreciation was the main mechanism through which inflation was transmitted to the domestic economy. With regard to the latter it was maintained that if the value of sterling could be tied to the currency of a stable, low inflation economy this would provide an 'anchor' for the UK's inflation rate. For this reason the government operated an unofficial exchange rate target of £1 = DM 3, later amended to DM 3.10 and then DM 3.20. It was at this time that the appropriateness of the UK's entry into the EMS's exchange rate mechanism became an issue of increasing topicality.

Just as the concentration on a single internal monetary target in the early years of the government led to an excessively tight monetary policy, so the emphasis on a single external target – the £:DM exchange rate – resulted in an over-relaxation of the monetary stance. The upshot was the 'Lawson Boom' which has exhibited many, though not all, of the marks of previous expansions. It has been likened to the ill-fated 'Barber Boom' 15 years previously. Some details of the boom are given in **Table 9.5**.

Moreover, the public sector has moved into considerable surplus as higher levels of economic activity have increased tax revenues even after privatisation revenues have been accounted for.

Indeed, a reduction in the PSBR, and most recently the objective of balancing the Budget, has been retained as the main relic of the MTFS. On this basis the fiscal position can be said to have remained relatively tight despite the reflationary effects of a series of income tax cuts in the 1986, 1987 and 1988 Budgets. The rise in productivity has also been cited as a significant change from the earlier boom (Minford, 1989). But whilst productivity rose by 19 per cent between 1985 and the third quarter of 1988, the rise in productivity from 1970 up to the third quarter of 1973 was 21 per cent.

Overheating

In many respects the similarities are more striking – the rapid expansion in consumer credit, a house price boom, a surge in consumer spending and the deterioration in the current account are all characteristic symptoms of overheating in the UK economy. If nothing else, they are certainly reminiscent of an earlier age.

By far the most important contributor to the boom has been the continued rise in consumers'

expenditure, whih has grown at an average rate of 6.2 per cent per year between 1985 and 1988, as shown in **Table 9.5**. In particular, the housing market once again provided a graphic indicator of the loosening of money and credit policy. House prices rose at an average of nearly 16 per cent per annum in both 1986 and 1987; by 1988 they had accelerated to 38 per cent. Inflation followed suit. After reaching a low of 2.6 per cent per annum in the third quarter of 1986, rising demand began to feed through to higher inflation figures during 1987 and especially in 1988, rising to 6.5 per cent by the year's end.

The unfolding of events at this time is instructive since it reveals the government's attempt to deal with a major policy dilemma and its abandonment of the pretence that it did not believe in demand management of a sort.

Policy entered a critical phase early in 1988 after interest rates had been cut in the wake of the Stock Exchange collapse of the previous October as shown in **Figure 9.2** and **Table 9.6**, below. Upward pressure on sterling forced further interest rate cuts as the government attempted to hold stirling at its DM3 target. Even after sterling had been 'uncapped' in March 1988, further interest

Table 9.6   *Representative[1] money market interest rates (%)*

	USA	Germany	Japan	UK		USA	Germany	Japan	UK
Annual Averages					Monthly Averages – 1988/89				
1978	8.2	3.7	4.4	9.2	1988 May	7.2	3.5	3.3	8.0
1979	11.2	6.7	5.9	13.7	June	7.5	3.8	3.5	8.9
1980	13.1	9.5	10.9	16.6	July	7.9	4.8	3.7	10.5
1981	15.9	12.1	7.4	13.9	August	8.4	5.3	3.8	11.4
1982	12.3	8.8	6.9	12.3	September	8.2	4.9	3.9	12.1
1983	9.1	5.8	6.4	10.1	October	8.4	5.0	4.0	12.0
1984	10.4	6.0	6.1	10.0	November	8.8	4.8	3.7	12.3
1985	8.1	5.4	6.5	12.2	December	9.3	5.3	4.1	13.1
1986	6.5	4.6	4.8	10.9	1989 January	9.2	5.6	3.9	13.1
1987	6.9	4.0	3.5	9.7	February	9.5	6.3	3.9	13.0
1988	7.7	4.3	3.7	10.3	March	10.1	6.5	4.0	13.0
					April	9.9	6.4	4.1	13.1

Note:
[1] USA – 3 months CD rate; Germany – 3 month interbank; Japan – Call money; UK – 3 month interbank.
Source: Barclays Economic Review (May 1989).

rate reductions were required in order to prevent too fast an appreciation. On the domestic front, however, there were signs of too rapid an expansion. Either the exchange rate target would have to be sacrificed or interest rates would have to fall further, but at the risk of fuelling further domestic demand. By mid-Summer the problem has resolved itself. The evidence of overheating had become incontrovertible as measured by any indicator of the level of economic activity – be it the current account, inflation, consumer credit, average earnings, or the government's sole remaining monetary target M_O. Compared with its target range of 1–5 per cent, M_O grew by 7.7 per cent between June 1987 and June 1988. Interest rates were raised progressively through the Autumn and the exchange rate permitted to rise as the government sought to slow the pace of expansion. Base rates reached 13 per cent in November and mortgage rates followed suit.

Nigel Lawson, the ex-Chancellor, emphasised on numerous occasions (for example, Lawson, 1988) that short-term interest rates are regarded as the only effective instrument of monetary policy and hence the best way of affecting demand. This clearly indicates that demand management, which is the deliberate manipulation of aggregate demand to influence the ultimate objectives of policy, is by no means dead; during much of the past decade it has been actively pursued. What is different is that it has been assigned to the **control of inflation** rather than the regulation of employment as in earlier decades. Furthermore, fiscal policy has ostensibly been used as a supply-side instrument rather than a demand-side one.

There are two sharply contrasting ways of looking at the experience of the UK economy in the ten years since Mrs Thatcher's first Conservative Government was elected. The first is that because of the shake-up that has been administered by the tight anti-inflationary policy of the early years (1979–81), the prudent fiscal policy and the continuing emphasis on free market supply-side measures, the economy has emerged as more robust and flexible. The consequence is that economic growth is now more sustainable. The second, more pessimistic interpretation is that in spite of the recent growth performance, much of the improvement represents a catching-up period after a time of severe recession and the result of the operation of policy in a way rather different from its original conception. Moreover, many of the inherent weaknesses still remain and will resurface given the right conditions.

However, both these two views are too extreme. The period has produced some positive benefits – for example, in the marked improvement in the trend growth of productivity and the competitiveness of the manufacturing sector. On the other hand, such achievements have been obtained at the cost of heavy unemployment and lost output. As is the case with all economic adjustments, the costs have not been shared equally. In addition, there is ample evidence of the resurgence of some of the underlying problems of the UK economy – the current account deterioration, rising inflation and the behaviour of earnings.

The decline of Keynesianism

Self-fulfilling beliefs

In the 1950s the average level of unemployment was about 250,000, only a tenth the level of the 1980s and about one-eighth that of the 1930s. The low level of unemployment was almost universally attributed to Keynesian economic management as economists complacently congratulated themselves as having rid the world of the scourge of unemployment. Any appraisal of economic policy in the 1980s must, therefore, start by asking why the techniques that worked so well in the 1950s were not even tried in the 1980s – and whether, if tried, they would have worked.

Full employment in the 1950s and 1960s was the result of the **private sector's response** to the government policy of the time, not directly of what the governments did. In particular, because the private sector believed in full employment it changed its behaviour and invested more. The critical act of government was to commit itself to a policy of **full employment**. Full employment implied that demand and expenditure (and hence future sales) would remain high. It would thus be profitable to invest to satisfy this demand. Moreover, a belief in full employment boosted such intangible forces as business confidence, and so caused a further rise in investment.

One category of investment does not depend in any way on expectations of future sales. This is housebuilding, which is of especial importance because some studies suggest that it was a major cause of the high levels of employment experienced in the late 1950s — that this was, in Keynesian terms, the injection which kept the economy at a high level of demand. However, the housebuilding boom depended in large part on the enormous personal sector demand for housing which was matched by a willingness to accept long-term mortgage commitments to finance house purchase. Keynesian economists argue plausibly that the belief in full employment was at least a necessary condition for people to be prepared to do this. If someone takes out a mortgage they are committing themselves to making repayments over a period of at least 20 years. No-one would do this if he or she feared that they were likely to lose their job in the near future, nor for that matter would any building societies (which had a monopoly of mortgage lending in the 1950s) lend to him or her. Moreover, house purchasers have to consider the prospects of resale, which depend upon both the state of the economy in general and upon other people's willingness to take out mortgages in particular. Hence, the **belief** in full employment was again one of the causes of extra demand.

These Keynesian arguments can be challenged, but it is generally accepted that they have some force and that belief in the efficiency of activist government policy boosted employment in the 1950s. The reasons for its apparent failure in the 1960s and 1970s are more controversial. Keynesians cite two factors — a decline in the belief in full employment and the adverse consequences of the belief in full employment.

The erosion of belief

Belief in the continuation of full employment, and in particular of the ability of government to maintain it, declined from about 1965 because:

(a) of criticism of the theory of demand management, especially those made by Friedman; this has led some prominent Keynesians (such as Hahn) mischievously and humourously to suggest that such views should be suppressed even if they are right and Keynesianism promoted even if wrong
(b) governments seemed to give less prominence to full employment as a goal of economic policy after 1964 (when the Labour government gave priority to the balance of payments)
(c) as unemployment rose after 1965, faith in the efficiency of full employment policies declined.

The Keynesian account is thus of a **cumulative process**. Full employment would continue only so long as people believed that it would. As faith declined so unemployment rose and faith declined further, and so on *ad infinitum*.

Most Keynesian analysts, however, give much more weight to the adverse effects of a belief in full employment rather than to the decline in the belief itself. In particular, because trade union leaders believed in full employment, they ceased to believe that the threat of unemployment need constrain wage demands. Hence they asked for large-scale wage demands. Employers acceded to these demands — in part because their belief in full employment created the expectation in their minds that they would be able to pass the wage increases on as price increases, and consequent high demand. Hence the belief in full employment led firstly to cost inflation, and so to upward movements of aggregate supply curves, and secondly to employers substituting capital for labour. The premise of activist demand management was that the demand for labour would fluctuate only according to output. This was no longer so. Some Keynesians regarded this as an argument for incomes policy.

What is relevant is that the achievement of full employment depended on a belief that it **could and would be achieved**. This was because investment was much higher as a consequence of the belief in the effectiveness of government policy. Such beliefs, however, also had adverse effects which made the continuation of full employment much harder to achieve — indeed perhaps impossible. In summary, belief that governments could achieve and maintain full employment was self-fulfilling in the 1950s, but problems also arose both because this confidence declined and because of the management and trade union movement's response to its belief in full employment.

It was certainly the case that full employment policies encouraged complacency and inefficient management of firms. Firms expected to sell their products irrespective of quality, design or reliability, so they had no incentive to produce reliable, high quality goods. Hence the two aspects of the 'English disease' arose as a consequence — bad management and aggressive unions which resisted innovation and demanded high wages.

Friedman's critique

The most important omission from the elementary Keynesian theory of demand management is **inflationary expectations**. In essence, the idea underlying this concept is very simple: if economic agents expect inflation, they will change their behaviour such that there will be inflation. Although originally introduced into economic analysis by Friedman, the concept is now central to all economic models whether Keynesian, monetarist, post-Keynesian, New Classical or anything else.

Let us suppose that the government decides to pursue an expansionary policy which can be represented by an outward shift of the aggregate demand curve for the whole economy. Output will rise, and so will inflation. In the Keynesian model this is the end of the story, whereas Friedman argues:

1. that the higher rate of inflation will generate higher expectations as to the future rate of inflation
2. that this will cause the aggregate supply (AS) curve to shift up and to the left
3. that ultimately the AS curve will come to rest such that output falls to its original level and inflation is ongoing at the rate determined by the point of intersection of aggregate demand and aggregate supply.

If Friedman is right, then obviously activist demand management will work in the short run but not in the long run. However, the reader may very well ask to pertinent questions, namely

- Why does a rise in inflationary expectations cause the AS curve to shift upwards?
- Why is this shift exactly enough such that output reverts to its original level?

The answer to the first question is most easily answered by considering underlying microeconomic behaviour. Firms make decisions about their prices on the basis of costs and demand (marginal and average revenue). However, all of these have to be based on their beliefs about these variables since in the real world they cannot be known with certainty. In many cases, prices are fixed for a period of time so these beliefs are **expectations about the future**. For example, when Hoover are deciding what price to charge for washing machines, they need to determine the demand for their product. This will depend on such matters as the price of substitutes. If Hoover believe that rivals are going to increase their prices then their demand curve moves further to the right. Hoover's expectations about price increases by rivals will thus determine the position of their demand curve and hence their price. If every firm expects every other firm to charge more, the belief is self-fulfilling. Moreover, a higher price for the same output is a definition of an upward shift in a supply curve, aggregate or otherwise.

The argument is even simpler in the labour market. The perceived shift in the demand for goods causes a shift in the demand for the labour which made them. A higher expected level of prices causes a fall in perceived real wages, and so leads to an inward shift in the supply of labour. Supply moves in and demand moves out, hence wages rise at each level of employment. All of these shifts can be represented at an aggregate level by a shift of the AS curve. Higher inflationary expectations thus lead to an upward shift of the AS curve.

Friedman's argument is that higher inflation leads to a higher expected level of inflation and so to an adverse shift of the AS curve. The extent of this shift of the AS curve depends upon how

Figure 9.3 *Aggregate demand, aggregate supply and inflation*

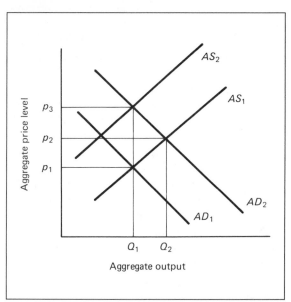

model there is an inverse relationship between inflation and unemployment. In Friedman's model the inverse relationship is between **demand** inflation and unemployment. The cost of a lower level of unemployment is demand inflation and hence an accelerating, rising level of total inflation – whenever there is demand inflation, inflation is necessarily higher than in the previous year (inflation falls only when demand inflation is negative).

In brief, Friedman's argument is that activist demand management can keep unemployment at a low level only by accepting an accelerating level of inflation. This is likely to be both unacceptable and probably uncontainable.

Since his earliest writings in the late 1940s, Friedman has emphasised a simple point: that the theory of (Keynesian) activist demand management was based upon an **assumption of omniscience**. Activist demand management assumes that governments know both the entire structure of the economy and the shocks that it will face. Friedman stressed the enormous amount of knowledge of behaviour required to write even the simple consumption function and other relationships discussed in Chapter 1 above. The government is unlikely, in Friedman's view, to know the value of the marginal propensity to save, with the result it cannot carry out the calculations necessary to manage the economy. Behaviour, Friedman argued, is much more complex and difficult to predict than the activists had assumed.

Similarly, to use stabilisation policy to offset shocks as described above, governments must be able to **predict them**. Friedman argued that any government which believed it had such knowledge was living in a fools' paradise. In this respect Friedman was echoing Keynes who had based his analysis on the threat posed by the 'dark forces of ignorance and uncertainty'. Keynes was, however, by temperamemt an activist and an optimist who believed that governments could reduce the consequences of the dark forces. Friedman, by nature a pessimist, believed that they could not.

Opponents of demand management have continued to stress these Friedmanite arguments. Laidler, for many years the most prominent of UK monetarists, recently described it as 'the bottom line' of his moderate Friedmanite-monetarist posi-

expectations of inflation respond to actual inflation. There can be little doubt that there is some response, since if inflation is high or rising it is unreasonable not to expect it to be higher in future than one would if inflation were low. Friedman's analysis is, however, a special case in that he assumes that the rise in the expected rate of inflation is exactly equal to the current rise in inflation. Thus if inflation rose from 4 to 5 per cent, expected inflation would follow suit (at least in the long run). If this is so, the shift in aggregate supply is exactly enough for output to fall to its original level, that is for aggregate supply to shift from AS_1 to AS_2 in **Figure 9.3**.

Friedman's analysis can be presented in another way:

Inflation$_t$ = Expected inflation$_t$ + Demand inflation

Expected Inflation$_t$ = Inflation$_{t-1}$

so Inflation$_t$ = Inflation$_{t-1}$ + Demand inflation

It is the linkage between **inflation and past inflation** which is one of the achievements of Friedman's model. By so doing, it explains inflation as a **continuing increase in prices**, rather than as a once-and-for-all rise in price. In the orthodox

tion, the foundation on which he rested his opposition to activist policy.

Friedman went on to argue that activist demand management policies would confuse the private sector and introduce an element of unpredictability into private sector decision-making – for example about tax rates. In Friedman's view this would have two adverse effects:

(a) it would render private sector behaviour less efficient: with less knowledge upon which to base their decisions, economic agents would inevitably make worse decisions; hence, the economy would be less efficient – in the terms of the analysis used in this book, the AS curve would shift upwards
(b) it would render private sector behaviour less stable and so contradict the goals of demand management; private sector behaviour would respond to contra-cyclical policy by being more erratic, and so income would vary more than without government action designed to reduce such fluctuations.

To summarise Friedman's argument: activist demand management is possible only with a degree of knowledge and predictive ability that is normally unattainable. However, for a variety of temporary reasons it seemed in the 1950s that such omniscience was the case. The 1960s and 1970s revealed the hollowness of this claim.

New Classical and radical critiques

So far in this chapter, the analysis has concentrated upon Friedman's critique of the theory and practice of Keynesian demand management. The contrast between these is marked when the analysis of the effect of an increase in aggregate demand on the economy is considered.

In **Figure 9.4** this is shown using both AD/AS analysis and Phillips Curves. The naive Keynesian model says that the expansionary policy, represented by a shift in the AD curve from AD_1 to AD_2, will move the economy from 1 to 2, that is it will reduce unemployment albeit at a cost in terms of inflation. Friedman argues that the result is only a short-run one. The higher inflation will generate expectations of higher inflation which will cause the AS or Phillips Curve to shift such that the economy finishes at point 3. For Friedman, then, acceptance of a higher rate of inflation buys only a transient fall in unemployment. The only way to reduce unemployment permanently is to accept accelerating inflation. Sophisticated Keynesians accept the essence of Friedman's analysis, but suggest econometric or theoretical reasons why the AS or Phillips Curve will not shift as far as in Friedman's analysis – thus the economy will finally come to rest at K. In this case there is still a long-run trade-off between unemployment and inflation, albeit a much more expensive one that in the naive Keynesian model.

Figure 9.4   *Aggregate demand, aggregate supply and Phillips Curves*

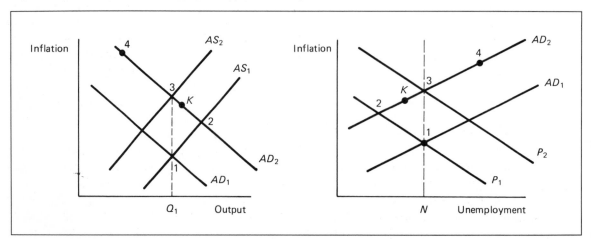

Many economists reject both the Keynesian and Friedmanite analysis. Indeed, they are both regarded as being very similar and open to the same objections. These critics take various positions, but all deny the Keynesian–Friedman model as 'orthodox' or some such similar term which they regard as pejorative. These critiques will now be analysed.

New Classical macroeconomics

The New Classical school focus upon the formation of inflationary expectations in Friedman's model. He argues that people usually expect inflation to be what it was in the previous period. This is regarded as irrational by the New Classical school because it introduces a systematic error. If inflation is rising, then in Friedman's world economic agents **always underpredict**. If inflation is falling, they **always overpredict**. On either statistical or common sense grounds it is easy to see that a better predictor could be devised. For example, if inflation has risen from 4 to 6 per cent, it is more plausible to expect 8 per cent in the following year rather than 6. Once this point is accepted then there is no reason for the 1–2–3 route shown in **Figure 9.4**. Indeed, 4 is just as likely as 2 as a response to an increase in aggregate demand.

Moreover, New Classical economists argue that it is irrational for workers or other economic agents to base their expectations of inflation upon past experience when they have available to them all of the information about the preferred macroeconomic model used by the government. For example, observation that the money supply is growing rapidly would be expected to trigger an upward revision to the expected rate of inflation. To behave in this way is rational, hence the belief in 'rational expectations'.

In its simplest and most plausible form, the New Classical critique argues that Friedman's model is just as mechanistic and illogical as the Keynesian analysis. Some New Classical economists, however, go on to argue that since it is known that the real wage will not rise even though money wages are being bid up, there is simply an instantaneous movement up the long-run Phillips Curve without

the short-run curve coming into play. This would happen only if the government were deliberately to introduce an unpredictable policy change, but this is rarely possible.

Radical critiques

Some New Classical economists argue for the 'clean kill' – that is, an instantaneous reduction in inflation with a minimal cut in unemployment. It should be possible for the government to send out unambiguous signals about its intention to cut the money supply with a view to reducing inflation, causing an instantaneous movement down the **AS** curve or the long-run Phillips Curve – in other words reducing inflation without creating unemployment in the process. But such a policy is unlikely to be practicable since it depends upon a government's credibility – economic agents have to believe that the government has both the power and the intention to execute such a policy. Even in 1979–82 the government faced major credibility problems even though its strategy was much less extreme than the 'clean kill' strategy.

Although there are other unorthodox right-wing critiques of the Keynesian–Friedmanite analysis, more attention has been paid to self-styled radical critiques. Radicals draw inspiration from Marx, Kalecki and the 'fundamentalist' interpretation of Keynes advanced by Shackle, Joan Robinson and Paul Davidson. There are many different streams of radical thought. Some radicals – part-Keynesians – stress the significance of speculation and argue that in consequence financial markets are inherently unstable. 'Black Monday' in October 1987 fitted their theories but the ease with which the world economy adjusted to the shock came close to refuting this line of thought. Other radicals stress that apparently economic decisions are frequently weapons in a class or sectoral conflict. Inflation may be the by-product of such conflict. If a group of workers wish to increase their share of real income they can do this only by bidding for higher nominal wages. The response by an opposed group will similarly be to raise its prices or to ask for higher wages. Such conflict theories are but some of a whole army of sociological theories of inflation. However, it is the premise of this book that economic models suffice without recourse to sociology.

A less radical but more influential approach emphasises the role of organised labour. It is argued that trade unions bargain for a money wage compatible with their real wage aspirations, after which employers simply add a mark-up to the wage cost in order to cover other costs and to provide an acceptable profit margin. This mark-up is not influenced by the demand for the end-product, hence an increase in demand will not cause money wages and prices to rise or fall relative to their previous levels. In this way of thinking the problem created by raising demand is not that it will fail to be matched by greater supply, hence creating inflation, but rather that UK firms are too uncompetitive to be the preferred source of the things demanded with the result that the excess demand gets side-tracked into imports. This leads to a justification for import controls, which were an integral part of the New Cambridge model once favoured by Radical Keynesians.

Financial policy in the ascendant

The loss of faith in incomes policy

In the 1980s the government has relied upon financial policy and has largely ignored direct and Keynesian instruments. The merits of this policy are reviewed in this section. The argument for an incomes policy is that it can reduce inflationary expectations and so reduce the unemployment cost of fighting inflation by shifting **AS** curves outwards. This effect depends upon economic agents having faith in the government to achieve its objectives. Such faith may be rare in the 1980s. Moreover, a full-blooded Thatcherite would argue that there is no hope that an incomes policy can shift the aggregate supply curve outwards, although the evidence on the effects of incomes policy is unclear. The Thatcherite view is that, if after 30 years of effort success had not yet been achieved, it was time to abandon the experiment of incomes policy. The essence of the Thatcherite view is that incomes policy has an adverse effect

on aggregate supply – that is, it causes the **AS** curve to shift inwards not outwards as the postwar orthodoxy suggested. The argument is simple:

1. incomes policies interfere with the workings of market forces
2. market forces ensure efficiency
3. therefore, **incomes policy reduces efficiency**; in other words they cause the aggregate supply curve to shift inwards.

Perhaps, the key feature of this argument is that incomes policies may be malign as well as benign. The full list of postwar incomes policies is set out in **Table 9.7**. The contrast between Thatcherism and the frequent use of incomes policy during the Keynesian era is clear to see.

The loss of faith in fiscal policy

The Thatcher era has also seen the (temporary?) end of the use of Keynesian fiscal policy. It has been argued that Keynesian demand management policies carry the seeds of their own destruction because after a while fiscal devices cease to influence aggregate demand. The argument is that, once individuals and companies realise that governments are seeking to use the tools of demand management to influence their behaviour, the private sector will change its behaviour. A special and much publicised example of this is the 'rational expectations' model but, in fact, the argument is both more general and more widely accepted.

It is clear that private sector behaviour does depend upon its perceptions of government policy as well as upon objective reality. Sometimes such behaviour can reinforce the workings of policy, as suggested above, because if businessmen believe that governments will maintain a high level of demand they will invest more, which leads to a high level of demand.

However, in most cases the effect on policy is counter-productive. The following example illustrates the use of one tool of fiscal policy: to vary income tax rates so as to vary personal disposable income (PDI) and hence, given an orthodox Keynesian consumption function, consumers' expendi-

Table 9.7 *Incomes policies*

1.	Cripps – TUC Pact	February 1948–1950
2.	Selwyn Lloyd Pay Pause	July 1961–March 1962
3.	Guiding Light	April 1962–October 1964

The Labour government 1964–70 had an incomes policy which changed its name and form

4.	Statement of Intent	December 1964–July 1966
5.	The Freeze	July 1966–December 1966
6.	Severe restraint	January 1967–July 1967
7.	Continued restraint	July 1967–April 1968
8.	Reserved restraint	April 1968–June 1970

The Conservative government (1972–4) had an incomes policy divided into 3 stages

9.	Stage 1	November 1972–January 1973
10.	Stage 2	February 1973–October 1973
11.	Stage 3	November 1973–February 1974
12.	Social Contract	March 1974–July 1975
13.	Compulsory non-statutory incomes policy	July 1975–May 1979

Source: Gowland (1989).

ture. The idea behind this is the manipulation of consumers' expenditure so as to offset fluctuations in investment and exports, and so maintain a stable full employment level of output. As a consequence, the private sector will have a fluctuating level of consumption. An example of this is shown in **Table 9.8**, in which consumers always have a pre-tax income of 100 and always choose to spend 75 per cent of their post-tax income. The government can then adjust tax rates so as to attain the level of consumers' expenditure necessary for the success of its demand management policy.

In each of 3 years, consumers' income is 100. The government's stabilisation goals require that consumers' spending be 42, 75 and 60 in the successive years. Believing that the consumption function is such that expenditure is 0.75 of PDI, the government sets taxes at 44 per cent, 0 per cent and 20 per cent. In consequence, personal disposable income is 56, 100 and 80 and so consumers' expenditure is 42, 75 and 60. Stabilisation policy is thus effective. However, the personal sector would prefer a stable path of consumers' expenditure, if only because of the **diminishing marginal utility**

of consumption. This principle states that a consumer will obtain less pleasure from consuming a ninth pint of beer than he or she obtained from the eighth. In consequence *ceteris paribus*, they would rather drink 8 pints of beer on each of two successive nights than 7 on one night and 9 on the other (since the extra benefit – an eighth pint – produces more pleasure than the cost, the foregone ninth).

By extension to the macroeconomic level it is reasonable to assume that, *ceteris paribus*, consumers would like to spend the same amount in real terms each year. Once consumers realise the nature of policy – and the consequent fluctuations in their incomes and consumption that it induces – they will react by adjusting their borrowing and saving plans. The personal sector will maintain a constant path of consumers' expenditure and pay for any extra taxes by drawing upon savings, which will be replenished when taxation is low. This case is illustrated in the lower part of **Table 9.8**. A consumption pattern of 10 in year 1 and 10 in year 2 gives more utility than 15 in year 1 and 5 in year 2 (diminishing marginal utility means that

Table 9.8   *Stabilisation policy*

	Income	Tax	PDI	Consumers' expenditure	Saving
1. Initially					
1	100	44	56	42	14
2	100	0	100	75	25
3	100	20	80	60	20
2. Once consumers react to policy					
1	100	44	56	59	−3
2	100	0	100	59	41
3	100	20	80	59	21

the benefits of consuming 6–10 are greater than 11–15). Consumers will thus borrow and save such that, so far as is possible, they can achieve this. Once they realise how government policy is working, they will adjust their behaviour such that if the policy is repeated it will not work, as set out in the lower part of **Table 9.8**. Consumers will spend 59 each year – and so maximise their utility – and vary their savings to achieve this.

If necessary they will dissave (borrow) in year 1 so as to achieve their welfare-maximising level of consumption. It is important to realise that consumers do not need to understand how government policy operates, but merely to observe that there are fluctuations in their tax bills which will cause their consumption to vary unless they respond by adjusting saving. In this case, when the government varies the size of one withdrawal (taxation) it is not income which adjusts (as in the simple model) but another withdrawal (saving) so demand management is ineffective. Hence, in the belief that direct controls and Keynesian instruments are ineffective, the government has relied upon financial policy since 1979.

The desirability of intermediate targets

The case for targets

From 1976 to 1985 UK governments pursued

monetary targets. After that, until his resignation Mr Lawson argued against any effective target. It was his critics who argued for a restoration of some target: either the money supply or the exchange rate through membership of the EMS.

The most basic case for targets is that they give information about the **future behaviour of objectives**. In the UK, monetary developments in 1986–87 suggested that inflation would accelerate, eventually. It did in late 1988. Advance knowledge should make it possible to take corrective action. If this is done, less drastic measures will be needed than if action is delayed. The dramatic 5 per cent rise in UK interest rates in May–October 1988 would not have been necessary if the authorities had raised rates earlier – perhaps a 1 per cent increase in 1986 and 2 per cent in 1987 would have sufficed.

In addition, three arguments have been put in favour of targets. The first is an argument that a money supply target acts as an automatic stabiliser – that is, it will reduce the deviation of output from its trend level. This can be accepted by many Keynesians since it is agreed that the action necessary to meet a monetary target will frequently reduce the impact of shocks on output. The difference, of course, is that Friedman and Brunner have argued that this reduction of the impact of shocks is the most that is attainable, whereas Tobin and other self-styled Keynesians believe that more is possible. However, less emphasis is now given to this aspect of Keynesian beliefs, since the implicit fine-tuning discretionary policy is very hard to implement successfully.

The shock analysed for illustrative purposes is a fall in exports caused, for example, by a world recession. This will reduce the overseas effect below what it would otherwise be. In this case it is necessary to influence one of the other items so that it is larger (or less negative) than it otherwise would be, and thus offset the monetary effects of the fall in exports. Any action that would do this would be expansionary in any model – whether lower interest rates, higher public spending or a relaxation of credit ceilings. Consequently, the reduction in output and employment caused by a fall in exports would be offset. The monetarist argument is that setting the economy on an automatic course is better than letting the authorities use their judgement.

Hence, it is universally accepted that observance of a monetary target will be stabilising. However, whereas Brunner and Friedman argue that this is the maximum attainable degree of stability, Keynesian writers would either rely on discretionary action or on automatic stabilisers of a fiscal kind.

The second argument concerning monetary targets is beguilingly attractive. The private sector needs information about the public sector's behaviour if it is to plan its activities optimally. Information about government monetary policy is the most useful information that private sector agents can have, so a government should commit itself to a specific path of monetary growth. This proposition is very similar to the arguments put forward for indicative planning in the 1960s. The counter-arguments of opponents of monetary targets are that more useful information can be given – for example, a commitment to price stability or full employment or that the benefits of more information are less than the costs imposed by monetary targets.

However, much more attention has been given, at least in the UK, to the more sophisticated argument of the role of the money supply in the formation of inflationary expectations. This argument can range from a purely economic argument, to one incorporating a large element of politics. Minford has argued that the function of monetary

targets is to show that the government means 'business about inflation'.

The third argument for targets is that they are necessary to constrain or discipline governments. Buchanan has been a frequent proponent of this view, but it is even more closely associated with Friedman. This view can be put in a rather illiberal, undemocratic fashion: governments, left to themselves, will pursue policies that cause inflation, perhaps to buy votes, so it is necessary to find devices which will constrain them. This method of presentation is, however, unfair to its proponents who, to use Buchanan's terminology, want to see the introduction of an 'economic constitution'. Governments have enormous potential political power but accept constraints upon it, either through a written constitution as in the USA, or tacitly as in the UK. Such constraints involve both an acceptance of 'rules of the game' (the opposition is not kept out of power by force) and of rights such as freedom of the press, as well as procedural safeguards such as trial by jury. Buchanan and Friedman argue that it is equally necessary to constrain the economic power of government by similar devices. In this form the argument is not unreasonable, although one may argue that the majority's right to use economic power is sufficiently circumscribed by a political constitution. Nevertheless, it is worthy of note that this form of argument is new to monetarism in the twentieth century; traditionally monetarists believed in discretion not fixed rules, for example, in their contests in the nineteenth century with supporters of the gold standard.

To summarise, monetarists believe that governments should accept a commitment to a monetary target and should be prepared to make sacrifices to achieve it. This is justified because of the impact of monetary targets on expectations and because their adoption constrains governments and tends to stabilise output. None of these is without foundation. The 'automatic stabiliser' proposition is incontestably valid; the dispute is whether discretion or an alternative rule could do better. Monetary targets do convey information and influence expectations, but it is as easy to overstate as to ignore this case for their introduction.

Nevertheless, an issue which needs to be addressed is 'why money?' Similar arguments could be constructed for interest rate targets; other quantity targets; exchange rate targets; or more complex rules. This is seen most clearly in the discipline case. Buchanan acknowledges that a balanced budget rule (or a maximum tax: GDP ratio) or fixed exchange rates may be better constraints on governments. So what are the relative merits of monetary and other targets?

Monetary targets

Since Wicksell, in the 1880s, economists have argued that some quantity target, such as money, is necessary as well as a price target such as the rate of interest. Otherwise, the price level is indeterminate in theory and hyperinflation is possible in practice. However, while the system requires some anchor to avoid this, the institutional structure of the UK provides this without any target. Hence, whilst this argument is both reasonable and theoretically important, it has little practical relevance.

It can be demonstrated that a money target is desirable if the economy is subject to shocks in domestic goods markets, and an interest rate target if it is subject to monetary shocks. Similarly, a money target is preferable if shocks come from foreign sources and an exchange rate target if they come from domestic sources. The predominant nature of uncertainty in the UK in the 1980s is probably from the foreign and goods rather than the domestic and monetary sectors.

There are 6 definitions of money currently in use in the UK and also over 40 in the USA. Some critics argue that it is impossible to target a variable which is so hard to measure, but this argument is specious. There are over 50 definitions of unemployment and money is less hard to measure than most variables. What is relevant is whether alternative measures tell similar stories. Using annual growth figures, the implications of each series is the same: money grew too fast from 1984–88. In general, except in the very short term, alternative monetary data do tell the same story, whether one's interest is in annual changes or in longer-run changes.

It is further argued that financial innovation has

so changed the nature of financial assets and the reasons for holding them, that a consistent measure of money is impossible. Mr Lawson has frequently cited this proposition, such as in the 1987 Budget speech. This argument is true, but irrelevant. Financial innovation makes all assets more liquid, and some assets which were not previously money have accordingly now become money. Thus the bias is that all measures of money understate its true growth. The UK money supply in 1980 should have excluded building society deposits, whereas it should now include them, so true UK money has grown faster than either M_3 (which excluded building society deposits) or M_4 (which includes them). Hence the official response to innovation should be slower growth in money.

The most interesting argument against monetary targets is the post-Keynesian critique. This argues that money is so powerful in its effects that control of the money supply is likely to have dramatic and unpredictable effects. It is better to let money adjust to shocks, especially to changes in speculative sentiment, than to seek to control it. Money is the best buffer. Milton Friedman argues on similar lines that the best buffer is no change in money. In other words, post-Keynesians accept Friedman's argument for a neutral financial policy, but disagree about the meaning of neutrality. In the UK context the argument is that although the effects of no control have been devastating, the effects of trying to control money would have been still more destabilising.

Friedman has always argued that excess money growth causes high and variable (nominal) interest rates. Monetary growth raises inflation and inflationary expectations. Both cause interest rates to rise and the monetary authorities, moreover, have to increase rates still further to reduce inflation. Friedman could argue that the period 1984–88 in the UK proves his point.

The EMS and monetary targets

In recent years arguments in favour of variable exchange rates (and so opposition to the EMS) have been based on domestic macroeconomic grounds. In its negative form, the argument is that exchange rate constraints may inhibit freedom to exercise domestic instruments to combat inflation and unemployment. The German authorities have found that trying to stabilise the DM tends to lead to excess monetary growth, because such intervention leads to a positive overseas impact on the money supply. In the UK the argument is usually more forcefully put; higher exchange rates reduce inflation, lower ones reduce unemployment. Hence a government needs the freedom to adjust exchange rates for domestic reasons – in late 1988 the UK authorities welcomed a higher exchange rate for anti-inflationary reasons. However, few would deny the merits of more fixed rates and fewer still that membership of the EC involves eventual membership of the EMS. However, it may not be necessary to choose between money and exchange rate targets. Indeed, the EMS may necessitate a monetary target.

In the UK money growth tends to be the best predictor of the exchange rate; monetary expansion leads to exchange rate depreciation and vice versa. Hence, exchange rate stability can probably be best achieved by monetary stability. Moreover, all European advocates of the EMS argue that it necessitates macroeconomic policy co-ordination. That is, if the EMS is to survive there must be co-ordination of monetary policies – probably a common DCE target. Otherwise, differential macroeconomic policies will produce differential inflation and so mean that EMS rates cease to be in equilibria. Given that the UK's trade pattern is different from that of the rest of the EC, it will be harder to maintain EMS membership than for existing members. Hence the need for macro co-ordination is greater. Indeed for good or ill, EMS membership probably implies not only a monetary target but a common one with Germany. Arguments about EMS membership are therefore essentially **political** – is a greater degree of integration with Europe preferable to domestic economic policy autonomy?

Direct controls on credit

In 1988, with inflation accelerating and a £15 bn balance of payments deficit, it was clear that either money or credit, or both, needed to be controlled. Moreover, since the PSBR was already in surplus and the Government had in 1985 ruled out the use of debt sales as an instrument of monetary policy, it followed that to control money it was necessary to control bank lending. Thus Keynesians and monetarists were agreed about **what** was necessary, but not about **why**. Many critics suggested that it would be either necessary or desirable to use quantity ceilings or other direct controls on credit, but the Chancellor opted for the alternative of control on interest rates. The choices are illustrated in **Figure 9.5**. The authorities wish to reduce credit from Q_1 to Q_2. They can either ration credit and aim for point 2, or raise interest rates to r_2 and aim for point 3.

In general the following considerations apply to the choice of methods.

Figure 9.5 *Alternative approaches to credit control*

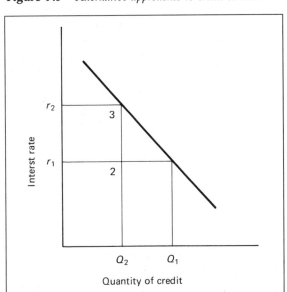

Quantity of credit

● **Direct controls are ineffective**: Any form of rationing creates an incentive to evade it (profitably!) – the classic black market. Direct controls on credit led, during the 1960s, to black markets (called parallel markets) and to disintermediation (see **pp. 89** and **100**). Direct controls on bank deposits (the Corset) led similarly to evasion in the 1970s. The simplest form of evasion involves the use of the overseas sector, and involves a loan (or credit card) from, say, the Midland Bank of Paris rather than the Midland Bank of York. Evasion is a serious problem with direct controls but with personal sector credit they could probably be effective **for a time**.

- **Direct controls are (Pareto) inefficient**: Direct controls lead to a loss of economic welfare.
- **Direct controls are inequitable or unfair**: Some lenders and borrowers are far more adversely affected than others.
- **Direct controls distort official statistics**: This may not seem important, but it is probably one of the two main arguments against direct controls on credit. A direct control will probably be partially effective, but to an unknown extent. Hence it is no longer clear whether policy is too tight or too slack. For example, if the authorities wish the level of credit to be £250 bn and use direct controls, official statistics will understate the size of credit. Black market transactions are never included in official data, and rarely ever under official purview in the short term. Hence, if the official data show £240 bn it is not clear if official policy is too tight, too slack or about right – it depends on whether the black market is more or less than £10 bn.

Given these circumstances, the reader may wonder why anyone supports the use of direct controls. There are two main reasons. One is that rationing of any kind leads to a lower price – in this case interest rates – than would otherwise be the case. This may be thought desirable in its own right or as a means to a preferred redistribution. Lower interest rates help the rich, mortgagees, the young and debtors generally at the expense of the poor, the old and creditors generally.

More usually, lower interest rates are welcomed because they lead to a higher ratio of investment to consumers' expenditure. Investment is usually more interest-sensitive than consumers' expenditure in empirical studies, and moreover in theory a rise in interest rates has an ambiguous effect on consumers' expenditure since the income and substitution effects operate in opposite direction.

The other argument is more interesting. This is that direct controls are relatively quick-acting, unlike interest rates. Indeed, their effect may wear off quickly. Nevertheless, for a short period a direct control is likely to work, especially if used skilfully by the authorities. This may be invaluable if the authorities have got policy seriously wrong, as Mr Lawson had in 1988. In similar circumstances direct controls proved useful in 1974 and 1978, whereas their absence made the conduct of monetary policy very difficult in 1979–80. This is the choice concerning direct controls on credit: the fast-acting instrument against the disadvantages of black markets. This choice is probably the most important short-term economic policy issue in the UK at present.

Are Budget surpluses beneficial?

In his 1988 and 1989 Budget speeches, Mr Lawson took considerable pride in large Budget surpluses. Indeed, there was much press comment about the possibility and desirability of running Budget surpluses of sufficient size for sufficient time to pay off the National Debt. In favour of such a policy it can be argued that:

(a) It will benefit **future generations** at the expense of **present ones**. After centuries of argument, it has been agreed amongst economists that the National Debt is a burden and does impose costs on future generations.

(b) It **eliminates the danger of crowding-out**, which occurs when government spending or borrowing reduces private spending or borrowing in an undesirable way. There is no evidence that it has ever been a serious problem in the UK, but it is still of some relevance. In particular, the withdrawal by the government from the long-term bond market has led to an upsurge of private corporate bond issues.

(c) It **raises the saving ratio**. Private sector saving has fallen in the UK in recent years. A Budget deficit – public sector saving – may be a substitute for it (see **p. 46**).

However, these advantages are offset by the disadvantages of Mr Lawson's unbalanced policy – tight fiscal constraint with very slack monetary policy, even after the interest rate increases in 1988.

Governments have usually used monetary and fiscal policy at the same time. For example, during the Barber expansion (1971–73), the money supply grew rapidly **and** there was a record Budget deficit. During the Jenkins squeeze (1968–69) both monetary and fiscal indicators measured the tightness of policy (the first Budget surplus for 50 years, the smallest money supply growth for 15 years). On occasions governments used one instrument earlier than another (monetary policy was tightened in 1974, fiscal policy in 1975), or eased one without adjusting the other (monetary policy alone was eased in 1977–78). Nevertheless, the tools were always in approximate balance, whereas since 1980 government policy has been unbalanced. However, it is necessary to examine the impact of an unbalanced policy, combining a loose monetary policy with a tight fiscal policy. (It is interesting to note that at the same time the USA pursued an equally unbalanced policy the other way around.) The effects of this lack of balance mean that the basic assumptions of macroeconomics must be relaxed – the economy can no longer be treated as if it were producing a single good. Instead, it is both necessary and possible to examine the form and duration that the stimulus to demand takes.

Monetary policy operates through **changing the demand for assets** (for an expansionary policy):

(a) An increase in the money supply creates an excess of supply over demand in the money market.

(b) Some of the excess money is switched to those assets which are substitutes for money (say, houses, antiques and Spanish villas).

(c) This extra demand means that there is excess demand for these assets. Hence either their price rises (antiques), or their quantity (Spanish villas), depending on the elasticity of supply. The two examples cited are unusual examples of (almost) perfectly inelastic and elastic supply respectively, and rather more often both price and output rise (houses).

Some monetarists argue that supply is virtually inelastic (classical monetarism); others, including French monetarists, that it is perfectly elastic. Friedman takes the compromise position: output responds in the short run but price in the long run. Hence, to examine the effects of the imbalance, one must seek to list the assets that private sector economic agents, companies and persons wish to purchase with their excess money holdings:

(a) Foreign assets – factories, shares, property; from 1980–88 these totalled £100 bn.

(b) Consumer durables – (in particular) cars and electrical goods. Most of these came from abroad, so there was little effect on prices, but an enormous balance of payments deficit was created (£15 bn in 1988.)

(c) Shares and financial assets – hence one reason why in the boom prior to October 1979, share prices rose faster in the UK than elsewhere.

(d) Houses

Undoubtedly, the monetary expansion caused the explosion in house prices. This generated a rise in housebuilding but it also caused serious social problems as well as impeding labour mobility.

More generally unbalanced demand management led to the concentration of growth in a few sectors of the economy and a few regions, notably the South East. This is an excessive price to pay for the advantages of a Budget surplus.

References

Allsop, C. and Mayes, D. (1985) Chapter 13 in D. Morris (ed.), *The Economic System in the UK*, 3rd edn. (Oxford University Press).

Bank of England (1971) 'Competition and Credit Control! The New Approach', *Bank of England Quarterly Bulletin* (December).

Blackaby, F. (ed.), (1978) *British Economic Policy 1960–74* (Heinemann).

Dornbusch, R. and Layard, R. (1987) *The Performance of the British Economy* (Oxford University Press).

Gowland, D.H. (1984) *Controlling the Money Supply*, 2nd edn (Croom Helm).

Gowland, D.H. (1989) *Whatever Happened to Demand Management?* (RJA Books).

Lawson, N. (1988) *The State of the Market* (IEA).

Minford, P. (1989) *The Sunday Telegraph*, 5 March.

Shields, J. 'Controlling Household Credit', *NIER* (August).

Walters, A. (1986) *Britain's Economic Renaissance* (Oxford University Press).

Cmnd 7858 (1980) *Monetary Control* (HMSO).

Index